ITALY
AND
HER INVADERS

PART THREE

OSTROGOTHIC INVASION. IMPERIAL RESTORATION

THOMAS HODGKIN

BOOK IV
THE OSTROGOTHIC INVASION.

I. A CENTURY OF OSTROGOTHIC HISTORY.
II. THE REIGN OF ZENO.
III THE TWO THEODORICS IN THRACE
V. FLAVIUS ODOVACAR.
V. THE FRIGIAN WAR
VI. THE DEATH-GRAPPLE.
VII. KING AND PEOPLE.
VIII. THEODORIC AND HIS COURT
IX. THEODORIC'S RELATIONS WITH GAUL.
X. THEODORIC'S RELATIONS WITH THE EAST.
XI. THEODORIC'S RELATIONS WITH THE CHURCH.
XII. BOETHIUS AND SYMMACHUS.
XIII. THE ACCESSION OF ATHALARIC.
XIV. JUSTINIAN.
XV. BELISARIUS.
XVI. THE LOVERS OF AMALASUNTHA.

BOOK V
THE IMPERIAL RESTORATION
535—553

I. THE FIRST YEAR OF THE WAR
II. BELISARIUS AT CARTHAGE AND AT NAPLES.
III. THE ELEVATION OF WITIGIS.
IV. BELISARIUS IN ROME
V. THE LONG SIEGE BEGUN.
VI. THE CUTTING OF THE AQUEDUCTS.
VII. THE GOTHIC ASSAULT.
VIII. ROMAN SORTIES.
IX. THE BLOCKADE
X. THE RELIEF OF RIMINI.
XI. DISSENSIONS IN THE IMPERIAL CAMP.
XII. SIEGES OF FIESOLI AND OSIMO.
XIII. THE FALL OF RAVENNA.
XIV. AFFAIRS AT CONSTANTINOPLE
XV. THE ELEVATION OF TOTILA.
XVI. SAINT BENEDICT (480 – 547)
XVII. THE RETURN OF BELISARIUS.
XVIII. THE SECOND SIEGE OF ROME.
CHAPTER XIX. ROMA CAPTA.
XX. THE RE-OCCUPATION OF ROME.
XXI. THE THIRD SIEGE OF ROME.
XXII. THE EXPEDITION OF GERMANUS.

XXIII. THE SORROWS OF VIGILIUS.
XXIV. NARSES AND TOTILA.
XXV FINIS GOTHORUM. THE LAST OF THE GOTHS

BOOK IV.

THE OSTROGOTHIC INVASION

CHAPTER I.

A CENTURY OF OSTROGOTHIC HISTORY.

I have now to record the establishment of a Teutonic kingdom in Italy, which, more than any other of the new states arising on the ruins of the Roman Empire, promised to promote the happiness of the human race, which seemed likely to draw forth all that was noblest in the manhood of the barbarian, all that was most refined in the culture of the Italian, and to weld them both into one harmonious whole; a kingdom the Arian ruler of which so wisely deferred to the feelings of his Catholic subjects, and held with so even a hand the balance between contending creeds that he all but solved the difficult problem how to construct 'a free Church in a free State'; a kingdom the preservation of which would (as I have already hinted) have helped forward the civilisation of Europe by five centuries, and would perhaps have contributed something towards the softening and ennobling of human life even at the present day. I have then to describe through what faults and flaws in its own structure, by what craft of foreign foes, by what treachery of ungrateful subjects, by what marvels of strategic skill this fair kingdom was shattered and brought to nought. Two names, which will ever defy oblivion, connect themselves with the two acts of this mighty drama: Theodoric with the establishment of the Ostrogothic monarchy, Justinian with its fall. But while Theodoric is all ours, no part of his career being outside the limits of our subject, there are vast spaces in the life and acts of the Byzantine Emperor which are foreign to our present purpose, and upon which we must not allow ourselves to enter.

I proceed to sketch in brief outline the history of the Ostrogothic people until the story of the nation begins to narrow into the biography of a man, their young king Theodoric.

The Ostrogoths were that member of the great Position of

The Ostrogoths were that member of the great East-German family of nations which first attained to widely extended dominion. Through the greater part of the third century after Christ theirs was the chief controlling influence in the vast plains between the Baltic and the Euxine which form the Lithuania and Southern Russia of modern history. Like the other German nations at that time, they were probably passing or had recently passed from the nomadic to the settled form of society, from dependence on flocks and herds to dependence on the tillage of the ground as their chief means of support. The head of this powerful but loosely compacted state was Hermanric the Amal, sprung from the seed of gods, still true to the martial religion of

Odin and Thor; a Goth of Goths, and a Teuton of Teutons. Under his orders moved to battle the hosts of the Visigoths who dwelt between him and the Danube, of the Gepidae who perhaps occupied the plains of Central Russia in his rear. The forecast of European history which then seemed probable would have been that a great Teutonic Empire stretching from the Danube to the Don would take the place which the colossal Slav Empire now holds in the map of Europe, and would be ready, as a civilised and Christianised power, to step into the place of Eastern Eome when in the fulness of centuries the sceptre should drop from the nerveless hands of the Caesars of Byzantium.

All these possible speculations as to the future were upset and the whole course of human history to the latest generations was modified by the rush of the swarthy dwarfish Huns over the shallows of the Sea of Azof and the impetuous charge of their light cavalry upon the unwieldy masses of the army of Hermanric. The defeat of the Ostrogothic army is acknowledged by the national historian. The death of the Ostrogothic king, who was in very advanced age, is not quite so honestly related. It is attributed to a wound received from rebellious subjects, but seems to have been in truth the death of a suicide, in despair at the sudden overthrow of his power.

The collapse of the power of Hermanric did not bring with it so disastrous rum to his people as would have been the case with a more highly organized state. The Hunnish monarch needed soldiers, and the Ostrogoths could supply them. He cared little about law and government, and therefore the Ostrogoths might keep such political institutions as they had. They were pushed somewhat westward, probably over the Carpathian mountains, and they no longer possessed the suzerainty over the vast and loose confederacy of nations who roamed over the plains of Sarmatia. Otherwise there was little change, only their king escorted the chariot of the conqueror instead of filling it. There are even indications that the Hun, regarded at first by his Gothic antagonist with blended feelings of fear and disgust, became somewhat less hateful as he was better known. Balamber, the monarch of the Huns at the time of their great migration, married Vadamerca, an Ostrogothic princess; and the bold attempt of *Winithar*, and, after his death, of the guardians of his infant son *Wideric*, to shake off the Hunnish yoke, seems to have met with but a faint and partial response among, their countrymen. *Hunimund* the son of Hermanric, who, as vassal of the conquerors, ruled over the great mass of the Ostrogothic people, is described as an active warrior, conspicuous for his manly beauty, and as having fought successfully against the Suevic nation, probably situated on his northern or north-western border.

The reign of Hunimund, which seems to have been a time of comparative prosperity for the Ostrogothic people, probably occupied the years between 375 and 415. Important events were then going forward in the West of Europe, events in which their Visigothic kinsmen and their old Vandal neighbours were distinguished as chief movers, but in which they had no share. About the year 415 Thorismund, son of Hunimund, succeeded his father. He is said to have been still 'in the flower of his youth,' which we should hardly have expected from a grandson of the aged and long since deceased Hermanric, nor from a son of Hunimund, who had just died after a reign of forty years. In the second year of his reign he marched with an army against the Gepidae, won a mighty victory over them, but, apparently in the moment of victory, was killed by a fall from his horse.

On the death of Thorismund some strange turn of fortune or popular caprice, the workings of which are evidently veiled in the narrative of Jordanes, obscured for a time the Amal kingship. We are told that, so great was the grief of the Ostrogoths for the loss of their young hero, that for forty years they would not allow any one to succeed in his place. His son Berismund, loathing the foreign dominion of the Huns and despising his nation for submitting to it, wandered off to the West and joined his fortunes to those of the Visigothic conquerors of Gaul, in which country he left descendants, one of whom was eventually to receive in marriage the daughter of the great Theodoric. At the end of the forty years' interregnum the Ostrogoths, who considered that by this time Thorismund had been sufficiently lamented, reverted to the Amal stock, and raised Walamir, grandson of the patriotic but unfortunate Winithar, to the vacant throne.

There can be no doubt that this story of the forty years' mourning for the brave young Thorismund is mere Saga. Nations do not suspend the working of an institution so essential to their safety and well-being as was the barbaric royalty for an interval longer than a whole generation out of mere sentimental considerations. What was the real nature of the revolution which is thus poetically veiled from us we can only conjecture. A German author has with some plausibility interwoven into this part of the history a detached notice preserved for us in the official letters of Cassiodorus concerning a certain Gensemund. The writer is praising the quality of loyalty, when exhibited towards the boyish heirs of a great chief by leaders who have been adopted into his family:

"Of this fidelity there is a distinguished example in the Gothic race. That Gensemund, whose fame is spread abroad throughout the whole world, though only adopted as a son-in-arms [by the deceased king], joined himself with such devotion to the Amial race that he rendered service of anxious fidelity to its heirs, although he himself was besought to wear the crown. He made his own merits available for others [his wards], and with unwonted moderation reserved for children the dignity which might have been bestowed on himself. Therefore his fame lives eternally in the songs of the Gothic race : he despised transitory greatness and earned deathless renown".

It is possible that the interpolated reign of this loyal hero may be the true explanation of the fabled forty years' mourning for Thorismund. But on the other hand it is to be remarked, (1) that no word from Cassiodorus himself assigns these events to this particular period; (2) that if Cassiodorus had told the story here it would have excluded the Saga which Jordanes has without doubt copied from him; (3) that the point of the story of Gensemund is that he *refused* the crown which, in order to make the hypothesis fully fit the facts which are to be accounted for, he must have worn for forty years; and (4) that as the new Amal kings were evidently men in middle life at the end of the so-called interregnum, a loyalty which exhibited itself by keeping the heirs of the deceased monarch so long from the throne would hardly have been recommended for imitation under the circumstances of Athalaric's minority.

A more probable explanation of this curious story seems to be that the Ostrogoths may really for a short time have hesitated about filling up the place left vacant by the death of their beloved young hero-king, that this hesitation may have caused them to split up into factions (since then, as so often since, Teutonic royalty and national unity were convertible terms), that this time of confusion may have been purposely prolonged by their Hunnish over-lords, in order to keep them in an enfeebled and depressed condition, but that at length, and not till after the kinsmen of Thorismund had reached and almost passed the prime of life, they succeeded in re-establishing the Amal royalty on something like its old basis.

The change which strikes us in the revived kingship of the Ostrogoths, and which makes these last qualifying words necessary, is that now for the first time we find the kingly power *divided*. That splitting up of the kingdom between a whole family of brothers which we so often meet with in the case of the Franks, and which was also apparently usual with the Huns, had not till now been practised in either branch of the great Gothic nation. Now, however, we find three kings—brothers—standing at the head of their people, and it is natural to suppose that this division of power was encouraged if not commanded by their Hunnish over-lord in order to keep the nation in a state of weakness and dependence. The three brothers are *Walamir, Theudemir*, and *Widemir*, the eldest of whom, Walamir, had some sort of supremacy over his younger brothers, which is rather hinted at than explained in the flowery language of Jordanes : "Of which three brothers, Walamir, by succession to his relatives, ascended the throne, the Huns still keeping a general supremacy over them, as over all the surrounding nations. And a fair sight was it then to see the union of these brothers when the admirable Theudemir fought under the orders of his brother Walamir, while Walamir helped each of the other two by the honours with which he adorned them [?], and Widemir, though serving, remembered that he served his brother".

Whatever may have been their mutual relations of supremacy and obedience, the three brothers served their Hunnish over-lord faithfully, followed his banners across the rivers and plains of Central Germany, and stood amid the 'crowd of kings' who waited for his nod on the Catalaunian fields. It was a hard thing for them to fight against their Visigothic kindred, but they dared not to refuse the orders of Attila, 'for the compulsion of the master', thinks Jordanes, 'must be obeyed, even though he should order parricide'. And on that great day, as we have before seen, Walamir the Ostrogoth, trusty, good-tempered, open-hearted, shared with the Gepid Ardaric the honour of being admitted to the inmost counsels of the moody barbarian.

Then came, close upon Attila's death, the glorious day of Netad, when the German tribes which had deemed themselves compelled to do his bidding, even though the deed were parricide, faced his sons in fight, and broke the Hunnish yoke from off their necks. Thus were the Ostrogoths once more free after eighty years of subjection, and pressing, as we may suppose, westwards and southwards, to fill up the vacuum caused by the extrusion of the Huns, they came into possession of the once flourishing but now, no doubt, grievously wasted province of Pannonia. There must have been some recognition, however faint, of the Roman right to this province, some relation of covenanted service (*foederatio*) to Empire, be rendered to Valentinian III in return for its occupation, for Jordanes distinctly says that 'they preferred to seek lands from the Roman realm, rather than at their peril to invade the lands of others, and thus they accented Pannonia... a country adorned with a great number of cities, from Sirmium at one end to Vindobona (Vienna) at the other.' At this time the relation of the Ostrogoths to the Empire was probably almost the same as that of their Visigothic brethren forty years earlier, when Walia obtained possession by treaty of the district of Septimania in Aquitaine.

As to the precise distribution of the Pannonian territory between the three brothers, Jordanes does not give a very clear account. He says that 'Walamir dwelt between the rivers Scarniunga and the Black Water. Theudemir next to Lake Pelso, and Widemir between the other two.' Unfortunately, it seems hopeless to attempt to identify the two rivers; and even as to the lake, there is a certain degree of hesitation between Neusiedler See in the north-west corner of Hungary, and Platten See, more than a hundred miles to the south-east of it. But till local antiquaries shall have produced some decided arguments in favour of another hypothesis, we may perhaps safely assert that Walamir occupied the provinces of Sclavonia and Northern Croatia which lie between the rivers Drave and Save, that Theudemir ruled a broad belt of country between the Danube and the Platten See, and that the triangle between the Platten See, the Save and the Danube was allotted to the youngest brother Widemir.

Their old lords the Huns would not accept the verdict of the day of Netad as final, but still considered the Ostrogoths as absconding slaves. The sons of Attila came with a great host against Walamir, before his brothers were apprised of his danger. He met them, we are told, with an army greatly inferior in numbers, but so bravely withstood their onset that only a comparatively small part of the invading army was able to escape to their new abodes near the mouth of the mighty stream which the Huns called in their own language Var, but which was just then beginning to be known in Europe by its modern name, the Dnieper. The news of this successful engagement came to the palace of Theudemir on the very day on which 'the boy of good omen,' THEODORIC, was born to him by his concubine, Erelieva. Notwithstanding the word which implies the inferior position of the mother of Theodoric, he was always treated as lawful heir to his father, and the widowed Erelieva seems to have maintained the position which would belong to Queen-mother in a half-civilised people. It is probable, therefore, that, though she was of inferior birth to her husband, the union between them was one sanctioned by the Church, somewhat resembling the morganatic marriages of modern Germany, but unlike those as conveying full right of inheritance to the offspring, at any rate where there was not a subsequent marriage to a woman of higher rank.

Something must be said as to the name of the infant over whose arrival the household of Theudemir were rejoicing when the messenger of Walamir dashed into the court-yard of the palace and shouted 'Victory!'. Like the two Visigoths, father and son, who reigned at Toulouse and fought with Attila, his name is indelibly written in the pages of history as Theodoric. This form of the name became current so early (we meet with it in the letters of Sidonius and the annals of Prosper), and obtained so wide a circulation, that it is useless now to seek to change it. But it is right to notice that the true form of the name, which is very fairly represented by the *Theuderichus* of the Byzantine historians, is THIUDA-REIKS, and signifies 'the people-ruler'. It is a curious coincidence that the name is nearly equivalent in meaning to that of the Athenian orator Demosthenes. One might have expected that the courtly and scholarly Cassiodorus, who so faithfully served Theodoric as secretary, would have availed himself of this resemblance in some one of the many harangues which he prepared for his master to deliver to the Roman Senate or to the envoys of foreign courts.

But this is an anticipation. We return to the young Teuton, with the yellow locks falling to his shoulders, playing with his toy broad-sword in his father's palace. There came a day, bitter without doubt and memorable to the childish heart, but fraught with future good, when he had to leave his mother and his brother, the Danube and the fresh air of the Pannonian highlands, his folk and the old warriors songs at night-fall about the great deeds of his Amal forefathers, and had to spend ten years of heart-ache, but also of keen interest and thought-stimulating wonder, in the purple presence-chamber of the Caesar at Constantinople. The change came to pass on this wise. When Theodoric was seven years old the Gothic Ostrogothic brothers found that the tribute, which under the delicate euphemism of *Strenae* (New Year's presents) they had been taught to look for from the Emperor Leo, was falling into arrear. They sent envoys to

Constantinople to enquire into the cause of the delay, and the report which these messengers brought back made the grievance greater.

There was a certain Gothic chieftain, the son of Triarius, (of whom there will be more to say hereafter,) at the Byzantine court. This man was a kinsman of the great Aspar, had perhaps been on friendly terms with Leo, when the future Emperor was only a sort of upper steward of their common patron, and therefore he, coming from some quite inferior stock, with no claim to Amal ancestry, was honoured with the friendship of the Romans and was punctually receiving his yearly honorarium, while the Amals were left to poverty and contempt. The insult was too exasperating; they rushed to arms, and ravaged Moesia far and wide. Then the Emperor repented of his previous inattention to their demands. Peace was arranged; the arrears of *strenae* were at once handed over, and their punctual payment in future was guaranteed. On their part the Ostrogoths must have undertaken to confine their rovings to the northern shores of the Danube; and in pledge of their future fidelity the eldest Amal heir, Theodoric, was to be sent as a hostage to Constantinople. Theudemir demurred to this proposal, that he should send his boy to live among unsympathising strangers; but when Walamir, who might have commanded as his lord, besought him as a brother, and urged the importance of ratifying a firm peace between Goths and Romans, he consented. So was the young prince brought to Constantinople, where, being a handsome noble-spirited boy, he soon endeared himself greatly to the Emperor Leo.

After the conclusion of the treaty with the Empire, which the Goths appear to have observed faithfully during the ten years of Theodoric's tarriance at Constantinople, there followed some obscure and uninteresting struggles with the barbarous nations on their northern and eastern borders. The Ostrogoths moved against the Sadages, an Alan or Hunnish tribe whose geographical position we need not trouble ourselves to discuss. Seeing them thus occupied, Dinzio, one of the sons of Attila who dwelt on their southern border, crossed the Danube with the warriors of four barbarous clans which still followed his standard and besieged Bassiana, once a Roman city of some importance, and containing a gynaeceum, or manufactory, in which a century before female slaves wove the purple robe of the Emperor and the linen tunics of his soldiery. Now, the Hunnish chieftain, finding it inaccessible to his storming parties, drew a line of circumvallation round it and proceeded to plunder the surrounding country. While he was thus engaged, the Ostrogoths, who had turned back from their expedition against the Sadages, attacked the Huns and drove them forth from Pannonia, so utterly defeated, says Jordanes, that the men of that nation ever after trembled before the Gothic name.

The next encounters of the Goths were with the Suevi or Suavi, a portion of that wide-spread confederacy of peoples which presents to us some of the most difficult problems of German ethnology. Caesar tells us of his encounters with the Suevic Ariovistus on the Rhine. Tacitus makes them stretch across Germany from the sources of the Danube to the Vistula, and paints for us the splendid but short-lived empire erected by the Suevic Maroboduus in that which we now call Bohemia. In a previous part of this history we have seen the Suevi pressing, with the Vandals, across the Rhine into Gaul, across the Pyrenees into Spain, and founding a kingdom in the latter country, which, though eventually destroyed by the Visigoths, is thought by some to have contributed a trace of separate Suevic nationality to the modern Portuguese : and we have also seen the Suevic chieftain Ricimer arrayed as a Roman patrician, disposing of the destinies of Rome at his pleasure, setting up and dethroning emperors, marrying the daughter of Anthemius, and bidding Avitus assume the tonsure of a priest. The Suevi with whom we are now concerned dwelt in the south-west corner of Germany, in the region which is now known as the Black Forest, and away eastwards along the Upper Danube, perhaps as far as the river Lech. They were already mingled with the Alamanni of the mountains, a process which was no doubt carried yet further when, some thirty years after the time now reached by us, Clovis overthrew the monarchy of the Alamanni, whom he drove remorselessly forth from all the lands north of the Neckar. The result of these migrations and alliances was the formation of the two great Duchies with which we are so familiar in the mediaeval history of Germany, Suabia, and Franconia. Suabia, which is a convertible term with Alamannia, represents the land left to the mingled Suevi and Alamanni; Franconia that occupied east of the Rhine by the intrusive Franks. The reason for calling attention to this geographical detail here is that in the passage of Jordanes which we have now before us we see most clearly the transition from the Suevi of Caesar and Tacitus to the Swabia from which the great Hohenstaufen Emperors took their ducal title.

The war between Ostrogoths and Suevi arose in this wise. Hunimund king of the Suevi made a raid on some portion of the Roman territory, and in order to reach it had to cross the lands of the Ostrogoths, whose wandering cattle his people appropriated. Cattle, it need hardly be said, were emphatically the wealth of these early Teutonic communities; and, just as the Fosters and Armstrongs of Northumberland resented and requited a cattle-lifting foray of the Kerrs or Scotts from the Scottish side of the Border, so did Walamir and his brothers watch their opportunity to repay the Sueves for their depredations. In the dead of night they came upon them encamped by the lake Pelso, slew many with the sword, made a prisoner of King Hunimund, and reduced the bulk of his army to slavery. After a time, however, and apparently after the death of King Hunimund, Walamir effected some sort of reconciliation with his son, and sent him back with his followers to their native Suavia. The generous forgiveness, which Jordanes praises, was probably due to the difficulty of obtaining subsistence for the added multitude and the danger of enslaving so large a people, as martial probably as their conquerors.

After a further lapse of time (we have now probably reached the year 470) the son of Hunimund, remembering the shame of the defeat rather than the boasted clemency of the conqueror, made a sudden assault upon the Ostrogoths, having leagued himself with their northern neighbours the Scyri. In the battle which ensued King Walamir was thrown from his horse and at once perished, pierced through and through with Suevic lances. Jordanes obscures the real issue of the contest by saying that in their rage for the loss of their king the Ostrogoths blotted out the name of the Scyri from under heaven : but it is evident that the true result of these operations was not only the death of Walamir but a severe defeat of his people.

Theudemir, the next oldest brother, assumed the chief kingship and fought a bloody battle with the Suevi and Scyri, who had also confederated with themselves the Gepidae, the Rugians, and a race designated by the conveniently vague term of Sarmatians. This great confederacy was defeated by the Ostrogoths, now prepared and united, upon the banks of the Bollia (perhaps the modern Ipoly). After the battle the field presented the usual spectacle of carnage on which Jordanes delights to dwell,— the wide waters of the marsh turned into a red sea, a lake of blood, and the plain for ten miles round covered with artificial hillocks formed from the unburied corpses of the slain. "The Goths saw this and rejoiced with unspeakable exultation, feeling that now at length their king Walamir was avenged".

Another campaign followed, a winter campaign in which Theudemir, crossing the frozen Danube, and marching perhaps through Moravia and Bohemia, took the Suevi and their confederate Alamanni in the rear, and, falling upon them thus unexpectedly, "conquered, wasted, and almost subdued them". Returning home the father's heart was gladdened by the sight of his son Theodoric, now a youth of about seventeen years of age, versed doubtless in Roman and courtly ways, if not imbued with Roman literature. The Emperor Leo had sent him back from the Bosporus to his home with rich presents and high good-will. Scarcely had the young lion-cub reached the lair of his fathers, when he set forth again for his first taste of blood. Gathering to himself some of his father's guards and men of his nation who loved him, to the number of 10,000 men (a precise reproduction of the old Germanic *Comitatus* as described to us by Tacitus), he stole away unknown to his father, crossed the Danube where it formed the south-eastern frontier of Pannonia, and attacked Babai king of the Sarmatians, who was just then swelling with the pride of victory, having recently defeated Camundus, the Roman Duke of Upper Moesia, and taken from the Empire the important city of Singidunum (Belgrade). The young Ostrogoth conquered, wrested Singidunum from the Sarmatian, did not restore it to his Roman patrons, but kept it under his own sway, and returned with his joyous *Comitatus* to his father, having furnished another subject for song to the Gothic minstrels. Either at this time, or else on his return from Constantinople, he seems to have been hailed by his nation as king, of course in subordination to his father and uncle. Thirty years later (500), when he was lord of Italy, Dalmatia and Rhaetia, he rode through the streets of Rome celebrating the *tricennalia* of this, his accession to the Gothic throne.

If the Emperor Leo had thought to attach the Ostrogoths firmly to the Empire by his friendly treatment of the young Theodoric, he was disappointed. A foretaste of that which was to come had been afforded by the retention of the Roman city of Singidunum in Gothic hands. Next year (not many months before the death of Leo) the Ostrogoths, who had for some time been coming to the conclusion that Pannonia was too strait for them, and who were hindered, perhaps by the increasing strength and solidity of the Rugian monarchy, from enriching themselves as they wished at the expense of their barbarian neighbours, clamoured to be led forth to war; whither they heeded not, but it was evidently understood that it must be war against some part of the Empire. Theudemir called his brother into council. It was decided that Widemir, as the weaker of the two, should invade Italy, then recently bereft of the stout heart of the unscrupulous Ricimer, and, under the rule of the feeble Glycerius, apparently sinking into a mere appanage of Burgundy. The issue of this invasion has been already told. Widemir died in Italy, and his son and namesake led his army into Gaul, where, waiving apparently his royal dignity, he united his forces with those of Euric, king of the Visigoths.

To Theudemir, as the stronger of the two brothers, was assigned the task of attacking the Eastern Empire. He crossed the Save with a formidable host, which imposed neutrality on the Sarmatian borderers. Making his son's new conquest, Belgrade, his base of operations, he marched a hundred miles up the valley of the Morava to Naissus, now the Servian city of Nisch, where he took up his headquarters. The young Theodoric, with two Gothic counts, probably old and wary officers, Astat and Invilia, as his counsellors, was sent on a rapid southward march. He pushed up the

Morava valley for another hundred miles to the source of that river, crossed the western ridge of the Balkans, and descended by the valley of the Axius (*Vardar*), having apparently, in order to circumvent the foe, deviated somewhat from the beaten track and traversed some passes previously deemed inaccessible. Stobi and Heraclea (*Monastir*) in Macedonia, possibly even Larissa in Thessaly, fell before him, and yielded a rich booty to his followers. Theudemir, apprised of these brilliant successes of his son, quitted his camp at Naissus and moved forward with the main body of his troops to Thessalonica. That terrible push from Vienna to Salonica, which the diplomacy of our days is so busy with, alternately affirming and denying that Austria contemplates its accomplishment, was actually made, with brisk efficiency, by Theudemir and his son in the spring of 473.

The Patrician Hilarianus who commanded in Thessalonica, seeing the siege of that city commenced by the barbarians, a wall of circumvallation built, and every sign that they were likely to succeed, opened negotiations with Theudemir. Handsome presents were given to the barbarian chiefs, the old figment of a covenant (*foedus*) between the Empire and her brave Gothic allies was furbished up again; the latter promised to abstain from further ravage, and received in return fertile lands and a group of cities at the head of the Aegean, among which figure the well-known names of Pella, Methone, Pydna, and Berea, for their possession.

Shortly after these events Theudemir, the last of the three Amal brethren, died, and his eldest son Theodoric, now twenty years of age, whom he had designated as his heir in the presence of a general assembly of the Goths, succeeded to the sole kingship. By some change, the cause and the date of which are entirely hidden from us, the settlements of the nation were transferred from the head of the Aegean to the western shore of the Black Sea, where in the region now called the Dobrudscha, then known as the Roman province of Scythia, the native land of Alaric and Aetius, we find them settled in the year 478, when we next cross the path of Theodoric.

CHAPTER II.

THE REIGN OF ZENO.

We have now followed the fortunes of the young Ostrogoth down to the time when he settled as a Gothic *foederatus* in the home provinces of the Eastern Empire. In order to understand his subsequent career, and even in order rightly to appreciate the scanty notices of his future rival, Odovacar, as ruler of Italy, we must grasp the connection of events in that city which was now virtually the capital of the world, the New Rome beside the Thracian Bosporus; we must, at the cost of some little repetition, trace the outline of the reign of the Emperor Zeno.

This Emperor, as the reader may remember, bore at first the barbarous name and style of Tarasicodissa, the son of Rusumbladeotus, a name which he changed to Zeno, in memory of one of his countrymen who a generation previously had climbed up to greatness in the Roman State. He came from Isauria, that wild upland region on the northern skirts of Mount Taurus, between Cilicia and Phrygia, which Paul and Barnabas traversed in their missionary journey to Derbe and Lystra, but which the Roman legionary for three centuries after Christ found it difficult to penetrate and impossible to subdue. The part which this obscure mountainous corner of Asia Minor played in the politics of the Lower Empire is truly extraordinary. We shall find that Zeno and his Isaurian country-men were, for near twenty years, the dreaded and hated lords of Constantinople. They depart and disappear for a time, but, two centuries later, another Isaurian, the hero-emperor Leo III, ascends the throne, commences and all but carries through a mighty religious reformation (the Iconoclastic), and transmits his throne to a son whose reign with his own makes up a period of sixty years, the most glorious and the most successful in the whole later history of the Roman Empire. The peculiar position thus occupied by the Isaurians is no doubt explained by the fact that these tameless mountaineers had in great measure preserved their freedom. They had not passed, like the wealthier inhabitants of the plains, between the mill-stones of the Byzantine despotism. Their country was the Switzerland of the Eastern Empire.

From the ranks of the Isaurian adventurers who made their way to the capital the Emperor Leo, who needed all the support which he could obtain against the party of the domineering Aspar, selected Tarasicodissa, who was perhaps the best-born among them, and bestowed upon him in marriage his elder daughter Ariadne. At the death of Leo, his grandchild, the younger Leo, a child of seven years old, son of Zeno and Ariadne, already associated with his grandfather in the Empire and proclaimed consul for the year, succeeded without opposition to the throne. Naturally his reign would have implied for some years to come the regency of his parents; but, to make sure, Ariadne instructed her child, when his father came to make obeisance before him in the Hippodrome, to place on his head the imperial diadem. The precaution was a wise one, for in nine months the child-emperor died. The charge brought against Zeno by one writer, distant from the scene, of having procured the death of his own child, must be dismissed as unworthy of belief since none of the Greek writers, not even those who canvass his actions the most bitterly, have dared to insinuate it.

It cannot be said that the new Emperor did anything to justify his predecessor's selection of him as a son-in-law. He was quite incapable in the field, 'not only a coward but a wretch, an emperor who could not bear even the picture of a battle', says one of our authorities. This author proceeds to say that Zeno's only notion of conquest was by buying off his foes, for which purpose he laid upon his subordinates the duty of raising as much money as possible by exactions and confiscations. Another historian gives a somewhat different account of the cause of Zeno's financial misgovernment. He says that this Emperor was not so cruel, passionate, or avaricious as his predecessor, but that he was ambitious and vain, with no real knowledge of affairs nor formed habits of business. He was thus exposed to endless peculation on the part of the officials of his exchequer, and at the same time squandered with lavish hand the carefully-hoarded treasures of his father-in-law among his greedy Isaurian friends. This incapacity for business, again, made him dependent on his underlings, especially on one Sebastian, who was Praetorian Prefect during a large part of his reign, and who possessed an extraordinary influence over his master. Like the eunuch Eutropius, ninety years before, Sebastian put up offices and governments for sale as in a market, and suffered no business to be transacted in the palace upon which he did not levy his toll. Some part of the gain of this unblushing traffic he graciously shared with the Emperor, but if the latter had bestowed an office on one of his own friends, the favourite would insist on buying it at a small price from the recipient, that he might re-sell it at a high figure to one of the attenders of his auction-mart.

An Emperor thus governing, of discreditable private character and strengthened by no deep roots of ancestral claim to the loyalty of his subjects, was sure to find his right to rule challenged by usurpers; and in fact the history of the reign of Zeno is chiefly a history of the rebellions against him. The course of these rebellions is drearily similar. With a certain tenacity of purpose, which perhaps explains Leo's selection of him, Zeno generally succeeds in holding on to power. Some popular officer delivers him from the rival of the moment, and becomes for the time 'the man whom the king delighteth to honour'. Then he too falls under suspicion, the Emperor or Empress intrigues against his life; he is forced to make himself the mouthpiece of the popular discontent. Another rebellion and another deliverance by a champion who is doomed to experience the imperial ingratitude, and so the dismal round recommences. Add to the already enumerated causes of discontent the fires, never long smouldering in this reign, of religious bigotry, the incessant battle-cries, 'Nestorian,' 'Eutychian,' 'The Council of Chalcedon,' 'The Council of Nicaea'; add also the intrigues of Verina, the Emperor's mother-in-law, one of the most odious women who ever stepped inside the purple chamber at Constantinople, and the reader will have some idea of the events which formed the staple of the reign of Zeno.

The rebellion of Basiliscus was the first of the series. It was on the ninth day after his accession to the office of Consul, when Zeno was sitting in the Hippodrome presiding over the games, that he received a message from his mother-in-law desiring him to come to her with all speed. He obeyed, and when he reached her chamber, Verina informed him that the generals, the senate, the people, all were united in the resolution to depose him, and that his only safety was in flight. Without a struggle he appears to have given up the prize of empire, took with him his wife Ariadne and his mother Lallis, and such of the imperial treasures as he could pile upon his horses and mules, and stole away by night accompanied by many of his Isaurian fellow-countrymen. Still wearing the rich imperial robes in which he had presided in the

Hippodrome, he crossed the Bosporus to Chalcedon, and was soon in the heart of Asia Minor. Thus did Basiliscus, Verina's brother, find himself at length in possession of the diadem which he had coveted with an insane desire. He associated his son Marcus with him in the empire, and in their joint names issued edicts for the regulation of Church affairs. These edicts were to the utmost extent of his power in the interests of the Monophysite party, of which he, and still more his wife Zenonis, were fanatical adherents. Peter the Fuller was reinstated at Antioch, Timothy the Weasel at Alexandria. Everywhere the opponents of the decrees of Chalcedon began to take heart, and its adherents, except the dauntless Acacius of Constantinople, began to despond.

But Basiliscus, raised to the throne by female influence and intrigue, was threatened by dangers from the same source. Verina had a lover, Patricius, upon whom, rather than upon Basiliscus, she had hoped that the choice of the insurgents would have fallen, but who was put to death by the new emperor. Zenonis, who was a woman of great beauty, had also a lover, the nephew of her husband, the handsome and effeminate Harmatius. This man, who knew more about the palaestra and the hair-dresser's shop than about the art of war, was, by the influence of his paramour, promoted to the high office of Magister Militum in Thrace. He also shared the honours of the consulship with Basiliscus. Puffed up with wealth and official importance, he began to imagine himself a great soldier, and rode about the streets of the capital, aping in arms and accoutrements the great Achilles. The populace followed him with their acclamations, and called him the new Pyrrhus, in allusion to his fresh pink-coloured complexion. But many doubtless thought, what the historian could safely write, that the new hero was more like Paris than Pyrrhus.

Meanwhile the dethroned Emperor Zeno had betaken himself to his native Isauria, and there maintained a feeble resistance to his rival. In the course of his wanderings he came to a castle situated upon a hill, and enquired the name of this place of refuge. When told that it was called (by a curious chance) Constantinople, he gave a deep sigh and said, "Verily man is God's plaything. The prophets foretold that the month of July should see me lodged in Constantinople, and so indeed I am, in this little hill-side fort of a Constantinople, instead of in my royal city". Brighter days, however, were at hand for the fugitive as the second July of his exile drew near. Ulus and Trocundus, the generals of Basiliscus who had been for some time besieging him, perhaps in the mountain fortress just referred to, changed sides and openly espoused his cause. The money and the promises of Zeno had no doubt some share in producing this result; but they had some excuse for their defection in the fact that letters had been received from the Senate at Constantinople informing the generals that the profligacy and folly of Basiliscus had become absolutely unbearable, and inviting them to aid in his deposition. In fact, what with political discontent and what with theological strife, the capital was almost in a state of revolution. Acacius had draped the altar and the clergy in black. Daniel, the greatest of the Stylitae, had descended from his column to harangue and muster the people. A vast multitude of men, women, and children had assembled at the gates of the cathedral to protest against the heretical doings of the Emperor. There was a talk of burning down the city, from which Basiliscus withdrew in terror, but Daniel and the monk Olympius followed him to his retreat, and forced him to listen to their passionate invectives.

Liberated from his long blockade and strengthened by his new allies, Zeno now set forth for the capital. Basiliscus sent Harmatius to meet the foe, having first exacted from him, possibly on account of some rumours of his doubtful loyalty, an oath 'by his holy baptism' that he would not betray him. Harmatius took with him not only the troops which ordinarily followed the standard of the Magister Militum in Thrace, but also a levy, probably a hasty levy, from the citizens of Constantinople. This fact, together with the statement that a terrible massacre of Isaurians took place at the time of the expulsion of Zeno, seems to indicate that the animosity against the Asiatic highlanders was especially bitter among the mob of the capital.

However, neither his baptismal oath nor the rancour of his civic followers availed to keep Harmatius from entering into a transaction with the dethroned emperor, his willingness for which was doubtless increased by the consciousness of danger from the discovery of his intrigue with Zenonis. He advanced to Nicaea, where Zeno and the two generals were quartered. Great terror was at first caused in the Isaurian army by his approach. Zeno was on the point of retreating, but Illus undertook and accomplished the delicate task of detaching Harmatius from his fidelity to his uncle. The terms were high: the rank of Magister Militum Praesentalis (commander of the household troops, ranking above the other Magister Militum) for life, and the dignity of Caesar for his son Basiliscus, which assured to that son the succession to the empire on Zeno's death. The bargain being concluded, the two armies, now united, marched against Constantinople.

Basiliscus, when he heard that his rival accepted as lawful emperor by the senate, the people, and even by the arch-intriguer Verina, saw that the game was hopeless, and took refuge in the church of St. Sophia, to which he had betaken himself nine years before on the failure of the Carthaginian expedition. Leaving his crown on the holy table, as a sign that he renounced the sovereignty, he passed on with his wife and children into the baptistery, and there sought for shelter. Not even in the hour of her downfall can the ecclesiastical chroniclers forbear to triumph over the heretical Empress, thus compelled to seek the shelter of the Church whose power she had dared to cope with. The patriarch Acacius came and upbraided the fallen Emperor with the impious innovations which he, the Eutychian, had sought to introduce into the Christian Church. According to Procopius he actually delivered the suppliant into the hands of his rival; but this is so contrary to the character of the man and to the religious instincts of the age, that we may safely reject such a story. Doubtless Acacius was a powerful agent, probably the most powerful in the counter-revolution which hurled Basiliscus from his throne. Probably also he was the medium of the negotiations which resulted in the fugitive's surrender of himself to his rival; but this is a different matter from the accusation that with his own hands he delivered him over, a suppliant at the Church's altar, to his enemy.

"The most religious emperor Zeno", says the Paschal Chronicle, "then gave orders that the curtain should be drawn over the amphitheatre. He mounted to his seat, exhibited the games of the circus to the citizens, and received their acclamations. Then he sent to the Great Church, stripped all the emblems of imperial dignity from the fallen Emperor, his wife and children, and induced them to come forth by a promise that their heads should be safe. Zeno then sent him away and those with him to the camp of Limnae in Cappadocia. And they were thrust into one tower of the camp, and the gate was built up, and the tower and the camp itself were guarded by soldiers and by a great multitude of Isaurians. And thus Basiliscus himself and his wife and children, perishing by Hunger, gave up their lives and were buried in same tower of Limnae".

Procopius and some other historians say that the banishment was in the depth of winter, that the unhappy exiles were insufficiently supplied with clothing as well as food, and that cold worked together with hunger for their destruction. Thus was Dante's terrible story of Ugolino and his children in the *Torre del Fame* anticipated by eight hundred years. That deed of horror and of perfidy was perpetrated by an archbishop, this by an emperor, whom, in the very act of describing his wickedness, the chronicler terms 'most religious', because he was not tainted with the heresy either of Nestorius or of Eutyches.

Thus had Harmatius surrendered his uncle and his paramour to a death of horror. He had not long to wait for his reward, in either sense. He received the post of *Magister Praesentalis*, his son was proclaimed Caesar, had a royal seat prepared for him by the side of the Emperor, and joined in distributing the prizes to the charioteers. Soon, however, Zeno began to reflect that a man who had displayed so much perfidy to his kinsman and benefactor, and had violated his solemn baptismal oath, was not likely to serve him more faithfully, when his son, the young Caesar, should have grown to manhood. He argued with himself that he had kept all his promises to his deliverer. *Magister Praesentalis* he was now, and that for life, but he had said nothing as to how long he was to live. His son had been declared Caesar, and, having once worn the imperial purple, should now be dignified with an office in the Church. The Emperor therefore gave orders that 'Harmatius the perjurer' should be slain. It was evidently no judicial sentence that was passed, but an order for a private assassination that was given. An agent for the bloody deed was soon found. Onoulf, son of Edica and brother of king Odovacar, was still in the imperial service. He had received much kindness from Harmatius when he came a poor barbarian to the capital of the East. His patron had procured for him the dignity of Count, then that of Prefect of Illyricum, and had made him handsome presents of money to enable him to give the banquets which his rank rendered necessary. At Zeno's order Onoulf laid wait for his patron at a palace ten miles from Constantinople, and stabbed him in the back when he was mounting a spiral staircase to the Hippodrome. The fickle populace, who had forgotten the shouts of admiration with which, they once hailed the rubicund 'Pyrrhus', as be dashed in brilliant armour along the streets, now applauded his death; and remembering the cruel manner in which he, in conjunction with the Gothic foederati, had punished an insurrection in Thrace during the reign of Leo, cutting off the hands of the peasants who were accomplices therein, they now rejoiced with rapture that one so arrogant and so hard-hearted had at last met with his deserts. The young Basiliscus, son of Harmatius, after his brief dream of Caesarship, was installed as Lector in the church of Blachernae, and appears before his death to have reached the dignity of bishop of the important city of Cyzicus, the metropolis of the Hellespontine diocese.

The next revolt against Zeno was of a different kind, and one which illustrates the peculiar ideas about hereditary succession which were introducing themselves into the originally elective sovereignty of the Empire. These ideas had assumed a somewhat different shape since Pulcheria, sister of Theodosius II, had, by the bestowal of her hand, raised Marcian to the throne and thus familiarised the Romans with the idea of a hereditary right to the purple conveyed through females. The Marcian who now, by assuming the diadem, gave a rallying-point for all the unsubdued discontent with Zeno and his Isaurians, was, on his mother's side, grandson of that Emperor Marcian. He was also son of an Emperor—of that Anthemius sovereign of the West whom Sidonius saw riding through the streets of Rome side by side with Ricimer. Yet upon neither of these relationships did he found his pretensions to the throne. He had married Leontia, the youngest daughter of the Emperor Leo, and set up the claim so often heard of in Eastern, and sometimes in Western, monarchies, that his wife, as being *Porphyrogenita*, born after her father had attained to supreme power, was of higher dignity than her elder sister Ariadne, born while Leo was still a private person serving in the household of Aspar. Marcian raised troops and attacked the palace of his brother-in-law. A bloody battle took place; the two brothers of Marcian, Procopius and Romulus, brought up supports at a seasonable moment; the palace and the diadem were almost won. But, inheriting the slack and indolent disposition of his father, Marcian betook himself to the banquet and the couch, let slip the golden opportunity, and adjourned till the morrow the victory which never came. For during the night Illus, the general of Zeno, who was now holding the high rank of *Magister Officiorum*, brought a large number of Isaurians across the straits from Chalcedon in market boats, the regular transports having been seized by the rebels. He also practised with his bribes so successfully on the fidelity of the insurgent troops, that, when morning dawned, Marcian found himself forsaken by most of his followers, and far from capturing the palace was forced himself to flee to the Church of the Apostles. Hence he was dragged away, and sent, like all the enemies of Zeno, into captivity in the recesses of Asia Minor. He became a monk; he escaped; he attempted another abortive insurrection. Hereupon, if not after his first downfall, he was ordained a presbyter; and henceforth Marcian, with his wife Leontia, who had escaped to the convent of 'The Sleepless Ones' disappears from history. It is clear that Zeno recognised, in the feeble character of his brother-in-law, less danger to his throne than from other claimants of less noble birth. Procopius and Romulus, the brothers of Marcian, were caught in Constantinople while bathing in the baths of Zeuxippus. They escaped, however, from their captivity, fled to the camp of the Gothic general, who, as we shall find in the next chapter, steadfastly refused to surrender them to their enemies, and finally made their way to Rome, where these sons and grandsons of emperors disappear into the undistinguishable crowd.

The last of the insurgents against the authority of Zeno was also the best and the noblest of his foes, countryman Illus the Isaurian. Sent with his brother Trocundus by Basiliscus to conduct the campaign in the Asiatic highlands against the fugitive Emperor, he had, as we have already seen, not only gone over himself to Zeno's side, but had been the broker through whose mediation the similar defection of Harmatius and the consequent ruin of the cause of Basiliscus had been secured. Such important services should have earned the life-long gratitude of the restored Emperor; but for some reason the ladies of the imperial family pursued him with unrelenting hatred. Three times was his life in danger through their machinations. Before a year had elapsed from Zeno's return, Paulus, a slave in the imperial household, was detected, sword in hand, watching for a favourable moment to slay the general. The Emperor abandoned the slave to the just resentment of Illus, upon whom next year was bestowed the dignity of Consul. While he was busied with the restoration of the Royal Porch, a magnificent work probably, which was to have commemorated his year of office, another assassin, this time a barbarian of Alan race, was found in his apartments, again with a naked sword in his hand. The murderer, being put to the torture, confessed that Epinicus the Phrygian, who, by the favour of the Empress-mother, had risen from an obscure position to the successive dignities of *Comes Privatarum Rerum, Comes Sacrarum Largitionum,* and *Praefectus Praetorio*, had hired him for the bloody deed. Again was a victim sacrificed to propitiate the anger of Illus. The Praetorian Prefect, stripped of all his honours and wealth, was handed over to the man whose death he had compassed, but who generously spared his life, and was satisfied with banishing him to his own native Isauria. Visiting him there not long after, Illus learned from the ex-prefect's lips that he in turn had been stimulated to the deed of blood by the arch-intriguer, the Empress-mother, Verina.

For the time Illus held his peace, and remained in honourable and self-sought exile from the court. Before long, however, he was recalled by his master, who, with all the ranks of the military and civil hierarchy, crossed the Bosporus and came more than six miles along the road from Chalcedon to welcome the returning general. Immediately, perhaps before he would even enter the capital, Illus disclosed to the Emperor the intrigues of Verina against his life, and declared that he could never be in safety so long as that woman remained in Constantinople. Zeno, who knew that he too was never safe from the conspiracies of his mother-in-law, abandoned her without reluctance to his general. She was sent off under the care of the brother-in-law of Illus with a large retinue to Isauria, compelled to take the veil in the cathedral of Tarsus, and then shut up in the fortress of Dalisandus. Epinicus, in return for his information, was, at the request of Illus, received again into the imperial favour, perhaps restored to his old office.

Among the followers of Illus who accompanied him into the capital on that day of his triumph none probably attracted more attention than the Egyptian grammarian, poet, and philosopher, Pamprepius. Rich gifts of intellect were hidden under the unprepossessing countenance of this dark Egyptian, who was possibly a full-blooded negro. His poetical attainments in his native country (perhaps acquired in emulation of his compatriot Claudian) were rewarded by the chair of Grammar in the University of Athens. Here too he studied philosophy under the mighty mystic, Proclus, the last and some say the greatest, of the Neo-Platonists; and, in the judgment of all Athens, Pamprepius ranked pre-eminently the first among the great master's pupils. Having left Athens in consequence of an insult received from one of the local magistracy, who was himself a dilettante philosopher, Pamprepius came to Byzantium and attached himself to the fortunes of Illus, which he powerfully influenced both for good and for evil. There was certainly a strain of nobility in the character of the patron. "Illus", says his fellow countryman Candidus, "conferred many benefits on the Roman state, by his brave deeds in war and by his generosity and righteous dealing in the city". There was also a vein of literary pursuit in him, such as we should by no means have looked for in an Isaurian highlander. When first introduced to the general, Pamprepius recited, with much grace of delivery, a long-meditated discourse, probably in the Platonic or Proclean style, on the nature of the soul. Illus was charmed with what he heard, proclaimed the swarthy Egyptian wisest of all the professors in Constantinople, and arranged that he should be engaged at a large salary, paid by the State, to teach the choicest spirits among the young men who resorted to the 'Museums', or, as we should call them, the colleges, of the capital. At the time when we behold him about to re-cross the Bosphorus in the train of his triumphant patron, Pamprepius has reached a higher elevation. He is now Quaestor, belongs therefore to the awful innermost circle of the Illustres, endorses the petitions of the subjects, directs them to the proper office which has to take them into consideration, and prepares the stilted sentences in which Tarasicodissa-Zeno may clothe his meagre thoughts when replying to supplications or promulgating laws.

But there was a worm at the root of this amazing heathen, good fortune of the Egyptian, although for the present all went well with him. Like his master Proclus, he was a *Greek*, or, as we should call it, a heathen in his creed; and made no secret of his Hellenic faith, even in Christian Constantinople itself. The avowed heathenism drew after it the imputation of darker practices, and of a knowledge of the future obtained by unhallowed arts, an imputation to which the windy theosophy of the Neo-Platonist not unnaturally exposed him, and which Pamprepius himself, by mysterious and enigmatical utterances, which could be claimed as prophecies if they turned out true, seems to have intentionally fostered. It would be going too far to attribute either to Illus or his client an attempt at the hopeless task of the restoration of heathenism: but it is probable that the general as well as the philosopher may have shown a deeper interest in the Dialogues of Plato than in the endless theological squabbles of Timothy the Weasel and Timothy Solofaciolus, and that his popularity with the mob of Constantinople may have suffered accordingly.

The insurrection of Marcian, which followed shortly after these events, was partly caused, according to the representations of the rebels, by the harsh treatment of the widow of Leo. Certainly Illus was bound to keep his master harmless from the consequences of a severity which he had himself insisted upon : yet he seems to have wavered for a moment. In his perplexity he turned to the dark Egyptian for counsel. The voice of Pamprepius was in favour of loyalty, and presaged the victory of Zeno. "Providence is on our side", he said oracularly; and when, notwithstanding the first successes of Marcian, his standard was eventually lowered, men looked with yet heightened reverence on the prophetic powers of the Neo-Platonist professor.

To Zeno's triumph on this occasion the valour and the skill of Illus, as we have seen, largely contributed. But if the Emperor prized his services, the Empress could not forget her mother's wrongs. Ariadne on this occasion belied the fair and honourable character which, as far as we can judge, she generally bore in a dark and troublous time. When the Master of the Offices (for this was the dignity now held by Illus) was mounting the stairs to view the races in the Hippodrome, a life-guards-man named Spanicius, hired by Ariadne for the purpose, drew his sword and endeavoured to cut off his head. The armour-bearer of Illus interposed and struck up the assassin's hand, but the escape was so narrow that the right ear of the intended victim was actually severed, and he ever after wore a skull-cap when he appeared in public.

It was vain to ask this time for the surrender of the instigator of the crime, and probably from henceforward it was only a question of time how soon Illus should revolt. But, according to our chief authority, the Emperor began the quarrel by insisting on the liberation of his brother Longinus. This person, whose previous history is almost hopelessly obscure, had been for ten years kept a close prisoner by Illus at a castle in Isauria. So strange a predicament for the brother of a reigning Emperor is perhaps explained by the private character of Longinus, which was detestably immoral. He may have inflicted on the general some wrong which in one less powerfully protected would have called for the punishment of death, a punishment which even in his case could be commuted for nothing less than life-long imprisonment. It would seem, however, that the Emperor's request was granted, and that both Longinus and the mother of Zeno arrived in Constantinople, having been voluntarily released by Illus.

The Emperor next proceeded to strip Illus of his military command, which he bestowed on one of the barbarian *foederati*, John the Goth. He then made a harangue to the people of Constantinople—there are some indications that Zeno was vain of his oratorical powers—setting forth his grievances against Illus, and ordering that all his relations and dependents should be banished from Constantinople. The possessions of these men the Emperor, ever thinking of his highland home, distributed among the cities of Isauria.

Illus, thus driven to open revolt, withdrew into his native Taurus-country and endeavoured to strengthen himself by alliances. The kings of Armenia and Persia promised help if he would effect a junction of his forces with theirs. Odovacar, 'the tyrant of Western Rome' was also appealed to, but for the present declined to join the confederacy, though two years later he showed symptoms, or Zeno thought that he showed symptoms, of a willingness to favour the cause of Illus. The insurgent general seems to have at first proclaimed Marcian Emperor, but the attempt to conjure with this name proving fruitless, he next sought out his former persecutor Verina in her exile. Their common hostility to Zeno brought these two old antagonists together. Verina, arrayed in imperial robes, was announced as the lawful disposer of the diadem, and mounting a high platform, in the presence doubtless of the assembled army, proceeded to invest with the insignia of empire a certain citizen of Dalisandus of obscure parentage, named Leontius, whom Illus had selected for the dangerous honour. Leontius nominated the high officers of the household and the state, distributed money to the people, and established his court at Antioch, which had not, apparently, been the residence of an Augustus since the days of Valens.

Zeno, whose position was somewhat insecure, Tmade for himself strange alliances with ecclesiastics and barbarians. He persuaded his fellow-countryman Conon, bishop of Apamea in Syria, to leave his episcopal throne and don the armour of a legionary. At the same time he bestowed the chief command in Isauria on Linges, the bastard brother of Conon, a man of high courage, and probably of great local influence. Of the share which the Goths under Theodoric and the wild Rugians from beyond the Danube took in this war as soldiers of Zeno it will be convenient to speak in the following chapter. After Leontius for little more than two months had possessed the semblance of sovereignty his fortunes began to decline. Illus, who had been worsted in the field, sent his wife, and provisions for a siege, to the fortress of Cherreus. These precautions, and the messages he sent to Leontius and Verina to quit Antioch and come to him with all speed, produced a discouraging effect on his army. The officers dispersed to seek shelter in friendly fortresses, while many of the more obscure abettors of the rebellion took refuge in the caves with which that part of Asia Minor abounds.

The castle of Cherreus also bore the name of its builder Papirius, apparently a kind of robber chieftain who had occupied it as a feudal baron occupied his turrets by the Rhine, in order to levy toll on passers-by and to keep his rustic neighbours in terrified subjection. Papirius was apparently now dead, but his son Indacus, a man of great courage and physical strength, who fought with his left hand and as a runner outstripped the fleetest horsemen, still held the castle and was faithful to the cause of Ulus. Here had Marcian been imprisoned, and here Verina. Hither did the empress-mother now return, a fugitive though no longer a captive. The fatigues and anxieties of the last few months had been too much for her strength, and on the ninth day after she reached the castle her turbulent and intriguing life came to an end. She was embalmed and placed in a leaden coffin, with the hope doubtless that one day a tomb befitting her dignity might he found for her beside the Bosporus. After thirty days died Marsus, a faithful friend of Illus, and he by whose intervention Pamprepius was first introduced to him. The castle was strong and provisioned for a long siege, and Illus, after entrusting the details of the daily defence to Indacus, shut himself up in his library and devoted his now abundant leisure to the study of his beloved manuscripts. Leontius took the turn in his fortunes less philosophically. He macerated himself with fastings, and passed his days in unmanly lamentations.

After the siege had lasted two years, the hopes of Illus and Leontius growing ever fainter, the besiegers, under the command of John the Goth, obtained possession of a fort on an opposite hill which in some degree commanded the castle, and plied their engines with great effect. The besieged called for a parley, and by the mediation of the Goth sent to the Emperor at Constantinople a letter reminding him of their past services and praying for forgiveness. The appeal, however, was ineffectual, and the siege dragged on for two years longer. At length, at the end of four years, A.D. 488, treachery accomplished what fair fighting could not achieve. The wife of Trocundus, the brother of Illus, privately communicated to the Emperor her willingness to betray her relative. She was sent for this purpose from Constantinople, probably with a delusive offer of pardon, entered the fortress, and succeeded in opening its gates to the imperial troops. Illus and Leontius were slain, and their heads were cut off and sent to the Emperor. Pamprepius was slain with them. All through the four years of siege he had fed his associates with hopes of ultimate triumph; and it is said that when they found that his prophecies were about to turn out false they themselves in their disappointment cut him to pieces. The authorities for this story are not of the highest class. One would gladly disbelieve a history so inconsistent with the character of the brave philosopher-soldier Illus.

No further rebellion disturbed the reign of Zeno. His brother, the shameless profligate Longinus, was now all-powerful. Master of the Offices in 484, Consul in 486 and again in 490, he was the head of the Isaurian faction in the capital, and doubtless intended to wear the diadem after his brother. The health of the Emperor was now visibly declining, and he was filled with a restless desire to know how it would fare with his family and his beloved Isaurians after his death. With this view he consulted Maurianus the Count, "a very learned man, who was acquainted with certain mystic rites and had predicted many future events", and asked to be informed of the name of his successor on the throne. The answer was ambiguous : "Your successors shall be your wife and one who has served as Silentiarius"—that title being given to the guard of honour, thirty in number, who watched in the purple chamber. On hearing this Zeno at once ordered the arrest of a certain Pelagius, formerly a Silentiarius but now a Patrician, and an eminent statesman, who seemed to him the most likely person to be thus indicated. Moreover, Pelagius, who was a man of high character and some literary fame (he had written in verse a history of the Empire from the time of Augustus), had dared to rebuke the misgovernment of Zeno and to oppose earnestly his project of declaring his fatuous brother Caesar. His property was ordered to be confiscated, and soon after he was strangled by his gaolers. When the Praetorian Prefect Arcadius heard of this act of iniquity he rebuked Zeno for it with a freedom worthy of better times. Upon this the Emperor ordered Arcadius also to be killed the first time that he should set foot within the palace, but the Prefect, receiving a hint of his danger, 'turned aside as if casually to pray in the Great Church [St. Sophia], claimed the right of asylum there, and so escaped bitter death.'

Next year (April 9, 491) the life of the wretched and suspicious tyrant was ended by an epileptic seizure. Longinus claimed the throne; but now the long-suppressed indignation of the citizens broke forth; civil war raged, and the Isaurians, who had for years contemplated this event and devised their plan of action, set the city on fire with long poles prepared for the purpose, tipped with flax and sulphur. A considerable part of the city and the Circus was burnt, but at length order was restored and the Isaurian faction owned themselves vanquished. Longinus was sent back to his native land, and many of the Isaurians accompanied him at their own request, doubtless because their lives were imperilled by the fury of the mob.

The prophecy of Count Maurianus came true. The Empress Ariadne was requested to bestow the diadem where she would, and she bestowed it, and her hand, on Anastasius, a native of Dyrrhachium, past the prime of life, not yet even a senator, but one of the *schola* of Silentiarii. With the events of his reign of twenty-seven years, which on the whole fully justified the choice of Ariadne, we have no present concern, but it will be well briefly to follow the fortunes of the Isaurian *émigrés* before we return to the history of Theodoric. When the exiles trooped back to their rough Asiatic homes, it may be imagined that they returned in no good-humour with the new ruler of the East. Soon they were in open insurrection, Conon the militant bishop again taking up arms on behalf of his countrymen; and it is probable, though not distinctly stated, that they proclaimed Longinus Emperor. Not he, however, but a certain Athenodorus, seems to have taken the command in the war with Constantinople which broke out next year, and which lasted till the end of 497. It remained but a local affair, for the insurgents apparently never pushed their incursions further than into Phrygia; but the Emperor, who had confided the conduct of the war to two generals of the same name, John the Goth and John the Hunchback, was accused by his critics of feebleness and faint-heartedness in its prosecution. After five years of it he grew weary, and secretly confided to Euphemius, Patriarch of Constantinople, that he would gladly see it at an end. As the Isaurians, with all their savageness, were orthodox Chalcedonian Christians, and Anastasius was not, Euphemius leaned somewhat towards the side of the rebels, and most improperly repeated what had been said to him to yet another John, the Patrician, father-in-law of the insurgent general Athenodorus. The Patrician hastened to Anastasius, expecting to be made the instrument of a negotiation, but found the Emperor, instead thereof, highly indignant at this betrayal of his confidence. Next year (498), prosecuting the war in a bolder and more imperial way, he obtained a complete victory over his enemies. Athenodorus and Longinus were taken prisoners and beheaded. Their heads, sent by John the Goth to Constantinople, were fixed high on poles and exhibited at Sycae opposite the city, "a sweet sight to the Byzantines", says a historian, "in return for the evils which they had endured from Zeno and the Isaurians". When the overthrow of the rebel cause was certain, Anastasius sent his Master of the Offices to the Patriarch with the insulting message, "Your prayers, O great man! have covered your friends with soot."

The remembrance of this Isaurian rebellion was maintained by a tribute called 'Isaurica', which was thenceforward collected (probably from the malcontent province) for the imperial treasury; and we are told that from this tax, amounting to £200,000 annually, were paid the subsidies to the barbarian foederati.

In the sketch which has been given of the reign of Zeno, its political aspect only has been dwelt upon. Its place in the development of religious doctrine must be alluded to, however briefly, for, as Gibbon truly remarks, "it is in ecclesiastical story that Zeno appears least contemptible". Throughout his reign the Emperor was a steady supporter of orthodoxy, and the patriarchs of Constantinople, who were thorns in the side of a Basiliscus and an Anastasius, served him as faithfully and as steadily as his own Isaurians. There was a great deal, however, of sheer misunderstanding of the Council of Chalcedon and much personal rancour against it in some of the Eastern dioceses, especially in Egypt and Syria. Acacius, patriarch of Constantinople, a man of great gifts and much force of character, induced the Emperor to attempt to remove these misunderstandings and to soften this rancour, by the issue of his celebrated *Henoticon*, or Letter of Union, a document which was of course drawn up by Acacius bimself. In this instrument the *Via Media* of Catholic orthodoxy, as distinct, on the one hand from the Nestorian doctrine that Christ's human nature was a mere robe worn by the Eternal Son, and on the other, from the Monophysite doctrine that the Godhead was weary, suffered, and died, was reaffirmed in terms which appear to the lay mind undistinguishable from the decrees of Chalcedon. A formal adhesion to the utterances of that Council was, however, not insisted upon, and, with some lack of candour, the one allusion to Chalcedon which was introduced was couched in purposely disrespectful terms.

Such was the tenour of the Henoticon of Zeno, a document which has met with but scant favour from ecclesiastical historians. Yet the object which it proposed to itself, the closing of a barren and profitless controversy, was one earnestly to be desired in the interests of a living faith. The mere statesman could not be blind to the fact that this Monophysite logomachy (which in fact paved the way for the conquests of Mohammed) was rending the Eastern Empire in pieces. And from the point of view of a Byzantine official, there was nothing monstrous in the idea of the Augustus preparing a symbol of religious belief for all his subjects, though no doubt, as a matter of ecclesiastical order, that symbol should have been submitted for discussion to a council of bishops. However, issued as it was on the sole authority of the Emperor, it all but succeeded in its object. Alexandria, Jerusalem, Antioch accepted it; and thus the four great patriarchates of the East, after the discords of forty years, were again united in apparent harmony. There was but one exception, but that was world-important. The Pope of Rome, now but a precarious subject of the Eastern Caesar, unwilling to acquiesce in any further exaltation of the Patriarch of Constantinople, and determined above all things that the decrees of Chalcedon, those trophies of the victory of the mighty Leo, should not merely mould but should be recognised as moulding the faith of the whole Christian world, refused to accept the Henoticon of Zeno, and soon began to clamour for its withdrawal. It will be necessary hereafter to sketch the outlines of the controversy thence ensuing, a controversy in which it is impossible to believe that either party saw any principle at stake other than the sublime principle of self-assertion, the sacred duty of choosing the chief seats in the synagogues and the uppermost places at feasts.

But whatever its motives, this controversy led to a schism between the two great sees of Eastern and Western Christendom, a schism which lasted thirty-five years, which had important results on the earlier fortunes of the Ostrogothic monarchy in Italy, and which undoubtedly prepared the way for the more enduring schisms of later years. The Henoticon of Zeno, which was meant to reconcile the Churches by the Bosporus and the Nile, laid the first courses of the wall of separation which now parts St. Petersburg from the Vatican.

CHAPTER III.

THE TWO THEODORICS IN THRACE.

SUCH as has been described in the last chapter was the wild welter of sedition, intrigue, religious rancour, military insubordination, imperial tyranny in which the young Ostrogoth was to spend the fourteen years following the death of his father and his own elevation to sole kingship over his people. What were his own aims? Confused and uncertain enough, doubtless; but they gradually grew clearer, and the clearer they became the more they drew him away from Byzantium. What did he require? First and foremost food for his people, who were suffering, as all the world was suffering, from that movement of the nations in which they had borne so large a share; who had wandered from the Middle Danube to the Balkans, and had not yet found an unravaged land where they could dwell in plenty. For himself, he wanted, sometimes, a great place in the Roman official hierarchy, in the midst of that *civilitas* which, in his ten years of hostage-ship, he had learned to love so well. To be saluted as Illustris; to command the sumptuously clothed 'silentiaries' in the imperial palace; himself to wear the *laticlave* and take his seat in that most venerable assembly in the world, the Roman Senate; to stand beside Augustus when ambassadors from the ends of the earth came to prostrate themselves before him,—this was what seemed sometimes supremely to be desired. But then, again, there were times when he felt that the love and loyalty of his own yellow-haired barbarians were worth all the pomp and flatteries of the purple presence-chamber. He was himself by birth a king, ruler of a dwindled people, it was true, but still a king; an Amal sprung from the seed of gods, and with the blood of countless generations of kings coursing in his veins. Was such an one to wait obsequiously outside the purple veil; to deem it a high honour—when the voice of the sensual poltroon who might happen to be the Augustus of the hour, and whom some woman's favour had raised from nothingness to the diadem, called him into ' thesacred presence'? No : the King of the Goths was greater than any Illustris of Byzantium. And yet how could he keep his kingship, how sway this mass of brave but stolid souls whose only trade was fighting, without putting himself at enmity with the Empire which, after all, he loved?

The perplexities of his position were not lessened by the fact that he was not the undisputed representative even of the Gothic nation in the eyes of the Eastern Romans. Over against him, the Amal king, stood another Theodoric the Goth, his senior in age, his inferior by birth, brought forward into notice by his connection with other barbarian chiefs, once all-powerful at court, and regarded probably by the Byzantine statesmen as the foremost 'Scythian' in their land. This was Theodoric the before-mentioned son of Triarius, surnamed Strabo (the Squinter), nephew of the wife of the great Aspar, distantly connected by blood with the Ostrogothic king, but not belonging to the Amal line. These two Theodorics cross and recross one another's paths like Una and Duessa in the 'Faery Queen'. By the Greek historians the older chieftain is generally spoken of as 'Theuderichus' simply, while the more nobly born is invariably called 'the son of Walamir.' This mistake, for such it must certainly have been, since the family historian asserts him to have been the son of Theudemir, was probably due to the circumstances of his first introduction to the Byzantine Court. Walamir being then king of the Goths, this child, which was brought as a pledge of his fidelity, was known as the son of Walamir; and, that title once given to him, the courtiers of Leo and Zeno were too supercilious or too careless to change it. With his own name and his father's name thus denied to him, and wavering, as he sometimes felt his own soul to waver, between the gorgeous bondage of the one career and the uncultured freedom of the other, he may well have sometimes doubted of his own identity. In order that we may be under no such confusion between the two leaders of the Goths, it will be well to drop the name which is common to both of them, for a while, and to call Theodoric son of Theudemir 'the Amal' and Theodoric Strabo 'the son of Triarius.'

Our first undoubted information as to the son of Triarius belongs to the latter years of the Emperor Leo. We may infer that ever since the fall of his great kinsman Aspar he had assumed, with his barbarians, an attitude of sullen opposition or of active hostility to the Empire. At length it became necessary to send an embassy to ascertain what terms would purchase his friendship. For this mission Leo selected Pelagius the Silentiary, the same officer, doubtless, who seventeen years later was foully murdered by the dying Zeno. The son of Triarius received Pelagius courteously, and sent a return embassy to Constantinople, expressing his willingness to live in friendship with the Romans, but claiming the concession of three points,—that the whole of Aspar's inheritance should be made over to him, that he should succeed to all his military commands, and that his people should have settlements assigned them in Thrace. Only the confirmation of the nephew in the military rank of his uncle was Leo willing to concede, and accordingly the war went forward. The son of Triarius divided his forces, and attacked both Philippi and Arcadiopolis. Against the first city he achieved no considerable success, but he pressed the blockade of the second so closely that the inhabitants, after feeding on horseflesh, and even on the corpses of their fellow-citizens, were compelled to surrender. Meanwhile, however, the Goths themselves were suffering all the miseries of famine. Food, not empire, was probably the prize for which many of these campaigns were planned.

And thus the high contracting parties came to an agreement, the terms being that the son of Triarius was to receive the highly honourable post of *Magister Equitum et Peditum Praesentalis*, and faithfully to serve the Emperor Leo against all his enemies, the Vandals only excepted; to receive for himself and followers a yearly subsidy of 2000 lbs. of gold, and further to be recognised as king of the Goths, while the Emperor bound himself not to harbour any rebels against the new king's authority. This last clause possibly points to some growing tendency on the part of the Triarian Goths to enlist under the banners of his better-born rival, the true Amal king. It has been well remarked that this proposal to accept a patent of *Gothic* royalty from the Roman Augustus distinctly indicates inferior ancestry, an absence of true royal descent on the part of the son of Triarius. With the kingship of Alaric, of Walamir, and of the young Theodoric, Roman emperors had had no concern. It was no doubt tacitly assumed that the Goths would find settlements in Thrace, and in consideration of their yearly subsidy would abstain from promiscuous raids upon their neighbours.

The death of Leo and the proclamation of Zeno brought about a change in the attitude of the son of Triarius towards the Empire. The opposition was probably sharper between the Gothic party once headed by Aspar, and the Isaurians, than between any other two factions; and the son of Triarius may have speculated on the elevation of Basiliscus rather than Zeno to the vacant throne. At any rate he now threw off the mask, divested himself, we must suppose, of his dignity as Commander of the Household Troops, and advanced in a threatening attitude to the long wall which defended the Thracian Chersonese. Against him Zeno sent some troops under the command of Heraclius, son of Floras, a brave general, but harsh, unpopular, and destitute of forethought. In his over-confidence he stumbled apparently into some trap prepared for him by the barbarians, was defeated, and taken prisoner. The Emperor sent an embassy to the son of Triarius to arrange for the liberation of his general, whose ransom was fixed at 100 talents (£20,000). This sum, with delicate consideration for the feelings of the captive, Zeno ordered to be paid by the near relations of Heraclius, saying that if any one else (himself for instance) found the money, it would seem as if the great Heraclius was being bought and sold like a slave.

The money was paid to the Goths, and an escort of barbarians was told off to escort him to the friendly shelter of Arcadiopolis. On the march, while Heraclius, who seems not to have been allowed the dignity of a horse, was walking along the road, one of the Goths smote him roughly on the shoulder. An attendant of the general returned the blow, and said, "Fellow I remember what you are. Do you not know who it is that you have struck?". "I know him quite well", was the reply, "and I know that he is going to perish miserably by my hand". With that, he and his companions drew their swords, and one cut off the head of Heraclius, another his hands. What became of the ransom we are not told. The story is not creditable to the good faith or the humanity of the barbarians; but it was stated in explanation, though not in justification of the deed, that Heraclius had once ordered some soldiers serving under him, who had committed a trifling military offence, to be thrown into a dry well, and had then compelled their comrades to bury them under a shower of stones. It was the memory of this cruel deed which now cost him his life.

Instead of Heraclius, Illus was sent to prosecute the war against the Gothic mutineers : but soon the face of affairs was changed by the success of the conspiracy in favour of Basiliscus, which was in fact hatched at the head-quarters of Illus. Zeno was now a fugitive, Basiliscus was draped in the purple, and the son of Triarius resumed his place in the Court of Byzantium. He was, however, indignant at finding himself, the veteran and the representative of the great Aspar, constantly postponed to the young dandy Harmatius, "a man who seemed to think about nothing but the dressing of his hair and other adornments of his person". Possibly this jealousy made him somewhat slack in upholding the tottering fortunes of Basiliscus. His namesake the Amal, on the other hand, cooperated zealously with Illus and the other generals in bringing about the return of Zeno, who contrived to send messengers to him at his quarters at Novi asking for help. A panegyrist of the great Theodoric in his later years ascribed to him the sole glory of restoring the fugitive and helpless Emperor to his throne; but this no doubt is the exaggeration of a courtier.

The upshot of the whole matter is that in the year 478 we find the son of Triarius again outside the pale of the commonwealth, wandering probably up and down the passes of the Balkan, in a state of chronic hostility to the Empire, while his rival, the young Amal king, holds the dignities of Patrician and *Magister Utriusque Militiae,* dignities usually reserved for much older men, and is, by some process in which Roman and barbarian ideas must have been strangely blended, adopted as the Emperor's son-in-arms. It is, however, a curious commentary on the double and doubtful position of the young Ostrogoth, that his duties as Magister Utriusque Militiae do not appear to have prevented him from continuing to reside with his people, in the Province of Scythia by the mouth of the Danube.

Soon after the restoration of Zeno to the throne, an embassy came to Constantinople from the Goths in Thrace allied with the Empire whom the Romans call *foederati*, and who were evidently the bands under the command of the son of Triarius. This description, which we owe to the accurate pen of Malchus, is interesting as showing that the term *foederati* was still employed, that these wandering hordes, formidable as they were to the peaceful husbandman, were still nominally the allies of Rome. Nay, the word carries us back a hundred years to the time when Theodosius enlisted the disheartened fragments of the Gothic nation under his eagles, and perhaps permits us to in the son of Triarius the natural successor of the Ostrogothic chiefs, Alatheus and Saphrax.

The request preferred by this embassy was that the Emperor would be pleased to be reconciled with *their* Theodoric, who wished for nothing better favour than to lead a quiet and peaceable life, and refrain from vexing the republic with his arms. On the other hand, they begged the Emperor to consider what harm Theodoric the Amal had done to the State, and how many cities he had destroyed when he too was in opposition. Let Zeno bury old grudges in the grave of Basiliscus, and only consider which cause was really most for the advantage of the Roman world.

On receiving this message the Emperor convoked a meeting of the Senate and desired the advice of that body as to his reply. The Senators answered that it was out of the question to think of taking both the Theodorics into his pay, inasmuch as the revenues, even now, scarcely sufficed to supply the regular soldiers with their rations. Which of the two the Emperor would select to honour with his friendship, was a matter for and with Augustus himself to decide. He then called in to the palace all the common soldiers a who were in the city and all the *scholae* (regiments of household troops); mounted the platform (*suggestum*), from which a Roman imperator was accustomed to harangue his men; and delivered a long oration of invective against the son of Triarius. "This man has always been the enemy of the Roman name. He has wandered, ravaging, through the plains of Thrace. He has joined in the cruel deeds of Harmatius, cutting off, like him, the hands of his captives, and has frightened all the agricultural population from their homes. He exercised a disastrous influence on the commonwealth in the affair of Basiliscus, and persuaded that usurper to make away with his Roman troops, on the plea that the Goths would suffice for his defence. And now he sends an embassy, nominally to sue for peace, but really to demand the office of Magister. If you therefore have any opinion on these matters, utter it boldly, for, indeed, for this purpose have I summoned you into the palace, knowing that that emperor is likely to succeed who calls his brave soldiers into his counsels". The soldiers, seeing which way their advice was asked for, all shouted for war with the son of Triarius; and, after a short interval of hesitation, a defiant answer was returned to his ambassadors. Zeno's resentment against him was further increased by the fact of the discovery of the secret practices of three of the Gothic chief's adherents in the city. These men (one of whom was 'Anthemius the physician') had not only written letters to him themselves, but had forged others (if in truth they were forgeries) from men holding high office in the State, bidding the son of Triarius be of good heart since he had many well-wishers in the city. The three traitors were punished with stripes and exile, the sentence of death being commuted at the express request of the Emperor.

War then, open war, was declared by Zeno on the Gothic *foederati*. It seems, however, soon to have suggested itself to the Emperor, that *his* Theodoric was every day growing weaker, while the son of Triarius was accumulating a larger and larger army; and he accordingly determined, if it were possible, to make peace with the latter on reasonable conditions. He sent therefore to offer him his own previous terms, restoration of his private property (including probably the estates of Aspar), a life unmolesting and unmolested, and the surrender of his son as a hostage for the fulfilment of this compact. But the books of the Sibyl were not now for sale at the same price as before. The son of Triarius refused to consent to these terms. He would not send his son as a hostage, nor could he (so he said), now that he had collected so vast a force, live upon the estates which, carefully husbanded, might have sufficed for his previous wants. No! He would keep his men about him, till some great success, or some great catastrophe, had decided the quarrel between him and Zeno.

The Emperor therefore had no resource but to prosecute the war with vigour. The dioceses of Pontus, Asia, and the East (representing the whole of Asia Minor and Syria) were emptied of their legions, which came flocking to Constantinople. Waggons were procured for the transport of arms, draught oxen were bought, corn and all other necessaries for a campaign were laid up in store, and the great Illus himself was expected to take the command.

For some reason or other, not Illus, but his brother-in-law Martinianus, a much weaker man, was named general. As the imperial army, consisting probably of a number of discordant elements without cohesion or mutual reliance, was rapidly becoming disorganized under the nominal command of this man, Zeno determined to accelerate matters by urging the Amal into action. He sent him a pressing message, urging him to do some deed against the son of Triarius, which might show that he was not unworthily styled Magister of the Roman army. Theodoric however, who was no doubt aware of the recent attempt to resume negotiations with his rival, refused to stir until the Emperor and Senate had both bound themselves by a solemn oath to make no treaty with the son of Triarius. He then arranged a plan of campaign, which involved a march with all his forces from Marcianople (Shumla) to the Gates of the Balkan. There he was to be met by the Magister Militum of Thrace with 2000 cavalry and 10,000 heavy armed soldiers. After crossing the Balkans he was also to be met in the valley of the Hebrus and near Hadrianople by 20,000 infantry and 10,000 cavalry, troops being drawn, if necessary, from Heraclea (Monastir) and all the cities and garrisons near Constantinople.

All these junctions of troops were promised : none of them were performed; and thus Theodoric, who punctually fulfilled his share of the bargain, found himself, after an exhausting march over the rugged Balkan country, with only his Goths, unsupported by the imperial troops, in presence of his enemy, who was encamped on the steep and unassailable cliff of Sondis. A pitched battle was impossible; but skirmishes constantly took place between the soldiers of both armies, when engaged in getting fodder for their horses. Every day, too, did the son of Triarius ride within earshot of his rival's camp, and pour forth a stream of insulting epithets on the head of "that perjurer, that enemy and traitor to the whole Gothic race, Theodoric. Silly and conceited boy! He does not understand the disposition of the Romans, nor see through their design, which is to let the Goths tear one another to pieces, while they sit by and watch the game at their ease, sure of the real victory, whichever side is defeated. And we the while, turning our hands against our brethren, like the men who in that story of theirs sprang from the seed of Cadmus, are to be left few in number, an easy prey to the machinations of the Romans. Oh, son of Theudemir! which of all the promises have they kept by which they lured you hither? Which of all their cities opened her gates to you and feasted your soldiers? They have enticed you to your own destruction, and the penalty of your rashness and stupidity will fall on the people whom you have betrayed".

These words, frequently repeated, produced their effect on the Amal's followers, who came to him, and said that indeed the adversary spoke reasonably, and that it was absurd for them to continue an internecine conflict with their kinsmen for the benefit of the common enemy. The son of Triarius, perceiving that his words were finding entrance, came next day to the crest of an overhanging hill, and thence shouted forth his upbraidings to Theodoric: "Oh, scoundrel! why art thou thus leading my brethren to perdition? Why hast thou made so many Gothic women widows? Where are now their husbands? What has become of all that abundance of good things which filled their waggons, when they first set forth from their homes to march under thy standard? Then did they own their two or three horses apiece. Now, without a horse, they must needs limp on foot through Thrace, following thee as if they were thy slaves. Yet they are free men, and of no worse lineage than thine. Ay! and the time hath been when these penniless wanderers would use a bushel to measure their aurei".

When the army heard these too truly taunting words, men and women alike came clamouring round the tent of Theodoric, "Peace, peace with our brethren! Else will we quit thy standards, and take our own road to safety". The king, who was truly head of a limited monarchy, recognising an expression of that popular voice to which he must defer, came down (doubtless with difficulty smothering his wrath) to the banks of the stream appointed for a conference, met and consulted with the man who had just been calling him a scoundrel and a boy, settled the conditions of peace, and then took and received a solemn oath, that there should be no war thenceforward between the son of Theudemir and the son of Triarius.

The reconciled Gothic chiefs sent a joint embassy to the Emperor, demanding, on the part of the son of Triarius, the fulfilment of all promises made to him by Leo, the arrears of pay due for past years, and the restoration of his relatives [the family of Aspar] if still alive, if not, an oath concerning them from Illus, and any of the Isaurian chiefs to whose keeping they might have been consigned. The claim of the Amal prince (mingled with complaints of the broken promises of the Emperor) was, that some district should be assigned him for a permanent dwelling-place, that rations of corn should be provided for his people till they could reap their own harvest, and that some of the imperial revenue officers, who were called *Domestici*, should be immediately sent to take account of (and no doubt to legalise) the requisitions which the Goths were then levying on the province. If this were not done, the Amal said, he could not prevent his men, famished and destitute, from supplying their needs in any way they could. This last request curiously illustrates Theodorics desire not to sink into a mere chief of lawless plunderers, nor to make an irretrievable breach with the Roman *civilitas*.

To the son of Triarius, Zeno does not appear to have vouchsafed any reply. He answered the Amal's complaints with a wrangling 'Tu quoque' :

"You said nothing at first about requiring the help of imperial troops to beat your rival; that was an afterthought, when you had already made up your mind to negotiate with him, and you hoped to betray our soldiers into a snare. So, at least, our generals thought, and that was why they would not carry into effect the proposed combinations. Nevertheless, if you will even yet be faithful to our cause, and will vanquish the son of Triarius, you shall receive £40,000 in gold and £35,000 in silver, paid down, a yearly revenue of £6,000, and the daughter of Olybrius (sprung from the mighty Theodosius) or some other noble Byzantine damsel to wife".

Though aided by high dignities bestowed on most of the Gothic emissaries, all these attempts to break the league between the two Theodorics proved fruitless, and the Emperor saw himself once more compelled to face the reality of war. He again called out his army and announced that he in person would share the hardships, and applaud the valour, of his soldiers. The announcement that, after a century of seclusion in his palace, the Roman Augustus was going to be once more, in the antique sense of the word, an *Imperator*, roused indescribable enthusiasm in the troops. The very men who had before paid large sums to the generals for exemption from military duty, now gladly paid for liberty to fight. The scouts who had been sent forward by the son of Triarius were taken prisoners : a portion of the Amal's guard, who had pressed forward to the Long Wall, were bravely repulsed by the soldiers who were guarding it. This was the outlook one day, and it shows us what immense recuperative energy yet lay in the Roman state-system, if only it had been guided by worthy hands. The next day, all was changed by the palace-bred sloth and cowardice of the Emperor. It was announced that Zeno would not go forth to the campaign. The soldiers heard the tidings with indignation. They gathered together in angry clusters, and began taunting one another with cowardice. Are you men?" they said; "have you arms in your hands, and will you patiently endure such womanish softness, by which city after city has been sacrificed, and now the whole fair Empire of Rome is going to ruin, and every one who pleases may have a hack at it?". The temper of the troops was so mutinous that by the advice of Martinianus (himself, as has been said, an incompetent commander) they were ordered to disperse into winter quarters, the pretext being alleged that there was a prospect of peace with the son of Triarius. The dispersion was successfully effected, but, as they went, the soldiers growled over their own folly in quitting the neighbourhood of the capital before they had bestowed the purple on some man worthy to wear it and able to save the state.

However, if Zeno failed to exhibit the courage of the lion, he possessed, and could use with some success, the cunning of the fox. The hope of dissolving the Gothic coalition by intrigue proved to be not illusory. He had tried it before, at the wrong end, when he dangled his bribes and his heiresses before the eyes of the loyal-hearted son of Theudemir. He now sent his ambassadors to the son of Triarius, to see upon what terms he could buy peace with him. They arrived at a critical moment. Theodoric the Amal had swooped down on the fertile country at the foot of Rhodope, was carrying off flocks and herds, expelling or slaying the cultivators and wasting their substance. The son of Triarius watched with grim delight these proceedings of the friend of the Romans, the son of Augustus: but at the same time professed to mourn that the punishment was falling on the guiltless peasants, not on Zeno or Verina, whose happiness would not be interfered with, though they were reduced to the extreme of misery. In this mood the ambassadors found him : but all his newly-kindled and virtuous indignation against the Court, as well as his recently professed horror of Goth warring against Goth, vanished before the splendour of their offers. The promise of regular pay and rations to 13,000 Goths to be chosen by himself, the command of two *Scholae*, the dignity of *Magister Praesentalis,* the regrant of all the offices which he had held under Basiliscus, and the restitution of all his former property, these were the terms which detached the fervid German patriot from his young confederate. As for his relations (the family of Aspar) the Emperor returned a mysterious reply: "If they were dead, it was of no use to say anything more about the subject ; but if they were alive they too should receive their old possessions and go to dwell in some city which he would point out to them". The negotiation was finally ratified on these lines. Money was sent for distribution among the Triarian Goths, and their leader stepped into all the dignities which were previously held by the Amal, but of which the latter was now formally divested. In this 'triangular duel' each combination had now been tried. 'Zeno and the Amal against the son of Triarius' had given place to 'the two Theodorics against Zeno', which in its turn was now replaced by 'Zeno and the son of Triarius against the Amal.'

Of the immediate effect of the announcement of this combination on the Amal king we have no information. We find him, however, early in the next year, exasperated by recent losses, bursting, an angry fugitive, into Macedonia, burning towns and killing garrisons without quarter. Stobi having been thus severely handled, he pressed on to Thessalonica. The inhabitants of that city, ever an excitable and suspicious people, conceived an idea that the Emperor and the Prefect meant to surrender them, unresisting, to the Barbarian. A kind of revolution took place in the city. The statues of Zeno were thrown down, and the mob were on the point of tearing the Prefect to pieces and setting his palace on fire. At the critical moment, the intervention of the clergy and of some of the most respected citizens averted these crimes. The populace, who were asked to confide the defence of their city to whom they would, took the keys of Thessalonica from the Prefect and handed them to the Archbishop, whose zeal against the Arian invaders they doubtless felt to be a sufficient guarantee for the tenacity of his defence. A civic guard was formed, a commander was chosen, and his orders were obeyed. In perusing the few lines which the Byzantine historian devotes to these events we might fancy ourselves to be reading the story of Paris in the early days of 'Madame Ligue.'

Meanwhile Zeno, finding himself not strong enough to crush Theodoric, determined at least to soothe him, and to avert, if possible, the conflagration of towns and the slaughter of garrisons. He sent an embassy (consisting of his relative Artemidorus and of a certain Phocas who had been his secretary when he himself filled the office of Magister Militum) to remind Theodoric of past favours and dignities conferred upon him, a barbarian by birth, in full reliance on his loyalty. All these advantages he had lost, through no fault of the Emperor, by giving heed to the crafty suggestions of a man who was their common enemy. But let him at least, in order not to make his case more desperate, refrain from inflicting on the cities of a powerful nation such injuries as it would be impossible to forgive, and let him send an embassy to obtain from the goodness of the Emperor such requests as he could reasonably prefer.[1] Theodoric, whose own better instincts were ever on the side of civilisation, issued orders that his soldiers should abstain from conflagration and from needless bloodshed, though they were still to live at free-quarters in Macedonia. His messengers returned with the Emperor's ambassadors to Constantinople, and were graciously received there. He himself moved with his army to Heraclea.

This city, the *Monastir* of our own day, was situated on the great Egnatian Way, a little less than half-way from Thessalonica on the Aegean to Dyrrhachium on the Adriatic. Built at the western edge of a noble plain, surrounded by the most exquisitely shaped hills, in a recess or bay formed by two very high mountains, between which magnificent snow-capped barriers is the pass to Akridha, and with one of the main branches of the Axius (*Vardar*) flowing through it, a broad and shifting torrent, crossed by numerous bridges, the city has been for centuries, under Caesar and Sultan alike, a highly important centre of civil and military administration for the great plain of Macedonia. Of that plain, indeed, it does not strictly form a part, being raised as it were a step above it towards the central highlands, but the great chain of Scardus stretching behind it (to which belong the snow-capped barriers mentioned above) far more decisively separates it from the western regions, which were then known as Epirus and Illyria, now as Albania.

The rich presents of the bishop of Heraclea to Theodoric and his followers preserved that city for the present from pillage. He made it his headquarters, and was in fact detained there for a considerable time by the sickness of his sister, a sickness which in the end proved fatal. This fact illustrates the domestic aspect of the events which we are now following. It was not an army merely, it was an aggregation of families that was roaming over the regions of Thrace and Macedon, and suffering, too often, the hardships so insultingly pourtrayed by the son of Triarius.

While Theodoric was at Heraclea the answer of Zeno arrived. Theodoric had urged that the ambassador should be a man of high rank and large powers, as he could not undertake to keep the masses of his followers from lawless pillage, if negotiations were unnecessarily protracted. In compliance with this request the Emperor selected as his ambassador, Adamantius the son of Vivianus, patrician, ex-prefect of the city, and consul. Adamantius was empowered to offer the Goths the district of Pantalia (a little south of Sardica, the modern Sofia) for their habitation, and a sum of £8000 as subsistence-money, till they reaped their first harvests in their new settlement. The Emperor's secret motive in selecting this region was, that the Amal would there act, to some extent, as a restraint on the son of Triarius (of whose precise location we are not informed), while, on the other hand, if he himself relapsed into disloyalty, he could be crushed by the converging forces of the Thracian and Illyrian provinces. Possibly Theodoric saw the imperial game: at any rate he was not eager to accept the Pantalian settlement.

For, meanwhile, another idea had been ripening in his brain. Thrace, Moesia, Macedon,—all these districts were impoverished by the marching to and fro of Romans and Barbarians for the last hundred years. Why should he not cross those soaring Scardus ranges on the western horizon, descend upon the rich and flourishing cities of Epirus Nova, which (except perhaps in an occasional visit from Gaiseric) had not known an invader for centuries, and there, carving out a kingdom for himself, bring the long wanderings of the Ostrogoths to an end? With this view he commenced a correspondence with Sigismund, a wealthy landowner near Dyrrhachium, who had formerly served in the imperial army, and, though a Goth, was supposed to be loyal to the Romans.

This Sigismund was nephew of a certain Edwin, (with what pleasure do we come upon these true Teutonic names in the Byzantine historian's pages!), a man who had great influence with the empress-mother Verina, and had held the high office of captain of the Domestici. To him, then, Theodoric sent, reminding him of the tie of relationship which existed between them, and begging his help in obtaining possession of Dyrrhachium and the rest of Epirus, that he might thus end his long rovings, and having established himself in a city defended by walls, might there receive whatever

Fortune should send him. Sigismund, notwithstanding his presumed philo-Romanism, elected to live under a ruler of his own nation rather than under the Emperor, and at once, repairing to Dyrrhachium, propounded to all his acquaintances there the friendly counsels of panic. The barbarian was certainly coming among them : the Emperor acquiesced in his doing so : arrangements for that end were at that very moment being concerted with Adamantius. He would advise them, as a friend and neighbour, to use the short interval still left, in removing their families and most precious possessions to the shelter of some other city or some island, before the Goths were upon them. By these suggestions, coupled with hints of the Emperor's displeasure, if the city were defended against his will, and judiciously aided by the continual fabrication of fresh and more alarming rumours, he persuaded not only the chief citizens, but even two thousand soldiers who were stationed there, to flock out of the city, and was soon able to send word to Theodoric inviting him to claim an unresisting prize.

The messenger arrived, just when the death of his sister had set Theodoric free to march from Heraclea. He called for a parley with the inhabitants of that city, who, notwithstanding the absence of outrages, had taken the alarm, and gone forth to a stronghold in the neighbourhood. To these refugees he offered that he would withdraw with all his people from the town, if they would supply him with a considerable quantity of corn and wine as provision for the journey. They declined, saying that their own stores in so small a fortress were scanty; and Theodoric in a rage burned the greater part of Heraclea, all deserted as it was. He then set forth upon his westward journey over the wild and rugged Scardus Mountains, which none of the enemy had dreamed of his attempting to cross. A few Gothic horsemen, sent forward to secure the heights, struck such terror into the garrison of a fortress, erected probably on a shoulder of the snow-crowned Mount Peristeri on purpose to guard the road, that they gave no thought to the defence of the position, but fled from it helter-skelter. Quite reassured as to the success of his expedition by this disgraceful cowardice, Theodoric marched on, with few or no precautions, in joyous boldness of heart, through the wild and lonely country which the Via Egnatia traverses in this part of its course. This was the order of march : Theodoric himself at the head, pushing cheerily forward, eager to see and to surprise the first city on the other side of the mountains; Soas, the greatest of all the generals under him, in the centre; and Theudimund, brother of Theodoric, commanding the rear. It was no slight sign of the King's confidence in the Roman unwillingness to fight or to pursue, that he dared to give to the waggoners and the drivers of the beasts of burden, the signal to follow him into this rocky region, where, even against unencumbered troops, brave men might easily, in a hundred places, have made a new Thermopylae.

Soon after crossing the highest part of the Scardus range (about 3000 feet high), Theodoric and his men came in sight of the broad expanse of what is now called the Lake of Ochrida, larger than any other piece of water between the Danube and the Aegean. At its northern edge rose conspicuous from afar a steep and isolated cliff, dominating the lake and all the surrounding country. Here, where now stands the castle of Ochrida, stood then the town and fortress of Lychnidus, unassailable by storm of armed men, and moreover well supplied with stores of corn, and with abundance of fountains springing up in its enclosure. At this place, therefore, the eagerness of the young Gothic chief was doomed to meet with disappointment. Even Eoman soldiers of the fifth century could maintain such a post as this: and Lychnidus refused to surrender. Its garrison did not, however, attempt to bar his way, and when, descending into the valley of the rock-chafed Genusus, after two days' march he reached Scampae, he found that city (the modem *Elbassan*) left bare of all inhabitants in the midst of its beautiful plain and rich olive-groves, a prey ready to bis hand. A day and a-half or two days more brought him to the shores of the Adriatic, half-islanded in whose blue waters, on its long and slender promontory, stood the main object of his quest, the usually rich and busy city of Dyrrhachium.

Dyrrhachium, which our Greek historian insists on calling by its old name of Epidamnus, and which we know as Durazzo, is a city of many associations for the classical student. In the pages of Thucydides it figures as the cause, or pretext, of the Peloponnesian War. Caesar faithfully records the severe check which he met with before its walls, and which had well-nigh turned the current of the Civil War and changed the whole after-history of Europe. Owing to the shortness of the crossing between Brundusium and Dyrrhachium the Epirote town was a place familiar to the memory of many a Roman general setting forth to administer an Eastern province, of many a Greek man of letters, with his face set westward, coming to seek his fortune in Rome. As far as Theodoric is concerned, but little of historical interest is added by his connection with the town. Apparently, the discouraging counsels of Sigismund had produced all their intended effect, and the place was already abandoned, for we are simply told that "pushing on from Scampae he took Epidamnus". But it may be allowable to conjecture that now, finding himself beside the waters of Hadria, knowing that he was within fifty miles of Apulia, and perhaps seeing the cloud-like form of Italy in the western horizon, he may then have dreamed the dream, which became a reality when all that fair land from Alps to Aetna was his own.

When news of this unexpected turn in affairs reached Adamantius, who, as has been said, was especially charged with the conduct of the treaty with Theodoric, he sent one of the mounted messengers, who, being under the orders of the Magister Officiorum, were called *Magistriani,* to expostulate with the Gothic king for resuming hostilities while negotiations were still pending. He entreated Theodoric not to take any further steps in the path of hostility to the Emperor; above all things not to fit out a naval expedition in the harbour of Dyrrhachium, but to send a trusty messenger who should assure him of a safe-conduct, going and returning, if he came in person to renew the conferences. In order to be nearer to the spot, he himself left Thessalonica and came westward, two days' journey, along the Egnatian Way to Edessa.

Edessa (now *Vodena*) has derived both its ancient and modem name from the wealth of waters with which it is encircled. It stands on a curving shelf of rock, overlooking the whole wide plain of Lower Macedonia; and the river Lydias, dividing itself behind the city into several branches, comes foaming over this rocky screen in innumerable cascades, which remind a traveller, familiar with Italian scenery, of Tivoli. Behind the city, tier on tier, rise three ranges of magnificent mountains, Scardus himself apparently dominating all. The fact that it commands the chief pass leading into these Macedonian highlands is no doubt the reason why the early Macedonian kings fixed their capital there; as it was also the reason why, in this awkward crisis of the Gothic campaign, Adamantius selected it as the scene of his council of war.

At this council he met Sabinianus, a man, as we shall see, of somewhat peculiar and stubborn character, but who, as a skilful general and a firm disciplinarian, towered far above the dead level of inefficiency, reached by most of the commanders of that time. He also met there Philoxenus, a Byzantine official of high rank, who had been employed in some of the earlier negotiations with Theodoric. After opening the imperial letters, appointing *Sabinianus Magister Utriusque Militiae per Ulyricum*, they proceeded to discuss the military position, which they found truly deplorable. Sabinianus had with him only a small band of soldiers, consisting chiefly of his own followers and dependants, while the bulk of the regular army, such as it was, was scattered through the cities of Thrace, or followed the banners of Onoulph, brother of Odovacar and murderer of Harmatius, who still held some high rank in the imperial service. They could only resolve to send notices of the appointment of Sabinianus in all directions, and summon the troops to his standard.

Meanwhile the horseman sent by Adamantius to Theodoric returned, bringing with him a Gothic priest who had been sent to ensure his safe passage through the barbarian ranks. They took the priest with them, and at once proceeded to Lychnidus (Ochrida), which still held out for the Empire; and were met at the gates by the magistrates and chief citizens of that strong and wealthy city by the lake. Negotiations followed for an interview with Theodoric, who was asked either to come himself to some place in the neighbourhood of Lychnidus, or to allow Adamantius to visit him at Dyrrhachium, sending his lieutenant Soas and another eminent Goth, to be kept as pledges for the ambassador's safe return. The two Goths were sent, but ordered not to advance beyond Scampia (*Elbassan*) till Sabinianus should take a solemn oath that, on the return of Adamantius, they too should be dismissed safe and sound. This was indeed negotiating at arm's length, but no doubt Theodoric, during his ten years' residence at Byzantium, had learned how far it was safe to trust to Roman honour. To this proposition, however, Sabinianus returned an answer, as to which we would gladly know whether it was a mere piece of contrariety, or whether it was founded on loyalty to the Teacher who said "Swear not at all". He declared that he had never in his life sworn about any matter, and would not now break a resolution of this kind, which he had formed long ago. Adamantius begged him to make some concession to the necessity of the times, and not to allow all the negotiations to collapse for want of those few words from him; but all that he would reply was, "I know my duty, and shall not deviate from the rule which I have laid down for myself".

Finding it impossible to overcome the scruples of this obstinate Non-Juror, Adamantius, whose heart was set on fulfilling his mission, started at evening; and by a series of difficult mountain-paths, on which, it was said, no horse-hoof had yet trodden, he worked round to a steep hill overlooking Dyrrhachium, but separated from it by a precipitous ravine through which a deep river ran. Halting here, he sent messengers for Theodoric, who came with a few horsemen to the river's brink. Adamantius, having posted some men on the crown of the hill to prevent a surprise, came down to his side of the river. Theodoric dismissed his attendants, and the two chiefs conversed with one another alone, the mountain torrent foaming and brawling between them. The Gothic King unfolded his complaints against the Roman Emperor, complaints which the Byzantine historian who records them considers well founded.

"I was willing enough", said he, "to dwell quietly outside the limits of Thrace, in my Moesian home, almost on the very confines of Scythia, obeying the Emperor and harming no man. Who brought me forth from my retirement, and insisted on my taking the field against the son of Triarius? The Emperor and his ministers. They promised that the Master of the Soldiery for Thrace should join me with an army : he never made his appearance. Then that Claudius, the steward of the Gothic funds, should meet me with the pay for my troops: he, too, was invisible. Thirdly, the guides who were assigned to me, instead of taking the smooth and easy roads which would have brought me straight to the enemy's camp, led me up and down all sorts of break-neck places, where, if the enemy had attacked me, with all my long train of horses and waggons and camp furniture, I must inevitably have been destroyed. Thus brought at a disadvantage into the presence of our enemies, I was obliged to make peace with them. And in truth I owe them great thanks for having saved me alive, when owing to your treachery they might easily have annihilated me".

Adamantius tried to answer these just complaints. He reminded Theodoric that he, when quite a young man, had received from the Emperor the dignities of Patrician and Magister Militum, dignities which were generally reserved for old and long-tried public servants. For these and many other favours he was indebted to the Emperor, whom he ought to look up to and reverence as a father. His recent conduct, however, was quite intolerable. By the artifice of sham negotiations he had contrived to break out of Thrace, in which the Romans, had they been so minded, could easily have penned him up between the rivers and mountains by which that province was girdled, and had attacked the splendid and flourishing cities of Epirus. It was impossible for the Romans to abandon these cities to him, and equally impossible for him permanently to resist the Romans. Let him therefore go into Dardania, where was a wide and pleasant and fertile country, absolutely longing for cultivators, and there see all his followers well nourished, while at the same time he lived in peace with the Empire.

Theodoric replied with a solemn asseveration that he himself would gladly accede to this proposition; but his army, worn out with long marches, must be allowed to repose for the winter in their present quarters. When spring came, he would be willing to deposit all his goods and all the non-combatant population in some city to be indicated by the Emperor, to surrender his mother and sister as hostages of his fidelity, and then to march with all speed into Thrace, with 6000 of his bravest warriors. With these and the troops quartered in Illyricum and such other forces as the Emperor might please to send him, he would undertake to destroy every Goth in Thrace. A strange promise certainly to be made by this, the ideal Teutonic hero. Of course, as his own followers were all now quartered in Epirus, this sweeping destruction was intended only for the bands which followed the son of Triarius; but even so, considering his recent alliance with that chief and the appeal to their common Gothic nationality on which that alliance had been based, one would be glad to think that the Byzantine historian had misreported the proposals of the son of Theudemir. The reward which he claimed for these services was that he should again receive his old office of Magister Militum, the insignia of which should be stripped off from the hated son of Triarius, and that he should be received into the capital, "there to live as a citizen after the Roman fashion". A striking evidence this of Theodoric's genuine appreciation of that '*civilitas*' which we shall hereafter find so persistently commended by his most famous minister. An indication that his thoughts were already turning, if not yet with any steadiness of purpose, towards Italy, is furnished by a still more startling proposal, that if the Emperor would but give the word, he would march off into Dalmatia in order to restore the exiled Nepos—a kinsman, be it remembered, of Zeno—to the Western throne.

To all these overtures Adamantius as yet could only reply, that he had no power to treat while Theodoric remained in Epirus. But let him abstain from offensive warfare, and all these matters should be laid before the Emperor for his decision. And thus they parted.

While these negotiations were proceeding between Adamantius and the Gothic King, the troops summoned to the standard of Sabinianus had been flocking in to the lake-mirrored fortress of Lychnidus, with an alacrity rare in those degenerate days. Word was brought to the Roman general that a large detachment of the barbarians was descending, in leisurely fashion, the Candavian range of hills which intervene between Dyrrhachium and Lychnidus. They were encumbered with baggage and a long train of waggons; and the rear of the army, commanded by Theudimund brother of Theodoric, had not yet reached the plain. To render the prize more tempting, it was stated that the mother of Theodoric and Theudimund was also with the rear-guard. The conscience of Sabinianus, too scrupulous to swear, could not resist the opportunity of striking so easy a blow, although the pending negotiations of Adamantius rendered such a course somewhat dishonourable. He sent a small body of infantry round over the mountains, with precise instructions when and where to attack the barbarians. He himself started after supper with the main body of his army, and fell upon the Goths at dawn. Surprised and panic-stricken, Theudimund fled with his mother into the plain, breaking down, as he went, a bridge by which they had crossed a very deep ravine. This precaution secured their own retreat, but prevented the escape of the rest of their countrymen. The latter at first, with the courage of despair, fought against the cavalry of Sabinianus. But when the other body of troops, the infantry who had been sent round, appeared over the crest of the mountain, there was no longer any hope of escape. Most of the Goths were cut to pieces, but more than 5000 were taken prisoners, the more nobly-born of whom were kept in ward, no doubt for the sake of their ransoms, while the rank and file were assigned as slaves to the soldiers, among whom also the booty was divided. Two thousand Gothic waggons fell into the hands of the Romans. Only a short time before, Sabinianus had issued requisitions on the Macedonian cities for a large number of those vehicles. These requisitions were at once countermanded, and indeed, after the wants of the army were fully supplied, so many waggons remained that the blaze of their burning soon lighted up the defiles of Mount Candavia, over which the general despaired of transporting them in safety.

On the return of Sabinianus to Lychnidus, he found Adamantius there, having just come back from his mission to Theodoric. Each sent an account of his operations to the Emperor, Adamantius pleading for peace, Sabinianus magnifying his recent success and beseeching Zeno to make no peace with the barbarian, who might certainly now be driven out of the province, if not utterly crushed. The large boasts of the general told on the unstable mind of the Emperor, who decided that war was more honourable than peace, and directed Sabinianus to carry on uncompromising hostilities against Theodoric with all the troops that he could muster. For some unexplained reason there was associated with him in this commission a man named Gento, a Goth by birth, who had married a wealthy Roman lady of the province of Epirus, and who possessed considerable local influence.

Adamantius, making a virtue of necessity, assembled the troops, addressed them in an eloquent harangue, praised their past valour, and exhorted them to a continued exercise of that peculiarly Roman quality, courage. He then read them the Emperor's proclamation, and stimulated them with the usual promises of special imperial favour for such soldiers as should distinguish themselves by their zeal. He was welcomed with shouts of applause, and had the gratification of making a very successful oration. "And so", says Malchus, surely with a slight touch of scorn, "Adamantius disappeared, not having done anything besides".

From this point onwards we have no further information from Malchus concerning the history of Theodoric, and our most valuable spring of knowledge thus dries up at once. The excuse for narrating so minutely the events of a few months in the life of the Ostrogothic king must be that, for no other part of a life extending over seventy-two years, and rich in momentous deeds, have we a history, for fulness, clearness, and vividness of colour, at all comparable to these fragments of the work of a Byzantine rhetorician fortunately preserved by the industry of a literary emperor. Compelled as we are to trace, by mere conjecture, the vague outlines of the history of Theodoric for the next nine years (479-488), we must conclude that for some reason or other his attempt to establish himself in Epirus proved a failure. Possibly he was too much weakened, and the provincials too much encouraged, by the battle of the Candavian Mountains, for him to maintain himself with force in the midst of a hostile population. Possibly also it was not altogether safe for him to relinquish entirely his communications with the Lower Danube, across which may have flowed the streams of Teutonic migration constantly refilling his wasted ranks.

The narrative returns for a brief space to his rival, the son of Triarius. At the time of the insurrection of Marcian (which occurred probably a few months after the Amal's invasion of Epirus), he marched with great alacrity to the gates of Constantinople. It was easy to see, however, that this promptness proceeded from no exuberance of loyalty towards Zeno, but rather showed an inclination on the part of the Goth to fight for his own hand. The Emperor sent to thank him for his eagerness, but also to beg him to return without entering the city, lest he should awaken a fresh spasm of panic in the minds of the citizens, only just settling down after the exciting scenes of the Marcianic war. The son of Triarius replied, almost in the words of his namesake, that he himself would gladly comply with the Emperor's command; but his army was large and unruly and he feared that they would not obey the signal of retreat without tasting the pleasures of the capital. Privately, he reckoned not only on the feeble state of the fortifications, but yet more on the hatred of the mob of Constantinople to the Isaurian monopolisers of the favour of the Court, a hatred so intense that even the Goths might be welcomed as deliverers. The Emperor knew that this was his calculation, but knew also something of the desperation with which his countrymen would cling (as, ten years later, they did cling) to their hold of the capital. On all grounds, therefore, it was of the utmost importance to get the Gothic army quietly away from the gates. Pelagius the Silentiary (the same man who was afterwards sacrificed to the jealousy of the dying Emperor) was sent, with great sums of money for the son of Triarius and his followers, with promises of larger presents to come, and threats of the consequences of disobedience, to adjure them to depart from the city. The avarice inherent in the Gothic mind was roused by the actual sight of the dazzling hoards, and the mission of Pelagius was successful in inducing the barbarians to return. Not so, however, with the demand for the surrender of Procopius the brother of Marcian, and Busalbus his friend. To this request the warrior gave a positive denial, saying "that he would obey the Emperor in all other matters, but it was not a righteous thing for the Goths, nor for any one else, to betray suppliants, who had fled to them for protection, into the hands of enemies who were thirsting for their blood". The two refugees accordingly lived for some time under his protection, cultivating a small estate. Eventually, as we have seen, they made their escape to Rome.

It is probably to this period that we must refer a statement made by Joannes Antiochenus that the trouble caused to the state by the pair of Theodorics marching up and down and sacking the cities of Thrace compelled the Emperor to form an alliance with the Bulgarians, whose name then appears for the first time in history. A Turanian people, possibly true Huns, without doubt one of the vast medley of tribes who thirty years before had followed the standards of Attila, the Bulgarians have, as is well known, in the course of centuries become thoroughly Slavonised, and looked to Russia, not to Turkestan, as the lode-star of their race. When the diplomatists of Europe, a few years ago, were revising the treaty of St. Stefano at Berlin, and discussing the respective claims of the big and the little Bulgaria, they were but working out the latest terms of an equation which was first stated amid the vexations that the pair of Theodorics caused to the statesmen of Constantinople.

Theodoric the Amal appears, at some such time as this, to have met the leader of the Bulgarians in single combat, to have wounded him, but not mortally, and to have forced his nation to submit to humbling conditions of peace.

Two years later (481) the son of Triarius, now apparently again in open enmity to Zeno, having obtained some successes against these Hunnish-Bulgarian allies of the Empire, drew near to the gates of Constantinople. He had all but succeeded in taking it, in which case perhaps the Eastern Empire would have survived her sister of the West only five years. But either the bravery of Illus, or a cleverly fomented conspiracy among his own followers, obtained for the capital a fortunate reprieve. The Goth moved across the harbour to Galata; made another attempt, which again failed; marched ten miles up the Bosporus, thinking to cross over into Bithynia; was worsted in a naval engagement, and then moved westwards into Thrace, meditating an expedition into the comparatively undevastated regions of Greece. He rode at the head of 30,000 Goths; and his wife Sigilda, his two brothers, and his son Recitach accompanied him. We see that in his case, as in that of the other Theodoric, of Alaric, and no doubt of many another Teutonic chieftain, the march of the general meant also the migration of his family.

Moving along the Egnatian Way, they had reached a place on the Thracian coast more than 200 miles from Constantinople, which, in memory of that savage Thracian king who in the days of Hercules used to feed his horses on human flesh, still bore the name of *The Stables of Diomed*. Here the chief, one day wishing to take some exercise, ordered his horse to be brought to his tent-door. In those days, before the invention of stirrups, a Roman noble generally mounted with the assistance of a groom. The son of Triarius, however, though probably past middle life, disdained such effeminate habits, and always vaulted to his seat unaided. This time, however, before he was fairly astride of his horse, the creature, which was wild and mettlesome, reared up in the air and danced about on its hind legs. Theodoric tried to get the mastery of the horse, but did not dare to grasp the bridle lest he should pull it over upon him. Rider and horse, thus swaying backwards and forwards, came up to the tent-door, before which a spear with a thong fitted to it was hanging, in the fashion of the barbarians. Jostled by his unruly steed against the spear, the chief was pierced by it in his side and forced to dismount. He took to his bed, and soon after died of the wound. Henceforward the undisputed right to the name Theodoric passes over to his Amal rival.

Sigilda, wife of the dead chief, buried her husband by night. Dissensions broke out in his family. His two brothers tried to grasp the leadership and to oust his son, relying perhaps in part on a rumour which strangely obtained currency, that the death which has been so minutely described was, after all, not accidental, but that Recitach, indignant at having received personal chastisement from his father, had repaid the insult by parricide. The lad, however, bided his time. Before long he deprived his uncles of life, and grasped the leadership of the thirty thousand followers of his father—a leadership which he employed to inflict yet more cruel sufferings on the provincials of Thrace than those which they had endured at his father's hands.

After this he must have been reconciled to the Empire (there is a wearisome inconstancy both in the friendships and the enmities of these guerilla chiefs), for the last information that we have concerning him is that the Emperor Zeno, perceiving that Recitach was becoming disaffected through envy of Theodoric, ordered the Gothic king to destroy him, which he accordingly did, although Recitach was his cousin, having an old grudge against him because of the murder of his ....? (A defect in the MS. leaves us in doubt as to the nature of this old grievance.) Theodoric fulfilled the bloody commission by piercing his young rival under the fifth rib when he was on his way from the bath to the banquet. The murder of Recitach is one of the few blots on the generally fair fame of Theodoric.

By the extinction of the house of Triarius, the Amal became the undisputed head of the Gothic nation in the Eastern peninsula. Thirty thousand men were added to his army, but these implied more than thirty thousand mouths for which he must find provisions. It was impossible for him, at the head of his roving bands of hungry warriors, to settle down into an orderly, hard-working magister militum in Thrace. For six years following the death of his elder rival, he vibrated to and fro with apparent absence of purpose between Romanism—using the word in a political sense—and barbarianism. In 482 he laid waste the two Macedonias and Thessaly, and plundered Larissa the capital of the latter province. In 483, "being almost appeased by the munificence of the Emperor Zeno" (says Count Marcellinus, nearly our only authority here), "and being made Magister Militiae Praesentis, and designated as Consul for the next year, he and his satellites kept for the time within bounds in the portion of Dacia Eipensis and Lower Moesia which had been allotted to him". His head-quarters appear to have been Novae, on the Lower Danube. It is noteworthy that he was here within fifty miles of Nicopolis, the town which, 130 years before, had formed the centre of the settlement of the Lesser Goths who followed the guidance of 'their Moses,' the pure-souled and pious Ulfilas. Probably this portion of Moesia had never ceased to be strongly Gothic in the character of its population.

The next year (484) saw him in the full glory of *Consul Ordinarius*, wearing the toga, doubtless with the peculiar Gabine cincture which marked the Consulate, giving his name to the year, and liberating a slave by a stroke on the day of his inauguration. There are indications that now, at any rate, if not in the previous year, he took up his abode in Constantinople, and that his enjoyment of the pomps and luxuries of the capital, while his followers were suffering the pangs of hunger in their Danubian settlement, was not viewed with approbation by the Goths. They felt the contrast all the more keenly, since his authority, as became a consul and a magister militum, was strenuously exerted to check their old habits of plunder.

It was in the year of Theodoric's consulship that he soiled his hands with the blood of his kinsman Recitach, and received the adhesion of his followers. It was in the same year that the revolt of Illus broke out. Theodoric was at first ordered to march for its suppression, but he had not proceeded further than Nicomedia in Bithynia, when the timid and suspicious Zeno recalled him and his Goths, and committed the imperial cause to the championship of his strange allies from the middle Danube, the Rugians, under the command of a son of Aspar. This evidence of distrust no doubt alienated the high-mettled Gothic king. In 486 he broke out into open revolt and ravaged a part of Thrace; and in the following year with a large army (swollen no doubt by all the Triarian Goths) he came up to the very gates of Constantinople, and took the town of Melantias on the Sea of Marmora and only fourteen miles from the capital. He found himself, like countless other generals before and after him, unable to take the city of Constantine; but, before he returned to his head-quarters at Novae, the citizens saw the flames ascending from many towns and villages, and knew that they were kindled by the followers of the man who but three years before had ridden through their streets as a Roman Consul.

This endless vacillation between friendship and enmity to Rome was an unfruitful and unstatesmanlike policy; and we may be sure that Theodoric recognised the fact as clearly as any one. But the time was now ripe for the execution of another project, which would find full employment for all the warlike energies of his people, and which, if it succeeded, would give him a fixed and definite position among the rulers of the earth, and would exempt him from the necessity of marching up and down through the thrice-harried Thracian plains, to extort from the wretched provincials food for his almost equally wretched followers.

The scheme shall first be told in the words of Jordanes, who without doubt is here quoting from Cassiodorus, the friend and minister of Theodoric : "Meanwhile Theodoric, who was hound by covenant to the Empire of Zeno, hearing that his nation, abiding as we have said in Illyricum, were not too well supplied with the necessaries of life while he was enjoying all the good things of the capital, and choosing rather, after the old manner of his race, to seek food by labour than to enjoy in luxurious idleness the fatness of the Roman realm while his people were living in hardship, made up his mind and spoke thus to the Emperor : "Though nothing is wanting to me for my service to your Empire, nevertheless, if Your Piety think fit, I pray you to hear freely the desire of my heart." Then, as was wont, leave was granted him to speak without reserve. "The Hesperian clime," said he, "which was formerly subject to the rule of your predecessors, and that city which was once the capital and mistress of the world,— why should they now be tossed to and fro under the usurped authority of a king of Rugians and Turcilingians? Send me thither, if it please you, with my people, that you may be relieved from the expense which we cause you here, and that there, if by the Lord's help I conquer, the fame of Your Piety may beam brightly forth. For it is fitting that I, your son and servant, if victorious, should hold that kingdom as your gift; but it is not fitting that he, whom you know not, should press his tyrannical yoke upon your Senate, and that a part of the Roman Republic should languish in the bondage of captivity under him. In brief, if I conquer, I shall possess the land as of your gift and by your grant: if I am conquered, Your Piety will lose nothing, but rather, as before said, will save the heavy charges which we now bring upon you". On hearing this speech the Emperor, though sorry to part with Theodoric, yet not wishing to sadden him by a refusal, granted what he desired; and, after enriching him with great gifts, dismissed him from his presence, commending to his protection the Senate and People of Rome".

This is the account of the transaction given by Jordanes. The Byzantine authorities put a slightly different colour upon it. *Procopius* says, "The Emperor Zeno, a man skilful in expedients of a temporary kind, exhorted Theodoric to march to Italy, and, entering the lists against Odoacer, to win the Western Kingdom for himself and the Goths. He showed him that it was better for him, now especially that he had attained the dignity of Senator, by the overthrow of a tyrant to obtain the rule over all the Romans and Italians, than, by continuing the struggle with the Emperor, to run so many risks as he must do. Theodoric then, being pleased with the bargain, departed for Italy"; and so on.

The author who generally goes by the name of *Anonymus Valesii*, and who clearly writes from Byzantine sources and with a particular regard for the Emperor Zeno, says, "Zeno therefore rewarded Theodoric with his favours, making him Patrician and Consul, bestowing on him a large sum and sending him to Italy. With whom Theodoric made a bargain that, if Odoachar should be conquered, he on his arrival should reign in his stead as a reward for all his labours."

There is evidently a certain conflict of testimony as to the quarter from which the idea of a Gothic invasion of Italy first proceeded. Odovacar, as we shall see, had made himself obnoxious both to the Byzantine and the Goth. Theodoric's prolonged stay in the Danubian regions was a perpetual menace to Constantinople; and, whatever Jordanes may feign as to the Emperor's sorrow in parting with his adopted son, Zeno certainly desired few things more earnestly than that he might never see his face again; and Theodoric knew this. When matters have reached this point, when the guest has over-stayed his welcome, and both he and the host are keenly conscious of the fact, it may be difficult to say which first gives the signal for departure; and perhaps the means of escape from a position which each finds intolerable, may present itself simultaneously to both by a process of "double independent discovery". Only, in the idea of leading his nation away from the shores of the Danube, haunted by them for a hundred weary years, descending the Alps into Italy and founding an Ostrogothic kingdom on the Hesperian shore, there is a touch of genius which disposes one to look for its conception, rather to the bright and vigorous young Amal king than to the tired brain of the imperial voluptuary.

More important than the question of priority of invention between Zeno and Theodoric is the uncertainty in which the rights of the contracting parties were, no doubt intentionally, left. The Goth asks the Emperor's leave to invade Italy. If Italy was recognised as permanently lost to the Roman Empire, if it was like Dacia or Britain, why was this leave necessary? He says that he will hold the new kingdom as his adoptive father's gift. Did that gift fasten any responsibilities to the receiver? Did it entitle the giver to be consulted in the subsequent disposal of the crown? Was it, to borrow an illustration from English law, like a gift 'for life' or 'to him and the heirs of his body', or 'to him and heirs general'? In feudal times a transaction such as this could hardly have taken place without the creation of a fief; but it is some centuries too soon as yet to talk of fiefs and vassals of the Empire.

All that we can say, apparently, is that Theodoric was despatched on his hazardous expedition with the imperial approval; that the future relations between the parties were left to accident to determine; but that there was, underlying the whole conversation, a recognition of the fact that Italy and Rome still formed part of the *Respublica Romana*; and out of this fact would spring claims which any *Imperator*, who was strong enough to do so, was certain to enforce.

Before we follow the march of Theodoric and his Goths across the mountains we must first consult our meagre authorities to ascertain what Odovacar has been doing, during the thirteen years that he has been undisputed lord of Italy.

CHAPTER IV.

FLAVIUS ODOVACAR.

The humiliation of Rome was completed by the events recorded in the preceding volume. There was still, no doubt, a legal fiction according to which Rome and Italy yet belonged to the Empire, and were under the dominion of the successor of Augustus, who reigned not in Old Rome by the Tiber, but in New Rome by the Thracian Bosporus. In fact, however, one will was supreme in Italy, the will of the tall barbarian who in sordid dress once strode into the cell of Severinus, the leader of the Herulian and Rugian mutineers, the conqueror of Pavia, Odovacar.

For thirteen years this soldier of fortune swayed with undisputed mastery the Roman state. He employed, no doubt, the services of Roman officials to work the machine of government. He paid a certain deference, on many occasions, to the will of his nominal superior, Zeno, the Emperor at Constantinople. He watched, we may be sure much more anxiously, the shifting currents of opinion among the rough mercenaries who had bestowed on him the crown, and on whom he had bestowed the third part of the lands of Italy. But, on the whole, and looking at the necessity of concentrated force in such a precarious state as that which the mercenaries had founded, we shall probably not be far wrong if we attribute to Odovacar the effective power, though of course he used not the name, of Autocrat.

The highest praise that can be bestowed on the government of this adventurer from the Danubian lands is that we hear so little about it. Some hardship, perhaps even some violence, probably accompanied the compulsory expropriation of the Romans from one-third of the lands of Italy. There is some reason for supposing, however, that this would be in the main only a loss of property, falling on the large landed proprietors. Where the land was being cultivated by *coloni*, bound to the soil and paying their fixed rent or their share of produce to the lord, no great visible change could probably be made. From motives of self-interest, and to gratify his warlike impatience of toil, the Rugian warrior, entering upon the ownership of his sors, would generally leave the tillage of the soil in the same hands in which he found it. To him, or rather to his bailiffs (*actores*), instead of to those of the luxurious Roman senator, the *coloni* would henceforward pay their dues, and that would be the whole visible outcome of the late revolution. It seems hardly likely that there can have been much gratuitous cruelty or actual bloodshed on the part of the soldiers of Odovacar, or we should surely have had some hint of it from one of the Byzantine historians. It ought, however, to be mentioned that Ennodius draws a somewhat gloomy picture of the financial oppression of Odovacar's reign; but his purpose of blackening the fallen king in order to glorify Theodoric is so obvious that we need attach but little weight to his testimony. Perhaps his best remark is that Odovacar's consciousness of his own lowly origin made him timid in the presence of his army, and prevented him from checking their excesses. There are also some expressions in the letters of Pope Gelasius which hint at "barbaric incursions" and "the continual tempest of war" that had afflicted Italy, but the language employed is extremely vague, and gives us rather the impression of words used to round off a rhetorical period than of a genuine cry of sorrow forced out of the writer by the sight of the misery of his people.

As far as Italy herself is concerned, this part of her annals is an absolute blank, not one of her own sons having said anything at all about it, at least not in a voice loud enough to reach posterity. This absolute extinction of the national consciousness, in a people which had once numbered among its sons a Livy and a Tacitus, is one of the strangest symptoms of the fifth century. But in truth it seems as if even for the chroniclers, who did in their way try to preserve some of the events of their age from oblivion, the Monophysite Controversy, to us so unintelligible and so wearisome, possessed a fascination which quite diverted their gaze from the portentous spectacle of a barbarian ruling in Italy. It would probably be safe to say that we have three allusions to Timotheus Aelurus, the militant Patriarch of Alexandria, for every time that the name of Odovacar occurs in the pages of the chroniclers.

In geographical extent, the dominions of Odovacar probably did not differ greatly from those of the Roman Emperors of the West during the last twenty-five years of their rule. It is true that Gaul was lost to him. The fair region which we now call Provence, nearly the earliest formed and quite the latest lost *Provincia* of Rome, that region in which the Latin spirit dwelt so strongly that the Roman nobles thought of migrating thither in 401, when Alaric first invaded Italy, refused to submit to the rule of the upstart barbarian. The Provençals sent an embassy to Constantinople to claim the protection of Zeno for the still loyal subjects of the Empire. Odovacar, however, sent his ambassadors at the same time, and again, as before, when the restoration of Nepos was in question, the representations of the new barbarian ruler of Italy prevailed. Zeno, we are told, rather inclined to the cause of Odovacar. The latter however, who perhaps thought that he had enough upon his hands without forcing his yoke on the Provençals, made over his claim to Euric, king of the Visigoths, whose influence was at this time predominant in Gaul.

Sicily, which had been for a generation subjected, first to the devastations and then to the rule of the Vandal king, was now by a formal treaty, which must have been nearly the last public act of Gaiseric, ceded to Odovacar, all but a small part, probably at the western end of the island, which the Vandal reserved to himself. A yearly tribute was to be the price of this concession; but, in the decay of the kingdom under Gaiseric's successors, it is possible that this tribute was not rigorously enforced, as it is also almost certain that the reserved portion of the island, following the example of the remainder, owned the sway of Odovacar.

The other great Italian islands, Sardinia and Corsica, as well as the Balearic isles, formed part of the maritime monarchy of the Vandals, and fell eventually, when it fell, under the sway of Byzantium.

North of the Alps, the dominion of Odovacar was probably more firmly established than had been that of any Italian ruler for a generation. It will be remembered that Raetia, the oblong block of territory which extended from the Alps to the Danube, formed, in the fourth and fifth centuries, a part of the 'Diocese' of Italia. It seems likely that under Odovacar, himself an immigrant from the Danubian lands, and able to draw to his standard many of the bravest and strongest of the adventurers who then roved through that portion of 'Varbaricum', the passes of the Alps may have been more strongly guarded, and Raetia may have been more of an outpost for Italy, than it had been since the wave of westward migration, at the beginning of the fifth century, changed all the landmarks on the north-western frontier of the Empire. In fact, such indications as we have of the policy of Odovacar would dispose one to think that his face was turned towards the North rather than the South. Peace with the Vandals, peace, if not a very cordial peace, with Byzantium, with an energetic policy towards the Burgundians, Alamanni, Thuringians, Rugians, on whose settlements he looked down from his Raetian stronghold—this was probably the policy of the new kingdom. It accorded well herewith that, like Honorius, though not from the same motive of personal timidity, Odovacar fixed his residence at Ravenna rather than at Rome.

There came a favourable opportunity for enlarging his kingdom by an extension to the east of the Adriatic. It will be remembered that Nepos, the exiled Emperor of the West, reigned for some years, apparently as legitimate Augustus, in the province of Dalmatia. As this province belonged to the Western Empire, he probably owned no subjection to his brother Emperor at Constantinople, nor confessed any other inferiority than such as the ruler of a small and precariously held state must have felt in the presence of the undoubted lord of Illyricum and the Orient. We have already met with his ambassadors at the Court of Byzantium vainly entreating one legitimate Emperor to restore the other to his rightful position; and we also more recently have heard the offer of Theodoric the Amal to restore Nepos, if Zeno so willed, to the Western throne. No effectual help, however, was ever really rendered by Zeno to his dethroned kinsman, and in the year 480, as has been already related, Nepos fell by the traitorous blows of the Counts Viator and Ovida at his villa near Salona. In the following year Odovacar transported an army into Dalmatia, conquered and slew Count Ovida,—perhaps Viator had already fallen in some robber's quarrel over the division of the plunder,—and thus avenged the death of Nepos. There can be no doubt that the result of this campaign was the annexation of Dalmatia to the dominions of Odovacar, though this fact is not expressly asserted by the annalists.

It is worthy of remark that the Byzantine historian Procopius, who probably gives the strict legitimist view of the reign of Odovaear, does not consider that reign to have commenced till the death of Nepos, and thus reduces to ten years an interval which, according to the de facto view generally adopted by historians, lasted at least fourteen.

From this survey of foreign affairs we pass, to consider the internal condition of his kingdom.

In the first year after he had attained to supreme power he put to death a certain Count Bracila at Ravenna. From the form of the name we should have supposed that this was some barbarian rival, anxious to win the favour of the soldiery and to serve Odovacar as Odovacar had served Orestes. But Jordanes, whose statements, in the great dearth of authentic information, we cannot afford utterly to despise, tells us that it was done "that he might strike terror into the *Romans*". Perhaps, as it had been with Stilicho the Vandal and with Ricimer the Sueve, so now was it with Bracila, the son of some unknown German princeling, that the cause of Rome was most stubbornly maintained by some conspicuous soldier not himself of Roman blood.

Possibly the Teutonic adherents of the new ruler, dwelling on the lands wrested from the old possessors and assigned to them, may still have been governed by their old tribal laws, and may have preserved some remains of their tribal organization. Analogy points to this as a probable conclusion, but we have absolutely no information on the subject. There is no doubt however that, for the great mass of the inhabitants of Italy, the old order of things remained unchanged. Justice was still administered according to Roman laws by Roman magistrates. The taxes of the Empire were still collected by Roman *Rationales*. There were still Praetorian Prefects, Counts of the

Sacred Largesses, Counts of the Domestics, Masters of the Offices, and all the rest of the administrative and courtly hierarchy introduced by Diocletian and fully developed under Constantine. Only, the centre and mainspring of all this elaborate organization was no longer a Roman imperator, but a nondescript barbarian chief, King in relation to his followers, Patrician in his dealings with the Senate, a man not wearing the imperial purple nor crowned with the diadem, a man who could do everything in Italy except say by what right he ruled there.

One proof that the time of Odovacar's kingship was no mere revel of barbaric licence and anarchy is furnished by the names of Roman administrators—men of high character and position—who served him in the affairs of the state. Chief among these we must place Liberius. We are not informed of the precise position which he occupied at this time, but from the terms, honourable both to the praiser and the praised, in which his faithful services to Odovacar are recounted by that king's successful rival, we may infer that it was a prominent one.

Another name with which we are already familiar, that of Cassiodorus, also emerges into notice in this reign. But, though some historians have been of a different opinion, it is now generally admitted that it was not 'Cassiodorus Senator', the minister of Theodoric and historian of the Goths, but his father who held office under Odovacar. The scanty details of the father's political career will be best reserved till we come to deal with the pedigree and the character of his illustrious son. It may be mentioned, however, that he seems to have successively filled the two great financial offices of Count of the Private Domains and Count of the Sacred Largesses.

Pierius, who was *Comes Domesticorum* or Captain of the Guard under Odovacar, was employed to superintend a certain transportation of Roman inhabitants from Noricum to Campania, which will be described in the next chapter. It is an interesting fact that there is still extant a deed of gift from Odovacar to this trusted minister. As the document throws some useful light on the internal condition of Italy at this period, and is really the only authentic record of the reign that we possess, it is transcribed in full at the end of this chapter.

Pelagius, who filled the high office of Praetorian Prefect, does not show so fair a record as some of the other ministers of Odovacar. We hear his name only from Ennodius, the biographer of Epiphanius, the saintly bishop of Ticinum, and he assures us that the province of Liguria groaned under his oppressive exercise of the right of *coemptio*, meaning probably the royal prerogative of buying provisions for the army at a fixed price below the market value. By this extortion, which Ennodius attributes to the long-concealed but at length forth-blazing ardour of the malice of Pelagius, but which probably proceeded simply from the poverty of the exchequer, the possessores of Liguria found that their taxes, already unendurable, were virtually doubled, and the province was brought to the brink of ruin. Epiphanius, that embodiment of good-nature, whose good offices as mediator were perpetually being invoked on behalf of some injured person or class, was appealed to by the half-desperate Ligurian 'possessors,' set off with alacrity for the court, and obtained, probably after a personal interview with Odovacar, a remission of the obnoxious imposts.

Nor was this the only concession made by exchequer of the barbarian king to the prayers of the Bishop. Epiphanius had devoted himself to the rebuilding of the churches of Ticinum and Pavia, both of which, as was previously told, had perished in the sack of the city by the revolted mercenaries. Notwithstanding the poverty of his ravaged diocese, and the opposition of 'that crafty serpent', the devil, to whose agency his biographer attributes the fall of the colonnaded wall of one of the churches, the Bishop succeeded in raising both edifices, in a marvellously short space of time, to their old height, and perhaps in restoring them to their former splendour. An accident which occurred in the progress of the work, the fall of the workmen with a large hoisting machine from the very cupola of the second church, raised the Bishop's fame to a yet greater height, since the people attributed it to his prayers, efficacious to delay the ruin and to check the falling stones in mid-air, that not a bone of one of the workmen was broken. Epiphanius, however, considerately remembered that the restoration of the ecclesiastical glories of his city would not repair the ruined fortunes of its inhabitants,—perhaps even he had been forced to solicit for the purpose contributions which were as hardly spared as the widow's mite,—and he therefore appealed for aid to Odovacar, who directed that Ticinum should enjoy a five years' exemption from tribute. The biographer adds that of all the citizens the Bishop who had obtained the boon reaped the least benefit from it, so modest was he in putting forward his own claims for exemption

Such benefits, granted by the barbarian and heretical king at the request of the Catholic bishop, are honourable to both parties. But there are not wanting indications that, in his attitude towards the head of Catholic Italy, towards the Bishop of Rome himself, Odovacar exhibited the same spirit of wise and dignified toleration which during the larger part of his reign was the glory of his great successor. Though the detailed history of the Popes lies outside of the scope of this work, some pages must be devoted to the position and character of the Pontiffs who witnessed the establishment of barbarian rule in Italy.

The stately Leo, the tamer of Attila and the hammer of Eutychian heretics, died on the 10th of November, 461, and was succeeded by *Hilarus* the Sardinian. The pontificate of Hilarus, which lasted nearly six years, was chiefly occupied with attempts to assert the Papal supremacy over the Churches of Gaul and Spain in a more despotic style than had yet been possible. These attempts were successful. It is a marvellous sight to see how, as the political power of Rome over the provinces of the Empire ebbs away, the ecclesiastical power of her bishop increases. The Tribune and the Centurion disappear, but the Legate of the Pope comes oftener, and is a mightier personage each time of his return. So, too, with the outward splendour of the Papal Court : it grows brighter as that of the Caesars wanes. A long page in the Lives of the Popes is filled with the catalogue of the costly gifts of gold and silver offered by Pope Hilarus, chiefly in the three oratories which he erected in the Lateran Basilica. The names of these vessels (to us scarcely intelligible), their shapes, their weights, are recorded with tedious minuteness by the enthusiastic scribe. But, as has been well observed, these gifts, purchased with the revenues of the spacious and ever-increasing Church domains, were almost a satire on the general poverty of the city. While the life of the citizens was growing harder and the civil edifices were every year putting on more of the appearance of squalor and desolation, the shrines of martyrs and saints were glowing with ever-fresh splendour before the eyes—shall we say the envious, or the awe-stricken eyes—of the Christian Quirites.

Pope Hilarus also made his mark on his times (467) by withstanding a faint attempt at toleration made by the secular power. The Emperor Anthemius was darkly suspected of plotting, in concert with a certain citizen of Rome named Severus, a restoration of the worship of the gods of the Capitol. This was perhaps mere calumny; but what was undoubted was that he was accompanied to Rome by Philotheus, an asserter of the Macedonian heresy and a denier of the divinity of the Holy Ghost. At the instigation of this Philotheus, Anthemius proposed to allow full liberty to all the sects to hold their conventicles in Rome. But the aged Hilarus, who was within a few months of his end (for he died in September 467, only five months after Anthemius' triumphal entry), thundered with so loud and clear a voice in St. Peters against the proposed act of toleration, that the Emperor was obliged to relinquish his design and to pledge himself by a solemn oath to the Pontiff never to resume it.

The successor of Hilarus, Pope Simplicius, presided over the Church fifteen years (468-483), and in that time saw some great events. He witnessed the deposition of Augustulus, and the accession to supreme power in Italy of a Teutonic mercenary. He heard also of an event far more important in the eyes of the chroniclers of the time, the publication of the Henoticon of the Emperor Zeno, that document wherein an emperor, by his sole authority, without the sanction of pope or council, endeavoured to fix the land-marks of Christian belief and to terminate the Monophysite controversy. The long pontificate of Simplicius was chiefly occupied by his struggles for ascendency against the able but somewhat unscrupulous Patriarch of Constantinople, Acacius. This struggle prepared the way for, and perhaps necessitated, the first great schism between the Eastern and Western Churches, which was opened under his successor.

In this struggle we are bound to remember that there was an element of self-defence mingled with all the aggressiveness of the Roman Pontiffs. Looking back through the dim vista of the middle ages at the steady and resistless growth of the papal power—a growth lasting over far distant centuries which, we are inclined to say, never conspired together for one single end as they did for this,—we perhaps sometimes overrate the distinctness of vision wherewith the individual pontiffs saw the goal to which they were tending, while we underrate the actual pressure of cares and perils in each successive generation by which they were surrounded. Thus, for instance, at the point of time which we have now reached, in the last quarter of the fifth century from the birth of Christ, it might sometimes seem a doubtful matter to contemporary opinion whether the Roman See would not have to descend from the high place of its dominion at the head of the Christian world.

It was true that the person of the Pope was exalted by the humiliation and the eventual disappearance of the Western Caesar; but the See was in some danger of sharing the fallen fortunes of the city in which it was placed. Whatever might be the precise degree of support which they derived from the theory of an apostolical succession from Peter and an heirship of his power of the keys, it will not be disputed that in fact the position of the Popes at the centre of gravity of the Roman world, in the one great city to which all roads converged, enormously smoothed the way for their advance to the undisputed primacy of tbe Church. The whole constitution of the new religious community imitated that of the great political system in which it found itself embedded; and, like it, depended on the recognition of great cities as centres of life and power for the countries in which they were situated. The Bishop of Antioch was head of all the Churches of Syria. The Bishop of Alexandria was head of all the Churches of Egypt. It was only natural, in the second and third centuries, that the Bishop of Rome should be head of all the Churches of the Roman Empire, which was practically conterminous with Christendom. Had Peter lived and died at Bethsaida, it is possible that the primacy of the Christian Church might have been claimed for the bishopric of Bethsaida: it is certain that the claim would not have met with so easy nor so worldwide acceptance.

Since, then, the position of the Roman bishops in the forefront of the Christian Church was Papal originally connected so closely with the political ascendency of their city, it was possible, now that political ascendency was lost, that ecclesiastical supremacy might go with it. And, if the Pope lost his primacy, to no see was he more likely to lose it than to the pushing, ambitious, powerful see of Constantinople; that see whose representatives were ever at the ear of the Emperor, moulding the ecclesiastical policy of his reign; that see whose splendour was beheld by all the strangers who visited the New Rome; that see which already, in the course of little more than a century, had acquired the primacy first of Thrace, then of Pontus and Asia; that see which had just succeeded in accomplishing the subjection of the Patriarch of Antioch, and was now profiting by the religious wrangles of the Egyptians to reduce to similar dependence him of Alexandria.

Of all the many able and somewhat unscrupulous men who ever stood in the *ambo* of the great church at Constantinople perhaps none was cleverer and none bolder than Acacius. We have already seen him opposing the usurper Basiliscus, restoring Zeno, and guiding the pen of that Emperor as he traced the characters of the great Henoticon, that instrument which, as he no doubt hoped, would be looked back to by posterity as a more triumphant 'End of Controversy' than the Tome which the great Leo himself had presented to the fathers of Chalcedon. Now that our point of view is transferred to Rome from Constantinople, we can perhaps see a little more clearly what reasons Acacius had, apart from any deep spiritual interest of his own in the subject-matter of the controversy, for desiring its settlement on the basis of the Henoticon. The Council of Chalcedon had by its twenty-eighth canon (a canon passed, it is said, after the departure of Leo's legates and of the majority of the bishops) rested the primacy of Old Rome solely on the political ground, making no mention of the commission to Peter, and had assigned the same prerogatives to the Bishop of New Rome, leaving apparently but an honorary precedence to the Bishop of the elder capital. Since this was the judgment of Chalcedon, a judgment which, when the grounds of it were considered, would evidently, in a very few years, through the political changes that were going forward, give the see of Constantinople priority over that of Rome itself, the authority of the Council of Chalcedon must be upheld, and therefore neither Basiliscus nor any other emperor should be allowed to lapse into mere Monophysitism. But, on the other hand, since the good-will of the occupants of the thrones of Antioch and Alexandria was necessary to the success of the designs of Acacius, since the doctrine of the single nature of Christ was popular in those capitals and the name of the Council of Chalcedon was abhorred by very many, it would be wise to readmit them to communion by a scheme which should avoid the actual mention of the double nature of Christ and the express ratification of the decrees of the Third Council. With this object the Henoticon was framed, and for a generation or two seemed likely to be successful. In this, as in most ecclesiastical controversies, words were the all-important things. The personal vanity of the combatants must be conciliated, their pretensions to knowledge of Divine things must be respected: if these could be saved harmless, the faith might take care of itself.

Of course, just as much interest as Acacius Bishop of Constantinople had in upholding the Henoticon, just so much had Simplicius Bishop of Rome in destroying it, and the troubles of the see of Alexandria afforded him a useful lever for the purpose. Timothy the Weasel was dead. His rival, the other Timothy, called Solofaciolus, died five years later. Acacius determined to put Peter the Stammerer, a well-known follower of the Weasel's, on the episcopal throne of Alexandria, the Henoticon being the basis of union between the two Churches, by the Bosporus and by the Nile. At first the plan succeeded. Peter the Stammerer subscribed the Henoticon, reigned as bishop at Alexandria, and was during his eight years' episcopate the useful tool of his Byzantine benefactor. But there was a rival candidate for the see, one John Talaias, who had been actually elected on the death of Timothy, but who had, so it was said, solemnly sworn to Zeno that he would never accept the dignity. He was also charged with simony and with misappropriation of the treasures of the Church. What was more undoubted, and perhaps more to the point, was that he was a friend and dependent of Illus, who was now falling into disgrace at Constantinople, and was indeed on the very verge of rebellion. All these circumstances made it easy for Acacius to nullify the election of Talaias and drive him into exile from Alexandria. He fled, however, to Rome, and there, in Pope Simplicius, found a willing listener to all his grievances against the Patriarch of Constantinople. Once, twice, even—four times did Simplicius write to Acacius insisting more and more peremptorily that he should withdraw from the communion of Peter the Stammerer, that rebel against the decrees of Chalcedon, and should not hinder the return of Talaias to his see. Acacius had not the courtesy to reply to any of these letters. While affairs were still in this position the fifteen years' pontificate of Simplicius came to an end. He died on the 2nd of March, 483, and his relics are still exhibited to the people once a year in his native town of Tivoli. The Pope who, born by the waters of 'headlong Anio' had doubtless as a boy often wandered through the vast villa of Hadrian, then still in its original glory, had lived to see Rome itself, the Rome of Horace and of Hadrian, pass under the yoke of a petty chieftain of Herulian mercenaries.

On the death of Simplicius, when the clergy and Odovacar, people of Rome were assembled in the church of St. Peter to elect his successor, one of the Roman ministers of King Odovacar made his appearance among them. This was Basilius, perhaps the same Caecina Basilius whom Sidonius had chosen for his patron twenty-six years before, when he visited Rome, and whose somewhat reserved but honest character he described in writing to his friends. He now filled the office of Praetorian Prefect to the barbarian King—another indication that in the civil government of Italy Odovacar retained the forms of the imperial hierarchy of office unaltered. Addressing the assembled multitude, Basilius informed them that they must not presume as to elect a new Bishop of Rome without the concurrence of his master. This announcement probably only meant that all such rights, not of nomination but of veto, as the emperors had wielded previously to 476, must now be deemed to have survived to Odovacar. But he then proceeded to read a decree forbidding the new Pope, whoever he might be, to alienate any of the lands or ornaments of the Roman Church, and in case of disobedience, threatening the buyer with civil penalties, and the seller—strange menace from a layman and an Arian—with the spiritual penalty of anathema. We know nothing of any special proceedings of Simplicius which may have prompted this decree. It seems to have been accepted without murmuring at the time, though, nineteen years after, it was denounced by a similar assembly held in the same place, as an unhallowed interference on the part of a lay ruler with the affairs of the church, and the assembled clergy with difficulty, while the decree was being read, contained their indignation at the insolent tone of the fallen layman who had dared to interfere with a priest's monopoly of anathema.

The new Pope, Felix II, threw himself heartily into the quarrel with Constantinople. He sent two legates, vitalis and Misenus, with a letter to the Emperor and the Patriarch of Constantinople, haughtily commanding them to desist from all further proceedings in the matter of the recognition of Peter the Stammerer. The legates were imprisoned as soon as they arrived at the Hellespont, their papers were taken from them, and they were threatened with death unless they would obey the Emperor's orders and recognise Peter as Patriarch of Alexandria. On the other hand, gifts and promotion were to be theirs if they complied with the imperial mandate. The legates, who were evidently weak and timid men, submitted to the coercion and the blandishments of the dread Augustus, and communicated with Acacius at a solemn festival at which the name of the Stammerer was read in the Diptychs, or tablets containing the roll-call of orthodox prelates in communion with the see of Constantinople. By this concession they of course surrendered the whole matter in dispute. Their master, Felix, was informed of this disloyalty by his faithful allies, the so-called 'sleepless' monks of Constantinople, who, perhaps from pure conviction, were passionate adherents of the Council of Chalcedon. On the return (484 A.D.) of his legates he held a synod at Rome (no doubt attended only by Italian bishops), and therein condemned the traitorous conduct of his legates, deposed them from their sees, and even excluded them from the holy Table. He went further, and the Council accompanied him. By an unheard-0f stretch of power they condemned Acacius as a promoter of heresy, pronounced him deposed from his episcopal office, and cut him off 'as a putrid limb' from the body of the Church.

Next came the question by whom this sentence was to be served on the object of it, on the great Acacius, in all his pride of place and strong in the favour of his sovereign. Tutus, a *Defensor* of the Church, was dispatched on this errand; and, notwithstanding the vigilance of the imperial guards, arrived in safety at Constantinople. There monkish fanaticism relieved him of the most dangerous part of his task. One of the Sleepless ones fastened the fatal parchment to the dress of Acacius as he was about to officiate in the church. Acacius quietly proceeded in the holy ceremony. Suddenly he paused: with calm, clear voice he ordered the name of Felix, Bishop of Home, to be struck out of the roll of bishops in communion with his Church. The ban of Rome was encountered by the ban of Constantinople. Some of the monks who had dared to affix such a stigma on the all-powerful Patriarch were killed by his indignant followers, others were wounded, and the rest were shut up in prison.

This scene in the great Church of the Divine Wisdom at Constantinople was the commencement of the first great schism between the Eastern and Western Churches,— a schism which lasted thirty-five years, and covered almost the whole period of the reign of Theodoric. Several overtures towards reconciliation were made. One by one all the chief actors in the scene were removed by death, Acacius in 489, Zeno in 491, Felix in 492. But the See of Rome was inflexible; she might 'spare the fallen', but she would 'war down the proud'. There could be no peace with Byzantium till the name of Acacius, who had dared to strike a Roman pontiff out of the diptychs, was struck out of the diptychs itself, nor till Peter the Stammerer's accursed name was also expunged: all which did not take place till the year 519.

It is possible that the quarrel between the two sees of Rome and Constantinople reacted on the political relations of Italy and the Empire. It is certain that these relations became rapidly more unfriendly soon after the mutual excommunication of the pontiffs, and continued so till the end of the reign of Odovacar.

At the outset it is probable that Zeno did not view the Teutonic mercenary's accession to power with any great dissatisfaction. In Augustulus he could have no interest: for his kinsman Nepos his sympathy was of a very languid character. His vanity was flattered by the fact that 'all the ornaments of the palace', including no doubt the diadem and the purple robe, were sent by Odovacar to Constantinople. The story of the embassies from Italy to Byzantium told by Malchus illustrates that aspect of the case in which it was possible for the Eastern Caesar to look upon the recent events in Italy with not unmingled dissatisfaction. It was not unpleasant to hear from the lips of a Roman Senator that Italy did not need a separate royalty, since Zeno's own imperial sway would suffice for both ends of the earth. And, however little the facts of the case might correspond with this deferential theory, Odovacar suing with some humility for the title of Patrician, Odovacar representing himself as in some sort a lieutenant of the Emperor, presented a not unwelcome spectacle to the imperial vanity. Add to this, that at any rate for the first three or four years of the reign of Zeno, Onoulf the brother of Odovacar, the client and the assassin of Harmatius, was a soldier of fortune about the Court, probably a connecting link between the Augustus and his brother. We can thus understand why, down to about 480 or 481, the Courts of Ravenna and of Constantinople may have regarded one another with no very unfriendly feelings.

The conquest of Dalmatia may have told both ways on this friendly relation. The barbarian's promptitude in avenging the death of her cousin Nepos would recommend him to the favour of the Empress Ariadne; but, on the other hand, by the addition of Dalmatia to his dominions he became a disagreeably near neighbour to the lord of the Lower Danube.

Then came, almost contemporaneously and not unconnected with one another, the schism between the two sees and the revolt of Illus. John Talaias, the fugitive patriarch of Alexandria, the client of the Roman popes, was, as we have seen, also a client of Illus, and may very probably have been the medium of communications between that general and Odovacar. Onoulf also, perhaps at this time, quitted the service of Zeno, since three years later we find him commanding his brother's armies in Noricum. But, as our information concerning this alienation between the Emperor and the King is very meagre, and is all furnished by one author (Joannes Antiochenus), it will be best to give it in his own words :—

"Illus therefore, having gone into open revolt, between proclaimed Marcian Emperor, and sent to Odovacar the *tyrannus* of Western Rome, and to the rulers of Persia and Armenia: and he also prepared a navy. Odoacer, however, replied that he could not ally himself with him, but the others promised alliance as soon as he could join his forces with theirs".

Joannes then describes the revolt of Illus, its early successes and subsequent decline, and continues :—

"In the consulship of Longinus (486, two years after the date of the previous extract), when Theodoric was again disposed for revolt and was ravaging the districts round Thrace, Zeno stirred up against Odoacer the nation of the Rugians, since he was apprised that the latter was making arrangements to ally himself with Illus. But when Odoacer's troops had obtained a brilliant victory [over the Rugians], and moreover had sent gifts to Zeno out of the spoils, he disclaimed his allies and professed satisfaction with what had been done".

The story of the Rugian war, taking us as it does out of Italy into the lands of the Middle Danube, and opening up some interesting glimpses into the life of the new barbarian states founded amidst the ruins of the Empire, must be told in the next chapter. But meanwhile it is important to note that already in the year 486 the friendly relations between Odovacar and Zeno had been replaced by scarcely veiled enmity; and thus the mind of the Emperor was already tuned to harmony with that fierce harangue against the usurped authority of a king of Rugians and Turcilingians which, according to Jordanes, Theodoric delivered before him some time in the year 488.

CHAPTER V.

THE RUGIAN WAR.

'The Emperor stirred up against Odoacer the nation of the Rugians'. To understand the meaning of this statement, and to complete our knowledge, scanty at the best, concerning this war, which occupied the attention of Odovacar during three years of his short reign, 486-488, we must turn back to the life of the saintly hermit of Noricum, *Severinus*.

The picture of the long-continued and hopeless misery of a people which the biographer of the Saint draws for us is very depressing. Those lands between the Danube and the Noric Alps which now form one of the most thoroughly enjoyable portions of 'the playground of Europe', the valleys round the Gross Glockner, the Salzkammergut, Salzburg with its castle rock and its noble amphitheatre of hills, Lorch with its stately monastery, Linz with its busy industries, all the fair domains of the old Archduchy of Austria down even to Vienna itself, were then in that most cruel of all positions, neither definitely subjected by the barbarian nor efficaciously protected against him, but wasted by his plundering bands at their will, though still calling themselves Roman, and possibly maintaining some faint show of official connection with Italy and the Empire. The Thuringians 011 the north-west and the Alamanni on the west appeared alternately under the walls of Passau, and seldom departed without carrying some of its wretched inhabitants into captivity. The latter nation of marauders pushed their ravages sometimes as far inland as to Noreia, in the very heart of Noricum. The Ostrogoths from Pannonia levied contributions in the valley of the Drave; and the Suevic Hunimund, the enemy of the Ostrogoths, marching across the unhappy province to meet his foe, sacked the city of Boiotrum, which he surprised while the inhabitants were busy over their harvest, and shed the blood of the priests in the baptistery of the basilica.

In the midst of this anarchy, the only semblance of firm and settled government seems to have been offered by the powerful monarchy of the Rugians, who occupied a compact territory north of the Danube corresponding to the eastern half of Bohemia, the west of Moravia, and a part of Lower Austria. And such order as they did preserve was probably but the reservation to themselves of an exclusive right to levy contributions on the Roman provincials. "I cannot bear", said the Rugian king Feletheus to Severinus, "that this people, for whom thou art interceding, should be laid waste by the cruel depredations of the Alamanni and the Thuringians, or slain by the sword or carried into slavery, when there are near to us tributary towns in which they ought to be settled". And this was the motive for bringing a great army of Rugians against the city of Lauriacum, in which were assembled the trembling fugitives who had escaped from the other barbaric invasions. Nor could all the exhortations of the Saint, though they seem to have prevented actual bloodshed, change the barbarian's purpose of removing the Provincials (who are always spoken of by the once mighty name of Romans) out of their city of refuge and dispersing them among various towns in his own dominions, where 'they lived in benevolent companionship with the Rugians', the benevolent companionship, doubtless, of the lamb with the wolf.

So long as he lived, no doubt Saint Severinus did much to soften, in individual cases, the hardships of this harassed and weary existence. In his monastery at Faviana he collected great magazines of food and stores of clothing, from which he used to relieve the hunger and nakedness of the captives or refugees who travelled along the great Danubian road. But though his heart was full of pity for his brethren, his presence was not always welcomed by them. The stormy petrel of Noricum, he was constantly appearing at some still undemolished Roman settlement and prophesying to the inhabitants, "The time of this *castellum* is come. In two days, or in three days, the barbarians who have devastated so many cities will appear before your walls". The practical counsel of the Saint was generally contained in one of two words. It was either 'Fast' or 'Fly'. Himself an anchorite who practised the austerest forms of self-discipline, never eating before sunset except on feast-days, and allowing himself only one meal a week in Lent, yet ever preserving, even under the stress of this abstinence, a cheerful and unruffled countenance, he loved to accompany his message of coming woe by an exhortation to the provincials to disarm the anger of the Lord by fasting and prayer. This counsel was not always acceptable. At Innstadt, for example, when the priests asked for relics for their church, and the merchants that leave might be obtained for them to trade with the Rugians, and when the Saint replied, "It is of no use; the time is come for this town, like so many other *castella*, to be desolated", a certain presbyter, filled with the spirit of the devil, cried out, "Oh, go away, holy man! and that speedily, that we may have a little rest from fastings and watchings". The Saint wept, for he knew that open scurrility is the evidence of secret sins; and then he prophesied of the woe that should come upon them, and how that human blood should be shed in that very baptistery in which they were standing. All which came true almost immediately after he had departed. Hunimund drew near to the city and took it, and the scurrilous priest was slain in that very basilica, to which he had fled for refuge".

Once or twice the Saint lifted up his voice for war, and promised victory; but as a rule, if he did not recommend the spiritual weapons of fasting and prayer, he counselled the inhabitants to withdraw before the barbarian forces. Thus he vainly urged the people of Joviacum (a town about twenty miles below Passau) to escape before the Herulian invasion, which he foreboded, should come upon them. The citizens of Quintana, who had already fled once, to Passau, were exhorted to flee again, to Lauriacum; and the few disobedient ones were massacred by the Thuringians. But always, during the last and dreariest years of his life, when the barbarian darkness seemed gathering most hopelessly over the doomed provincials the Saint foretold that the Romans should be delivered from their enemies, and led up out of Noricum, as Moses led the Israelites out of Egypt. "And then", said he, "as Joseph asked his brethren, so do I beg of you, that ye carry my bones up hence. For these places, now so crowded with cultivators, shall be reduced into so mighty a solitude that the enemy, hunting for gold, shall break open even the sepulchres of the dead".

Severinus preserved the mystery as to his origin and parentage till the end, unimparted even to his nearest friends. His pure Latin speech showed that there was no admixture of the barbarian in his. blood, and it was generally believed that he had spent some time as a hermit in the East before he suddenly appeared in the towns of the Danubian Noricum. He would sometimes casually allude to the cities of the East, and to immense journeyings which he had in past times performed there. But he did not permit himself to be questioned as to his past history. Near the close of his life, an Italian priest of noble birth and weighty character, Primenius by name, fled to Noricum, fearing to be involved in the fate of Orestes, of whom he had been the confidential adviser and friend. After many days bad passed in friendly intercourse between them, Primenius one day hazarded the enquiry, "Holy master, from what province first sprang that light which God has deigned to bestow on us in thee?". The man of God turned aside the question with a joke: "If you think I am a runaway slave, get ready the ransom, that you may offer it on my behalf when I am claimed". Then, more seriously, he discoursed on the unimportance of race or birthplace in comparison with that Divine call which, he earnestly asserted, had led him to those regions to succour his perishing brethren.

The young recruit whom Severinus had blessed him and on his journey to Italy, and to whom he had prophesied the splendid future which lay before him, beyond the Alpine horizon, was not unmindful of that early augury. King Odovacar sent to the Saint a friendly letter, promising him the fulfillment of any petition which he might choose to make. On this invitation Severinus asked for the forgiveness of a certain exile named Ambrose, and the King joyfully acceded to the request. On another occasion several noble persons were speaking about the King in the Saint's presence, and "according to custom", says the biographer, "were praising him with man's flattery". We note the presence of these 'many noble persons' of Noricum, Roman citizens no doubt, in the Saint's cell, and their high praises of the barbarian ruler of Italy, as interesting signs of the times, even if their panegyrics were, as the biographer hints, somewhat conventional and insincere. The Saint enquired, "Who was the king thus greatly lauded?". They replied, "Odovacar". He answered, "Odovacar who shall be safe between thirteen and fourteen years", predicting thus with accuracy the duration of the new king's unquestioned supremacy in Italy.

But the chief relations of the hermit of Noricum were naturally with the Rugian kings, and through his biography we gain an insight into the inner life of one of these new barbaric royalties, of which we should otherwise know nothing. *Flaccitheus*, king of the Rugians (perhaps from about 430 to 460), was greatly alarmed at the vast multitude of Goths, apparently full of enmity against him, who were settled on his border in Lower Pannonia. Asking the advice of the holy man, whom he consulted like a heavenly oracle, he told him in much perturbation that he had requested from the Gothic princes a safe-conduct into Italy, and that the refusal of this request filled him with alarm as to their intentions. Severinus replied, "If we were united by the bond of the One Catholic Faith I would gladly give thee advice concerning the life to come. But since thy enquiry relates only to the present life, I will tell thee that thou needest not be disquieted by the multitude of these Goths, since they will shortly depart and leave thee in safety. Live a peaceful life; do not undergo the curse laid upon him "who maketh flesh his arm", lay no snares for others, while taking heed of those laid for thyself: so shalt thou meet thine end peacefully in thy bed".

The divine oracle soothed the anxious King, who went away greatly comforted. Soon afterwards, however, a crowd of barbarian, probably Gothic, marauders carried off a number of the Rugians, whose King again came to the Saint for counsel. By divine revelation Severinus warned him not to follow the robbers, to beware of crossing the river, and to avoid the snares which in three several places his enemies had laid for him. "Soon shall a faithful messenger arrive who shall assure thee of the truth of all these sayings". And in fact, very shortly afterwards, two Rugian captives, who had escaped from the dwellings of the enemy, arrived at the King's court and confirmed the Saint's predictions in every particular. The devices of the enemies of the Rugian king being thus frustrated, his affairs went on prospering, and in due time Flaccitheus died in rest and tranquillity.

To him succeeded his son *Feletheus* or *Feva*, who at first followed his father's example, and was guided in all things by the counsels of the holy hermit. But before long the influence of his wife, the cruel and guilty Giso, began to assert itself, always in opposition to the healthful spirit of divine grace. This woman (evidently an Arian), among her other infamous actions, even sought to re-baptize certain Catholics, but was obliged to desist when her husband, out of reverence for Saint Severinus, forbade the sacrilegious deed. This queen was wont to cause certain of the 'Romans' (that is, provincials) to be carried across the Danube and there kept in bitter bondage. This had she once done with some of the inhabitants of Faviana, whom, when carried captive, she condemned to slavery of the most degrading kind. Severinus, grieving for his neighbours, sent messengers entreating her to restore them to their homes. But she, flaming out in violent wrath, returned a message of angry contempt to the hermit: "Go, oh slave of God! skulk into your cell to pray, and let me issue such orders concerning my slaves as I think fit". The Saint, when he received this answer, said, "I trust in our Lord Jesus Christ, who will make her do of necessity that which her evil will refuses to do at my request".

That very day the judgment of God came upon the arrogant queen. There were certain barbarian goldsmiths who were kept close prisoners in the palace and obliged to work all day at ornaments for the royal family. The little prince Frederic, son of Feletheus and Giso, out of childish curiosity (and perhaps attracted by the glitter of the gold) ventured in amongst these men. The workmen at once caught up a sword, and held it to the child's throat. "No one", said they, "shall now enter this room unless our lives and our liberty are assured to us by oath. If this be refused we will first kill the child and then ourselves, for we are made desperate by the misery of this dungeon". The cruel and wicked queen at once perceived that the vengeance of God had come upon her for her insults to the holy man. She sent horsemen to implore his pardon, and restored to their homes the Roman captives for whom he had that day interceded. The goldsmiths received a sworn assurance of safety, upon which they let the child go, and were themselves dismissed in peace. The revered servant of Christ recognized the good hand of his God in this interposition, which had actually accomplished more than he asked for, since not only the Roman captives but the oppressed barbarian gold-workers had obtained their freedom. The queen and her husband hastened to his cell, exhibited the son whom they acknowledged themselves to have received back from the very gates of death through his intercession, and promised obedience to all his commands in future.

One instance of the prescience of the Saint may be noticed here, because it incidentally throws some light on the condition of the soldiers who guarded the boundaries of the Empire. What happened to the legions on the Danubian *limes* may easily have occurred also to those stationed *per lineam valli* in our own island (England). "At the time", says Eugippius, "when the Roman Empire still held together, the soldiers of many towns were supported by public pay for the better guardianship of the limes". This obscure sentence perhaps means that local troops were drafted off to the limes, and there received, as was natural, imperial pay and equipments. "When this custom ceased, the squadrons (*turmae*) of cavalry were obliterated; but the Batavian legion (stationed at Passau) lasted as long as the limes itself stood. From this legion certain soldiers had gone forth to Italy to bear to their comrades their last pay, and these men had been slain on the march by the barbarians, no one knowing thereof. On a certain day, while Severinus was reading in his cell, suddenly he closed the codex and began to weep and sigh. Then he told the by-standers to run quickly to the river's brink, which, as he affirmed, was in that very hour stained with human gore. And immediately word was brought that the bodies of the aforesaid soldiers had just been swept on shore by the force of the stream".

At length the time (482) drew near for the saint to die. Of the very day of his death, as of so many of the events which had made his life memorable, it was believed that he had an intimation from Heaven. Not long before it arrived he sent for the king and queen of the Rugians. "Giso", said he to the queen, "dost thou love this man" (pointing to the king) "or silver and gold best?". "My husband better than all wealth", said she. "Then", he said, "cease to oppress the innocent, lest their affliction be the cause of the scattering of your power: for thou dost often pervert the mildness of the king. Hitherto God has prospered your kingdom. Henceforward you will see…." The royal couple took leave of him and departed.

Next stood Ferderuchus by his bed-side—Fer-deruchus the king's brother, who had received from Feletheus a present of the few Roman towns remaining on the Danube, Faviana among them. Severinus spoke of his own imminent departure, and besought the prince not to draw down upon himself the Divine wrath, by touching the stores collected during the saint's lifetime for the poor and the captives. Ferderuchus eagerly disclaimed the intention imputed to him, and professed a desire to follow the pious footsteps of his father Flaccitheus. But Severinus replied, "On the very first opportunity thou wilt violate this my cell and wilt be punished for it in a manner which I do not desire". Ferderuchus repeated his protestations of obedience and departed. The Saint knew his covetous nature better, perchance, than he did himself. The end followed speedily. At midnight Severinus called his monks to him, exhorted them to persevere according to their vocation, kissed each one of them, made the sign of the cross, and died, while they were reciting around him the 150th Psalm. Scarcely was his worn body laid in the slight shell which the brethren had prepared for it, mindful of his prophecy concerning their speedy migration southwards, when Ferderuchus, poor and impious, and made ever more ruthless by his barbarous avarice, bore down upon the monastery, determined to carry off the stores of raiment collected there for the use of the poor. When these were swept away he proceeded to take the sacred vessels from the altar. His steward did not dare to execute this part of his master's commands himself, but deputed the work to a soldier named Avitianus, whose unwilling sacrilege was punished by an immediate attack of St. Vitus's dance. Alarmed and penitent, the soldier turned monk, and ended his days in solitude on a distant island. Meanwhile the covetous Ferderuchus, unmindful of the dying saint's exhortations and of his own promises, continued to ransack the monastery, and finally carried off everything except the bare walls, which he could not convey across the Danube to his own land. But vengeance soon overtook him; for before a month had elapsed, being slain by Frederic his brother's son (the boy who once wandered into the workshop of the goldsmiths, now grown up to manhood), he lost both booty and life.

These events occurred in the early part of 482, and they are connected—but precisely how connected it is impossible to say—with the war which Odovacar, five years later, waged against the Rugians. The biographer of Severinus, after describing the defeat of Ferderuchus by his nephew and the death of the former, says, "For which cause king Odovacar made war upon the Rugians". But as the sacrilegious inroad of Ferderuchus seems to have followed close upon the death of the Saint, which certainly happened in 482, and is expressly stated to have been followed in its turn by the expedition of Frederic, and as Odovacar's Rugian war did not break out before the end of 486 (being in fact assigned by two chroniclers to the year 487), it is clear that the death of Ferderuchus was not immediately avenged by the Italian king. Possibly (but this is a mere conjecture) some brotherhood in arms may have connected Odovacar and Ferderuchus in old days, when the former was still an adventurer in Noricum, and he may have been bound by Teutonic notions of honour to avenge, sooner or later, the death of his comrade. Possibly the increased sufferings of the provincials at the hands of the Rugians, after the death of Saint Severinus, may have called upon a king, who now in some sort represented the majesty of Rome, to redress their wrongs. At any rate, in these elements of strife, and in the fact that between the Alps and the Danube no other barbarian power existed which could vie with the monarchy of Feletheus, we find some explanation of the sentence in which John of Antioch informed us that "the Emperor Zeno stirred up against Odoacer the nation of the Rugians".

The events of the war are soon told. Possibly the Rugians made some movement against Odovacar in 486. It is certain that in 487 he returned the blow, invaded their territory, put the young general Frederic to flight, and carried Feletheus (or Feva) and his wicked wife prisoners to Ravenna.

Afterwards, probably in the following year, Odovacar was informed that Frederic had returned to his own land, upon which he sent his brother Onoulf with a large army against him. Frederic was again forced to flee, and betook himself to Theodoric the Amal, who was then dwelling at Novae (probably the place which is now the Bulgarian town of Sistova), on the Lower Danube.

After this conquest of *Rugiland* (so Paulus Diaconus informs us that the country of the Rugians was called) the emigration of Roman provincials into Italy took place, as foretold by Severinus. Onoulf ordered it; Pierius, Count of the Domestics (who received from Odovacar the deed of gift mentioned in the last chapter), superintended the taking the doing of it. A certain aged priest named Lucillus, to whom Severinus had predicted his decease, and who had then replied, "Surely I shall go before thee", was still living, and directed the removal of his remains, which, mindful of the Saint's injunction, the emigrants were set upon carrying up out of the land of bondage. They went at evening, chanting psalms, to the Saint's resting-place. The usual mediaeval marvels of the charnel-house followed,—the body found undecaying, though un-embalmed, after six years' entombment, even the hair and the beard still untouched, a sweet odour filling all the neighbourhood of the tomb. The body, with its cerements unchanged, was placed in a chest, which had been prepared some time before in anticipation of the removal, set upon a waggon (*carpentam*), and drawn by horses over the mountainous passes which separate Noricum from Italy. In the sad procession which followed the relics of the saint walked all the Roman inhabitants of Noricum, leaving the ruined towns by the Danube for the new homes allotted to each of them in Italy.

After long journeyings, the body of the Saint reached a village (*castellum*) called Mons Feletis (possibly Felitto in Campania, about fifteen miles east of Paestum), and there it abode during at least four of the troublous years that followed, healing the sick, giving speech to the dumb, and working the usual wonders that attested the genuineness of a Saint's relics in the fifth century. But, after a time, a devout and illustrious widow named Barbaria, who had known the Saint by report during his life, whose husband had often corresponded with him, and who now greatly venerated his memory, finding that his body, though brought with all honour to Italy, yet lacked a permanent resting-place, sent to Marcian the presbyter and the congregation of monks which had gathered round the sacred relics, inviting them to lay their precious deposit within her domain. The Pope, Gelasius, gave his consent. All the dwellers in Naples poured forth to receive in reverence the body of the Saint, and it was duly laid, according to her invitation, 'in the Lucullan Castle', where a monastery was founded, presided over, first by Marcian and then by Eugippius, the biographer to whom we owe these details. The usual miracles were wrought by the sacred bones. A blind man was restored to sight. The chief of the Neapolitan choir was cured of a most stubborn headache by leaning his forehead against the dead man's bier. Demons were cast out, and innumerable other miracles of bodily and mental healing perpetuated the fame of Saint Severinus of Noricum till the fear of the Saracen marauders caused tomb and monastery to be transported to the safer asylum of Naples.

But who was the illustrious lady who invited the monks to settle on her land? and what is the Lucullan Castle where Severinus was laid? It is impossible to prove, but we may venture a conjecture that this widow Barbaria, evidently a lady of high rank, is none other than the mother of Romulus Augustulus. She too sprang from Noricum, her husband Orestes had doubtless often corresponded with Severinus concerning the affairs of the provincials in that country. Yet they might well have known the Saint by fame only, not by personal intercourse, since, about the same time that Severinus suddenly appeared by the banks of the Danube (shortly after the death of Attila), Orestes, accompanied doubtless by his wife, must have left his native country, Pannonia, and come to seek his fortune in Italy. These, however, are but slight coincidences; but when it is remembered that it was to 'the Lucullan Castle' that Augustulus was consigned by the barbarian conqueror, our conjecture rises many degrees in probability. It is true that nothing is said as to his being accompanied by his mother, but this companionship, in itself probable, is rendered yet more so by a letter written by command of Theodoric to *Romulus and his mother,* which we find in the official correspondence of Cassiodorus.

As for the Lucullanum (whose site was left somewhat doubtful when it was previously mentioned in this history), it seems to be agreed by the best antiquaries of Naples that it corresponds, as nearly as the alteration of the coast-line will permit, with the Castel dell' Ovo, that remarkable island or peninsula which juts out from the shore of modem Naples between the Chiaja and the Military Harbour. Perhaps some of the mainland in the modern quarter of Santa Lucia, lying westward of the present Royal Palace, went to make up the pleasure-grounds and to form the fishponds of the luxurious conqueror of Mithridates, that Lucullanum which was the gilded prison of the last Roman Emperor of Rome.

NOTE C. ODOVACAE'S NAME IN AN INSCRIPTION AT SALZBURG.

A READER of this boob, visiting Salzburg, might, unless forewarned, think that he had stumbled upon an important contribution to our scanty knowledge of the acts of Odovacar.

In the side of the Monchsberg, a steep cliff immediately above the church and cemetery of St. Peter, there are two caves which tradition connects with the memory of Maximus, who is said to have suffered death at the hands of the barbarians in the year 476 or 477. There is still visible in the cave this inscription on a stone: "Anno Domini 477 Odoacer, rex Ruthenorum, Gepidi, Gothi, Hungari et Heruli".

There was also a wooden tablet (now, I think, removed to the Museum) bearing a long inscription, the most important sentences of which, for our purpose, are the following: "Quo [Attila] mortuo regnante Zenone im- peratore anno Domini 477 Odoacer, natione Rhutenus, Romam cum Herulis ingreditur, Latinos annis 14 opprimens…".

In spite of the minuteness of their details, and of the very interesting place with which they are connected, these two inscriptions are of no historical value. Both of them give the date according to the computation of Dionysius Exiguus, from the birth of our Lord; that fact alone makes it impossible that they could be in any sense contemporary documents. (The Dionysian computation was not adopted even in Italy till about 530). Nor, if the date were treated as an alteration of later times, will the substance of the inscriptions stand the test of criticism any better. Both introduce the Hungarians into the list of the assailants of Juvavia, and the Hungarians did not appear in Europe till the ninth century. Both make Odovacar a Ruthene instead of a Rugian, the Ruthenians having apparently emerged not long before the Hungarians. The inscription on the wooden tablet makes Severinus bishop of *Ravenna*,—a ridiculous blunder. It would require fuller data than I possess, to decide when these inscriptions were really placed in the caves, but probably not earlier than the fall of the monarchy of the Avars in 796 (soon after which time German civilization began to rear Salzburg on the ruins of Juvavia), perhaps much later.

The same remarks which have been made as to the inscriptions apply to a work entitled 'Historia de origine, consecratione et reparatione speluncae seu eremitorii ejusque capellae in monte prope coemeterium sancti Petri in civitate Salisburgensi, ex antiquissimis monumentis et manuscriptis in lucem protracta' (printed in 1661).

The historian of Roman Salzburg, Dr. Ignaz Schumann von Mannsegg (in his monograph *Juvavia* published 184a), comments on this MS. at considerable length (pp. 247-361), while admitting that it is not entirely accurate. But it also mentions Hungarians among the invaders, and is evidently a comparatively late production, not at all deserving the attention which Dr. Schumann has given to it. The only reason for alluding to it at all is that it speaks of Odovacar as an ordinary barbarian king and invader ('Eodem anno 476 ille Rugiorum princeps Odoacer exercitum suum ingen tem et fortissimum per hasNoricales terras in Italiam duxerat, etc.). And if this little treatise had any contemporary authority at all, we might be forced by it to reconsider the theory, now admitted by all scholars, that Odovacar was not in form a foreign invader, but rather a ringleader of mutinous soldiers in the pay of the Empire.

The caves in the Monchsberg, and the cemetery of St. Peter below them, are extremely interesting, and probably do carry us back to the earliest days of Christian Juvavia. It is quite possible that monks under the presidency of a certain Maximus may have congregated there after a partial destruction of the city by the Huns in 452. Quite possible too that Maximus and fifty of his companions may have been hurled down the steep sides of the Monchsberg, and so met their death at the hands of some of the barbarians who were at that time the scourge of Noricum. But it may be said positively that Odovacar had nothing to do with this massacre, and it may be almost as strongly asserted that ' the heretic Widemir (the Ostrogoth), whom the MS. 'de Origine' tries to connect with it, was also guiltless, and very likely entirely ignorant of the cruel deed.

CHAPTER VI.

THE DEATH-GRAPPLE.

In the preceding chapter we saw that Frederic, Theodoric the last scion of the Rugian stock, after his unsuccessful revolt fled before the army commanded by the brother of Odovacar, and sought refuge at the Court of Theodoric. Perhaps the injury done to one who was certainly an ally, and who may have been a kinsman, quickened the preparations of Theodoric. Or perhaps his bargain with the Byzantine Court having been concluded, he had been given to understand that he and his foederati, who had now received a commission to invade Italy, must look for no more rations or pay from the imperial treasury. Certain it is that, at what seems to us a most unseasonable time for such a march, in the late autumn of 488, he broke up his court or camp or settlement at Sistova, that high fortress on the south of the Danube overlooking what is now the flat and marshy Wallachian shore, and started with his nation-army on the long and difficult journey to Italy.

Seldom, since Moses led the Children of Israel through the wilderness, has a more ill-compacted host tempted to penetrate through hostile countries and to win, by the edge of the sword, a new possession. In the case of Alaric, and of others of the great Teutonic chiefs, we have already had our attention called, by Claudian and other authorities, to the *family* aspect of their marches, migrations rather than campaigns. But of this journey of Theodoric the emphatic language of contemporaries justifies us in saying, that it was preeminently a nation, in all its strength and all its helplessness, that accompanied him. His own family, mother, sisters, nephews, evidently were with him, as before on the march to Dyrrhachium. And as with the chief, so with the people. Procopius says, 'With Theodoric went the people of the Goths, putting their wives and children and as much of their furniture as they could take with them into their waggons.' Somewhat more minutely, but with too much of his usual vapid rhetoric, says Theodoric's panegyrist, Ennodius, "Then, after you had summoned all your powers far and wide, the people, scattered through countless tribes, come together again as one nation, and a world migrates with you to the Ausonian land, a world every member of which is nevertheless your kinsman[2]. Waggons are made to do duty as houses, and into those wandering habitations all things that can minister to the needs of the occupants are poured. Then were the tools of Ceres, and the stones with which the corn is ground, dragged along by the labouring oxen. Pregnant mothers, forgetful of their sex and of the burden which they bore, undertook the toil of providing food for the families of thy people. Followed the reign of winter in thy camp. Over the hair of thy men the long frost threw a vail of snowy white; the icicles hung in a tangle from their beards. So hard was the frost that the garment which the matron's persevering toil had woven (for her husband) had to be broken before he could fit it to his body. Food for thy marching armies was forced from the grasp of the hostile nations around, or procured by the cunning of the hunter".

The question has been often asked, what must we suppose to have been the number of this moving multitude? The calculation can be only conjectural, but the data that we have point to a high figure. In the campaign in Epirus, as the reader may remember, the defeat of the mere rearguard of the Ostrogothic army led to the capture of 5000 prisoners (a yet larger number having been cut to pieces), and put 2000 waggons at the disposal of the Byzantine host. In the same campaign a body of 6000 men, the most valiant in the army, are spoken of by Theodoric as a sort of flying column with which he was willing to march into Thrace and annihilate the forces of the son of Triarius; while that rival, on making his peace with the Empire, had obtained the promise of rations and pay for 13,000 men, to be selected by himself from the number of his followers. Looking at these facts, remembering that probably many of the Triarian Goths had joined Theodoric's standard after the extinction of the family of their leader, and that some, perhaps many, Rugians must have followed the fugitive Frederic into his camp, we shall probably be safe in estimating the fighting strength of Theodoric's army at 40,000 men, and the total number of the nation on its travels at 200,000If anything, this conjecture is too low, since we find it stated that the Gothic army which besieged Rome only fifty years later (but they had been years of peace and unexampled prosperity) consisted of not less than 150,000 fighting men.

Accepting the moderate computation here suggested, we can imagine, or rather we cannot imagine, the anxiety which must have gnawed the soul of Theodoric when he had cut himself loose from his communications in Moesia, when his progress was barred by enemies upon whose neutrality he had, perhaps rashly, reckoned, when weeks lengthened into months, winter months, and still his long array, with all the sick, the children, the delicate women, with 200,000 mouths needing daily food, stood upon the snow-covered Illyrian uplands, and could not yet descend into the promised land, could not yet even see their final foe.

The first 300 miles were probably much the easiest part of the journey. They would be travelling along the great Danubian highway, perhaps the most important of all the roads connecting the eastern and western portions of the Roman Empire, and one which, even in those days of feebleness and decay, and after all the ravages of Goth and Hun, was still probably kept in a fair state of repair. Possibly too, as Theodoric was still in the territory of the now friendly empire, supplies for his followers would be forthcoming, if not from the imperial magazines, at any rate on moderate terms in the markets of the provincials. But when he reached Singidunum (Belgrade), the scene of that boyish victory of his over the Sarmatian king, his difficulties began, if they had not begun before. It is pretty clear from the facts, even if it were not expressly stated by Procopius, that, after the Ostrogoths performed their celebrated march to the Aegean under Theudemir (in 473), the Gepidae moved across the Danube (from Dacia into Pannonia) and occupied either the whole of the broad lands thus evacuated, or at any rate the south-eastern corner of them, including the important and still not utterly ruined cities of Singidunum and Sirmium. Now, into this corner of the land, this long strip of country (the modern province of Slavonia) between the rivers Drave and Save, Theodorics road led him, and through it he must lead his way-worn and hungering followers; but the Gepid barred the way. An embassy was sent, we may imagine, with such an appeal as Moses made to Sihon king of the Amorites which dwelt at Heshbon: "Let me pass through thy land : we will not turn into the fields, or into the vineyards; we will not drink of the waters of the well: but we will go along by the king's high way, until we be past thy borders". Like that appeal, however, this of Theodoric's, though it might have been based on the claims of kindred and on memories of the far-distant days when the Gepids manned one boat and the Goths two in the first migration, if made, was disregarded, and the nation-army, all encumbered as it was with baggage and diluted with non-combatants, had to fight for its right of way.

The decisive engagement came off at the river Ulca, concerning which we are told that 'it is the defence of the Gepidae which protects them like a mound, gives them an audacity which theywould otherwise lack, and strengthens the frontier of the province with a wall that no battering ramscan crumble'. It is not easy from this description to identify the river in question. The Save, which at this time must have formed the southern boundary of the Gepid territory, would have seemed a probable suggestion, but we have no hint that it ever was called by any name like Ulca. On the whole, the least improbable conjecture seems to be that we have here to do with the Hiulca Talus, a great sheet of water (possibly connected with streams above and below, and therefore not quite incorrectly termed a river) which, according to the striking description of Zosimus, mirrored the towers of the high hill-city of Cibalis, an important place, the exact site of which has not yet been discovered, but which was 101 Roman miles higher up the valley of the Save than Singidunum. If this identification be correct, the landscape on which Theodoric and his countrymen looked on this day of unwelcome conflict, was one which had already been the theatre of great events, for here it was that Constantine the Great fought the first battle in that long duel with his brother-in-law Licinius which finally gave to the Christian Emperor the undisputed mastery of the Eastern and Western worlds. Here too, only seven years later, was born one of the ablest of his successors, the ferocious but statesmanlike Valentinian.

The ambassadors who were sent to theGepid king, Traustila, returned with an unfavourable reply. No passage through his dominions would be conceded to the Ostrogoths; if they still desired it they must fight for it with the unconquered Gepidae. Then indeed was the distress of the wandering nation at its height. Famine, and the child of famine, pestilence, urged them on : behind them lay the frozen road marked by their blood-stained footprints, before them a yet worse and steeper road, one which even a fugitive would have shunned, leading over a quivering morass and up to the frowning ranks of their enemies. The Gothic vanguard charged across the morass; many were swallowed up in its muddy waters; those who reached the opposite side were falling fast beneath the shower of lances which the mighty arms of the Gepidae hurled against their frail wicker-work breastplates. In that apparent shipwreck of the fortunes of a noble nation, the calm valour of Theodoric saved his people. Like Henry IV at Ivri, he shouted, "Whoso will fight the enemy let him follow me. Look not to any other leader, but only charge where you see my standard advancing. The Gepids shall know that a king attacks them : my people shall know that Theodoric saves them". Then he called for a cup, and performed with it some old Teutonic rite by way of augury, the nature of which is not described to us, and on he dashed, urging his horse to a gallop. We may conjecture that his keen eye had discerned some causeway of solid ground through the morass, along which he led his followers. However this may be, his charge was completely successful. "As a swollen river through the harvest-field, as a lion through the herd", so did Theodoric career through the Gepid ranks, which everywhere melted away before him. In a moment the fortune of the day was turned. They who a little while ago were vaunting victors were now fugitives, wandering without cohesion over the plain, while the Amal king moved proudly on, no longer now at the head of his troops, but encompassed by thousands of stalwart guards.

A great multitude of the enemy were slain, and only the approach of night saved the trembling remnant. What was more important, the store waggons of the Gepidae fell into the hands of the Goths; and so well were they supplied with corn from all the cities of the neighbourhood, that the satisfied wanderers congratulated themselves on the pugnacity of their hosts, which provided them a feast such as they could never have obtained from their hospitality.

How long the campaign against the Gepids other lasted we know not. We hear vaguely from the panegyrist of innumerable other combats with the Sarmatians and others, the mention of which may or may not be due to some confusion with Theodoric's boyish exploits in the same region. What seems certain is, that either in this guerilla warfare, or in mere foraging expeditions through a country which was of course perfectly familiar to the chief and to all but the mere striplings in his army (since they had migrated thence only sixteen years before), winter, spring, and the greater part of summer wore away. It was not till the month of August that the Ostrogothswho may perhaps have marched by different routes, some up the valley of the Save, others by that of the Drave, and who may then have concentrated at Aemona (Laybach), finally crossed the Julian Alps, and descended by the road trodden by so many conquerors—Theodosius, Alaric, Attila —past the Pear-tree and the Frigid Stream, into the plains of that Italy which they were to win bybloody battle, to hold for sixty-six years, to love *so* fondly, and to lose so stubbornly.

We are told that the flocks and herds which accompanied them on their march, soon showed, by their improved condition, the superiority of the tender pastures of Italy over the scanty herbage of the Alpine uplands.

At the eleventh mile-stone from Aquileia (*Ad Undecimum*) the host reached the confluence of the river Frigidus with the Sontius (Isonzo), and here probably it was that Odovacar and his army stood ready to meet them and dispute their passage. South-westwards, in the sea-like plain, rose the ghostly ruins of Aquileia, over which near forty years of desolation had passed. No fleets of merchantmen lined her broken wharves; no workman's hammer resounded in her ruined Mint; the Baths, the Amphitheatre, the Forum, were all silent. Only, perhaps, a few black-robed priests and monks still clustered round the repaired basilica, keeping warm the embers of religious life in the province of Venetia, asserting the continuity, and preparing the way for the revival, of the power of the Patriarchate of Aquileia.

Odovacar had taken a strong post on the Isonzo, and had fortified it strongly. In his well-defended camp a large army of various nationalities was mustered under his orders. Ennodius speaks of 'so many kings' trooping to the war under Odovacar's banners. Pompous and inflated as his style is, it is difficult to suppose that this detail is absolutely devoid of truth. Perhaps, in the motley host who first acclaimed Odovacar as king, there may have been chiefs and princelings who retained some of their old semi-royal position towards their followers, while towards him they were but generals under a generalissimo. Perhaps also the nations on the Danube, Alamanni, Thuringians, Gepidae, had sent their contingents to defend the menaced throne of the conqueror of the Rugians.

Of the battle of the Isonzo, which was fought on the 28th of August, we have no details. Odovacar had all the advantages of position, of preparation, and of a force which must surely have been more easily handled than the long train, encumbered with women and with waggons, which emerged from under the shadow of the Tarnovaner Wald. But it is probably true, as Ennodius declares, that the vast mass of the defending armament wanted a soul. Its leader, who throughout this war shows not a single instinct of generalship nor trace of that soldierly dash which first made him conspicuous among his fellows, had probably grown torpid during his thirteen years of royalty, amid such animal delights as Italy could offer to a barbarian autocrat. And on the other side were three powerful champions, Youth in the leader, Loyalty in the led, and Despair in both. The deep river was crossed, the *vallum* climbed, the camp taken: a crowd of fugitives scattered over the plain announced to the villages of Venetia that the day of Odovacar's supremacy was drawing to a close.

Odovacar fled from the Isonzo to the line of the Adige, thus abandoning the whole modern province of Venetia to the invader. So large and so fair a slice of Northern Italy owning his sway, justified that invader in looking on himself as from that day forward a ruler in Italy, not the mere leader of a wandering host. Near the close of his reign, when a question arose how far back the judge might go in enquiring into the wrongful ouster of a Roman from his farm, Theodoric made his 'Statute of Limitations' commence with the victory of the Isonzo. 'If,' he said, 'the expropriation took place after the time when by the favour of God we crossed the streams of the Sontius, when first the Empire of Italy received us, then let the farm be restored to its former owner, and that whether thirty years have since elapsed or not. Further back than that, into the wrongs inflicted at the time of the Herulo-Rugian land settlement, Theodoric did not consider himself bound to travel or to enquire.

Odovacar's next stand was to be made at Verona; and here 'in the Campus Minor,' as before at the Isonzo, he entrenched himself in a *fossatum*, a large square camp, doubtless surrounded with those deep fosses of which the archaeologist who has studied the Roman military works in Britain and Germany can form some not wholly inadequate conception. On the top of the mound, formed of the earth thrown up out of the ditch, would probably be planted a line of sharp stakes. Here the attacked king stood at bay, having the line of the deep and rapid Adige behind him, to compel his followers to fight by the impossibility of escape. There had been some vaunting words uttered by Odovacar in the parleys which preceded the combat; and 'if the tongue could have achieved victory instead of the right arm' says Ennodius, 'his array of words would have been invincible'. But in truth his army was a very formidable one in point of numbers: and when Theodoric, on the night before the battle, pacing up and down, saw the wide extent of the camp-fires gleaming like earthly constellations upon the hills between him and Verona, his heart well-nigh died within him. But, as his panegyrist truly says, there was a certain calm and noble stability in the nature of the Ostrogothic king. He was not easily elated by good, nor depressed by adverse fortune, and his serene assurance of victory communicated itself to his countrymen.

At dawn of the 30th of September the trumpets of the two armies sounded for battle. While Theodoric was arming himself with breastplate of steel, was buckling on his greaves, and hanging to his side that sword which his Roman admirer calls 'the champion of freedom,' his mother Erelieva and his sister Amalfrida came to him, not to depress his courage by womanly lamentations, but, anxious as to the result of the day, to try to read in his beloved face the omens of victory. He reassured their doubting hearts with cheering words :

"Mother, this day it behoves me to show to the world that it was indeed a man-child whom you bore on that great day of the victory over the Huns. I too, in the play of lances, have to show myself worthy of my ancestors' renown by winning new victories of my own. Before my soul's eye stands my father, the mighty Theudemir, he who never doubted of victory, and therefore never failed to achieve it. Bring forth, oh my mother and my sister, my most splendid robes, those on which your fingers have worked the most gorgeous embroidery. I would be more gaily dressed on this day than on any holiday. If the enemy do not recognise me, as I trow they shall, by the violence of my onset, let them recognise me by the brilliancy of my raiment. If Fortune give my throat to the sword of the enemy, let him that slays me have a grand reward for his labour. Let them at least say, "How splendid he looks in death," if they have not the chance to admire me fighting".

With these words of joyous confidence, instinct with the life of the coming age of chivalry, Theodoric leaped on his charger and was soon in the thickest of the fray. It was time for him to make his appearance. Even while he was saying his farewells, the Ostrogoths were slightly wavering under the onset of the enemy. The charge of Theodoric and his chosen troops restored the fortunes of the day. There are indications, however, that the victory, perhaps owing to the position of the Rugo-Herulian troops which made escape all but impossible, was more stubbornly contested than that of the Isonzo, and that the Ostrogothic loss was heavy. Before the end of the day, however, the troops of Odovacar were all cut to pieces, or whelmed beneath the swift waves of the Adige, save a few bold swimmers who may have escaped, Horatius-like, by swimming the stream. In these fierce battles of Teuton against Teuton, we hear nothing of quarter asked or night of granted. Apparently Odovacar, in order to urge his troops to more desperate efforts, must have broken down the bridge behind them leading to Verona. He himself escaped, but not westward. He sped across the plain, towards the south-east, and took refuge in the impregnable Ravenna. One authority, of a late date, says that he first fled to Rome, and finding the gates of the city closed against him, wasted the surrounding country with fire and sword. In the face, however, of the clear testimony of the contemporary writer, whom scholars call the Chronographer of Ravenna, and who evidently watched the successive acts of the bloody drama with minute and eager interest, it seems safer to affirm that the beaten king fled at once from the battle-field to the secure shelter of Ravenna and her dykes.

Theodoric meanwhile repaired to Mediolanum, that great city which had been so often in the third and fourth centuries the residence of emperors, and which was still the most important city of the Province of Liguria, as its successor, Milan, is of the modern Lombardy. Here he received the submission of a large part of the army of his rival. Great as had been the number of the slain, it was still a goodly host which stood before him, their arms bright and dazzling as a German's arms were bound to be on a day of parade, and which, probably by the clash of spear on shield, acclaimed him as victor and lord. The Amal's heart may well have beat high at the sight, and it doubtless seemed to him that the labour of conquest was over and that he was undisputed lord of Italy.

But this early success was a delusion. Easily as these Teutonic bands turned about from one lord to another, there was still too much vitality in the cause of Odovacar for him to be abandoned so utterly by his followers as seemed to be the case at Milan in October 489. Treason to the new lord was already preparing itself in the hearts of the surrendered army, and the manager, for a time the successful manager, of this treasonable movement, which seemed likely to change the whole course of the war, was Tufa. This man, evidently a person of mark in the Rugo-Herulian army, perhaps one of the 'kings' whom Ennodius describes as commanding it, had been solemnly, in an assembly of the chiefs, appointed Magister Militum by Odovacar on the 1st of April in this year (489). The part which he now played, whether it were the result of deep and calculated treachery or simply of unreasoning impulse, vibrating backwards and forwards between the old master and the new, reminds a modern reader of the conduct of Marshal Ney in 1815, setting forth from Paris with the assurance to Louis XVIII that he would in a week bring back the Corsican usurper in an iron cage, and, before the week was over, deserting to Napoleon with all his troops. But assuredly, if Tufa may pair off with Ney, we are under no temptation to carry the parallel further. The glorious young Amal king is as much above the gouty Bourbon epicure, as the incapable resourceless Odovacar is below the mighty Napoleon.

Theodoric, who seems to have been thoroughly blinded by his confidence in Tufa, sent him, probably within a few days after the interview at Milan, to besiege his old master at Ravenna. Tufa advanced along the great Emilian Way, as far as Faventia, about eighteen miles from that city. There he began the blockade of the capital, but when Odovacar came forth, came to Faventia itself, and had an interview with his former subordinate, Tufa changed again, abandoned the cause of Theodoric, and had the baseness to surrender the 'Comites Theodorici,' probably some Ostrogothic nobles, members of the *Comitatus* of Theodoric, into the hands of Theodoric's enemy. They were loaded with chains and brought into Ravenna, and there it is but too probable that they were foully murdered by Odovacar, an event which, more than any other, embittered the contest of the two rivals.

This defection of Tufa, accompanied probably by a large part 01 the troops committed to his charge, caused a violent revulsion in the fortunes of Theodoric. The Ostrogoth, who had been dreaming of dominion, now found himself again called upon to plan for the mere safety and subsistence of himself and his people. Milan seemed to him too exposed, too accessible from Ravenna, to be safely selected as his winter-quarters. He chose instead the city of Ticinum (Pavia), which resting on two rivers, the Ticino and the Po, would offer more difficulties to an advancing army. Here too still dwelt the saintly bishop Epiphanius, towards whom, notwithstanding the difference of his creed, the young Ostrogoth seems to have been drawn, as Ricimer and Euric had been drawn, by the transparent beauty and holiness of his character. He said at once, 'Here is a bishop who in all the East has not his equal, whom even to have seen is a high privilege.' And, according to the biographer, he added that the city must be safe where such a good man dwelt, that here was a wall which no soldiers could storm, no Balearic slingers could over-shoot. Whether he indulged in quite such soaring flights of rhetoric or not, it is clear that he did select Pavia not only for his own quarters in the winter of 489-490, but also as a place of safe deposit where he might leave his venerable mother, and where all the other non-combatants of the Gothic army might be collected, for what remained to them of the war, a period, as it turned out, of three years. During this period, Epiphanius played his difficult part with that success and which is sometimes the reward of a perfectly simple and unselfish character, surrounded by unscrupulous and greedy men. Though he evidently inclined to the side of Theodoric, he succeeded in maintaining friendly relations with Odovacar. He obtained from both princes the one boon on which his heart was set, the liberation of 'prisoners and captives,' and this not for his own Roman compatriots only. Often did an Ostrogoth or a Turcilingian, whose wife and children had fallen into the hands of the enemy, obtain, through the prayers of the Bishop, that redemption which gold would have been powerless to procure. To the not over-welcome guests in his own city the generosity of Epiphanius was conspicuous. It was a singular state of affairs, as his biographer truly, if somewhat bombastically, points out. "Those forces of Theodoric, which the whole East had scarcely been able to support, were now contracted within the limits of a single town. You saw that town swarming with the gatherings of tribesmen, the heads of mighty clans cooped up in narrow hovels. Whole homesteads seemed to have migrated from their foundations, and scarcely was there standing room for the new inhabitants". In these strangely altered circumstances of his diocese the Bishop applied himself to relieve, to the utmost of his ability, the bodily needs of the new-comers, forgetting, or teaching himself to forget, that it was by them and such as them that the estates of his bishopric had been laid waste, and his own income pitiably diminished. And living, as he had now to live, for three years, constantly under the eyes of "a most clever people, quickly touched by the lightest breath of suspicion, in troublous times such as make even gentle hearts cruel through fear", he showed himself so uniformly kind and true that he retained their unwavering esteem and confidence. As has been already said, the princes, who were at deadly war with one another, agreed in venerating Epiphanius.

The campaign of the year 490 was marked by the formation of great transalpine alliances which, though we hear but vaguely concerning them, must have exercised an important influence on the fortunes of the war. Gundobad, king of the Burgundians, of whom we have heard nothing since, sixteen years before, he left his client Glycerius defenceless against Nepos and stole back to his own kingdom by the Rhone, now seeing the tide apparently on the turn against Theodoric, and fearing probably that, if he conquered, the Ostrogoth of Italy and the Visigoth of Gaul would join hands and the Burgundian would have an evil time between them, invaded Liguria with a large army. Whether he came as an ally of Odovacar to effect a seasonable diversion in his favour, or simply to rob and ravage on his own account, is not clear from history, very possibly was not altogether clear to the mind of the Burgundian. What is undoubted, is that Theodoric, in some way, either by force or favour, caused him to abandon his opposition, that a treaty was concluded between them which in after years was ripened into a firm and lasting friendship, but that, in the meantime, Gundobad, in returning across the Alps, took with him a long train of captives who were to languish in exile for at least four years, while their native fields in Liguria were well-nigh relapsing into a wilderness for lack of cultivators.

The natural counterpoise to the Burgundians in the political scale was the power of the Visigoths, and those remote kinsmen of the people of Theodoric interfered on his behalf in this campaign. Odovacar seems to have occupied the months of spring and early summer in winning back the country between Ravenna and Cremona, aided perhaps by the attacks of Gundobad on Liguria which called all Theodoric's energies to the western end of the valley of the Po. Milan was then visited by Odovacar, and roughly handled by him in retribution for the readiness with which its bishop, Laurentius, and its principal citizens had welcomed Theodoric in the preceding year. At length, on the river Addua (Adda), ten miles east of Milanthe great battle of the year was fought. We only know that in it Theodoric was helped by his Visigothic kinsmen, and that, after another terrible slaughter on both sides, victory again rested on the standards of Theodoric. In this battle Odovacar lost his Count of the Domestics, the officer who had superintended the emigration of the provincials from Noricum to Campania, and to whom he had given the lands in Melita and Syracuse, his faithful friend and counsellor Pierius. Odovacar himself fled, and again shut himself up by the lagoons of Ravenna, never more to emerge from their shelter.

It is apparently to the same year, 490, that we must refer a mysterious movement against the followers of Odovacar all over Italy, of which we have some dark intimations in the Panegyric of Ennodius. He speaks of it as in some sort a counter-blow to the treachery of Tufa.

"It pleased them [Tufa and his confederates] to promise a kingdom to Odovacar when he again stretched out a peaceful hand towards them. But, as soon as their deed was brought to light, the miscalculation which their hostile minds had made became apparent. You [Theodoric] appealed to that Providence which watched over all your steps, and, that the greed of those deserters might not go unpunished, you unfurled the banners of revenge and made the people, whose friendship to you was now thoroughly proved, the confidant of your secret designs. Not one of your adversaries got scent of the scheme, though more than half the world had to share it with you. Over the most widely severed districts [of Italy] was arranged a sacrificial slaughter. What but the will of the Most High can have brought this to pass, that in one instant of time the score which had been so long accumulating against the slaughterers of the Roman name should be wiped away?". It has been truly pointed out by the best of our German guides, that these words point to a kind of 'Sicilian Vespers' of the followers of Odovacar all over Italy: and, from the sanctimonious manner in which the Bishop claims Heaven as an accomplice in the bloody deed, we may perhaps infer that the Roman clergy generally were privy to the plot.

The action of the drama for the next three years is almost entirely confined to Ravenna, which city, Caesena and Rimini, were the only places in Italy that still held out for Odovacar. Theodoric seems to have recognised the impossibility of taking Ravenna by assault. His only hope was to reduce it by blockade, and that was a slender hope, so long as he was not master of the Adriatic and vessels could enter the harbour of Clapis, bringing provisions to the besieged king. However, he occupied a position 'in the Pineta,' in that magnificent pine-wood which every traveller to Ravenna knows so well, skirting its eastern horizon and shutting out the sight of the sea. Here, at three miles distance from the city, he entrenched himself with a deep and widely extended *fossatum*, and waited for events. His taking up this position, eastward, that is sea-ward of the city, probably implied a determination to cut off, as much as possible, all succours from the sea, while his flying squadrons no doubt blocked the communications with the Emilian Way and effectually prevented assistance by land. The blockade, by one means or other, must have been a tolerably one, since corn, in the markets of Ravenna, rose to the famine price of six solidi per modius, equivalent to seventy-two shillings a peck, or £115 4s. a quarter. This was, it is true, not quite equal to the price (£192 a quarter) paid in the camp of Jovian during the disastrous retreat of the Roman army from Persia. But, on the other hand, in the good days that were coming for Italy under the peaceful reign of that very Theodoric whose *fossatum* now caused such terrible distress to the Queen of the Adriatic, the ordinary price of one modius of wheat was to be not six solidi but one-sixtieth of a solidus, equivalent to 6s. 4d. a quarter.

Before the year 490 ended, Theodoric, considering himself now *de facto* lord of Italy, sent Faustus, a Roman noble, chief of the Senate and Consul for the year, to claim from Zeno the imperial robes, perhaps also the imperial diadem, which Odovacar, in his politic modesty, had sent to Constantinople after the downfall of Augustulus. Faustus, however, probably arrived only in time to stand by the wretched and crime-polluted death-bed of the Emperor, to hear his ravings about the guardsman who was to be his successor, and to behold his remorse for the murder of Pelagius. In April of the next year Zeno was a corpse, and Anastasius the Silentiary reigned in his stead. From him Theodoric was one day to receive the recognition which he desired, but he was not to receive it yet.

The chief event of the year 491 was a desperate sally made from Ravenna by the besieged king. Odovacar had by some means or other procured a reinforcement of Heruli fresh from their Carpathian homes. With these recruits, seeing that Theodoric was dwelling securely behind his *fossatum*, and believing him to have relaxed his guard, he one night issued forth from Ravenna and attacked the entrenchment of the Goths. The battle was long, and great was the number of the slain on both sides. But, at length, Odovacar had again to acknowledge himself defeated. His Magister Militum, a certain Libila (or Levila), was slain, perhaps drowned in attempting to cross the sluggish and slimy Ronco. The Heruli, as Ennodius exultingly remarks[1], after making proof of Theodoric's prowess in their own home, had now an opportunity of repeating the experience on Italian soil. This engagement occurred about the 10th (or 15th) of July. Odovacar again retired into his lair; and Theodoric, a month later, returned to his temporary capital at Pavia. It is possible that the Burgundian invader was not yet finally disposed of: and no doubt the home-loving Ostrogoth longed again to behold the faces of his mother and his children. Of course, the blockade was continued with unabated vigour.

In the year 492 we have again a strange dearth of events in the early part of the year; the only incident which our careful diarists at Ravenna have to record being that, on the 26th of May, 'an earthquake took place at night before the crowing of the cocks'. Possibly both parties sought to strengthen themselves for each campaign by drawing fresh recruits from beyond the Alps, in which case the difficulty of crossing the snow-covered passes might well postpone the conflict of the year till June or July. Theodoric, however, now took a step, which probably should have been taken before, in order to make his blockade perfect. He went southward to Ariminum, about thirty miles distant (one sees the Rock of S. Marino which overhangs Rimini, cutting the horizon as one looks southward from the church towers of Ravenna), and he appears to have reduced that town to his obedience. What was more important, he made himself master of a fleet of cutters (called *dromones*, 'runners,' in the Latin of that age). With these he arrived at the Lions Harbour, a port about six miles from Ravenna, where in later days he built a small palace—perhaps a country retreat—in a camp which, probably from this circumstance, was called *Fossatum Palatioli*. Here we must leave him, watching with ships and soldiers against the entrance of any provisions into Ravenna, while the scene shifts for a moment to the banks of the Ticino and the Adige.

Few men, one would think, in the Ostrogothic army had more powerful motives for loyalty than Frederic prince of the Rugians. His father and mother had been led into captivity by the armies of Odovacar, he himself, twice defeated and expelled by the same armies, had sought the palace of Theodoric a helpless fugitive. As a member of Theodoric's Comitatus, he had now entered Italy, and had fought by his side in three, perhaps in four, bloody battles. He was, if he could exercise patience and fidelity for a few months longer, about to taste delicious and long-delayed vengeance on the enemy of his race. Yet, with characteristic fickleness, at this crisis, or perhaps some months earlier, Frederic deserted the standards of Theodoric and entered into a treasonable correspondence with the double traitor Tufa, who, with some sort of army under his orders, was still roving about the plains of Lombardy. Perhaps some remembrance of their common Rugian nationality working in the mind of Frederic drew him away from the Ostrogothic chief, and towards the followers of Odovacar. Perhaps Theodoric had not assigned a sufficiently high place in his counsels to the son of a king whose word had once been the mightiest in all the regions of the Middle Danube. More probably, Frederic saw simply a better chance of plunder and of eventual kingship, by fighting for his own hand, and with barbarian naturalness went straight towards what seemed to be his own interests, without troubling himself for fine words to justify his treason.

The Rugians occupied Pavia ; this we know from the distress which they caused to the soul of the saintly Epiphanius. Possibly enough, they may have laid their hands on some of the moveable property of the Ostrogoths in that City of Refuge : but the women and children and the rest of the non-combatants must have escaped unharmed, for we should certainly have heard of it had there been any general massacre. For nearly two years the Rugians made Pavia their head-quarters. "A race", says Ennodius, "hideous by every kind of savagery, whose minds, full of cruel energy, prompted them to daily crimes. In fact, they thought that a day was wasted which had passed unsignalised by any kind of outrage". The sweet discourses of the prelate, however, softened even these wild men's hearts. "Who could hear without astonishment that the Rugians, who will scarcely condescend to obey even kings, both feared and loved a bishop, a Catholic and a Roman? Yet so it was; and when the time for their departure came, they left him even with tears, although they were returning to their parents and families."

The mention of a period of nearly two years for the stay of the Rugians at Pavia, coming as it does after the description of three years of Gothic tarriance in that city, brings us down nearly to the end of 494 for the date of their final expulsion. As we shall see, Odovacar had disappeared from the scene before that date. The Rugians therefore probably continued fighting on their own account, and required a separate castigation from Theodoric. But of all this we have no record.

We do know however that, in the year with which we are now dealing (492), the two traitors Tufa and Frederic quarrelled about the division of the spoil. A battle ensued between them in the valley of the Adige, betwixt Trient and Verona. After many thousands of men had been killed on both sides, the death of Tufa put an end to the battle. Frederic, as has been said above, probably remained to trouble his benefactor some little time longer, but henceforth he disappears from history. Ennodius is jubilant, and not without cause, over this merciful arrangement of Providence, by which the two traitorous enemies of the King were made to counter-work one another's evil designs, and Frederic first earned, at the expense of Tufa, the triumph which his own defeat was afterwards to yield to Theodoric.

The year 493, the fifth year of the war, the fourth of the siege, the second of the complete blockade of Ravenna, opened upon a terrible state of things in the hunger-stricken capital. Men were staying the gnawing of their stomachs by eating hides and all kinds of unclean and horrible victuals, and still they were dying fast of famine.

At length the stubborn heart of Odovacar was quelled. He commenced negotiations for a surrender, and on the 25th of February he handed over his son as a hostage for his fidelity. On the following day Theodoric entered Clapis in state, that seaport being probably assigned to the Ostrogothic army for their head-quarters. On the next day, 27th of February, peace was formally made between Theodoric and Odovacar, John the Archbishop of Ravenna acting as mediator.

The life of the defeated king was to be safe. Nay more, he and his conqueror were, at any rate in appearance, to be joint rulers of the Western Empire. The arrangement was so obviously destitute of any of the elements of stability, so sure to breed plots and counter-plots, so impotent a conclusion to the long blockade of Ravenna, that we might hesitate to accept its accuracy, but that a recently-discovered fragment of the well-informed John of Antioch confirms the statement of Procopius too emphatically to allow us to reject it.

It was not till the 5th of March that the victorious Ostrogoth rode through the gates of Ravenna, and took possession of the city which for the remaining thirty-three years of his life was to be his home. Before he entered the Archbishop went forth to meet him, 'with crosses and thuribules and the Holy Gospels' and with a long train of priests and monks. Falling prostrate on the ground, while his followers sang a penitential psalm, he prayed that 'the new King from the East' would receive him into his peace. The 'request was granted, not only for himself and the citizens of Ravenna, but for all the Roman inhabitants of Italy. The terms of the real peace had no doubt been strenuously debated with the Teutonic comrades of Odovacar; but a ceremony like this, pre-arranged in all probability between the King and the Archbishop, was judged proper, in order to impress vividly on the minds both of Italians and Ostrogoths that Theodoric came as the friend of the Catholic Church and of the vast population which, even in accepting a new master, still clung to the great name of Roman.

For ten days there were frequent interviews between the two chieftains; then, on the 15th of March, the Ostrogoth invited his rival to a banquet in the Palace of the Laurel-Grove, at the south-east corner of the city. Odovacar came attended by his faithful *comitatus*, but was probably led to a seat of honour and thus separated from his friends. Two men knelt before him to prefer some pretended request, and clasped his hands in the earnestness of their entreaty. Then rushed forth some soldiers who had been placed in ambush in two alcoves on either side of the banquet-hall. But when they came in sight of the victim something in his aspect, either his kingly majesty or possibly his white hairs, *or* simply the fact that he was defenceless, struck such a chill into their hearts that they could not attack him. Then strode forth Theodoric and raised his sword to strike him. [e] "Where is God?", cried Odovacar in a vain appeal to Divine justice. "This is what thou didst to my friends", shouted Theodoric, kindling his rage by the remembrance of his comrades, slain by his rival after their base betrayal by Tufa. The blow descended on Odovacar's collar-bone, and stayed not till the sword had reached his loin. Theodoric himself was surprised at the trenchancy of his stroke, and said with a brutal laugh, "I think the wretch had never a bone in his body".

The assassinated king was at once buried in a stone coffin close by the Hebrew synagogue. His *comitatus*, powerless to save him, fell in the same fatal banquet-hall. His brother (possibly Onoulf) was shot down with arrows while attempting to escape through the palace garden. Sunigilda, the wife of Odovacar, was closely imprisoned, and died of hunger. Their son Thelane, whom his father in prosperous days had designated as Caesar, and who had more recently been given over as a hostage for his fidelity, was sent off to Gaul, doubtless to Theodoric's Visigothic ally King Alaric, and, having subsequently escaped thence to Italy, was put to death by order of the conqueror. So did the whole brood perish, and Italy had but one undoubted master, the son of Theudemir.

"No! It was not well done by thee, descendant of so many Amal kings! Whatever a mere Roman emperor, a crowned upstart of yesterday, might do in breaking faith with his rivals, a Basiliscus or an Armatius, thou shouldest have kept thy Teutonic truth inviolate. And so, when we enter that wonderful cenotaph of the Middle Ages, the church of the Franciscans at Innsbruck, and see thee standing there, in size more than human, beside the bearers of the greatest names of chivalry, Frankish Charles and British Arthur, and Godfrey with the Crown of Thorns; one memory, and hardly more than one, prevents our classing thee with the purest and the noblest of them,—the memory of thy assassinated rival Odovacar".

CHAPTER VII.

KING AND PEOPLE.

Now that Theodoric has safely brought his people into the promised land of Italy, has conquered and slain his enemy, and seated himself at Ravenna, undoubted king and ruler of the land, it may be well to pause for a little space, and, before we contemplate the new State which he founded there, to ask ourselves what was understood in the Gothic host by that word, kingship, in virtue of which he ruled them. We shall find indeed, as we proceed, that the spirit and maxims of the new kingdom, its form, and the machinery of its administration, were Roman rather than Gothic. Still, even in order to grasp this fact more clearly, it will be well to devote a few pages to a subject upon which volumes have been usefully written, that of *German Kingship*.

'God save the King!'— words how lightly spoken by revellers at a banquet, or by shouting crowds as a monarch moves slowly through their midst! Yet in this familiar formula are enshrined two words of mysterious power, which have come down with the stream of national life, 'through caverns measureless to man,' from those distant highlands wherein the eye of science strains, and strains in vain, to discover the origins of the human race and of human society. To argue from the ancient origin of these two names of power that there is any necessary connection between them; to maintain, as the advocates of the divine right of kings once did, that religion forbids men to govern themselves under republican forms, however clear it may be that the State will best be so administered, is an absurdity of which few men will now be guilty. But, nevertheless, it is permitted us to gaze, with a wonder in which there is something of love and something of reverence, on this wonderful word, so different in form in the various languages of the earth,—Melech, Basileus, Rex, Thiudans, King,—yet so essentially the same in power, which constrains the many members of one vast community, her strong men,, her wise men, her holy men, to bring the best of their gifts to the treasury, and to devote the strength of their lives to the service of one man, in mind and body no different from themselves, but—a King.

Reverence for the kingly office seems to have been deeply implanted in the heart of the Germanic branch of the great Aryan family; and it has been, in the World-life, the especial function of the Germanic peoples to carry kingship and faithfulness to the king, or—to borrow two words from the Latin tongue—Royalty and Loyalty, farther down into the ages than any other group of free nations. How early the old Homeric royalties of Greece and the kings of Rome disappeared from the scene we all know. On the other hand, the long-lived royalties of Assyria, of China and of Persia, were mere despotisms, giving no free play to the national character, and stiffening the peoples that were subjected to them with immobility. To reign on such terms, to be the master of millions of slaves, was comparatively an easy task, when once the nation had become used to the clank of its fetters. But to maintain for generations, to prolong into the strangely different world of modem society, that peculiar combination of kingly authority and popular freedom which was characteristic of most of the Germanic royalties in the first century after Christ, and which contained the seeds of the institution which we now call Constitutional Monarchy,—this has been a great and marvellous work, and one which could only be accomplished by a race with exceptional faculties for governing and being governed.

We have the authority of Tacitus, that acute observer of the life of states and nations, for asserting that German kingship was, in his day, for the most part thus compounded of the two apparently antagonistic principles of Authority and Liberty. He contrasts the *libertas Germanorum* with the *regnum Arsacis*, when deciding that Rome has suffered more from the free barbarians beyond the Rhine than from the compact despotism of the monarchy beyond the Euphrates. When describing the sway of the Gothic kings, he says that, "though somewhat stricter than that of most other German rulers, it still stretched not to the infringement of liberty". Only one race, the Suiones, who dwelt in the islands of Baltic and on the Swedish promontories, were "under the absolute rule of one man, to whom they were bound to pay implicit obedience". The great power attained in this tribe by even the slaves of royalty, the fact that the nation could not be trusted with the custody of its own arms, which were kept, in time of peace, in a locked-up arsenal guarded by a slave, were emphatic proofs of the absence of the popular element in the government of this nation, and strengthened by contrast the general picture of German freedom.

It is, however, from Tacitus also that we receive our impressions of the extraordinary manifoldness of political life amongst the German nations. In its way, his sketch of Germania in the first century reminds us of the mediaeval *Reich*, with its wonderful assortment of kingdoms, duchies, ecclesiastical states, republican free towns, all congregated together, like the clean and unclean beasts in the ark, under the rule, often only the nominal rule, of some Hapsburg or Luxemburg emperor. Of course, in the Germania, even this semblance of unity is wanting; but the variety of political life is there. Observing the language of Tacitus with attention, we soon discover from his pages that the kingly form of government was not universal among the Germans. *Rex vel princeps, rex vel civitas,* are alternative expressions, frequently used by him. The mere fact that the chief ruler of a barbarian state is not always called by the same name by the historians of a civilized country, who have occasion to mention his existence, is not one upon which it would be safe to lay much stress. We must be conscious that we talk with great looseness of Indian chiefs, of Zulu kings, and so forth, and that we have no very clear idea of a difference in rank and power between Cetewayo and the father of Pocahontas, when we speak of the former as a king and of the latter as a chief. Something of the same vagueness may be observed in the Homan writers, taken as a class, from Caesar to Ammianus, when they speak of the leaders of the Teutonic tribes who warred on Rome. But with Tacitus the case is different. His eye was quick for all political facts. His mind was always revolving the advantages and disadvantages of different forms of government. Even when describing the wild freedom of Germany, he is half-thinking about Rome and her vanished liberties; when face to face with Parthia, he is comforted by the thought that at least he is not under the lawless despotism of an Eastern king.

Every word therefore of Tacitus respecting the political institutions of our Teutonic forefathers is precious; and these hints of his about the *Rex*, or the *Civitas* show us that there were German tribes not under the sway, however lenient, of one sole king.. Some modern writers speak of these tribes as Republican, and the expression, though not used by Tacitus himself, brings before us more vividly than any other the nature of the rule under which the Cherusci, the Batavi, and many other German tribes, were living at the Christian era. In time of war these republican tribes elected a leader (*Heritogo*, in modern German *Herzog*, translated in Latin by *Dux*, in English by *Duke*), who was necessarily a man of tried bravery. In peace they may have been presided over by some officer, also elective, who acted as supreme judge, and as president of their assemblies; but even the name of this president has perished. In any case, however, the distinguishing mark of these magistracies was their non-hereditary character. The general or the judge was chosen for some special emergency; perhaps in some cases he held his office for the term of his natural life: but he held it only by the free choice of his countrymen, and had no claim to transmit any power to his son.

In the royal tribes, on the other hand, the birth, of the supreme ruler was everything. Doubtless the king was rich, doubtless he must be personally brave (or else his warriors would soon find a fitter leader), doubtless he had a large following of devoted henchmen; but none of these things alone would qualify him to be chosen king. He must be sprung from some kingly family—the Amals, or the Balthae, or the Asdings, or the Merovings—who had been kings (or at any rate nobles) from a time to which the mind of man runneth not to the contrary; some family which, while the nation was still heathen, boasted that it was sprung from the seed of gods, and which still linked itself with the remembrance of the heroes of old, even after the missionary-priest had dispeopled Walhalla and sent Odin and Gaut to dwell for ever beside Jupiter and Venus in the penal lake of fire.

Yet, being born of the kingly family, it was by no means needful that he should be what we call 'the head of the house' by lineal descent. It is hardly necessary to say, to those who know anything of the history even of mediaeval monarchy, that the strict principles of primogeniture and representation, which would make the crown descend in a line as definitely fixed as the course of succession to an English estate settled 'in tail male,' were quite unknown to the Germanic nations. Of course a veteran Gothic warrior-king, gathered to his fathers in a good old age, and leaving a warlike eldest son in the vigour of his years, would generally be succeeded by that son.

That is the natural course of things, and in all such cases monarchy and primogeniture easily become entwined together. Still, even in these instances, the nation chose, the nation raised the first-born on the shield, and acclaimed him as king. And if the dead king's children were minors, or if the eldest son was a *nithing*, incapable in council or a coward in the field, if there was some national hero standing near to the throne, and overshadowing by his fame the relatives who came before him in the strict order of descent, in all such cases the elective element in Germanic kingship asserted itself, and, by no fraud upon the postponed claimants, by no usurpation of the preferred claimant, the worthiest, kingliest, wisest, Amal or Balth, was called to the throne.

No doubt this manner of bestowing the crown—inheritance tempered by election—had its dangers, leading, as it did easily, to the wars and heartburnings of a disputed succession. It may very probably have been a presentiment of these dangers which led Gaiseric to promulgate a law of succession for the Vandals, according to which the oldest of his descendents at each vacancy, in whatever line of descent, was to be called to the empty throne; a provision, however, which did not work well in practice nor avert the dreaded danger. But in the main, for communities such as were the German tribes, living in the midst of foes, and in need, before all things, of strong and wise leadership, we may believe that the principle of choice out of one particular family worked well, and tended, by 'the survival of the fittest', to bring about an improvement in the strain of royal blood, and to make the kings more and more fit by stature, strength, and capacity of brain, to stand forth as unquestioned leaders of men.

Around the king's person, parting him off in some degree from the great mass of the free but undistinguished warriors of the nation, but also constantly checking and curbing his power, and compelling him 'so to rule as not to transgress the bounds of liberty,' stood the nobles. Who can say whence they sprang? For they too, like the king, have an old-world origin, and if a warrior is noble, it is because the oldest man in the host cannot remember a tradition of the days when the ancestors of that warrior were anything else but noble. Partly, perhaps, they are descended from younger branches of the kingly house : partly they represent the vanished royalty of smaller tribes, whom the great nation, as it rolled onwards, has incorporated with itself: partly, it may be, here or there, they are the descendants of some great chief of a pre-existing people, Finnish or Basque or Celtic, whom the invading Teutons have found it easier to win over and to assimilate than to destroy.

But in any case, whatever its origin, the important thing to notice about this old Teutonic nobility is, that it is essentially a counterpoise to the kingly power. In after days, when the new Teutonic kingdoms are reared 'in Welshland', a new nobility will arise, the so-called 'nobility by service,' represented by the 'king's thegns' among our own ancestors. These men, the king's butlers and seneschals and chamberlains, will shine by the borrowed light of their master, and naturally for a time will do nothing to check and everything to magnify his power. While they and the obsequious ecclesiastics who stand with them round the new-raised throne are hymning the praises of Our Lord Clovis or Chlotachar, the old nobility, which used to remind him, sometimes with a certain roughness, that he was only the first among his equals, will have had its ranks thinned by the wars and the migrations, will find itself in the midst of a new and hostile order of things, unpopular with the Roman provincials, anathematized by the clergy, vexed by the exactions of the king's officers, and continually postponed to the new and pliable 'service-nobles' of the Court, and thus, silently and sullenly, will vanish away.

A conspicuous feature in the social life of the ancient Germans, and one which probably aided the development of kingly power (though assuredly it was not the origin of that power), was the institution which the Latins called *comitatus*, and which the Germans now speak of as *Gefolgschaft*. We have no name exactly corresponding to it, but our historians are endeavoring to introduce the term *Comrades* to describe the members of a Comitatus. The description of such a band given by Tacitus remains the most accurate and the most vivid picture that we possess of it.

"When the young nobles have received their arms and are enrolled in the ranks of the warriors, they take their places by the side of the hardy veterans, nor do they blush to be seen among the 'comrades'. Each receives his rank in the 'comradeship' according to the judgment of him whom they follow, and great is the rivalry among the comrades which shall attain to the highest place beside his chief, and of the chiefs which shall have the most numerous and the most eager comrades. This is their dignity, this their strength : to be ever surrounded by a great cluster of picked youths is in peace a distinction and in war a defence. Nor is this so in a chief's own tribe only, but among neighbouring states also; his name and his glory are spread abroad if his comradeship excel in numbers and valour. Such chiefs are in request for embassies, are loaded with presents: by their mere renown they often virtually end a war. When the day of battle is come, it is disgraceful for the chief to be excelled in bravery by the comrades, disgraceful for them not to equal the chief's valour. Yea, and base for all the rest of his life is he accounted by himself and others who has escaped alive from the battle, leaving his chief behind him. Him to guard, him to defend, in his glory to merge every brave deed of his own, this is the one great point of honour with the comrade. The chiefs fight for victory, the comrades for their chief. If the community in which they were born grows sluggish with too long peace and restfulness, most of the young nobles seek of their own accord those nations which may then be waging war elsewhere, both because this race hates rest, and because renown is more easily won on well-balanced battlefields; nor can a great comradeship be well kept together except by violence and war. Each comrade claims from the chief's generosity that great war-horse of his, that gory and conquering spear. For the rest, the seat at the banquet, the bountiful though coarse repast, are taken as sufficient pay. The material for the chief's generosity is provided by war and rapine. You would find it harder to persuade them to till the ground and wait a year for the harvest, than to challenge a foe and earn honourable wounds. For it seems ever to them a dull and stupid thing to accumulate, by the sweat of your brow, that which you might make your own by the shedding of blood".

This passage has given rise to many dissertations which are not perhaps the most fruitful part of German archaeology. Who might become the head of a *comitatus*, what precise relation existed between the 'comrades' and their chief, what states were founded by the leaders of a *comitatus*, and other questions of the like nature, have been discussed with much ability and some bitterness, but seem after all to resolve themselves only into the setting of one man's guess against another's. More important is it to keep the poetical aspect of this Germanic institution vividly before us. All admit that it has in it the promise of chivalry, the germs of the feudal relation between lord and vassal. We have already had occasion, in tracing the achievements of the young Theodoric, to see how vigorous was the institution in his day, four centuries after it had been described by Tacitus. It had undoubtedly a considerable influence in developing the idea and the power of royalty among the German races. Probably also the life of adventure and hardship which it promoted, favored the growth of great qualities of mind and body among the royal families from whom some of the rulers of mediaeval, and a few of the rulers of modern Europe have descended. For to what depths of degradation they might sink when the stimulating influence, of the *comitatus* was withdrawn, and the barbarian king could wallow undisturbed in the swinish delights of his barbarian royalty, is abundantly shown by the dreary story of the sons of the Merovings.

Around the king and his 'comrades', and around the outer circle of the nobles, gathered the great mass of the nation, the free but not noble warriors, who were known as 'free Franks' in the army of Clovis, and as *ceorls* on the soil of England. Of the social life of these men, of their days passed in alternations of fierce excitement and sturdy idleness, of their carousings and their mad devotion to the dice-box, Tacitus draws for us a striking and well-known picture. Our present business is to follow them to what our fathers called the *Folcmote*, other tribes the *Folks-Thing* or the Mall, and Tacitus the *Concilium*, the assembly from which in direct lineal succession our own Parliament is descended. So long as the tribe is contained in narrow limits, each new and full moon sees the assembly of the tribesmen. As it grows into a wide-spreading nation, the times of meeting are necessarily reduced, till, in the vast Frankish Empire, they occur only twice or thrice in the year. The men come armed, and the mere fact of being free and a warrior is enough to give a right to attend the Folc-mote, though, for full voice and vote, it is necessary that a man should also have land—which means a home—of his own. Among all these armed men the *Things-fried,* the peace of the great meeting, prevails; and however hot the discussion may be, none may dare to lift a hand against his opponent in debate. They do not assemble punctually,—'this,' says Tacitus, 'is the fault of their German freedom,'—but often waste two or three days in waiting for those who come not on the appointed day. Then, at length, when it pleases the multitude to begin, they sit down, all arrayed in their armour. The priests, inconspicuous generally in the German polity, but prominent on these occasions,—perhaps in order to guard the *Things-fried* by religious reverence,— call for silence, and the clash of the barbarians talk and song ceases. The king, if there be a king, if not, the head of the state, begins the debate. The warriors follow in no exact order of precedence. Age, noble birth, mighty deeds in war, the gift of eloquence, all give a speaker the right to be heard: but none, not even the king, orders; all must seek to persuade. If the speaker's advice displeases, he is interrupted by the indignant clamour of his hearers : if it meets their approval, they brandish their mighty spears and so give to the barbarian orator his most coveted applause.

And what is the business thus debated of? Many matters doubtless, belonging to the peaceful life of the tribe, which Tacitus has not described to us. He mentions the accusation, or, as we should call it, the impeachment, of great offenders, upon whom the punishment of death may be inflicted. This man, who was a traitor to the tribe, is hung from a tree; that one, who was only a *Nithing* and a coward, is plunged into a morass with a hurdle over him to prevent his struggling out of it; another, who is found guilty of some lighter offence, is fined so many horses or oxen.

The judicial work of the assembly at an end, its administrative work begins. They elect the chiefs who are to dispense justice and keep some kind of barbarian order in each shire or village. Then, no doubt, there are often questions of boundary to settle, some rudimentary works of civilisation to be talked over, the clearance of this forest, the dyking out of that encroaching stream. But after all, the debates of these warriors turned most naturally towards war. Over and over again, in these German Folc-motes, was the question raised, "When and how and where must we make a stand against this all- pervading tyranny of Rome? Shall we make war on such and such a subject-tribe and punish them for their submission to the common enemy? Or shall we strike boldly at the great enemy himself? Shall we swim the Rhine, shall we swarm over the easily crossed *Pfahlgraben*, and win great spoil in the rich cities beyond?".

To complete the picture of the social state of the German tribes we should need to inquire into the condition of the slaves, and of the men, if there were such, who occupied a position akin to that of the Roman *colonus*, bound to till the land of a lord and to make him certain payments out of the produce, and yet not entirely dependent on his caprices. That there were slaves following in the train of these stalwart barbarians there can be no doubt: nay, we are informed by Tacitus that "even a German warrior, in his overmastering passion for play, would sometimes sell himself, and doubtless his wife and children also, into slavery".

So far therefore, the grand outline of popular freedom exhibited to us by the German folc-mote, at which every warrior has a right to be present, requires some modification. Like the free commonwealths of Greece and Rome, the German state does rest, to some extent, on a basis of slavery. It is clear, however, that slavery was not, as in some of those commonwealths, the cornerstone of the fabric. The most careful inquirers are of opinion that slavery, or serfdom, constrained the movements of but a small part of the population of ancient Germany[1]: and it is noteworthy that when Tacitus speaks of the idle life, during peace, of the German warrior, he says that household cares and the tillage of the fields were left [not to the slaves but] to the women, the old men, and the less robust members of the family.

To go back to our main subject, the power of the kings in that Germany which Tacitus described: it is manifest that it was subject to some strong controlling forces. A body of nobles, nearly as proud of their birth as the king himself, watched his movements and jealously resented every word or gesture which would seem to imply that he was a master and they his slaves. The frequently held popular assemblies, even if attended, as was probably the case in quiet times, by but a small part of the nation, kept alive the tradition of the rights of the people. It was a very different thing to dictate an unpopular order, as the Caesar of Rome might do, in the privacy of his *secretarium*, leaving the odium of its execution to the officer who sped with it to some distant province; and to have to defend that order oneself, as must the leader of the free warriors of Germany, in the next assembly of the people, to see the spears brandished in menace rather than in applause, to hear the harsh murmur of martial voices uttering in no courtly tones their disapprobation of the deed.

So far we have been dealing with the political life of our Teutonic forefathers at the time when Tacitus wrote. From that date till Theodoric's establishment of his Italian kingdom four centuries had passed; an interval of time which may count for comparatively little in a changeless Oriental monarchy, but which counts for much in European states, when the busy brain of an Aryan people is kindled by some new and great idea, or is brought forcibly into contact with other civilizations than its own. Four centuries before the date at which these words are being written, the Canary Islands were believed to be the uttermost limit of the habitable world in the direction of the setting sun. All the myriad influences which America has exerted upon Europe—to say nothing of those which Europe has exerted upon America—Peruvian gold, voyages of the Buccaneers, Negro-slavery, the Rights of Man—have had but those four hundred years to work in.

During the four centuries which we are now specially considering, from Domitian to Zeno, the ever at heart and mind of Germany were ever in contact with the wonderful fascination of the world-Empire of Rome. First, for two or three generations, they had to fight the almost desperate battle of defence against Roman aggression. Then, when Quadi and Marcomanni, by their stubborn resistance to the noble Marcus, had renewed the old teaching of Arminius, and shown the barbarians that Rome was not invincible; still more when, in the miserable anarchy of the third century, Rome herself seemed to have lost the power of self-preservation, and to be falling from ledge to ledge down the precipice of ruin, the Germans began to entertain the idea of something more than self-defense, and with ever- increasing pertinacity to renew the attempt to carve out for themselves settlements (not necessarily independent settlements) in the fair ' Welchland' on the other side of Rhine and Danube.

165-181.

All these wars, all this stir and movement among the peoples, tended to increase the power of the kingship. A weapon which was to pierce the Empire's defensive armour of castles and legions needed to be sharpened to a point and tipped with steel; and that steel point was royalty. Moreover, in the very act of the migration, many old associations would be loosened, the kinships which had dwelt in the same secluded valley for generations, and which mistook

'the rustic murmur of their bourg
        For the great wave that echoes round the world',

would be shaken out of their boorish conservatism, which, with all its dulness, nevertheless had been a certain bulwark against royal encroachments. Above all, the members of the old nobility, conspicuous for their deeds of headlong valour, would, many of them, leave their bones to whiten on the Roman battlefield, and more and more, as they fell in war, would their places be filled up by the young and dashing 'comrades' of the king, men perhaps of noble birth themselves, but magnifying the office of their chief, and prouder of their loyal service to him round whose standard they gathered than of their own descent from the gods of Walhalla.

Let the reader apply these general principles to some of those incidents in the Germanic migration which have been already recorded: let him think of Fridigern, of Athanaric, of Eriulph, the chiefs of the Visigoths, of Hermanric the mighty and wide-ruling king of the Ostrogoths: then let him remember how Alaric's elevation on the shield and the acclamation of his name as king gave at once a point and a purpose to the previously desultory warfare of the Goths, and led, by no obscure connection of causes and effects, to the occupation of the Eternal City itself by the forces of the barbarians. One instance of a Folc-mote, at least of a council of war, which might possibly bear that character, we noticed in the pages of Claudian. It was that held before the battle of Pollentia, in which the poet represents an old chief as pleading for peace and harshly silenced by the vengeful voice of Alaric. We do not need the doubtful authority of the poet to assure us that, if assemblies of the people were held during these marchings and counter-marchings on the soil of Italy, this would generally be the result. All military instinct would be in favour of obeying rather than arguing with the young and brilliant leader of the Goths; and the necessities of the 'war power,' which made a temporary autocrat of so constitutional a ruler as President Lincoln, might well make Alaric the Balth the unquestioned disposer of the lives and fortunes of his people.

The vassalage into which so many German kings were forced under the yoke of Attila the Hun probably tended towards the effacement of popular freedom. Before Attila, Ardaric and Walamir might tremble, but to their subjects they would be terrible, as representing not only their own power, but all the consolidated might of that heterogeneous monarchy.

As for the polity of the Vandals, we saw, in tracing the history of the conquest and land- settlement of Africa, how vast a preponderating influence was thereby assigned to the king. It is true that, by careful examination, some traces of the old Teutonic freedom may still be discovered among the warriors of Gaiseric, but they are indeed rare and feeble. Peace and war, treaties, persecutions, all seem to be decided upon and carried through by the overwhelming authority of the king.

And thus we come to the subject with which we are now specially concerned, the kind and degree of kingly authority wielded by the Amal Theodoric. It must be stated at once that this was absolutely unlike the limited and jealously watched authority of the German kings described by Tacitus. After the Ostrogoths crept forth from under the world-shadowing might of Attila, they fell into a position of more or less dependence upon the power of Eastern Rome; a power materially far less formidable than that of the terrible Hun, but more potent in its influence on the minds and thoughts of men. It is impossible to prove what effect the forty years between the death of Attila and the death of Odovacar had upon the 'Walamir-Goths but it is almost certain that many old German ideas and customs were lost during that time of close intercourse and frequently-renewed alliance with Byzantium. For the fact that they did not become altogether Romanised and sink into the position of a mere military colony of the Empire, their old hereditary loyalty to the Amal kings was mainly answerable. The reader will remember in what insulting terms Theodoric the son of Triarius taunted the squalid retinue of his rival for their fall from their once high and prosperous estate. He was correct in saying that it was their loyalty to Theodoric the Amal that had brought them into that abyss of wretchedness. But the instinct of the nation was right. Theodoric was indeed the people's hope, and their loyalty to him brought them safely through so many dangers and trials and seated them at length as lords in the fairest lands of Italy.

But when the great enterprise was thus at length crowned with success, the author of it was no longer a king after the old Germanic pattern, bound to consult and persuade his people at every turn. As an uncontrolled, unthwarted ruler he had led them from Novae to Ravenna. As an uncontrolled, unthwarted ruler he was thenceforward to guide the destinies of the nation in his palace by the Adriatic.

There is no trace of anything like a single meeting of the Folc-mote during the reign of Theodoric. All action in the State seems to proceed from the king alone, and though he condescends often to explain the reason for his edicts, he does this only as a matter of grace and favour, not of necessity, and in doing so he employs the same kind of language which is used in the Theodosian code. There is, as we shall see, at his death a faint acknowledgment of the right of the people to be consulted as to his successor; but here again there is no more recognition of the elective character of the monarchy, if so much, as in the case of the successive wearers of the purple at Byzantium. In short, though Theodoric never assumed the title of emperor, his power, for all practical purposes, seems to have been exactly the same as an emperor's; and we get a much more truthful idea of his position by thinking of him as the successor of Theodosius and the predecessor of Charles the Great, than by applying to him any of the characteristics of Teutonic royalty which we find in the Germania of Tacitus.

But though the kingship of Theodoric was thus greatly changed from the old model of his forefathers' royalty, there is one case of an early German ruler, described to us by Tacitus himself, whose career is in some respects very similar to that of the Amal hero. Maroboduus, king of the Marcomanni, a very few years after the birth of Christ led his people across the Erzgebirge, and established a strong kingdom in Bohemia and Bavaria and on the Middle Danube. A disciplined army of 70,000 men, hovering upon a frontier only 200 miles from Italy, caused even the great Augustus to tremble for the peace of his Transalpine provinces. No German had ever seemed more formidable to Rome, but he was formidable only because he was despotic. It is evident that in his kingship the rein was drawn far tighter than was usual in the Germanic states of that day, and this harsher system of government, though it made him for the time a more dangerous foe to Rome, prevented his dynasty from striking root in the affections of his people. When Arminius attacked him after about twenty years of rule, 'the name of king,' that is, of despotic king, 'alienated the sympathy of his own countrymen from Maroboduus, while the cause of Arminius was popular, as he was fighting for liberty.' By this war Maroboduus was greatly weakened, and had to sue for the degrading help of Rome to avert absolute overthrow. Only two years later the

Gothic chieftain Catualda, who had once been driven from his country by the might of Maroboduus, ventured on an expedition of revenge, which, by the help of the disloyal nobles of the Marcomannic kingdom, was completely successful; and forced Maroboduus, a hunted exile and outlaw, to seek the protection of Tiberius, who received this disarmed enemy of the Roman people into his territory, and permitted him to spend the eighteen remaining years of his life in the friendly shelter of Ravenna. Strange vicissitude of fortune, which caused the first great absolute monarch of a German nation to grow old, amid the contempt of his people, in the very same capital which witnessed the splendid reign and honoured death of the greatest of German despots, Theodoric.

Happily the reign of the Amal king ended in no such disastrous collision with the free spirit of his people as that which brought the might of Marobodaus to the ground. Yet, if there were any traditions of a healthy national life still lingering among the warriors whom he had settled in Italy, these must have been continually wounded by what they saw and what they heard at the Court of Ravenna. True, they still were summoned to appear, at any rate those who lived in the north of Italy, once a year in the presence of their King, and to receive a donative from his hand. They were not turned into Roman legionaries; they fought still in the old national order, with the great Gothic broadsword and under the command of their own captains of thousands. But when they stood in the presence of their countryman, the great Amal, they found him surrounded with all the pomp of Byzantine royalty. The diadem which the Western Emperors had worn was upon his head, silken robes, dyed with the purple of the murex, flowed over his shoulders, *silentiarii* in bright armour kept guard before the curtain which separated the awful *secretum* of the sovereign from the profane crowd of suitors and suppliants, the Prefect of the Sacred Bedchamber, some Roman courtier intent on currying favour with his new lord by an exaggerated display of servile devotion, stood ready to stop on the threshold any of his old 'comrades,' of however noble blood, who would venture unbidden into the presence of the King.

The donative and the ration-money were given and were welcome to the spendthrift Goth, who had perhaps already diced away his lands to some fellow-soldier after they had sung together the old Gothic songs and drunk too deeply of the new delights of the wine of Italy. But before receiving the money, the old and grizzled warrior had perhaps to listen to some eloquent harangue from the lips of the fluent Roman quaestor, Cassiodorus, about the delights of being admitted to the royal presence and the living death which those endured who beheld not the light of his countenance—a harangue which almost made the donative loathsome, and which, if anything could have done so, would have quenched his loyal enthusiasm, when at last the veil was drawn asunder and the well-known form, conspicuous in so many battle-fields from the Bosporus to the Ticino, moved forth to receive their acclamations.

The picture here drawn of Gothic dissatisfaction at the exaltation 01 the royal prerogative is chiefly a conjectural one, but the fact is that almost all our information as to the feelings of the Gothic element in Theodoric's new state has to be derived from a few faint and widely-scattered hints, combined and vivified by the historical imagination. The information which reaches us as to the manner of the kingdom—and it is abundant—comes all from the Roman side. The rhetorical Cassiodorus, the courtly Ennodius, the dispirited Boethius, are all Romans. Even the Goth Jordanes is more than half-Roman at heart, and derives all his materials from Cassiodorus. We are therefore really without a picture of the Ostrogothic kingdom of Italy from the true

Ostrogothic point of view. Only, in reading the phrases in which these rhetoricians and churchmen magnify the might of their master, we are sure that they must have grated on the ears of all that was self-respecting and genuinely Teutonic in the countrymen of Theodoric.

To a certain extent we, who have imbibed from our childhood the idea that kingship is never so great a blessing to the world as when it is rigorously—almost jealously—controlled by the national will, can share the feelings of disgust with which our imaginary Gothic warrior listened to the fulsome flatteries of his Roman fellow-subjects. It is difficult for the most loyal admirer of Theodoric not to turn away with something more than weariness from the volume of state correspondence in which, for page after page, the great King, by the pen of his secretary, praises his own virtue, his own wisdom, his own moderation, .his own love of equal justice for Goth and Roman. Partly we become reconciled to this apparent want of modesty by remembering that, though the King is supposed to speak, it is well understood that the clever Quaestor really speaks for him. All the world knew that in these letters it listened, not to Theodoric praising himself, but to Cassiodorus praising Theodoric. The will of the King is undoubtedly expressed in these letters, and we may be sure that his share in them was by no means limited to a mere formal assent, or the languid addition of his stencilled signature at the bottom. Yet when Theodoric knew that the substance of the royal will was therein contained, he probably gave himself little trouble about the form. For that, the learned Quaestor was responsible. A brave Gothic warrior would have blushed to enumerate his own good qualities with so many swelling words of vanity. But if this was the custom of the country, it must be complied with; and probably the King saw his short, business-like, verbal instructions expanded into the turgid state document, with similar feelings to those with which an Englishman receives from his lawyer the great expanse of sheepskin covered with legal verbiage, that is required to give validity to a purchase which was settled in an interview of an hour.

After all, the great justification for the somewhat despotic form assumed by the government of Theodoric must be found in the object which he proposed to himself, and which, with signal success, he achieved. What was that object? It was in one word, *Civilitas*; the maintenance of peace and tranquillity, and the safeguarding of all classes of his subjects from oppression and violence at the hands either of lawless men or of the ministers of the law. The golden words of Ataulfus, as recorded by Orosius, seem to have expressed exactly the aim which Theodoric kept constantly before him. Not to obliterate the Roman name, not to turn *Romania* into *Gothia*, but to correct the inherent lawlessness of the Gothic character by the restraint of those laws without which the state would cease to be a state, to restore the Roman name to its old lustre and increase its potency by Gothic vigour; this was the dream which floated before the mind of Ataulfus, this was the dream which became a reality for forty years under Theodoric and his descendants.

The state papers of the Ostrogothic monarchy, as will be seen by any one who glances through the abstract of the letters of Cassiodorus, are filled almost to satiety with the praises of this great gift, *Civilitas*. It was attained, however, not by the fusion, but rather by the federation, of the two peoples, over both of whom Theodoric was king. Whatever may have been his hope as to the ultimate effect of his measures, and probably the vision of a united Italian people did sometimes fascinate the mind of the King, or at any rate of his ablest minister, they well knew that at present the absolute assimilation of the two nations was impossible.

The Goth could not be taught in one generation that reverence for the name of Law, that disposition to submit to authority, however harshly displayed, which had become an instinct with the Roman people. The Roman could not in one generation become imbued with that free heroic spirit, that love of danger and of adventure, which rang in every Gothic battle-song. This had perhaps never been precisely the endowment even of his forefathers, for even the Fabricii and the Valerii were inspired to do great deeds rather by a lofty sense of duty, self-respect, loyalty to their comrades and their country, than by the mere animal delight in fighting which fired the sons of Odin. And whatever the Roman's prowess had once been, it had now utterly left him, and generations of intermixture with a new stock were needed to bring back the iron into his blood.

Meantime, then, the two nations were to be governed with a strong and impartial hand, not as one people, but for one end, the happiness of all. The Gothic sword was to preserve the soil of Italy from foreign foes, while the Roman practised the arts of peace and administered the laws which had come down from his forefathers. The situation was like that which existed in Normandy under William Longsword, like that which his descendant William the Bastard strove to establish in England after the Conquest; striving unsuccessfully because his English subjects, at any rate after the revolt of 1068, refused to give him that willing obedience which undoubtedly was rendered during the larger part of his reign by the Roman population to Theodoric. Or, to choose an illustration from our own times, the relation of the Ostrogothic King to the two classes of his subjects was like that of an enlightened and conscientious Governor-General of India to the Europeans and Hindoos under his sway. Fusion of the two nations is at present an impossibility. It is impossible to legislate for the European indigo-planter exactly as if he were a native Rajah, or for the headman of a Hindoo village as if he had the same ideas as a Queen's soldier from Devonshire. The best rulers keep the fusion of the two nations before them as an event possible in the far-distant future, and meanwhile strive so to govern that the thought of a common interest in the prosperity of the whole country, the idea of a true *Res Publica*, may take root in the minds of both races, that no violence be practised by the European against the Hindoo, and no chicane by the Hindoo against the European, that 'Ephraim shall not envy Judah, and Judah shall not vex Ephraim.'

This equal balance held between the two diverse nations requires, however, a steady hand the scales. A Folc-mote of the Goths would have made short work of the liberties of the Romans; a meeting of citizens in the Roman Forum, lashed to fury by the harangue of some windy orator, would soon have pulled down the statues of the Gothic king. And thus we are brought by these considerations to the same conclusion to which, as we have seen, all the events in the history of his nation tended. German kingship as wielded by Theodoric had to be despotic. The crown of the arch must be made strong and heavy to repress the upward thrust of the two opposing nationalities.

This being so, the laws and usages of the Gotho-Roman state throw not much light on the development of Teutonic institutions. It is the dying Empire, as we shall see, rather than dawning Feudalism, which is displayed in the correspondence of Theodoric's secretary. The *Edictum Theodorici*, to which reference will be made in the next chapter, is not, like the codes of other German races—the Burgundian, the Salian, the Ripuarian—an exposition in barbarous Latin of the customary law of the tribes who had come to seat themselves within the borders of the Empire; but it is rather a selection of such parts of the Theodosian code and of the Roman *Responsa Prudentum* as were suitable for the new monarchy, a few unimportant changes being made in some of their provisions by the supreme will of the king.

Gothic law we may be sure there was, to be administered where Goths only were concerned; but it has left little trace in any written documents, no doubt because in the great majority of cases Romans were concerned either alone or together with Goths, and here the irresistible tendency of the magistracy which Theodoric had taken over from the Empire was to make Roman law supreme.

There are two offices, however, which we may notice here, before we pass on to consider the Roman side of Theodoric's administration, since they are both purely Teutonic, and were no doubt always held by men of barbarian origin. One is that of the Count of the Goths, the other that of the Saiones.

1. The *Comes Gothorum* (we know not his Gothic title) was no doubt in practice always a general high in office, perhaps usually a great provincial governor. But his chief duty was to decide, doubtless according to the old traditional law of his people, any disputes which might arise between one Goth and another. Should the controversy he between a born Goth and a born Roman, in that case he was to associate with himself a Roman jurisconsult and decide the strife 'according to fair reason'. In estimating what 'fair reason' required, we may probably conclude that the Roman law, with its vast store of precedents, the accumulated experience of ages, aptly quoted and enforced by a quick-witted jurisconsult, would be almost uniformly victorious over the few and crude maxims of German Right, born in the forest or the pasture-land, and dimly present in the brain of some stalwart Count of the Goths, more able to enforce his conclusions with his sword than with his tongue.

2. The Saiones were apparently a class of men peculiar to the Ostrogothic monarchy. More honoured than the Roman lictor (who was but a menial servant of the magistrate), but hardly perhaps rising to the dignity of a sheriff or a marshal, they were, so to speak, the arms by which Royalty executed its will. If the Goths had to be summoned to battle with the Franks, a Saio carried round the stirring call to arms. If a Praetorian Prefect was abusing his power to take away his neighbour's lands by violence, a Saio was sent to remind him that under Theodoric not even Praetorian Prefects should be allowed to transgress the law. If a new fort had to be built on some dolomite peak commanding the ravines of the Adige, and shutting out the barbarians of Northern Tyrol, a Saio was dispatched to urge and guide the exertions of the provincials. The Saiones seem to have stood in a special relation to the king. They are generally called 'our Saiones,' sometimes 'our brave Saiones,' and the official virtue which is always credited to them (like the 'Sublimity' or the 'Magnificence' of more important personages) is 'Your Devotion.'

One duty which was frequently entrusted to the Saio was the *tuitio* 0f some wealthy and unwarlike Roman. It often happened that such a person, unable to protect himself against the rude assaults of sturdy Gothic neighbours, appealed to the King for protection. When the petition was granted, as it probably was in almost all cases, the person thus taken under the *tuitio regii nominis* acquired peculiar rights, and any maltreatment of his person or injury to his property was treated as more than an ordinary offence against *civilitas*, as a special act of contempt towards the royal authority. He seems to have had, at any rate in certain cases, a peculiar privilege of suing and being sued directly in the Supreme Court (*comitatus*) of the King, overleaping all courts of inferior jurisdiction. But the chief visible sign of the King's protection, and the most effective guarantee of its efficiency, was the stout Gothic soldier who as Saio was quartered in the wealthy Roman's house, ready to fight all his battles, and to make all other Goths respect the person and the property of him to whom Theodoric had pledged the royal word for his safety. A payment, of the amount of which we are not informed, but which probably varied according to the wealth of the Roman and the lineage of the Goth, was paid, *commodi nomine,* by way of douceur, by the defended to the defender.

The relation thus established was one which, being itself a somewhat barbarous remedy for barbarism, might easily degenerate from its original intention. Sometimes the protected Roman, having this robust Goth in his house, sharing his hospitality and ready to do his bidding, used him not merely for his own defence but for the oppression of his poorer and weaker neighbours. Sometimes the Saio, tired of ever guarding the soft, effeminate noble committed to his care, and perhaps stung by the silent assumption of superiority in knowledge and culture which lurked in all the Roman's words and gestures, would turn against his host and even violently assault his dainty person. Thus, to his eternal disgrace, did Amara, who actually drew a sword against the Senator Petrus, whose defender he was. He wounded his hand, and, had not the Roman been partly sheltered by a door, would have severed it from the wrist. Yet, notwithstanding this evil deed, he had the audacity to claim from Petrus, *commodi nomine*, the Saio's usual gratuity. Rightly did the indignant King order that Amara should be removed from the post of defender, the duties of which he so strangely discharged, that his place should be given to his countryman Tezutzat, and that he should refund twice the sum which he had exacted for his gratuity.

Slight indications like this of the footing upon which the two nations lived may help us to understand the difficulty of the problem set before Theodoric the common ruler of both of them, and to appreciate more highly the skill which for thirty years he displayed in solving it.

CHAPTER VIII.

THEODORIC AND HIS COURT.

We have endeavoured in the previous chapter to look at Theodoric king of the Goths and the Romans with the eyes of such of his old barbarian comrades as survived the hardships of the march and the perils of four bloody battles, and found themselves quartered in the pleasant lands of Italy, with every possession that heart could desire except their old freedom. Let us now hear what the Roman inhabitants of the land, the orators and churchmen, who alone could translate his deeds into literature and so transmit his fame to posterity, have to tell us concerning him.

No stirring It may be stated at once that no great events mark his and no great historian illustrate his reign. Seldom has there been a better illustration of the proverb, 'Happy is the nation that has no annals'; for in the comparative poverty of our historical information one thing is clear, that the period during which Theodoric bore sway, a period equivalent to the average length of a generation of mankind, was a time of great and generally diffused happiness for the Italian population, one that stood out in emphatic contrast to the century of creeping paralysis which preceded, and to the ghastly cycle of wars and barbarous revenges which followed that peaceful time.

But, had the events of this reign been many we could have said little about them. By some strange fatality, the Ostrogothic King, with all his generous patronage of arts and literature, never lighted on the 'sacred bard' who should keep his fame green through the centuries, nor on the fluent historian who should weave the various actions of his time into a connected history. Or, if such a work ever was written—and possibly the later books of Cassiodorus' history of the Goths would have answered to this description—the foolish sieve of Time, which so often retains the sand and lets the pure gold fall through into oblivion, has not preserved it to our days.

Much valuable and interesting information however, as to both home and foreign affairs, can be obtained from the official correspondence of Cassiodorus, the manner of the composition of which has been glanced at in the previous chapter. But the only continuous account of the history of his reign—except a few meagre sentences of Jordanes—is contained in the mysterious fragment which is quoted by historians as *Anonymus Valesii*, and which is always printed (for no very obvious reason) at the end of the history of Ammianus Marcellinus.

This unknown scribe, with whom we have already made some acquaintance, takes his literary name from Henri de Valois, a French scholar of the seventeenth century, who first introduced him to the modern world. According to an opinion now generally accepted, he is none other than that Maximian Bishop of Ravenna whose mosaic portrait we still see on the walls of S. Vitale, where, arrayed in alb and pallium and with a jewelled cross in his hand, he consecrates the new church in the (imaginary) presence of Justinian and his Court. Whoever the writer be, he writes as an ecclesiastic and as an inhabitant of Ravenna. A vein of something like legendary adornment runs through his narrative, nor should we be justified in quoting him as an absolutely accurate witness for events, some of which may have happened twenty or thirty years before his birth, and the latest of which (as recorded by him) probably happened in his boyhood. But, as has been before hinted, there is every reason to think that for some of his names and dates he relies upon the absolutely contemporary but now perished 'Annals of Ravenna'; and on the whole, as historical authorities go, he is, notwithstanding his anonymousness, a very fair voucher for the truth of the facts which he records.

As the extract is not long, and is of considerable importance, it will be well to translate it entire:—

THE ANONYMUS VALESII ON THEODORIC.

'Now Theodoric had sent Faustus Niger on an embassy to Zeno. But as the news of that Emperor's death arrived before the return of the embassy, and as the entry into Ravenna and the death of Odoacer had intervened, the Goths confirmed Theodoric to themselves as king, without waiting for the orders of the new Emperor.

'He was a man most brave and warlike, the natural son of Walamir king of the Goths. His mother was called Ereriliva, a Gothic woman but a Catholic, who took at baptism the name Eusebia.

'He was an illustrious man and full of good-will towards all. He reigned thirty-three years, and during thirty of those years so great was the happiness attained by Italy that even the wayfarers were at peace[1] For he did nothing wrong. Thus did he govern the two nations, the Goths and Romans, as if they were one people, belonging himself to the Arian sect, but arranging that the civil administration of the Romans should continue as it was under the Emperors. He gave presents and rations to the people, yet though he found the Treasury quite bankrupt, by his own labour he brought it round into a flourishing condition. Nothing did he attempt against the Catholic faith. He exhibited games in the Circus and Amphitheatre, so that he received from the Romans the titles Trajan and Valentinian (as he did in truth seek to bring back the prosperous times of those emperors); and on the other hand, the obedience rendered by the Goths to the Edictum Theodorici showed that they recognised its author as in all things their Mightiest.

'Unlettered as he was, so great was his shrewdness that some of his sayings still pass current among the common folk, a few of which we may be allowed here to preserve.

'He said, "He who has gold and he who has a devil can neither of them hide what they have got."

'Also, "The Roman when in misery imitates the Goth, and the Goth when in comfort imitates the Roman."

'A certain man dying left a wife and a little boy too young to know his mother. The child was taken away by a friend of the fathers into another province, and there educated. Returning as a young man to his mother, he found that she had betrothed herself to a suitor. When however she saw her son she embraced him, and blessed God for restoring him to her : so he abode with her thirty days. At the end of that time her lover returns, sees the youth and asks "Who is this?" She replied, "My son." When he found that she had a son, he began to claim back again his earnest-money, and to say, "Either deny that this is your son, or else go hence." Thus compelled by her lover, the woman began to deny the son whom she had previously owned, and ordered him out of the house as a stranger to her. He answered that he had returned, as he had a right to do, to his mother in the house of his father. Eventually the son appealed to the King against his mother, and the King ordered her to appear before him. "Woman!" said he, "you heare what this young man urges against you. Is he thy son or no?". She answered, "He is not my son, but as a stranger did I entertain him". Then when the woman's son had told all his story in the King's Court, the King said to her again, "Is he thy son or no?". Again she said, "He is not my son". Said the King to her, "And what is the amount of your possessions, woman?". She answered, "As much as 1000 solidi" [£600]. Then the King swore that nothing would satisfy him, unless the woman took him (the young man) for her husband instead of the suitor. With that the woman was struck with confusion, and confessed that he was indeed her son. And many more stories of the same kind are related of him.

'Afterwards he received from the Franks a wife named Augofleda; for he had had a wife before his accession to the throne who had borne him two daughters. One, named Arevagni, he gave in marriage to Alaric king of the Visigoths in Gaul, and the other, named Theodegotha, to Sigismund son of King Gundebaud [the Burgundian].

'Having made his peace with the Emperor Anastasius through the mediation of Festus for his unauthorised assumption of the royal title, [the Emperor] also restored to him all the ornaments of the palace which Odoachar had transmitted to Constantinople, contested 'At the same time there arose a strife in the the Papacy, city of Rome between Symmachus and Laurentius, both of whom were consecrated [bishops]. By Divine ordering Symmachus, the worthier of the visit to two, prevailed. After peace had been restored King Theodoric went to Borne, the Church's capital, and paid his devotions to the Blessed Peter as devoutly as any Catholic. To meet him, Pope Symmachus and all the Senate and people of Rome poured forthwith every mark of joy, outside the gates of the city. Then Theodoric entering the city came to the Senate, and at the Palma delivered an address to the people of Rome, promising that by God's help he would keep inviolate all that the preceding Roman sovereigns had ordained.

'Celebrating the thirtieth anniversary of his accession he entered the city in triumph, rode to the palace, and exhibited to the Romans the games of the Circus. He also gave to the Roman people and to the poor a yearly supply of grain to the amount of 120,000 modii [3750 quarters], and for the restoration of the palace or the repair of the walls of the city he ordered 200 lbs. [of gold = £8000] to be paid annually from the proceeds of the duty on wine.

Moreover, he gave his sister Amalafrigda in marriage to Transimund king of the Vandals.

'He made Liberius, whom in the beginning of his reign he had appointed Praetorian Prefect, Patrician, and gave him as his successor in the former office—[The name seems to have dropped out.] Therefore Theodorus son of Basilius [and Odoin his Count (?) conspired against him. When he had discovered this plot he ordered his head to be cut off in the palace which is called "Sessorium." For(?) at the request of the people he directed that the words of the promise which he had made them in his popular harangue should be engraved on a brazen tablet and fixed in a place of public resort.

'Then returning to Ravenna in the sixth month he gave Amalabirga his sister's daughter in marriage to Herminifrid king of the Thuringians. And thus he pleased all the nations round about him; for he was a lover of manufactures and a great restorer of cities.

'He restored the aqueduct of Ravenna which Trajan had built, and after a long interval of time again introduced water into the city. He made the palace perfect, but did not dedicate it, and he finished the porticoes round the palace.

'Also at Verona he erected baths and a palace, and carried a portico from the gate to the palace. The aqueduct, which had been long destroyed, he renewed, and introduced water through it. Moreover he surrounded the city with new walls.

'At Ticinum [Pavia] also he built a palace, baths, and an amphitheatre, and carried new walls round the city. On many other cities also he bestowed many benefits. Thus he so charmed the neighbouring nations that they came under a league with him, hoping that he would be their king. The merchants too from divers provinces came flocking together to him, for so great was the order which he maintained, that, if any one wished to leave gold or silver on his land, it was deemed as safe as if within a walled city. An indication of this was the fact that throughout all Italy he never made gates for any city, and the gates that were in the cities were not closed. Any one who had any business to transact did it at any hour of the night as securely as in the day.

'In his time men bought wheat at 60 modii for a solidus [about 12s. a quarter], and for 30 amphorae of wine they paid the same price [2s. 4d. per gallon].

'Now King Theodoric was an unlettered man, and so unsuccessful as a student that after years of reigning he was still utterly unable to learn the four letters of his own signature to one of his edicts Thiud, if in Gothic, THEO if in Latin. Wherefore he ordered a golden plate to be engraved, having the four letters of the royal name pierced through it, so that when he wished to sign any document he could place the plate upon the paper, and drawing his pen through the holes could give it the appearance of his own signature.

'Then Theodoric, having conferred the honours of the consulship on [his son-in-law] Eutharic, triumphed at Rome and Ravenna. But this Eutharic was a man of very harsh disposition, and a bitter enemy of the Catholic faith.

'After this, when Theodoric was staying at Verona through fear of hostile movements among the barbarians [north of the Alps], a strife arose between the Jews and Christians of the city of Ravenna. For the Jews, disliking those who were baptized, often by way of derision threw persons into the water of the river, and in the same way they made sport of the Lord's Supper. Hereupon the people being inflamed with fury, and being quite past the control of the King, of Eutharic, and even of Peter who was then bishop, arose against the synagogues and soon burned them. Then the Jews rushed to Verona, where the King was, and by the agency of Triwan the Grand Chamberlain, himself a heretic and a favourer of their nation, they got their case against the Christians presented to the King. He promptly ordered that, for their presumption in burning the synagogues, all the Roman population of Ravenna should pay a contribution sufficient to provide for their restoration; and those who had no money to pay were to be flogged through the streets of the city while the crier proclaimed their offence. Orders to this effect were given to Eutharic-Cilliga and to the Bishop Peter, and thus it was done'.

The 'Anonymus' then begins to narrate the story of the religious troubles and persecutions which clouded the last years of Theodoric, and which will be described in a later chapter.

Let us try to bring to a focus the somewhat confused and inartistic picture which is here drawn for us by the most valuable of all witnesses to character, an unfriendly contemporary.

Evidently there was peace and prosperity, at any rate comparative prosperity, throughout Italy in the reign of Theodoric. Absolute freedom from hostile invasion—except, as we shall see, some trifling ravages of the Byzantines in Apulia—was a great thing; a thing to which Italy may almost be said to have been a stranger during the ninety years that had elapsed, since the clarions of Alaric first sounded in the plains of Pollentia. But yet more important for Italy, in her then condition, was the presence in the royal palace of a strong will, wielding irresistible power and guided by benevolence towards all classes of the people. Long enough had the name and the reality of power been disjoined the one from the other. Long enough had flatterers and rhetoricians pretended to worship the almost divine majesty of the Emperor, while every one knew that in reality some menacing barbarian freebooter, or some yet more intolerable barbarian life-guardsman, was master of the situation. Now, the man who was hailed as king was once more in truth a king of men. He knew, every Goth in his disbanded army, every Roman possessor in the most secluded valleys of the Appennines, knew, that Theodoric was and would be undisputed master. He could be terrible to all extortionate and unjust governors, because behind him there loomed no figure greater than his own ; he could be just, because the welfare of his subjects was in truth his own highest interest; he could be gentle, because he was irresistible.

The same picture of firm and just rule is brought before us by a few sentences of Procopius, who again, as a man employed in the Byzantine army, may be considered as a witness unfriendly to the Gothic rule.

'Theodoric' says he, ' was an extraordinary lover of justice, and adhered rigorously to the laws. He guarded the country from barbarian invasion, and displayed both intelligence and prudence in the highest degree. Of injustice towards his subjects there was hardly a trace in his government, nor would he allow any of his subordinates to attempt anything of the kind, save only that the Goths divided among themselves the same proportion of the land of Italy which Odoacer had given to his partisans. So then Theodoric was in name a tyrant, but in deed a true king, not inferior to the best of his predecessors, and his popularity grew greatly, contrary to the ordinary fashion of human affairs, both among Goths and Italians. For generally, as different classes in the State want different things, the government which pleases one party, has to incur the odium of those who do not belong to it.

'After a reign of thirty-seven years he died, having been a terror to all his enemies, and left a deep regret for his loss in the hearts of his subjects.'

The fact that such results were achieved by an unlettered chieftain, the scion of an only half-civilised German tribe, must be accounted a signal victory of human intelligence and self-restraint, and justifies, if anything can justify, the tight rein which, while curbing himself, he kept upon the old Teutonic freedom. Obviously however, with the best good-will on the part of the King, these results could not have been obtained in detail unless he had been well served by ministers—from the necessity of the case chiefly Roman ministers—like-minded with himself. To these men, the Sullys and the Colberts of the Gothic King, let us now turn our attention.

The first man who served as Praetorian Prefect under Theodoric, holding that great office for the first seven years of his reign, was Liberius. This man—who was of course Roman, not Teutonic, by origin—had occupied an important place among the ministers of Odovacar. Unlike the treacherous Tufa, he remained faithful to the last to his barbarian chief, and took an active part in directing the operations against Theodoric. On the downfall of his old patron, he showed no unmanly fear as to his own fortunes, no servile haste to propitiate the new lord of Italy, but, with calm sadness, intimated that he accepted the judgment of Heaven, and since he could no longer be loyal to Odovacar, he was willing to serve with equal loyalty that monarch's conqueror. Theodoric was wise enough to accept the proffered service, and, as we have seen, to confer upon the true-hearted Roman the still vast powers of the Praetorian Prefect.

Unhappily these seven first years of the reign of Theodoric—perhaps its most interesting portion —are an almost absolute blank. Liberius left no such copious record of official work behind him as was left by the fluent Cassiodorus. But we are informed incidentally that one of the chief cares of the new ministry was, as we might have expected, finance. He introduced a wise economy into every department of the State, and while the Exchequer found itself every year in a more flourishing condition, the tax-payer was conscious that, at any rate, there was no addition to his previous burdens. It seems probable that some, at least, of that praise which arose from a prosperous and contented Italy should be attxibuted to these early measures of Liberius.

One work of great delicacy and importance, which was successfully performed by him, was the assignment of the Tertiae, or third part of the soil of Italy, to the new-comers. Broadly, as has been already said, the new land-settlement was probably a transfer of these Land-thirds from the men of Odovacar to the men of Theodoric. But there may have been reasons, unknown to us, which prevented this from being the sole principle of distribution, and which obliged the commission, of which Liberius was the head, to proceed in many instances to a new division as between Roman and Goth. Here we are told he showed great tact and skill, settling neighbour by neighbour in such a way that not rivalry but friendship sprang out of their new relation, introducing probably the Gothic settlers chiefly into those parts of the country where the land really cried out for more numerous cultivators* and ever impressing upon his Roman countrymen the great principle of the new government, that the Goth was there for the defence of the whole land, and that, by sacrificing one-third, the Roman cultivator might reckon on enjoying the remaining two-thirds in security.

It was probably through the hands of Liberius that the tedious negotiations with Byzantium passed, those negotiations which ended at length in the recognition of Theodoric as legitimate ruler of Italy. The chief persons employed in these negotiations were Faustus and Festus, two Roman noblemen of about equal rank, and whom it is not easy to distinguish from one another. Faustus was a successor, though not the immediate successor, of Liberius in the office of Praetorian Prefect; and Festus, who was dignified with the high title of Patrician, was apparently at about the same time Prefect of the City. It may be useful, as a note of distinction between them, to observe that Faustus was the unsuccessful ambassador to Constantinople in 493, Festus the successful one in 497. Further, that while Faustus, in the disputed Papal election of 498, took the part of the ultimately successful candidate, Pope Symmachus, Festus, who desired to obtain a pontiff favourable to the Henoticon of Zeno, sided with the Anti-Pope Laurentius.

It was in one of the lucid intervals of this prolonged struggle for the chief place in the Roman Church that Theodoric visited the ancient capital of the Empire. 'Murders, robberies and infinite evils' had afflicted the citizens of Rome, and even the nuns had been cruelly maltreated in this street warfare, which was to decide whether Symmachus or Laurentius was henceforward to have the power of binding and loosing in the kingdom of heaven. But, as has been said, there was a lull in the storm, during which the Ostrogothic King wisely determined to visit the city. Constantinople, the New Rome by the Bosporus, he had gazed upon near forty years before with eyes of boyish wonder. Now he was to see for himself the mysterious and venerable city by the Tiber; that city which had so long cast her spell upon his people, but of which he, a barbarian from the Danube, was now unquestioned lord. Having knelt devoutly at the shrine of St. Peter, in the long pillar-lined basilica (so unlike its modern representative) reared amid the gardens of Nero, he was met outside the gates of the city by the procession of Pope, senators and people, who, with shouts of loyal welcome, pressed forth to greet him. Then came, as the Anonymus Valesii has told us, the speech in the Forum, the games in the Circus, probably also in the Colosseum, and the solemn renewal of the grain largesse to the Roman populace, which had perhaps been interrupted since the days of Odovacar.

It seems probable that this may have been the occasion chosen by the King and his enlightened minister for the formal publication of the *Edictum Theodorici*. It is true that the somewhat obscure language of the Anonymus Valesii does not prove, as was once supposed, that it was promulgated at this time. The solemn privilegium, to which he refers, engraved on a brazen tablet and posted in the Forum, was quite a different document, and little more than a promise to observe the laws of his predecessors, such a promise as William the Norman gave to govern according to the laws of King Edward. But there is a certain amount of concurrent testimony in favour of this date, and no valid argument against it. Upon the whole, it may fairly be stated as a probable conjecture, though not an ascertained fact, that Theodoric's visit to Bome was the occasion of the publication of the Edict, and that Liberius was its author.

This Edict, of which a slight sketch is given in the note at the end of this chapter, is (as was stated in the last chapter) utterly unlike the codes which formulated the laws of the other barbarian monarchies. There is hardly a trace in it of German law or German ideas: it is Roman and imperial throughout. We may remember how Sidonius complained of a certain renegade Roman governor, as 'trampling under foot the laws of Theodosius and setting forth the laws of Theodoric.' But here it is a German, a Theodoric himself, who, wisely no doubt for the most part, and with statesmanlike insight into the necessities of the case, treads the laws of his Amal forefathers in the dust and exalts on high the laws of Theodosius.

It may have been—though there is nothing but one darkly enigmatic sentence in the Anonymus to confirm the conjecture—the publication of this obviously Romanising edict, and the evident desire of Theodoric to draw as close as possible to his Roman subjects, which brought the Gothic disaffection to a head. Odoin, a barbarian Count, planned a conspiracy against his lord. We have no details of the plot or of its discovery. We only know that it failed, and that in the Sessorian Palace, just within the southern wall of Rome (hard by the Basilica della Croce, where rests Helena, mother of Constantine and discoverer of the Holy Cross), the treacherous Goth knelt down to receive the blow of the executioner, and the headless trunk of Odoin showed to all the world that the mild and righteous Theodoric could also be terrible to evil-doers.

It may have been during this tarriance at Rome that Theodoric commenced his great works of draining the Pontine Marshes and repairing the Appian Way, works commemorated in an inscription still preserved in the Piazza at Terracina. At the last-named place, situated about sixty miles from Rome, where a spur of the Volscian mountains juts out into the blue Tyrrhene Sea, stand yet on the brow of the hill the massive ruins of the so-called Palace of Theodoric. It may be doubtful how far this name is correctly given to them : but if the great Ostrogoth ever did dwell here, and look forth from these windows over the sea, which his wise rule was covering with the whitewinged messengers of commerce, and over the plain where the peaceful army of his labourers was turning the wilderness of the Pontine Marshes into a fruitful field, it was probably during this visit to Eome, in some weeks of villeggiatura, away from the sun-baked capital, that he thus sojourned at Terracina.

We see, from the statement of the Anonymus Valesii, that it was also during the King's residence in Rome that he took in hand the repair of the walls and of the imperial residence on the Palatine. So large a sum as £8000, spent yearly on these objects, would make a marked difference in the condition of both sets of buildings. We learn, from a letter of Cassiodorus that 25,000 *tegulae*—the square flat bricks which the antiquary knows so well—were used yearly in the restoration of the walls. We may well wonder, not that some tiles have been discovered bearing the name and titles of 'Our Lord Theodoric, the benefactor of Rome', but that the number of these is not much larger[1].

Upon the whole we may probably conclude that this Roman visit, which lasted for six months, was one of the happiest periods in the life of Theodoric. There was peace abroad and at home. The barbarian stranger had borne the ordeal of an entry into the fastidious city by the Tiber, once the capital of the world, successfully, though it was an ordeal before which born Romans, like Constantius and Honorius, had well-nigh quailed. He had addressed the people in the Forum, he had shared the deliberations of the Conscript Fathers in the Senate House, and it seems safe to say that he had produced a favourable impression upon both assemblies. As he journeyed along the Flaminian Way to his chosen home by the Hadriatic, he felt himself more firmly settled in his seat, more thoroughly king of all the Italians as well as of all the Goths, than he had done before. The headless corpse of Odoin was well atoned for by the remembrance of the enthusiastic shouts, both of welcome and farewell, of the Roman people.

During this sojourn in Rome, Liberius, who was now probably a man advanced in years, was honourably dismissed from the laborious though dignified post of Praetorian Prefect, and received the rank of Patrician, which was generally conferred on those who were retiring from this office with the favour of their sovereign.

His successor as Praetorian Prefect, though perhaps not his immediate successor, was Cassiodorus, father of the writer so often named in this history. And here, in order to disentangle a needlessly complicated discussion, a few sentences must be devoted to the Cassiodorian pedigree.

From a sketch of the history of his ancestors, which Cassiodorus (the author) included in the official letter announcing to the Senate his father's elevation to the Patriciate, we learn that, for at least three generations the family had taken an active part in public life.

The first Cassiodorus who is here mentioned attained to the rank of an Illustris, and held a leading position in the province of Bruttii, which, with the neighbouring island of Sicily, he defended, apparently with a troop raised at his own cost, from an invasion of the Vandals. This may very probably have occurred in the year 440, when, as we learn from the Chronicle of his descendant, 'Gaiseric sorely afflicted Sicily'.

His son, the second Cassiodorus, was a Tribune (or, as we should say, Colonel) in the army of Valentinian III, and a *Notarius* in the secret cabinet of the Emperor. In both capacities he seems to have attached himself zealously to the party of the brave and statesmanlike Aetius, the man to whom all true Roman hearts then turned with longing. In company with the hero's son Carpilio he went on an embassy to the court of Attila, one doubtless of the innumerable embassies with which the Emperor sought to soothe the anger of the terrible Hun in the years between 440 and 450. According to his descendant, Cassiodorus exercised, over the quarrelsome Mongol, something of the same magnetic influence that was afterwards obtained by Pope Leo. He dared to meet the omnipotent victor in argument; he calmly braved his wrath; he convinced him of the reasonableness of the Roman demands; he inspired him with respect for the State which could still send forth such ambassadors: finally, he brought back with him the peace which was well nigh despaired of. We are not bound to believe all this highly-coloured picture, which seems to be at least suggested by the embassy of Leo, perhaps simply adapted from that well-known scene. But we may fairly presume that his conduct earned the approbation of his superiors, since Aetius offered him the rank of an Illustris, and some charge upon the public revenues, if he would remain at court. Cassiodorus, however, preferred returning to his beloved Bruttii, and there, under the shadow of the purple hills of Calabria, ended his days in quietness, undisturbed apparently by the ruins of the falling Empire.

His son, the *third* Cassiodorus, entered more boldly into public life. When still a young he discharged the duties of *Comes Privatarum Rerum* and *Comes Sacrarum Largitionum (*the two offices which represent the duties of our Commissioners of Woods and Forests, and Chancellor of the Exchequer), and in both capacities he earned the good opinion alike of his own countrymen and of his barbarian master Odovacar.

In the struggle between Rugian and Ostrogoth he seems not to have taken a part, but, as soon as Theodoric's throne was set up at Ravenna, he and then at once offered his services to the new monarch, and they were gladly accepted. The inhabitants of Sicily, who looked upon the Gothic rule with doubt and suspicion, were won over by their neighbour to the side which he had made his own; and, on the other hand, his wise and soothing words restrained Theodoric from the revenge to which some hostile acts of the Sicilians might otherwise have impelled him. For these services he had been rewarded with the post of Corrector of Lucania and Bruttii, chief governor, that is to say, of his own native province. He had large herds of horses on his estates—the Calabria of that day by the dense shade of its forests afforded great advantages to the horse-breeder—and out of these he made such generous presents to Theodoric that his son in later years, speaking by the mouth of the King, said (no doubt hyperbolically), 'he has mounted our whole army.'

This was the man who, having passed through all the lower ranks of the official service with credit and success, was now, in the first or second year of the sixth century, raised to the high honour of Praefectus Praetorio; an honour which had been already held for the extraordinary term of eighteen years by his kinsman Heliodorus, at Constantinople, when Theodoric himself was a guest of the Eastern Emperor. His own tenure of office was not long—we may conjecture it to have ended by the year 504—nor, except from the general terms of laudation in which it is referred to by his son, have we any information respecting it. We are fairly entitled to infer that he carried forward the policy of mild firmness and equal justice to both nations, which had been inaugurated by Theodoric and Liberius, and that his short administration contributed its share to the peaceful happiness of Italy.

Its chief event however, and that which has made it worth while to dwell upon the family honours in so much detail, was the fact that it his son to the notice of

Theodoric, and was the means of starting that son on an official career which lasted for nearly forty years, and will for ever connect his name beyond any other name in literature with the varying fortunes of the Ostrogothic monarchy.

Magnus Aurelius Cassiodorus Senator, the fourth of the family whose fortunes we have to trace, was born at Squillace in Calabria about the year 480. The year was a memorable one, since it witnessed the birth of three of the foremost men of their age—Cassiodorus, Boethius, and Benedict, the politician, the philosopher, and the saint. The place—let it be sketched for us by the loving hand of the greatest of its sons :—

'Scyllacium, the first city of Bruttii, founded by Ulysses the overthrower of Troy, is a city overlooking the Hadriatic Sea [more strictly the Gulf of Tarentum], and hangs upon the hills like a cluster of grapes; hills which are not so high as to make the ascent of them a weariness, but high enough to give a delicious prospect over the verdant plains and the deep blue back of the sea. This city sees the rising sun from its very cradle. The coming day sends forward no Aurora as herald of its approach, but with one burst uplifts its torch, and lo! the brightness quivers over land and sea. It beholds the rejoicing Sun-god, and so basks in his brightness all the day, that with good reason it might challenge the claims of Rhodes to represent itself as his birthplace. Its sky is clear, its climate temperate. Sunny in winter, it yet enjoys cool summers, and this moderation reflects itself in the character of its inhabitants. For a burningly hot country makes its children sharp and fickle, a cold one heavy and cunning; the best characters are produced by a more temperate clime.

' Scyllacium has an abundant share of the delicacies of the sea, possessing near it those Neptunian doors which we ourselves constructed. At the foot of Mount Moscius we hewed out a space in the bowels of the rocks, into which we caused the streams of Nereus to flow. The sight of the fishes sporting in their free captivity delights all beholders. There man feeds the creatures on which he himself will shortly feed ; they swim eagerly to take the morsels from his hand : sometimes, when he has fished to satiety, he sends them all back into the water.

'Fair is it to see the labours of the husbandmen all round while tranquilly reposing in the city. Here are the cluster-drooping vineyards, there the prosperous toil of the threshing-floor, there the dusky olive shows her face. Thus, as Scyllacium is an unwalled town, you might at choice call it a rural city or an urban farm; and, partaking of both characters, its praises have been sounded far and wide'.

Such was Scyllacium and such Bruttii in the days of Theodoric's minister. It may be feared that a modern traveller would not find all the delights in the modern Squillace and the modern Calabria which then existed, still less that delicate and lovely civilisation which ten centuries before had tinged every shore and headland of 'the Greater Greece'. Still, as then, the purple chain of Aspromonte divides the sparkling waters of the Eastern and the Western seas. Still do cities, beautiful at a distance, crown the finely-modelled hills that project into the plain. But the temple, with its pure white marble columns, has disappeared: a squalid comune replaces the Greek republic, instinct with life and intelligence, or the well-ordered Roman civitas. Instead of the white-robed Hellenes, wild-looking peasants, clad in goatskins, with their guns in their hands, slouch along through the cactus-bordered ways. The Saracen, the Spaniard, and the Bourbon have laid their heavy hands on the lovely region and brutalised its inhabitants. May better days be in store for it and for them in the Italy of the future!

The son who was born to Odovacar's minister at Squillace was named, as we have seen, Senator. It seems a strange thing to give a title like this as a personal name ;

but there is no doubt that it was done in this case. Cassiodorus speaks of himself as Senator, and is so addressed by others. His letters are written by 'Senator, a man of illustrious rank'; and in his Chronicle, when he has to record his own consulship (A.D. 514), his entry is 'Senatore, viro clarissimo consule'

It is evident that the young Senator received the best education that Italy could furnish in his day, and imbibed with enthusiasm all that the rhetoricians and grammarians who conducted it could impart to so promising a pupil. All through life he was essentially a literary man. We may perhaps in this aspect compare him to Guizot, a man of letters who rose to be first minister of a mighty monarchy, but whose heart was always given to the studies which engrossed him, when still a professor in the University of Paris. There are some indications in Cassiodorus' works that, next to Rhetoric, next to the mere delight of stringing words together in sonorous sentences, Natural History had the highest place in his affections. He never misses an opportunity of pointing a moral lesson by an allusion to the animal creation, especially to the habits of birds. Of course most of the stories which he thus introduces are mere imaginations, and often of a very laughable kind; but, had he fallen on a happier and more scientific age, it is reasonable to think that there might have been found in him some of the qualities of a Buffon or an Audubon.

It seems probable that, immediately on the elder Cassiodorus receiving the post of Praetorian Prelect, Senator, still quite a young man, obtained an appointment as his Consiliarius, or legal assessor, a post generally filled by young men with some legal training,—we shall find Procopius holding it in the tent of Belisarius,—and one which no doubt gave valuable experience to any man who hoped some day to sit himself on the judgment-seat.

It was while he was thus acting as Consiliarius to his father that he pronounced in presence of Theodoric an oration in his praise, which by its eloquence so delighted the King that he appointed him, still quite a young man, to the office of Quaestor, which brought with it what we should call cabinet-rank. The rank of Illustris gave him the privilege of sharing the secret and friendly conversation of the monarch, and entitled him to pronounce in his master's name solemn harangues to the ambassadors of foreign nations, to the Senate, sometimes perhaps to the citizens and the army. Allusion has already been made to the spirit in which Theodoric probably regarded the necessary labour of translating his own weighty, sledge-hammer sentences into the tumid Latin of the Lower Empire. But, however Theodoric may have regarded that work, there can be no doubt that Cassiodorus thoroughly enjoyed it. To have the charge of the correspondence of so great a king, to address to the officials of Italy, or even to the Sacred Majesty of Byzantium, a series of flowing sentences interspersed with philosophical reflections, excellent if not new, and occasionally to illustrate one's subject with a 'delicious digression' on the habits of birds, the nature of the chameleon, the invention of letters, or the fountain of Arethusa,—this was happiness indeed; and, though the emolumenta of the office were large, one may believe that Cassiodorus would have been willing to pay, instead of receiving them, for the privilege of doing the very work which was more to his liking than that done by any other Italian between the mountains and the sea.

Cassiodorus has been aptly likened to one of the *improvisatori* of modern Italy. The *Variae* are State papers put into the hands of an *improvisatore* to throw into form, and composed with his luxuriant verbiage, and also with his coarse taste. The shortest instructions begin with an aphorism or an epigram. If they are more important or lengthy, they sparkle and flash with conceits or antitheses, and every scrap of learning, every bit of science or natural history, every far-fetched coincidence which may start up in the writer's memory, however remote in its bearing on the subject, is dragged in to exalt or illustrate it, though the subject itself may be of the plainest and most matter-of-fact kind. You read through a number of elaborate sentences, often tumid and pompous, sometimes felicitous and pointed, hut all of the most general and abstract sort; and nestling in the thick of them, towards the end of the letter or paper, you come upon the order, or instruction, or notification, for which the letter or paper is written, almost smothered and lost in the abundance of ornament round it.

Yet let us not be unjust to the rhetorician-statesman. We can all see, and seeing must smile at, the literary vanity which peeps out from every page of his letters. All who consult those letters for historical facts must groan over the intolerable verbosity of his style, and must sometimes wish that they could have access to the rough, strong sentences of the Gothic King, instead of the wide expanse of verbiage into which his secretary has diluted them. Yet literary vanity was by no means the only motive of his service. Like his father, and like Liberius, he had perceived that this so-called barbarian was the best and wisest ruler that Italy had had for centuries, and that the course of true civilisation could be best served by helping him to work out his own scheme of a State, defended by German arms but administered by Roman brains. Perhaps too he saw, what we can see so plainly, the heavy price which Italy as a land had paid for Rome's dominion over the world. The desert expanse of the Campagna, though

'A less drear ruin then than now,'

may have spoken to him, as it does to us, of the disastrous change since the days when Rome was a little town and those plains were covered with the farms of industrious and happy husbandmen. Above all, as the instincts of a true statesman may have showed him, a return, at that time of day, to the imperial order of things meant dependence on the Eastern Emperor, on grasping, grovelling, eunuch-governed Byzantium. 'Let the old Roman Empire go, and let Italy live: and if she is to live, none so fit to guide her destinies as Theodoric.' It would be unsafe to assert that this thought, thus definitely expressed, found an entrance to the mind of Cassiodorus or any other patriotic Roman of the sixth century. But it was the limit towards which many thoughts were tending (ignorant, as ours are, of the future that is before us but conscious that some bit of the past has to be put away); and the subsequent history of Italy, traced in characters of blood from Belisarius to Barbarossa, showed how well it had been for her if that idea, of dissevering her from the wreck of the ruined Empire, might but have been realised.

It was with this hope doubtless, of reconciling the proud and sensitive Roman to the hegemony of the sturdy Goth, that Cassiodorus, near the middle of his official life, composed in twelve books that history of the Goths with which we have already bmade acquaintance through the extracts taken from it by the hasty and ignorant Jordanes'. In this book, as he himself says, speaking of it through the mouth of his king, 'he carried his researches up to the very cradle of the Gothic race, gathering from the stores of his learning what even hoar antiquity scarce remembered. He drew forth the kings of the Goths from the dim lurking-place of ages, restoring to the Amal line the splendour that truly belonged to it, and clearly proving that for seventeen generations Athalaric's ancestors had been kings. Thus did he assign a Roman origin to Gothic history, weaving as it were into one chaplet the flowers which he had culled from the pages of widely-scattered authors.'

In other words, he collected what ' hoar antiquity among the Gothic veterans had to tell him of the old Amal kings, the fragments of their battle-songs and sagas, and persuaded or forced them to coalesce with what his classical authors, Dio and Trogus and Strabo, had to tell him about the early history of the dim Northern populations. By identifying the Goths with 'the Getse—an error for which he is not originally responsible—and by claiming for them all the fantastic imaginations of the poets about the 'Scythians'—a word of as wide and indefinite a meaning as the 'Indians' of modern discoverers—he succeeded in constructing for the fore-elders of Theodoric a highly respectable place in classical antiquity. He 'made the Gothic origin Roman', nay, rather pre-Roman, carrying back their earliest kings to Hercules and Theseus and the siege of Troy, and thus giving that connection with the cycle of Homeric legend which an upstart nation valued, as an upstart family with us values a pedigree which shows that it came over with the Conqueror.

All this seems a little childish to us now, and indeed the chief work of a modern enquirer is to unwind that which Cassiodorus wound together so carefully, to disentangle what 'hoar antiquity ' told him (the only thread that is of any value) from the flimsy and rotten threads which he collected from various authors in his library. But, for the man and the age, the work was doubtless a useful and creditable one. Many a Roman noble may have accepted a little more readily the orders of the so-called barbarian, who turned out to be not so great a barbarian after all, now that Cassiodorus, nearly the most learned man of his day, had proved that Goths fought against the Greeks at the siege of Troy, and that possibly even Theodoric might be the remote descendant of Telephus. And the great King himself, who from those early days at Byzantium had always half-loved and admired the Roman State, though he felt that his rude Goths had in them something nobler;—to him this reconciling history of his clever secretary, which showed that he might be a true-hearted Goth and yet listen with delight to the verses of Homer, and gaze with rapture on the statues of Praxiteles, since these too were kinsmen of his forefathers, must have been a welcome discovery, and must have given him fresh courage to persevere in his life-work of conveying the blessings of *civilitas* to both nations of his subjects.

Strange is it to reflect that, after all, there was a truth underlying this odd jumble of Scytho-Geto- Gothic-Greek traditions,—a truth which scarcely till the beginning of this century was fully brought to light. Philology has now made it clear that Goth, Roman, and Greek were not really very distant relations, and the common home of the Aryan nations in the Asiatic highlands or elsewhere is something like a scientific compensation for the lost belief that all European nations were represented by their progenitors at the siege of Troy.

If Cassiodorus, with a true conviction that he was thus best serving his country, brought his loyal service to Theodoric, there can be no doubt that the heart of Theodoric also warmed towards him. He found in him the very minister whom he needed, to help him in fashioning his own great ideas of government, and to put them in the most acceptable shape before the Roman people. Often, we may be sure, in the 'gloriosa colloquia' which the subject so lovingly commemorates, did King and Quaestor talk over the difficulties of the state, the turbulent freedom of the Goths, the venality and peculation of the Roman officials, the want of any high aim among the nobles or great purpose among the citizens, still proud of the name of Romans, but incapable of being stirred by anything nobler than a chariot-race, a battle between the Blues and Greens, or at best a contested Papal election. Often too would the remedies for these evils be discussed. Cassiodorus, like so many fluent rhetoricians, would perhaps think that it only required a sufficient number of his eloquent essays to establish civilitas in the new state, to make the Romans honest and the Goths law-abiding. Theodoric, with the Northern patience and the Northern melancholy, would refuse to accept any such optimist view of the situation; and sometimes, while feeling that the work was long and his life was shortening, would heave a sigh at the remembrance that Providence, so gracious to him in all else, had denied him the gift of a son, strong and valiant, to carry on his great enterprise.

Amalasuntha, the only legitimate child of Theodoric, was a woman endowed with much of her fethers courage and strength of will, and more than her father's love for the civilisation and literature of Rome. Possibly foreseeing that this tendency to copy the manners of the less war-like people might bring her into collision with the martial Goths after his decease, Theodoric determined to marry her to no Roman noble, but to a Goth of the purest blood that he could meet with. He already had one daughter (the child of a concubine) married to a Visigothic king and living in Spain. From his connection with that country he heard that there was dwelling there a scion of the old Ostrogothic house, Eutharic son of Wideric, grandson (or more likely great-grand-son) of King Thorismund the Chaste, and therefore a lineal descendant of the mighty Hermanric, who once ruled all the lands between the Baltic and the Euxine. Eutharic was well reported of for valour and prudence and comeliness of person.

The King summoned him to his court, gave him his daughter's hand in marriage, and four years later conferred upon him the honour of the consulship. The Gothic prince-consort visited Rome in order to celebrate his assumption of the consular *trabea* with becoming magnificence. Senate and people poured forth to meet him. The games which he exhibited in the amphitheatre were on a scale of surpassing magnificence. The wild beasts, especially those from Africa, amazed and delighted the mob, many of whom had seen no such creatures before. Even Symmachus the Byzantine, who was present at the time in Rome on an embassy from the Eastern Emperor, was obliged to confess his stupefied admiration of the scene. When his sojourn in Rome was ended, Eutharic returned to Ravenna, and there exhibited the same shows, with even greater magnificence, in the presence of his father-in-law.

Of the prince thus romantically brought into the family of Theodoric we know very little, but that little makes us believe that he might have been found a useful counterpoise to the Romanising tendencies of Amalasuntha. The Anonymus Valesii, in the extract before quoted, calls him 'a man of harsh disposition and an enemy to the Catholic faith.' This perhaps means no more than that he stood firmly by the customs of his Arian forefathers, and was not inclined to bandy compliments with the priests and prefects whom he found standing round the throne of his father-in-law. But, whatever were his good or bad qualities, he died, before the death of Theodoric gave him an opportunity of making his mark on history. Amalasuntha was thus left a widow, with a son and a daughter, Athalaric and Matasuentha, the former of whom must have been born in 518, as we are told by Procopius that he was eight years old at the death of his grandfather.

From the family of Theodoric we return to the description of his ministers and friends. The elder Cassiodorus seems to have retired from office soon after his son had entered public life, and to have spent the rest of his years in the ancestral home in

Bruttii, which was dear to four generations of Cassiodori. For some years the great office of Faustus, Praetorian Prefect was administered by Faustus, Prefect, to whom a large number of letters in the Variarum tire addressed. An act of oppression, however, against a neighbour in the country alienated from him the favour of the just Theodoric and caused his downfall. A certain Castorius, who seems to have got into debt, perhaps into other kinds of trouble, had his farm unjustly wrested from him by the all-powerful Prefect. On making his complaint to the King and proving the justice of his cause, he obtained a decree for the restitution of his own farm and the addition of another, of equal value, from the lands of the wrong-doer. 'Grimoda the Saio' and 'Ferrocinctus the Apparitor,' apparently one Goth and one Roman officer, were charged with the execution of this decree, which further declared that if 'that well-known schemer' should attempt anything further against Castorius he should be punished with a fine of fifty pounds of gold (£2000). With some allowable complacency Theodoric was hereupon made by his quaestor to exclaim, 'Lo a deed which may henceforward curb all overweening functionaries! A Praetorian Prefect is not allowed to triumph in the spoliation of the lowly, and on the cry of the miserable his power of hurting them is taken from him at a blow.'

The Illustrious Faustus received leave of absence from the sacred walls of Rome for four months : and it may be doubted whether, when he returned thither, he any longer wore the purple robes of the Praetorian Prefect.

Soon after this signal display of the King's justice an invitation was sent to the elder Cassiodorus, inviting him, in very flattering terms, to return to Court, where probably he would have been asked to reassume the great office which he had previously held. Apparently, however, the hill of Squillace had greater charms for him than the palace of Ravenna. We have no evidence that he again took any active part in public affairs.

A pleasing contrast to the rapacious and triguing Faustus was afforded by one who had been faithful through good and evil fortune, the King's friend *Artemidorus*. This man, one of the nobles of Byzantium, a friend and relation of the Emperor Zeno, had been strangely attracted by the young barbarian, to whom he was sent as ambassador, on the eve of his march into Epirus. He left, for his sake, the splendid career which awaited him in the Eastern Empire, followed him through all his campaigns, and sat, an ever-welcome and genial guest, at the royal table. Not aspiring to high dignity, nor desirous to burden himself with the cares of State, he found for several years sufficient occupation for his artistic, pleasure-loving nature, in arranging the great shows of the circus for the citizens of Ravenna. At length, however (in 509), Theodoric persuaded him to undertake the weightier charge of Prefect of the City, and sent him in that capacity to Rome to govern the capital and preside over the Senate. The lighthearted Byzantine seems to have discharged the duties of this serious office more creditably than might have been expected.

Very different from this brilliant, joyous Greek was the other close friend of Theodoric, the rugged Gothic soldier *Tulum*. Sprung from one of the noblest Gothic families, he mounted guard as a stripling in the King's antechamber. His first experience in war was earned in the campaign of Sirmium, and here he showed such vigour and courage, and such a comprehension of the art of war, as procured for him in early manhood the place of chief military counsellor to Theodoric. A marriage with a princess of Amal blood still further consolidated his position. He was admitted to the friendly conversation of the King in his moments of least reserve, and, surest mark of friendship, often dared to uphold against his master the policy which he deemed best for that master's interests. In the Gaulish campaign of 509, in the campaign, or rather the armed neutrality, of 524, he was again conspicuous. Returning from the last by sea he suffered shipwreck, probably somewhere on the coast of Tuscany. The ship and crew were swallowed up by the waves. Tulum, with his only child, took to an open boat, and he had to depend on his own strength and skill to save them both by rowing. Theodoric, who was awaiting his arrival, saw with agony the imminent danger of his friend. The aged monarch would fain have rushed into the waves to rescue him, but, to his delight, Tulum battled successfully with the billows, and soon leaping ashore received his master's affectionate embrace.

We may perhaps conjecture that at the close of Theodoric's reign Tulum and Cassiodorus stood in friendly rivalry, the one at the head of the Gothic, the other at the head of the Roman party, among the nobles who were loyal to the new dynasty.

Of two other names by which the Court of Theodoric was rendered illustrious, Symmachus the orator and historian, with his son-in-law Boethius, the Marquis of Worcester of his age, it will be well to speak later on, when we have to discuss the melancholy history of their end. Enough to say here that, during the greater part of this period, they appear to have been on friendly terms with the King, though not zealously and continuously engaged in his service like Cassiodorus and Liberius.

The usual residence of Theodoric was Ravenna, with which city his name is linked as inseparably as those of Honorius or Placidia. The letters of Cassiodorus show his zeal for the architectural enrichment of this capital. Square blocks of stone were to be brought from Faenza, marble pillars to be transported from the palace on the Pincian Hill: the most skilful artists in mosaic were invited from Rome, to execute some of those very works which we still wonder at in the basilicas and baptisteries of the city by the Ronco.

The chief memorials of his reign which Theodoric has left at Ravenna are a church, a palace, and a tomb. Of the last it will be the fitting time to speak when the great Amal is carried thither for burial.

The marvellous basilica which now bears the name of S. Apollinare Nuovo was originally dedicated to St. Martin, and from its beautiful gold-inlaid roof received the title S. Martinus in Caelo Aureo. An inscription under the windows of the tribune, still visible in the ninth century, recorded that King Theodoric had built that church from its foundations in the name of our Lord Jesus Christ. Notwithstanding the words of the ecclesiastical biographer, who ascribes the work to an orthodox bishop, Agnellus, it is difficult not to believe that to Theodoric's order are due those great pictures in mosaic which give the church its peculiar glory. On the opposite sides of the nave, high attics above the colonnades are lined with two long processions. On the north wall, the virgin martyrs of the Church proceed from the city of Classis, each one bearing her crown of martyrdom in her hand, to offer it to the infant Christ, who sits on Mary's lap, attended by four angels. Between the virgin martyrs and the angels intervene the three wise men from the East, who, with crowns on their heads, run forward with reverent haste to present their offerings to the holy Child. The star glows above them in the firmament. On the south wall a corresponding procession of martyred men, also bearing crowns in their hands, moves from the palace at Ravenna onwards to the Christ in glory, who sits upon his judgment-seat and is also guarded by four angels. The dignity of both groups is their most striking characteristic. Not all the quaint stiffness of the mosaic can veil the expression of solemn sadness in the faces of the martyrs, who look like men who have come out of great tribulation and have not yet seen the face of Him for whom they suffered. Nor does the same deficiency in the mode of representation prevent our seeing the look of radiant triumph on the faces of the virgins. Here are Agnes with her lamb, the child-martyr Eulalia of Merida, Lucia of Syracuse, Agatha of Catana, all the most celebrated maidens who suffered for the faith in the terrible days of Diocletian. No wrinkled and faded convent-dwellers are these. Fresh, young, and beautiful, apparelled like the daughters of a king, they move on with a smile of triumph upon their lips to see the wondrous Child for whose sake they, scarcely yet emerged from childhood, gave up their tender bodies to torture and to death.

Besides the human interest of these figures, there - is the local interest derived from the fact that we have here contemporary views of the Ravenna of the sixth century. Ciassis is represented as a walled city, with colonnades, domes and pediments. Hard by, three ships, one with sails fully spread, the others under bare poles, are entering the narrow lighthouse-guarded passage from the sea. The palace of Theodoric, as represented on the other side, consists of four tall Corinthian columns with arches springing from their capitals, a pediment above, and in a horizontal space of white the word PALATIUM. On one side of this, the main entrance, is a long low colonnade with an upper storey over it. The objects which most catch the stranger's eye are the curtains between the pillars. Looped up half-way, and with large square patches of purple upon them, they have a singularly modern aspect, but are no doubt a pretty faithful representation of the veil which guarded the privacy both of the Eastern Emperor and the Gothic King.

The palace itself, as we learn from local records, occupied a large space on the eastern side of the town. It adjoined the beautiful church of S. Martinus in Caelo Aureo, which was perhaps used as a royal chapel. Only one fragment of it, but one of pretty well-ascertained genuineness, exists to the present day. It is a high wall, built of the square brick-tiles with which we are so familiar in Roman work, and with eight marble pillars in the upper part supporting nine arched recesses, one of them of considerable width. It is the mere shell of a ruin : the house behind it is entirely modern. A porphyry vase, or rather high trough, let into the lower part of the wall used to be shown as the former coffin of Theodoric, but this notion is now generally abandoned, and the prevalent idea seems to be that it was once a bath. The palace we are told was surrounded with colonnades, and had many dining apartments (triclinia) within it. We learn from the Anonymus Yalesii that this edifice, which no doubt took many years to build, was completed but not 'dedicated' at the time of Theodoric's death.

Here then, on the eastern side of his capital, dwelt for more than thirty years the great Ostrogoth, looking forth towards the dark Pineta where he had had that terrible night of battle with Odovacar, and seeing, it may be, from some high tower in his palace, the blue rim of the Hadriatic. Beyond that sea, but of course invisible, lay his own fair province of Dalmatia; beyond that again those, wasted plains of Moesia, where he had wandered so often, the fugitive lord of a brigand people.

Statues in abundance were reared in his honour, at Rome, at Ravenna, at Ticinum, in all the chief cities of Italy. We hear of one statue made by Boethius with so much art that it ever turned towards the sun, and hence was called Regisol; but this is probably a mere legend of the Middle Ages. In another sculptured group, erected on a pinnacle of his palace, and conspicuous to mariners from afar, Theodoric, grasping shield and spear and clothed in a coat of mail, sat on a brazen horse covered over with gold. The two cities Rome and Ravenna completed the group. Rome was apparently standing, guarding him in calm dignity, with shield and spear; while Ravenna seemed gliding rapidly forward to meet her lord, her right foot passing over the sea and her left resting on the land. The statues of the horse and his rider, Charles the Great, after his coronation in Rome, carried across the Alps to Aix-la-Chapelle, declaring that he had seen nothing like them in his whole realm of Francia.

Pavia and Verona were also places honoured with the occasional residence of Theodoric. At both he built a palace and public baths. Of neither of these two palaces is any remnant now to be seen. A grim square fortress of the fifteenth century, much injured by the French Republicans, stands (it is believed) on the site of Theodoric's palace at Pavia. So too at Verona: the palace, of which there were still some noble remains incorporated into the castle of the Viscontis, was blown up by the French in 1801, and an absolutely modern building stands upon its site. This, like the castle at Pavia and so many buildings in Italy of great historic name, is now occupied as a barrack.

It seems probable that Theodoric's residence at both these places depended on the state of Transalpine politics. When the tribes of the Middle Danube were moving suspiciously to and fro, and the vulnerable point by the Brenner Pass needed to be especially guarded, he fixed his quarters at Verona. When Gaul menaced greater danger, then he removed to Ticinum. It was apparently the fact that Verona was his coign of vantage, from whence he watched the German barbarians, which obtained for him from their minstrels the title of *Dietrich of Bern*. Thus strangely travestied, he was swept within the wide current of the legends relating to Attila, and hence it is that the really grandest figure in the history of the migration of the peoples appears in the Nibelungen Lied, not as a great king and conqueror on his own account, but only as a faithful squire of the terrible Hunnish king whose empire had in fact crumbled into dust before the birth of Theodoric.

CHAPTER IX.

THEODORIC'S RELATION'S WITH GAUL.

The respite from foreign invasion during the reign of Theodoric was chiefly due to his commanding position at the head of the new Teutonic royalties of Europe. That position was in great measure strengthened and consolidated by a system of matrimonial alliances with the chief of the royal families of the barbarians. The somewhat entangled sentences in which they are described by the anonymous authority quoted in the last chapter, deserve therefore a more careful study than we might at first, when repelled by their uncouth form and by the harsh sound of the barbarian names with which they are filled, be disposed to give to them.

We see from them that Theodoric was himself the brother-in-law of the king of the Franks and the king of the Vandals, and that the owner of the Visigothic, and the heir-apparent of the Burgundian royalty were married to his daughters. Our informant might have gone further, and told us that a niece of Theodoric was married to the king of the Thuringians. Here was a vision of a 'family compact,' binding together all the kingdoms of the West, from the Scheldt to Mount Atlas, in a great confederacy, filling all the new barbarian thrones with the sons, the grandsons, or the nephews of Theodoric, a matrimonial State-system surpassing (may we not say?) anything that Hapsburg or Bourbon ever succeeded in accomplishing, when they sought to make Venus instead of Mars build up their empires. We shall see however that, when it came to the tug of war between one barbarian chief and another, this family compact, like so many others in later days, snapped with the strain. Yet it was not at once a failure; for one generation at least the position of Theodoric, as a kind of patriarch of the kingly clan, was one of grandeur and influence, and did undoubtedly promote the happiness of Europe.

With the Vandal sovereigns of Carthage his relations were, till near the close of his reign, friendly. Gaiseric's son, Huneric (477-484), that fierce and cruel persecutor of the Catholics, had ended his short reign before Theodoric started on his march for His cousins and successors, Gunthamund (484-496) and Thrasamund (496-523), though still Arians, abated sensibly the rigour of the persecutions at home and pursued a fair and moderate policy abroad. The corsair-state of the fierce adventurer Gaiseric had lost something of its lawless vigour. It was passing into the rank of gular monarchies, and becoming flaccid and respectable. Sicily, which had been subjected for many years to their depredations, and then under Odovacar had paid a tribute something like our own Danegeld as the price of quietness, was now free both from invasion and from tribute. On the death of his first wife (possibly soon alter 500) Thrasamund married Amalafrida, the widowed sister of the Ostrogothic king. A thousand Gothic nobles with five thousand mounted servants followed Amalafrida to her African home, and the fortress of Lilybaeu, *(Marsala),* at the extreme western corner of Sicily, was, with more generosity perhaps than statesman-like prudence, handed over to Thrasamund as the dowry of his elderly bride.

With two of the three great powers that still divided Gaul, the Visigoths, Burgundians, and Franks, Theodoric's relations were more varied and less uniformly amicable.

The Visigoths now held, not only the fair quadrant of France between the Loire and the Pyrenees, but also the greater part of Provence, besides the whole of Spain, except the north-western angle, which was still occupied by an independent Suevic monarchy. This powerful people, mindful of the old 'brotherly covenant,' was friendly to the Ostrogothic ruler of Italy, as it had been to its Ostrogothic invader. Their king Alaric II, the son-in-law of Theodoric, had mounted the throne in the year 485. He was a man of whom we hear no unfavourable testimony, but who seems not to have possessed the harsh energy of his father Euric, far less the dash and originality of his mighty namesake Alaric the Great.

Between the dominions of Theodoric and his Visigothic son-in-law lay the goodly land which owned the sway of the Burgundians. Their domain, considerably more extensive than when we last viewed it on the eve of Attila's invasion now included the later provinces of Burgundy, Franche-Comté, and Dauphiné, besides Savoy and the greater part of Switzerland—in fact the whole of the valleys of the Saone and the Rhone, save that for the last hundred miles of its course the Visigoths barred them from the right bank and from the mouths of the latter river.

Gundobad, whom we met with twenty-one years ago in Rome hanging on to the fortunes of his uncle Bicimer, wearing the robe of the Patrician, and even creating an emperor of his own, the insignificant Glycerius, returned, as we then saw, to his own country in 474, probably on the death of his father Gundiok, leaving his hapless client-emperor in the lurch. According to the frequent usage of these Teutonic nations, the kingdom of Gundiok was divided between his four sons; but these four had now been reduced by death to two, Gundobad and Godegisel. Gundobad, the first-born and the more powerful, ruled at Lyons and Vienne, while Godegisel held his court at Geneva.

But the family of one of the dead brothers was destined to exert a more powerful influence over the fortunes of Gaul than either of the surviving kings. Hilperik, whose capital had been Lyons, and who died apparently between 480 and 490, had, as some authors conjecture, married a wife Caretene, whose virtues and whose Catholic orthodoxy are recorded in an inscription still to be seen in her husband's capital. Caretene, whose fervour of fasting and whose gentle persuasive influence on her harsh husband are alluded to in the letters of Sidonius, as well as in this inscription, was allowed by her Arian husband to bring up her children—they were only daughters —in the Catholic faith which she herself professed. One of these daughters, Hrothchilde, whose name history has softened into Clotilda, was dwelling, as an orphan ward, at the court of her uncle Gundobad, when there came thither on business of State frequent embassies from Clovis king of the Franks.

The ambassadors on their return home used to praise to their master the grace and accomplishments of the young princess. He sent to ask for her hand, which, in the year 492 or 493, was accorded, not perhaps very willingly, by the Burgundian king.

This marriage of the king of the Franks (whether we call him Chlodovech, Hlodwig, Luduin, Louis, or Clovis) with the young Catholic orphan of the house of Hilperik of Burgundy prepared the way for the Frankish Empire, and for events which changed the face of Europe. For she, mindful of the training received from the devout Caretene, and hostile to the Arian faith of her father and uncles, determined to win over her heathen husband, not merely to Christianity, as the other Teuton conquerors understood it, but to orthodoxy. Later ages have believed that she entered the palace of Clovis filled with thoughts of terrible revenge against Gundobad and his family. When, a generation later, her own sons inflicted terrible calamities on the royal house of Burgundy, the idea perhaps occurred to some courtly bard of representing these cruelties as mere retaliation for the atrocities which their mother's father and his house had suffered at the hands of Gundobad. Accordingly, Hilperik was alleged to have been slain with the sword; his wife, with a stone tied round her neck, to have been thrown into the water; his two daughters to have been banished; his sons (of whose very existence there is no other trace) to have met death from the hands of the same cruel relative. There is some reason to think that all this, though set forth in the pages of Gregory of Tours, who lived but a century after the death of Hilperik, is mere untrustworthy legend. If Caretene was really the wife of Hilperik, we see from the epitaph at Lyons that she survived him at least fifteen years, dying in the year 506. Moreover a letter to Gundobad from Avitus, the Catholic bishop of Vienne, no flatterer of the king, but rather, if the anachronism may be permitted, leader of the Constitutional Opposition in the Burgundian realm, while condoling with his sovereign on the death of a daughter, refers to his earlier domestic afflictions, and reminds him with what 'ineffable piety' he had mourned the deaths of his brothers [Hilperik and Godomar]. It seems in the highest degree unlikely that such a letter could have been addressed by its author to the avowed murderer of Hilperik.

When Clovis married Clotilda he was aged twenty-seven, and had been reigning for twelve years. Seven years before, he had by his overthrow of the Roman kinglet Syaorius advanced from Flanders into the valley of the Seine; and, at the accession of Theodoric, we must probably think of his dominions as touching the Visigothic kingdom at the Loire, and the Burgundian kingdom on the Catalaunian plains, comprising in fact already one third, but not the fairest nor the richest third, of Gaul. This portentous growth of the Frankish power in twelve years was but an augury of the yet mightier extensions which should take place when the prayers of the Catholic Clotilda should be accomplished, and her husband should accept the faith of the great mass of the Roman provincials.

The statesmanlike vision of Theodoric saw the necessity of including the Frankish lord of Soissons in his system of family alliances. At the very outset of his reign he sought for and obtained the hand of Audefleda, the sister of Clovis, who bore him one daughter, his only legitimate child Amalasuntha. Providence, as we have seen, denied him a son, while a whole clan of martial sons and grandsons filled the palace of the Frankish king. This difference had much to do with the very different duration of the political systems reared by the two kings.

The course of our narrative takes us back for a short time to consider the internal affairs of Italy after Odovacar's death. We are told by one chronicler that 'all his army wherever they could be found, and all his race, perished with him'; by another, that 'all his colleagues who ministered to the defence of the kingdom were put to death'. These statements are almost certainly exaggerated, if not altogether untrue. Certainly the after-life of Theodoric shows that he was not a man given to needless bloodshed. But he did issue one edict, an edict which he was wise enough to be persuaded to cancel, and which shows, it must be admitted, that the fierce bitterness of the struggle had not yet entirely faded from his mind.

This edict was to the effect, that only those among the Roman population who could prove that they had been loyal to the cause of Theodoric should enjoy the full rights of citizens. His recent opponents, even had their services been rendered compulsorily to Odovacar, lost the power of disposing of their property by will and of bearing evidence in courts of justice. A most monstrous enactment, and one which showed that its author was still more familiar with the simple pastoral life led by his people in the plains of Moesia, than with the necessities of an old and complex civilisation, in which such a party-measure as this could Epiphanius not fail to work frightful injustice. The good Epiphanius, who had been busily engaged in repairing the ravages of war, and inviting the best the citizens of surrounding towns to settle at Ticinum, heard the general lamentation of Italy, and was besought to make himself its exponent at the Court of Theodoric. He consented, on condition that Laurentius of Milan would share the burden with him. The two bishops journeyed together to Ravenna, and were received with all veneration by the King.

And here let us observe for a moment, that we have in this embassy an excellent illustration of the way in which barbaric conquest forced the Church onwards in the path of temporal dominion. The edict against the adherents of Odovacar was a purely civil edict. Whether wise or foolish, it in no way specially concerned the Church, nor trenched upon ecclesiastical privilege. Neither was it, like the revenge wreaked by Theodosius on the citizens of Thessalonica, an outrage upon humanity, a gross and obvious breach of the law of Cod. It was a very harsh and ill-conceived measure, but it related to matters which were entirely within the domain of the civil governor; and as such, we cannot imagine that either Ambrose or Eusebius would have felt himself entitled to remonstrate against it, nor that Theodosius or Constantine would have tolerated such an interference. Now, however, that a Barbarian, instead of a Roman, sits in the seat of power, the moderating influence of the ecclesiastic in purely political matters is eagerly invoked by the governed, and not repelled by the governor.

Epiphanius, being invited to state his case, congratulated 'the most unconquered prince' on the success which had crowned his arms. He reminded Theodoric of the promises which he had made to the Almighty when, under the walls of Ticinum, he had been attacked by the bands of the enemy, who greatly exceeded his own troops in number, but whom by heavenly aid he had then been enabled to overcome. By heavenly aid, for the very air seemed to serve his purposes. When Theodoric required serene weather for his operations, they were over-arched by an unclouded sky; when rain would help him more effectually, torrents fell. Now let him profit by the example of his predecessor. Odovacar fell because he ruled unrighteously. Might the present King—such was the prayer of Liguria—confirm to innocent men the blessings of the laws, even at the risk of some, who little deserved it, obtaining his protection. 'To forgive sins is heavenly; to punish is an earthly thing.'

The Bishop was silent and the 'most eminent King' began to speak. When he opened his lips every heart was wrung with a fearful anxiety to know what would be his decision.

'Oh, venerable Bishop!' he said, 'though your merits command my respect, and your many kindnesses to me in the time of confusion deserve my gratitude, yet the hard necessities of reigning make that universal forgiveness which you praise impossible. I have the divine warrant for the position which I here take up. Do we not read of a certain king, who, because he neglected to take the destined vengeance on the enemy of his people, was himself rejected by God. That man weakens and brings into contempt the divine judgments who spares his enemy when he is in his power. As for the patience of our Redeemer, of which you speak, that comes after the severity of the law has done its work. The wise surgeon first cuts deep to remove the gangrened flesh, before he applies the healing liniment. By allowing criminals to go unpunished, we exhort the innocent to commit crime.

'Nevertheless, since heaven itself bends to your prayers, the powers of earth must not disregard them. I consent that not a single head shall fall, since you may prevail with God that the minds of the most hardened offenders shall be turned from the perverseness of their way. Some few, however, of the chief incendiaries must be removed from their present dwellings, lest they rekindle the flame of civild discord.'

Theodoric then ordered the Quaestor Urbicus—a man who, we are told, surpassed Cicero in eloquence and Cato in integrity—to prepare a royal letter embodying these concessions, which of course must have included the repeal of the civil disabilities of the vanquished party. The absolute honesty of Urbicus did not prevent him from so wording the decree that even the excepted cases were included in the amnesty, a difference which we must suppose that Theodoric's imperfect knowledge of Latin prevented him from observing.

After the interview was ended, Theodoric called Epiphanius aside to express to him the sorrow with which he beheld the desolate state of Italy after the war, weeds and thorns filling all the fields, and especially 'that mother of the human harvest, Liguria, which used to rejoice in her numerous progeny of husbandmen', now robbed of her children, and lying, through vast spaces of her territory, untouched by the plough, and with her vines trailing in the dust. All this was the work of the Burgundians, who, after the foray mentioned in the preceding chapter, had carried back great numbers of the Ligurians captives across the Alps. Theodoric, however, had gold, and would willingly unlock his stores for their ransoming, if Epiphanius, whose pleading voice none could resist, would himself intercede with Gundobad for their restoration.

Epiphanius with tears of joy welcomed the commission conferred upon him by bis prince. He could not help acknowledging how much the new sovereign surpassed the previous emperors, the rulers of his own race, not only in justice and in warlike deeds, but in pity for the sufferings of his people. They had too often carried, or suffered the people to be carried, captive, whereas he was bent on redeeming them. If Victor, Bishop of Turin, might be joined with Epiphanius in the commission, he felt that he could safely answer for the result. The King assented, and 'the awful pontiff,' having said farewell and received the money for the ransom, departed upon his mission. It was the month of March; the Alpine passes were of course still covered with snow; but the brave old man faced the hardships of the road as cheerfully as when, twenty years before, he set forth upon his celebrated embassy to Euric. 'Not once' we are told, ' did his feet slip upon the frozen snow, whose soul was founded upon the Rock.' He was so intent on fulfilling his mission that he tolerated with impatience even the halts for refreshment, and when his companions were appalled at the difficulties of the way, he alone knew no fear. At the fame of his approach, young and old, men and women, flocked from distant hamlets to get a sight of the venerable peace-maker. They brought with them generous offerings of food for the travellers. Epiphanius and his companions accepted what was absolutely necessary for their own wants, but bestowed the greater part on the poor of the district. As one of those companions was Ennodius himself, the biographer of the Saint, we have the satisfaction of knowing that every incident characteristic of life and manners in the story of this legation is from the pen not only of a contemporary, but of an eye-witness.

When the deputation reached Lyons, Rusticus, the successor of Bishop Patiens, and a man who had always served the interests of the Church, when still an official of the State and not a bishop, came forth to meet them, and gave them a sketch of the crafty character of the King, which put Epiphanius on his guard and caused him to rehearse the speech which he was about to deliver before him.

When, however, King Gundobad heard of the Bishop's approach he at once said to his servants, 'That is a man whose character and whose countenance I have ever associated with those of the blessed martyr St. Laurence; enquire when he is willing to see me, and invite him accordingly'.

The day of audience came. The courtiers flocked in crowds to see the man whose eloquence had conquered so many conquerors. Victor was invited to commence the proceedings, but he courteously threw off upon his companion the weight of the harangue.

'Most worthy Sovereign,' said Epiphanius, 'only an unutterable love for you has forced me thus to wage war upon time and nature, to dare the perils of the avalanche, to thread my way through forests paved with snow, to leave my foot-prints on the ice-fields, where even the foot is clasped by the all-binding frost. But when I see two excellent kings thus situated, one asking what the other has not yet granted, how can I refrain from setting before them the testimony of the heavenly word, "It is more blessed to give than to receive". Divide this promise between you; weigh it out in equal scales; nay, rather do thou press in and claim more than the half of it for thyself, by letting the captives whom he wishes to redeem, go forth free of charge. Despise the ransom-money which he offers, and which he has sent by me. That money, if scorned, will make thine armies wealthy; if accepted, it will make them beggars.

'Hear, oh King, the words of that Italy for whom you once fought. "How often," she says, "did you on my behalf oppose your mailed breast to the enemy! How often did you toil in counsel that I might be kept free from invasion, that my sons might not be carried captive, whom now you have carried captive yourself!" Even when they were being dragged from their homes, the matron, wringing those helpless hands that were chained to her neck, thought of thee as one who would avenge her. The fair young girl, struggling to preserve her honour, thought of thee as one who would applaud her victory. The simple husbandmen, those hardy children of the soil, accustomed to ply the heavy mattock, now, when their necks were tied together with thongs and their hands were bound in manacles, said, "Are not you our Burgundians? See to it, how you shall answer for this before your pious King. How often have the hands which you presume to bind, paid tribute to your lord and ours! We know right well that he never ordered these wicked deeds." Yea, many and many a one had to pay for his confidence in thee with his life, being struck down for some too haughty word to his captors.

'Oh! restore these honest hearts to their country; then will they still be thine. Fill that Liguria, which thou knowest so well, with happy cultivators, and empty her of thorns and thistles. So may a long succession of thy sons stand at the helm of the Burgundian state, and thou live again in their glories. It is not strangers who ask this of thee. The lord of Italy is joined to thee now by the tie of kindred : let the wedding-gift to Sigismund's bride be the freedom of the captives; the wedding-gift of thy son to her and to Christ.' Having thus spoken he and Victor arose and went to the King, laid their heads upon his breast, and wept.

The reply of Gundobad, who was, we are told, 'wealthy in speech and rich in all the resources of eloquence,' practically amounted to an enunciation of the maxim of modern Gaul, '*Á la guerre comme á la guerre*'. 'It might suit this bright Christian star to inculcate the law of kindness towards an adversary, and of moderation even in warfare, but the statesman had to remember the quite different maxims by which the world is governed. The rule of warriors is, that everything which is not lawful in peace becomes lawful in war. Your business is to cut up your adversary's power root by root, and so gradually detach him from his kingdom. This had Gundobad done to his adversary. He had repaid him scorn for scorn; when mocked with the semblance of a treaty, he had forced his secret opponent to show himself an open foe. Now however, by divine permission, a peace had been established between them, which, he hoped, would be a long-lasting one. If these holy men would return to their homes he would consider what course it might be best to take, for the welfare of his kingdom and the safety of his soul, and would decide upon his answer.'

When the bishops had departed the King called to him his councillor Laconius, a man of high—evidently ERoman—birth, grandson of Consuls, of pure and pious life, one who was always ready to second every kind and generous impulse which he perceived in his sovereign. 'Go,' said the King to him, 'hoist all your sails to the winds. After hearing that holy man Epiphanius, and seeing his tears, I am ready to grant all you desire. Prepare a decree in my name which shall make this bargain as tight as possible. All the Italians who through fear of the Burgundian marauders, under stress of hunger, or by compact on the part of their prince have come hither as captives, shall be at once liberated, free of charge. Those, however, whom our subjects in the ardour of battle carried captive on their own private account, must pay a ransom to their masters, for it would only make future battles more bloody, if the soldier had not a hope of profiting by the ransom of his captives.'

With joyful alacrity Laconius prepared the documents setting forth the royal indulgence and brought them to the Bishop, who embraced the bearer of so precious a gift. Soon the news spread abroad, and you would have thought Gaul was being emptied of its peasants, so great a number flocked from all the cities of Sapaudia to thread the passes of the Alps for their return. Stripped of all exaggeration, the recital of Ennodius testifies that he himself, who was sent by the Bishop to the governors of the fortresses with the orders of release, in one day procured the liberation of 400 captives from Lyons alone, and that in all more than 6000 persons returned to their own land. Apparently the treasure confided by Theodoric to Epiphanius was all needed for the ransom of those who were in private hands, and was even supplemented by the pious offerings of Avitus, bishop of Vienne, and Syagria, a devout lady—possibly a daughter of the slain 'King of Soissons'—who was looked upon as a living treasury for the Church's needs.

A visit to Geneva, to the Burgundian King Godegisel, was needed in order to obtain the same concession from him which had been already granted by his brother of Lyons. Then Epiphanius set forth accompanied by the rejoicing host of his redeemed captives. They went apparently by the way of the Col de Lauteret and the Col de Genèvre. As they went, the multitude sang hymns of praise to God and the Bishop, who seemed to their excited imaginations another Elijah, just ready to ascend to heaven in a chariot of fire. The Bishop returned to Ticinum in the third month after he had quitted his home.

The mind of Epiphanius, however, was still beset with cares for the fortunes of the restored captives. They had returned as beggars to their native land, and the lot of those who had once held high station among them was especially hard. It seemed as if they were to be still as miserable, but less pitied than when they were in the hand of the enemy. An appeal to Theodoric was the natural remedy; yet Epiphanius would not make that appeal in person, lest it might seem as if he were claiming from the King those thanks, and that distinguished reception, which were the rightful meed of his services in Gaul. He seconded, however, the prayers of the petitioners, and by his letters on their behalf obtained that relief for each which was necessary. The precise mode in which Theodoric helped these returned exiles to stock their farms and recommence the operations of husbandry we are not informed of, interesting as such a detail would have been.

About two years afterwards he again journeyed to Ravenna, to obtain a relief from taxes for his which had suffered, and apparently was still suffering, from a plague of great waters. His admiring biographer thus addresses him in the recollection of that journey: 'Never did thy limbs, though weakened by disease, prove unequal to the task imposed upon them by thy soul. Cold, rains, the Po, fastings, sailings, danger, thunderstorms, the bivouac without a roof on the banks of the river, the doubt of reaching harbour in that inundated land, were all sweet to thy virtue which rejoiced in its triumph over these obstacles'. Arrived at the court of Theodoric, he pleaded with him to show his confidence in the security of his dynasty, by a remission of taxation which would assuredly one day benefit his successors; and said, in words which Theodoric seems to have adopted for his own, 'The peasant's wealth is the wealth of a good ruler'. The King replied that, although the 'immense expenses' of the State made it difficult to forego any part of the revenue, and notwithstanding the necessity of bestowing regular gifts on the Gothic defenders of the kingdom, he would, in testimony of his esteem and gratitude to the petitioner, remit two-thirds of the taxes for the current year. The remaining third must be paid, else would the straitness of the treasury bring about in the end greater evils than those which Epiphanius was now seeking to remove.

With this concession in his hands, the Bishop hastened to return home. He had a suspicion that his end was not far off; a thought which did not occur to any of the multitudes who flocked to visit him. His own presentiment, however, was a true one. The snowy air of Ravenna had prepared the way for a fatal attack of catarrh which seized him on his way home, at Parma. The people of Ticinum saw with consternation the return of their beloved bishop as a dying man. They stood in the forum, whispering and panic-stricken, and thinking that the end of the world was at hand if Epiphanius was to be taken from them. On the seventh day after his entry into Ticinum he died, having on his lips the triumphant song of the wife of Elkanah—'My heart rejoiceth in the Lord, mine horn is exalted in the Lord: because I rejoice in thy salvation.' He died in the fifty-eighth year of his age and the thirtieth of his episcopate: certainly one of the noblest characters of his time, and a man who deserved a better biographer than the one who has fallen to his lot, the wordy and vapid Ennodius.

The death of Epiphanius occurred in the year 497. We retrace our steps one year, to notice a very important event 0f 496. In that year, at some place unknown, but near the banks of the Rhine, and probably not far from Strasburg, Clovis met the Alamannic hosts in battle. Both nations were yet heathen, both perhaps equally barbarous. Both had felt the heavy hand of Julian, while the Empire still stood. Both had pressed in, when the Empire could no longer keep them at bay; the Frank, as we have seen, through the woods of Ardennes and across the flat lands of Picardy, to the Seine, to the Loire, and to the Catalaunian plains; while the Alamanni oversprang the too long dreaded *limes*, stormed the camp of the Saalburg on the heights of Taunus, and settled themselves in the lovely land, still crowded with Roman villas and rich with Roman vines, which was watered by the Neckar and the Main, and which sloped down to the right bank of the Middle Rhine. Which now of these two nations was to speak this word of power in the regions of the Ehine? That was the doubtful question which the issue of this day was to decide. Clovis had been intending to cross the Rhine, but the hosts of the Alamanni came upon him, as it seems, unexpectedly and forced a battle on the left bank of the river. He seemed to be overmatched, and the horror of an impending defeat overshadowed the Frankish king. Then, in his despair, he bethought himself of the God of Clotilda. Raising his eyes to heaven he said, 'Oh Jesus Christ, whom Clotilda declares to be the Son of the living God, who art said to give help to those who are in trouble and who trust in thee, I humbly beseech thy succour! I have called on my gods and they are far from my help. If thou wilt deliver me from mine enemies, I will believe in thee, and be baptized in thy name.' At this moment, a sudden change was seen in the fortunes of the Franks. The Alamanni began to waver, they turned, they fled. Their king, according to one account, was slain; and the nation seems to have accepted Clovis as its over-lord.

Clovis hastened back to his queen, and told her the story of his vow. At the Christmas festival, he stood in the white robes of a catechumen in the basilica of Rheims, and heard from the mouth of Saint Remigius the well-known words, 'Bow thy neck in meekness, oh Sicambrian! Adore what thou hast burned, and burn what thou hast adored'.

The mere conversion to Christianity of a Teutonic ruler of a Roman province was an event of comparatively little importance. It was but a question of time, a generation sooner or a generation later, when all the men of this class should renounce their hope of the banquets of Walhalla for an inheritance in the Christian City of God. But that the king of the Franks should be baptized into that form of Christianity which was professed by Clotilda and Remigius, that he should enter into devout and loyal communion with the Catholic Church was an event indeed of worldwide significance, well worthy of the congratulations which it called forth from Pope and Metropolitan, from Anastasius of Rome and from Avitus of Vienne. The title 'Eldest Son of the Church' borne by the kings of France, while she still had kings, perpetuated, to our own day, the remembrance of the rapture with which the hard-pressed and long-suffering Catholics of the Empire greeted the fact that at length force, barbarian force, was coming over to their side. They had been oppressed and trampled upon long enough. Carthaginian Hilderic had cut out the tongues of their confessors. Euric of Toulouse had shut up their churches and turned cattle into their church-yards. But now the young and irresistible conqueror beyond the Loire would redress the balance. Clovis, and his sons, and the nobles who would inevitably follow their example, from above, with the great mass of patient orthodox Roman provincials from below, would yet make an end of the Arian oppression.

In the presence of this new arrangement of forces, with the certainty that henceforth every bishop and every priest throughout Western Europe would be a well-wisher, open or concealed, of the Frankish monarchy, there should undoubtedly have been a close league for mutual defence formed between the four great Arian and

Teutonic monarchies, the Visigothic, the Burgundian, the Ostrogothic, and the Vandal. The statesmanlike mind of Theodoric must have perceived this truth. To some extent, as we shall see, he endeavoured to act upon it, but, from one cause or another, with no great persistency or success. Both he and his Burgundian kinsman belonged to the class of tolerant Arians: in fact, Gundobad seemed at times more than half ready to turn Catholic himself. Possibly they felt themselves out of sympathy with the narrower and bitterer Arianism which reigned at the courts of Toulouse and Carthage. And, what was of more importance, diplomatists were wanting to them. Precisely the very men who would in any other matter have acted as their skilful and eloquent representatives, travelling like Epiphanius from court to court, and bringing the barbarian sovereigns to understand each other, to sink their petty grievances, and to work together harmoniously for one common end, precisely these men were the Catholic prelates of the Mediterranean lands to whom it was all-important that no such Arian league should be formed. It has been forcibly pointed out by a historian of the Burgundians that, whereas all over the Roman world there was a serried array of Catholic bishops and presbyters, taking their orders from a single centre, Rome, feeling the interests of each one to be the interests of all, in lively and constant intercourse with one another, quick to discover, quick to disclose the slightest weak place in the organization of the new heretical kingdoms, of all this there was not the slightest trace on the other side. The Arian bishops took their fill of court favour and influence while it lasted, but made no provision for the future. They stood apart from one another in stupid and ignorant isolation. Untouched apparently by the great Augustinian thought of the world-encompassing City of God, they tended more and more to form local, tribal Churches, one for the Visigoths, another for the Vandals, another for the Burgundians. And thus in the end the fable of the loosened faggot and the broken sticks was proved true of all the Arian monarchies.

It seemed as if the first to fall would be the kingdom of the Burgundians. In the autumn of 499, Gundobad was aware that his younger brother, Godegisel of Geneva, was engaged in a treacherous correspondence with Clovis, the object of which was the expulsion of Gundobad, and the elevation of Godegisel as sole king of the Burgundians, probably on condition of ceding some territory to his Frankish ally. Sorely perplexed and doubtful of the result, he was, as has been said, almost prepared to avert the blow by himself joining the Catholic Church. The two leading bishops in his dominions—Stephen of Lyons and Avitus of Vienne—besought him to convoke his prelates to a conference, at which they might by disputation establish the Catholic verity. Could the King have seen the letter written three years before by Avitus to congratulate Clovis on his conversion, the letter in which he speaks of Gundobad as 'king indeed of his own people but your dependant,' and declares, 'we are affected by your good-fortune; whensoever you fight, we conquer', he might have been less disposed than he was to maintain friendly relations with this eloquent and brilliant prelate but secret enemy of his crown and people. As it was, he said to the bishops, with some force of argument, 'If your faith is the true one, why do not your colleagues prevent the King of the Franks from declaring war against me, and leaguing himself with my enemies? Where a man covets that which belongs to another, there is no true faith'. Avitus cautiously replied, 'I know not why the King of the Franks should do this; but I know that the Scripture says that states often come to ruin because they will not obey the law of God. Turn with your people to that law, and you will have peace'. Not in this sentence only, but throughout this curious colloquy, there ran an under-current of assurance, that if Gundobad would reconcile himself to the Church, the Church would guarantee his safety from the attacks of Clovis. The King on this occasion replied with some heat, 'How? Do I not recognise the law of God? But I will not worship three Gods!'

However, the bishops obtained their request: and it was fixed that a public disputation should take place at Lyons on the festival of St. Justus (2nd September, 499); the same festival, half-religious, half-popular, of which Sidonius gives so lively an account in connection with his epigram on towel. The King only stipulated that the discussion should not take place before a large assembly of the people lest there should be a breach of the peace.

The debate, which lasted two days, took the usual course of such disputations where neither party can enter, or wishes to enter, in the slightest degree into the difficulties and the convictions of its opponent, but each is simply bent on shouting its own shibboleth. Avitus made a long speech, Ciceronian in its style, proving the Athanasian Creed out of Holy Scripture. Boniface, the Arian champion, replied with the taunt of polytheism, to which already the King's words had given the cue. Next day Aredius, a high functionary of the Court and a Catholic, met the bishops of his party and besought them to discontinue the discussion, which was only embittering religious hatred, and was, besides, disagreeable to the King. They looked upon him as a lukewarm and timeserving believer, and refused to take his advice. The King renewed his complaints of the hostile machinations of Clovis, and now for the first time mentioned the dreaded defection of his brother. The bishops answered, that if Gundobad would only turn Catholic it would be easy to arrange an alliance with Clovis. They then proceeded to reply to the charge of polytheism. Boniface, who is represented as vanquished in the argument, could only shriek out his invectives against the worshippers of three Gods, till he had shouted himself hoarse. Then the orthodox bishops proposed an appeal to miracle. Both parties should repair to the grave of St. Justus, and ask the saint which confession of faith was the true one, and a voice from the grave should decide the question. The Arians replied that such a course would be as displeasing to God as Saul's attempt to raise Samuel from the tomb, and that they for their part would rest their case on nothing else than the appeal to Holy Scripture.

Thus the *Collatio Episcoporum* broke up. Nothing had been accomplished by it. Gundobad had not been persuaded, perhaps had not seen, among his own chief nobles, sufficient pliability of faith to make him venture on declaring himself a convert. He, however, took Stephen and Avitus into his inner chamber, embraced them, and begged them to pray for him. As they left him they meditated on the words 'No man can come unto Me, unless the Father which hath sent Me draw him.' Politically, there was nothing left but for the Arian and Athanasian to fight it out on the soil of Burgundy.

Early in the year 5oo the storm broke. Gundobad, who had perhaps marched northwards in order to anticipate the junction of the two armies, was met by Clovis, and seems to have shut himself up in the strong Castrum Divionense. This place, the modem Dijon, now made memorable to the traveller by the exquisite tombs of Jean-sans-Peur and Philippe-le-Bon, almost the last rulers of a separate Burgundy, was then an *urbs quadrata*, showing still to the barbarians what was the likeness of a camp-city of the Romans. The wall, strengthened with thirty-three towers, which surrounded the city, was thirty feet high, and, as we are told, fifteen feet thick. Large hewn stones formed the foundation and the lower courses, but the upper portions were built of smaller stones, probably of what we call rubble masonry. A stream, which to some extent added to the strength of the camp, flowed in under a bridge at the northern gate, traversed the city, and emerged from it at the southern gateway. Here, apparently, Gundobad made his stand—his unsuccessful stand. The Frankish host, aided by the men of Geneva, overcame the Burgundians of Lyons. Gundobad fled to Avignon, on the very southernmost border of his dominions, and there, clinging perhaps to the protection of his Visigothic neighbour, he remained for some months in obscurity.

Godegisel and his Frankish ally marched through the length and breadth of the kingdom, and the younger brother dreamed that he had reunited the whole of the dwellings of his people under his own sway. Discontent, however, was working beneath the surface; and, possibly on the departure northward of Clovis and his host, it broke out. Gundobad with a few followers, whose number daily augmented, crept cautiously up the valley of the Rhone, and at length, appearing before his old capital Vienne, besieged his brother therein. Godegisel, whose supply of provisions was small, ordered all the poorer inhabitants to be expelled from the town. Among them was an ingenious man, a Roman doubtless by birth, who had had the charge of the chief aqueduct of Vienne. Going to the tent of Gundobad he confided to him the existence of a certain ventilation hole, by which troops could be introduced through this aqueduct into the heart of the city. Gundobad followed the engineer's advice. He himself headed the detachment of troops which went through the aqueduct; and in a few hours Vienne was his own again. With his own hand he slew the treacherous Godegisel, and, we are told, 'put to death, with many and exquisite torments, the senators [no doubt Roman nobles] and Burgundians who had been on his side.' The Frankish troops, which had been left to guard the newly-erected throne, he did not dare either to keep, or to dismiss to their homes. He accordingly sent them to his ally, the King of the Visigoths, who kept them for some time in honourable captivity at Toulouse.

The inactivity of Clovis during these later events, by which the whole fruits of the victory of Dijon were wrested from him, is left quite unexplained in the meagre annals of the time. There is some slight indication of Visigothic influence having been thrown on the side of Gundobad: but, though we have no evidence to adduce in support of it, we can hardly repress the conjecture that Theodoric, the father-in-law of Sigismund, heir of the Burgundian kingship, Theodoric, who from the provinces of Raetia and Liguria could, when summer was advanced, so dangerously operate on the flank of an army of Clovis descending the Rhone valley, must have been the real counterpoise to the Franks in the year 400, during Gundobad's war of Restoration. Whatever the cause, the restored King, who now wielded the whole might of the Burgundian nation, and was more powerful than any of his predecessors, was during the remaining sixteen years of his reign left unmolested by the Frank; nay even, as we shall see, was invited to join in the schemes of Frankish conquest, though on terms of partnership not unlike those which the Horse accepted from the Man, in the old fable.

In the early years of the new century, probably about 503 or 504, Clovis was again at war with his old enemies, the Alamanni. As the Frankish historian, Gregory, is silent about this campaign, we can only speak conjecturally as to its causes and its course. We can see, however, that king and people revolted against their Frankish overlord, that there were hints of treachery and broken faith, that Clovis moved his army into their territories and won a victory, much more decisive, though less famous, than that of 496. This time the angry King would make no such easy terms as he had done before. From their pleasant dwellings by the Main and the Neckar, from all the valley of the Middle Rhine, the terrified Alamanni were forced to flee. Their place was taken by Frankish settlers, from whom all this district received in the Middle Ages the name of the Duchy of Francia, or, at a rather later date, that of the Circle of Franconia.

The Alamanni, with their wives and children, a broken and dispirited host, moved southward to the shores of the Lake of Constance, and entered the old Roman province of Raetia. Here they were on what was held to be, in a sense, Italian ground; and the arm of Theodoric, as ruler of Italy, as successor to the Emperors of the West, was stretched forth to protect them. Clovis would fain have pursued them, would perhaps have blotted out the name of Alamanni from the earth. But Theodoric addressed a letter to his victorious kinsman, in which, while congratulating him on having aroused the long dormant energies ot his people, and won by their means a triumph over the fierce nation of the Alamanni, having slain some and forced others humbly to beg for life, he warned him not to push his victory too far. 'Hear,' said he, 'the advice of one who has had much experience in matters of this nature. Those wars of mine have had a successful issue, over the ending of which, moderation has presided.' Throughout the letter the tone is hardly so much of advice as of command, to the Frankish conqueror, to pursue his ruined foe no further.

The Alamanni gladly accepted the offered protection and dominion of Theodoric. The king of the Ostrogoths became their king, and they, still in their old heathen wildness, became his subjects, conforming themselves doubtless but imperfectly to the maxims of the Roman *civilitas*, but, for one generation at least, leaving the mountain-passes untraversed, and doing rough garrison duty for their king, between the Alps and the Danube. Eastern Switzerland, Western Tyrol, Southern Baden and Wurtemberg, and Southwestern Bavaria probably formed this new Alamannis, which will figure in later history as the *Ducatus Alamanniae* or the Circle of Swabia.

The next stroke from the heavy hand of Clovis fell upon the Visigothic kingdom, and it was a crushign one. In the year 507 the Frankish King announced to his warriors, possibly when they were all assembled at the Field of Mars, 'I take it very ill that these Arians should hold so large a part of Gaul. Let us go and overcome them with God's help, and bring their land under our rule.' These abrupt denunciations of war have not unfrequently been resorted to by Frankish sovereigns. We heard one of them in our own day, when, at the New Year's festivity of 1859, the Emperor of the French suddenly informed a startled Europe that his relations with his brother of Austria were not as good as he could desire.

In this case, rapid as was the action of Clovis, there was apparently time for a brief and lively interchange of correspondence between Italy Gaul. Theodoric, hearing of the threatened outbreak of hostilities, employed the pen of his eloquent Quaestor Cassiodorus to compose a series of letters, to all the chief persons concerned, to Alaric, to Clovis, to Gundobad, nay, even to the semi-barbarous kings of the tribes still tarrying in Germany, the Heruli, the Warni, the Thuringians, in order to avert by all possible means the dreaded encounter.

To his Visigothic son-in-law Theodoric uttered His letter a note of warning: 'Strong though you are in your own valour and in the remembrance of the great deeds of your forefathers, by whom even the mighty Attila was humbled, yet since your people's strength and aptitude for war may, by long peace, have been somewhat impaired, do not put everything to the hazard of a single action. It is only constant practice which can make the actual shock of battle seem anything but terrible to man. Let not, then, your indignation at the conduct of Clovis blind you to the real interests of your nation. Wait till I can send ambassadors to the King of the Franks, and till I have endeavoured to make peace between two princes, both so nearly allied to me, one my brother and the other my son, by marriage.' To 'his brother Gundobad' Theodoric expressed his regrets that 'the royal youths' should thus rage against one another, his desire that they might listen to the counsels of reverend age, as represented by himself and Gundobad, and his proposal that a joint embassy from the three nations (Ostrogoths, Visigoths, and Burgundians) should be addressed to Clovis, in order to re-establish peace between him and Alaric. The German chieftains, he reminded of the benefits and the protection which they, in past times, had received from Euric, the father of the now menaced prince. He expressed his conviction that this lawless aggression threatened equally every throne of a neighbour to Clovis, and begged them to join their ambassadors to his, in a summons to the Frankish King to desist from the attack on the Visigoths, to seek redress for his alleged wrongs from the law of nations [but where were the courts then, or where are they now, in which that law is administered?]; if he would not obey these counsels, then to prepare himself for the combined onset of them all.

The letter to 'Luduin' (as Theodoric, or Cassiodorus, styles the King of the Franks) reiterates the same thoughts, dwells on the miseries which war inflicts upon the nations, declares that it is the act of a hot-headed man to get his troops ready for war at the very first embassy, and urges, almost commands, the Frank to accept his mediation. The letter contains the following passage, which certainly went far to pledge Theodoric to armed championship of his son-in-law: 'Throw away the sword, ye who wish to draw it for *my disgrace*. It is in my right as a father, as a friend, that I thus threaten you, He who shall suppose that such monitions as ours can be treated with contempt—a thing which we do not anticipate—will find that he has to deal with us and our friends, as his adversaries.'

Yet, in spite of all this correspondence and all these embassies, directed by one who had been a man of war from his youth, and who had a true statesman's eye to the necessities of the position, Alaric the Visigoth stood alone, and fell unaided. The Franks crossed the Loire; directed their march to Poitou : at the Campus Vogladensis, ten miles from Poitiers, the two armies met. Alaric would have played a waiting game, trusting to the eventual arrival of succours from his father-in-law; but the ignorant impetuosity of his troops, who vaunted that they were at least the equals in arms of the Franks, forced him to accept the offered battle. Alaric fell, slain, it seems, by the hand of Clovis himself. His troops fled from the field of hopeless rout. Amalaric, the grandson of Theodoric, and the only legitimate child of the late King, was hurried away to Spain by his guardians. A few cities still held out for the Visigoths, but almost everywhere, from the Loire to the Pyrenees, the Frank roamed supreme. The religious fervour of Clovis was satisfied. That pious monarch would no longer be chagrined by seeing so large a part of Gaul in the hands of the Arians.

What was the cause of this sudden collapse of the great Arian confederacy and of Theodoric's entire failure to redeem his pledge, by championing his son-in-law? It seems probable that it is to be sought in the unexpected defection of Gundobad, who did not even remain neutral in the conflict, but positively allied himself with the Frankish invader. The reasons for this change of attitude are not fully known to us. Ever since the *Collatio Episcoporum*, Gundobad had been on increasingly friendly terms with the Catholic Episcopate, especially with the courtly Avitus. His first-born Sigismund, perhaps both his sons, had formally joined the Catholic communion. Some of the courtiers had followed their example. Gundobad himself, though to the day of his death he refused to abjure the faith of his forefathers, showed a willingness to do everything for the creed of his Roman subjects, except to make that one ignominious confession of hereditary error. He might perhaps also allege that in the catastrophe of 500 he had been left to fight his battles alone, and that he was under no obligation, for Alaric's sake, a second time to see the terrible Sicambrian devastating the Rhone-lands. Whatever the cause, it is clear that Burgundia went with Francia against Vesegothia in the fatal campaign; and it is highly probable that Theodoric did not know that this was to be her attitude till the very eve of the contest, and when it was too late for him to take measures for forcing his way past the territories of a hostile nation to the relief of his son-in-law.

At the death of Alaric the situation was further complicated by a division in the Visigothic camp. The child Amalaric, now a refugee in Spain, was, as has been said, the only legitimate representative of the fallen king. But Alaric had left a bastard son named Gesalic, now in early manhood, who, according to the lax notions about succession prevalent among the Teutonic peoples, might fairly aspire to the kingdom, if he could make good his claim by success. He appears, however, to have been but a feeble representative of his valiant forefathers. He lost Narbonne to Gundobad, and after a disgraceful rout, in which many of the Visigoths perished, he fled to Barcelona, whence, after four years of a shadowy reign, he was eventually expelled by the generals of Theodoric.

The great city of Arles, once the Roman capital of Gaul, maintained a gallant defence against the united Franks and Burgundians, and saved for generations the Visigothic rule in Provence and Southern Languedoc. Of the siege, which lasted apparently from 508 to 510, we have some graphic details in the life of St. Caesarius, Bishop of Arles, written by his disciples. This saint, who was born in Burgundian Gaul, had for years lain under suspicion of being discontented with the Gothic yoke, and had spent some time in exile at Bordeaux under a charge of treason. Released, and permitted to return to his diocese, he was busying himself in the erection of a convent, where holy women were to reside under the presidency of his sister Caesaria, when the Franks and Burgundians came swarming around the city; and the half-finished edifice, which was apparently outside the walls, was destroyed by the ferocity of the barbarians.

The siege dragged on and became a blockade. A young ecclesiastic, struck with fear of captivity and full of youthful fickleness, let himself down the wall by a rope, and gave himself up to the besiegers. Not unreasonably the old suspicions as to the loyalty of Caesarius revived. The Goths, and the Jews, who sided with the Goths, surrounded the church, clamouring that the Bishop had sent the deserter, on purpose to betray them to the enemy. 'There was no proof,' say his biographers, 'no regard to the stainless record of his past life. Jews and heretics crowded the precincts of the church, shouting out "Drag forth the Bishop! Let him be kept under strictest guard in the palace!" Their object was that he should either be drowned in the Rhone, or at least immured in the fort of Ugernum [one of the castles by the river, not far from Arles], till by hardship and exile his life was worn away. Meanwhile his church and his chamber were given up to be occupied by the Arians. One of the Goths, in spite of the remonstrances of his comrades, dared to sleep in the saint's bed, but was smitten by the judgment of God, and died the nest day.

'A cutter (*dromo*) was then brought, and the holy man was placed in it that he might be towed up [to the above-named castle] past the lines of the besiegers. But as, by divine interposition, they were unable to move the ship, though tugging it from either shore, they brought him back to the palace, and there kept him in such utter seclusion that none of the Catholics knew whether he was dead or alive.

At length however there came a change. A certain Jew tied a letter to a stone and tried to fling it to the besiegers. In it he offered to betray the city to them on condition that the lives, freedom, and property of all the Jews were spared; and he indicated the precise spot in the walls, to which the besiegers were to apply their ladders. Fortunately, next day the enemy did not come so near the walls as usual. Hence the fateful letter was found, not by the Burgundians, but by the Goths, and thus the selfish cruelty of the Jews, hateful both to God and man, was exposed. Then was our Daniel, St. Caesarius, drawn up from the den of lions, and the Jews his accusers, like the satraps of Darius, were sent to take his place.'

The brave defence of Arles enabled Theodoric still to intervene to save the remnants of the Visigothic monarchy in Gaul. This he could doubtless do with the more success now that the embarrassing claim of Gesalic was swept away. In the spring of the year 508 he put forth a stirring proclamation to his people, prepared by Cassiodorus. 'We need but hint to our faithful Goths that a contest is at hand, since warlike race like ours rejoices at the thought of the strife. In the quiet times of peace, merit has no chance of showing itself, but now the day for its discovery draws nigh. With God's help, and for the common good, we have decided on an invasion of Gaul. We send round our faithful Saio, Nandius, to warn you to come in God's name fully prepared for our expedition, in the accustomed manner, with arms, horses, and all things necessary for the battle, on the 24th of June'.

The Ostrogothic army advanced to the relief of the courageous garrison of Arles. Conspicuous among the generals, perhaps chief in command, was Tulum, who had recently shown in the war of Sirmium that a Gothic lord of the bedchamber could deal as heavy blows as any trained soldier among the Byzantines or the Huns. The possession of the covered bridge which connected Arles with the east bank of the Rhone was fiercely contested, and in the battles fought for its capture and recapture, Tulum showed great personal courage, and received many honourable wounds.

But the united armies of Franks and Burgundians required much defeating ; and still the siege of Arles was not raised, though its stringency may have been somewhat abated, and though all Provence to the eastward of the city was probably secured to Theodoric.

We have reason to believe that in the next year a bold and clever stroke of strategy was executed by the Ostrogoths. An army under Duke Mammo seems to have mounted the valley of the Dora-Susa, crossed the Alps near Briançon, and descended into the valley of the Durance, plundering the country as they proceeded. They thus threatened to take the Burgundians in rear as well as in front, and put them under strong compulsion to return to defend their homes, in the region which we now know as Dauphiné.

The decisive battle was perhaps not delivered till the early part of 510. Then the Goths under Count Ibbas completely routed the united armies of the Franks and Burgundians. If we may believe the boastful bulletin transcribed by Jordanes, more than 30,000 Franks lay dead upon the field. Certainly many captives were taken by the united forces of the Visigoths and Ostrogoths, since all the churches and houses of

Arles were filled with their unkempt multitudes. St. Caesarius gladly devoted the proceeds of the communion-plate, which he sold, to the redemption of some of these captives; and when cavillers objected to so uncanonical a proceeding, he replied that it was better that the communion should be celebrated in delf, than that a fellow-man should remain in bondage one hour longer than was necessary.

To complete the history of the good prelate, it may be mentioned that some years later the cry of disloyalty was again raised against him, and he was taken to Ravenna, under a guard of soldiers, to give account of himself to his new sovereign, Theodoric. As soon as the King saw the firm and venerable countenance of the Bishop, he seems to have instinctively felt that this was a man to be conciliated, not intimidated. He rose from his seat to greet him, doffed his crown to do him reverence, asked him concerning the toils of his journey, and affectionately enquired what tidings he could give him of the people of Arles, and what, of his own Goths who were garrisoning it. As soon as Caesarius had left the royal presence, Theodoric, we are told, imprecated woe on the malicious accusers, who had caused a man of such evident holiness to be annoyed by so long and so needless a journey.

'When he entered to salute me,' the King is said to have exclaimed, 'my whole frame trembled. I felt that I was looking on an angelical countenance, on a truly apostolic man. I hold it impiety to harbour a thought of evil concerning so venerable a person.

After the interview the King sent to the saint a silver dish weighing 6olbs., together with 300 golden solidi (£180), entreating him to use the salver daily and to remember his son Theodoric who had presented it. The saint, who never had an article of silver on his table except an egg-spoon, at once sold the dish (which would probably be worth 240 solidi, or £144) and applied the proceeds to his favourite charity, the liberation of captives. Mischief-makers informed the King that they had seen his present exposed for sale in the market; but when he learned the purpose to which Caesarius was applying the proceeds, he expressed such admiration of the virtues of the saint, that all his courtiers followed suit and repaired to the Bishop's dwelling to shake him by the hand. But already the crowd of poor sufferers, in his oratory and in the atrium of his lodgings, was so great that his wealthier admirers found it no easy matter to gain entrance to his presence.

The result of the battle of Arles was to put Theodoric in secure possession of all Provence, and of so much of Languedoc as was needful to ensure his access to Spain, whither, peace having been concluded with Clovis and Gundobad, Ibbas and the Ostrogothic army now marched, to cut up by the roots the usurped dominion of Gesalic. That feeble pretender was soon driven forth from his capital, Barcelona, and wandered, an exile, to the Court of Thrasamund the Vandal, Theodoric's brother-in-law. Notwithstanding this tie of kindred with his pursuer, Thrasamund received the fugitive kindly, and enabled him to return to Gaul, having provided him with large sums of money, with which he enlisted followers and disturbed the peace of the Gothic provinces. Theodoric upon this wrote a sharp rebuke to his brother-in-law, telling him among other things that he was certain he could not have sought the counsel of his wife; the wise and noble Amalafrida, before taking a step so fatal to all friendly relations between the two kingdoms. The Vandal King frankly confessed his fault, and sent ambassadors with large presents, apparently of gold plate, to soothe the anger of his brother-in-law. Theodoric cordially accepted the apology, but not the presents, saying that, after reading the words of Thrasamund, it was sweeter to give back his presents than to receive costly gifts from any other sovereign.

As for Gesalic, weak and cowardly intriguer, his attempted rebellion was again with ease suppressed. After a year spent in troubling the peace of Gaul he returned to Spain, was defeated by Ibbas in a pitched battle twelve miles from Barcelona, again took flight—this time for Burgundy—was captured a little north of the river Durance, and was put to death by his captors.

After the overthrow of the Visigothic kingdom, Clovis received from the Emperor Anastasius letters bestowing on him the dignity of Roman ConsulIn the church of St. Martin at Tours, he appeared clothed in purple tunic and mantle, the dress of a Roman and of a sovereign, and with the diadem on his head. Then, mounting his horse at the door of the atrium of the church, he rode slpwly through the streets to the cathedral, scattering gold and silver coins as he went, and saluted by the people (the Roman provincials doubtless) with shouts of 'Chlodovechus Consul! Chlodovechus Consul!'

After having murdered the rest of the Salian and Ripuarian princes in Gaul, and left himself in a solitude which he sometimes affected to deplore, (but this was only in the hope of tempting any forgotten kinsman who might be lingering in obscurity, to come forth and meet the knife of the assassin), Clovis, the eldest son of the Church, died at Paris in the forty-fifth year of his age and the thirtieth of his reign, and was buried in the Basilica of the Holy Apostles, which had been reared by him and Clotilda. Already, in the founder of the Merovingian family, we see indications of that shortness of life which was to be so remarkable a characteristic of its later generations. At his death his kingdom was divided between his four sons, Theodoric, Chlodomir, Childebert, and Chlolochar. The three last only were sons of Clotilda.

For the rest of his reign, Theodoric the Amal ruled Spain and Visigothic Gaul as protector of his grandson Amalaric, but in his own name, and with power nearly as uncontrolled as that which he exercised in Italy itself. The chief limitation to that power consisted in the great influence wielded by Theudis, an Ostrogoth whom he had appointed guardian of Amalaric, perhaps *Praefectus Praetorio* of Spain. Theudis married a wealthy Spanish lady, surrounded himself with a body-guard of 2000 men, and affected some of the state of independent royalty. There was no open breach between him and his master, but when, towards the end of his reign, Theodoric invited the too powerful minister to visit him at Ravenna, Theudis, who was doubtful as to the return journey, ventured to refuse obedience to the summons, and Theodoric did not consider it prudent to enforce it. The aged king probably knew that he was not transmitting a perfectly safe inheritance to his Visigothic grandson.

We return to contemplate the declining fortunes of the Burgundian monarchy. Gundobad had certainly reaped little benefit from his desertion of the Arian confederacy and his alliance with Clovis. He had quite failed to secure the coveted lands at the mouths of the Rhone : he had even, it would seem, lost Avignon, though he may have gained the less important city of Viviers (Alba Augusta) in exchange. A strong chain of Ostrogothic fortresses barred the passage of the boundary river, the Durance, and he was now cooped up between two mighty neighbours, one of whom ruled from the Rhine to the Pyrenees, and the other from the Danube to Gibraltar. Whether the mutual relations of these two states were friendly or hostile, he was but too likely to come to ruin between them.

However, Gundobad died in peace in the year 516, having outlived Clovis five years; and was succeeded by his son Sigismund, son-in-law of Theodoric, and a convert to the Catholic faith. The new king, a man of an unstable hysterical temperament, left scarcely a fault uncommitted which could hasten the downfall of his throne. After alienating, probably, the affections of his Burgundian warriors by abjuring the faith of his forefathers, he lost the hearty good-will of the Catholics by engaging in a quarrel with their bishops, on account of their excommunication of his chief treasurer for marrying his deceased wife's sister. The resolute attitude maintained by the bishops, who put 'the most excellent king' in a kind of spiritual quarantine till he should come to a better mind, coupled with an opportune attack of fever, brought Sigismund to his knees in abject surrender, and he was reconciled to the Church, but doubtless with some loss of royal dignity.

The natural ally of the Burgundian against his too powerful neighbour the Frank, was evidently the Ostrogothic King. Instead of recognising this fact, Sigismund exhausted the vocabulary of servitude in grovelling self-prostration before the Emperor Anastasius, a sovereign whose power was too remote from the scene of action to be of the slightest service to him, when the time of trial should come. At the same time, he irrevocably alienated Theodoric by a domestic crime, which reminds us of the family history of another distinguished convert, Constantine, and, perhaps with less justice, of a passage in the life of another pillar of orthodoxy, Philip II of Spain. The daughter of Theodoric had borne to Sigismund a son who was named Segeric. This youth contemplated, we are told, his eventual accession to both thrones, the Burgundian and the Ostrogothic, and, though we have no reason for asserting that his maternal grandfather designed to make him his heir, such a union of the kingdoms would have had much to recommend it to the statesmanlike mind of Theodoric. But Sigismund, after the death of his Amal wife, had married again. His second wife, a woman not of noble birth, but of orthodox creed, inflamed the fathers jealousy against his son, who had flouted her as unworthy to wear the clothes of her late mistress, and whom she accused of not being willing to wait the ordinary course of nature for the succession to his inheritance. The wretched Sigismund listened the poisonous insinuation, and, without giving his son an opportunity of justifying himself, cut him off by a coward's stroke. One day when Segeric was flustered with wine (we remember how Sidonius speaks of the deep potations of the Burgundians), his father advised him to enjoy a siesta after the banquet. Suspecting no evil he fell asleep. Two slaves by the King's command entered the chamber, fastened a cord round his neck, and strangled him.

Scarcely was the foul deed done than it was repented of. The miserable father, finding that his son had been falsely accused, threw himself upon the corpse, and bitterly bewailed the blind folly which had bereft him of his child. Truly, and with Teutonic frankness, did the servant who witnessed his repentance, say, 'It is not he, but His thou, oh King, who needest our pity.' He fled to his beloved monastery at Agaunum, to that spot so well known to the modern traveller, where 'a key unlocks a kingdom,' as the Rhone, between nearly meeting mountain barriers, emerges from Canton Valais into Canton Vaud. Here, in the narrow defile, on the site of the imaginary martyrdom of the 'Theban Legion' (who, with Maurice at their head, were fabled to have gladly suffered martyrdom at the hands of Maximian rather than offer sacrifice to the gods of the Capitol), a house of prayer arose, and was so richly endowed by Sigismund, that it passed, though incorrectly, for his original foundation. In this retreat the King many days of misery, fasting and 'weeping. Here he ordered a choir to be formed, whose songs were to arise to Heaven night and day, that there might be a ceaseless ascription of prayer and praise to the Most High. One cannot condemn the religious turn which was taken by the bitter self-condemnation of the unhappy Sigismund, even though it induced him to issue the somewhat harsh order for the extrusion of all women and all secular persons from the vicinity of Agaunum. But one may condemn the clouds of adulation which Avitus, at the installation of the new choir, sent rolling towards the royal murderer from the pulpit of the basilica of Agaunum. He called him 'pious lord,' he praised his devotion, praised his liberality to the Church, regretted that she could find no words adequate to his virtues, but assured him that on that day, by the institution of the perpetual choir, he had surpassed even his own good deeds. And this, to the assassin of his own son, to the man whose conscience was at that very hour tormented by the Furies, the avengers of his child. Not with such poisonous opiates did Ambrose soothe Theodosius, after the massacre of Thessalonica. But then Ambrose had not been always a priest. While administering justice in the Roman prsetorium, he had learned, it may be, some lessons of truth and righteousness which gave an increased nobility even to his ecclesiastical career.

The crime of Sieismund, however glossed over by the pulpit eloquence of Avitus, did not wait long for its punishment in this world. In 523, the year following the murder of Segeric, came the crash of a Frankish invasion, more disastrous even than that of 500. Three sons of Clovis joined in it, Chlodomir, Childebert, and Chlotochar (Lothair), incited thereto, according to the story current a century later, by the adjurations of their mother Clotilda, who urged them to revenge the wrongs which her family had suffered from Gundobad, more than thirty years before. We have seen how much reason there is to look with doubt, or even with absolute disbelief, upon this long-credited story. It is true that the one successor of Clovis who was not born to him of Clotilda, Theodoric, king of Metz and lord of the Arverni, took no part in the enterprise; but that abstention is sufficiently accounted for by the fact that his wife Suavegotta was the daughter of Sigismund.

On the other hand, the other and greater Theodoric, (after whom no doubt the son of Clovis was named), enraged at the murder of his grandson, adopted an attitude of something more than friendly neutrality towards his nephews, the Frankish invaders of Burgundia. Procopius, if we could trust his narrative of these distant affairs, draws for us a curious picture of the almost commercial arrangement between Ostrogoths and Franks for an 'invasion on joint account' of the contracting parties. He says, 'Afterwards, the Franks and Goths made an alliance for the injury of the Burgundians, on condition that they should subdue the people and divide their land; the nation which should fail to assist its confederate in the campaign, paying a certain stipulated quantity of gold, but not being shut out from its share in the division of the territory'. He then describes how Theodoric gave instructions to his generals to delay their march, and not enter Burgundian territory till they should hear of the victory of the Franks; and how the weight of the conflict thus fell upon the Franks alone, who gained a hard-fought victory. As they chid their allies, when they at length appeared, for their tardy arrival, the latter pleaded in excuse the difficulty of the Alpine passes. The stipulated amount was paid by them, and Theodoric was admitted to his equal share of the conquered territory, receiving general praise for the dexterity with which he had contrived to secure a large accession of territory, without bloodshed, by the payment of a moderate sum of money.

Whatever may have been the compact which Procopius has thus curiously distorted,—for certainly his account resembles more the transactions between Byzantium and Ctesiphon than the probable arrangements between two warlike Teutonic nations,—it must be admitted that in its immediate result the campaign of 523 was greatly to the advantage of Theodoric. With no hard fighting, he pushed his frontier in the Rhone-lands northwards from the line of the Durance to that of the Drome, thus adding to his dominions all that he did not already possess of Provence, and no inconsiderable portion of Dauphiné besides. The leader of the Ostrogothic army which achieved this bloodless conquest was Tulum, the hero of the campaign of 509 and the valiant succourer of Arles.

Meanwhile Sigismund fought and lost a battle with the Frankish invaders, probably near the northern frontier of his kingdom, fled to his favourite retreat of Agaunum, and was given up to the enemy by his Burgundian subjects, whose love he had no doubt lost when he slew his son.

All seemed lost, but was not lost yet. As the Frankish hosts were retiring, probably on the approach of winter, Godomar, the younger and more energetic son of Gundobad, collected some troops and assumed the government, probably as a kind son of regent on behalf of his captive brother. That brother with all his family was at once murdered by Chlodomir, with that ruthless indifference to human life which is an especial note of the Merovingian house. Sigismund, his wife, and his two sons were all thrown down a deep well in the neighbourhood of Orleans; and, as some faint justification of the crime, later generations trumped up the story, that after this manner had his father Gundobad dealt by Hilperik, the father of Clotilda, and his sons. But the wicked deed did not avail to stay the reaction against the Franks, and perhaps even strengthened the position of Godomar, the now recognised King of the Burgundians.

The new King by his valour and energy restored for a time the almost desperate fortunes of his people. The Frankish brothers, joined this time by Theodoric of Auvergne, invaded the country. Godomar met them in battle at Véséronce on the Rhone, about thirty miles east of Lyons. Chlodomir was slain by a javelin. The Burgundians, when they saw the long and carefully-tended hair of the dead man, drawn back from his forehead and descending to his shoulders, knew that they had slain a royal Meroving. They cut off the head and exhibited it on a spear-point to the Frankish victorious, warriors, who, discouraged by the death of their leader, broke their ranks and fled from the field. The little children of Chlodomir were cruelly murdered by Childebert and Chlotochar, who, intent upon this partition, left his death unavenged and Burgundia in peace.

This then was the condition of affairs in Gaul when Theodoric the Ostrogoth died. The friendly Frankish monarchy of the Visigoths was all but rooted out of the land. That of the Burgundians still lived on, but had been shorn by Theodoric himself of some of its territory in the south, and really awaited but the first vigorous effort from the Franks to crumble into ruin. The dominions of the chief royal house of the Salian Franks, which at the accession of Clovis reached but from Utrecht to Amiens, now touched the Pyrenees at the southwest, and the Main and Neckar in the east. The Thuringians, under their king Hermanfrid, Theodoric's nephew by marriage, were the only power in Germany that seemed to have a chance of maintaining their independence against the Franks, and they too, soon after the death of Theodoric, were to be incorporated with the new world-empire of the Merovingians.

Looking thus over the map of Western Europe at the beginning of the sixth century, is it possible for us not to cast one glance at that country whose chalk cliffs, seen from the shores which owned the sway of Clovis, looked then near and fair as now they look from France when lit up by the sun of a summer morning. Yet this is how the contemporary Procopius speaks of the island of *Brittia*, which can hardly be any other than our Britain. After describing the wall bunt across it by the ancients, which, according to him, ran from north to south, and separated the fruitful and populous east from the barren, serpent-haunted western tract, in which no man could live for an hour, he proceeds to tell a well-known story, which he scarcely likes to repeat, since it sounds like fable, and yet which is attested by such numberless persons who themselves witnessed the strange phenomenon that he does not like entirely to reject it:—

'The coast of the continent over against Brittia is dotted with, villages, in which dwell fishermen, husbandmen, merchants, who serve the kings of the Franks but pay them no tribute, being excused by reason of the service which I am about to describe. They understand that they have it in charge to conduct by turns the souls of the dead to the opposite shore. Those upon whom the service devolves, at nightfall betake themselves to sleep, though waiting their summons. As the night grows old, an unseen hand knocks at their doors, the voice of an unseen person calls them to their toil. Then they spring up from their couches and run to the shore. They understand not what necessity constrains them thus to act: they know only that they are constrained. At the water's edge they see barks not their own, with no visible passengers on board, yet so deeply loaded that there is not a finger's breadth between the water and the rowlocks. They bend to their oars, and in one hour they reach the island of Brittia, which, in their own barks, they can scarce reach in a night and a day, using both oar and sail. Arrived at the other side, as soon as they understand that the invisible disembarkation has taken place, they return, and now their boats are so lightly laden that only the keel is in the water. They see no form of man sailing with them or leaving the ship, but they hear a voice which seems to call each one of the shadowy passengers by name, to recount the dignities which they once held, and to tell their father's names. And if women are of the party, the voice pronounces the names of the husbands with whom they lived on earth. Such are the appearances which are vouched for by the men who dwell in those parts. But I return to my former narrative.'

So thick was the mist and darkness that had fallen upon the land where Severus died, where Constantine was saluted Imperator, and where Pelagius taught that man was born sinless. And truly, the analogy of that which happens to the spirits of the dead, well describes the change which had come over Britain. Our historians tell us indeed that Anderida fell two years before Theodoric won his kingdom. They conjecture that Eburacum fell during the central years of his reign, and that Cerdic, the pirate ancestor of Queen Victoria, conquered the Isle of Wight, where his descendant now abides in peace, four years after the death of the great Ostrogoth. But to the questions, so intensely interesting to us, how all these things happened, how the struggle was regarded by those engaged in it, what manner of man the Roman Provincial seemed to the Saxon, and the Heathen to the Christian, what were the incidents and what the nature of the strife,—to all of these questions we can scarce obtain more answer than comes back to us from the spirits of those with whom we once shared every thought, but who, summoned by the touch of an unseen hand, have left us for the Land of Silence.

CHAPTER X.

THEODORIC'S RELATIONS WITH THE EAST.

For five-and-twenty years—that is to say, for three-quarters of its whole duration—the reign of Theodoric ran parallel to that of Anastasius, the handsome but elderly officer of the household whom, as we have already seen, the favour of Ariadne, widow of Zeno, raised to the imperial throne. The character of the man who was still, probably, in the view of all the provincial populations, the only legitimate ruler in the lands west of the Euphrates, could not but seriously affect, for good or for evil, the fortunes of Theodoric and of the new realm which he was founding; and, upon the whole, it may be said that the influence exerted upon them by Anastasius was for good.

There are few sovereigns of whom more contradictory characters are given than those which the historians of the period—chiefly ecclesiastical historians—have drawn of Anastasius. Avaricious and generous; base and noble : one who sold the offices of the state to the highest bidder; one who found the custom of so selling them in existence and resolutely suppressed it; a destroyer of the resources of the provinces; a careful cherisher of those resources,—such are some of the contradictory qualities assigned to him in the pages of these writers. Even his personal appearance has not altogether escaped from this perplexing variety of portraiture. While Cedrenus tells us of the lofty stature, the vivid blue eyes, and the white hair of the noble-looking Silentiarius, to whom Ariadne gave her hand and the imperial crown, Zonaras declares that his two eyes were of different colours, the left black and the right blue, and that hence he derived his surname of Dicorus.

As to his religious opinions, some authors say (or hint) that he was a Manichean, others an Arian, others an Eutychian,—a set of statements about as consistent with each other as if a modem statesman were represented as at once an Agnostic, an Ultramontane, and a Calvinist. The truth appears to be that Anastasius was not at first an eager partisan of any of the theological fashions (it were giving them too high honour to call them faiths) which distracted the dioceses of the East. He was himself inclined to Eutychianism,—that form of doctrine which exalted the Divinity of Jesus Christ at the expense of his true Humanity; but if I read his actions aright, he wished to reign in that spirit of toleration for all faiths which had been the glory of the reign of Valentinian I more than a century before him, and which was to be the glory of the reign of his great Gothic contemporary Theodoric. Events, however, were too strong for him. Scarcely anything is harder than to preserve perfect fairness and toleration towards men who are themselves intolerant and unfair. Thus, as time went on, Anastasius began to press more heavily on the adherents of Chalcedon than on their opponents. The bishops of that way of thinking began to find themselves driven from their sees, perhaps on insufficient pretences. The mob of Constantinople, sensitive on behalf of the faith of Chalcedon, took the alarm. There were tumults, bloodshed, even armed rebellion. The majesty of the purple was degraded. Anastasius became a partisan, and a partisan of the unpopular cause. Before he died, he, whose chief ambition it had apparently been to serve the state well as a civil ruler, and to let theology take care of itself, had the sad conviction that he was known to most of his subjects only as the hard and bitter persecutor of that form of theology which attracted their ignorant but enthusiastic allegiance.

Hence, no doubt, from the position occupied by this Emperor in Church affairs flow those strangely diverging currents of testimony as to his character which have been commented upon above. We have unfortunately hardly any information as to the civil transactions of his reign from a secular historian. No Priscus, and no Procopius, tells us how the transactions of this Emperor in peace and war were viewed by the statesmen of his day. We have only from the ecclesiastical writers the history of the wild war-dance performed round his venerable figure by monks and priests, archimandrites and patriarchs, some shouting 'Anathema to the Council of Chalcedon!' and others 'Anathema to Eutyches, to Zeno, to Acacius! Away with the men who communicated with Peter the Stammerer! Away with the Manichean Emperor!'. The shriek of the latter, the Chalcedonian party, reaches the ears of posterity in the more piercing tones, because it has in the end won the prize of a character for orthodoxy, but we can also distinguish some notes of the war-cry of its enemies, and they help us in some measure to understand why and how the aged and tolerant Emperor was forced into acts which his calumniators represent as worthy of Herod or Diocletian.

To Anastasius as a financial administrator the historian can, with but little hesitation, assign a high place among the rulers of the Empire. Procopius, who styles him 'the most provident and most economical of all the Emperors,' tells us that at his death the imperial treasury contained 320,000 pounds of gold (£14,400,000), all collected during the twenty-seven years of his reign. Yet, at least in one instance, the Emperor had not increased but lessened the weight of taxation on his subjects. This was the case of the tax called Chrysargyron, which bad been first imposed, some say, by Constantine, and which seems to have been a licence-tax levied once in four years on all who lived by any kind of trade. From the manner of its collection it pressed with extreme severity on small hucksters and others of the poorest class; and it also seemed to give the State's sanction to vice, since it was levied upon prostitutes and others who traded only upon immorality. These perhaps paid their Chrysargyron more readily than any other class, feeling that they thereby purchased indemnity for their evil courses. The tax had long been denounced by statesmen and divines, and now (in the year 501) Anastasius determined that it should cease. When he had gone through the form of obtaining the sanction of the Senate to its abolition, he burned in the Circus, in the presence of all the people, the rolls containing the names of the persons liable to the tax. Still, however, as Anastasius well knew, there was one class of men who viewed the abolition with regret. These were the clerks in the office of the Chrysargyron, whose employment, one of the most distinguished in the whole civil service, was taken from them by the reform. Fearing that under his successors the tax might, on the representation of these men, be revived, he took a precaution which, though ingenious, showed some of that not very imperial quality of slyness which we can discern also in his ecclesiastical proceedings, and which partly accounts for the bitterness with which his outwitted theological opponents have persecuted his memory. Inviting the officers who had been charged with the collection of the Chrysargyron to meet him at the palace, he delivered an oration, in which he professed to regret his hasty abolition of the tax, and his rash destruction of the documents connected with it. After all, said he, it was desirable to have some records of the manner of collecting an impost which, at any time, the necessities of the State might compel him to revive. If therefore the worthy numerarii before him had among their private papers any such documents, the Emperor would thank them to bring such papers to him, and would reward them handsomely for doing so. On a given day the revenue officers met the Emperor again. The papers were given up and paid for. 'Are there any more?' he asked. 'None, gracious lord,' replied all the officers, and swore it by the Emperor's life. 'Then now shall all be destroyed,' said the Emperor, who burned them at once in the presence of all, and threw even the ashes of the rolls into running water. So intent was he on the thorough performance of the act by which he

' took the tax away,
And built himself an everlasting name' .

Some of the other financial measures carried by Anastasius are spoken of in more doubtful terms. One of them seems to have been the commutation of the of the tithes payable in kind from the cultivator to the treasury for a fixed money-payment, which, according to Evagrius, was calculated on an oppressive scale. Of course if the commutation was unfair the measure cannot be defended; but, in itself, the principle of allowing the possessor to sell his corn to the nearest purchaser, and bring the tenth part of the gold representing it into the treasury, was a good one.

Another reform was the abolition, at least the partial abolition, of the curial system. We are told that he took away the collection of taxes from the local senates, and sent instead officers called Vindices to each city, charged with the execution of this duty : 'Whereby the revenues in great part came to grief, and the glory of the cities departed. For [under the old system] the nobles were inscribed each in the album of his city, and thus every city had its own council, with defined and well-ascertained powers'. So says Evagrius, writing a century after the accession of Anastasius, when it was perhaps not easy to discriminate exactly between his work and that of his successors. From the history of the Curies, as far as we have been able to trace it, one would be inclined to say that the abolition of these local senates must in itself have been a wise and righteous measure. Their 'glory' was but a bright robe covering deep and cruel wounds. Overcharged with terrible responsibilities, and with scarcely any real power, they stood helpless in presence of the imperial despotism, with whose rapacity they were unable to cope; and thus the privilege of having one's name inscribed in their rolls, once an eagerly-sought distinction, had become a most intolerable burden. The Curies were in fact bankrupt, and the curiales were no longer shareholders in a flourishing enterprise, but contributories struggling to evade their liability.

In these circumstances, to sweep away the Curies with their system of ruthlessly enforced 'joint and several liability' for the taxes of the district was probably an act of mercy. Still it was a step towards centralisation. The Vindices were not local officers, but received their commission direct from the imperial treasury. In the days of financial pressure which were approaching, when Justinian's wars, his wife, and his architects had well- nigh beggared the Empire, and when the chief concern of the ruler was how to wring the last *solidus* out of the exhausted tax-payer, it may be that the vindex of the Emperor was found more efficacious than the old-fashioned duumvir of the Curia. But the blame for this oppression must rest, not on Anastasius, who remodelled the taxing-machine of the State, but on Justinian, who wasted the revenues provided by it.

Other traits of the character of this Emperor seem to disclose a generous and sympathetic nature. Even his enemies attest his habit of abundant almsgiving, both before and after his elevation to the throne. And to any city in his dominions which had suffered from hostile invasion he was wont to grant a remission of all taxes for the space of seven years.

Among the great works which signalised the reign of Anastasius was the construction of a wall, more than fifty miles long, drawn from the Sea of Marmora to the Euxine, at a distance of about thirty-five miles from the capital. The wall was apparently strengthened by a fosse, which was really a navigable canal uniting the two seas. This Great Wall of Anastasius played an important part in the defence of Constantinople for many centuries, giving as it did to the capital, so long as it was kept in good repair, all the strength of an insular position.

The Isaurian war (which has been described in a previous chapter), waged against the brother and the countrymen of Zeno, occupied five years at the beginning of the reign of Anastasius. Then, after a peaceful interval of five years, came four years of war with Persia. The peace between the two great monarchies of the Eastern world, which had lasted for sixty years, was at length broken by the King of Kings. Kobad, who mounted the Persian throne in 487, was under great obligations, both moral and pecuniary, to his barbarous neighbours on the northern frontier, the Ephthalites, or so-called White Huns, by whose aid he had been twice enabled to win or to recover his crown. To enable him to discharge the material obligation, he applied to Anastasius for a sum of money, which was, according to one account, to be a loan, according to another the repayment of an old debt, for expenses incurred on the joint account of the two civilised Empires in defending the passes of the Caucasus from the barbarians. Under whatever name the request was made it was refused by Anastasius, and Kobad prepared for war. In the first year of the war the Persians, after a stubborn resistance, took the great city of Amida, the capital of the Roman territory on the upper waters of the Tigris. An army, or rather four armies under virtually independent commanders, were despatched by Anastasius to the seat of war. From want of co-operation and want of generalship these four armies effected little or nothing, blundering into a victory here and a defeat there, but on the whole losing ground before the able strategy of Kobad. It might perhaps have gone hard with the opulent cities of Syria but for the fortunate circumstance that Kobad himself was forced to return to defend his territory against the barbarians on the Oxus; and in his absence his generals fought as badly as those of Eome. The siege of Amida was vigorously pressed by the generals of Anastasius, and the Persians must in a very few days have surrendered it from want of provisions, when messengers came from Kobad proposing a peaceful settlement. If Anastasius would pay £40,000 Amida should be restored to him, and all should be again as it was before the war. The Roman generals accepted these terms, and did not discover till too late that Amida, which their master had bought for 1000 pounds of gold, was really theirs by right of conquest. However, the peace, which was concluded for seven years, lasted for one-and-twenty, and was doubtless a great advantage to both Empires.

The recovered city of Amida was so generously assisted by the Emperor that it soon seemed to flourish even more than it had done before the war broke out. Upon the whole, the Persian war, if it had not brought any great glory, had not brought shame on the arms of Anastasius.

In the year in which the Persian war ended (505), occurred the first passage of arms between the of Anastasius and those of Theodoric. This will therefore be the most suitable opportunity for reviewing the notices, scanty and scattered as they are, of the intercourse between the two monarchs.

We know from ecclesiastical history that in the year 493 Faustus, who was then Master or the Offices, was sent along with Irenaeus (like himself an Illustris) to Constantinople on the King's business, and that, on their return to Rome, Faustus did his utmost to heal the schism between the Churches by representing to Pope Gelasius the injury to the cause of orthodoxy which resulted from his insisting on the damnation of Acacius, whose memory was dear both to sovereign and people at Byzantium.

The only result of their representations, however, was a long and somewhat haughty letter from Gelasius to the Emperor, excusing himself for not having written before, assuring him that Gelasius as a Roman loved and venerated the Roman sovereign, but reminding him that there were two powers by which the world was governed, the sacred authority of pontiffs and the power of kings.

'Of these two, so much the weightier is the office of the priest inasmuch as he has to give account for kings also in the day of the Divine judgment. You know, most clement son, that though you excel all the rest of the human race in dignity, you must nevertheless meekly bow the neck to the chief stewards of the Divine mysteries when you receive the sacraments at their hands, and in the affairs of the Church it is for you to obey, not to command ... It is vain to say that the populace of Constantinople will not bear the condemnation of their late bishop. You have repressed their turbulence at the games : can you not in this matter, which concerns the good of souls, exert the same authority? Let them call the Apostolic See proud and arrogant: they are herein only like a sick man who blames the doctor that uses sharp measures for his restoration to health. If we are proud who do but obey the teaching of the Fathers, what are they to be called who resist us and fight against Divinity itself?'

Certainly the pretensions advanced by Pope Felix were not abated by his successor. We do not hear what reply the Emperor made to this lordly letter. We can hardly be wrong in supposing that the two ambassadors just mentioned, Faustus and Irenaeus, were sent by Theodoric to announce his final triumph over Odovacar, and to claim the ratification of the bargain made with Zeno, that Italy, if thus conquered, should be, perhaps, abandoned by the Empire, at any rate recognised as the possession of Theodoric. Apparently, however, the embassy was not successful. Anastasius was offended at Theodoric's haste in declaring himself king of the Romans as well as the Goths in the land of Italy, and perhaps refused to be bound by the undefined promises of his predecessor.

Again therefore, in the year 497, was an embassy sent to Constantinople. This time the royal envoy was the Patrician Festus, and he was accompanied by two bishops, Germanus and Cresconius, who bore a letter from the Pope. Gelasius was now dead, and the chair of St. Peter was filled by an Anastasius, namesake of the Caesar of Byzantium—a man of gentle and peaceable disposition, eager to end the quarrel which reflected so little and pacific credit on either of the two Churches. The letter of Anastasius the Pope to Anastasius the Emperor bore willing testimony to the virtues and the piety which the latter had displayed in a private station, and, though still not surrendering the indispensable damnation of the unfortunate Acacius, offered to recognise the validity of all orders conferred by the laying on of his hands. The ecclesiastical difference seemed in a fair way of being settled, and probably the conciliatory temper of the bishops smoothed the path for their colleague the Patrician. For (to quote again the words of the Anonymus Valesii transcribed in a former chapter[1]) 'Theodoric made his peace with the Emperor Anastasius, through the mediation of Festus, for his unauthorised assumption of the royal title. The Emperor also restored to him all the ornaments of the palace which Odoachar had transmitted to Constantinople.'

Thus, then, peace and friendship are established, on paper as well as in fact, between Ravenna and Constantinople, and Theodoric is formally recognised as, in some sense or other, legitimate ruler in Italy. What was the precise relation thus established between the two monarchs I must give up the attempt to explain. I see no statement of a formal abandonment by the Empire of the sacred soil of Italy; yet neither do I see any formal recognition by Theodoric that he was governing it in the Emperor's name, or that the latter was his superior. To me the whole matter seems to have been purposely left vague, as is so often the case when Fact and Law are felt by all parties to be hopelessly at variance with one another. A spectator of modern politics, who feels his inability to explain the precise legal relation of the Hapsburg monarch to the Sultan in respect to Bosnia, of the Queen of England to the same potentate in respect to Cyprus and Egypt, or even the exact nature of the tie which unites the Emperor of Germany to his crowned partners, or vassals, of Bavaria and Saxony, need not be ashamed to confess that he cannot absolutely decide whether Theodoric was dependent or independent of the Emperor of the New Rome.

Whatever may have been the exact title assumed by Theodoric, or the moral limits of his power, there is no doubt that geographically it extended far beyond the country which we call Italy. Of his Gaulish dominions enough has been already said. Raetia, including the eastern half of Switzerland, the Tyrol, and Bavaria south of the Danube, theoretically formed part of his kingdom, though in practice, as we have seen, the somewhat loosely subordinated Alamanni soon occupied most of the lands between the Alps and the Black Forest. In Noricum, Pannonia, and Illyricum, the whole that is of the modern Austrian Empire south and west of the Danube, Theodoric was regarded as the legitimate successor of the Emperors of the West. It is a question, which we have no means of solving, how far Rugians, Heruli, and Gepidae may practically have limited his dominions in this direction; but it is important to remember that, at any rate after the compact of 497, the Emperor of the East had no claim to rule directly in those countries any more than in Ravenna. Illyricum evidently was Theodoric's in fact, as well as in right. All that island-studded coast of Dalmatia, Diocletian's vast palace at Salona, and the highlands behind, which we now call Bosnia and Herzegovina, were really held by the strength of the Goths, and administered in accordance with the erudite rescripts of Cassiodorus. The frontier of the two monarchies was apparently that settled in the year 395 between the two sons of Theodosius; and thus Dyrrhachium, the birth-place of the Emperor Anastasius, was only some fifty miles south of that part of the Dalmatian coast-line which owned the sway of the great Ostrogoth.

This being the extent of Theodoric's rights in the Illyrian lands, he determined in 504 to vindicate them by a campaign against his old enemies the Gepidae. Doubtless he had not forgotten that hard fight by the river Ulca, when his people found their passage barred by the inhospitable King; but now, with his new rights, he found an additional grievance in the fact that Sirmium, one of the greatest cities in the whole Illyrian Prefecture, was held by the Gepid barbarians. The ruins of this great provincial capital lie near to Mitrovitz on the Save, in the extreme east of the modern province of Sclavonia. Nevertheless, from the point of view then taken, Bishop Ennodius was right in speaking of it to the King as 'the threshhold of Italy, in which the senators aforetime used to watch lest the neighbouring nations gathered round should inflict their deadly wounds on the body of the Boman people'. It was no alleviation of the calamity, says the Bishop, that the loss of this city had not happened under Theodoric's rule. It ought again to belong to Italy, and, till it was recovered, his honour felt a stain.

There seems to have been division in the councils of the Gepid nation, one part following Trasaric the son of Trastila (the king whom Theodoric had defeated at the river Ulca), and the other following: a certain Gunderith. Trasaric asked Theodoric's help against his rival, perhaps promised him Sirmium as a recompense. In course of time the Gothic King found that the promises of the Gepid were only made to be broken, and sent an army consisting of some of his noblest young Gothic warriors against him. Pitzias was leader of this expedition: the next in command was named Herduic. Tulum, a young Gothic noble employed in the household of the King, first made himself famous in this campaign. So too did a Gothic stripling named Witigis, who earned a reputation for valour in this campaign which was hereafter to be more fatal to his countrymen than the most pitiful display of cowardice could possibly have proved.

It is impossible to extract any details as to this war of Sirmium from the vapid rhetoric of Ennodius or the jejune sentences of Jordanes. All that can be said is that though the Gepids had procured the assistance of the Bulgarians—that new and terrible nationality which had lately shown itself on the banks of the Lower Danube— Theodoric's generals obtained a victory—an easy victory we are told—over the allied barbarians. Trasaric was expelled from Sirmium, and his mother, the widow of the inhospitable Trastila, was taken captive by Pitzias. In his treatment of the recovered city the general was careful to show that he looked upon it as a lost prize regained, not as an alien possession conquered. All tendency to ravage on the part of the soldiers was sternly checked, and the Sirmian citizens, when the standard of Theodoric was planted in their citadel, could again rejoice in the long-lost luxury of 'the Roman peace'.

This appearance of a Gothic army so near the frontier line of Theodoric and Anastasius not unnaturally brought their forces into collision. There was a certain Mundo, a son or grandson of Attila, who had fled from the face of the Gepidae, and was wandering through the valleys of what we now call Servia, at the head of a band of marauders, of whom, as Jordanes contemptuously says, he called himself king. Against this prince of freebooters the Emperor sent the general Sabinian, son and namesake of Theodoric's old antagonist. Ten thousand men marched under his standards, and a long train of waggons carried the arms and rations of the soldiers. Mundo, on the point of being overpowered, invoked the assistance of the Goths, and Pitzias descended from the mountains of Bosnia to his aid. The battle was joined in the valley of the Morava, at a place called Horrea Margi. If we may believe Jordanes, the Ostrogothic reinforcements consisted of only 2000 infantry and 500 cavalry. If we may believe Ennodius, the Bulgarians were again opposed to them, employed by the subtle Greeks as a bulwark to break the first fury of their onset. Perhaps, on putting the two accounts side by side, and observing that Marcellinus the chronicler (who acknowledges the defeat of the Imperial troops by Mundo without any reserve) makes no mention of the Ostrogoths on one side nor of the Bulgarians on the other, we may conclude that the arrangement between the confederates was that Mundo the Hun should deal with Sabinian and the troops of the Empire, while Pitzias with his disciplined Goths broke the fierce onset of the Bulgarians.

The Gothic general saw from afar the barbarian host rushing to the battle, and lashed the eager spirits of his own young warriors into fury by his impassioned words. 'Remember, my comrades, by whose order you have marched hither. We fight for the fame of our King, and let each man deem that his eyes are upon us. If a whole shower of lances darkened the sky the valiant warrior would still be visible. Plunge your breasts into that line of steel, that by your carelessness of life the victory may be assured. Have these men forgotten Theodoric? Is there not one living still who remembers how his mighty arm smote them long ago? Or do they think that Theodoric is unlike his people? They shall find that we can fight as well as our King.'

The battle, by the account of the conquerors themselves, was a hardly-fought one. Neither Bulgarians nor Goths would believe that it could be possible for a foe to resist the fury of their onset. But at length the desperate shock and countershock were over. It was seen that the Bulgarians were beaten, and with loud lamentations they, who boasted that they had never before turned their backs before an enemy, streamed from the lost battle-field.

Sabinian fled in terror when he saw the discomfiture of his confederates. Pitzias, we are told, that he might not incur the imputation of avarice, forbade his soldiers to strip the bodies of the slain, and left them to the dogs and the vultures. The very chivalry of these days was barbarous. We hear no more of Mundo, but Theodoric's courtier takes pride in declaring that 'the Roman realm has returned to its ancient limit. Once again, as in the days of old, the Sirmians are taught to obey : the neighbours who have hitherto been keeping back our possessions from us' (apparently the Eastern Emperors) 'are now made to tremble for their own territories'.

Three years after the war with Mundo, we find the ships of Byzantium making a piratical raid on the Apulian coast. Our information as to this affair comes entirely from a chronicler of the Eastern Empire (Marcellinus Comes), and he very honestly condemns an operation so unworthy of a Roman Emperor. His words are these : 'Romanus Count of the Domestics, and Rusticus Count of the Scholarii, with one hundred armed ships and as many cutters bearing eight thousand armed men, went forth to ravage the coasts of Italy. They proceeded as far as the very ancient city of Tarentum, and then, recrossing the sea, bore back to Anastasius Caesar [the news of] this inglorious victory which, with pirate-daring, Romans had snatched from Romans'.

As we hear no more of raids or revenges between the two states we may perhaps conclude that the complaints of Theodoric and the condemnation hinted by his subjects, caused Anastasius, himself at heart a lover of peace, to lay aside his unfriendly attitude and to resume the peaceful intercourse which had been for three years interrupted. If so, we may possibly place about this time a letter—the first in the collection of Cassiodorus—which was borne by two ambassadors from the Court of Ravenna to that of Constantinople. In that letter, Theodoric, or rather Cassiodorus writing in his name, complains, in well-chosen and weighty words, of the interruption of friendly relations with 'the most clement Emperor'. He praises the condition of Peace : Peace, the fair mother of all noble arts, the nurse of the succeeding generations, by whom the race of man is prolonged, who is the softener of savage manners. Theodoric himself learnt 'in your republic' how to govern Romans with a mild and equal sway. His kingdom is meant to be an imitation of the Emperor's : the Senate who are the Emperor's friends are his also; and his love for the venerable city of Rome is or ought to be another powerful link between them. The two republics, which under earlier sovereigns were always looked upon as forming one body, ought to be not only not discordant but bound to one another by bonds of love, ought not merely to love, but actively and vigorously to help one another. With words of courtly greeting to the 'most glorious charity of your Mildness,' but words which seem carefully framed to convey compliments only, without any recognition of real superiority, Theodoric concludes by referring the Emperor to his ambassadors for fuller information as to his feelings.

Either on this occasion, or another of his numerous embassies to the Eastern Court, Theodoric sent Agapetus (Patrician and Illustris) to represent him. In the letter charging him with this appointment he is informed that, for such a commission as his, it is necessary that 'a man of eminent prudence be selected, one who can dispute with persons of the keenest subtlety, and so manage as not to lose his cause in an assembly of literati, where the best-trained intellects of the world will come against him. Great art is required in dealing with these artful men, who think that they can anticipate every argument that you can employ.'

It is possible that among these word-fencers whom the ambassadors of Theodoric had to contend with, there may have been a man whose name is memorable in the history of the Latin tongue, Priscian the Grammarian. We possess a poem of his in praise of Anastasius, written in flowing hexameters, much above the ordinary level of the Latinity of his times. The descent of the Emperor from Pompey the Great, his Isaurian victories, his abolition of the Chrysargyron, his establishment of public granaries, his repression of the factions of the Circus, are all duly commemorated. One of the titles given to the Emperor (besides Isauricus and Parthicus) is Gotthicus, a circumstance which seems to point to a date after the outbreak of hostilities with Theodoric for the delivery of the oration. And in the poem occur the following remarkable lines, which indicate that then, at any rate, notwithstanding all the optimism of Cassiodorus, there were some Romans disposed to look upon the Emperor, not the King, as their natural sovereign and protector:—

'But of all acts our grateful praise that claim,
Two, mighty Prince! most illustrate your name.
The first, your choice of rulers for the land,
And then, your goodness to the exiled band.
All of her sons whom Elder Rome may send
You greet, you succour, as a fostering friend.
Step after step they mount in your employ,
Till grief for their lost country turns to joy.
Fortune and life to you, great lord, they owe,
And night and day for you their prayers shall flow'

But whatever disposition Anastasius may have felt to trade upon the doubtful loyalty of the Romans towards a Gothic ruler, the increasing discontent of his own subjects towards the end of his reign found him employment enough, without his engaging in any further contests with Theodoric. We must now plunge therefore into those dreary theological faction-fights which were briefly referred to at the commencement of the chapter.

The state of ecclesiastical parties in the Empire throughout this whole period was most peculiar, and was enough to strain the powers and the patience of the wisest and the most enduring of rulers.

There was Egypt, venerating the memory of Cyril above all other ecclesiastics, cherishing, if not venerating, the name of Eutyches, set upon maintaining to the uttermost the doctrine of the unity of the nature of Jesus Christ, who, they maintained, as God was born, as God was crucified.

Syria, which had given birth to the opposite doctrine, that of Nestorius (whose denial that Mary was rightly called 'the Mother of God' had brought about all this controversy), fluctuated still between Nestorianism and Monophysitism in the strangest and most bewildering uncertainty.

At Constantinople the populace, led by a rabble of fanatical monks, were attached with incomprehensible fervour of loyalty, not to Eutychianism, not to Nestorianism, but to the very name of the Council of Chalcedon, which excommunicated both, and proclaimed the narrow Via Media of orthodoxy between them. Middle ways do not generally thus enlist the passions of a religious mob in their behalf. But so it was, that throughout the reign of Anastasius, if at any time words were used by a person in a prominent position which seemed to reflect on 'the Synod of the Six Hundred and Thirty' (the number of fathers who met at Chalcedon), blood might be expected soon to flow in the streets of Constantinople.

The upper classes seem at this time to have been generally Monophysite, or at least strongly attached to the Henoticon of Zeno. They probably felt the danger of dismembering the Empire which would be incurred by crushing the fanaticism of Alexandria by the fanaticism of Constantinople.

And Rome, the seat of Peter, and still in a certain sense, notwithstanding her barbarian rulers, the capital of the Empire? Bome seemed at this time to have no ears for the original controversy; so set was she on maintaining the damnation of Acacius, who had dared to excommunicate a pope. Of course she was out of communion with Monophysite Alexandria, but then she was equally out of communion with orthodox Constantinople, which held fast by the Council of Chalcedon and venerated the Tome of Leo, but which would not strike the name of Acacius out of her diptychs. Bishop after bishop of that see suffered persecution and exile for maintaining the faith of Chalcedon against the Monophysite Emperor; but as they would not admit that Acacius was inevitably damned, Rome, the champion of Chalcedon, would have none of them.

Anastasius, as has been already said, was probably at heart, like most of the Byzantine nobles, a Monophysite. But he was strongly suspected, and probably with truth, of the much more dangerous heresy of caring very little about the whole matter, and preferring justice and mercy and the practice of the Christian virtues to all this interminable wrangle about such questions as whether Christ ought to be said to subsist in two natures or to consist of them. While he was still in a private station, he had been accused of attending the conventicles of the heretics and yet retaining his seat in the great Catholic Basilica. Euphemius the bishop had sent for him, and sharply rebuked him for such dangerous dalliance with error, concluding the interview by a threat that, if the offence were repeated, he would cut off his hair and expose him to the derision of the mob. This story, it should be said, rests on the doubtful authority of Suidas. It seems improbable that even the Patriarch of Constantinople would dare to use such a menace to an officer of the household, past middle life and held in high honour by the people.

However, the doubt, the suspicion as to the orthodoxy of the elderly Silentiarius, devout and charitable as all tongues proclaimed him to be, remained in the mind of the Patriarch Euphemius. When Ariadne presented him to the Senate as the future Emperor, Euphemius long resisted his election, and at length, it is said, only withdrew the objection on receiving from Anastasius a written confession of his faith, in which he declared that he held as true all the decrees of the Council of Chalcedon. No doubt if such a humiliating condition were enforced upon him, the remembrance of it would rankle in the mind of the new Emperor, who is said to have made the recovery of the document, either from Euphemius or his successor, the main object of his ecclesiastical policy for some years. There is some variation, however, in the accounts of this matter given by the different historians, and, as we so often find to be the case, the further they are removed from the transaction the more detailed does their information about it become. Probably the importance of the affair has been overrated by ecclesiastics.

Anastasius, however, had reason enough to look coldly on Euphemius, not only as the personal enemy who had threatened to subject him to bitter humiliation, but also as the partisan, and hardly the secret partisan, of his rival the Isaurian Longinus. In the year 496, after the close of the Isaurian campaign, when, according to the triumphant Emperor, 'the prayers of the Patriarch had covered his friends with soot'; by one of those exertions of high-handed power which were becoming almost the rule at Constantinople, Anastasius deposed Euphemius from his see, and sent him into exile at Euchaita, a city of Pontus. The demand for his deposition came undoubtedly from the Emperor, but it was apparently carried into effect in a regular manner by a synod of bishops, before whom Anastasius laid the proofs of the Patriarch's treasonable complicity with the Isaurian insurgents. It was, at any rate ostensibly, for political not for theological offences that Euphemius was cast down from his high place.

The new Patriarch of Constantinople was Macedonius, a gentle and sweet-souled man, too good for the days of wrangle in which he lived. Euphemius, before his departure for the solitudes of Pontus, desired to have the sworn promise of his successor that he should not be molested on his journey. Macedonius, who had the permission of the Emperor to grant this safe-conduct, was told that his predecessor was in the baptistery of the basilica, waiting for the interview. With generous thoughtfulness he called to a deacon and desired him to take off from his shoulders the bishop's mantle, that he might not seem to flaunt before the eyes of the fallen Patriarch the ensigns of a dignity which was no longer his. He also himself borrowed money from the Usurers to provide for the travelling expenses of Euphemius and his retinue. The banished man lived on for nineteen years in exile; apparently had to change his place of abode on account of the invading Huns; and died in 515 at Ancyra in Galatia.

During the fifteen years that Macedonius governed the Church of Constantinople there was a division, growing gradually wider and wider, between him and his Emperor. At the time of his elevation he signed the Henoticon, and perhaps anathematised the Council of Chalcedon. Gradually however, under the influence of the monastic and popular enthusiasm which prevailed in the capital, he 'hardened into a stern, almost a fanatic partisan of that very Council.' With the usual fairness of religious disputants, the man who battled on behalf of the Via Media with Eutychians was accused of himself inclining to Nestorianism. One charge made against him in this connection and much insisted upon was that, in order to support his heretical views, he had altered a letter in a celebrated passage of the New Testament which has often since been the battlefield of controversy.

The increasing estrangement between the Emperor and the Patriarch, the increasing irritation of the Chalcedonian mob at the proceedings of their sovereign (who everywhere, but especially in Syria, was pressing more and more heavily on those bishops who did not accept the Henoticon), was brought to a crisis by the proceedings of a band of strangers and schismatics, who one Sunday burst into the Chapel of the Archangel in the Imperial Palace, and dared to chaunt the Te Deum with the addition of the forbidden words, the war-cry of many an Eutychian mob, 'Who wast crucified for us'. The Trisagion, as it was called, the thrice-repeated cry to the Holy One, which Isaiah in his vision heard uttered by the seraphim, became, by the addition of these words, as emphatic a statement as the Monophysite party could desire of their favourite tenet that God, not man, breathed out his soul unto death outside the gates of Jerusalem. What one party asserted with the loud voice of defiant psalmody the other party were of course bound to deny, maintaining their denial, if need were, by force. On the next Sunday the Monophysites sang the verse which was their war-cry in the great Basilica itself. Shouts were heard from the angry mob; to shouts succeeded taunts; to taunts blows and strifes. The magistrates, acting perhaps at the instigation of the Emperor, loudly and fiercely upbraided Macedonius as the author of all this tumult. But there were men, well-known faction leaders, on the other side, whose presence goaded the Chalcedonian populace to fury. Chief among these was Severus, who had been throwing all Syria into confusion by his zeal for the condemnation of the synod, and who was to be rewarded for his turbulence by being seated on the episcopal throne of Antioch. It was soon seen on which side the voice of the multitude was given. A vast crowd of citizens, accompanied by and in the their wives and children, and headed by the abbots of the orthodox monasteries, surged through the streets of Constantinople, shouting, 'Christians, lo, the day of martyrdom! Let no one abandon our father!'. They hurled their insults at the Emperor himself, denouncing him as a Manichean, as unworthy to reign.

Anastasius, terrified at the turn which things had taken, ordered the great gates of the palace on every side to be barred, and the ships made ready for his flight. So he sat solitary in the vast enclosure, trembling at the brutal clamours which reached him from without. At length he determined to bend to the storm. Though he had sworn that he would never again look upon the face of Macedonius, he sent some trusty retainers to the Patriarch to beg him to come and salute him. As Macedonius, in that his hour of triumph, glided through the streets, the mob shouted with joy, 'Our father is still with us!', and, ominous sound for the Emperor, the soldiers of the household regiments, through whose ranks he passed, echoed the cry. When the Patriarch entered the presence chamber, he frankly rebuked the Emperor for his alleged enmity to the Church. An apparent reconciliation was effected. The mild character of the Patriarch (who had not only forgiven but sent away with a handsome present an assassin who sought his life) made the restoration of peace an easy task.

The reconciliation, however, was but superficial. The dignity of the Emperor had been too deeply wounded for it to be real. Yet, from fear of the populace, he did not dare to bring the venerated Patriarch openly to trial. He caused him to be hurried out of his palace, rowed across the Bosporus to Chalcedon, and thence escorted to the same little town of Euchaita whither his predecessor had been conveyed fifteen years before. A council was hastily summoned, and the absent Patriarch was deposed from his see.

After four years of exile at Euchaita, he was driven by a Hunnish invasion to Gangra, a town in Paphlagonia, where he shortly after died. One of his faithful followers declared that on the night of his decease the injured Patriarch appeared to him, having in his hand a roll, and saying, 'Depart hence, and read what is here written to Anastasius'. In the roll was written, 'I indeed depart to my fathers, whose faith I too have kept. But I shall not cease to importune the Lord until thou comest, that the cause between us two may be brought to judgment.'

Anastasius in fact survived Macedonius three years, but he lived somewhat too long for his fame. The irregular and illegal deposition of the Patriarch is one of the worst acts that can be laid to his charge; and the remaining seven years of his life were poisoned by the results which flowed from it—an ever-increasing unpopularity with his Byzantine subjects, and an ever-dwindling hope of seeing the fires of religious faction dying out and peace restored to the Empire. Again, in the year after the expulsion of Macedonius, the terrible war-cry of the corrupted Trisagion sounded through the streets of Constantinople. It was on a memorable day that the flames of religious war were thus rekindled. The 6th of November in every year was kept as a solemn fast, in memory of that awful day in 472 when the heaven at Constantinople was blackened with the ashes of Vesuvius, while half the cities of Asia Minor were rocking with the violence of an earthquake. On the Sunday which preceded the fortieth of these anniversaries, Marinus, the able but grasping Praetorian Prefect, and Plato the Prefect of the city, were standing in their place of honour in the Great Church of Constantinople, when the singers (as it was believed by their command) thundered forth the words, 'Holy, Holy, Holy, Lord God Almighty,' with the terrible addition breathing defiance, menace, and insult, 'Who wast crucified for us.' The orthodox took up the strain and chaunted the verse in the way used by their forefathers. Again psalmody gave place to blows : men wounded and dying lay upon the floor of the church; the ringleaders of the tumult were led off to the dungeons of the city. Next day the scene of strife was transferred to the atrium or oblong porch in front of the Church of St. Theodore, and a yet greater slaughter of the champions of the Catholic faith took place there. On the third day, the 6th of November, the day ot the solemn procession, the orthodox mob streamed from all parts into the great forum. There they swarmed and swayed to and fro all that day and all that night, shouting forth, not the greatness of the Ephesian Diana, but 'Holy, Holy, Holy,' without the words 'Who wast crucified.' They hewed down the monks—a minority of their class—who were on the side of the imperial creed, and burned their monasteries with fire. They carried the standards of the army and the keys of the various gates of the city to the Forum, where a sort of camp was established, with monks for its officers. A poor monk from the country was found hiding in the palace of Marinus. Having persuaded themselves that it was by his advice that the deadly words had been added to the hymn, they cut off his head and carried it about on a pole, shouting, 'See the head of an enemy of the Trinity!' The statues of Anastasius were thrown down. The Emperor's nephew Patricius, and Celer Master of the Offices and general-in-chief in the Persian War, were sent to the   populace with soothing words; but, notwithstanding their senatorial rank, they were greeted with a shower of stones. Ominous cries claimed the Empire for Areobinda, related by marriage to the family of Valentinian III, and a general who had achieved some successes in the Persian War. The houses of Marinus the Prefect and of Pompeius, a nephew of the Emperor, were burned. At length, after two days of continued riot, the triumphant mob, fresh from their work of destruction, brandishing gospel and cross as the ensigns of their war, and shouting 'Holy, Holy, Holy,' without the heretical addition, streamed into the Circus Maximus and stood before the Podium of the Emperor. There on his imperial throne, but without the diadem or the purple, sat the aged monarch (he who was now eighty-one years of age), and seemed by his helpless attitude to enquire what was their will. The mob shouted that the two Prefects, Marinus and Plato, should be thrown to the wild beasts. No lighter punishment, in the judgment of those accurate theologians, would suffice for the crime of these men, who had added four words to the Trisagion. Anastasius, whose own voice was no doubt 'changed to a childish treble' could not himself answer the hoarse hymn-shouters, but he bade the criers make proclamation to the people that he was ready, if they wished it, to lay down the burden of empire; but, inasmuch as all could not be masters, it would be necessary that his successor should be chosen. Perhaps this was an adroit device to divide the victorious Chalcedonians, united in opposition to Anastasius, but not united in their choice of Areobinda or any other successor. Perhaps the mob were touched with pity and relenting at the sight of those white hairs uncrowned and bowed low before them. Whatever the cause, the multitude were appeased. They melted away out of the streets and Forum and back into their homes, having received from the Emperor nothing but fair words, perhaps promises and oaths to respect the faith of Chalcedon.

The promises, if they were given, were not kept; for, though the Emperor seems to have abstained from again shocking his subjects in the capital by the sound of the heretical Trisagion, he continued, with the help of Timotheus, his Monophysite Patriarch of Constantinople, to rule the Church in the interests of the heretical party, no longer, it would seem, contented with exacting the signature of Zeno's Henoticon, but insisting on an express anathema to the Council of Chalcedon. For refusing this anathema the gentle Flavianus, who had tried to please all parties, and had satisfied none, was thrust out from the see of Antioch, where the busy Monophysite Severus reigned in his stead. All over the East, especially in Syria, was heard the wail of the orthodox for sees widowed of their Catholic bishops and handed over to heretical intruders.

The discontent caused by these high-handed proceedings furnished a pretext which enabled a military adventurer named Vitalian to shake the throne of Anastasius. Though the son of an officer in the imperial army, Vitalian was of Gothic extraction. He was a man of diminutive stature, and had a stutter in his speech : he had all the fire and the courage necessary to lead a band of mutineers and barbarians to victory, and along therewith the address to feign an interest (which he can hardly have felt) in the theological controversy, and to link his cause with that of the prelates deposed for their adherence to the Council of Chalcedon. This was the pretext for rebellion which was flaunted before the eyes of the Byzantine populace, and which has to some extent imposed on later ecclesiastical historians, who have looked upon him as the champion, certainly the ruthless champion, of the Fourth Council of the Catholic faith. The recently-discovered fragments, however, of the history of Joannes Antiochenus (who evidently drew from nearly contemporary sources) show that the rebellion had a much more ignoble origin. Vitalian had a grievance in his removal from the office of distributor of the rations to the foederati; the mutinous soldiers alleged that they had a grievance in the withholding of some arrears of pay; the Huns, who formed perhaps the bulk of the army, needed no excuse at all for their willingness to swarm across the

Danube under the guidance of their savage chiefs Saber and Tarrach and the like, and to devastate the cultivated plains of Moesia and Thrace.

The war was waged chiefly in the neighbourhood of Varna (then called Odessus); but twice, nay three times, Vitalian, by a bold dash through the passes of the Balkan, or by assembling a fleet and sailing along the Euxine coast, succeeded in penetrating to the very suburbs of Constantinople. The first time, Anastasius affixed to the city gates brazen crosses with a long statement of the true origin of the insurrection, to disprove Vitalian's assumption of the character of a champion of the faith. At the same time he promised—and this has an important bearing on our main subject—that 'he would bring men from Old Rome to settle matters concerning the faith.' To remove the discontent of the taxpayers he announced that he remitted a fourth part of the tax on cattle for the provinces of Bithynia and Asia, and deposited the paper containing this pledge on the Holy Table in the Great Church.

For the time Vitalian retired, and the wave of war rolled back across the Balkans. The insurgent general was declared a public enemy by the Senate, and an army of 80,000 men was despatched against him, under the command of the Emperor's nephew Hypatius. The Roman army was encamped behind its waggons at a spot called Akrae, on he sea-coast a little north of Varna. The arrows of the Huns dealt death among the draught oxen, their savage onset broke the line of the waggons, and then (we are gravely told), in the mist raised by their enchantments, the panic-stricken and flying Romans fell into a deep ravine, where they perished, to the number of 60,000. Their dead bodies piled one upon another filled the rocky chasm. Hypatius fled to the shore and tried to hide himself in the sea, but his head, 'like a sea-bird's', was seen above the waves : the barbarians dashed into the breakers and captured their valuable prize, the nephew of an Emperor. Vitalian pushed on with a fleet of 200 ships to the suburbs of Constantinople, and overpowered the imperial general John, who rushed into his master's presence and implored him to grant the enemy's terms, however hard they might be. Dispirited by so terrible a defeat of his troops and by the capture of his nephew, Anastasius consented to treat, conferred on Vitalian the dignity of Magister Militum of Thrace, paid him the enormous sum of £200,000 as ransom for Hypatius, and, it is to be feared, made some promises, even swore some oaths, which were not meant to be kept, that he would restore to their episcopal thrones the exiled adherents of Chalcedon.

The slippery character of Anastasius made it well-nigh impossible for him ever to end a dispute. Vitalian felt sure that the Emperor was plotting against him, and next year resolved to anticipate the blow by another dash for Constantinople. A battle by land and sea followed, under the very walls of the capital. Now at length fortune turned against the fiery little Gothic rebel. A rough Thracian soldier named Justin, who had fought his way up from the lowest ranks to the position of Captain of the Guard (Excubitorum Praefectus), thrust his ship boldly forwards into the hostile fleet, which was commanded by Vitalian himself, grappled a ship, made prisoners of all the soldiers on board, and struck such terror into the sailors of Vitalian that they turned and fled. Seeing this, the army on land fled likewise, leaving heaps of their comrades slaughtered on the field. Soon the whole force of Vitalian, Huns, mutinous Romans, Goths, had melted away like snow in summer; and the arch-rebel himself, so lately an important personage in the state and the arbiter between contending creeds, slunk away into obscurity, in which he remained for the rest of the reign of Anastasius.

At the end of the year 514, while the rebels' power was still unbroken, the Emperor, in fulfilment of his promise to Vitalian to settle the dispute concerning the faith in concert with the Bishop of Old Rome, sent two letters to Hormisdas, who now sat in the chair of St. Peter, saying that the common fame of the Pope's gentleness and moderation induced him to break the long silence caused by the harshness of his predecessors, and to suggest that a council, at which the Pope should preside, and in which he should act as mediator, should be held at Heraclea on the shore of the Propontis (about 60 miles west of Constantinople), in order to settle the affairs of the Church and heal the troubles which had arisen in the province of Scythia. The day for the Council's assembling was to be the 1st of July, 515. Hormisdas sent a prompt and courteous reply, declaring that peace was his desire, as it had been that of his venerable predecessors. The time for the Council was too near, perhaps had been purposely fixed at too early a date, to make it possible for the Pope and his bishops to attend it; but the ice had now been broken, and negotiations between Rome and Constantinople could go forward, whether the Council were ever to assemble or not. On the 8th of July Hormisdas again sent a short note to the Emperor, commending his zeal for the restoration of unity to the Church, and referring him to the five legates whom he was at the same time despatching from Rome, for fuller information as to the terms upon which he would assist at a new Council.

The legates (two bishops, a presbyter, a deacon, and a notary) were headed by Ennodius, Bishop of Ticinum, whom we already know so well as biographer of Epiphanius and turgid panegyrist of Theodoric. The letter of instructions (*Indiculus*) addressed to these legates is still preserved; a long and circumstantial document and curiously characteristic of its author and of the times. Throughout the letter runs that almost exaggerated fear of Greek subtlety, that sense of inferiority to Greek diplomacy, which we trace also in the works of Cassiodorus. We have seen how, in instructing Theodoric's ambassador to Constantinople, the accomplished secretary had warned him of the difficulty of dealing with men 'who think they can foresee everything'. It was with a determination to foresee everything that Hormisdas supplied Ennodius and his colleagues with this marvellous paper, which sought to anticipate every possible opening of the game by the Emperor, and to indicate the proper reply upon the ecclesiastical chessboard. A few extracts may indicate the character of these instructions.

'When you are come into the parts of Greece, if the bishops come out to meet you, receive them with all due respect. If they prepare a lodging for you, do not refuse it, lest the laity should think that the hindrance to concord comes from you. But if they ask you to a meal decline with a gentle apology, saying, Pray that we may be permitted first to meet at the Mystic Table, and then this hospitality of yours will be all the sweeter." When by the favour of God you are come to Constantinople, lodge in the quarters assigned to you by the most clement Emperor, and allow nobody to visit you till you have had your first audience with him. Afterwards you may receive the visits of the orthodox, and of those who seem to have the cause of union at heart. Use caution in conversing with them, and you may obtain useful hints for your own guidance.

'When you are presented to the Emperor, hold out our letter and say, "Your Father salutes you, daily entreating God and commending your kingdom to the intercessions of the holy apostles Peter and Paul, that God who has put this desire into your heart, to work for the happiness of the Church, may carry it on unto perfection."

'If he wishes to enter on the subject of the embassy before opening our letter, you shall use these words, "Command us to hand you the writings." If he shall say, "What do the papers contain?" reply, "Salutations to your Piety and thanks to God for making you desire the unity of the Church. Read, and you will see." Make no mention of the matter in hand till he has received the letters and read them.'

'After he has done this, add, "Your servant Vitalian, having received, as he said, permission from your Piety, sent his messengers to your Father the holy Pope. To him also we have letters, but, as is fitting, have first directed our course to your Clemency, that we may receive your command to bear our message to him." Should the Emperor ask to see our letters to Vitalian, you must answer, "Your holy father the Pope gave us no such commandment : we cannot do anything of the kind unbidden. Yet that you may know that they contain nothing but that which furthers your own desire for the unity of the Church, associate with us some person in whose presence the letters which we deliver to Vitalian may be read aloud". If he says again that he ought to read them himself, answer again that the Holy Father did not so order you. If he says, "Is all your message contained in the letters? are there not perhaps some verbal communications beside?" you must answer, "Be that far from our conscience. That is not our custom. We come only in God's service. The Holy Pope's commission is a simple one, and his desire is known to all men, being only this, that the decrees of the fathers be not tampered with, and that heretics may be banished from the Church. Our legation relates to nothing else but this".'

We need not closely follow the imaginary interview through all its succeeding stages, which are chiefly theological, not political. At a certain point, it was expected that the Emperor would say, 'We have received and still hold the Synod of Chalcedon and the letters of Pope Leo'. At this confession of faith the legates were to kiss his breast, and to return thanks to God for giving him this conviction of the Catholic faith, preached by the Apostles, without which no man can be orthodox. If he was to try to throw the blame of the schism on the late Pope Symmachus, predecessor of Hormisdas, they were to reply that they had the letters of Symmachus in their hands, which contained nothing but exhortations to persevere in the faith of Chalcedon. They were then to have recourse to prayers and tears, saying, 'Lord Emperor! think upon God: place before your eyes his coming judgment. The holy fathers who taught thus have but followed the Apostles' faith, by which was builded up the Church of Christ. '

After a good deal more imaginary debate the legates were again to shed tears, and to allude in a humble and delicate way to the controversy which distracted the Church of Constantinople itself. The Emperor would perhaps say, 'You are talking about Macedonius; I understand your finesse. He is a heretic: it is quite impossible that he should be recalled'. Then the legates were to reply, 'We, Lord Emperor, mention no one by name. But let your Piety consider, from your own point of view, how much better it would be that there should be a discussion on this point, and that his heresy, if he be a heretic, should be judicially settled, rather than that the orthodox should think him to be unjustly deposed.'

This brought them to the question of the legitimacy of the consecration of Timotheus, whom the legates were immovably to refuse to recognise in any way as legitimate Patriarch of Constantinople. They were not to allow themselves to be presented by him to the Emperor, and if he was standing by the throne they were to ask for a secret interview, in which they would deliver the papal commission.

Finally, they were to announce to Anastasius that the terms upon which Hormisdas would consent to waive a point of personal dignity, and come to preside at a council held out of Rome, were, (1) public recognition of the Council of Chalcedon and the letters of Leo; (2) public anathematisation of the heretics Nestorius, Eutyches, and the like, who had, on one side or the other, deviated from Chalcedonian orthodoxy, and express inclusion of the name of Acacius among these heretics; (3) the recall of all bishops sent into exile for their fidelity to the Eoman see; and (4) the removal of the cases of all bishops banished for any ecclesiastical offence, to Rome, there to be tried by the Apostolic See. In fact these terms, however gently and persuasively and tearfully urged, involved a surrender at discretion of all the points at issue between Emperor and Pope.

How the actual interview between the aged Anastasius and the verbose Ennodius and his colleagues passed off we are unable to say, but, as they could not arrive in Constantinople till October, 515, it is easy to imagine that they found the Emperor in a mood little disposed for conciliation. The Pope's correspondent Vitalian had doubtless before that time met his crushing defeat at the hands of Justin. Now that he was a fugitive, and his wild Hunnish marauders were scattered to the winds, the bland excuses, the accurately measured tears, and the punctilious breast-kissings of the Roman envoys might even be found somewhat burdensome by the Byzantine Caesar.

Still, the negotiations were not wholly dropped, though the proposed Council faded more and more into oblivion. In a long letter sent back by the hands of Ennodius, Anastasius declared his adhesion to the teaching of Leo and Chalcedon, but suggested that it was hard that living men should be kept out of the Church on account of the dead, and that to anathematise Acacius would cause the effusion of much human blood.

In July of the following year he sent two high officers of his Court, Theopompus Count of the Domestics (an Illustris) and Severianus Count of the Consistory (a Clarissimus), with letters both to the Pope and the Senate. The first letter was chiefly filled with excuses, somewhat hollow excuses, for his tardy action in the matter of the reunion of the Churches. The length of the journey and the unusual severity of the preceding winter are made to bear the burden of this delay. The other letter throws an interesting light on the difficult question of the relations existing between the Caesar of Byzantium, the Gothic King, and the Senate of Rome. It begins :—

28 July, 'The Emperor Caesar Flavius Anastasius, pious, fortunate, victorious, ever august, renowned conqueror of the Germans, of the Franks, of the Sarmatians, father of his country, says Hail! to the proconsuls, the consuls, the praetors, the tribunes of the commons, and to his Senate. If you and your children are in good health it is well. I and my army are in good health also.'

In using this well-known classical formula, the Emperor says 'I and my army' where Cicero would have said 'I and Terentia,' to indicate the close bond of union which in theory always existed between the Imperator and his dutiful soldiers. The use of the possessive pronoun before Senate must, one would think, have jarred upon the ears of Theodoric, when he heard the document read in his *Comitatus* at Ravenna.

The rest of the letter was couched in terms which would not be displeasing to the Gothic King. The Emperor begged the Conscript Fathers to join their prayers with his, prayers which might reasonably be expected to avail 'both with the most glorious King and with the very blessed Pope of the fair city of Rome for the restoration glorious of peace. And again, near the close of the letter, they are asked to use their utmost efforts for this end, 'both with the exalted King to whom the power and the responsibility of ruling you is committed, and with the venerable Pope, to whom is entrusted the capacity to intercede for you with God.' It would be difficult to express more clearly that Constantinople recognised, as in some sense legitimate, the rule of Theodoric.

The Senate replied to the Emperor in a letter full of suitable quotations from Scripture on the beauty of peace and the blessings of charity. The sentiments which they express are excellent, and it is only when one sees the title at the beginning, and thinks of those grey old war-wolves who used to be the terror of Italy and the world, that one feels a slight sense of incongruity in the thought that this meritorious, if somewhat vapid, pastoral was addressed to a Roman Imperator by a Roman Senatus. They accept the designation of your Senate, and say that 'the mind of our lord and most unconquered King, your son Theodoric, who orders obedience to your commands,' tends in the same direction as that of Anastasius.

The real pivot of the negotiation however was, of course, neither King nor Senate, but Pope. Hormisdas, who was offended, somewhat unreasonably one would think, at the Emperor's having sent only laymen, though laymen of high rank, as his ambassadors, had come to the conclusion that the Greeks talked of peace with their lips, but did not care for it in their hearts, and while sending Ennodius on a second embassy to the Emperor, charged him with a letter, written in somewhat sharper tone than those which had preceded it, insisting on the absolutely indispensable damnation of Acacius. Acacius had rolled himself in all the mire of Peter the Stammerer, Dioscorus, and Eutyches. Acacius had spread the poison of Monophysite heresy, which before had only infected Alexandria, far and wide through the Churches. The wound of the Church could not be healed without his damnation. As for the angry feeling which such a proceeding might raise among the mob, sovereigns could bend their subjects to their will. Who heard anything about the wishes of the populace when Marcian, of religious memory, established the faith of Chalcedon? And so the letter ended with an earnest, almost imperious call to the Emperor to acquiesce in the monitions of his spiritual father.

Ennodius and his colleague Peregrinus reached Constantinople at the beginning of July. The Emperor, who for all his eighty-six summers was by this time thoroughly aroused by the obstinacy of the Pope, and who perhaps had ceased to care greatly about the question of reunion, entirely refused to accept the terms of Hormisdas, and forced the legates out of the city, charging the two Prefects with a band of Inland Revenue officers to accompany them on ship-board, and to see that they landed at no city of the Empire. Notwithstanding this pressure, however, they contrived to hand to their monkish partisans in the capital the copies of a protest which they had prepared for circulation through all the Eastern Churches.

To Hormisdas the Emperor addressed a short answer but dignified letter, which, after some rather commonplace reflections upon the mercy and long-suffering of the Most High, he thus concluded:— 'We think, therefore, that those who have themselves received mercy, ought not to show themselves merciless. But from henceforth we shall keep silence as to the request which we made of you, thinking it absurd to show the courtesy of prayers to men who stubbornly refuse all that is asked of them. We can bear insults and contempt, but we cannot allow ourselves to be commanded.'

So ended the correspondence between Anastasius and Hormisdas. In the following year the aged Emperor died. Strange portents, according to the ecclesiastical historians, marked his death. A terrible thunderstorm was raging, and Anastasius, to whom it had been foretold that he should die by such a storm, crept into an inner apartment and was there found by his servants dead; but whether struck by a flash of lightning, or slain only by his own fears, none could tell. On the same day Elias, the deposed Patriarch of Jerusalem, had a revelation that the Emperor. was dead, and that he himaelf was to follow in ten days to bear witness against him before the throne of God. A short time before the death of the Emperor, according to the foolish story of some late writers, a man clothed in white raiment was seen by him in a vision, turning over the leaves of a book which he held in his hand. With a frown the supernatural visitor said, 'In punishment for thy impiety, behold I strike off fourteen', and therewith cancelled fourteen years of the Emperor's life, who, it seems, might otherwise have attained the age of a hundred and one.

All this stir in heaven and earth over the death of a sovereign who had entered his eighty-eighth year, may, at any rate, be taken as a proof that he had not sunk into dotage, but had still energy enough to inspire energetic hatred. We picture him to ourselves with his tall figure still unbowed by age, with his steel-blue eyes not dimmed, nor the vigour of his intellect abated. Two testimonies which we possess concerning him outweigh many of the fierce censures of his ecclesiastical opponents : the acclamation 'Reign as you have lived!' with which the populace hailed the news of his accession, and the phrase 'sweetest-tempered of sovereigns' which the notary Lydus, years after his death, when nothing was to be gained by praising him, dropped by his half-forgotten grave.

Yet, with many noble qualities, Anastasius hardly attained to greatness. He allowed himself to be forced from a position of calm impartiality between warring sects, into one of bitter partisanship on behalf of a single sect, and that the one which has eventually been judged heretical. And in his dealings both with the external and internal enemies of the Empire, he certainly showed himself more a Greek than a Roman in his lack of the kingly quality of truthfulness.

On the very day of the death of Anastasius, Justin, Captain of the Guard, and lately the conqueror of Vitalian, was raised to the throne, nominally by the Senate, but really by the household troops. The means by which this rough and illiterate Thracian soldier attained to the first place in the civilised world were simple, if not in the highest degree praiseworthy. Amantius, an eunuch and Grand Chamberlain, who had been allpowerful in the later years of Anastasius, desired to maintain his hold of power by placing on the throne a certain Theocritus, whom he deemed to be entirely devoted to his interests. For this purpose he deposited a large sum in the hands of Justin, to be distributed as a donative to the soldiers of the guard, who were under his orders. Justin, however, who was an adherent of the faith as formulated at Chalcedon, perceived that he would better serve the interests of orthodoxy, and his own, by seating himself upon the vacant throne rather than Theocritus, and used the gold of Amantius for that purpose.

It was an unusual sight to see in the palace of the emperors a peasant-born soldier who could neither read nor write, and who, like Theodoric the Goth (if indeed the story be true of Theodoric), must needs affix his sign-manual to the state-papers by drawing the stylus dipped in purple ink through four holes for letters prepared in a metal plate. His wife Lupicina also, who took the name Euphemia, was not of illustrious origin, being a barbarian slave whom her future husband bought as his concubine. All, however, in the eyes of the populace was condoned by the undoubted orthodoxy of the new Emperor, by the delight of having again a ruler who adhered to the Council of Chalcedon.

On the first Sunday after Justin's elevation the crowded into the Great Church, and when the Patriarch John—the successor of Timotheus and believed to be in sympathy with Chalcedon— appeared at the Ambo, they shouted out, 'Longlife to the Emperor! Long life to the Patriarch! Anathema to Severus [Monophysite Patriarch of Antioch]. Why do we remain excommunicated? Carry out the bones of the Manicheans. He who does not shout is a Manichean. Mary the mother of God is worthy of the throne. Bishop! speak or leave the church. Proclaim the faith of Chalcedon. The Emperor is a Catholic : what are you afraid of? Long life to the new Constantine! To the new Helena! *Justine Auguste tu vincas*.' This official formula of salutation to a new Emperor was uttered in the Latin tongue, all the rest of the excited utterances of the crowd being in their vernacular Greek. With difficulty the Patriarch persuaded them to hold their peace till he should have kissed the altar and celebrated mass. This done, the shouters resumed their self-imposed toils. At length the Patriarch mounted the Ambo and said, 'You know, brethren, how many labours I have undergone in past years for the faith. There is no need for disturbance. We all receive the four great Councils, including that of Chalcedon'. 'No,' said the shouting crowd, 'that is not enough. Anathematise Severus : proclaim a feast in honour of the Council of Chalcedon. We will stay here all night if you do not. You shall not depart till you have anathematised Severus.'

At length, with an appearance of yielding to the wishes of the mob, but probably with a consciousness of having prepared the whole scene himself in concert with his master, the Patriarch announced that it should be as they wished. In unison with a large number of bishops from neighbouring dioceses, present in the basilica, he formally anathematised Severus, and announced that on the following day (16th July) there should be a solemn ceremony in honour of the Holy Fathers of the Council of Chalcedon.

On the morrow, when this rite was ended, there was a renewal of the same disorderly cries 'Anathema to the Nestorians. I do not know who is a Nestorian. Anathema to the Eutychians. Dig up their bones. Cast the bones of the Manicheans out of doors. *Justine Auguste tu vincas*.' Mingled with these shouts were heard ominous growls at Amantius the Manichean, which indicate pretty plainly who had been tuning the voices of these tumultuary theologians. In fact, the Eunuch, whose gold had been so adroitly used against him, was very shortly after these days of clamour put out of the way by the new Emperor.

There was a moment of real sublimity in the ceremony of the 16th of July. This was when the Patriarch ascended the Ambo, with the diptychs in his hands, and read from them, amid the deep silence which had fallen upon the shouting crowd, the names of the four Councils which the Church of Constantinople held in highest reverence, Nicaea, Constantinople, Ephesus, and Chalcedon. Then followed the names of the bishops who had departed this life in the faith and fear of God, and with whom the Church still maintained her mystic and invisible communion. Towards the close of this mighty roll of names came Leo, Pontiff of Rome, and Euphemius and Macedonius, Archbishops of the kingly city of Constantinople. At this sound, which announced to their ears the termination of the controversy of a life-time, the populace burst into a loud and joyful shout, 'Glory be to Thee, 0 Lord'. So, after nearly forty years of imperfect acquiescence or actual opposition, did the Church of Constantinople return to unhesitating allegiance to the faith as formulated at Chalcedon.

Not yet, however, was Rome fully appeased, nor could she yet welcome the Eastern Church as wholly purged from her error. The theological question was settled, but the more important personal question remained open. Nay, even the recent triumph of the orthodox populace was stained with some disrespect to the chair of St. Peter, since Rome could not admit that even Euphemius and Macedonius, however manfully they might have struggled against a Manichean Emperor, could rightly have their names recited in the Church's diptychs.

Letter Communications were soon opened between Constantinople and Rome. The new Emperor wrote a short letter to the Pope in which he announced that, by the favour of the indivisible Trinity, of the nobles of the palace and the most holy Senate, and by the choice of his brave army, he had been elected to the Empire; and he dared to add that he had been most unwilling to accept the honour. Hormisdas replied, and letters passed backwards and forwards for some months between the two capitals. The chief part in the correspondence on the side 01 Byzantium was played, not by the illiterate Justin, but by his nephew, a man in early middle life, holding the high office of Count Domestics, and who showed already great talents for theological disputation. This literary assessor of Justin was Justinian.

In the letters sent from Constantinople a faint-hearted attempt was made to save Acacius from damnation. Hormisdas saw that the Emperor really desired reunion; and firmly, but with more gentleness than he had used towards the heretical Anastasius, insisted that those who were sincere in anathematising Eutyches must also anathematise Acacius. The real stress of the contest probably bore, not so much on the name of Acacius, whom both Emperor and people were willing to surrender to damnation, as on the names of the beloved and venerated Euphemius and Macedonius, whom the Pope insisted, not indeed on formally branding with his anathema, but on silently omitting from the diptychs.

At length affairs were ripe for the reception of an embassy from the Pope, and eight months after Justin's elevation to the throne the papal legates arrived at Constantinople. They were charged with letters to the Emperor, the Empress, the Patriarch, the Archdeacon and clergy of Constantinople, to Count Justinian and other courtiers, and to two noble ladies—perhaps members of the family of Anastasius—who were named Anastasia and Palmatia, and who had apparently, in the evil days of the preceding reign, signalised themselves by their zeal for the faith of Chalcedon. The legates had also an *Indiculus* for their own private use, telling them how far to go and where to stand firm in their debate with the Emperor, and a Libellus or formula of submission and profession of faith to be signed by all those who wished to re-enter into communion with the Holy See.

The Pope's messengers had no reason to complain of want of cordiality in their reception at Constantinople. At the tenth milestone from the city they were met by a brilliant throng of courtiers and nobles. At the head of the procession were Vitalian, the little eager soldier who had borne arms for the faith of Chalcedon, Pompeius the nephew of the late Emperor, and Justinian the nephew of the reigning Emperor. Thus did the evening and morning stars of the monarchy meet to do them reverence.

On the next day they stood in the presence of Justin and the Senate. The Patriarch of Constantinople, though favourable to reunion, would not compromise his dignity by appearing in person, but was represented by four of his suffragan bishops. To an invitation from the Emperor that they should argue the matters recently in debate between the two sees, the legates replied that they had no instructions to argue, but only to produce the Pope's letters and the Libellus, which must be signed by all bishops who desired to be reconciled to the Apostolic see. The Libellus was read; the representatives of the Patriarch pronounced it to be consistent with the truth. The Emperor and the ithe Senators burst out into impatient exclamations, 'If it be true, sign it at once, and make an end of the matter.' A day, however, had to elapse, and then the Libellus was put before the Patriarch, who was now present in the palace. He, even in accepting it, dexterously contrived to save some shreds of the dignity of his see. A Libellus was generally subscribed by those who had fallen from the faith, and was thus an admission of guilt. He wrote a clever prologue, turning it into a letter of friendship, addressed 'to his most blessed brother and fellow-servant Hormisdas.' He declared that he held the two Churches of the old Rome and the new to be one Church, and one seat of the Apostle Peter; and then, after these precautionary words and a statement of his acceptance of the four great Councils, he adopted uncompromisingly the whole of the Libellus, with its strong assertion of the office of Peter and the Apostolic see as guardians of the Catholic religion, and its condemnation of the usual string of heretics, beginning with Nestorius and ending with Timothy the Weasel and Peter the Stammerer. Then came the clause of special interest, the key of the whole battle-field. 'Similarly we anathematise Acacius, formerly Bishop of Constantinople, who made himself accomplice and follower of these heretics, together with all who persevered in their fellowship and communion'. In these last words lay a covert if not an express anathema for all the recent bishops of Constantinople.

Next came the solemn act of erasing from the diptychs, and thus striking out of the communion of the Church the names of Zeno and Anastasius the emperors, as well as of Acacius and his four successors in the see of Constantinople, including those two honoured names which had so recently been replaced there, the names of Euphemius and Macedonius. This was done, not only in the Patriarchal Basilica but in all the churches of Constantinople. The legates recorded with wonder and gratitude to God and St. Peter that none of the evil consequences which had been threatened, neither tumult nor shedding of blood, followed this act, which must, one would think, have torn the hearts of many thousands of the people of Constantinople who had loved and well-nigh worshipped the excommunicated prelates.

After such an immense surrender as this, the rest of the work of reunion all over the East, except at Monophysite Alexandria, was comparatively easy, nor need we trouble ourselves with any further details of what had now become a mere matter of formal negotiation. Thus then ended the first great schism between the Eastern and Western Churches. Followed as it has been in later ages by other and more enduring divisions, which have produced results of world-historical importance, this schism will hardly be deemed unworthy of the space which has here been devoted to it. While it lasted, it secured fair play, at least, for the young kingdom of Theodoric. Its termination was an event of evil augury for the Ostrogothic power; and the peace of the Church, by no very remote chain of causes and effects, involved war for Italy.

Looked at merely as a question of spiritual strategy, and without any reference to the spirit and maxims of Christianity, the action of the Popes during the forty years of the struggle must be pronounced most masterly. It was necessary to show to all the world that no act of importance could take place in any of the Churches of Christendom without their consent. Acacius had presumed to endeavour to carry through Zeno's scheme of comprehension without the sanction of the Pope, and therefore, though personally orthodox, Acacius must suffer eternal torment. That end was now attained as far as ecclesiastical censures could secure it; and it might be expected that it would be long before another Patriarch of Constantinople would incur the same tremendous penalty. It is a new warfare in which the Popes are engaged, those venerable men whose faces in almost endless series look down on the visitor to Rome from the walls of S. Paolo. Legates are their proconsuls, monks their legionaries, the Churches of foreign lands their provinces, the sentence of eternal damnation the pilum with which those provinces shall be won. They plan their campaigns with the skill of a Scipio, and they fight them through with the fortune as well as with the relentlessness of a Sulla. This at least is their general character; but in their career of conquest, as in that of the Republic which preceded them, there are occasional vicissitudes of defeat. We have just been tracing the history of the Acacian war, crowned by the victory of Constantinople. Thirty years later we shall have to witness the defeat and surrender of Vigilius at the same place; a calamity for the pontifical arms as great and as bitterly resented as that which befell the Roman legions on the disastrous day of Caudium.

CHAPTER XI.

THEODORIC'S RELATIONS WITH THE CHURCH.

It was a singular coincidence that for nearly thirty years at the close of the fifth and beginning of the sixth century, the three greatest monarchies sovereigns of the civilised world were ruled by sovereigns whose religious opinions differed from those of their subjects.

We have seen the troubles which befell Anastasius, because the mob of Constantinople could never be satisfied that he held the right opinion as to the union of the Divine and the Human in the person of Jesus Christ.

Across the Euphrates, Kobad had to atone for his acceptance of the reformed Zoroastrianism of Mazdak by three years of imprisonment in 'the Castle of Oblivion.' He regained the kingdom only by the arms of the White Huns, and when once again seated on the throne and wearing the diadem of the King of kings, he found it prudent to effect a compromise between his personal and his official consciences. As a man he still held the wild communistic faith of Mazdak, but as king he ruled upon the old lines and respected the rights of property both in jewels and in wives.

In Italy, Theodoric, unshaken in the Arianism which had been, probably for a century, the faith of his forefathers, ruled over a people the vast and at majority of whom were Trinitarians, but ruled so justly that, as we have seen, even orthodox bishops loudly praised his fairness and moderation. So thoroughly was it understood that the Catholic had at least an equal chance with the Arian of obtaining the royal favour that, in a story which was current not long after his death, he was even represented as putting to death a Catholic deacon who had embraced the creed of the court in order to ingratiate himself with his sovereign. Historians are probably right in rejecting this story, which would indeed have been a striking example of 'an intolerant love of toleration', but the fact that it should have obtained currency, is a striking proof that his subjects recognised the earnest desire of their sovereign to keep a perfectly even balance between the two warring creeds. In this respect Theodoric stands out in marked contrast to most of the other Teutonic rulers. While the barbarian Gaiseric and his son plunge with blind zeal into the theological fray, cut out the tongues and rack the limbs of Catholic bishops, while the hypocrite Clovis makes his pretended zeal for the Catholic faith an excuse for invading the fair lands of his kinsman and ally, Theodoric with this noble sentence on his lips, 'We cannot command the religion of our subjects, since no one can be forced to believe against his will,' pursues, perhaps unconsciously, the truly statesmanlike, truly reverent, policy of Valentinian I, and, leaving each man to answer to his Maker for his thoughts concerning Him, uses the power of the State only for the punishment of those deeds whereby the State is endangered.

This absolute impartiality in matters of religion extended even to the Jews; and herein is one of the strongest proofs that it was not a mere counsel of convenience, but that it sprang from conviction deeply rooted in the sovereign's mind. It would have been easy, for him, as an Arian, to curry favour with the orthodox party by showing that he could be as bitter as any of them against the Jewish enemies of the faith.

Instead of this, any offence against Civilitas was punished with equal severity, whether Jew or Christian complained of its perpetration. At Rome, at Milan, at Ravenna, the Jews were at various times attacked by furious mobs, their Synagogues burned, and their persons ill-treated. Of course, there was the usual crop of stories to justify the popular fury, stories like those which three centuries before had stirred up the same kind of mobs to do violence to the impious Nazarenes. The Jews in the Trastevere had beaten their Christian servants, the Jews at Ravenna had performed some insulting parody of Christian baptism. But the decision of Theodoric was firm. The order of the State should be upheld, and those who transgressed it, whether Jews or Christians, should be punished. The Synagogues were to be rebuilt at the cost of the persons by whom they had been destroyed, and the authors of the tumult were to be severely punished.

True, the Gothic King, or his Secretary for him, in one of the letters announcing these decisions, made a pathetic appeal to the Jews to escape from , the future punishment of their misbelief—an appeal which would hardly appear at the end of a similar state-paper issued in our own times. "But why, oh Jew! dost thou seek by thy supplications to us for temporal quietness, if thou art not able to find the rest which is eternal?"- But the long oppressed nation did not resent a word or two of disapprobation for their theology, while their material rights were safe-guarded by so firm a hand. They gave their strong, hearty, and unwavering loyalty to the Gothic rule in Italy : and, when we come to the story of the final contest between King and Emperor, we shall find that, as certainly as the Catholic priest is on the side of Justinian, so certainly is the Jewish merchant on that of Witigis or Totila.

From the impartial, almost friendly attitude which Theodoric assumed towards the Catholic Church through the greater part of his reign, he naturally exercised a great moral influence in addition to the political rights which belonged to him as head of the State, at that time of trouble and anxiety, both for Church and State, a contested Papal election.

In tracing the history of the schism between the Eastern and Western Churches, we have come down to the pontificate of Hormisdas. Remounting the stream of Papal history, we find that the occupant of St. Peter's chair at the accession of Theodoric was the vigorous and uncompromising Gelasius. In the pontificate of Gelasius the controversy with Constantinople was conducted with at least as much vigour and asperity as had marked the spiritual war under the generalship of Felix. Happily, however, we may now turn from this monotonous controversy to behold the Pope trampling out the dying, but not quite dead, embers of Paganism. There was still a party at Rome, with the Senator Andromachus at their head, who wished to keep up the old heathen orgies of the Lupercalia, that strange rite made memorable by Mark Antony's share in it, on the day when, after running naked through the Forum, he knelt down and offered the diadem to Caesar. This custom had not been suppressed along with the other heathen observances, and now Andromachus and his party wished to perpetuate it.

They pleaded that none of the earlier Popes had objected to the rite. It used to be thought that the touch of the Lupercalian's thong falling on the shoulders of the Roman matrons brought with it a peculiar good fortune. It could, at any rate, do no harm to keep alive so ancient a custom. Gelasius replied, with bitter scorn, that though earlier pontiffs might not have been strong enough to suppress the heathen observance, he was, and would exercise his power. If Andromachus and his party really believed the Lupercalia to be a religious act, let them take the shame of it on themselves,

themselves rush about like naked madmen through the streets, and not, as was now the custom, put off the shame of it upon others, their inferiors in rank. The observance of the Lupercalia had not brought luck to Rome in past times, had not saved her from the sword of Alaric or the ships of Gaiseric. Nay, even in later days, the terrible scenes which marked the strife between Anthemius and Ricimer had not been averted by this silly and licentious rite. He could not lay down the law for Pagans, but to Christians he spoke in a voice to which they must hearken. No baptized person, no Christian, should dare to take part in the impious orgy: if he did, he should be without hesitation cut off from the communion of the faithful. We know not the result, but it cannot be doubted that such a mandate, coming from such lips, was sufficient to destroy the Lupercalian festival.

Gelasius was succeeded by the gentle Anastasius and, on the death of this conciliatory Pontiff, Festus the ambassador who had just visited Constantinople with a commission both from the Pope and the King, and who had succeeded in making peace on behalf of the latter for his 'pre-assumption of the kingdom,' endeavoured to further the cause of unity by procuring the election of a Pope who would look favourably on the Henoticon of Zeno. Both at Old and New Rome, symptoms may be discerned of a disposition on the part of the aristocrats to press this creation of statesmen, this politically concocted 'end of controversy', on the rulers of the Church; while the lower classes and the monks, seeing perhaps less of the necessities of the position, stood immutably faithful to the Tome of Leo and the Council of Chalcedon.

The candidate whom Festus, in the interests of his scheme of church union, desired to see made Pope, was the Arch-Presbyter Laurentius, who was elected a few days after the death of Anastasius in the great Liberian Basilica. On Laurentius same day, however, a larger body of clergy, assembled in the Lateran Church, had elected as Pope the deacon Symmachus, a native of Sardinia, whose consecration was accomplished before that of his rival.

Here then was the city plunged anew into all the miseries and the turmoil of a contest for the chair of St. Peter. Blood had already begun to flow in the streets of Rome, when the wise resolution was taken, to refer the whole matter in dispute to the arbitration of Theodoric. The rival candidates appeared accordingly in his palace at Ravenna, and claimed his award. Political reasons would probably have inclined him to support the candidate of Festus, who had so successfully served him at the court of Anastasius, but his instinctive love of justice prevailed. 'The candidate first elected, if also the candidate elected by most voices, ought to be Pope'. He who fulfilled these conditions was Symmachus.

A council, the first of many on this business, was called at St. Peter's on the 1st of March in the following year (499). Symmachus, who had convened the council, was recognised as regularly elected Pope; and decrees were made against the practice of canvassing for votes in anticipation of a vacancy in the Holy See, and for the regulation of future contested elections in the case of the Pope's dying suddenly without having been able to arrange for the election of his successor.

The victory of Symmachus, however, was only apparent. Though Laurentius, who seems to have been a man of peaceable disposition, was willing to acquiesce in his defeat, and even accepted the bishopric of Nocera from his rival, his partisans, who perhaps constituted the majority of the Senate, could not brook their defeat by the popular party. We hear no more of the Henoticon, the original cause of the quarrel : everything seems merged in the passionate determination of the Senators, by fair means or foul, to depose Symmachus from the Papacy. It seems probable that the means used were foul rather than fair, when, in addition to the ordinary charge of alienation of church-property (doubtless in order to meet the expenses of the election) and a singular one of celebrating Easter apart from the multitude of believers, an accusation of gross immorality was also brought against Symmachus by Festus and his fellow-worker Probinus. The vagueness of these charges, the illegal means by which it was sought to support them, and the earnest denial of their truth by Ennodius (an honest man, though an intolerably tedious writer), all seem to justify the belief that this was one of those cruel attacks on private character which are made, only because the high position of the victim causes accusation and condemnation to be one, in the charitable judgment of the crowd.

Again disturbances broke out, again there was bloodshed in the streets and squares of Rome. We are not able to fix the precise date of this recrudescence of the strife, but it seems probable that it was in the later months of 500, just after the sojourn of the King in Rome, during which undoubtedly both parties kept truce in the presence of that stalwart maintainer of *civilitas.*

The King, who during that visit had probably been in frequent intercourse with the leaders of the Senatorial party, may have imbibed some of their prejudices against Symmachus, who was formally accused before him of immorality. At any rate he summoned him to Rimini, and the Pope, who seems to have understood that only the trifling question about his manner of keeping Easter would be examined into by Theodoric, obeyed the summons. One evening, however, as he wandered by the sea-shore, he saw some travellers ride by along the Flaminian Way. Among them were the Roman women whom he was accused of having seduced. The truth flashed upon his mind. They were going to the King's Comitatus, and he was to stand his trial before it for adultery. Terrified at the prospect, he stole away secretly in the dead of night, with one attendant, to Rome, to his old refuge at the Basilica of St. Peter.

Offended by the Pope's flight, and rendered yet more suspicious of his guilt, Theodoric now took the bold step of appointing a 'Visitor' to summon a council, to hear thereat the charges against Symmachus, and meanwhile to undertake the government of the Church in his stead. This was undoubtedly a high-handed proceeding; one which, in the distracted state of the Church, success, and the maintenance of strict impartiality by the King's delegate, might have excused, but which otherwise it would be difficult to justify. The Visitor, Bishop Peter of Altino, preserved no semblance of judicial impartiality, and consequently his mission was doomed to failure. Instead of visiting the Pope at the shrine of St. Peter's, he at once threw himself into the arms of the Senatorial party, turned several of the clerical adherents of Symmachus out of their churches and intruded Laurentians in their room.

This strong partisanship, exhibited by the nominee of an Arian king at the bidding of the laymen of the Senate, touched the hierarchical spirit of the bishops who were summoned to the Council, and caused a certain reaction in favour of Symmachus, who hitherto had perhaps had only the lower clergy and the populace of Rome in his favour. Some of the bishops on their way to Rome had an interview with Theodoric, in which they frankly told him—so say the Acts of a later Council, which undoubtedly represent the high ecclesiastical view of the question—'that he, the accused Pope, and not the King, was the person who ought of right to convene the Council, since by God's command this was the peculiar privilege of the Pope, derived from the dignity of Peter's primacy, that he could not be judged by those of lower degree.'

This was in fact the position taken up by Symmachus, when at length, soon after Easter in 501, the Council which was to try his case assembled in the Julian Basilica. Yet, he intimated, he might be willing to waive his right, and appear before the Council to answer the charges against him, but only on condition that Peter the Visitor should be disavowed, and the churches which he had taken from the adherents of Symmachus should be restored to them. The Council, which was composed chiefly of elderly men, did not dare thus to reverse the acts of Theodoric. Nor did they, on the other hand, though partially reassured by a letter which the King had shown the bishops at Ravenna, proving that Symmachus himself had expressed a desire for the assembling of the Council, dare to sit in judgment on the successor of St. Peter without his consent. After fumbling at the question for some time with feeble trembling hands, they gave it up, and requested the king to convoke a council at Ravenna. The Council then broke up, and several of its members left Rome.

This futile result disgusted the King, who was not perhaps greatly interested in the question whether Symmachus or Laurentius should win, but earnestly desirous that the strife should be ended somehow, and peace restored to Rome. He wrote to the bishops who remained at Rome, praising their patience, but complaining with some acerbity of their faint-hearted colleagues. He entirely refused to have the matter referred to him at Ravenna. "Had it been his wish to interfere in the dispute", he said, "he doubted not that he and the great officers of his household would have been able to find a solution of the difficulty, which would have been approved by posterity. But as it concerns God and the clergy he had decided to summon the bishops; and they must settle it". Three letters were written by Theodoric in this strain, urging the bishops to do their duty and not to leave undecided a controversy which was daily imperilling the peace of 'the Royal City'. "If you like to decide it withont enquiry, on account of the rank of the accused person, do so; though I must remind you of that saying of Aspar's" (and here Theodoric indulged in a remembrance of his Byzantine days) "when he was recommended by the Senate to make himself Emperor: "I fear", said he, "lest by me this thing should be drawn into a custom in the Empire". Even so I fear lest if you leave this matter unenquired into, immorality should become common among priests. Still, on you be the responsibility; only decide the case".

At the same time, Theodoric sent three stout Goths, Arigern the count and the chamberlains Gudila and Bedewulf, to Symmachus, to protect him on his passage through the city, and probably also to remind the Sardinian priest that the King of the Goths and Romans was not accustomed to have his orders disobeyed by any subject, however exalted. The persuasion, of whatever kind it may have been, was effectual; the protection, as it turned out, was really needed. The Pope set forth on the morning of the 1st of September to meet the Council of his judges assembled in the church of Santa Croce, hard by that Sessorian palace in which, a year before, the head of Odoin the traitor had rolled on the marble pavement. To reach the place of judgment Symmachus must needs traverse the whole breadth of Rome, from the north-western Janiculan hill to the southeastern Coelian. The sight of the Pope going forth on this humiliating errand touched the hearts of his plebeian supporters. A multitude gathered in his train, who followed him weeping and lamenting. These evidences of the popularity of their hated antagonist kindled the rage of the Senators of the opposite party. To them the question between Laurentius and Symmachus was probably no more than as one of those disputes in the circus between the Blues and Greens, in which the victory of a charioteer favoured by the mob goaded the dainty Senator to madness. Whatever the cause, the party of Laurentius, including some priests as well as Senators, fell upon the mournful procession of Symmachus, dealing such cruel blows that many fell wounded to the earth, and only the energy of the three Gothic henchmen succeeded in winning for their protégé a way back through the crowd to his asylum at St. Peter's shrine.

This street-brawl secured the victory to Symmachus. With good reason could he now entrench himself behind his sacred prerogative, and say, "I Peter's, am in God's hands and the King's. Let them do with me what they will. I appear not before the Council". The sympathies of Theodoric, which had been for a time turned against Symmachus, by what looked like an evasion from justice, were now heartily restored to him by this gross breach of *civilitas* on the part of his accusers; an outrage which was made personally insulting to himself by the fact that it was committed on a man who was under the *tuitio regii nominis* and escorted by three Gothic officers. Henceforward nothing more was heard from the King about compelling the Pope to answer his accusers. He only pressed upon the Council (which now willingly pronounced a verdict clearing the Pope of the charges brought against him) that they should not merely decide this theoretical question, but practically end the dispute by assigning the churches and other ecclesiastical buildings in Rome to the persons who were canonically entitled to them, and compel the obedience of all the clergy to Symmachus, now the undoubtedly lawful Pope. All this difficult but necessary work the feeble old bishops would gladly have thrust off upon him, but he answered with truth and spirit, "That is your affair, not mine. Had it been my business, I and my good chiefs would have settled it long ago".

The final decision of the whole controversy was attained in the Council called the Synodus Palmaris, which was held 'in the Portico of St. Peter's, which is called Palmaria.' This Council, which was called by its enemies, 'The Synod of the Incongruous Absolution,' was fiercely attacked by them on divers grounds, both of substance and of form. It was defended by Ennodius in a long apology, in which, through a thick veil of almost unmeaning rhetoric, and amidst a profusion of Scripture texts pelted forth at random upon his antagonists, it is just possible to discern some of the main outlines of the controversy. According to the taste of the age the Apology closes with three long imaginary addresses from St. Peter, St. Paul, and the city of Rome. In these addresses the good bishop reaches a higher level than in the rest of his composition, and the rhetorician once or twice speaks like an orator. His warm praises of Theodoric's rule impress us more in this tractate than in the panegyric which was composed to be recited before him. We understand also more fully the feeling of depression with which a Christian Roman of that day looked back upon the past history of his country, when we hear Rome lamenting that all her greatest sons, the Curii, the Torquati, and the Camilli had been borne by her only to languish for ever in Tartarus because the Church had not regenerated them, that the Fabii and Decii who had saved others could not be saved themselves; that Scipio, who was ever a fervent lover of the right, was joined with the greatest criminals in the world to come because he was ignorant of Christ.

It took some time for the troubled waters to subside. We hear that Laurentius, who had come back to Rome, continued the strife for four years; but Symmachus was now strong in the approbation of councils, and the support of Theodoric, and, as far as we can see, his opponents, playing faintheartedly a losing game, did not again venture on any actual breach of the public peace.

The whole controversy has, it will at once be seen, an important bearing on events of a much later date. Some of the questions mooted are the same as those which came up for solution at the Council of Constance. In so thorny a controversy it is hardly possible to frame any proposition which may not be attacked from one side or the other; but perhaps we shall be safe in asserting these :—

I. The right of the King, as head of the State, to convene a Council by his own authority was asserted on the one side and denied on the other.

II. But the tacit assent of the Pope cured the informality of the Council, even in the eyes of ecclesiastics.

III. It was not formally denied that the Pope, like other subjects of the King, was subject to his jurisdiction for such an offence as adultery. But—

IV. It was strenuously denied that a Council (consisting as it did of his ecclesiastical inferiors) could sit in judgment on a Pope. And in the end this contention practically prevailed.

We can see at once the great difference between the third and fourth points. To subject a pope to the jurisdiction of the bishops in his obedience was like bringing a captain to trial before the soldiers of his company—a proceeding necessarily subversive of all discipline. But that was not saying that the Pope, who was still no temporal sovereign but a subject,—either of the Emperor or the King—need give no account to the Head of the State, for acts which he had committed in defiance of its laws. The successor of St. Peter was responsible for the exercise of his spiritual authority to no man. But if Symmachus committed adultery or murder, he must answer for the deed to our lord Theodoric in his palace at Ravenna.

The history of the strife exhibits in a favourable light the sound sense and statesmanship of the Ostrogothic King. He has no desire to meddle in matters ecclesiastical. His one anxiety is to see that *civilitas* be maintained and its assailants punished. A free Church in a free—or at all events in a well-ordered—State is practically his maxim. He makes one or two mistakes, but shows his statesmanship in this more than anything, that he knows how to retrieve his mistakes, and is not, by a foolish craving after consistency or blind self-love, enticed into the common blunder of letting the first error drag him on into a series of other errors each greater than its predecessor.

The only other act of the Pontificate of Symmachus which need be noticed here is his in the proceedings of another council, the fifth, which was held at St. Peters on the 6th of November, 502. Addressing the assembled fathers of the Church, he recommended that the authors of the recent schism, who had been led away by love of dominion and had cast off the yoke of the Church, should be left to the mercy of God if they were not too hardened to accept of it. After proclaiming this somewhat dubious amnesty, he brought before the notice of the Council the encroachment on the rights of the Church of which Odovacar had been guilty twenty years before. In order to bring the matter more vividly before them, the deacon Hormisdas a man who was himself one day to be Pope, read the decree once issued by the illustrious Basilius in the name of the most excellent King Odovacar. The particulars of that certainly somewhat daring piece of legislation have been already detailed. The holy fathers gasped with indignation when they heard once more the language of a layman, though a king, arrogating to himself the absolute nomination of a successor to the Papal throne, and, what was even more audacious, inflicting the penalty of anathema on the alienators of ecclesiastical property. Speaker after speaker interrupted the reader, pointing out successive violations of the canons by this decree: and when each one had finished, again the calm voice of the deacon Hormisdas was heard, perhaps indicating by sarcastic emphasis his own dislike of the document of which he was the unwilling expositor. After heartily condemning the decree and declaring that, as wanting the Papal sanction, it was utterly invalid, the Council proceeded to re-enact, in a regular manner, the really valuable portion of it,—that which forbade the alienation of the property of the Church; making, however, an exception on behalf of houses in Rome, which the clergy, if they found themselves unable to bear the expense of keeping them up, were at liberty to sell, accounting scrupulously for the proceeds of the sale.

After sixteen years, the eventful pontificate of Symmachus came to an end. When he died, Cassiodorus was in Rome, dehghting in the shadowy glories of his year of office as Consul. He was admirably adapted for the task which naturally devolved upon him, of allaying the bitter spirit of contending factions, of soothing the wounded self-love of the Senate which had probably never been heartily reconciled to the victory of Symmachus, and inducing it to co-operate peaceably with the popular leaders among tbe clergy in the election of a new pope.

The scandals of a contested election were avoided, and, after an unusually short vacancy of seven days, the Papal seat was again filled; the newoccupant being Hormisdas the Campanian, the reader of the obnoxious decree of Odovacar: a man who, as the event showed, was to be not only himself a pope, but also the father of a pope.

The chief events of the pontificate of Hormisdas have already been told in the chapter describing Theodoric's relations with Constantinople. He was well fitted to conduct such a struggle as that in which he was engaged with Anastasius, and to reap, with cold complacency, the uttermost fruits of the victory which was offered him by Justin.

There was again a short vacancy and an undisputed succession. On the 13th of August, 523, John, a Tuscan, first of the long line of Popes who have borne the name, if they have not all imitated the saintliness, of the beloved Disciple, sat in the chair of St. Peter.

The new Pope came to his dignity at a difficult and anxious time. Four years had now elapsed towards since the close of the schism, and during those the years, while Justin's relations with the Roman Church had been excellent, his relations with the Italian King appear to have been growing steadily worse. How the chasm began to yawn between Romans and Goths, and how Theodoric, challenged to decide, declared himself on the side of his own nation, will be told in the next chapter. It is sufficient here to note that the year of John's accession to the Papacy is also the year when, by Theodoric's orders, Boethius was shut up in prison.

The next year, honoured by the Emperor Justin's assuming for the second time the consular title, was marked by a decided step taken by that Emperor in the direction of intolerance. Hitherto Justin, while persecuting severely the Manicheans and all heretics of that class, had left the Arians untouched, and seems even to have alleged, as a reason for his tolerance, that they professed the same religion as Theodoric. Now, however, this exception in their favour was suddenly and harshly terminated. Everywhere the churches of the Arians were reconsecrated with Catholic rites, and they themselves were made to understand that the time had gone by when they could be allowed to continue to disbelieve in the Homoousion.

Theodoric, irritated by the insult to himself, and disgusted by such an ungrateful return for policy of his impartial tolerance, now began to lose his temper, and under the influence of ill-temper not only departed from the principles of a life-time, but committed one of the greatest mistakes in policy which it was possible to perpetrate. He, whose one great glory it had been to make no distinction between creed and creed, began to entertain the idea of a persecution of the Catholics in Italy, by way of reprisal for the persecution of Arians in Thrace. And, in order to change the purpose of the Emperor, he committed the astounding folly of sending the Pope to Constantinople. No two pieces on the political chess-board ought, for the safety of his kingdom, to have been kept further apart from one another than the Pope and the Emperor: and now, by his own act, he brings these pieces close together. Summoning Pope John to Ravenna, he signified his pleasure that the head of the Catholic Church should visit Constantinople as his ambassador, and should inform Justin that, unless he restored their churches to the Arians, the sword of Theodoric would ravage the whole of Italy. The Pope, sick and infirm, besought with tears to be excused from so degrading and unsuitable a mission, but the King, in whom the blood of all his Amal ancestors was now boiling, would take no denial, and the unhappy priest, cowed into submission, consented to set forth. The mission was in outward show a brilliant one. Three exconsuls, Theodorus, Importunus, and Agapetus, and one patrician, a second Agapetus, went in the train of the Pontiff. Miracles marked their course. At Corinth, a nobleman's horse which had been lent for the Pope's use, absolutely refused thenceforward to be ridden by a woman, the owner's wife, whose tractable steed it had been till that day. The nobleman, making a merit of necessity, sent the creature, possessed of such nice spiritual discernment, to the Pope, and besought him, with many prayers, to regard it as his own. At the entrance into Constantinople, a blind man imploring his aid, and touched by the Pontiff's hand, received his sight.

Everywhere there were joyous excitement and expectation at the arrival of the successor of St. Peter in the New Rome; an event, men said, which had never happened since Silvester came to visit its founder Constantine. Justin, with all his Court, and, so it seemed, the whole city of Constantinople, streamed forth with crosses and candles to meet the ambassadors at the twelfth milestone. Prone on the ground the Emperor, whom all other men adored, adored the weary Pontiff. Sick and anxious as he was, it was impossible for John not to feel that it was a great day for the Papacy. When Easter-day came the Pope, taking the place of honour at the right hand of the Patriarch of Constantinople, celebrated Mass according to the Latin use in the great Cathedral. Nay, so far, according to one rather doubtful story, did Justin carry his devotion to his distinguished guest, that, though now in the eighth year of his reign, and once crowned already by the Patriarch of Constantinople, he solicited and obtained the honour of a second coronation from his papal visitor.

As to the success of John's intercession with Justin it is not easy to speak positively. The authorities who are most nearly contemporary assert very clearly that the prayers and tears of the Pope and his colleagues prevailed, and that the Emperor granted all their requests except that for the reconversion to Arianism of the new-made Catholics, which was deemed a thing impossible. Thus, they say, was Italy liberated from the fear of the vengeance of Theodoric. Modern papal historians like Baronius, eager to vindicate the Pope from the stain of advocating religious toleration, vehemently contend against this statement, and ask with some force, "Why then the rage of Theodoric on the Pope's return, if he had done, with one inconsiderable exception, all that he was ordered to do". Perhaps we may fairly conclude that the Pope deserved the anger of both parties; of the Catholics for asking for and obtaining things which were in his view unlawful, and of the King for throwing out hints and commencing negotiations inconsistent with his loyalty as a subject. The maxim—

' To thine own self be true,
And it must follow, as the night the day,
Thou canst not then be false to any man,'

was one the spirit of which had been disregarded by Pope John, and he paid the penalty.

On his return to Eavenna, early in 526, the Pope found the King in no friendly mood, broken probably in health and sore against all the supposed 'abettors of Boethius and Symmachus in their treasonable practices with Constantinople. John himself and his three ex-consular colleagues were thrown into prison, and there lingered several months. The hardships of the prison life were too much for the already enfeebled health of the Pontiff, and he died in confinement on the 25th of May, 526, ninety-seven days before the death of the King himself.

Thus did Theodoric, whose whole reign had been pervaded by the attempt to harmonise Goth and Roman, and to rule without partiality over Catholic and Arian, cruelly wound the feelings of his Roman subjects by degrading the person of the Pope, and end his career by making the one man to whom the eyes of all Catholics turned with reverence—a martyr. Toleration is a noble principle, but it cannot be taken up and laid down at pleasure. He who would earn the glory of a tolerant king must be tolerant even in the presence of intolerance : tolerant even to the end. If we may take a simile from horsemanship, it is of no use for the rider to keep his temper with a timid, shying horse through ten vagaries, if at the eleventh he loses patience and brings the whip down in heavy wrath. All his previous self-restraint goes for nothing, and his ill-temper spoils the temper of his steed.

CHAPTER XII.

BOETHIUS AND SYMMACHUS.

THE greatest mistake, if not the greatest crime, which sullied the fame of Theodoric, was the order given by him for the execution of Boethius and Symmachus. Coming as these executions did so near in time to the imprisonment and death in prison of Pope John, they easily acquired an ecclesiastical colour which did not of right belong to them: and thus these two noble, if somewhat mistaken men, who really perished as martyrs to the great name of Rome and the memory of the world-conquering Republic, have been surrounded by a halo of fictitious sanctity as martyrs to the cause of Christian orthodoxy.

To clear the ground, it will be well first of all to suffer our previous guide, the *Anonymus Valesii*, to tell us the tragic story, as it was recounted in ecclesiastical circles at Ravenna about a generation after the event.

After describing Theodoric's residence at Verona, the resort thither of the Jews of Ravenna with their complaint about their ruined synagogue and the stern order for restitution made by the King, the Anonymus thus continues:—

'From this event the devil found occasion to subvert the man [Theodoric] who had been [up to this time] governing the republic well and without cause for complaint. For he presently ordered that the oratory and altar of St. Stephen, at the fountains in the suburb of Verona, should be overthrown. Then he commanded that no Roman should bear any arms, not even allowing them to carry a knife.

'Also a poor woman, of the Gothic nation, lying under a porch not far from the palace of Ravenna, gave birth to four dragons: two were seen by the people to be carried along in the clouds from the west to the east, and then to be cast into the sea: two were captured, having one head between them. There appeared a star with a torch, which is called a comet, shining for fifteen days, and there were frequent earthquakes.

After these things the king began, upon the least occasion that he could find, to flame out in wrath against the Romans. Cyprian, who was then Reporter to the High Court of Justice, afterwards Count of the Sacred Largesses and Master [of the Offices], urged by cupidity, laid an information against Albinus the Patrician, that he had sent letters to the Emperor Justin hostile to the rule of Theodoric. This accusation he, upon being summoned, denied, and thereupon Boetius the Patrician, who was Master of the Offices, said in the King's presence: "False is the information of Cyprian, but if Albinus did it, both I and the whole Senate did it with one accord. It is false, my lord oh King!". Then Cyprian, with hesitation, brought forward false witnesses not only against Albinus, but also against his champion Boetius. But the King laid snares for the Romans, and sought how he might slay them: he put more confidence in the false witnesses than in the Senators. Then were Albinus and Boetius taken in custody at the baptistery of the church (at Ticinum?). But the King called for Eusebius, Prefect of the city of Ticinum, and passed sentence against Boetius unheard: and soon after sent and ordered him to be killed on the Calventian property. A cord was twisted for a very long time round his fore-head, so that his eyes started from his head: and then at last in the midst of his torments he was slain with a club.

The King's return in high wrath to Ravenna, and his ill-conceived scheme of sending the Pope to Constantinople to plead for toleration to the Arians, are next described.

The Anonymus then continues: 'But while these things are going on, Symmachus the Head of the Senate, whose daughter Boetius had to wife, is led from Rome to Ravenna. But the King, fearing lest through grief for the loss of his son-in-law he should attempt anything against his kingdom, caused him to be accused and ordered him to be slain. Then Pope John returning from Justin was badly received by Theodoric and ordered to consider himself in disgrace. After a few days he died, and as the people were going in procession before his corpse, suddenly one of the crowd fell down, stricken by a demon, and when they had come with the bier to the place where he was, suddenly he stood up whole, and walked before them in the procession. Which when the people and senators saw, they began to cut off relics from the garment [of the Pope]. Thus, amid the extreme joy of the people, was his corpse led out beyond the gates of the city.

'Then [another] Symmachus, a Jew, and an official in the royal scholae, at the bidding, not of the king, but of the tyrant, issued orders on the fourth day of the week, the seventh before the kalends of September [26 August], on the fourth indiction, in the consulship of Olybrius, that on the following Lord's Day the Arians should take possession of the Catholic basilicas. But He who suffers not his faithful worshippers to be oppressed by the aliens, soon inflicted on him the same sentence as on Arius the author of his religion. The king was attacked with diarrhoea, and after three days of incessant purgings, on the same day on which he promised himself to invade the churches, he himself lost both kingdom and life. Before he drew his last breath he appointed his grandson Athalaric to the kingdom. During his lifetime he made for himself a monument of squared stone, a work of wonderful bigness, and sought for a gigantic stone, which he placed as the crowning of the edifice'.

(Here the Anonymus Valesii abruptly ends.)

The information here given us may be illustrated, if not greatly increased, by the hints as to the life and character of Boethius, which we obtain from his own writings and those of his contemporaries.

Anicius Manlius Severinus Boethius was born at Rome probably in, or very soon after, the year 480. His family was one of the most illustrious in Rome. He belonged to the gens Anicia, which, originally sprung from Praeneste, first emerges to notice in Roman, history in the third century B.C., played a respectable, though not important, part in the times of the Republic, and, simply by living on through the wars, proscriptions, and massacres of the Empire, became a large and mighty kinship in the fourth century after Christ, when so many of the great names of the Republic had gone out for ever. To this clan belonged Probus, Olybrius, Symmachus, whose names have come under our notice in connection with the history of the later empire. Possibly also both Faustus and Festus, the two rival ministers of Theodoric, styled themselves Anicii.

Thus his name Anicius indicated a real and genuine connection with one of the noblest families of the Lower Empire. Manlius was meant to carry back his lineage to the Manlii Torquati of the Republic; but here the connection was probably of that vague and shadowy kind which is met with in manufactured genealogies. Severinus was no doubt given to him in honour of one of the holiest names of the fifth century, the saintly hermit of Noricum.

A Boethius, probably the grandfather of Severinus Boethius, was, as we have already seen, murdered side by side with his friend Aetius, on that disastrous day when 'the last of Romans' fell, by the orders of the last Theodosian princeling Valentinian III. In the next generation Aurelius Manlius Boethius, after being twice Praefectus Urbi, and once Praetorian Prefect, attained the dignity of Consul in 487, during the domination of Odovacar. As this nobleman died in early middle life, his son, the one who was to immortalise the name, was left an orphan while still a boy. Powerful relations, however, undertook his guardianship, the most noteworthy of them being Symmachus, who, when Boethius reached manhood, gave him Rusticiana his daughter to wife.

The names of Symmachus and Boethius are so inextricably intertwined by the fate which made their deaths part of the same dark tragedy, that it will be well to interrupt here the story of Boethius in order to give the main facts of the life of his father-in-law.

Quintus Aurelius Memmius Symmachus, was sprung, like his younger contemporary, from the great Anician house. The most conspicuous of his ancestors was Symmachus the orator, consul under the great Theodosius in 391, leader of the senatorial party at that day, and one of the last great names of Rome's slowly dying Paganism. The story might well have been told in the earlier volumes of this history, of his eloquent remonstrance with the young and uncompromising Gratian, against the removal of the altar of Victory from the Senate-house, and of his earnest entreaties to Theodosius and his colleagues to undo the impious work and restore the altar to its place.

A hundred years had wrought great changes in the attitude of the Roman nobles towards the unseen world. The Symmachus with whom we have now to deal—a man in many respects resembling his great ancestor, like him head of the Senate and enthusiastic for its glory—has become an earnest member of the Christian Church, and shows his fidelity to Rome by upholding the standard of Catholic orthodoxy against the Arian Theodoric.

Not, however, that we have any reason to suppose that, during the greater part of his life,. Symmachus occupied an unfriendly position to the Ostrogothic government. He supported his namesake, Pope Symmachus, in his controversy with Laurentius, and, during the greater part of that struggle, was no doubt fighting on the same side as the King. He had held the dignity of Consul in 485 under Odovacar. He became *Praefedits Urbi* under Theodoric, thus attaining the rank of an Illustris; and he also received the proud title of Patricius. By right of seniority he had risen by the year 524 to the venerable position of Head of the Senate, corresponding pretty closely with the high, but unofficial pre-eminence enjoyed in England by 'the Father of the House of Commons'. A man 0f correct and stately eloquence, of irreproachable character; the Cato of his age, but with the old Stoic virtues softened and refined by his Christian faith; a diligent student, and the author of a Roman history in seven books, a man also full of fine local patriotism for the great city which was his home, and willing to spend some of his vast wealth freely in the repair of her public buildings—such is the Symmachus of the age of Theodoric as he is represented to us by his admiring contemporaries.

The friendship of the elder and younger nobleman, crowned at length by the union which made Boethius the son-in-law of Symmachus, is a pleasing picture in an age in which we meet with little else than the rottenness of civilisation and the roughness of barbarism.

To the career of the younger Senator we now return. Boethius was an ardent student of Greek philosophy, but we have no evidence that he ever visited Greece. The notion that he actually studied at Athens seems to have been chiefly derived from the misunderstanding of a figurative expression of Cassiodorus as to his familiarity with Greek science. He early attained high rank in the State. Consul at about the age of thirty, and apparently even before that time dignified with the honour of the Patriciate, he was evidently, in those years of adolescence and early middle age, in high favour with the Ostrogothic King. His heart, however, was not in the stately presence-chamber of king or prefect, not with the shouting and excited crowd who lined the dusty hippodrome, but in the delightful retirement of his library. Here, in this temple of philosophy, adorned as its walls were with ivory and glass, did he hold converse deep into the night with the heavenly visitant, who was to come to him again in far other environment and cheer the squalid solitude of his dungeon.

The chief literary object of Boethius was to familiarise his countrymen with what he deemed best in Greek speculation; carrying on the work which had been commenced by Cicero, and applying it to some writers whom it was harder to treat in a popular manner than those whom Cicero had expanded. He translated, Cassiodorus tells us, Pythagoras for the theory of music, Ptolemy for astronomy, Nicomachus for arithmetic, Euclid for geometry. But the chief work of these prosperous days, and that by which he most profoundly influenced the thoughts of after-times, was his commentaries on the logical treatises of Aristotle. The Categories, the Syllogism, the Analytics, and the Topics, with some minor treatises, thirty books in all, were translated by this indefatigable scholar, heir to one of the greatest names and one of the finest fortunes in Rome, but intent on placing philosophical truth within the reach of his fellow-countrymen. It seems to have been in great measure through the translations and commentaries of Boethius that the mediaeval Schoolmen made their acquaintance with the philosopher of Stagira. From him, at least in part, they derived the materials for the long war of words between the Nominalists and Realists; though Boethius himself, 'rushing into the battle at once with the valour of his race and his own personal intrepidity, gravely and peremptorily decides a question in which the doctors of Europe for centuries were to engage', by avowing himself a Realist. Boethius's own belief in the absolute existence of the Aristotelian conception, Genus, Species, Difference, Property, and Accident is firm and immutable, and the ardour of his conviction impressed itself on many generations of his readers.

On the whole the encyclopaedic labours of Boethius, though in the very highest degree honourable to the worker, have perhaps been of somewhat doubtful benefit to the world. It has been admirably said, by one well fitted to understand his intellectual position, 'Qualities, quantities, magnitudes, multitudes—who does not see that these names were building a prison for Boethius, of which the walls were far higher and more impenetrable than those of the one to which Theodoric consigned him? There was positively no escape, above, below, through ceiling or pavement, for one confined within this word-fortress: scarcely an aperture, one would have thought, for air or light to enter in'. And great as the authority of Boethius was for many centuries on the science of music as known to the ancient world, it seems to be thought, by those best qualified to judge, that his own knowledge of the subject was somewhat inaccurate, and that by going back to the Pythagorean scale he really retarded the scientific development of the art.

But Boethius was more than a mere student, however laborious; more than a populariser of the work of other men, however successful. He was also a highly skilled mechanician—a character which since the days of Archimedes had not been greatly affected even by the philosophers of Greece, and which a mere Roman noble might have been in danger of despising as beneath his dignity. Whenever Theodoric and his ministers were in want of advice on a mechanical, or (to use the modern term) on a chemical question, Boethius was the person to whom they naturally had recourse. If Gundobad the Burgundian was to be flattered and awed by an exhibition of Italian skill, Boethius must construct the wonderful water-clock which was to mark out the length of each successive solar day, the orrery (as we should call it) which was to imitate the movement of the solar system. If a skilful player on the cithara was to be sent to the court of Clovis the Frank, Boethius must select the performer. If the life-guards complained that the paymaster was putting them off with coins of inferior weight and fineness, Boethius was called upon, as Archimedes in a similar case by Hiero of Syracuse, to detect the fraud. That these friendly and familiar relations between the subject and his King should terminate in the dungeon, the cord, and the bludgeon, is one of the saddest pages in the history of courts.

In addition to his other occupations, Boethius entered the thorny labyrinth of theological controversy. A debate, which was carried on for many generations, as to the identity of Boethius the philosopher with Boethius the theologian, is now finally settled by the language of the fragment so often referred towhich asserts that 'he wrote a book concerning the holy Trinity, and some dogmatic chapters and a book against Nestorius. He also wrote a bucolic poem'.

A nobleman with these various endowments, philosopher, musician, astronomer, mechanician, poet, theologian, and the best writer of Latin prose of his century, was certainly a considerable figure on the stage of history. We have now to consider him in his character of politician—a character which one is disposed to think it would have been well both for him and for Italy that he had never assumed. He tells us, in a review of his past career, that it was in obedience to the teachings of Plato that he entered the domain of politics. Plato had said that states would be happy if either philosophers were kings or kings philosophers. He had also declared that the wise ought to take a share in political affairs, in order to prevent the disaster and ruin which would fall upon the good if the helm of the State were to be left in the hands of dishonest and immoral men.

'Guided by this authority', says he in his colloquy with Philosophy, 'I sought to translate into practical and public life the lessons which I had learned from thee in the secrecy of the study. Thou, and the God who breathed thee into the souls of the wise, are my witnesses, that nought moved me to the acceptance of office but the desire to promote the general welfare of my fellow-citizens. Hence came those bitter and implacable discords with scoundrels, and hereby was I strengthened to do what all must do who would keep a clear conscience, despise the anger of the great when I knew that I was championing the right.

'How often have I met the rush of Cunigast when coming on open-mouthed to devour the property of the poor! How often have I baffled Trigguilla the royal chamberlain in some course of injustice which he had begun and all but completed!

How often have I interposed my influence to protect the poor creatures whom the unbridled avarice of the barbarians was for ever worrying with false accusations!

'Never did any one turn me aside from right to wrong-doing. When I saw the fortunes of the Provincials being ruined at once by private robbery and by the public taxes, I grieved as much as the sufferers themselves. At a time of severe famine, when a rigorous and unaccountable order of 'coemption' was like to strike the whole province of Campania with poverty, I commenced in the public interest, and with the knowledge of the King, a struggle against the Praetorian Prefect, which was crowned with success, and led to the abandonment of the coemption'.

The reader will notice that in the above Boethius fairly enough attributes to Theodoric knowledge and approval of his attempts to preserve the Provincials of Campania from oppression. And indeed, on comparing this passage with those letters of Cassiodorus, which describe the disgrace of Faustus, we can hardly doubt that the latter nobleman is the Praetorian Prefect here referred to, and that Boethius co-operated with Cassiodorus to obtain at least a temporary suspension of the powers of so grasping and tyrannical a governor.

Boethius then mentions the case of 'Paulinus, a man of consular rank, for whose wealth the dogs of the palace were hungering and had in fancy already devoured it, but who was rescued by me from their hungry jaws'.

So far we have heard nothing that is not in entire conformity with the uniform tenour of the Various Letters of Cassiodorus, nothing as to which we may not believe that the conduct of Boethius was wise, statesmanlike, and in perfect accord with the wishes of Theodoric and his great minister. Both Goths like Trigguilla, and Romans like Faustus, were continually, with Pacha-like voracity, scenting the prey of the subject Provincials, and it needed all the watchfulness and all the courage of the central government at Ravenna to detect and to punish their crimes.

It was no doubt partly in reward of such services, and in order to mark the King's appreciation of the character and attainments of his distinguished courtier, that honours and offices were bestowed on Boethius and his family. His own consulship made the year 510 illustrious. In 522 his two sons, Symmachus and Boethius, one bearing his own name, and the other that of his honoured father-in-law, notwithstanding their extreme youth, were arrayed in the consular robes. The proud father, little dreaming of the ruin which was already nigh at hand, addressed Theodoric from his place in the Senate in a brilliant speech of panegyric. Afterwards, probably on the 1st of September in the same year, Boethius was promoted to the highly important and confidential post of Master of the Offices, which dignity he held when the storm of the royal displeasure burst upon him.

We thus come to the case of Albinus. Again Boethius himself shall describe it to us, and while reading his words, it will be well to compare them with the shorter but generally harmonious account given by the Anonymus Valesii.

'That Albinus the Consular might not undergo punishment upon a foregone conclusion of his guilt, I set myself against the wrath of the informer Cyprian. Great indeed were the animosities which I thereby sharpened against myself [namely, of Cyprian's party]; but I ought to have been all the safer with the rest [of the Senators], who knew that from my love of justice I had left myself no place of safety with the courtiers. But, on the contrary, who were the informers by whom I was struck down? [They were Senators themselves.] Basilius, long ago turned out of the King's service, was driven by pressure of debt to calumniate my name. Opilio and Gaudentius, when, on account of their numberless and varied frauds, they had been ordered by a royal decree to quit the country, not choosing to obey, sought the shelter of the sanctuary. This came to the King's ears, and he ordered that, unless by a given day they had left Ravenna, they should be driven forth with a brand of infamy on their foreheads. What more stringent measure could have been adopted? Yet on that very day they laid their information against me, and that information was accepted. Was that a fitting reward for my services? Did the foregone conclusion to condemn me turn those accusers into honest men? Had Fortune no shame, if not for the innocence of the accused, at least for the villainy of the accusers?

But perhaps you ask in fine, of what crime is it that I am Accused. *I am said to have desired the safety of the Senate.* "In what way?" you ask. I am accused of having prevented an informer from producing certain documents in order to prove the Senate guilty of high treason. What is your advice then, oh my teacher? Shall I deny the charge in order that I may not bring disgrace upon you? But I did wish for the safety of the Senate, and shall never cease to wish for it. Shall I confess? That would be to play into the hands of the informer. Shall I call it a crime to have desired the safety of that venerable order? I can only think of their decrees concerning me as a reason why that should be a crime. But imprudence, though ever untrue to itself, cannot alter the nature of things, and, influenced as I am by the teachings of Socrates, I do not think it right either to conceal the truth or to admit a falsehood.

'How this may be [what may be my duty to the Senate now that it has deserted me,] I leave to be settled by thy judgment and that of the sages. In order that the truth and the real connection of the whole affair may not be hidden from posterity, I have drawn up a written memorandum concerning it. For, as for those forged letters, by which I am accused of having hoped for Roman freedom, why should I say anything about them? Their falsity would have been manifest if I had been allowed to use the confession of the informers themselves, winch is alwavs considered of the greatest weight. For what chance of freedom, pray, is still left to us? Would, indeed, that there were any such chance. [Had I been examined in the King's presence] I would have answered in the words of Canius, who, when accused by Caius [Caligula] of being privy to the conspiracy against him, answered, "If I had known of it, thou shouldest have never known".'

Boethius then expresses his wonder that a good God can suffer the wicked thus to triumph over the righteous. As an earlier philosopher had said, "If there be a God, whence comes evil hither? And if there be none, whence comes good?".

'But let it be granted that it was natural for evil-minded men, who were thirsting for the blood of the Senate and of all good citizens, to seek to compass my ruin, because they saw in me the champion of both classes. But did I deserve this treatment at the hands of the Senate also? Since you [0 Philosophy] ever present beside me, directed all my sayings and doings, you will remember, I think, that day at Verona, when the King, eager for a general slaughter, laboured to transfer the charge of treason brought against Albinus, to all the Senate. At what great peril to myself did I defend the innocence of the whole order! You know that in all this I am putting forth nothing but the truth, and am indulging in no vain boastings. My innocence has been more hardly dealt with than confessed guilt. Scarcely would an avowed criminal find all his judges unanimous against him, nor one disposed to make allowance for the frailty of the human mind, or to remember the inconstancy of Fortune. If I had been accused of wishing to burn the sacred edifices, to slay the priests with impious sword, to plot the murder of all good citizens, I should at least have been confronted with my accusers, and have either confessed my guilt or been convicted before I was punished. But now, at a distance of about 500 miles from my judges, dumb and undefended, I have been condemned to death and the forfeiture of my estate. For what? For too earnest love towards the Senate [my judges]. Assuredly they deserve that no one should ever again suffer on such a charge : a charge which even they who made it, saw to be so far from dishonourable that they were obliged to darken it with the admixture of some wickedness.

'They therefore falsely alleged that, in my pursuit of office, I had stained my conscience with sacrilege. Whereas thou, present in my breast, hadst driven base cupidity from thence, and under thy holy eyes there was no room for sacrilege. Thou hadst daily instilled into mine ears and thoughts the great Pythagorean maxim, "Follow God". How could I, whom thou hadst thus been fashioning into the divine likeness, seek to gain the favour of the baser spirits [of the under-world]? Moreover the innocent retirement of my home, the companionship of my honoured friends, the very presence of my father-in-law, a man holy and reverend as thou art, should have defended me from the suspicion of such crimes. But, alas! my very friendship with thee lent colour to the charge, and it was for this cause that I seemed likely to have practised divination, because I was known to be imbued with the teachings of Philosophy.'

It will not be needful to repeat to the reader any more of the sad ejaculations of Boethius. Failing that memorandum as to his defence, which Boethius he composed, and the loss of which leaves a lamentable gap in our knowledge of his case, we may take these few paragraphs as his plea against his accusers at the bar of history. With all its passionate declamation it does make some points of the story clearer.

(1) It is plain that Boethius was in no sense a martyr to orthodoxy. He was a Catholic, and Theodoric was an Arian, but that difference of creed had evidently no direct connection with the disgrace and death of the philosopher.

(2) Nor was it directly a case of Goth against Roman. The names of Gothic enemies which he mentions—Trigguilla, Cunigast, perhaps 'the dogs of the palace'—are all connected with his earlier life. In this latest act of the drama the 'delatores' against him are all Romans, Cyprian, Basilius, Gaudentius, Opilio. And this agrees with the hints of the Anonymus Valesii, who says that the informer was moved by cupidity; and with the language of Procopius, who declares that the wealth, the philosophic pursuits, the charity and the renown of Symmachus and Boethius, had stirred up envy in the breasts of spiteful men who laid a false charge against them before Theodoric, that they were plotting a revolution. Though the government is equally responsible on either hypothesis, it was Roman fraud, not Gothic force, which set the powers of government in motion.

(3) It was by the Senate that Boethius was condemned to death and proscription. Here, too, the ultimate responsibility is not removed from the king, before whose frown the slavish Senate trembled. As we do not accept it as any apology for the sanguinary deeds of a Tudor prince, that his Parliament was found willing to invest them with the forms of law, so too the condemnation of Boethius, if unjust, stains the memory of Theodoric equally, whether passed by the Conscript Fathers in Rome or by his own *Comitatus* at Ravenna. But how shall we think of the case if evidence were laid before them which the Senate, with all their good-will to the prisoner, could not ignore? At any rate the interposition of the Senate shows that we have not to do with a mere outbreak of lawless savagery on the part of the Gothic King.

(4) The case was strangely complicated by an accusation against Boethius, that he practised forbidden arts and sought to familiar spirits. Ridiculous as this accusation seems to us, we can easily see how the pursuits of so clever a mechanician as Boethius would in the eyes of the ignorant multitude give plausibility to the charge. The Theodosian code teemed with enactments against *Mathematici*, meaning, of course, primarily the impostors who calculated nativities and cast horoscopes. From many allusions in the 'Consolation' we infer that astronomy was to Boethius the most attractive of all the sciences. He would have been centuries in advance of his age if he had been able to divest his study of the heavenly bodies of all taint of astrological superstition. The insinuation that a profound mathematician must needs possess unlawful means of prying into the future, was of course absurd; but it is not the barbarous ignorance of the Goth, but the superstitious legislation of generations of Christian Emperors, that must bear the blame of this miscarriage of justice.

There is one more witness, (a sad and unwilling witness,) who must be examined, and then the evidence in this mysterious case will be all before the reader. Cassiodorus, in all the twelve books of his letters, makes, I believe, no reference, direct or indirect, to the death of Boethius and Symmachus. This silence tells against Theodoric. Had the execution of the two statesmen been a righteous and necessary act, it is hardly likely that Cassiodorus would have so studiously avoided all allusion to the act itself, and to the share which he, the chief counsellor of Theodoric, may have had in the doing of it. As it is, we may almost imagine, though we cannot prove, that the minister, finding his master bent upon hot and revengeful deeds, such as could only mar the good work of their joint lifetimes, retired from active co-operation in the work of government, and left his master to do or undo at his pleasure, unchecked by a word from him.

Yet the evidence of Cassiodorus tells also somewhat against Boethius. The reader has seen in what tints of unrelieved blackness the philosopher paints all those who were concerned in his downfall. The letters of Cassiodorus, written after Theodoric's death, collected and published when their author was retiring from politics, give a very different impression of these men.

Cyprian, the accuser of Albinus, who was forced to become the accuser of Boethius also, appears, to have been a Roman of noble birth, son of a consul, to have been appointed *referendarius* in the king's court of appeal, and in that capacity to have had the duty of stating the cases of the litigants, first from one point of view, then from the other. The fairness with which he did this, the nimbleness of mind with which he succeeded in presenting the best points of each case without doing injustice to the other, often excited the admiration of the suitors themselves. Then, when Theodoric was weary of sitting in his court, he would often mount his horse and order Cyprian to accompany him in a ride through the whispering pine-wood of Ravenna. As they went, Cyprian would often, by the King's command, describe the main features of a case which was to come before the Comitatus. In his hands, the dull details of litigation became interesting to the Gothic King, who, even when Cyprian was putting a hopelessly bad case before him, moderated his anger at the impudence of the litigant, in deference to the charm of his counsellor's narration.

Cyprian, after some years' service as Referendarius, was sent on an important embassy to Constantinople, in which he successfully upheld his master's interests at the Imperial Court. He was afterwards, apparently after the execution of Boethius, appointed to the high office of chief Finance Minister of the kingdom.

One would have said that this was the record of a fair and honourable official career, and that he who pursued it was not likely to be a base and perjured informer. Rather does it suggest to the mind the painful position of a statesman who, Roman himself, knew that many other Romans were not dealing faithfully by his Gothic King, but, by underhand intrigues at Constantinople, were seeking to prepare a counter revolution. His situation would thus be like that of a minister of Dutch William or Hanoverian George; bound in honesty to the king whose bread he is eating to denounce the treasons of the Jacobite conspirators around him, even though they be his countrymen and the king a foreigner. He names Albinus, whose guilt he is certain of. Boethius, the all-honoured and all-envied, steps forward, and thinks, by throwing the shelter of his great name over the defendant, to quash the accusation. With regret, but of necessity, Cyprian enlarges his charge, saying, 'Well, if you will have it so—and Boethius too.'

Let us turn to the characters of the other accusers. It is true that Basilius, 'long ago turned out of the King's service,' may be the same as the Basilius who was accused along with Praetextatus of being addicted to magical arts and whose case was handed over to the Prefect of the city for trial. Basilius, however, is a somewhat common name, and we must not be too certain of this identification. But as to Opilio, we have and strong evidence from Cassiodorus, which makes it almost impossible that the passionate invective of Boethius can be absolutely true. Opilio was evidently the brother of Cyprian, and probably grandson of the consul of 453, who was also called Opilio. In 527, four years after these events, he was raised by Amalasuntha, probably on the advice of Cassiodorus, to the responsible office of Count of the Sacred Largesses, which had been previously held by his brother. In the letters announcing his promotion to this office, the loyalty and truth of character, both of Opilio and Cyprian, are enthusiastically praised. 'Why should I describe the merits of his ancestors when he shines so conspicuously by the less remote light of bis brother? They are near relations, but yet nearer friends. He has so associated himself with that brother's virtues that one is uncertain which of the two one should praise the more highly. Cyprian is a most faithful friend, but Opilio shows unshaken constancy in the observance of his promises. Cyprian is devoid of avarice, and Opilio shows himself a stranger to cupidity. Hence it comes that they have known how to keep faith with their sovereigns, because they know not how to act perfidiously towards their equals. It is in this unfettered intercourse that the character is best shown. How can such men help serving their lords honourably, when they have no thought of taking an unfair advantage of their colleagues?'

Doubtless these official encomiums are to be received with caution, but, after making all due abatement, it is impossible to suppose that Cassiodorus would have deliberately republished letters, full of such high praises of men, whom all his contemporaries knew to be, in truth, the base scoundrels described by Boethius.

In connection with this subject we must take also some words of the philosopher with reference to one of his colleagues in office. When he is musing on the vanity of human wishes, and showing why the honours of the State cannot satisfy man's aspirations after happiness, he says, or rather Philosophy says to him, 'Was it really worth while to undergo so many perils in order that thou mightest wear the honours of the magistracy with Decoratus, though thou sawest in him the mind of abase informer and buffoon?'. Now Decoratus—the name is too uncommon to make it probable that there were two contemporaries bearing it—was a young nobleman of Spoleto, a man of some eminence as an orator, loyal, faithful, and generous. He died in the prime of life, and the King, who deeply regretted him, sought to repay some part of the debt owing to Decoratus by advancing in the career of office his younger brother Honoratus. Such is the picture of his character which we collect, not only from two letters of Cassiodorus, but also from one of Ennodius, and from the more doubtful evidence of his epitaph. Are all these men's characters to be blasted, because of the passionate words of Boethius in his dungeon? Do not these words rather return upon himself, and can we not now see something more of his true character? To me they indicate the faults of a student-statesman, brilliant as a man of letters, unrivalled as a man of science, irreproachable so as he remained in the seclusion of his library; but utterly unfit for affairs; passionate and ungenerous; incapable of recognising the fact that there might be other points of view beside his own; persuaded that every one who wounded his vanity must be a scoundrel, or at best a buffoon;—in short, an impracticable colleague, and, with all his honourable aspirations, an unscrupulous enemy.

The reader has now before him all the evidence that is forthcoming with reference to this most important but most perplexing State-trial. A historian shrinks from pronouncing his own verdict in such a case. His admiration and sympathy are due in different ways both to the author of the sentence and to its victim; and he can only extenuate the fault of Theodoric by magnifying, perhaps unduly, the fault of Boethius. But, after all the analysis that we have been engaged in, some short synthetical statement seems needful for the sake of clearness.

It was probably some time in the year 523 that Theodoric was first informed that some of the leading Senators were in secret correspondence with the Emperor. The tidings came at a critical time. In the previous year the great Ostrogoth had heard of his grandson Segeric's death, inflicted by order of his father, the Catholic King of Burgundy. In May or June of this year came the news that his own sister, the stately Queen of the Vandals, Amalafrida, was shut up in prison by the Catholic Hilderic. Must then 'the aspiring blood of Amala sink in the ground?' Was there a 'conspiracy everywhere among these lesser lords of the Germans, both against the creed of their forefathers, and against the great Ostrogothic house which had been the pillar of the new European State-system? Such were the suggestions that goaded the old hero almost to madness. He had now just reached the seventh decade of life; and the temper so well kept in curb all through his middle years, since the day when he slew Odovacar, was beginning to throw off the control of the feebler brain of age.

Then came the scene of the denunciation of Albinus. It happened apparently at Verona, most likely in the High Court of Justice (*Comitatus*) of the King. Boethius generously steps forward to shield Albinus. Cyprian, driven into a corner, reluctantly accuses Boethius also. Of what was it that Albinus and Boethius were accused? This, which should be the plainest part of the whole transaction, is in fact the darkest. None of our authorities really enable us to reconstruct the indictment against the Senators. Boethius shrilly vociferates that he was accused of nothing but 'desiring the safety of the Senate', which, taken literally, is absurd. But we have seen abundantly how indefinite and anomalous was the tie which bound both the Senate, and in some sort Theodoric himself, to the Empire. Is it possible that the letters which were sent by the senatorial party urged Justin to turn this shadowy senior-partnership into real supremacy, and especially *claimed for the members of the Senate that they should be judged only by the tribunals of the Empire, not by those of Theodoric?* Some such demand as this would explain the words of Boethius about 'desiring the safety of the Senate'. At the same time it was a proposal which, in the actual circumstances of both realms, meant really treason to Theodoric.

It seems probable that some letters of this similar purport were actually signed by Boethius as well as by Albinus and forwarded to Constantinople. Boethius says that the letters which were produced against him were forged. Perhaps, in reality, they were tampered with, rather than forged from beginning to end. It was a case in which the alteration of a few words might make all the difference between that which was and that which was not consistent with a good subject's duty to Theodoric. If any such vile work were done, the author of it may have been Gaudentius, the chief object of the vituperations of the philosopher for whom we can produce no rebutting evidence from the pages of Cassiodorus.

Whatever the accusation, and whatever the proofs, they appear to have been all forwarded to Rome, where the Senate, with base cowardice and injustice, trembling before the wrath of the King, unanimously found Boethius guilty of treason, and perhaps of sacrilege also. He was never confronted with his accusers, but was all the time lying in prison at Pavia or Calvenzano. Albinus disappears from the narrative, but was probably condemned along with Boethius.

For some reason which is not explained to us Boethius was kept in confinement for a considerable time, probably for the latter half of 523 and the earlier half of 524. The King was evidently greatly enraged against him. Probably the recent consulships bestowed on the sons of the conspirator and the flowery panegyric which he had then pronounced on Theodoric quickened the resentment of the King by the stings of ingratitude and, as it seemed, successful deception. It is possible that the reason for this long delay may have been a desire to wring from Boethius the names of his fellow-conspirators; and if so, we dare not altogether reject the story told by the Anonymus Valesii of the tortures applied to him in the prison. In itself this writer's narrative is not of a kind that commands implicit faith, and one is disposed to set down the story of the twisted cord and the protruding eyes as a fit companion to that told a few lines before of the woman who gave birth to the dragons, and of their airy passage to the sea. The author is evidently misinformed as to some circumstances of the trial, since he makes the King, not the Senate, pass sentence on Boethius, and represents the sentence as soon carried out, whereas the philosopher undoubtedly languished for a considerable time in prison after his condemnation.

The death of Boethius occurred probably about the middle of 524. We have no means of ascertaining the date more accurately. Then came the ill-judged mission of the Pope to Constantinople; and before his return, apparently early in 525, the citation of the venerable Symmachus to Ravenna, and his execution. From the whole tenor of the narrative it is safe to infer that this was much more the personal act of Theodoric than the condemnation of Boethius had been. The evidence, if evidence there was, of conspiracy was probably far slighter. Fear was the King's chief counsellor, and, as ever, an evil counsellor. The course of argument was like that of Henry VIII in his later years, or the Committee of Public Safety in the French Kevolution. 'Symmachus has lost his son-in-law; Symmachus must be disaffected to the monarchy; let Symmachus be prevented from conspiring—by the executioner.' It is clear, from the stories which were floating about in the next generation, that this act was the one which was most severely blamed by contemporaries, and the one which lay heaviest on the King's own conscience.

In short, from such information as we can collect, it seems right to conclude,—

(1) That the death of Boethius, though a grievous blunder, was, according to the principles of self-preservation acted upon by all rulers, not a crime.

(2) That if torture were employed, which is too probable but not proved, such a proceeding was an infamy.

(3) That the death of Symmachus was both a blunder and a crime.

But while condemning the conduct of Theodoric we may also lament the error of judgment which led the high-minded but visionary Boethius into the field of politics. He had doubtless noble dreams for the future of a reorganized and imperial Italy; dreams which entitle him to reach over eight centuries and clasp the hand of the Florentine poet, the author of the *De Monarchia*. But in that near future to which politicians must confine their gaze, the restoration of the Empire meant the carnival of the tax-collectors of Byzantium; the ascendancy of the Church meant the inroads of the fierce and faithless Frank. These evils would have been avoided and centuries of horror would have been spared to Italy, if the inglorious policy of Cassiodorus, the statesman of the hour, might have prevailed over the brilliant dreams of Boethius, the student and the seer.

I have purposely reserved to the last, till these matters of political debate were disposed of, the mention of the great work which has made the imprisonment of Boethius for ever memorable—his 'Consolation of Philosophy'. The title of the hook is ambiguous; but it need hardly be said that Philosophy is not the consoled one but the consoler. She indeed, at the end of the dismal tragedy, might well seem to need comfort for the loss of her favourite disciple. But in this book he, still living, describes how she braced and cheered him in his dungeon, when he was tempted to repine at his unmerited downfall, and to murmur at the triumph of the bad, at the apparent forgetfulness of the just Ruler of the world.

The scheme of the book is on this wise. The 'author of the bucolic poem', sick and in prison, employs his lonely hours in writing verses, and thus he sings :—

'I, who once touched the lyre with joyful hand,
Now, in my grief, do tread sad ways of song.
Lo! at my side the tearful Muses stand
To guide my heartfelt elegy of wrong.

No tyrant's wrath deters these guests sublime
From journeying with me all my downward way;
These, the bright comrades of my joyous Prime,
And now, my weary Age's only stay.

Yes: weary Age. For Youth with Joy has fled,
And Sadness brings her hoar companion.
Untimely honours silver o'er my head,
Untimely wrinkles score my visage wan.

Oh! happy they from whose delightful years
Death tarries far, to come, when called, with speed.
But deaf is Death to me, though called with tears :
These tearful eyes he will not close at need.

While still my bark sped on with favouring breeze,
Me, Death unlooked-for all but swept away.
Now, when all round me roar the angry seas,
Life, cruel Life, protracts her tedious stay.

How oft you named me happy, oh my friends.
Not happy he, whose bliss such ruin ends.'

Scarce has the mourning philosopher thus uttered his grief in song, when he lifts up his eyes and sees a mysterious form standing beside him. A woman, she seems, of venerable face, with gleaming eyes, with every sign of youthful vigour about her, and yet with something in her countenance which tells of life protracted through untold centuries. Her very stature is mysterious and indefinite. Now her head seems to touch the skies, and now she is only of the ordinary height of men. The raiment which she wears was woven by her own hands of finest gossamer thread, and is dark with age. On the lower hem of her robe is embroidered the letter P, on the upper one T. *(These letters, as we afterwards learn, stand for Practical and Theoretical Wisdom.)* Upon the robe is embroidered the likeness of steps leading up from the lower letter to the higher. In her right hand she bears some rolls of parchment; in her left a sceptre.

This is Philosophy, come to reprove and to comfort her downcast disciple. With sublime wrath she dismisses the Muses from the bed-side of the patient, pouring upon them names of infamy, and declaring that they are aggravating the disease which they pretend to heal. Boethius is her disciple, nourished on the doctrine of Eleia and the Academy, and by her Muses, not by their Siren voices shall his soul be cured. The Muses venture no reply, but with downcast looks and blushing faces silently depart.

Then Philosophy, sitting on the edge of his bed and looking into his face with sad eyes, sings a song of pity and reproof. 'Alas!' she says, 'for the darkness which comes over the mind of man. Is this he whose glance roved freely through the heavenly labyrinth, who watched the rosy light of dawn, the changes of the chilly moon, who marked the course of the winds, the return of flowery spring and fruitful autumn, and who knew the reason of all these things? Yet now here he lies, with his mind all bedimmed, with heavy chains upon his neck, casting downward his gloomy countenance, and forced to contemplate only the stolid earth beneath him.'

'The time is come,' she continues, 'for the healing art of the physician. Look fixedly at me, and tell me, dost thou know me?' A deadly lethargy oppresses Boethius, and he makes no reply. Then she wipes his streaming eyes : the touch of her hand revives him; he gazes earnestly into her face; he recognizes his own and oldest friend, his Muse, his teacher, Philosophy. But why has she come to visit him in this his low estate? She assures him that she never leaves her votaries in their distress, and reminds him by the example of Socrates, Anaxagoras, Zeno, and many more, that to be misunderstood, to be hated, to be brought into prison, and even to death itself by the oppressor, is the customary portion of those who love her. She is come to heal him, but, that she may practise her skill, it is needful that he shall show her all his wound. Then Boethius, in a few pages of autobiography, gives that narrative of his fall from the sovereign's favour which has been already put before the reader. The remembrance of all his wrongs, the reflection that even the people condemn him and that his good name is trodden under foot of men, forces from him a cry of anguish, and in a song, well-nigh of rebellion against the Most High, he says, '0 God, wherefore dost thou, who rulest the spheres, let man alone of all thy creatures go upon his wicked way, heedless of thy control?'

Philosophy, with face sadder than before, hears this outburst. 'I knew,' she says, 'when I first saw thee that thou wast an exile from thy home, but how far thou hadst wandered from the City of Truth I knew not till now. Tell me, dost thou believe in an all-wise and all-good Governor of the world?'. 'I do', he answered, 'and will never cast away this faith'. 'But what is the manner of his governing?' Boethius shakes his head, and cannot understand the question. 'Poor clouded intellect!' says Philosophy to herself. 'Nevertheless his persuasion that there is a righteous Ruler is the one point of hope. From that little spark we will yet reanimate his vital heat. But the cure will need time.'

'I see,' said Philosophy, 'that it is the sudden change of Fortune that has wrought this ruin in thy intellect. But it is of the very essence of Fortune to be ever changing. If she could speak for herself she would say, "All those things which you now mourn the loss of were my possessions, not yours. Far from groaning over their departure, you should be thankful to me for having let you enjoy them so long". Think what extraordinary good fortune you have had in life; friends to protect your boyhood, an honoured father-in-law, a noble wife, a marriage-bed blessed with male offspring. Remember that proud day when you went from your home with a son, a consul, on either side of you, begirt by crowds of senators. Remember your oration in the Senate-house in praise of the King, and the glory won by your eloquence. Remember the shouting multitudes in the circus, who acclaimed your lavish gifts'. 'Ah, but that is the very pity of it,' says Boethius : 'the remembrance of these past delights is the sharpest sting of all my sorrows'. 'Courage!' replies his heavenly visitor : 'all is not yet lost. Symmachus, that wise and holy man, whose life ou would gladly purchase with your own, still lives, and though he groans over your injuries has none to fear for himself. Rusticiana, whose character is the very image of her father's, lives, and her intense sympathy with your suffering is the only thing which I can consent to call a calamity for you. Your sons, the young Consulars, live too, and at every turn reflect the mind either of their father or their grandfather. After all, even in your present low estate there are many who would gladly change with you. Some secret grief or care preys on almost every heart, even of those who seem most prosperous'.

Then the gifts of Fortune are passed rapidly under review. Money, jewels, land, fine raiment, troops of servants, power, fame, are all subjected to that searching analysis, by which at any time for the last 2500 years philosophers have been able to prove their absolute worthlessness, that analysis in spite of which still, after so many centuries, the multitude of men still persist in deeming them of value.

The cure now begins to work in the soul of Boethius, and Philosophy feels that she may apply stronger remedies than the mere palliatives which she has used hitherto. She therefore leads him into a discussion of the *Summum Bonum*, the supreme good, which all men, more or less consciously, are searching after and longing to possess. There are many things apparently good, which cannot be this one highest good. Wealth cannot be the *Summum Bonum*, for it is not self-sufficing. Nor office, since it only brings out in stronger relief the wickedness of bad men; since it confers no honour among alien peoples, and the estimation in which it is held is constantly changing even in the same country. Nor can friendship with kings and the great ones of the earth be the *Summum Bonum*, since those persons themselves lack it. Glory, popularity, noble birth, all are found wanting. The pleasures of the flesh, yea and even family joys, cannot be the *Summum Bonum*. At this point a certain religious awe comes over the interlocutors. Philosophy sings a hymn of invocation to the Supreme Being, and then leads Boethius up to the conclusion that the Summum Bonum, or Happiness in the highest sense, can be none other than God himself, and that men, in so far as they attain to any real participation therein, are themselves divine. In a somewhat Pantheistic strain, Philosophy argues that all things tend towards God, and that evil, which appears to resist him, is itself only an appearance.

'Still,' cries the prisoner in agony, 'my difficulty has not really vanished. I see that the bad do prosper here, and the good are often cruelly oppressed. How can I reconcile these facts with the faith, which I will not abandon, that the world has a Just and Almighty Ruler?' Philosophy, one must admit, answers but feebly this eternal question. She repeats the Stoical commonplaces, that the wise man (or the good man) alone is free, alone is strong; that the evil man, though he sit upon a tyrant's throne, is in truth a slave, that liberty to work wickedness is the direst of all punishments, and that if wicked men could only, as it were, through a little chink of light see the real nature of things, they would cry out for the sorest chastisement, for anything to cleanse them from their intolerable corruption. The thought of a world to come in which the wicked, triumphant in this world, shall receive the just reward of their deeds, is somewhat timorously put forward, and does not become, as in the Christian Theodicy, the central point of the reply to the impugner of God's ways

Philosophy is perhaps nearer to grasping the key of the position, when she enters into a long disquisition on the distinction between Providence and Fate. Providence is the supreme, all-ruling, all-directing Intelligence, whose ways will be manifestly justified in the end : Fate, the instrument in the hand of Providence, more closely resembles what we understand by the Laws of Nature. To Fate belongs that undeviating order, that rigid binding together of Cause and Effect, which produces what to men seems sometimes hardness or even injustice in the ways of their Creator. Philosophy argues, therefore, that every fortune is, in truth, good fortune, since it comes to us by the will of God. The wise man, when he finds that what men call evil fortune is coming upon him, should feel like the warrior who hears the trumpet sound for battle. Now is the day come for him to go forth, and prove, in conflict with adverse Fate, the strength of that armour with which years of philosophic training have endowed him.

Rested and strengthened, Boethius now invites his heavenly guest to cheer him with one of those discussions in which of old he delighted, and to explain to him how she reconciles the divine foreknowledge of all future events with the freedom of human actions. God's knowledge of the future cannot be a mere opinion or conjecture : it must be absolute, certain and scientific. 'Yet, if He thus foresees my actions for this day, they are fixed, and my power of changing them is only apparent. Thus Necessity is introduced, Free-Will goes, and with it Moral Responsibility. It is useless to utter prayer to God, since the order of all things is already fixed, and we cannot change it. The thought of Divine Grace, touching and moulding the hearts of men, and bringing them into communion with their Maker, goes likewise. All is rigid, mechanical, immutable'.

Philosophy's answer to this question is long and subtil, but in the end brings us nearly to the same conclusion which is probably reached, more or less consciously, by the ordinary Theist of today. In all acts of perception, she says, the perceiver himself contributes something from the quality of his own mind : and thus perceptions differ according to the rank held by the perceiver in the intellectual universe. Animals see material things around them, but they do not see in them all that man sees. Where the horse sees only the quartem-measure in which his oats are brought to him, the trained intellect of man sees a circle, roughly representing the ideal circle of mathematics, and is conscious of all the properties inherent in that figure. As our manner of seeing is superior to that of the brutes, so we must train ourselves to think of God's manner of seeing as superior to ours. He can see all future events, both necessary and contingent, and yet not, by seeing them, impart to all the same necessity. Before him, as the Eternal Being, Past, Present and Future lie all outstretched at the same moment. He sees all events which have happened and which shall happen, as if now happening; and thus his foreseeing no more necessitates the actions foreseen than my looking at a man ploughing on yonder hill compels him to plough, or prevents him from ceasing his occupation.

'And yet, in a certain sense, there is a necessity laid upon men, from the very thought that they are thus doing all in the sight and presence of God : a necessity to lead nobler lives, to avoid vice, to raise their hearts to the true and higher hope, to lift up their humble prayers on high'.

Here, abruptly, the Consolation of Philosophy ends. We must suppose that when Boethius has reached this point, the step of the brutal gaoler is heard at his dungeon-door, the key turns in the lock, the executioner enters, and the Consolations of Philosophy end with the life of her illustrious disciple.

Such is an outline of the argument of the work upon which Boethius employed the enforced leisure of his prison hours. It will at once be seen that it deals with subjects which have ever been of primary interest to the human race. Sometimes the argument reminds us of the book of Job, sometimes of the Tenth Satire of Juvenal, sometimes of Pope's 'Essay on Man'. The author's Latin prose is, upon the whole, pure, correct, and intelligible, a delightful contrast to the verbosity of Cassiodorus and the turgid ineptitudes of Ennodius. The snatches of song, in a vast variety of metres, with which the discourse is pleasantly enlivened, show an intimate acquaintance with the tragedies of Seneca, from whom sometimes a poetical phrase, sometimes the central idea of a whole canzonet, is borrowed. The extent of this indebtedness, however, has been sometimes overstated. The poems belong to Boethius himself, though he has written them with the echoes of Seneca's lyre vividly in his ear; and some of the most beautiful thoughts are entirely his own.

In the argument of the book Boethius shows himself, as we should have expected, a persistent eclectic. Though Aristotle is his great master, he draws in this book largely from Plato; and often we come upon passages which remind us of the Stoic doctrines which were the favourite subject of ridicule to Horace.

The religious position of the author has always been a subject of perplexity, and is not less so, now that we know that he is the same person who wrote tractates on subtle points of Christian controversy. He speaks throughout as a Theist, a Theist unshaken and unwavering, notwithstanding all the things that seem to make for Atheism in the world, but hardly as a Christian. There is no hint of opposition to any Christian doctrine; but on the other hand there is no sign of a willingness to accept the special Christian explanation of the central difficulty of the world. Instead of subtle arguments about the nature of the *Summum Bonum*, or a proof that bad men cannot be said truly to be at all and therefore it is idle to trouble ourselves about their prosperity, a Christian martyr would inevitably have turned to the remembrance of the Crucifixion, the mocking soldiery, the cursing Jews, and would have said, at the sorest of his distress, 'He has suffered more for me.' And the same thought would naturally have comforted any man, who, though not a martyr yet holding the same faith, was assailed by any of the lesser miseries of life, and troubled by seeing the apparent ascendency of evil. By him who accepts the fact which the Christian witnesses proclaim it may surely be said with boldness, 'The true Theodicy is the Theopathy.' The Son of God suffering for sin, admits the difficulty of the apparent triumph of evil, but suggests an explanation, which Faith leans upon, though Reason cannot put it into words.

Of all this we have in Boethius not a hint. Perhaps it was precisely because he was something of a scientific theologian, and knew the shoals and currents of that difficult sea in which it was so hard to avoid making shipwreck, one side or another, on the rocks of heresy, that he preferred to sail the wide ocean of abstract Theism. More likely, the feeling of a certain incompatibility between Christianity and polite literature, a feeling which not all the literary eminence of Jerome and Augustine had been able entirely to dispel, a feeling which threw so many of the later historians, Ammianus, Zosimus, Procopius, on the side of heathenism, prevented Boethius from more distinctly alluding than he has done to the Christian solution of his difficulties.

Whatever the cause, the undogmatic character of the 'Consolation' had probably something to do with its marvellous success in the immediately following centuries. The Middle Ages were at hand, that era of wild and apparently aimless struggle between all that is noblest and all that is basest in our common humanity. Many refined and beautiful natures were to go through that strife, to feel the misery of that chaos, in which they were involved. Some, far the larger part, clinging to the religious hope alone as their salvation from the storm, would retire from the evil world around them into the shelter of the convent.

But there were some, few perhaps in number in each generation, but many in the course of the centuries, who would elect not to quit the world but to battle with it, not to fly the evil but to overcome it. To such souls the 'Consolation' of Boethius sounded like a trumpet-call to the conflict. It was not the less welcome, may be, because it did not recall the familiar tones of monk and priest. The wisdom of all the dead pagan ages was in it, and nerved those strong, rather than devout, hearts to victory.

To trace with anything like completeness the influence of Boethius on the mind of the Middle Ages would require another chapter as long as the present. The mere list of editions and translations of his works, chiefly of his greatest work, in our national library, occupies fifty pages of the British Museum Catalogue. Two names, however, of his English translators, a king and a poet, claim a notice here. King Alfred, probably in the years of peace which followed the Treaty of Wedmore, found or made leisure to interpret the 'Consolation' to his countrymen. 'Sometimes[1],' as he himself tells us, 'he set word by word, sometimes meaning for meaning, as he the most plainly and most clearly could explain it, for the various and manifold worldly occupations which often busied him both in mind and in body. The occupations are very difficult to be numbered which in his days came upon the kingdom which he had undertaken; and yet when he had learned this book and turned it from Latin into the English language, he afterwards composed it in verse, as it is now done'. The King then explains to his subjects how 'the Goths made war against the Empire of the Romans, and with their kings, who were called Rhadgast and Alaric, sacked the Roman city and brought to subjection all the kingdom of Italy. Then, after the before-mentioned kings, Theodoric obtained possession of that same kingdom. He was of the race of the Amali, and was a Christian, but persisted in the Arian heresy. He promised to the Romans his friendship, so that they might enjoy their ancient rights. But he very ill performed that promise, and speedily ended with much wickedness; which was that in addition to other unnumbered crimes, he gave order to slay John the Pope. Then there was a certain consul, that we call *heretoga*, who was named Boethius. He was in book learning and in worldly affairs the most wise. Observing the manifold evil which the King Theodoric did against Christendom and against the Roman Senators, he called to mind the famous and the ancient rights which they had under the Caesars, their ancient lords. Then began he to enquire and study in himself how he might take the kingdom from the unrighteous King, and bring it under the power of the faithful and righteous men. He therefore privately sent letters to the Caesar at Constantinople, which is the chief city of the Greeks and their king's dwelling-place, because the Caesar was of the kin of their ancient lords: they prayed him that he would succour them with respect to their Christianity and their ancient rights. When the cruel King Theodoric discovered this, he gave orders to take him to prison and therein lock him up'.

After this prelude the royal translator proceeds to describe the sorrow of Boethius and the manner in which it was soothed. It is perhaps a concession to the monastic depreciation of women that the heavenly comforter is introduced as a *man* who is called Wisdom (sometimes Wisdom and Reason), instead of the noble matron Philosophy.

Few men would have had more sympathy with all that was great in Theodoric than Alfred his fellow-Teuton, had he known the true character of the Amal King, and the nature of the task that he had to grapple with. But three centuries of ecclesiastical tradition had produced so distorting an effect on the image reflected, that, as will be seen, the Theodoric whom Alfred beheld, resembled in scarcely a single feature the Theodoric known to his contemporaries. But notwithstanding this blemish, Alfred's translation of Boethius is a marvellous work. Few things seem to bring us so near to the very mind and soul of the founder of England's greatness as these pages, in which (not always understanding his author and sometimes endeavouring to improve upon him) the King follows the guidance of the philosopher through the mazes of the eternal controversy concerning Fate, Foreknowledge, and Free-will.

Travelling over five centuries, we find the illustrious and venerable name of Geoffrey Chaucer among the translators of Boethius. In the note prefixed to the work he says, 'In this book are handled high and hard obscure points, viz. the purveyance of God, the force of Destiny, the Freedom of our Wills, and the infallible Prescience of the Almighty; also that the Contemplation of God himself is our Sum mum Bonum.' Chaucer's notion of the duty of a translator seems to be stricter than King Alfred's; but it may be doubtful whether he has not presented the book in a less attractive guise than the royal translator.

With the revival of learning in the fifteenth century it was inevitable that the surpassing lustre, of the fame of Boethius should suffer some eclipse. When learned men were studying Aristotle and Plato for themselves, the translator and populariser of their philosophies became necessarily a person of diminished importance. Still, however, so fine a scholar as Sir Thomas More cherished the teachings of the Consolation of Philosophy, and was cheered by them in the dungeon to which he was consigned by a more tyrannical master than Theodoric.

In the following century a Jesuit priestby an imaginary life of Boethius, somewhat revived his fame, and as a statesman who resisted a heretical sovereign to the death, he was held up as a model for the imitation of English and German Catholics.

In later days the writings of Boethius have ceased to live, except for a few curious students. Yet, whoso would understand the thoughts that were working in the noblest minds of mediaeval Europe would do well to give a few hours of study to the once world-renowned 'Consolation of Philosophy.'

CHAPTER XIII.

THE ACCESSION OF ATHALARIC.

THE sun of Theodoric, which for thirty years had shone in mild splendour over the Italian land, set in lurid storm-clouds. Boethius slain, Symmachus slain, Pope John dead in prison, these were the events which every tongue at Rome and Ravenna was discussing with fear, with anger, or with lawless hope; and assuredly the dying King, though he might say few words concerning them, thought of little else : and all his thoughts about them were bitter. According to a story which was told to Procopius (perhaps by one of the lacqueys of the Court whom he may have met at Ravenna), one day at the banquet a large fish's head was set before Theodoric. To the King's excited fancy, the object in the dish assumed the semblance of the pallid face and hoary head of Symmachus, newly slain. Then, as he thought, the teeth began to gnaw the lower lip, the eyes rolled askance and shot glances of fury and menace at his murderer. Theodoric, who, if there be any truth in the story at all, was evidently already delirious, was seized with a violent shivering-fit, and hurried to his bed, where the chamberlains could hardly heap clothes enough upon him to restore his warmth. At length he slept, and when he woke he told the whole circumstance to Elpidius his physician, bewailing with many tears his unrighteous deed to Symmachus and Boethius. In this agony of mind, says Procopius, 'he died not long after, this being the first and last act of injustice which he had committed against any of his subjects : and the cause of it was that he had not sufficiently examined into the proofs, before he pronounced judgment upon these men.'

The ecclesiastical tradition as to the death of Theodoric, preserved for us by the Anonymus Valesii, makes the cause of it dysentery; a form of disease which, ever since the opportune death of the arch-heretic Arius, seemed peculiarly appropriate for heterodox disturbers of the Church. For the secular historian it is enough to remember that Theodoric was now seventy-two years of age and broken-hearted. They may leave him alone, the orthodox Romans, the righteously indignant friends of Senator and Pope. For that noble heart, Hell itself could scarcely reserve any sorer punishment than the consciousness of a life's labour wasted by one fierce outbreak of Berserker revenge.

The body of the dead King was laid in the mighty mausoleum which he had built for himself outside the north-eastern corner of Ravenna. There the structure still stands, massive if not magnificent, no longer now the Tomb of Theodoric, but the deserted Church of S. Maria della Rotonda. It is built of white marble, and consists of two stories, the lower ten-sided, the upper circular. The whole is crowned with an enormous monolith weighing two hundred tons and brought from the quarries of Istria. It is hard even for the scientific imagination to conjecture the means by which, in the infancy of the engineering art, so huge a mass of stone can have been raised to its place. In the centre of the upper story of the building stood, in all probability, the porphyry vase which held the body of the great Gothic King. The name Gothic must not lead the visitor to expect to see anything of what is technically called Gothic architecture in the building. The whole structure is Roman inspirit; square pilasters, round massive arches, a cupola, somewhat like that of Agrippa's Pantheon. The edifice, however, of which upon the whole it most reminds us is the great Mausoleum of Hadrian, such as it must have appeared in the centuries when it was still an imperial tomb and before it became a Papal fortress. And probably this was the example which hovered before the mind of Theodoric, whose work was not undertaken in a spirit of mere vainglory. Believing that he was founding a dynasty which would rule Italy for centuries, he would construct, as Hadrian had constructed, a massive edifice in which might be laid the bones of many generations of his successors.

As it turned out, the great Mausoleum became a Cenotaph. Theodoric himself was buried there, but when Agnellus, three hundred years after his death, wrote the story of the Bishops of Ravenna, it was matter of public notoriety that the tomb had long been empty; and the belief of the chronicler himself was that the royal remains had been cast forth contemptuously out of the Mausoleum, and the porphyry urn in which they were enclosed, a vessel of wonderful workmanship, placed at the door of the neighbouring monastery.

Why should there have been this mystery about the disposal of the body of the great Ostrogoth? Thereto is attached a little history, which, if the reader has patience to listen to it, links together in curious fashion the name of the Pope who sent St. Augustine to convert the Saxons, and that of the Pope who in our own day wielded and lost the power of a king both at Rome and at Ravenna.

To begin with Pope Gregory the Great. In his Dialogues, written sixty-eight years after the death of Theodoric, he informs us that 'a certain Defensor of the Roman Church named Julian married a wife whose grandfather was employed after under King Theodoric in the collection of the land-tax in Sicily. This tax-collector was once returning to Italy and touched at the island of Lipari, where dwelt a holy hermit to whose prayers he wished to commend himself. The hermit said, "Know ye, that King Theodoric is dead". "God forbid," replied the tax-gatherer and his friends. "We left him in good health and have heard no snch tidings". "For all that," said the hermit, "he is dead: for yesterday, at three in the afternoon, I saw him between John the Pope and Symmachus the Patrician. All ungirded and unshod, and with bound hands, he was dragged between them and cast into yon cauldron of Vulcan" [the crater of Lipari]. When they heard it, they carefully noted the day and the hour : and found, on their return to Ravenna, that at that very time Theodoric breathed his last'.

So wrote Pope Gregory. We overleap 1260 years and find ourselves in 1854 in 'the Legation of Ravenna,' which province is sullen and discontented at being replaced under the Papal sway by the arms of Austria after the revolutions of 1848-49. Works of industry, however, are progressing, and at Ravenna a party of 'navvies' are employed excavating a dock between the railway station and the Canale Corsini, one or two hundred yards from the Mausoleum of Theodoric. There are indications that they are on the site of an old cemetery; and the Papal Governor, together with the Municipality, appoints a Commission to watch over the excavation in the interests of archgeology : but the Commission, like some other parts of the ecclesiastical government of the Legations, is not likely to be worn out by excess of energy.

One day rumours are heard of some important discovery made by the workmen and not reported to the Commission. Enquiries are commenced: two workmen are arrested: by coaxing and threatening, the whole grievous history is elicited from them. A few days previously the navvies had come suddenly upon a skeleton, not in but near one of the tombs. The skeleton was armed with a golden cuirass : a sword was by its side and a golden helmet on its head. In the hilt of the sword and in the helmet large jewels were blazing. The men at once covered up the treasure, and returned at nightfall to dig it up again and to divide the spoil. At the time when the slow-moving Commission set its enquiries on foot the greater part of the booty had already found its way to the melting-pot of the goldsmith or had been sent away out of the country. By keeping the prisoners in custody, their share of the spoil, a few pieces of the cuirass, was recovered from their relatives in the mountains. These pieces, all that remains of the whole magnificent 'find,' are now in the Museum at Ravenna. Great precautions were taken afterwards by the Commission: a trusted representative was always present at the excavations by day; the city police tramped past the diggings at night. But the lost opportunity came not back again: no such second prize revealed itself either to the labourers or the members of the Commission.

Now, to whom did all this splendid armour belong in life? and whose heart was once beating within that skeleton? Of course the answer must be conjectural. It was given by the archaeologists of the day in favour of Odovacar; and the bits of. the golden cuirass in the Museum at Ravenna are accordingly assigned to him in the Catalogue. But Dr. Ricci, an earnest and learned archaeologist of Ravenna, argues with much force that the scene of Odovacar's assassination took place too far from the Rotonda to render this probable, and that there but more has never been a dweller in Ravenna to whom the longed to skeleton and the armour can with more likelihood be assigned than Theodoric himself.

We may imagine the course of events to be something like this. During the reign of his grandson the body of the great King in its costly armour remains in the royal Mausoleum, guarded perhaps by some of his old comrades-in-arms, or by their sons. Troubles begin to darken round the nation of Theodoric; the Roman population of Ravenna stir uneasily against their Arian lords; monks and hermits begin to manufacture or to imagine such stories as that told to Gregory concerning the soul of the oppressor being cast into the crater of Lipari. The inmates of the monastery of S. Mary, close to the Rotonda, hear and would fain help this growth of legend, so fatal to the memory of the Ostrogothic King. Suddenly the body with its golden cuirass and golden helmet disappears mysteriously from the Mausoleum. No one can explain its vanishing; but the judgment of charity will naturally be that the same divine vengeance which threw the soul of the King down the volcano of Lipari has permitted the powers of darkness to remove his mortal remains. The monks of Santa Maria, if they know anything about the matter, keep their secret; but some dim tradition of the truth causes the cautious Agnellus, writing three centuries after the event, to say, 'as it seems to me he was cast forth from the tomb.' So the matter rests till, thirteen centuries after the deed was done, the pick-axe of a dishonest Italian 'navvy ' reveals the bones of Theodoric.

All this is of course mere conjecture, and is not put before the reader as anything but a somewhat romantic possibility. The bitterness, the undeserved bitterness with which the Catholic Church has taught the Italians to regard the memory of Theodoric, is but too certain a fact, and some curious traces of it remain even to this day. On the western front of the beautiful church of S. Zenone at Verona is a bas-relief representing a king hunting stags, and being himself on the point of capture by a demon with horns and hoofs, who, with a cruel grin on his face, stands waiting for his prey. Some lines underneath showed that this kingly victim of the evil one was meant for Theodoric. For generations the urchins of Verona have been accustomed to rub the two figures of king and demon, imagining that there is thus obtained a sulphurous smell, which bears witness to their present abode.

From these idle tales of religious rancour we turn to consider the fortunes of the kingdom when bereft of its mighty founder. Shortly before his death Theodoric presented his grandson Athalaric, son of Eutharic and Amalasuntha, to the leaders of the Gothic people, and declared that he was their future king. The declaration was made specially to the Gothic nobles; but in the speech which the old King made on that occasion, and which was listened to as if it were his last will and testament, there was an earnest exhortation to the Goths to show not only loyalty to the new sovereign, but kindly feelings towards the Senate and people of Rome, and to cultivate friendly relations with the Eastern Emperor.

The presentation to the Gothic warriors was a sort of recognition of their slumbering right to choose the successor to the throne. But in fact, limited as that choice was to the family of the King, there could be no doubt how it would be exercised on this occasion. It is true that Athalaric was but ten years old, and his nominal kingship necessarily implied a woman's regency. But Amalaric, the only other grandson of Theodoric, though he had now probably attained his majority, must needs dwell in Spain or Narbonnensian Gaul as ruler of his father's Visigoths. The only other male of the Amal line, the late king's nephew Theodahad, was too profoundly hated and despised for any one to press his claims, even against the child-king his cousin.

Athalaric then succeeded to his grandfather's throne; and the succession of Athalaric meant, as has been said, the rule of Amalasuntha. She was a woman in whom a strength of character almost masculine was joined to rich gifts of the intellect and a remarkable power of appreciating Roman culture. Her earnest desire was to rule the young kingdom righteously; and had she only been able to carry her Gothic countrymen with her, she might have made for herself one of the noblest names in history. As it was, the deep-seated discordance between her thoughts and theirs revealed itself at length in acts of tyranny on her side and of rebellion on theirs, which caused the ruin of the Gothic monarchy. But of these open dissensions between the Regent and her subjects the time is not yet come to speak.

As the sympathies of Amalasuntha were all on the side of Roman literature and civilisation, it is reasonable to suppose that Cassiodorus, the most distinguished representative of that rich inheritance, would have great influence in her government. It is possible that he may have directed her studies while she was still but a princess; it is certain that he was the chief minister of her policy when she was a sovereign. There was no necessary breach of continuity between the policy of the father and that of the daughter. Cassiodorus was the trusted minister of both. But we can perceive, from the tone of his correspondence, that the anti-Roman turn which had been given to the policy of Theodoric during his last three years of suspicion and resentment, was reversed, and that something of a new impulse away from barbarian freedom and towards Roman absolutism was given to the vessel of the State.

Cassiodorus at the time of the death of Theodoric held the rank of Master of the Offices. How long he may have retained it we do not know, but it is pretty clear from his own statement that his power and influence at the Court were not strictly limited by the terms of his official commission. Other Quaestors were appointed; Cassiodorus drew up the letters assigning to them their duties : but he was himself the one permanent and irremovable Quaestor, equipped with an inexhaustible supply of sonorous phrases and philosophical platitudes, 'ready', as was said of the younger Pitt, 'to speak a State-paper off-hand.' After having for eight years, in one capacity or another, guided the counsels of Amalasuntha, he was promoted to the great place of Praetorian Prefect, and thus assumed the semblance as well as the form of power. That dignity he appears to have held for four or five stormy years, until his final retirement from public life.

From the official correspondence of Cassiodorus we infer that some anxiety was felt by the loyal subjects of the Amal dynasty as to the acceptance by the Goths of so young a sovereign as Athalaric. The emphasis with which the minister dwells on the alacrity of the Goths in taking the oath of allegiance implies that Amalasuntha and her friends breathed more freely when that ceremony Tuium. was accomplished. And the honours and compliments showered on the veteran Tulum, who was introduced to the Senate with the splendid rank of a Patrician, suggest the idea that he was looked upon by some of his old companions in battle as a more fitting occupant of the throne than a lad of ten years old. A mysterious allusion made by the courtly scribe to the warrior Gensemund of a by-gone age, a man whose praises the whole world sang, and who apparently might have been king, but preferred to guide the suffrages of his countrymen to the heir of the Amal house, makes this conjecture almost a certainty.

One of the first difficulties as to which the advice of Cassiodorus was needed by Amalasuntha arose out of the news which reached her from Africa. A slight allusion was made in the last chapter to the troubles which had fallen on Amalafrida, sister of Theodoric. Her husband Thrasamund, one of the best of the Vandal kings, died in 523, and was succeeded by his cousin the elderly Hilderic. This man, though a son of Huneric, the most rancorous of all the persecutors of the Catholic Church, shared not his father's animosity against the orthodox. It was generally believed that his mother Eudoxia had influenced him in favour of her form of faith; and Thrasamund on his death-bed had exacted from him an oath that he would never use his kingly power for the restoration of their churches to the Catholics. The oath was given; but Hilderic, who could say with Euripides' hero

'My lips have sworn, my mind unsworn remains,'

devised a clever scheme for escaping from its obligation. The promise had been that he would not use his kingly power for the forbidden purposes. Therefore after Thrasamunds death, but before Hilderic had put on the Vandal crown or been proclaimed king in the streets of Carthage, he issued his orders for the return of all the Catholic bishops from exile; he opened the churches, which for more than two generations had never echoed to the words 'being of one substance with the Father'; and he made Boniface, a strenuous asserter of orthodoxy, bishop of the African Church.

Hilderic's entire reversal of the policy of his predecessor brought him speedily into collision with that predecessor's widow. The stately and somewhat imperious Amalafrida, who had been probably for twenty years Queen of the Vandals, was not going tamely to submit to see all her husband's friends driven away and his whole system of government subverted. She headed a party of revolt; she called in the assistance of the Moors, ever restless and ever willing to make war upon the actual ruler of Carthage; and battle was joined at Capsa, about three hundred miles to the south of the capital, on the edge of the Libyan desert. Amalafrida's party were beaten, and she herself was taken captive. So long as her brother Theodoric lived she was kept a close prisoner. Now the great head of the Amal line was laid low, the Vandal king had the meanness and the cruelty to put his venerable prisoner to death.

The insult was keenly felt at the Court of Ravenna, and produced a fatal alienation between the two kingdoms. A letter of angry complaint was written by Cassiodorus, and ambassadors were sent to demand an explanation. No satisfactory explanation could be given; for the story which Hilderic endeavoured to circulate, that Amalafrida's death was natural, seems to have borne falsehood upon its face. What followed we are not able to say. Probably there was a threat of war, replied to by menaces of reprisal from the still powerful Vandal fleet against the Italian coast. At least we know of no other opportunity to which we can so suitably refer Cassiodorus' own account of his services to the kingdom at a time when it was threatened by foreign invasion. 'When the care of our shores,' he makes his young sovereign say, occupied our royal meditations, he [Cassiodorus] suddenly emerged from the seclusion of his cabinet, and boldly, like his ancestors, assumed the character of a general. He maintained the Gothic warriors at his own charges, preventing the impoverishment of our exchequer on the one hand, and the oppression of the Provincials on the other. When the work of victualling the ships was over, and the war was laid aside, he again distinguished himself as an administrator by his peaceful settlement of the various suits which had grown out of the sudden termination of the contracts for the commissariat.'

We seem to read in this passage of a threatened Vandal invasion of Bruttii and Lucania, of Cassiodorus' preparations for defending his native province, and of the sudden collapse of hostilities about which neither nation was really in earnest. It was not from the Ostrogothic nation that the impending ruin of the dynasty of Gaiseric was to proceed.

Five years after these events another of the Arian and Teutonic monarchies of Europe received its death-blow. The reader may remember that, after the defeat and captivity of Sigismund, his brother Godomar raised from the dust the torn banner of the Burgundians, and maintained the independence of his native land against the Frankish invaders. Now Godomar's turn also was come. Chlotochar and Childebert again entered the land. They besieged Autun. Godomar, after one or perhaps two campaigns, took to flight. Theudibert, the remaining brother of the Frankish partnership, was persuaded to forget his relationship to the family of Sigismund when the invasion seemed likely to prove successful. In the year 534 the kingdom of Burgundy, which had lasted for all but a hundred years since its settlement in Savoy, was finally swallowed up in the vast nebulous mass of the Frankish monarchy, Theudibert, Chlotochar, and Childebert dividing the spoils between them.

This is all that needs to be said about the affairs of Western Europe during the reign of Athalaric. With the Papacy the relations of the Gothic monarchy seem to have been outwardly amicable. The 'martyred' John was succeeded by Felix III; he by Boniface II, a man of Gothic extraction ; and he by another John, the second of the name. There is nothing in the short reigns of these pontiffs, at peace with Constantinople and outwardly at peace with Ravenna, which need occupy our attention.

Only, the election of the first of the series, Felix III, should be noticed, since it seems to have been ordered by the dying Theodoric and confirmed by his grandson. This we learn from a letter addressed by Cassiodorus to the Roman Senate. There had evidently been at least the threat of a contested election, but the minister, speaking in the name of Athalaric, exhorts all parties to forget the bitterness of the past debate. He thinks that the beaten party may yield without humiliation, since it is the King's power which has helped the winning side. The letter suggests the idea of a contest, the decision of which has been voluntarily referred to Theodoric, and the whole tone of it is extremely difficult to reconcile with any story of the death of Pope John I which represents him as a martyr, wilfully allowed by a persecuting king to perish in a dungeon. Had this been the version of the story generally accepted at Rome, it is hard to believe that in a very few months the relations between King and Pope would have been so friendly as we find them in this letter

From this short sketch it will be seen that few events of great importance occurred in Italy during the eight years of the reign of Athalaric. Constantinople, not Ravenna, was now once more the place to which the chief action of the great drama was transferred, and already all Roman souls were aflame with the reports of the splendour, the reforms, and the victories of Justinian.

CHAPTER XIV.

JUSTINIAN.

SOME time after his accession to the Empire, the elderly Anastasius was troubled with a restless curiosity to know who should be his successor. He had three nephews, Hypatius son of one of his sisters, and the brothers Probus and Pompeius, who were possibly children of his brother. Inviting them one day to dine with him at the palace, he caused three couches to be spread upon which his nephews might take their siesta. Under the pillow of one of the couches he had secretly slipped a paper with the word REGNUM written upon it. 'Whichsoever of my nephews,' thought he, 'chooses that couch, he shall reign after me.' Unfortunately when the time for the noontide slumber came, Hypatius chose one couch, the two brothers in their love for one another chose to occupy the second together, and the pillow that had 'regnum' beneath it was left undimpled. Then Anastasius knew that none of his nephews should wear the diadem after him.

It was not one of the three delicately nurtured princes, but a man who had begun life in very different fashion, who was to be clothed with the out-worn purple of Anastasius. In the reign of Leo, three young peasants from the central highlands of Macedonia, tired of the constant struggle for existence in their poverty-stricken homes, strode down the valley of the Axius (Vardar) to Thessalonica, determined to better their lot by taking service in the army. They had each a sheep-skin wallet over his shoulder, in which was stored a sufficient supply of home-baked biscuit to last them till they reached the capital: no other possessions had they in the world. Being tall and handsome young men, Zimarchus, Ditybistus, and Justin—so the peasant-lads were named—had no difficulty in entering the army: nay, they soon found places in the ranks of the guards of the palace, an almost certain avenue to yet higher promotion. Once indeed Justin had a narrow escape from death. For some offence— probably against military discipline—which he had committed, he was ordered into arrest and condemned to death by his captain John the Hunchback, under whose orders he had been sent upon the Isaurian campaign. But a figure of majestic size appeared to the Hunchback in his dreams and threatened him with sore punishment if he did not release the prisoner, who was fated to do good service to the Church in days to come. After this vision had been seen for three successive nights, the general thought it must be from above and dismissed Justin unharmed.

Now, in the aged Emperor's perplexity, when with fasting and prayer he had besought from Heaven an indication as to who should be his successor, it was revealed to him that the destined one was he who should be first announced to him in the sacred bed-chamber on the morrow morning. The first person to arrive was Justin, who had now attained the high rank of Count of the Guardsmen; come to report the execution of some orders given to him on the previous night. The aged Emperor bowed his head and recognised his destined successor. So firmly was this belief implanted in his mind that when, at some great ceremonial in the palace, Justin, eager to set right some mistake in the procession in front of the Emperor, brushed too hastily past him and trod upon the skirts of the purple mantle, the Emperor uttered no hasty word, but mildly said, 'Why such haste?' which men understood to mean, 'Canst thou not wait till thy turn comes to wear it? It will come before long'

These are the legendary half-poetical adornments of the prosaic story which was told in a previous chapter, concerning the elevation of the orthodox Justin, by means of the misappropriated gold of Amantius, on the death of the Monophysite Anastasius. Whatever the precise chain of causes and effects which brought it to pass, the result was that an elderly Macedonian peasant, unable to read or write, but strictly orthodox as regards the subtle controversy between Leo and Eutyches, was seated on the throne of the Eastern Caesars. The difficulty arising from the presence of an unlettered emperor on the throne was evaded by making a wooden tablet containing the needful perforations through which the imperial scribe drawing his pen dipped in purple ink might trace the first four letters of his name. Proclus, the Qusestor, composed his speeches and acted as his prompter on all state-occasions. Upon the whole, the elderly Emperor, good-tempered, clownish, and of tall stature, seems to have played this last scene in his strangely varied life without discredit, if also without any brilliant success.

It was seen, however, in the negotiations with the Roman See as to the close of the schism, and it became more and more visible to all men as time went on, that the real wielder of all power in the new administration was the Emperor's sister's son Justinian. More than thirty years of age at his uncle's accession, and having, probably through that uncle's influence, already filled some post in the civil service of the Empire; a man always eager for work and a lover of the details of administration; such a nephew was an invaluable assistant to the rustic soldier who had to preside over the highly cultured and polished staff of officials through whom he must seem to govern the Empire.

The influence of Proclus the Quaestor gradually paled before that of the all-powerful nephew, whose servant he willingly became. A more formidable rival was the stout soldier Vitalian, who had upheld the standard of orthodoxy in the evil days of Anastasius, and whose restoration to office was an indispensable part of the reconciliation with the See of Rome. He probably looked for the reversion of the imperial dignity after the death of its aged possessor, and when he found himself raised to the rank of Magister Militum and created Consul (for the year 520), he might almost seem set forth to the people as Emperor Elect. To prevent any such mistake for the future, Justinian, or some one of his friends, caused him, in the seventh month of his consulship, to be attacked in the palace by a band of assassins. He fell, pierced by sixteen wounds: his henchmen, Paulus and Celerianus, fell with him, and the triumph of the party of Justinian was secure.

In the correspondence with Rome, Justinian had called Vitalian 'his most glorious brother', and the fact that the two men had solemnly partaken together of the Holy Communion should, according to the feelings of the age, have secured for the Master of the Soldiery an especial immunity from all murderous thoughts in the heart of his younger rival. The dark deed was not in accordance with the general character of Justinian, who showed himself in the course of his reign averse to taking the lives even of declared enemies : but there seems little reason to doubt that in this case he at least sanctioned, if he did not directly instigate, the murder of a dangerous competitor.

In the following year (521) Justinian celebrated his own consulship with a splendour to which, under the reign of the frugal Anastasius, the Byzantine populace had long been strangers. A sum of 280,000 solidi (£168,000) was spent on the machinery for the shows or distributed as largesse to the people. Twenty lions, thirty panthers, and a multitude of other beasts, appeared at the same time in the Amphitheatre. Horses in great numbers, and equipped in magnificent trappings, were driven by the most highly skilled charioteers of the Empire round the Circus. Already, however, even in the midst of the general rejoicing a note of discord was struck between the future Emperor and his subjects. So great was the excitement of the people, raised no doubt by the. victory of one or other of the rival factions in the Circus, that the Consul found it necessary to strike out of the programme the last race which should have been exhibited.

A successor thus announced to the people before-hand was almost certain of the diadem. In fact Justinian was associated in the Empire four months before the death of his uncle, and appears to have succeeded to sole and supreme power without difficulty.

Delivered by the death of Justin from one associate in the Empire, Justinian lost no time in providing himself with another, of a kind such as Augustus would indeed have marvelled to behold using his name and wielding his decorously veiled supremacy.

During the reign of Anastasius a certain Acacius, who had charge of the wild beasts of the Amphitheatre for the Green party, died, and, as he had saved nothing out of his small salary, his widow and three daughters were left nearly destitute. The widow became the wife or the paramour of another menagerie-keeper, for whom she tried to retain her late husband's situation. But though the three little girls, Comito, Theodora, and Anastasia, appeared like sacrificial victims with fillets on their heads, and stretched out their little hands beseechingly to the spectators, the Greens, who were entirely guided by their manager Asterius, took away the place from their stepfather and gave it to another man. The Blues, the rival faction, were more accommodating, and having lately lost their keeper by death, gave his post to the husband of the widow of Acacius. In one of those little fillet-crowned heads was born on that day an undying resentment against the Green party, and an undying attachment to the Blue.

The child Theodora grew up into a lovely woman, rather too short of stature, but with a delicate red-and-white complexion, and with brilliant quickly-glancing eyes, which told of the keen, restless, nimble intellect within. She evidently had something of the charm which belongs to a clever and beautiful Frenchwoman. Unfortunately, however, she was utterly destitute of womanly virtue or womanly shame. The least moral performer of the opera bouffe in Paris or Vienna is a chaste matron by comparison with the life of unutterable degradation which Theodora is said to have led in girlhood and early womanhood, as a prostitute and a dancer on the stage at Cyrene, at Alexandria, and throughout the cities of the East.

Returned to Constantinople, this bright and fascinating though abandoned woman kindled an irrepressible passion in the breast of the decorous and middle-aged student Justinian. His aunt Lupicina, who had taken the more stately name of Euphemia, and who had been first the slave and then the wedded wife of Justin, firmly and, for the time, successfully opposed his scheme of marrying Theodora. Though lowly born herself, she would not consent that her husband's heir should be the instrument by which the unspeakable degradation of hailing such a woman as Augusta should be inflicted on the Roman Empire. Before long, however, the Empress Euphemia died, and then Justinian, whose passion had but grown stronger by delay, at once married the daughter of the menagerie-keeper. Laws which had come down from the old days of the Republic, forbidding the union of a Senator with a woman of notoriously bad character, were abrogated by the feeble old Emperor on the imperious request of his nephew. Theodora was raised to the dignity of a Patrician, and when at length Justinian wore the imperial diadem he insisted on sharing it with her, not as Empress-Consort, to borrow the terms of a later day, but as Empress-Regnant must Theodora sit upon the throne of the Roman world. All ranks in Church and State crouched low before the omnipotent prostitute. The people, who had once acclaimed her indecent dances on the stage, now greeted her name with shouts of loyal veneration, and with outspread hands implored her protection as if she were divine. The clergy grovelled before her, calling her Mistress and Sovereign Lady, and not one Christian priest with honest indignation protested against this degrading adulation.

Raised to the throne of the world, Theodora assumed a demeanour in some degree corresponding to her elevation. Though not absolutely faithful to her husband, she disgraced his choice by no such acts of open licentiousness as those by which Messalina had insulted the Emperor Claudius. It would seem as if her own nature underwent a change, and as if Pride now took possession of the character which hitherto had been swayed only by Lust. Heartless she had always been, in the midst of her wild riot of debauchery; and heartless she remained in the stupendous egotism which made Justinian and all the ranks of the well-ordered hierarchy of the Empire the ministers of her insatiable pride.

In all things it seems to have been her fancy to play a part unlike that of her husband. He was strictly orthodox and Chalcedonian, she was a vehement Monophysite. He was simple and frugal in his personal habits, however extravagant as a ruler; she carried the luxury of the bath and the banquet to the highest point to which an opulent Roman could attain. He seldom slept more than four hours out of the twenty-four; she prolonged her siesta till sunset and her night's sleep till long after sunrise. He was merciful by temperament; she delighted in the power of being cruel. He showed himself easy of access to all his subjects, aud would often hold long and confidential conversations with persons of undistinguished rank; she surrounded herself with an atmosphere of unapproachable magnificence, and while rigorously insisting that her subjects should present themselves in her audience-chamber, made the ceremony of audience as short, as contemptuous, and as galling to every feeling of self-respect as it was possible to make it. A pitiable sight it was to see the consuls, the senators, the captains and high functionaries of that which still called itself the Roman Republic waiting, a servile crowd, in this harlot's ante-chamber. The room was small and stifling, but they dared, not be absent. Her long slumbers ended, and the ceremonies of the bath and the toilette accomplished, an eunuch would open the door of the hall of audience. The wretched nobles pressed forward, or, if behind, stood on tip-toe to attract the menial's notice. He singled out one and another with contemptuous patronage. The favoured one crept in behind the eunuch into the presence-chamber, his heart in his mouth for fear. He prostrated himself before the haughty Augusta; he kissed reverently the feet which he had once seen briskly moving in lascivious dance on the public stage; he looked up with awe, not daring to speak till spoken to by the supreme disposer of all men's lives and fortunes.

Such is the miserable picture presented to us by Procopius of the degradation of the great Roman commonwealth under its Byzantine rulers. Alas, for the day when the Senate, that assembly of kings, received with majestic gravity the over-awed ambassador of King Pyrrhus! Alas, for the selfish corruption of the *optimates*, and yet more for the misguided patriotism of a Caius Gracchus or a Livius Drusus, which had turned the old and noble Republic into an Empire, foul itself and breeding foulness!

Let it be said for Justinian, who had brought this shame upon the State, that he gave his days and nights freely to what he deemed to be its service. If he was insatiable in drawing all power into his own hand, he at least shrank not from the labour, even the drudgery, which the position of a conscientious autocrat involves. Especially, at the very beginning of his reign, did he devote himself to that which his experience as a high officer of state under his uncle had shown him to be necessary, the reform of the laws of the Empire. Speaking without technical precision, one may say that the jurisprudence of Rome at this period consisted, like our own, of two great divisions, Statute Law and Case Law. The Statutes as contained in the Theodosian Code were insufficient, and the Cases contained in the *Responsa Prudentum*, the Institutions and the Sentences of great jurists such as Glaius, Paullus, and Ulpian, were redundant, bewildering, and often contradictory. Before Justinian had been a year on the throne he had appointed a commission, consisting of nine officials of high rank, to inquire into and codify the Statute Law. The leading spirit in this Commission and the chief mover in all the legal reforms of Justinian was the far-famed Tribonian, who was raised successively to the dignities of Quaestor and Master of the Offices; a man whose love of money and far from spotless integrity could not avail to dim the splendour of a reputation acquired by his vast learning, and made bearable by his gentle courtesy to all with whom he came in contact.

After little more than a year of labour the Commissioners had completed the first part of their duties, and the Code of Justinian in twelve books was issued by the sovereign authority, expanding and superseding the Code of Theodosius and all previous collections of imperial rescripts.

The next piece of work was a harder one. Tribonian and his fellow Commissioners were directed to arrange in one systematic treatise, called the *Digest,* all that Roman lawyers of eminence had said concerning the principles of the law, as the varying circumstances of civil society had brought point after point under their attention. In fact their duty was similar to that which would be laid upon an English lawyer if he was called upon to codify the 'judge-made law' of England, incorporating with it all that is of importance and authority in the text-books, and where there is a conflict of opinion deciding which opinion is to prevail. This immense work, which 'condensed the wisdom of nearly two thousand treatises into fifty books, and recast three million "verses" from older writers into one hundred and fifty thousand,' was accomplished in three years by Tribonian and his colleagues. Work done in such fierce haste as this could hardly be all accurate, but probably no injustice which it could cause was so great as that which it removed by letting day-light into the thick jungle of those three millions of legal sentences.

The Digest, which was divided into fifty books, is not arranged in any scientific order, but follows apparently more or less closely the order of that which had for centuries been the great programme of Roman jurisprudence, the so-called Perpetual Edict of the Praetors.

The Code and the Digest being finished, Tribonian and his two most eminent colleagues were directed to prepare a short scientific treatise on the amended law of Rome, for the benefit of students. Thus came into being the Four Books of the *Institutes,* that book by which the fame of Justinian has been most widely spread over the civilised world in the two hemispheres. The far-reaching relations in time of such a book as this are vividly apprehended when we remember that as it rests on the treatise of Gaius—which Niebuhr discovered in palimpsest in the Cathedral Library of Verona—it is itself rested upon by our own eighteenth century Blackstone, who of course had the name and the arrangement of this book in his mind when he composed his Institutes of English Law. Justinian's name and titles head the majestic manual. Of course Tribonian and the two professors, his colleagues, are really responsible for the literary execution of the work. Still, the historical student is never so well disposed to take a lenient view of the faults of the great Emperor as when he finds Caesar Flavius Justinianus, Alamannicus, Gothicus, Vandalicus, and so forth, crowned with names of victory over many barbarous races, but cheering the young student to the commencement of his task, and promising not to encumber his mind at first with details, lest he should disgust him at the outset, and cause him to abandon his studies in despair.

Notwithstanding his attempt to put the stamp of finality on his two great works, the Code and the Digest, neither Justinian himself nor his indefatigable Quaestor could keep their hands from all further law-making. The *Novellae Constitutiones*, generally spoken of under a title which has since acquired such a strangely different meaning, that of *Novels*, were promulgated at intervals for nearly thirty years (535-664), and in some respects seriously altered the unalterable Code.

Except for some over-activity in issuing fresh laws after the publication of his Code, the fame of Justinian as a legislator is unassailable. The hour had come for clearing broad and traversable highways through the stately but sky-hiding forest of Roman jurisprudence. With Tribonian for his engineer-in-chief, Justinian undertook this necessary work, and did it nobly. Rightly and justly therefore is the name of the peasant's son from the valley of the Yardar mentioned with reverence, wherever, from the Mississippi to the Ganges, teachers of the law expound the greatest of Rome's legacies to the nations, the *Corpus Juris Civilis*.

But it is a trite axiom in politics and in every-day life, that good legislation does not necessarily imply good administration. Many a man whose journal records the most excellent maxims for the conduct of his life, has been a torment to his family and friends. Many a public company, with admirably-framed Articles of Association, has chosen the pleasant road to an early bankruptcy. Many an Oriental state has proclaimed, and is proclaiming at the present day, the most excellent principles of government, not one of which it ever dreams of reducing into practice.

As an administrator Justinian does not occupy nearly so high a position as that to which his legislative triumphs entitle him. He certainly had one of the most necessary qualifications for a ruler, the power of selecting fitting instruments for his work. The man who chose Tribonian for his legal adviser, Belisarius and Narses for his generals, the designers of Saint Sophia for his architects, can assuredly have been no mean judge of human character. He had also the power of forming truly grand conceptions, and is superior herein to two monarchs, with each of whom some points in his character tempt us to compare him—Louis XIV of France and Philip II of Spain. These merits, however, were more than counterbalanced by two great faults—intense egotism and financial extravagance. Coming as he did from the lower ranks of society to the administration of an old and highly-organized state, he was determined to leave his mark on every city of the Empire, on every department of the State. Some changes, like those involved in the codification of the Roman law, required to be made, and here the imperial egotist's passion for change worked well for the State. But besides this, many old and useful institutions were swept away, simply in order that the name of Justinian might be magnified. Local self-government received from him some of its severest blows.

The postal service, one of the best legacies from the great days of the Empire, he allowed to be ruined by greedy and shortsighted ministers, who sold the post-horses and divided the proceeds between their master and themselves. The venerable institution of the consulship, which still linked the fortunes of New Rome with the dim remembrance of the republican virtues of Brutus and Publicola, must be swept away. The schools of philosophy at Athens, touched certainly with the feebleness of age, but still showing an unbroken descent from Socrates, and deserving to be spared, if only for the sake of their late illustrious pupil Boethius, were closed by imperial decree, and the seven last Platonists were driven forth into exile, obtaining at length by the intercession of the King of Persia permission to exist, but no longer to teach, in that which had once been the mother city of all philosophy.

The mania of the empurpled Nihilist for destroying every institution which could not show cause for its existence by ministering to the imperial vanity, would have been less disastrous if it had not been coupled with an utter indifference to expense. Whatever dispute there may be as to other parts of the character of Justinian, there can be none as to his having been one of the worst of the many bad financiers who wore the diadem of the Caesars.

In reading the two histories in which Procopius records the vast operations of this monarch, both in peace and war, we are inclined to ask, 'Did the question once in his whole reign occur to the mind of Justinian, whether he was justified in spending the money of his subjects on this campaign which he meditated, or on that palace or basilica for which the architect had furnished him with plans?'.Certainly the results of his financial administration speak for themselves : the carefully and wisely hoarded treasure of Anastasius all spent, the very wars themselves starved, and in some cases protracted to three or four times their necessary length by the emptiness of the exchequer, and the people of his realms left at Justinian's death in a state of exhaustion and misery greater, if that be possible, than the subjects of Louis XIV of France after that monarch's seventy years' quest of glory.

The treasure of Anastasius had perhaps been melting away during the nine years of the reign of Justin. During this time the war with Persia War was begun, a war about which something will be said in the following chapter. Before Justinian had been five years on the throne the financial financial oppression of his subjects, particularly in thecountry districts, was becoming intolerable. Owing to changes in the mode of collecting the land-revenue and the abolition of the *cursus publicus*, the inhabitants were impoverished by the oppressive rights of pre-emption claimed by the government, and worn out with forced labour in moving produce from the interior of the country to the sea. Women with babes at their breasts were forced to take part in this cruel toil, and often did they, their husbands, and brothers fall dead by the road-side, where they were left, unpitied and unburied. There was no time for funeral rites; the Emperor's corn must be delivered in so many days at the sea-port, where, without fail, some venal officer or some slave of one of the palace slaves stood ready to take his tithe of the tithes collected at the cost of so much agony.

The very names of the new taxes imposed on various pretexts, about twenty in number, were terrible to the bewildered people. And this was what they had earned by those delirious shouts of joy which hailed the accession of Justin and the death of

Anastasius, the tender-hearted Anastasius, who with such infinite trouble had rooted out one obnoxious tax, the Chrysargyron, in the room of which Justinian had planted a score.

Despairing of earning a subsistence in the country, the dispirited peasantry nocked into the towns, above all into the capital city. In Constantinople there was at least food to be had, for the corn-rations were still distributed to the people; and in Constantinople there was the delicious excitement for an absolutely idle populace, of the races in the Hippodrome. We have already made some little acquaintance with the contending colours of these circus-factions. Once four in number, they had now, by the disuse or obscurity of the Red and the White, become practically reduced to two, the Blue and the Green. And such was the excitement produced among the favourers of these two colours, by the victory or defeat of their respective champions, that the contemporary Byzantine historian can call it nothing less than a madness, a curse, and a disease of the soul. They would pour out their money; they would expose themselves to blows and the most contemptuous insults, yea, even to death itself; they would rush into the thickest of a fray, well knowing that in a few minutes the city-guards would be upon them, and would drag them off to the dungeon and to death. All this they heeded not if only the Blues might take their revenge on the bodies of their antagonists for the victory of a Green charioteer, if only the Greens might pay off a long score of insults by breaking the heads of a mob of presumptuous Blues. Murder was of course the frequent consequence of these faction-fights; and it was perhaps not always murder in hot blood, but sometimes secret and premeditated. Even women, though not allowed to visit the theatre, were bitten with the madness of the strife; and brothers, friends, the companions of a life-time were turned into irreconcilable enemies by these absolutely senseless quarrels. Certainly of all the strange exhibitions of his character which Man has given since he first appeared upon our planet, few have been more unutterably absurd than the fights of Blues and Greens in the Hippodrome of Constantinople.

It was evident, soon after his accession, that the husband of Theodora meant to favour the Blue party, and in a few years, a long list of grievances was recorded in the hearts of the opposite faction against him. Such was the state of feeling in the multitude—the Blues jubilant with imperial favour, the Greens sore at heart and indignant against their oppressor, a multitude of the country-folk, having not as yet taken sides definitely with either colour, but remembering and cursing the tyrannical acts which had driven them from their immemorial homes—when on the morning of the Ides of January, 532, the august Emperor took his seat in the podium and commanded the races to begin. Race after race, till twenty-two races had been run, was disturbed by the clamours of the angry Green faction. Their fury was chiefly directed against the Grand Chamberlain and Captain of the Guard, Calopodius, to whom they attributed their ill-treatment. At length Justinian, worried out of his usual self-control, began to argue with the interrupters; and so the following extraordinary debate took place, in shrill shouts to and from the Imperial podium.

The Green party. 'Many years mayest thou live, Justinianus Augustus. *Tu vincas.* O only good one, I am oppressed. God knows it, but I dare not mention the oppressor's name lest I suffer it'.

The Emperor's answer to the people came back from the lips of a stalwart *Mandator* who stood, beside his throne, while a busy short-hand writer (*Exceptor*) at once began to take down all the words of this strange dialogue, that they might be enrolled in the official Acta of the Empire.

Mandator. 'Whom you mean, I know not.'

The Greens. 'O thrice August one, he who oppresses me will be found at the shoemakers' shops'.

Mandator. 'I know not whom you are speaking of'.

The Greens. 'Calopodius the Guardsman oppresses me, O Lord of all.'

Mandator. 'Calopodius has no public charge.'

The Greens. 'Whatever he may be, he will suffer the fate of Judas. God will reward him according to his works.'

Mandator. 'Did you come hither to see the games, or only to rail at your rulers?'

The Greens. 'If any one oppresses me, I hope he will die like Judas.'

Mandator. 'Hold your peace, ye Jews, ye Manicheans, ye Samaritans.'

The Greens. 'Do you call us Jews and Samaritans? We all invoke the Virgin, the Mother of God.'

Some sentences of scarcely intelligible religious abuse between the two parties to the dialogue follow. Then says the Mandator—'In truth, if you are not quiet I will cut off your heads'

The Greens. 'Be not enraged at the cry of the afflicted. God himself bears all patiently. [How can I appeal to you in your palace?] I cannot venture thither, scarcely even into the city except by one street when I am riding on my mule.'

Mandator. 'Every one can move freely about in this city, without danger.'

The Greens. 'You talk of freedom, but I do not find that I can get it. Let a man be ever so free, if he is suspected of being a Green, he is taken and beaten in public.'

Mandator. 'Gallows-birds! have you no care for your own lives, that you thus speak?'

The Greens. 'Take off that colour [the emblem of the Blues] and do not let justice seem to take sides. I wish Sabbatius [the father of Justinian] had never been born. Then would he never have begotten a murderous son. It is twenty years since [one of our party] was murdered at the Yoking-place. In the morning he was looking on at the games, and in the evening twilight, O Lord of all, he had his throat cut.'

The Blues here interposed with angry denial.

'All the murders on the race-course have been committed by you alone.'

The Greens. ' Sometimes you murder and run away'

The Blues. 'You murder and throw everything into confusion. All the murders on the race-course are your work alone.'

The Greens. 'Lord Justinian! They stir us up to strife, but no one kills them. Remember, even if you do not wish to do so, who slew the wood-seller at the Yoking-place, O Emperor!'

Mandator. 'You slew him.'

The Greens. ' Who slew the son of Epagathus, O Emperor?'

Mandator. 'Him too you slew, and then tried to throw the blame on the Blues.'

The Greens. 'Again! and again! Lord have mercy on us! Truth is trodden under foot by a tyrant. I should like to throw these things in the teeth of those who say that God governs the world. Whence then this villainy?'

Mandator. 'God cannot be tempted with evil.'

The Greens. ' "God cannot be tempted with evil." Then who is it that allows me to be oppressed? Let any one, whether Philosopher or Hermit, read me this riddle.'

Mandator. 'Blasphemers and accursed ones! when will ye be quiet?'

The Greens. 'If your Majesty will fawn upon that party, I hold my peace, though unwillingly. OThrice August one, I know all, all: but I am silent. Farewell, Justice : you have no more business here. I shall depart hence, and then I will turn Jew. It is better to become a Heathen than a Blue, God knows! '

The Blues. 'We hate the very sight of you. Your petty spite exasperates us.'

The Greens. 'Dig up the bones of the [murdered] spectators.'

With that the whole faction of the Greens streamed out of the Hippodrome, leaving the Emperor and the Blue party sole occupants of the long rows of stone *subsellia*.

The day was drawing towards a close when this multitude of enraged Orientals poured forth into the streets of Constantinople. Soon it was evident that the tumults which had embittered the later days of Anastasius were to be renewed, on a larger scale, and with more appalling circumstances, by reason of the crowds of hungry, idle, and exasperated rustics who had flocked into the town. Fire began to be applied to the buildings round the Hippodrome, and to the porticoes of the Palace in which the household troops were lodged. All through the earlier stages of the sedition Justinian kept quiet in his palace, with the nobles who had assembled there according to custom on the Ides of January, to offer their congratulations and to receive from his hands the tokens of their various promotions for the new year. Probably his expectation was, that the insurrection, if unopposed, would wear itself out; or that, at the worst, the fury of the attacked Blues would check the fury of the attacking Greens.

Soon, however, an ominous symptom appeared. The Blues began to sympathise with the Greens, and to join in the wild orgie in which their rivals were engaged. In a recent attempt to deal out even-handed justice between the two factions, the Prefect of the City had arrested seven notorious murderers, chosen indifferently from both parties. Four had been sentenced to death by beheading, three by hanging. The sword had done its work surely, but the gallows had broken under the weight of their victims, and two of the culprits, one a Blue, the other a Green, had thus escaped for a time the sentence of the law. The good monks of the neighbouring monastery of St. Conon had found them not quite dead, had put them on board ship, and had carried them to the church of St. Lawrence. The Prefect of the City insisted that the law should have its due, but popular sympathy was aroused on behalf of the wretches who had so narrowly escaped death. A common interest in the fate of their friends seems to have brought the two factions, hating one another with such deadly hatred, into momentary accord. As the old watch-words of party were suddenly become obsolete, they invented new ones. Not the loyal cry, 'August Justinian, may you conquer!' but 'Long live the friendly Greens and Blues!' was to be the battle-shout of the united factions, and 'Nika' (Victory) their secret pass-word.

With this reconciliation of the Circus-factions the sedition assumed a more important and a political character. The name of the chamberlain Calopodius drops out of the story, and those of the Quaestor Tribonian, of the Praetorian Prefect, John of Cappadocia, begin to be beard. Tribonian, with all his matchless knowledge of the law, was suspected, perhaps justly suspected, of sometimes framing the new laws so as to suit the convenience of those litigants who approached him with the heaviest purse in their hands. John of Cappadocia was undoubtedly a man absolutely devoid of principle, coarse, unlettered, vicious, but one whose daemonic force of will and whose relentless heart were all put at the disposal of his master for the purpose of wringing the maximum of taxes out of a fainting and exhausted people.

When the cry for the removal of these ministers came, Justinian at once yielded to it, and replaced them by men who stood higher in favour with the people. But still the riot went on. The futile endeavours of the soldiers to cope with it only increased its fury; and, sure mark that all the lowest and most lawless elements of society had broken loose, Fire was the favourite weapon in the combat. The Senate-house, the Palace of the Praetorian Prefect, the Baths of Zeuxippus, the Baths of Alexander, were all burnt. At last, either because the mob had grown wild and desperate with destruction, or because the wind which had sprung up respected not the distinctions which they would have made, the sacred buildings themselves were given to the devouring flame. The great church of Saint Sophia, and its neighbour the church of Saint Irene, fell in blackened ruin. Between these two edifices, the dwellings of Divine Wisdom and Peace, the charity of a devout man of earlier time, Sampson by name, had reared a hospital for the reception of the sick and aged poor. This noble illustration of the spirit of Christianity shared the fate of its statelier neighbours, and, alas for the madness of the populace, all the sick folk who were lying in the wards of the hospital perished in the flames.

Thus for five days raged the demon Fire through the streets of Constantinople. Through the short January day thick clouds of smoke rolled round basilica and portico. At night two red and flaring lines mirrored themselves in the Golden Horn and the Bosporus. The ineffectual efforts of the soldiers to suppress the riot did but increase the mischief. The Octagon was set fire to by them in their endeavours to expel the rebels, and the flames thus kindled consumed the church of St. Theodore and the vestry adjoining it.

Still for some time the insurrection lacked an aim and a leader. Justinian was despised, but no name was suggested instead of his. On the first or second day, it is true, the rioters marched to the house of Probus (no doubt the nephew of Anastasius and brother of Pompeius), searched the house for arms, and shouted as they searched, 'Probus for Emperor of Romania!', but not succeeding in their quest, nor prevailing on Probus to accept the Probus will offered diadem, they cast fire into his house and the added it to the general destruction.

On Sunday, the fifth day of the insurrection, Justinian sought to propitiate the mob by following the example of Anastasius and making an appeal to their compassion. Taking his place in the seat of honour in the Circus, he held on high the roll of the Holy Gospels. The populace streamed once more into the Hippodrome, to hear what their sovereign would say to them. Laying his hand on the sacred books, he swore a solemn oath : 'By this power I swear that I forgive you all your offences, and will order the arrest of none of you, if only you will now return to your obedience. The blame is none of yours, but all mine. For the punishment of my sins I did not grant your requests when first you addressed me in this place'. The humiliation was as great as that of Anastasius, but not so efficacious in disarming the fury of the mob. Some shouted 'Justiniane Auguste, tu vincas!' but many were silent, and there was even heard the insulting cry, 'O ass, thou art swearing falsely!'

With his dignity ruffled and his easy temper disturbed Justinian returned to the palace. There, apparently, all the nobles who had assembled on the Ides of January were still mustered, not having dared to return to their homes through the raging populace. The Emperor's eye fell on Hypatius and Pompeius, the nephews of Anastasius, and in an angry voice he ordered them to leave the palace. Procopius doubts whether to refer this strange order to suspicion of a conspiracy on their part, or to the influence of a mysterious destiny. The humbler theory, that it was due to mere ill-temper and annoyance, may perhaps be deserving of consideration. The two cousins naturally suggested that it was unfair to throw them at such a critical moment in the very path of conspirators and rebels; but Justinian insisted, and forth they went, slinking under cover of the twilight to their homes.

Next day, when the news of their departure from the palace was noised abroad, the whole multitude flocked to the house of Hypatius, intent on proclaiming him Emperor. In the campaign against Vitalian, eighteen years before, Hypatius had held the highest command, and the course of events seems to have pointed him out as, upon the whole, the most eminent of the nephews of Anastasius. When the multitude announced their intention of proclaiming Hypatius in the Forum, his wife Mary, a woman of great ability and noble character, with tears and cries besought them not to lead her husband to certain death. Hypatius also earnestly pleaded that he had no desire for the dangerous honour. But the people were inexorable. Mary's entwining arms were thrust aside, and Hypatius was borne by the shouting multitude to the Forum of Constantine, where he appears to have been soon after joined by his cousin Pompeius. As no diadem was at hand, a collar of gold was placed on the head of Hypatius. He was raised high up on the steps of the statue of Constantine, clothed in the white *chlamys* which was to mark his military rank, and all the vast multitude shouted with one accord, 'Hypatie Auguste, tu vincas!'

There was a discussion among the adherents of the new Emperor whether they should at once march to the palace of Justinian and grapple with their foe. Had they done so, Justinian would probably have been faintly remembered in history as a sovereign who made some attempt to reform the Roman laws and perished in a tumult after a reign of five years. And in truth this was the view which he himself was prepared to take of the chances for and against him. In a council held in the palace his voice apparently was for flight by the sea-gate, outside of which his ships were moored. But then was heard the manly voice of Theodora, insisting on resistance to the death.

"When man has once come into the world, death sooner or later is his inevitable doom. But as for living, a royal fugitive, that is an intolerable thought. Never may I exist without this purple robe; never may the day dawn on me in which the voices of all who meet me shall not salute me as Sovereign Lady. If then, O Emperor, you wish to escape, there is no difficulty in the matter. Here is the sea: there are the ships. But just consider whether, when you have escaped, you will not every day wish that you were dead. For my part, I favour that ancient saying, "There is no grander sepulchre for any man than the Kingship".'

The stirring words of Theodora prevailed. Belisarius, a young officer who had acquired great renown in the Persian war, was commissioned to attack with his small but disciplined body of troops the vast mob of Constantinople; and at the same time a middle-aged Armenian named Narses, an eunuch who had attained the rank of Grand Chamberlain in the imperial household, stole out of the palace with a heavy purse of money in his hand, to persuade and bribe the leaders of the Blue faction back to their old allegiance.

While this council was resolving on resistance to the uttermost, that of Hypatius resolved on procrastination. The advice of a Senator named Origen had determined them to leave the palace of Justinian unattacked, trusting that its occupant would soon be a fugitive, and to make for the old palace, which still bore the name of Flaccilla, the wife of Theodosius. On their way to this building the whole multitude halted for a time in the Hippodrome. Hypatius, who was still a most unwilling of claimant of the purple, at this juncture sent one of the noble guard named Ephraemius to Justinian with this message: 'Thy enemies are all assembled in the Circus; thou canst do with them what thou wilt'. Unfortunately Ephraemius met the Emperor's physician and confidant Thomas, who had heard of the rumoured flight, but had not heard of the later resolution to defend the palace. 'Whither are you going?' said Thomas to the glittering Candidatus : 'there is no one in the palace; Justinian has fled'. This message, brought to Hypatius, seemed to show that there was nothing for him but to reign; and he accordingly accepted the situation, mounted to the podium, and probably harangued the Roman people assembled in the Circus as their lawful Imperator.

Better had it been for Hypatius to be crouching, as he crouched eighteen years before, by the Scythian shore, up to his neck in the water and only his head showing, 'like a sea-bird's,' above the waves. He was in less danger then from the savage Huns than now from the insulted Emperor whom he had failed to dethrone. Belisarius heard that the rebels were all in the Hippodrome. With the instinct of a born general he saw in a moment his one chance of victory. With his band of disciplined soldiers, most of them barbarians, he mounted the broad and stately *cochlea* (spiral staircase) which led from the palace to the Emperor's box in the Hippodrome. A barred door prevented his entrance. He shouted to the soldiers, some of his own veterans, who were in attendance on Hypatius, 'Open the door, that I may get to the usurper!'. The soldiers, who wished to commit themselves to neither side, feigned not to hear. Then did Belisarius well-nigh despair of success, and, returning to the palace, he told the Emperor that his cause was ruined. But there remained another gate called the Brazen Gate, on the side to which the populace had set fire, and to it, amid falling timbers and over smoking ruins, Belisarius and his soldiers forced their way. This entrance adjoined the portico of the Blues, and perhaps was for this reason better adapted to the purposes of Belisarius; for at the same time the leaders of the Blue party who had received the bribes of Narses were beginning to shout, 'Justiniane Auguste, tu vincas!'. Then was heard the war-cry of Belisarius; the flashing swords were seen; suspicions of treachery, which soon grew into panic fear, fell upon the multitude. The one desire of every citizen was to escape from the Hippodrome, a desire impossible of fulfilment; for, lo! at the same moment Mundus, another of Justinian's generals, hearing the uproar and rightly divining the manoeuvre of Belisarius, pressed in to the Circus by another gate, called, as if in prophecy, the Gate of the Dead. The two generals did their bloody work relentlessly, so that no civilian, either citizen of Constantinople or stranger, either partisan of the Blues or the Greens, who chanced that day to be in the Hippodrome, left it alive.

It was estimated that 35,000 persons fell in this tumult. Justinian announced his victory as it had been won over some foreign toe, in exulting letters to all the great cities of his Empire. The triumph was won by ruthless disregard of human life, by an utter refusal to attempt to distinguish between the innocent and the guilty: but it was not a wholly barren one for the State. After this terrible lesson, it was long before the populace of Constantinople attempted to renew the disturbances which had disgraced the later years of Anastasius.

Hypatius and his cousin Pompeius were dragged out of the imperial box in the Circus and brought into the presence of Justinian. They fell prostrate before him, and began to sue for pardon on the plea that it was by their persuasion that the enemies of Justinian had been collected in the Hippodrome. 'That was well done,' said the

Emperor (who had not yet heard of the message sent by Hypatius), 'but if the multitude were so willing to obey your orders, could you not have done it before half the city was burnt down'. He ordered them away to close confinement, upon which Pompeius, a man with whom all things till then had gone smoothly, began with tears and groans to bewail his hard fate. The more rugged Hypatius sharply rebuked him: 'Courage, my cousin: do not thus demean thyself. We perish as innocent men: for we could not resist the pressure of the people, and it was out of no ill-will to the Emperor that we went into the Hippodrome'.

On the following day they were slain by the soldiers, their goods were confiscated, and their bodies were cast into the sea. After a few days, however, Justinian relented towards them, having heard the true story of the message of Hypatius. Thomas, the doctor who had so ill served the interests of his august patient, was ordered to be beheaded. The property of the two unfortunate Patricians was restored to their relatives, and commands were issued for the burial of their bodies. Only that of Hypatius, however, could be recovered from the keeping of the Bosporus, and over this when buried, Justinian, with all his clemency, could not deny himself the pleasure of carving an insulting epitaph:

'Here lies the Emperor of Luppa'. The insult is too subtle to reach the ears of posterity.

The blackened heaps representing the stately buildings of Constantinople reminded a spectator . who saw them of the masses of lava and cinders surrounding the cones of Vesuvius and Lipari. Soon however, by the command of the Emperor, troops of workmen were busily engaged in clearing away the rubbish and laying the foundations of new churches, baths, and porticoes. Thus was employment found for the ruined provincials who still swarmed in the city : and before long a new and fairer Constantinople rose from the ruins of the old.

So ended the celebrated sedition of the Nika. Its chief interest for us is that it brings us face to face with two men who gathered great fame in Italy, Belisarius and Narses.

CHAPTER XV.

BELISARIUS.

The peace between the Roman and the Persian Empires which was concluded in 505, after lasting for twenty-one years, was broken upon a strange cause of quarrel. The Persian king, Kobad, now far advanced in years, in order to secure the succession to the throne for his favourite son Chosroes, proposed to the Emperor Justin that that monarch should adopt him as his son. Justin was prepared to assent, but, listening to the dissuasions of the Quaestor Proclus, who feared that Chosroes might found on such an adoption a claim to the Roman as well as the Persian diadem, he eventually refused this act of courtesy. There were already some grievances against the Romans rankling in the mind of Kobad. They would not pay their promised quota towards the defence of the passes of the Caucasus from the Northern barbarians. They had built, contrary to agreement, the strong city of Daras close to the Persian frontier, almost overlooking the lost and bitterly-lamented city of Nisibis. When tidings came that the Macedonian peasant who called himself Augustus would not recognise the descendant of so many kings as his son, or would at most only confer upon him that military adoption as 'son-in-arms' which was a compliment paid to Gepid and Ostrogoth princes, the old monarch of Ctesiphon was furious. He must have war with Rome; and war accordingly was waged by him and his son after him, for five years, among the Mesopotamian highlands and on the fertile plains of Syria.

With the details of this war we have no concern except in so far as they are connected with the entrance upon the stage of history of the young hero-general, Belisarius. Born about the year 505, probably of noble parentage, in the same Macedonian mountain-country from which Justin and his nephew had descended to Thessalonica, Belisarius was serving in the body-guard of Justinian, and had the first manly down upon his lip when, in the year 526, he and another officer of his own age were entrusted with the command of the troops which were to invade the Persian (or Eastern) portion of Armenia. Fields were laid waste and many hapless Armenians were carried into captivity, but no successes in battle were earned by the young generals.

Soon after, Belisarius was made commandant of the newly-erected fort and city of Daras: and while in this command he made a selection which has had more to do with his subsequent renown than many victories. He chose 'Procopius of Caesarea who compiled this history' to be his Judge-Advocate. The office which I attempt to indicate by this suggested English equivalent was known among the Romans by names which we have borrowed from them, those of Counsellor and Assessor. For a Roman general like Belisarius, exercising by virtue of his office judicial power over civil as well as military persons, but having received himself no legal education, it was absolutely necessary to have a trained jurist ever by bis side, who might so guide his decisions that they should be conformable to the laws of the Empire. Occasions would also often arise in connection with the diplomatic duties that Belisarius had to discharge towards the rulers of the lands invaded by him, in which the presence of a learned Byzantine official would be of great assistance to a comparatively unlettered soldier. Such an adviser, legal assessor and diplomatic counsellor, was Procopius: not the general's private secretary, but, it may be said, in a certain sense, his official colleague, though in a very subordinate capacity.

Whether Procopius held precisely this relation to Belisarius during all the fifteen years that they were campaigning together, in Mesopotamia, in Africa and in Italy, it is difficult to say. It is slightly more probable that the official tie may have been sundered, and that the learned civilian may have remained on as a visitor and trusted friend in the tent of his chief, by whom he was occasionally employed on semi-military enterprises which required especial tact and exercise of the diplomatic faculty. It seems clear that, during all the period above mentioned, something more than official relations existed between the two men; that the counsellor loved and admired the general, and that the general respected and liked the counsellor. We shall have hereafter to trace, or if we cannot trace, to conjecture, the disastrous influences by which a friendship so honourable to both parties, and cemented by so many years of common danger and hardships, was at last broken asunder; and owing to which Procopius in his old age became the passionate reviler of the hero whom in his youth and middle life he had so enthusiastically admired.

The position occupied by Procopius in the history of literature is interesting and almost unique. After so many generations of decline, here, at length, the intellect of Hellas produces a historian, who, though not equal doubtless to her greatest names, would certainly have been greeted by Herodotus and Thucydides as a true brother of their craft. Procopius has a very clear idea how history ought to be written. Each of his books, on the Persian, the Vandal, and the Gothic wars, is a work of art, symmetrical, well proportioned, and with a distinct unity of subject. His style is dignified but not pompous, his narrative vivid, his language pure, and the chief fault that we can attribute to it is a too great fondness for archaisms, especially for old Homeric words, which are somewhat out of place in the pages of a prose author. He exhibits a considerable amount of learning, but without pedantry: and resembles Herodotus in his eager, almost child-like interest in the strange customs and uncouth religions of barbarian nations. He picks up from hearsay all that he can as to a land like Thule (Iceland or the North of Norway) lying within the Arctic Circle, and only regrets that, though earnestly desirous of the journey, he has never been able to visit that land in person and be an eye-witness of its wonders.

In politics Procopius shows himself an ardent lover of the glory of the great Roman Empire, of which he feels himself still thoroughly a citizen. In his most important work (the *De Bellis*) he preserves a truly dignified tone towards the Emperor, whose great achievements he praises without servility: but he often contrives to introduce in the speech of a foreign ambassador or the letter of a hostile king some tolerably severe Opposition-criticism on the home or foreign policy of the omnipotent Justinian. Very different from the manly and moderate tone of this his standard work are the sickening adulation of the *De Aedificiis* and the venomous tirade of the *Anecdota*, both of which books must belong to the old age of Procopius, the former being apparently written to the Emperor's order and therefore crowded with insincere and extorted compliments, while the latter was never to leave the author's desk while he lived, and therefore received all the pent-up bitterness of his insulted and indignant soul.

The attitude of Procopius towards the religious questions which agitated the Eastern world is as peculiar as his literary position. While all, or nearly all of his contemporaries are taking sides in the bitter theological controversies of the day, he stands aloof and looks coldly on the whole shrill logomachy. That he can speak the language of the Christian faith, when Court etiquette requires him to do so, is proved by some passages in the *De Aedificiis* which have an entirely Christian sound. But, though he will not go to the stake for his faith, nor indeed forego any chance of Court favour for the sake of it, it is clear that his real convictions are not Christian, but that he is a philosophical Theist of the school of Socrates and Plato: and we may be almost certain that he derived his religious creed as well as his rhetorical style from those philosophers of the University of Athens, whom Justinian banished and silenced in his lifetime. In his own writings he wavers in some degree between a devout Theism and a half sullen acquiescence in the decrees of a blind, impersonal destiny : but, upon the whole, Theism rules his mind, and he sometimes speaks, even with a reverent love, of the dealings of Providence with mankind. Probably the following passage from an early chapter of his Gothic history tells us as much as he himself knew about his innermost thoughts on religious subjects. After describing an embassy from the Pope to the Emperor 'on account of the doctrine about which the different Churches of Christendom dispute among themselves', he continues,—

' But upon the points in dispute. I, though well acquainted with them, shall say as little as possible, for I hold it to be proof of a madman's folly to search out what the Nature of God is like. For, by man, not even the things of a man can in my opinion be accurately apprehended, far less those which pertain to the Nature of God. I shall therefore pass over these subjects in safe silence, only remarking that I do not disbelieve in those things which other men reverence. For I would never say anything else concerning God, except that He is altogether good and holds all things in His own power. But let every one else, whether priest or layman, speak on such subjects according to his own presumed knowledge'.

There have been times in, the history of the world, with reference to which an inquiry of this kind as to the religious opinions of their describer would be irrelevant and almost impertinent. No one who knows the spirit of the sixth century will say this of Procopius. His attitude of aloofness from special theological controversy secures his impartiality between warring sects. His philosophical Theism is the key to much that would otherwise be perplexing in his own writings. As a 'Hellenising' rather than a Christian historian he stands in a direct line of succession from authors with whose works we have already made considerable acquaintance, Ammianus, Eunapius, Priscus, and Zosimus: and it would be an interesting inquiry, had we space for it, to ascertain where his Heathenism agrees and where it differs from theirs. Upon the whole, in the age of change and transition in which he lived, Procopius would seem to have clung fast to two great facts in the World-History of the Past, the wisdom of Greece and the greatness of Rome, and not to have accepted that clue to the interpretation of the Present and the anticipation of the Future which was offered him by Augustine's vision of the City of God.

From this sketch of the character of the biographer we return to survey the actions of his hero, the young imperial guardsman, Belisarius. The campaigns of the three years from 527 to 529 seem to have consisted of desultory and indecisive skirmishes: but in the last year Belisarius was appointed *Magister Militum per Orientem*; and this concentration of power in the hands most capable of wielding it was soon Persian followed by a brilliant victory. In 530, in the midst of negotiations for peace, the Persian Mirran or commander-in-chief, Perozes, made a dash at the new, much-hated fortress of Daras. In point of strategy he seems to have shown himself superior to the imperial general, since he was able to concentrate 40,000 men for the attack, while Belisarius could muster only 25,000 for the defence. Deeming the battle as good as won Perozes sent an arrogant message to the Soman commander: 'Prepare me a bath in Daras, for I intend to repose there tomorrow.' But when the Persian troops advanced to the attack they soon perceived that they were in the presence of a master of tactics and that their victory would not be an easy one. Under the walls of Daras Belisarius had ordered his troops to dig a long but not continuous trench, with two side-trenches sloping away from it at an obtuse angle at either end. His irregular troops, consisting chiefly of Huns, Heruli, and other barbarians, were stationed in the intervals which had been purposely left between the various parts of this line of defence. Behind them, ready to take advantage of any victory which might be won by the irregulars, lay the disciplined masses of the main body of the imperial army.

On the first day of the battle the Persians advanced, but retreated, seeing the imminent danger they were in of a flank attack if they threw themselves upon any point of the half-hexagon. Again they advanced and won some slight advantage, but failed to maintain it. The sun was now near setting, and the attention of both armies was distracted by the brave deeds of Andreas, a gymnastic-master and the bathing attendant of a Roman general, who engaged two Persian champions in succession and slew them both. In the second encounter the spears of the two combatants were both shivered on the opposing breastplates; the horses met in full career and fell to the earth from the violence of onset. Then ensued a struggle which of the two champions should first rise from the ground; a struggle which the gymnastic skill of Andreas terminated in his favour. He struck the Persian who had risen on one knee, with another blow he felled him to the earth, and so slew him amid the tumultuous applause of the Eoman soldiery.

That night was passed by both armies in their previous positions. In the early morning (while the Persian general was marching up 10,000 additional troops from the city of Nisibis), messages were interchanged between the generals. Belisarius, avowing that he held it to be the highest mark of generalship to obtain peace, invited the Mirran even now, at the eleventh hour, to relinquish an attack which, made as it was in the midst of negotiations for peace, had in it something of the nature of treachery, and to retire within the Persian frontier. The Mirran replied: 'If you were not Romans we would listen gladly to your arguments : but you belong to a nation which neither promises nor oaths can bind. We have met you now in open war, and will either die here or fight on till old age overtakes us, that we may force you to do us justice.' Said Belisarius: 'Calling us hard names alters not the truth of facts. God and justice are on our side.'

The Mirran answered: 'We too know that the gods are on our side, and with their help we shall tomorrow be in Daras. As I said before, let my bath and my breakfast be prepared within the fortress.' Belisarius put the letters on the point of his standards, as a symbol to all the army that he fought against men who were truce-breakers and perfidious.

Before beginning the action, the Mirran did his best to re-assure his soldiers as to the unexpected check of the previous day, and the strange new signs of cohesion and discipline exhibited by their Roman antagonists. His oration, as reported by Procopius, is, if we may rely on its genuineness, the most striking of all testimonies to the genius of the Boman general in turning a disorderly mass of discordant nationalities into a harmonious whole, animated by one spirit, and mighty either for onset or resistance. Belisarius, in his brief speech to his soldiers, insisted on the paramount necessity of order and discipline, the secret of their previous day's success and the means of securing on that day a far more splendid triumph. Especially he bade them not to be discouraged by the superior numbers of the enemy. The Persians possessed some brilliant *corps d'élite* (such as the troops known as the Immortals): but the great mass of the army, according to the Roman general's statement, consisted of squadrons of clumsy rustics, labourers rather than soldiers, good at undermining walls or plundering the bodies of the slain, but whose only notion of fighting consisted in covering themselves with their huge shields, keeping their own bodies safe for a time, but powerless to injure the enemy.

The battle began at noon, the Persians, who dined late, having purposely chosen this time for the attack, because they deemed that the Romans, debarred from their usual midday meal, would be faint with hunger. A cloud of arrows from both sides soon darkened the air. In number the missiles of the Persians greatly exceeded; but a favouring wind gave a deadly energy to the fewer darts of the Romans. The Mirran had drawn up his army in two divisions, intending continually to recruit his first line with drafts from the unwearied troops behind them. On the Roman side, the trench with its two flanking lines was still the framework of the position: but Pharas the Herulian, anxious to do great deeds, and not seeing his opportunity in the crowded lines at the left-hand angle of the trenches, asked and obtained leave to make a long flank march and to occupy an eminence in the rear of the Persian right.

Two generals, under the Mirran, commanded the Persian army, Pituazes on the left, Baresmanas on the right. The onset of Pituazes at first met with some success : perhaps the withdrawal of Pharas had unduly weakened the Roman line at the point assailed by him. Soon, however, the generals who were posted behind the main trench saw their opportunity to make a charge on the advancing Persians: and at the same time the appearance of Pharas on his hill in their rear turned the repulse into defeat. Belisarius, who saw that no further danger was to be apprehended from this quarter, withdrew Sunica, a Hunnish commander who had been stationed on the left of the main line, and swung him and his 600 Hunnish horsemen round to strengthen the Roman right, at this time sorely pressed by the advancing Persians. In fact, the Roman troops at the end of the main line were already in full flight. But the Huns on the flanking trench, under Simas and Ascan, joined by their brethren under Sunica and Aegan, now swooped down upon the pursuing Persians. Sunica himself, at the critical moment of the battle, struck down the standard-bearer of Baresmanas. The Persians found that they were being assailed both on the right and the left. They wavered a little in their headlong pursuit: the fugitive Romans finding themselves not followed, turned and faced them : they were soon hopelessly cut off from the rest of the Persian army. Sunica slew Baresmanas and dashed him from his horse to the ground. Great fear fell on all the Persians when they saw their standard fallen, their general's horse riderless. Five thousand of their soldiers, thus surrounded, were cut to pieces : and the rest of the Persians, seeing the slaughter, dashed down their great shields and fled in panic from the field.

Belisarius, mindful of his great inferiority in numbers and fearful of an ambuscade, forbade a distant pursuit of the enemy. The battle, which was a decisive one, had in truth been gained by tactics not unlike those which had in old times been practised by the Parthians against their enemies, namely, by taking advantage of the disorder into which the very fact of pursuit betrays an apparently successful squadron. We can see that the mode of fighting is as dissimilar as possible to the old steady advance of the heavy-armed legions of Pome. Belisarius's army, Roman only in name, consists largely of Huns, Herulians, and other stalwart barbarians drawn from along the northern frontier of the Empire. Courage they have in abundance : they need but discipline to make them irresistible, and that the subtle brain and commanding presence of Belisarius, a born general and king of men, supply in perfection.

How entirely the success of the imperial arms was due to the personal ascendency of Belisarius over his troops was clearly shown in the campaign of 531, when, for want of proper subordination on their part, the battle of Sura was lost by the Romans. In the deliberations in the Persian Court at the beginning of that year, Perozes, the late Mirran, appeared shorn of his dignity, and no longer wearing the circlet of gold and pearls which had before wreathed his brows. This was the punishment inflicted by the King of Kings on the general who had lost the battle of Daras. While Advice of the King and his counsellors were discussing the possible routes for invading the Empire by the old battle-fields of Armenia and Upper Mesopotamia, Alamundar, king of the Saracens, who had been all his life waging a guerrilla war against the Empire on its Arabian frontier, proposed a new plan of campaign. He would avoid the strong border fortresses on the Upper Euphrates and its affluents, cross the river lower down, traverse the wide desert north of Palmyra, and so, reaching that frontier of the Empire upon which there were no fortresses, because the desert was supposed to be its bulwark, strike boldly at Antioch itself. The plan thus proposed, coming from the lips of the king of the Saracens, was a too fatal forecast of the woes which should fall upon the Empire from that very quarter, when the sons of the desert should no longer be serving as vassals of the Persian king, but should be overthrowing empires on their own account, and fighting under the standard of the Prophet.

The counsel of Alamundar pleased Kobad and his nobles, and accordingly 15,000 men were ordered to cross the Middle Euphrates at Circesium, their new general being a Persian noble named Azareth, and Alamundar himself being their guide across the desert. The expedition at first obtained some successes, and the citizens of Antioch, fearing for the safety of their city, streamed down the valley of the Orontes to the coast of the Mediterranean. But tidings of the invasion having reached Belisarius, he ventured to leave the upper frontier comparatively undefended and to make a forced march with an army of 20,000 men to the little lake of Gabbula, about sixty miles east of Antioch, where the enemy were mustered. On hearing of his approach they abandoned the enterprise in despair, and began to retreat towards the Persian frontier. Belisarius followed, slowly pushing them down the Belisarius western hank of the Euphrates, avoiding a pitched invading battle, and each night encamping in the quarters retreat, which the enemy had occupied the night before. He had in this way reached the little town of Sura, nearly opposite the city of Callinicus. The latter, though on the other side of the Euphrates, was a Roman city, for down to this point both banks of the great river were still included in the Empire. Here the invaders were intending to cross the Euphrates and make their way back across the desert to their own land. Nor was Belisarius minded to stop them. True, they still carried with them some of the spoil which they had gathered in the plains of Chalcis, but the shame of a thwarted enterprise more than outweighed this advantage.

But now arose a strange delusion in the Roman army, shared alike by the most experienced officers and by the rawest recruits just drawn from following the plough in the valleys of Lycaonia, to face, for the first time, the realities of war. They all thought that they could read the fortunes of the game better than the general: and they dared to impute to that dauntless spirit the greatest of all sins in a soldier's code of morality—cowardice. In vain did Belisarius remonstrate against this infatuated determination to jeopardy the substantial fruits of the campaign for the sake of the mere name of victory. In vain did he remind them that they were exhausted by the rigour of their Paschal fast:—it was the day before Easter Sunday, and no orthodox Byzantine would touch any food from daybreak to nightfall. All was in vain. The soldiers only shouted more loudly what they had before murmured in secret, 'Belisarius is a coward! Belisarius hinders us from beating the enemy!'. Seeing that the troops were getting out of hand, and knowing that some of their officers were openly siding with the men, Belisarius with a heavy heart yielded to their clamour, pretended that he had only opposed, in order to test, their eagerness, and made his arrangements for the coming battle.

The Romans, with their faces to the south, touched the shore of the Euphrates with their left, and at this end of their line was stationed the bulk of the Roman infantry. In the centre, Belisarius himself commanded the cavalry, at that time the most important portion of the army. On the right, the Roman position was strengthened by book the steepness of the ground. Here fought those Saracen tribes who were friendly to the Empire, and mingled with them were some soldiers who bore the name of Isaurians. In reality, however, they were the Lycaonian rustics to whom reference has already been made. Like the name of Switzer after the great battles of Granson and Morat, so was Isaurian in the armies of the Empire, a title of honour sometimes claimed by men who had little right to it.

On the other side, Azareth and his Persians by the Euphrates faced the Roman left and centre: while the Saracens under Alamundar faced their countrymen on the Roman right.

For some time the battle hung in suspense. Both armies were fighting with missile weapons, and the Roman archers, though less numerous, drew a stronger bow and did more deadly execution than the Persian. After two-thirds of the day had thus elapsed, an impetuous charge of Alamundar caused the Roman right to waver. Ascan the Hun, by the prodigies of valour which he performed, checked for some time the rout of this portion of the army, but after he and the 800 braves who were with him had fallen, there was no longer a show of resistance in this part of the field. The Lycaonian rustics, who were lately so loud in teaching lessons of valour to Belisarius, fell like sheep before the knife, scarcely lifting a weapon in self-defence. The Saracens, pursued by their brother Saracens and the mighty Alamundar, streamed in disorder across the plain.

Belisarius, when he saw the death of Ascan, was forced to flee with his cavalry to the infantry beside the Euphrates. Dismounting from his horse, he fought as a foot-soldier in the ranks, and bade his companions do the same. Turning their backs to the river, the little band of Romans with tightly- locked shields formed a solid wedge, against which the masses of Persian cavalry dashed themselves in vain. Again and again the unavailing charge was attempted. At length night fell, and under its friendly shelter Belisarius and the brave remnant of his army escaped across the river to Callinicus, where they were safe from the Persian pursuit. When Easter Sunday dawned, the Persians as masters of the field buried the bodies of the slain, and found to their dismay that as many of their own countrymen as of the Romans lay upon the plain.

The event of the battle, though abundantly vindicating the wisdom of Belisarius in desiring to decline it, did not greatly alter the course of the campaign. The Persian generals continued their retreat: and when they appeared in the presence of Kobad, the aged monarch asked them what Roman city they had added to his dominions, or whether they had brought him any of the spoil of Antioch. 'Not so, 0 King of Kings,' answered Azareth, 'but we return from winning a victory over Belisarius and the Roman army'. 'At what cost'?' said Kobad. 'Let the arrows be counted'. It was an ancient custom in the Persian state that the army, when about to start for a campaign, should defile before the king, and that each soldier should cast an arrow into a basket at his feet. The baskets were sealed with the king's seal, and kept in a place of safety till the return of the host. They then again marched in order past the king, each soldier as he passed-drawing forth an arrow from the basket. The arrows undrawn told the tale of the soldiers who returned not from the enemy's land. Now, after the day of Sura so numerous were these, the arrows of the dead, that Kobad taunted the triumphant general with his too dear-bought victory; and never after was Azareth entrusted with any high command.

Four months after the battle of Sura, Kobad died; his long and eventful life being ended by a rapid attack of paralysis. His third son, the celebrated Chosroes or Nushirwan, succeeded to the throne, though not without a struggle, in which he put to death every male of his father's house. Possibly these domestic troubles made him the more ready to end the war with the Roman Emperor. After some little diplomatic wrangling a peace, proudly called 'The Endless Peace' was arranged between the two Empires. The fortresses taken on either side were to be restored; Daras was not to be occupied as a military post; and Justinian was to pay Chosroes 11,000 pounds' weight of gold (£440,000) as a contribution towards the expenses of guarding the Caucasus frontier from the barbarians. Upon the whole, the terms were a confession on each side that the game was drawn.

Meanwhile, shortly after the battle of Sura, Belisarius had been recalled to Constantinople by his master, who already meditated employing the talents of this brilliant officer in an entirely new field. It was probably at this time that the young general met and married the woman who was thenceforward to exercise so mighty an influence over his fortunes. Antonina, whose father and grandfather had been charioteers, and whose mother had been a woman of loose character connected with the theatre, could not be considered on the score of birth an equal mate for the young guards-man. In years also she had the disadvantage, being according to Procopius twenty-two years, and certainly not less than twelve years, her husband's senior. She was a widow, and had two grown-up children, when Belisarius married her. The strong and abiding affection which bound the great general to this strangely chosen wife, his deference for her clear and manly judgment, his toleration of her strange vagaries, and even of the stain which she more than once brought upon bis honour, all seemed like a reflection of his imperial master's passion for Theodora. At present, however, the two great ladies, the comic dancer and the actress's daughter, were not on friendly terms with one another. At a later period, the friendship of Theodora for Antonina was to be a factor strongly influencing the fortunes of Belisarius both for good and for evil.

The service upon which Justinian meditated employing Belisanus was to lie in the lands of the West, as far from Constantinople in that direction as the plains of Mesopotamia were in the other. He was to renew the attempt, in which Basiliscus had failed so disastrously sixty-five years before—the attempt to pull down the great Vandal kingdom and restore the provinces of Africa to the sway of the Emperor.

Two months after the battle of Sura a revolution took place at Carthage which furnished Justinian with an admirable pretext for such an enterprise. We have seen that Thrasamund was succeeded by Hilderic, the elderly grandson of Gaiseric, with Catholic sympathies derived from his mother Eudocia, daughter of Valentinian III. Not only by his religious divergence from the ancestral creed was Hilderic ill-fitted for the Vandal throne. His subjects, though they had lost much of their old warlike impetuosity, still loved at least to talk of battle and the camp: while Hilderic, in the exceeding softness and tenderness of his nature, could not bear that any one should even speak of warlike matters in his presence. For eight years the Vandal nation and the family of Gaiseric bore, with increasing impatience, the rule of such a king. At length, in June, 531, his cousin Gelimer, the great-grand-son of Gaiseric, a man who had himself almost passed middle life, a warrior and head of a brotherhood of warriors, unwilling to wait any longer, thrust the feeble Hilderic from the throne and mounted it himself, with the full consent of the Vandal nobility. The two nephews of Hilderic, one of whom, Hoamer, had been called, on rather slight martial cause, the Achilles of the Vandals, shared his captivity.

On hearing these tidings Justinian, who had commenced a friendly correspondence with Hilderic before his own accession to the throne, wrote to remonstrate with Gelimer, and to insist that the aged monarch should continue to wear at least the title, if not to wield the power, of a king. Throughout the correspondence the Emperor assumed the attitude of one who watched over the execution of the testament of Gaiseric, Gaiseric once the irreconcilable enemy of Rome, but now, by a constitutional fiction, her traditional friend and ally.

To the remonstrances of Justinian, Geiimer replied by blinding the Vandal Achilles and by subjecting Hilderic and his other nephew to a yet closer captivity. A letter of stronger remonstrance from Constantinople was answered by a brief and insolent note, in which 'King Gelimer informed King Justinian that nothing was more desirable than that a monarch should mind his own business'. Irritated by this reply, Justinian began seriously to meditate an expedition to chastise the insolence of the Vandal. Negotiations were commenced with Chosroes which resulted in 'the Endless Peace' with Persia, and a pretext was made for recalling Belisarius to Constantinople that the plan of the coming campaign might be discussed with him.

All these schemes were for a time cut short by the terrible insurrection of the Nika, in which the timely presence of Belisarius at the capital saved the throne of Justinian. That chapter closed, the Emperor began again to discuss with his counsellors his designs of African conquest. The proposed war was universally unpopular. The terrible loss of treasure and life in the unsuccessful expedition of Basiliscus was in every one's mouth. Each general dreaded the responsibility of so distant and uncertain an enterprise. The soldiers, who seemed to themselves to have come from the uttermost ends of the earth toward the sun-rising, murmured at the thought of visiting the equally distant lands of the sunset, before they had had time to taste any of the pleasures of the capital. The great civil officers groaned over the prospect of the toil they would have to undergo and the odium they must incur in collecting money and stores for so remote an expedition.

The chief of these civil officers, the ablest, the most illiterate, and the most unscrupulous man among them, the Praetorian Prefect, John of Cappadocia, delivered an oration in full consistory, earnestly dissuading the Emperor from his enterprise. 'You wish, O Augustus, to reach with your arms the city of Carthage. That city lies at a distance from us of 140 days' journey if you go by land. If you sail to it you must cross a wide waste of waters and reach the utmost limits of the sea. Should misfortune overtake your army, it will be a whole year before we hear the tidings of it. And even if you conquer Africa, O Emperor, never will you be able to hold it while Italy and Sicily own the sway of the Ostrogoth. In a word, success in my opinion will bring you no lasting gain, and disaster will involve the ruin of your flourishing Empire.'

For the time Justinian was shaken by the unanimous opposition or his counsellors, and was willing to relinquish the project. But the insulting words of Gelimer rankled in his breast; the glory of restoring the province of Africa to the Empire and her Church to the Catholic communion was too alluring to be abandoned : and when a Bishop from a distant Eastern diocese announced that he had come to Constantinople, commissioned by the Almighty in a dream, to rebuke the slackness of Justinian and to say, 'Thus saith the Lord, I myself will be his partner in the war and I will subdue Libya under him, the ardour of the Emperor could no longer be restrained : soldiers and ships were collected, and Belisarius was ordered to be in readiness to take the command of the expedition on the earliest possible day. He was invested, for the second time, with the rank of Magister Militum per Orientem: he was surrounded by a brilliant staff, and Archelaus the Patrician, formerly Prastorian Prefect, was attached to the expedition as Paymaster of the Forces.

Belisarius was accompanied by his two trusty counsellors, Antonina and Procopius. The latter tells us honestly that he had shared the general dread and dislike of the enterprise, but he too had had his favourable dream which had put him in better heart and caused him to enter upon the service with eagerness.

The army consisted of 10,000 infantry and 5000 cavalry, and was composed ot regular Roman soldiers and *foederati*, the latter probably preponderating. Huns and Heruli occupied prominent positions, not only in the ranks but in the general's tent. The fleet conveying this army comprised 500 ships, the largest of which was of 750 tons burden, and the smallest 45. The large number of 20,000 sailors (forty to each ship, great and small) manned this fleet. There were besides ninety-two fast war-ships, of the kind called dromones, rowed by 2000 Byzantines. These ships had only one bank of oars, and were roofed over to protect the rowers from the enemy's darts. We may perhaps consider that they occupied a similar position in the Byzantine fleet to that held by the torpedo-boats of today in a modern navy.

About Midsummer-day, in the year 533, the armament, the subject of so many hopes and fears, sailed from the quay in front of the Imperial Palace at Constantinople. Epiphanius the Patriarch came on board the general's ship, offered the accustomed prayers, and, for greater good-fortune, left a newly-baptized soldier, a convert to Christianity, under the flag of Belisarius. Calms detained the fleet for some days in the Hellespont, and, while there, two drunken Hunnish soldiers slew a man with whom they had quarrelled. Belisarius hung them up at once in sight of the whole army on a hill overlooking Abydos. Their comrades murmured; but the general, in a short, vigorous speech, reminded them that their only hope of success in the enterprise which they had undertaken lay in the observance of strict justice, without which neither God's favour nor man's could be looked for by them. And as for the plea of drunkenness, no man, whether Roman or barbarian, should be allowed to plead that as an excuse for his crime, which was rather its aggravation. The soldiers heard the general's words, looked upon the gallows from which their comrades were hanging, and conceived a salutary fear of offending against the laws which found so prompt a defender.

The winds were not favourable, and at Methone there was another long detention of the fleet. The misery of sickness was added to the misery of inaction, and that sickness was caused by the dishonest cupidity of a Byzantine official. John of Cappadocia, who had contracted to supply the fleet with a certain number of pounds' weight of biscuit, had sent the dough to be baked at the furnace which heated one of the public baths at Constantinople. He had thus economised baker's wages and fuel, and he had prevented the shrinking in volume which resulted from a proper application of the process. But the so-called twice-baked bread, only once baked and that imperfectly, was a loathsome and corrupting mass when the sacks containing it were opened at Methone. The commissaries at first insisted on supplying it to the men. A pestilence was the natural result, from which five hundred soldiers died. As soon as the matter came to the ears of Belisarius, he at once reported the Prefect's dishonesty to Justinian, stopped the issue of the unsound stores to the troops, and purchased the bread of the district for distribution among them.

At length the fleet reached Zante and there took in water. Still so idly flapped their sails that it took them sixteen days to cross from Zante to Catania in Sicily, and during this passage many of the ships' crews suffered severely from want of water. On board the general's ship, however, there was abundance; for the provident Antonina had stored a large quantity of the precious fluid in some glass amphorae, which she had then deposited in an improvised wooden cellar, constructed in the hold of the ship and carefully covered over with sand. Thus the general and his staff, including the grateful Procopius, had always plenty of cool draughts of water, while their comrades on board the other ships were parched with thirst.

About two months had probably elapsed from the time of the fleet's departure from Constantinople before it reached Sicily. Owing to the unhealed quarrel between the Vandals and Ostrogoths, resulting from the death of Amalafrida, and owing also to the relations of intimate alliance which the Romanising Amalasuntha had established with Justinian, Sicily afforded the imperial troops not only a safe but a friendly resting-place, where they could refit and revictual their ships at pleasure. Without this advantage, which the madness of the Vandals had thrown in their way, it may be doubted if the Byzantine expedition could possibly have succeeded.

Belisarius, however, notwithstanding this point in his favour, was racked with doubts and fears as to the issue of the campaign. His absolute ignorance of the numbers and position of the Vandal army, his want of all information as to the best points for landing, or the condition of the roads, were most unsatisfactory to a general who, with all his splendid personal courage, looked upon war as a science and knew what the postulates of that science demanded. And then, he knew not whether he should be allowed to join battle with the Vandals by land. They had a powerful fleet and might attack him, as they had attacked Basiliscus, by sea. Ominous murmurs were being uttered by the disheartened soldiery— and some of them reached his ears—that, though they would do their duty in an engagement on land and would show themselves brave men there, if they were attacked at sea by the ships of the enemy they would at once seek safety in flight.

Oppressed by these cares, Belisarius sought the quarters of his counsellor Procopius. He wished that the secretary should visit the city of Syracuse, ostensibly in order to buy stores for the army, but really to obtain all possible information as to the doings of the Vandals, the near neighbours of Sicily. Procopius gladly accepted the mission, and after some days presented himself at the general's quarters at Caucana, the meeting-place of the troops on the south coast of the island, about fifty miles from Syracuse. The Secretary's face showed that he brought good tidings, and he had a living voucher for their truth. Almost immediately on his arrival at Syracuse he had met with a person who had been a friend of his from childhood, but who, on account of his interest in some shipping propery, thad quitted the East and was now settled in the Sicilian capital. When Procopius cautiously propounded his questions about Carthage, his friend replied, 'I have the very man who can give you the needed information. This servant of mine returned but three days ago from Carthage: ask him'. The servant declared that no preparations worth speaking of were being made by the Vandals to meet the Byzantine armament. They did not even know that it had left Constantinople. Gelimer was at an inland place called Hermione, a considerable distance from Carthage. And, most important of all, by a piece of rare good-fortune for the Romans, all the best Vandal soldiers had sailed away to Sardinia, under the command of Tzazo, Gelimer's brother, to put down the rebellion of one Godas, a Goth who had been sent thither by the Vandal King to collect tribute, but who was now trying to open communications with the Emperor on his own account, and affected the airs of an independent sovereign.

All this was better news than Procopius had dared to hope for. That Belisarius might be satisfied of its truth, he took his friend's slave down with him to the port, which was still called 'the Harbour of Arethusa,' continued an eager conversation with the man till they were on board ship, and then gave a sign to the captain to weigh anchor and leave the harbour with all speed. The owner of the kidnapped slave, Procopius's friend from childhood, stood on the shore bewildered and inclined towards anger : but his old schoolfellow shouted out to him that he must not be grieved, for that it was absolutely necessary that the man should be brought into the general's presence; but after he had shown the Roman army the way to Carthage he should soon be sent back to Syracuse bringing a large reward,

Cheered by the tidings brought by this messenger Belisarius ordered the mariners to hoist sail. They passed the islands of Malta and Gozo, and the next day, a brisk east wind having sprung up, they reached the coast of Africa. It was now about the beginning of September, and nearly three months since they had sailed forth from the harbour of Constantinople.

The point of the African coast which the fleet had made was called Caputvada, and was about 130 miles in a straight line south by east of Carthage. The coast of Africa here runs nearly due north and south, and the corner where it turns from its usual east and west direction, the very conspicuous promontory of Cape Bon (called by the Greeks and Romans Hermaeum), lies 130 miles due north of Caputvada, and about thirty east of Carthage.

Before landing, Belisarius called a council of war on board his ship. The Patrician Archelaus, his civil Assessor and Paymaster-General, was earnest in his advice that they should not land there, but sail round to the great pool close to the harbour of Carthage, where there would be shelter and ample berthing-room for all the ships, and where they would be quite close to the scene of operations. There was much to be said on behalf of this view, and it was well said by Archelaus, who, as master of the commissariat department, especially insisted on the difficulties that would beset the provisioning of the troops upon a land-march if the fleet, their base of supply, should be dashed to pieces against the Libyan coast. Belisarius, however, who felt that he could trust his troops by land and could not trust them by sea, refused to give the Vandals another chance of bringing on a naval engagement, and gave his decisive voice in favour of disembarking at Caputvada and proceeding from thence to Cartbage by land. The soldiers were ordered at once to fortify the position at Caputvada with the usual fosse and vallum of a Roman camp. In doing so they discovered a copious spring of excellent water, welcome for its own sake, but doubly welcome because it was looked upon as something supernatural and a token of Divine favour on the enterprise.

As it proved, this *fossatum* or entrenched camp was not needed by the Romans. The extraordinary apathy, or panic, or over-confidence of the Vandals still left the imperial army free from attack. The neighbouring city oi Syllectum, at the persuasion of the Catholic bishop and the leading citizens—men doubtless of Roman nationality—gladly opened her gates to the Emperor's generals. An even more important defection was that of the Vandal Postmaster of the Province, who placed all the post-horses of his district at the general's disposal. One of the king's messengers (*veredarii*) was captured, and Belisarius sought to make use of him to circulate Justinian's proclamation, which, in the usual style of such documents, stated that the invading army came, not to make war on people of the land, but only on the tyrant and usurper Gelimer. The *veredarius* handed copies of the proclamation to some of his friends, but not much came of his proceedings. Sovereigns and statesmen generally overrate the importance of such manifestoes.

For eleven days Belisarius and his army moved steadily northwards, covering a distance of about thirteen miles a day. A force of 300 men under the command of his steward, John the Armenian, preceded the main body of the army at a distance of about three miles. The Huns rode at the same distance to the left. Thus, if danger threatened from either quarter, the general was sure to have early notice of it. His right wing was of course sufficiently protected by the sea, where his ships slowly accompanied the march of the land forces. Belisarius sternly repressed the slightest disposition on the part of his soldiers to plunder, and insisted on every article of food required being punctually paid for. He was rewarded for this exercise of discipline by the hearty good-will of the provincials, who evidently gave no information of his movements to the enemy. The soldiers, too, had their reward for their painful self-denial when, about sixty miles from Carthage, they reached the 'Paradise' which surrounded the beautiful palace of the Vandal kings at Grassé. Here were springing fountains, a great depth of shade, and fruit-trees in overpowering abundance. Into these lovely gardens poured the dusty, travel-worn Byzantines, and found them indeed a Paradise. Each soldier made himself a little hut under the boughs of some fruit-tree and ate his fill of its luscious produce: yet, strange to say, when the bugle sounded and the army had to leave the too brief delights of Grassé, it seemed as if there was still the same wealth of fruit upon the trees that hung there when the first soldier entered.

Now at length, on the 13th of September, four days after leaving Grassé, when the army reached Ad Decimum, came the shock of grim war to interrupt this pleasant promenade through the enemy's land. When Gelimer heard the tidings of the enemy's landing, his first step was to send orders to Carthage that Hilderic and his surviving relatives and friends should be put to death: his next, to desire his brother Ammatas, who commanded at Carthage, to arm all the Vandal soldiers and prepare for a combined attack on the invaders. The place chosen for this combined attack was a point ten miles from Carthage (Ad Decimum), where the road went between steep hills, and it seemed possible to catch the enemy as in a trap. Three divisions were to co-operate in the movement. While Ammatas, sallying forth from Carthage, attacked the Roman van, King Gelimer himself with the main body of the army was to fall upon their rear, and at the same hour his nephew Gibamund, moving over the hills from the west, was to fall upon their left flank.

The plan was skilfully conceived, and Procopius himself expresses his astonishment that the Roman host should have escaped destruction. Some part of the credit of their deliverance was due to the arrangements made by Belisarius for obtaining early information of what was going on in front of him and on his left flank, but more to the Chance or Fate or Providence (Procopius scarcely knows which to style it) that caused Ammatas to issue too early from Carthage and deliver his attack too soon. He came about noonday, and dashed impetuously, with only a few of his followers, against the Roman vanguard, led by John the Armenian. Ammatas slew with his own hand twelve of the bravest of the imperial soldiers, but he then fell mortally wounded, and his death changed the whole fortune of the day. His men fled, and John's pursuing soldiers wrought grievous havoc among the Vandals issuing from Carthage, who, in no regular order, were scattered along the road from the city to the battle-field. Procopius says that lookers-on conjectured that 20,000 Vandals were thus slain, but the estimate was probably an exaggerated one.

Equally unsuccessful was Gibamund's attack on the left flank of the Roman army. According to the arrangement of Belisarius above described, the troops that he fell in with were the covering squadron of Huns. The Vandals had often heard of the headlong bravery of these old enemies of the Gothic nations, but had not before met them in battle. Now, a Hun belonging to a noble family, which had by long usage a prescriptive right to draw first blood in every battle, rode alone close up to the Vandal ranks. These, surprised or terrified, did not assail the solitary champion, who returned to his comrades, shouting loudly that God had given these aliens to them as food for their swords. The Hunnish squadron advanced, and the Vandal detachment, two thousand men in number, fled panic-stricken from the field.

Very different at first was the fortune of the main body of their army led by Gelimer himself. Procopius's description of this part of the action is somewhat confused; but it seems clear that the hilly nature of the ground hid the movements of Belisarius and Gelimer from one another. The Roman general had inadvertently drawn out his line too wide; and the Vandal King, equally by accident, slipped in between Belisarius and the centre of his army. He was thus enabled to make a most dangerous flank attack on the Roman centre, and in fact to gain the victory, if he had known how to keep it. If after his defeat of the infantry he had moved to the left against the small body of cavalry that surrounded Belisarius, he might easily have overwhelmed them. If he had pushed forward he would have annihilated John's forces still scattered in all the disorder of pursuit, and saved Carthage. He did neither. As he was leisurely descending a hill, his possession of which had given him the victory over the Roman centre, he came upon the dead body of Ammatas, still unburied and gashed with honourable wounds. Grief at this sight drove every thought of battle from the mind of Gelimer. He burst out into loud bewailings, and would not stir from the place till he had given his brother befitting burial. Meanwhile Belisarius was rallying his fugitive soldiers; was learning the true story of the vanguard's encounter with Ammatas; put heart into his beaten army, and before nightfall had got together day a large body of men with whom he dashed at full speed against the unprepared and unmarshalled Vandals. Now at length the battle was really won. Gelimer's soldiers fled westwards from the field in wild disorder, and the Romans of all three divisions encamped that night among the hills of Ad Decimum, victorious.

Gelimer's ill-timed display of sorrow for his brother was attributed by Procopius to a Heavensent infatuation. A modern historian is probably more disposed to turn it into ridicule. But after all, there is a touch of Northern chivalry and tenderness even in the absurdity of the proceeding. Hardly would any rhetoric-loving Greek or materialistic Roman have been tempted to lose a battle in order to take the last farewell fittingly of the relics of a brother.

On the next day Antonina and the rearguard of the troops came up, and the whole army moved on over the ten miles which separated them from Carthage, and encamped at nightfall at the gates of the capital. The whole city gave itself up to merriment: lights were lit in every chamber, and the night shone like the day. The Vandals, hopelessly outnumbered and recognising that the sceptre had departed from their nation, clustered as timid suppliants round the altars; but Belisarius sent orders into the city that the lives of all of that people who peaceably submitted themselves were to be spared. Meanwhile, still fearing some stratagem of the enemy, and doubtful also of the self-restraint of his soldiers, he refused for that night to enter the illuminated city. Next day, having Carthage satisfied himself that the enemy had indeed vanished, and having harangued his soldiers on the duty of scrupulously respecting the lives and property of the Carthaginian citizens, fellow-subjects with themselves of the Roman Emperor, and men whom they had come to deliver from the degrading yoke of the barbarian, he at length marched into the city, where he was received with shouts of welcome by the inhabitants. The hundred years of Vandal domination were at an end. The Emperor, Senate, and People of Rome were again supreme in the great colony which Caius Gracchus had founded on the rums of her mighty antagonist. And yet, strange contradiction, suggestive of future labours and dangers for the great commander, at that very time Rome herself, her Senate and her People, obeyed the orders of the Gothic princess, Amalasuntha.

The exhortations of Belisarius to his troops bore memorable fruit. Never did soldiers march into a the troops, conquered town in more friendly guise. Although it was notorious that generally even a little handful of imperial soldiers marching into one of the cities of the Empire would fill the air with their boisterous clamour, and would terrify the peaceful inhabitants with their military braggadocio, now the whole army entered in perfect order and without an unnecessary sound. No threats were heard, no deed of insolence was done. The secretaries of the army, gliding about from rank to rank, distributed to each man his billet, and he departed tranquilly to his appointed lodging. In the workshops, the handicraftsmen plied their accustomed tasks; in the agora, the buyer and the seller bargained as of old. No one would have dreamed from the appearance of the city that a mighty revolution had that very day been consummated in the midst thereof.

On the morning of this eventful day many Byzantine merchants whom Gelimer in his rage had arrested, and whom he meant to have put to death on the very day of the battle of Ad Decimum, were cowering in a dark dungeon in the King's palace, expecting every moment to be ordered forth to execution. The gaoler entered and asked them what price they were willing to pay for their safety.

'My whole fortune,' each one gladly answered.

'You may keep your money,' said he. 'I ask for nothing but that you should help me if I too should be in danger of my life'. With that he removed a plank from before their prison window. With blinking eyes they looked forth to the blinding sky over the blue Mediterranean, and saw the imperial fleet drawing near to the city of their captivity. The chain which had stretched across the harbour was broken by the citizens' own hands, and they were crowding down to the port to welcome their deliverers. At that sight the prisoners knew that their chains also were broken. The gaoler opened the prison doors and went down into the streets in their company.

When noon was come, Belisarius, who had already entered the palace and seated himself on the throne of Gelimer, commanded that the mid-day meal should be served to him and to his officers in the Delphic chamber, the great banqueting-hall of the palace. Among the generals and officers sat the secretary Procopius, and mused on the instability of Fortune, as he found himself and his comrades waited upon by the royal pages, and eating, from the gold and silver plate of the Vandal, the very same luxurious meats and drinking the same costly wines which had been prepared for the repast of Gelimer himself.

A similar example of sowing without reaping was furnished by the cathedral church of Carthage, named after her great martyred bishop, St. Cyprian. Many a time, says Procopius, during the stress of the Vandal persecution, had the saint appeared in visions to his disciples and told them that they need not distress themselves, since he himself in time would avenge their wrongs. On the eve of his great yearly festival, which, as it chanced, was the very day that Ammatas rode forth from Carthage to fall among the hills of Ad. Decimum, the Arian priests, who had of course the sole right to minister in the cathedral, made great preparations, sweeping out the church, making ready the lights, bringing their costliest treasures out of the sacristy. Then came the decisive victory, by which African Arianism was for ever overthrown. The orthodox Christians flocked to the church, lighted the lamps, displayed the treasures, and rejoiced that they had at length received the long-delayed fulfilment of the promise of Saint Cyprian.

Gelimer, after the defeat of Ad Decimum, formed a camp at Bulla Regia, in the province of Numidia, and about a hundred miles west of Carthage. Here were collected the remains of the Vandal army, a still formidable host, and here were stored the vast treasures of the kingdom, those treasures which ninety-five years of sovereignty in the rich and fertile province of Africa had enabled the family of Gaiseric to accumulate.

While he was in this camp, meditating how best to recover possession of his capital, a letter was despatched from his brother Tzazo, the commander of the expedition to Sardinia. Tzazo, who had as yet heard nothing of the disasters of his people, wrote in a cheerful tone, announcing the easy victory which he had gained over the rebels, and prognosticating that even so would all the other enemies of the Vandals fall before them. By the irony of Fate, the messengers brought this letter to Carthage and had to deliver it to the hands of Belisarius, who read it and dismissed them unharmed.

Meanwhile Gelimer, who had perhaps gained information of the contents of the letter, wrote to his brother. 'Not Godas, but some cruel decree of destiny wrenched Sardinia from us. While you, with all our bravest, have been recovering that island, Justinian has been making himself master of Africa. With few men did Belisarius come against us, but all the ancient valour of the Vandals seemed to have departed, and with it all our old good-fortune. They turned faint-hearted when they saw Ammatas and Gibamund slain, and fleeing, left horses and ships and the province of Africa, and, worst of all, Carthage itself, a prey to our enemies. Here then we sit encamped in the plain of Bulla. Our only hope is in you. Leave Sardinia to take care of itself, and come and help us. It will be at least some comfort in our calamities to feel that we are bearing them together.'

When Tzazo and his Vandals received these grievous tidings in Sardinia, they broke forth into lamentations, all the more bitter because they had to be repressed whenever any of the subject islanders were near. Then, with all speed, they set sail, reached the point of the African coast where the Numidian and Mauritanian frontiers joined, and marched on foot to the plain of Bulla, where they met the rest of the army. The two brothers, Gelimer and Tzazo, fell on one another's necks and of the two remained for long locked in a silent embrace, neither of them able to speak for tears, but clasping one another's hands. Their followers did thesame, and for a space no word was uttered. Neither the victory in Sardinia nor the defeat at Ad Decimum was spoken of by either host. The lonely and desolate spot where they met, and which was all that they could now call home, told with sad and sufficient emphasis all the tale of the last fatal month.

After the battle of Ad Decimum active hostilities on both sides had ceased for a time. Belisarius had been busily engaged in the superintendence of a great number of workmen whom he had engaged to repair the numerous breaches caused by time and neglect in the walls of Carthage, to dig a fosse around it, and plant stakes upon the vallum formed of the earth thrown up out of the fosse. Gelimer had attempted nothing beyond a guerrilla war, conducted by some of the African peasants, with whom he was personally popular, and stimulated by a bounty for the head of every Roman brought into his camp.

Now that, by his iunction with Tzazo, he found himself at the head of forces considerably outnumbering the Roman army, Gelimer took a bolder line; marched to Carthage; broke down the aqueduct, an exceedingly fine one, which supplied the city; and encamped at Tricamaron, a place about twenty miles distant from the capital, from whence he could block more than one of the roads leading thither. The secret negotiations which he set on foot with the Arians in Carthage and in the army of Belisarius were discovered by the general, who at once hung Laurus the chief traitor, on a hill overlooking the city. With the fierce and ungovernable Huns, who had listened to Gelimer's proposals, it was not possible to take such severe measures. In the battle which all men knew to be now impending they had determined to take no active part till Fortune should have declared herself, and then to join the victorious side.

At length, about the middle of December, Belisarius marched forth from Carthage to fight the battle of Tricamaron. Gelimer, who had placed the Vandal women and children in the middle of his camp, in order that their cries might stimulate their husbands and fathers to a desperate defence, harangued his troops, adjuring them to choose death rather than defeat, which involved slavery and the loss of all that made life delightful both for themselves and for these dear ones. Tzazo added a few words, specially addressed to the army of Sardinia, exhorting them, who had yet suffered no defeat, to prove themselves the deliverers of the Vandal name. The battle began stubbornly. Twice was the desperate charge of the Roman cavalry, under John the Armenian, beaten back; and the third charge, though more successful, led to a fierce hand-to-hand encounter, in which for some time neither side could get the better of its antagonists. But then, in the crisis of the battle, Tzazo fell. Gelimer, again unmanned by a brother's death, forgot his own valour-breathing words and hurried swiftly from the field. The Huns now struck in on the side of the Romans. The rout of the Vandals was complete, and they fled headlong from the field, leaving camp, treasure, children and wives, all at the mercy of the enemy.

The utter demoralisation which spread throughout the conquering army at the sight of this splendid prize would have ensured their overthrow, had Gelimer and a few faithful followers hovered near to take advantage of it. Intent on stripping off the golden armour of the Vandal officers, enraptured at finding themselves the possessors of money, of jewels, of comely and noble-looking slaves, the host of barbarians who bore the name of a Roman army abandoned all thought of military obedience, forgot even the commonest maxims of prudence in the presence of a beaten foe, and were intent upon one only aim, to convey themselves and their spoil back within the walls of the city as soon as possible. Murder went as ever hand in hand with lust and greed. Not one of the Vandal warriors who was captured was admitted to quarter. When day dawned, Belisarius, standing on a neighbouring hill to survey the scene, succeeded by his shouted adjurations in restoring some degree of order, first among: the soldiers of his own household, and then, through their means, in the rest of the army. So were all the soldiers with their captives and spoils at length safely marched back to Carthage. The numerous Vandal suppliants in the churches of the district were admitted to quarter, and preparations were made for shipping off the greater number of them as prisoners to Constantinople. Experienced officers were sent to Sardinia, to Corsica, to the Balearic Isles, to Ceuta and other Mauritanian towns, and easily brought all these recent possessions of the Vandals into the obedience of the Emperor. At Lilybaeum only in Sicily (now Marsala) were they unsuccessful. Here the Goths, though friendly to the Romans, entirely refused to recognise that conquest gave Justinian any right to claim Amalafrida's dowry, and declined to surrender the city.

When Gelimer escaped from the field of Tricamaron, Belisarius ordered John the Armenian to follow after him night and day, and not to rest till he had taken him prisoner. For five days did this pursuit continue, and on the following day it would probably have been successful but for a strange misadventure. There was among John's soldiers a barbarian named Uliaris, a brave soldier, but flighty, impetuous, and a drunkard. On the morning of the sixth day, at sunrise, Uliaris, who was already intoxicated, saw a bird sitting on a tree and tried to shoot it. He aimed so clumsily that his arrow, missing the bird, pierced his general from behind in the nape of his neck. John Armenian languished a few hours in great pain and then expired, desiring that the offence of his unwilling murderer might be forgiven. Belisarius, who was at once sent for, wept bitterly at the grave of his friend, whose character and achievements had seemed to mark him out for a high career; and fulfilled his dying wishes by pardoning Uliaris.

But meanwhile the hard-pressed Gelimer had succeeded in escaping from his pursuers to a steep mountain called Pappua, on the very verge of the Numidian province. Here he with his nephews and cousins, the remnant of the proud family of Gaiseric, dwelt for three months, dependent on the hospitality and loyalty of the half-savage Moors who inhabited this district. A terrible change it was for the dainty Vandals, the most luxurious of all the races that overran the Roman Empire, to have to live cooped up in the fetid huts of these sons of the desert. The Vandal was accustomed to sumptuous meals, for which earth and sea were ransacked to supply new delicacies. The Moor did not even bake his bread, but subsisted upon uncooked flour. The Vandal dressed in silken robes, wore golden ornaments, and daily indulged in all the luxury of the Roman bath. The squalid Moor, swarming with vermin, wore both in winter and summer the same rough tunic and heavy cloak; he never washed himself, and his only couch was the floor of his hut, upon which, it is true, the wealthy Mauritanian spread a sheep-skin before he laid him down to rest. In the delights of the chase, the theatre, and the hippodrome had passed the pleasure-tinted days of the Vandal lords of Africa. Now, instead of this ceaseless round of pleasure, there was only the dull and sordid monotony of a Moorish hamlet on a bleak mountain.

After the death of John, Pharas the Herulian with a band of hardy followers had been told off for the pursuit of Gelimer, and had followed him sas far as the foot of the mountain. His attempt to carry the position by storm had failed. The Moors were still faithful to the exile, and the steep cliffs could not be climbed without their consent. Pharas therefore was obliged to turn his siege into a blockade; and during the three winter months at the beginning of 534 he carefully watched the mountain, suffering none to approach and none to leave it. At length, knowing what hardships the Vandal King must be enduring, he wrote him a skilful and friendly letter, asking him why, for the sake of the mere name of freedom, he persisted in depriving himself of all that made life worth living. He concluded thus : 'Justinian, I have heard, is willing to promote you to great honour, to confer upon you the rank of a Patrician, and to give you houses and lands. Surely to be fellow-servant with Belisarius of so mighty an Emperor is better than to be playing the king in Pappua, really serving the caprices of a few squalid Moors, and that in the midst of hunger and every kind of hardship not only for yourself but for your unhappy kindred.'

Gelimer's answer was characteristic. 'I thank you for your counsel, but I will not be the slave of a man who has attacked me without cause and upon whom I yet hope to wreak a terrible revenge. He has brought me, who had done him no wrong, to this depth of ruin, by sending Belisarius against me, I know not whence. But let him beware. Some change which he will not like may be impending over him also. I can write no more: my calamities take from me the power of thought. But be gracious to me, dear Pharas, and send me a lyre, and one loaf of bread and a sponge.'

The end of this singular letter was a hopeless puzzle to the Herulian general, till the messenger who brought it explained that Gelimer wished once more to experience the taste of baked bread, which he had not eaten for many weeks, that one of his eyes was inflamed owing to his inability to wash it, and that having composed an ode on his misfortunes he wished to hear how it sounded on the lyre.

After all, a trifling incident broke down the stubborn resolution of Gelimer. A Moorish woman had scraped together a little flour, kneaded it into dough, and put it on the coals to bake. Two boys, one of them her son and the other a Vandal prince, nephew of Gelimer, looked at the process of cooking with hungry eyes, and each determined to possess himself of the food. The Vandal was first to snatch it from the fire and thrust it, burning hot and gritty with ashes, into his mouth. At that the Moor caught him by the hair of his head, slapped him on the cheek, pulled the half-eaten morsel out of his mouth, and thrust it into his own. Gelimer, who had been watching the whole scene from beginning to end, was so touched by the thought of the misery which his obstinacy was bringing upon all belonging to him, that he wrote to Pharas, retracting his former refusal, and offering to surrender if he could be assured that the terms mentioned in the previous letter were still open to him.

Pharas sent the whole of the correspondence to Belisarius, who received it with great delight, and sent a guard of foederati named Cyprian to swear that the terms of surrender named by Pharas should be kept. Gelimer came down from his hill; the mutual promises were exchanged, and in a few days the Vandal King was introduced into the presence of his captor at a suburb of Carthage named Aclae.

When Gelimer met Belisarius, to the surprise of all the bystanders, he burst into a loud peal of laughter. Some thought that the sudden reverse in his fortunes, the hardships, and the insufficient food of the last few months had touched his brain; and to a matter-of-fact historian this will perhaps still seem the most probable reason for his conduct. Procopius, however, assigns a more subtle cause. The Vandal King, suddenly, at the end of a long and prosperous life, cast down from the height of human happiness, perceived that all the prizes for which men contend here so earnestly are worthless. They are making all this coil about absolute nothingness, and whatever happens to them here is really worthy only to be laughed at. The story, as told by Procopius, and some other passages in the life of Gelimer, suggest that the character of the Vandal King might be so studied as to throw some light on that most enticing yet most difficult problem, Shakespeare's conception of the character of Hamlet.

Meanwhile the conqueror—as well as the conquered—was feeling some f
'The stings and arrows of outrageous Fortune.'

Some of his subordinates, envious of his glory, sent secret messages to the Emperor that Belisarius was aiming at the diadem. No doubt his having seated himself on the throne of Gelimer on that day when he entered the palace of the Vandal King lent some probability to the utterly baseless charge. The general, by good fortune, obtained a duplicate of the letter written by his enemies : and thus, when a message came back from Justinian, 'The Vandal captives are to be sent to Constantinople : choose whether you will accompany them or remain at Carthage,' he knew what answer was desired. To return was by his own act to dispel the accusation of disloyalty: to stay would have been at once to take up the position which his enemies would fain assign to him of a pretender to the crown. He wisely and as a good citizen chose the former course.

On his return to the capital, Belisarius was rewarded for his splendid services to the Senate and People of Rome by the honours of a triumph, which, says Procopius, had for near six hundred years never been enjoyed by any but an Emperor. Even now he had not quite the full honours of an ancient Roman triumph. He walked from his palace, whereas a Scipio or a Fabius would have ridden in his chariot. But before him walked the throng of Vandal captives, ending with Gelimer and his kinsmen, all that remained of the mighty Asding name. When the Byzantine populace saw those strong and stately forms, they marvelled the more at the skill of the general who had brought all their power down into the dust. Gelimer himself, as he passed through the streets, and when he came into the Hippodrome and saw Justinian sitting on his throne and the ranks and orders of the Roman people standing on either side of him, neither laughed nor wept, but simply repeated again and again the words of the kingly Hebrew preacher, 'Vanity of vanities: all is vanity.'

When he reached the throne of Justinian, the attendants took off the purple robe which floated from his shoulders and compelled him to fall prostrate before the peasant's son who bore the great name of Augustus. It may have been some mitigation of his abasement that his conqueror, the triumphant Belisarius, grovelled with him at Justinian's feet. When the triumph was ended, Gelimer was admitted probably to a private audience of the Emperor. The rank of Patrician which had been promised him could only be his on his renouncing the Alian heresy, and this he steadily refused to do. He received, however, large estates in the Galatian province, and lived there in peace and of the with his exiled kinsfolk. The children and grand-children of Hilderic, who had the blood of Valentinian and Theodosius in their veins, and who also no doubt professed the Catholic faith, were especially welcomed and honoured by Justinian and Theodora, received large sums of money, and seem to have been invited to remain at the Byzantine Court.

Besides the other magnificent spoils which were exhibited at this triumph, the thrones and sceptres, the costly raiment, the pearls and golden drinking-cups, many of which had formed part of Gaiseric's spoil of Rome eighty years before, there were also carried in the procession the vessels of the Temple at Jerusalem which had once adorned the triumph of Titus. But, as has been already described a Jew who was acquainted with a friend of the Emperor said : 'If those vessels are brought into the Palace they will cause the ruin of this Empire. They have already brought the Vandal to Rome, and Belisarius to Carthage : nor will Constantinople long wait for her conqueror if they remain here.' The superstitious side of Justinian's nature was affected by this suggestion, and he sent the sacred vessels away to Jerusalem to be stored up in one of the Christian churches.

The next year, when Belisarius entered upon his consulship, he had a kind of second triumph, which was in some respects more like the antique ceremony. He was borne on the shoulders of the captives: then he rode in his triumphal car and scattered gifts to the crowd from out of the Vandal spoils. Silver vessels and golden girdles and money from the great Vandal hoard were scattered by the new Consul among that Byzantine populace which claimed the title of the Roman People.

The fall of the Vandal monarchy was an event full of meaning: for the future history of Africa. There can be little doubt that in destroying it Justinian was unconsciously removing the most powerful barrier which might in the next century have arrested the progress of Mohammedanism : and thus, in the secular contest between the Aryan and Semitic peoples, the fall of the throne of Gaiseric was a heavy blow to the cause of Europe and a great gain to the spirit of Asia.

The reasons which produced this overthrow cannot here he enumerated at length. It is clear, however, that in the Vandal monarchy there was less approach towards amalgamation between the Teuton invaders and the Roman provincials than in any of the other kingdoms founded by the Northern invaders. The arrogance of Gaiseric and his nobles and the ferocity of their persecution of the Catholics had opened a chasm between the two nations, which could perhaps never have been bridged over. Then upon this state of affairs supervened the weakening of the fibre of the conquering race and its loss of martial prowess, through the progress of luxury and through the increase of something which was perhaps not wholly undeserving of the name of culture. The quarrel with the Ostrogoths deprived the Vandals of their natural allies, and gave to

Belisarius the best possible base for his invasion of Africa. The character of Gelimer, impulsive, sentimental, unstable, additionally weighted the scale against his subjects. And finally, that which some would be disposed to call mere accident, the invasion of Sardinia, the absence of storms while the Roman fleet was voyaging along the coast, the failure of the concerted operations at Ad Decimum, all combined to turn the doubtful enterprise of Justinian and his general into an assured and splendid victory.

CHAPTER XVI

THE ERRORS OF AMALASUNTHA.

The imperial conquest of Africa foreboded at no very distant date trouble for the Gothic lords of Italy. Truly had John of Cappadocia advised the Emperor that he could not expect long to retain the lands which owned Carthage as their capital while the intervening lands of Italy and Sicily were in alien, possibly hostile, hands. Already the grievance of the unsurrendered fortress of Lilybaeum was an indication of the coming estrangement between the hitherto friendly monarchies; a hint to any reflecting Gothic statesman that his nation had not done wisely in so immensely facilitating the imperial triumph over its old Vandal ally.

Ambassadors were speedily sent by Justinian to bring his grievances—which related not to Lilybaeum alone—before the Court of Ravenna: but these ambassadors were also charged with private messages to the Ostrogothic princess more important than their formal demand for the surrender of the Sicilian fortress. These private messages related to the increasingly strained relations between Amalasuntha and her own subjects, relations which had already caused her, a Gothic ruler, to utter strange cries for help to the Roman Emperor.

The daughter of Theodoric was a woman endowed with many splendid gifts, but she was placed in a difficult, one is inclined to say in a hopelessly false, position, and the very splendour of her gifts only made her failure to fill that position more notorious. The mere fact that she was a woman made it almost impossible that she should command the hearty loyalty of her Gothic subjects. That which John Knox inveighed against as 'the monstrous regiment of a woman' though common among the Celtic nationalities, was almost unknown to the Teutons. Tacitus, near the close of the 'Germania', speaks of the remote tribe of the Sitones as differing from other German races in that they were governed by a woman : 'so far had they degenerated not only from liberty but even from slavery'. That peculiar development of the Teutonic spirit of honour to women which we call chivalry, and which was to make the stalwart knights of the Middle Ages proud to serve under a Lady Paramount, aud the counsellors of Elizabeth support her throne with an enthusiastic loyalty of devotion such as few of the kings her predecessors had experienced,—all this was yet in the far future. For the present the Gothic warriors felt themselves distinctly degraded by having to obey the commands of a woman, though nominally only a Regent, and though she was the mother of their King.

It probably availed little against this disparaging view of a woman ruler, that she was possessed of great intellectual accomplishments, that she could speak Latin and Greek as fluently as the ambassadors who came to discourse with her in either tongue, and yet had not lost the full use of the rich Gothic vocabulary of her ancestors. The sensibility to the culture of the vanquished lords of Italy, which Amalasuntha showed in her friendships, in her speech, in her daily occupations, was all, matter for distrust and suspicion to those of her Gothic countrymen who wished to stand fast by the old ways. Still this might have been borne with as a woman's whim; but when they perceived that she was bringing up the King of the Goths, the descendant of all the Amal warriors, to the same studious habits, their dislike deepened into indignation. The great Theodoric had said, in his proclamation to the Goths, even when Cassiodorus held the pen, 'What is not learned in youth is unknown in riper years. Bring forth your young men and train them in martial discipline'. A young Amal hero should be learning (like the Persian lads of old) 'to ride and to draw the bow, and to speak the truth'. He should be out daily with the young nobles, his equals in age, practising every kind of manly exercise. Instead of this, the unhappy Athalaric had daily to visit the school of a grammarian, to learn what Priscian had just written about the eight parts of speech, or what Boethius (that traitor Boethius) had translated from the Greeks about the science of arithmetic. His only companions were three old men, of Gothic bloody it is true, but whom the princess had selected because 'she perceived them to be more intelligent and reasonable than the rest of their countrymen', a doubtful recommendation in the eyes of their more impetuous and younger fellow-nobles.

At length, a chance event brought matters to a crisis, and emancipated Athalaric from female rule. For some act of disobedience Amalasuntha flogged her royal son, who came forth from the bed-chamber into the apartment of the men, sobbing bitterly. A Gothic king, flogged by a woman and crying over the chastisement; that was too much for the warriors to endure. They clustered together, and some voices were heard openly proclaiming the cruel calumny that Amalasuntha wished to kill her boy that she might marry a second husband, and with him lord it over both Goths and Italians. Soon a deputation, composed of men of such high rank that the princess could not refuse to listen to them, sought an interview with Amalasuntha. In a formal harangue the chief speaker represented that the young King's education was not being conducted in a way that was either suitable for himself or just towards his subjects. 'For letters,' said they, 'are very different from valour : and the teachings of aged men generally lead only to cowardice and meanness. A lad, therefore, who is one day to dare great deeds, and to win high renown, ought to be at once liberated from the fear of schoolmasters and to practise the use of arms. Theodoric, who was himself devoid of literature, and yet so mighty a king, would never permit the children of the Gothic warriors to be sent to a grammarian's to study: for he always said "If they once learn to fear the tutor's strap, they will never look unblenching on sword and spear." Therefore,O Lady, let the pedagogues and the old courtiers take their leave, and give to your son suitable companions of his own age, who may stir him up to manly exercises, so that when he comes to man's estate he may know how to rule after the fashion of the barbarians'.

Amalasuntha turned pale with anger as she listened to this bold harangue : but, with all her gifts of oratory, she knew when to be silent and when to feign acquiescence in the dictates of a power that was too strong for her. Such a time was now come. She professed to listen to the counsels of the nobles with pleasure, and promised to comply with their request. Athalaric was relieved from his lessons and from his gray-headed companions, whose place was taken by a band of Gothic striplings. Possibly his mother, irritated at the overthrow of her schemes for his education, ceased to take any further interest in the formation of his character, and used no care in the selection of these young comrades. It is certain that Athalaric's training went at one rebound from the extreme of strictness to the extreme of laxity. We do not hear of the martial exercises in which he was to be practised, but we do hear that his young companions soon initiated him into habits of intoxication and other forms of vice. His health, perhaps undermined by the too severe application which had been demanded of him as a child, soon began to give way under his unbridled licentiousness, and before he was sixteen years of age it was manifest to all, and even to Amalasuntha herself, that the young King of the Goths would never attain to man's estate.

Meanwhile the movement of disaffection towards the princess, once begun, had not been stayed by her concessions. The old Gothic party were now in declared hostility to the Regent, and at length audaciously ordered her to quit the royal palace. Athalaric, who was now of an age at which he might have exerted some influence on public affairs, was aware of the painful position in which his mother was placed; but, mindful of her former severity and caring more for his vicious pleasures than for any thought of filial duty, he refused to take her part in any way, and rather seemed to take pleasure in showing how lightly he regarded her counsels. That little golden circlet which, since the world began, has sundered so many hearts bound together by the ties of natural affection, had fatally and finally severed this woman from her son.

Still the daughter of Theodoric did not quail before her enemies, though they were every day growing more clamorous, and every day her position as ruler in her son's name was growing weaker by his more evident hostility. She singled out the three nobles who were most eminent in the party opposed to her authority and ordered them to leave the court and betake themselves to separate places of abode as widely parted from one another as the length and breadth of Italy would allow. The historian unfortunately does not give us the names of these dismissed nobles, but we can hardly be wrong in supposing that if Tulum was alive he was one of them. The chief among the Gothic generals, a man who had only just passed the prime of life, and a kinsman by marriage of the family of the Amals, he must, if still living, have played an important part in all the discussions as to the education of the young King; and from what we know of his character we may infer that his influence would not be exerted on Amalasuntha's side.

The dismissed nobles kept up communications with one another and were now, almost in their own despite, converted into conspirators against the princess. Being informed of this she prepared to strike a bolder stroke. She sent messengers to Justinian to inquire if he would be willing to receive her in case of her departure from Italy. The Emperor promised her a warm, an eager welcome, and ordered that a palace at Dyrrhachium should be prepared for her reception. The national royal treasure, amounting to the enormous sum of 40,000 pounds's weight of gold, was placed on board a ship which was sent by the princess, under the charge of some of her trustiest adherents, to anchor in the harbour of Dyrrhachium. That she should have been able, in the precarious condition of her authority as Regent, thus to deal with what was really the national reserve of gold, shows how absolute was the power transmitted by Theodoric to his successors.

Having thus provided herself with a refuge in case of the failure of any of her plans, Amalasuntha gave secret orders to some of her Gothic courtiers, daring men and entirely devoted to her interests, to seek out the three disgraced nobles in their various places of retirement and put them to death. There was no pretence of judicial process: it was but a triple murder committed under the shadow of the royal authority.

The plans of the unscrupulous princess succeeded better than they deserved. In each case the assassin's blow was fatal; and Amalasuntha, now deeming herself secure, ordered the treasure-ship back from Dyrrhachium, and no longer thought of fleeing across the Hadriatic. Such was the state of affairs when the ambassadors of Justinian arrived in Italy to discuss the question of Lilybaeum. An irreconcilable breach had been made between Amalasuntha and the patriotic party among the Goths. The son in whose name she exercised the regal authority was visibly sinking into a drunkard's grave. The nobles, perhaps startled by the sudden display of ruthless energy on the part of one whom they had despised both as a woman and as a pedant, were pausing to consider what step should next be taken, and waiting till the death of the nominal king should make the situation clearer, by compelling Amalasuntha to ask from the nation a formal sanction of her right to reign.

Ostensibly, the mission of the Senator Alexander, who now arrived at Ravenna on an embassy from Constantinople, was to set forth the various grievances which Justinian had sustained from the Goths. Lilybaeum, which had belonged to Gelimer, now by the fortune of war the slave of the Emperor, was clearly that Emperor's property, but was detained from him by Gothic officers. Ten Hunnish deserters from the army of Africa who had escaped to Campania had been received into the Gothic service by Uliaris, the commandant of the garrison of Naples. In some renewed border-wars with the Gepidae, the army of Sirmium had taken and sacked the city of Gratiana, which was in the imperial province of Moesia, and with which they had no business to meddle. The letter brought by Alexander rehearsed all these grievances and concluded with a growl of menace: 'Pray consider what is the necessary end of proceedings such as these'. Amalasuntha, or Cassiodorus under her dictation, prepared a suitable reply. She suggested that it was unfair in a great prince like Justinian to try to fasten a quarrel upon a boyish sovereign unversed in public affairs; and dwelt on the services which the Goths had performed to the Empire at the time of the Vandal expedition, by giving the troops a free market in Sicily and supplying the cavalry, who had really been the winners of the imperial victories, with the horses which were essential to their success. As for Lilybaeum, it was a mere rock of no pecuniary value, which had once belonged to the Goths and ought to belong to them again.

This was apparently all that passed on this occasion between the Emperor and the Regent-mother. The real purport of the embassy was very different. In a secret interview Alexander enquired if Amalasuntha still purposed throwing herself on the protection of Justinian, and received in return a formal proposal, made under the seal of absolute secrecy, to surrender the Gothic kingdom in Italy to the Emperor. Seldom has even diplomacy itself veiled a sharper contrast between the real and the apparent, than when this princess, in public proudly refusing to surrender one rocky promontory in Sicily, was in the secretum, of the palace bargaining away, for a promise of personal safety, the whole of Sicily, Italy, and Illyricum to the stranger.

But even below this intrigue lay another which was being carried on under cover of zeal for the welfare of the Church. With Alexander had started two ecclesiastics, Hypatius Bishop of Ephesus, and Demetrius Bishop of Philippi, who had been sent ostensibly to discuss some point of church doctrine with Pope John II. Their real mission was to enter into conversation on affairs of state with an important personage who was then in or near Rome, the heir presumptive of the Gothic crown, Theodoric's nephew, Theodahad.

It has been already hinted that this man, the son of Amalafrida and the nearest male heir to Theodoric after Athalaric, was not by virtue of his own qualities an eligible candidate for the throne. On the contrary, he, like the bulk of the Merovingian kings, is an illustration of the way in which a degenerate Romanised Goth might unite the vices of the two contrasted nations and the virtues of neither. Greedy and cowardly, with a varnish of philosophic culture over the laziness and dulness of the barbarian, a student of Plato and a practitioner of every kind of low chicanery, fond of Latin literature, but with no trace of the old Roman valour, devoid of gratitude and destitute of honour; such was the man who would now in, a very short time bo the sole male representative of the great Amal dynasty. By the favour of his uncle he had received, probably from the confiscated estates of the friends of Odovacar, broad lands in the province of Tuscia, and was already by far the largest proprietor in that part of Italy. But to Theodahad, as Procopius satirically observes, to have neighbours of any kind seemed a sad misfortune. The whole fair province of Tuscia, the broad valley of Arno in the north, the villages which lie within sight of cloudy Badicofani in the centre, the Campagna lands in the south beyond the Ciminian mount, extending within sight of the towers of Rome, all must be one vast latifundium belonging to the Gothic prince. While he was sitting in the portico of his palace, apparently immersed in the study of Plato or reading the lines in which Horace described himself as

'Happy enough with his one Sabine farm',

he was all the while scheming how, by a judicious mixture of fraud and force, to extrude some Gothic soldier or Roman provincial from the nearest 'Naboth's vineyard' that had not yet been grasped by his all-compassing cupidity. Twice in his uncle's lifetime had he been sharply rebuked for these over-reaching practices. 'Avarice,' as Cassiodorus was commissioned to tell him, 'was a vulgar vice, which the kinsman of Theodoric, a man of the noble Amal blo0d, was especially bound to avoid.' If Theodahad should not at once yield to the king's mandate, a stout Saio was to be despatched to compel restitution to the rightful owners. Undeterred by the disgrace of having to listen to such reproofs as these, perhaps presuming on the minority of his young cousin and the weakness of a female reign, Theodahad had been of late years pursuing even more eagerly his course of chicanery and violence; and at the time which we have now reached a large deputation of the inhabitants of Tuscia was at the court of Ravenna declaring 'that Theodahad was oppressing all the inhabitants of that country, taking away their lands on no pretence, and was not only thus offending against private individuals, but was even trenching largely on the royal *patrimonium.*'

The knowledge of his own unpopularity, and the estrangement which these acts had produced between himself and his royal relatives, gave to Theodahad a feeling of insecurity which was no doubt increased by the wonderful and unexpected victories of the Empire in Africa. The downfall of the Vandal throne probably gave to all persons connected with the new barbaric royalties a sense of the precariousness of their splendid positions; a presentiment that their power was but for a little time, and that soon the Roman Emperor would be again, what he had been for so many centuries, the unquestioned lord of civilised Europe. Whatever may have been the cause, when the ecclesiastical deputies from Constantinople, Hypatius and Demetrius, obtained their secret interview with Theodahad they found him willing, even eager, to enter into negotiations with their master. Let a large sum of money be paid down, and let the rank of Senator be conferred upon him, and he would hand over the whole of Tuscia to the Emperor, and spend the remainder of his days as a courtier at Constantinople.

When the ambassadors returned to make report of their mission, it might reasonably seem to Justinian that the whole kingdom of Italy was about, to fall into his hands without toil or bloodshed, only by a little judicious expenditure of treasure. All that was needed appeared to be to continue the negotiations which had been commenced with Amalasuntha and Theodahad, to keep the two intrigues from being entangled with one another, and at the right moment to make bold and liberal drafts on the Count of the Sacred Largesses at Constantinople. For this purpose a rhetorician of Byzantium, named Peter, a Thessalonian by birth, and one of the ablest diplomatists in the imperial service, was chosen. Peter, who had been Consul eighteen years before, was at this time in full middle life, a man of good diplomatic address, subtle, gentle, and persuasive. He knew, however, as was shown by his conduct of these negotiations, when to make felt the iron hand which at this time was always present within the velvet glove of Byzantine diplomacy!

The appointment of Peter as ambassador, nominally to renew the demand for Lilybaeum, really to cany these secret negotiations to a successful issue, probably took place ip the autumn of 534. When he arrived upon the scene some months later, he found that events had marched with terrible rapidity, and a totally different state of affairs awaited him from that which had been contemplated by the Emperor in his instructions.

In the first place, the enquiry into the acts of Theodahad demanded by bis Tuscan neighbours had taken place. The prince had been found clearly guilty of the charges brought against him, and had been condemned to make restitution of all the lands that he had wrongfully appropriated either from private individuals or from the royal domain. Theodahad, smarting under the shame of this sentence and powerless henceforward to remove his neighbour's landmark, had become the bitter enemy of the Regent.

Almost immediately after the termination of this affair came the event, so long looked for, yet so bewildering when it came, the death of the hapless, young king- Athalaric, in the eighteenth year of his age, worn out with drunkenness and de- increased bauchery. All the schemes of Amalasuntha were thus threatened with immediate overthrow. The success which had hitherto attended them was probably due to the fact that, so long as she could use the king's name, the whole army of functionaries who worked the machinery of the State, inherited from the Western Emperors, were at her service and ready to obey her bidding. But now, to get that name of royalty without which no Roman official was safe in obeying her orders, she must face her Gothic subjects, and at least go through the form of being freely chosen by them. So much, notwithstanding all the centralising and despotic tendencies of Theodoric's system, the instinct of a German nationality still required. Without this election, even her scheme of resigning the sceptre to Justinian could not be realised: and yet to obtain it she must face an assembly of those free Gothic warriors whom for the last eight years she had been persistently thwarting and humiliating; nay, she must see the clouded countenances of the relatives of those three nobles whom she had murdered, and whose death, according to old Teutonic notions, still called for vengeance at the hands of their kinsmen.

It must have been the pressure of necessities such as these that drove the princess to an act so extraordinary that Procopius could only account for it by the explanation, which is no explanation, that Amalasuntha was 'fated to perish'. She determined to share the throne with Theodahad, trusting to his sense of gratitude for this elevation to leave her still virtually sole sovereign. Sending for him, she assured him with a winning smile that she had long looked upon her son's early death as inevitable, and had felt that all the hopes of the house of Theodoric must be centred in him. Seeing, however, with regret that he was not popular either with the Goths or Italians, she had devoted herself to the task of putting him straight with his future subjects, in order that there might be no obstacle to his accession to the throne. This had been the object of the late judicial investigation; and, painful as the process might have been to himself, this result was now accomplished. She therefore now invited him to ascend the throne with her; but he must first bind himself by an awful oath that he would be satisfied with the name of kingship, and would leave her as much of the actual substance of power as she possessed at that moment.

Theodahad listened, professed entire acquiescence in all that the Regent had done in the past, and promised that the sole direction of affairs should remain in her hands for the future. The scheme was then made public: some sort of assent was probably obtained from the Comitatus or from an armed assembly of the Goths; and Amalasuntha and Theodahad were hailed as joint sovereigns of the Goths and Romans in Italy.

As to the main outlines of this transaction there can be no difference of view. Amalasuntha associated Theodahad with herself in the kingdom as a brother, not as a husband. The new King was already married, and the letters written for his wife Gudelina by Cassiodorus to the sovereigns of Byzantium give us the idea that she was a woman of eager and ambitious temperament, who possibly urged on her husband to labours and to crimes from which his more sluggish nature would have shrunk. A point as to which there may reasonably be some divergence of opinion is, how far the popular assent was needed, even in form, for the new bestowal of the crown. It may be observed that I have abstained from speaking of Amalasuntha as Queen before the death of her son; and my conjecture is that there was some formality of popular election after, the death of Athalaric, in compliance with which his mother and her colleague ascended the throne. There is something to be said, however, for a more strictly monarchical view of the transaction, according to which Amalasuntha may have become Queen in her own right as heiress to her son, and then, by a mere exercise of her sovereign power, may have associated Theodahad with her in the kingdom.

The facile pen of Cassiodorus was at once called into requisition to write the epistles which etiquette required from the new sovereigns. In two letters to Justinian, Amalasuntha and Theodahad announced the beginning of their joint reign, and recommended themselves to the favour of a sovereign the maxim of whose Empire had always been friendship with the Amals. In two letters to the Senate, the sister praised the noble birth, the patience and moderation, the prudence and the literary talent of her brother (not even the pen of Cassiodorus could write the words 'the courage of Theodahad'): and the brother exalted the serene wisdom of his sister, who, after causing him to make acquaintance with her justice, had weighed him in the scale of her accurate judgment and found him worthy to share her throne. As the Divine Wisdom has allotted to man two hands, two ears, two eyes, so was the Gothic kingdom to be thenceforward administered by two sovereigns, who, partaking of all one another's counsels, would rule the land in perfect harmony.

Words, vain words, with no trace of reality behind them! We seem to perceive the influence of Cassiodorus on the mind of his pupil, in Amalasuntha's over-estimate of the power of mere words, not only to veil unpleasant facts, but to smooth them away out of existence, and by the magic of a well-turned period to breathe noble instincts into a base and greedy soul. The Queen soon found that in trusting to the generosity or the gratitude of Theodahad she was leaning on a broken reed. In fairness to her partner it must be confessed that she had brought the affairs of her kingdom into such a state of almost hopeless bewilderment, that only a very brave, zealous, and loyal colleague could have extricated her from her difficulties : and Theodahad was none of these. The kinsmen of the three murdered nobles, already a powerful party, and including some of the noblest of the Goths, now found themselves reinforced by one who bore the title of King. They, or he—it is not easy to assign the exact share of responsibility for these deeds—broke out into open violence and slew some of the chief adherents of the Queen. Amalasuntha herself was hurried away from Ravenna to one of the two lonely islands which rise out of the waters of the lake of Bolsena. This lake, named fromk the ancient Etrurian city of Vulsinii, is now the picture of desolation. Malaria rules upon its shores, and scarcely a sign of human habitation appears upon them outside of the villages of Bolsena at its head, Montefiascone and Marta at its foot. The handiwork of Nature is beautiful, the blue lake lying under its forest of oak, and the hills to the north of it stretching up to dark, volcanic, Monte Amiata on the horizon: but man has done nothing to improve it. A strange awe seizes one as one looks down upon the white rocks of the little islet of Marta, now entirely uninhabited, but with a few steps cut in the rock which are said to have led to the prison of Amalasuntha. One seems to see the boat rowed by Theodahad's servants bearing the hapless Queen who had so lately ruled from Sicily to the Danube : one feels how her weary eyes rested on the hills around, the Tuscan hills, all owned by the hateful traitor Theodahad: and one knows that her clear and manly intelligence must have at once perceived that she was brought to this desolate rock only to die.

  For the moment Theodahad spared the life of his victim. It perhaps suited him to have a hostage for his own safety in the negotiations which he was about to recommence with Byzantium. He despatched an embassy, at the head of which were two Senators, Liberius and Opilio (the latter of whom had been Consul eleven years before with the Emperor Justin), to report the imprisonment of Amalasuntha, to deprecate the Emperor's anger, and to promise that she should receive no injury. An accusation against her that she had plotted against her partner's life was made the excuse for the violence used towards her, and was apparently supported by a letter of confession and self-reproach extorted from the helpless Queen.

  When the ambassadors arrived at Constantinople, all, with one exception, described the recent deeds of Theodahad in such terms as they deserved, Liberius especially, who was a man of high and honourable character, vindicating the conduct of Amalasuntha from all blame. Opilio alone (who was probably father of Cyprian the accuser of Boethius) insisted that reasons of state had justified all that had been done by Theodahad.

  Meanwhile the ambassador Peter, travelling in the opposite direction, had been gradually learning the events which changed the whole object of his journey. Soon after starting, he met the ambassadors who told of Athalaric's death and the elevation of Theodahad. When he came in sight of the Hadriatic he met Liberius and Opilio, from whom he heard of the Queen's imprisonment. He prudently went no further westward, but communicated the tidings to the Emperor and waited for fresh orders. When those orders arrived they were, to hand to the Queen a letter in which Justinian assured her that he would exert himself to the utmost for her safety. Peter was directed to make no secret of this letter, but to exhibit it to Theodahad and all the Gothic nobles, among whom the Emperor calculated that it would sow dissensions which might further his schemes of conquest.

Before Peter arrived at Ravenna the tragedy of Amalasuntha's fate was ended. The party of the three nobles found it an easy task to work upon Theodahad's fears and to persuade him that there was no safety for him or for them so long as the Queen lived. He consented to their murderous counsels; they repaired to Vulsinii, crossed the lake, climbed the white cliffs, and murdered the unhappy daughter of Theodoric in her bath. Theodahad loudly protested that the deed was done without his knowledge or approval, but as he loaded the murderers with honours and rewards, none heeded his denial.

Peter at once sought an audience with Theodahad and informed him that, after the deed of wickedness which had been done, there must be war without truce or treaty between him and the Emperor. Contrary, however, to the custom war usual both in ancient and modern times, he seems after this declaration to have remained still at the Gothic Court, evidently intending to see what diplomatic advantage he might yet obtain from the fears of the guilty King.

So perished Amalasuntha, Queen of the Goths and Romans, a woman worthy not only of a less tragic death, but of a more successful life, had she only possessed, in addition to her rare intellectual gifts, the humbler qualities of tact, insight into the minds of others, and some power of sympathising even with the unreasonable prejudices of those around her. She led a pure life, had a high and queenly spirit, and was earnest in the pursuit of wisdom, seeming as it were a kind of Gothic Minerva, sprung from the Gothic Jove. But half of her splendid qualities might have been wisely exchanged for the gift of reading the thoughts of the rough barbarians who guarded her throne, and above all, for sufficient remembrance of what is in the heart of a child, and sufficient imagination of what is in the heart of a boy, to keep her from the alternate errors of over-strictness and over-laxity by which she ruined the health and character of her son Athalaric.

BOOK IV

THE IMPERIAL RESTORATION
535—553

CHAPTER I

THE FIRST YEAR OF THE WAR

It was a 'truceless war' which Justinian's ambassador had denounced against the cringing Theodahad when he heard of the murder of Amalasuntha. And in truth all the schemings and machinations of the Byzantine Court had been rewarded beyond their deservings by as fair and honorable an excuse for war as ever prince could allege. Lilybaeum and Gratiana, Sicilian forts and Hunnish deserters, had all faded into the background. The great Emperor now appeared upon the scene in his proper character as Earthly Providence, preparing to avenge, on an ungrateful and cowardly tyrant, the murder of the noble daughter of Theodoric. The pretext was better than that put forth for the Vandal War, the foe infinitely baser. At the same time it might perhaps be discovered that, notwithstanding the ambassador's brave words about a truceless war, the Earthly Providence was not unwilling to arrange terms with the murderer if it could secure any advantage for itself by doing so.

In the summer of 535, nine years after Justinian's accession to the throne, the armies were sent forth from Constantinople, and the Gothic War began.

Troops, the number of whom is not stated, but probably not more than 3000 or 4000, were sent by land to invade the great Gothic province of Dalmatia, on the east of the Adriatic. This province was larger than the old kingdom of Dalmatia, since it included also a good deal of Bosnia and Herzegovina. Its capital was still Salona, that great city close to which rose the vast palace of Diocletian (now represented by half of the modern town of Spalato), the city where Nepos reigned after he had been driven from the halls of the Palatine, where his rival Glycerius chanted mass in the basilica, where Odovacar avenged his murder by the death of Ovida and Viator.

The commander of the Dalmatian army was himself a barbarian by birth, a Gepid of the name of Mundus; a man whose fiery valor was not chilled by age, and who was heartily loyal to the Emperor. It was Mundus who, during the sedition of the Nika, when the throne of Justinian seemed rocking to its overthrow, had penetrated with a band of Heruli to the Hippodrome, where Hypatius at that moment was being saluted as Emperor, and had, in cooperation with Belisarius, by a ruthless massacre of the insurgents, succeeded in stamping out the rebellion. At the outset of the present campaign his operations were completely successful. The Goths who met his invading army were defeated, and he marched on to Salona, which he entered unopposed.

The chief interest, however, was excited by the Italian expedition, commanded by Belisarius, the successful combatant with Persia, the conqueror of Africa—Belisarius who had been drawn a few months before in his triumphal car through the streets of Constantinople, and who now, sole Consul for the year, was setting forth to gather fresh laurels in the country where the Marcelli and the Fabii gathered theirs eight centuries ago.

The chief generals under Belisarius were Constantine, Bessas, and Peranius.

Constantine was a native of Thrace, a brave and strenuous lieutenant of the great commander, but rapacious, fierce, and not imbued with the soldierly instinct of subordination, as was eventually proved by the strange events which ended his career. Bessas also came from Thrace, but was of Gothic descent, and we are expressly told that he was one of the race who had of old dwelt in Thrace, but did not follow Theodoric. He too, though brave and warlike, showed on a critical occasion a selfish and grasping nature, which preferred its own ignoble gains to military duty and the most obvious interests of the Empire.

Peranius came from the far east of the Empire. He was the eldest son of Gurgenes, king of Iberia, part of that province between Caucasus and Ararat which we now call Georgia. In the course of the endless tussle between the Roman Emperor and the Persian King, Iberia was invaded by the Persian army; and Gurgenes, finding himself unable to defend his dominions, and disappointed of the expected help from Justinian, fled to the mountains which divided his country from Colchis, and there seems to have maintained a straitened but honorable independence. As the dynasty was Christian, its princes naturally inclined to Constantinople rather than to Ctesiphon. Thus it was that Peranius entered the service of the Emperor, in which he soon rose to all but the highest position.

The subordinate officers were—of the cavalry, Valentine, Magnus, and Innocentius; of the infantry, Herodian, Paulus, Demetrius, and Ursicinus; none of whom require at present any special notice on our part. The commander of the Isaurian contingent was named Eunes. Belisarius was attended by a large body-guard of tried and daring soldiers; and, in a capacity perhaps resembling that of a modern aide-de-camp, Photius, Antonina's son by a former marriage, accompanied his renowned step-father.

The total number of the army which was setting Number of forth to reconquer Italy was only 7500 men, scarcely more than the equivalent of one legion out of the thirty which followed Caesar's footsteps. How it figured on the muster-rolls of the Empire it is not easy to say. We are told that there were 4000 soldiers 'of the Catalogues and the Foederati', 3000 Isaurians, 200 confederate Huns, and 300 Moors. The 'Catalogues' must in some way represent the dwindled Legions; as the *Foederati*, drawn perhaps from the medley of Teutonic and Slavonic peoples who roamed along the banks of the Lower Danube, represent the *Socii* of the early days of Rome. It will be observed by the reader how large a proportion the gallant Isaurian highlanders, those Swiss of the Byzantine empire, bore to the whole army, and we shall have frequent occasion in the course of the war to notice the service rendered to Belisarius by their mountaineering skill and headlong bravery.

After all, the armament, though it gloried in the title of Roman, and was sometimes called Greek in derision by its enemies, was Roman or Greek only in name. It was essentially a barbarian band. Every great exploit which we hear of in connection with it was performed, as a rule, by some Gepid, or Herul, or Isaurian. But the barbaric strength and stolid stalwart courage of the soldiers were directed by generals who still cherished some of the traditions of scientific warfare which had been elaborated in the twelve centuries of the Roman Republic and Empire; and at the centre of the whole machine was the busy brain of Belisarius, a man of infinite resource and patience as well as courage, and certainly one of the greatest strategists that the world has ever seen.

The student who remembers how the battles of Republican Rome were generally won, namely, by the disciplined valor of the heavy-armed foot-soldiers of the Legion, experiences some surprise when he finds that the victories of Belisarius were chiefly won by his cavalry, armed with the bow and arrow, a force which, as has been already observed, may perhaps be compared to the mounted rifles of a modern army, but which certainly five centuries before was more celebrated in the tactics of Parthia than in those of Rome.

At the outset of the first campaign it may be interesting to quote from a later page of Procopius the reasons which Belisarius himself, in conversation with his friends, assigned for the long series of victories which he had then achieved over the Goths.

In public the Romans naturally expressed their wonder at the genius of Belisarius which had achieved such a victory, but in private his friends [no doubt including Procopius himself] enquired of him what was the token which, in the first day of successful engagement with the enemy, had led him to conclude that in this war he should be uniformly victorious. Then he told them that, at the beginning, when the engagement had been limited to a few men on each side, he had studied what were the characteristic differences of each army, in order that when the battles commenced on a larger scale he might not see his small army overwhelmed by sheer force of numbers. The chief difference which he noted was that all the Romans and their Hunnish allies were good *archers* on *horseback*. The Goths, on the other hand, had none of them practiced this art. Their cavalry fought only with javelins and swords, and their archers were drawn up for battle as infantry, and covered by the cavalry. Thus the horsemen, unless the battle became a hand-to-hand encounter, having no means of replying to a discharge of weapons from a distance, were easily thrown into confusion and cut to pieces, while the foot-soldiers, though able to reply to a volley of arrows from a distance, could not stand against sudden charges of horse. For this reason Belisarius maintained that the Goths in these encounters would always be worsted by the Romans.

As yet, however, there was little opportunity for the display of military skill on the part of Belisarius, for his first laurels were all easily gathered, in the region of politics rather than of war. His instructions were to land in Sicily, nominally again making of that island only a house of call on his way to Carthage: if he found that he could occupy the island with little trouble he was to do so, but if there was likely to be tough opposition he was to leave it for the present and proceed to Africa. The former alternative was that which he adopted. He found the Sicilians all ready and eager to become subjects of the Emperor. Catana, Syracuse, and every other city in Sicily, opened her gates to him. Only in Panormus (Palermo) was there a Gothic garrison strong enough to oppose the wishes of the inhabitants; and to the siege of Palermo he now addressed himself.

This eager defection of the islanders from the Gothic rule was a deep disappointment to their late lords, and was long and bitterly remembered by them. Sicily was still rich in the wealth that had been stored up there since the days of Gelon, rich in all manner of fruits, above all rich in corn, of which it sent large exports every year to Rome. For this reason the Roman inhabitants had prayed Theodoric that they might be left to themselves, and not vexed by the presence of large bodies of Gothic troops. Their request had been listened to; they had been left for the most part to their own sense of honor to defend the connection which had benefited them so greatly and had imposed such light burdens upon them. And this was their return. Not a city defended, not a skirmish fought, no pretence of overwhelming necessity forthcoming; but as soon as the insignificant armament of Belisarius hove in sight, every emblem of Gothic domination torn down and the islanders vying with one another in demonstrations of servility towards Belisarius and his master. So keenly was this ingratitude felt by the Goths that, as we shall see, twelve years afterwards, when there was a talk of peace between them and the Empire, and the Gothic King seemed to be in a position to dictate its terms, one of his indispensable conditions was that there should be no interference with the revenge of his nation on ungrateful Sicily.

Belisarius, having reconnoitered Palermo, decided that the fortifications on the landward side were too strong to be attacked with any hope of success. Of these fortifications no vestige now remains, and indeed the very site of the ancient city, successively Carthaginian, Greek, and Roman, is hopelessly obliterated by the busy prosperity of the modern capital of Sicily. Three features of the landscape only can we indisputably claim as identical with those which met the eyes of Belisarius. They are (1) the beautiful, almost land-locked bay (reminding the traveler of the bay of Naples), from which the city derived its Greek name, *All-Anchorage*; (2) the rich plain stretching inland, and now known as The Golden Shell (Concha d'Oro); (3) the grand natural fortress of Monte Pellegrino, 2000 feet high, a few miles out of the city, rising, like the Rock of Gibraltar, square and steep out of the sea to northward of the bay. Here Hamilcar Barca maintained for three years a sturdy opposition to Rome near the close of the First Punic War. But the Gothic garrison of Sicily resorted to no such desperate measure of defence against the army of Belisarius. Trusting in the strength of their walls, they refused to surrender the city and bade him begone with all speed.

The line of wall skirting the harbor was that which attracted the attention of the Byzantine general. It was detached from the ordinary line of circumvallation, it was left altogether bare of soldiers, and, high as it was, when he had collected his navy in the harbor he found that their masts overtopped the battlements. With his usual fertility of resource he at once hoisted the ships' boats filled with soldiers up to the yard-arms of the vessels, and told his men to clamber from the boats out on to the parapet. The maneuver, though somewhat resembling that tried by the Venetians at the Latin siege of Constantinople *(AD* 1204) would have been too perilous to be executed in the face of an active foe. As it was, practiced against an unguarded wall, it was completely successful. Soon the Byzantine soldiers, from their position of vantage on the high sea-wall, were shooting their arrows down into the ranks of the enemy in the city. The Goths were cowed by the unexpected sight, and offered terms of capitulation which Belisarius at once accepted.

Thus was all Sicily now subject to the Emperor's rule, and soon found itself paying heavy tax and toll to the imperial exchequer. The conquest of Sicily, peaceful comparatively as was its character, had occupied about seven months. On the last day of the year the Consul Belisarius, who had commenced his year of office while his victories over the Vandals were fresh in every one's mouth, closed it by a solemn procession through the streets of Syracuse, greeted by the loud and genuine applause of his soldiers and the Sicilians, upon whom his lavish hands scattered a welcome largesse of Justinian's *aurei*.

Meanwhile, the tidings which were coming from Sicily to Rome, cleverly enlarged upon at repeated audiences by the ambassador Peter, threw the wretched Theodahad into an agony of terror. Already in imagination he saw himself walking, as Gelimer had walked, a captive before his conqueror Belisarius, and heard the well-deserved cry, 'Death to the murderer of Amalasuntha!' thundered forth by the populace of Byzantium. In a private conference with Peter he consented to make peace with Justinian on the following humiliating conditions : (1) Sicily was to be abandoned to the Emperor; (2) Theodahad was to send to Justinian every year a golden crown weighing not less than 300 pounds; (3) he was to furnish 3000 warlike Goths whenever Justinian should require their services; (4) except with the Emperor's leave, the Gothic King was not to sentence any senator or any priest [Catholic priests, of course, were here meant] either to death or confiscation of goods; (5) he was not to confer the dignity of Patrician, or any office involving senatorial rank, upon any of his subjects without the same gracious permission; (6) at the Hippodrome, the Theatre, and all places of public resort the people were always to shout 'Vivat Justinianus!' before they shouted 'Vivat Theodatus'; (7) never was a statue of bronze or any other material to be raised to Theodahad alone, but wherever he stood Justinian must stand beside him on his right side.

The conditions were degrading enough and well exemplified the Byzantine habit of making the subjection of an inferior as galling and as wounding to his self-love as possible. That undefined relation of dependence on the Empire which Odovacar and Theodoric had ignored rather than contradicted, and into which Amalasuntha had been gradually sinking, was here proclaimed as offensively as possible by the Augustus, and admitted as abjectly as possible by the *Thiudans*. Though the word belongs to a later century, Theodahad would have become by this compact virtually the vassal of Justinian. Still, even this relationship, though marking a great fall from the proud 'moral hegemony' of Theodoric, might in the course of centuries have worked not unfavorably for the happiness of Italy. Leaning on the arm of her elder sister of Byzantium, the new Romano-Gothic state might have gradually reconciled Teutonic force with classical culture. In the convulsions which shook the Eastern world in the seventh century, her loyalty might have been a stay and staff to the Eastern Caesar. Greece and Italy united, and occupying their natural place at the head of European civilization, might have formed front against the Saracen in the East, against the Frank in the West. At the least, had such a confederacy been possible, the Hesperian land would have escaped the extortions of Byzantine blood-suckers on the one hand, the ravages of half-savage Lombards on the other.

But it is useless to speculate on what might have been. The portentous cowardice of Theodahad rendered him unable even to wait for an interchange of embassies with Constantinople to know whether his terms were accepted or rejected. He had not yet dispatched his own ambassador, when he sent for Peter, who on his leisurely journey had now reached Albano, the second station on the Appian Way, that delightful little town which, nestling under the high volcanic cone of Monte Cavo, looks down on the one side over its own peaceful little Alban Lake, and on the other over the broad Campagna to the faintly-seen towers of Rome. Peter came, when summoned, to yet another private audience with the King. The following strange dialogue then passed between them:

Theodahad. Do you think, Ambassador, that the Emperor will be pleased with the compact into which we have entered?

Peter. I conjecture that he will.

Theod. But if he should chance to quarrel with the terms, what will happen then?

Peter. Then, noble sir, the next thing will be that you will have to fight.

Theod. Is that fair, dear Ambassador?

Peter. Where is the unfairness, my good friend, in each of you following the bent of his own genius?

Theod. What do you mean by that?

Peter. I mean this. All your pleasure is in acting the part of a philosopher; but Justinian finds his, in acting as beseems a noble Roman Emperor. For a man who practices the precepts of philosophy to devise the death of his fellow-creatures, especially on so large a scale as this war involves, is quite unbecoming; and for a Platonist, it is preeminently necessary to keep his hands clean from human blood. But for the Emperor to vindicate his rights to a land which once formed part of his Empire is in no way unbecoming.

The result of this dialogue (in which it suited both King and Ambassador to ignore the fact that the hands of the former were already stained with the blood of his benefactress) was, that Theodahad swore to the Ambassador to sell his crown to Justinian if he should be required to do so; and for some reason which is not expressly stated, but probably because of her admitted ascendency over the mind of Theodahad, his Queen Gudelina was made a partner in the oath. Peter on his part was made to swear that he would not disclose the last and highest offer till he had fairly put the lower offer before the Emperor, and found that it was hopeless to press it. What prudent man would thus bid against himself even in the purchase of a field? With such utter fatuity did these children of the barbarians play their little bungling game against the veteran diplomatists of Constantinople.

Peter was accompanied on the return embassy by Rusticus, a Roman, a priest (probably of the orthodox Church), and an intimate friend of Theodahad. They arrived at Constantinople; they stood in the presence of the Emperor; they set forth the first offer of Theodahad. Had Peter sent a private messenger to his master, or did he now, by ever so slight and scarcely perceptible a gesture, imply that, were he in Justinian's place, he would not accept the offered vassalage? We know not, but it is certain that Justinian declared that the terms, abject as was their humbleness of surrender, did not at all please him. Then Rusticus produced the Gothic King's letter, which had been reserved for this stage of the negotiations. It was a strange letter to be written by a member of the race whose forefathers swept like night over the shores of the Aegean, by a grandson and great-nephew of the brave Amal kings who stood unflinching by the side of Attila "in that world-earthquake" on the Catalaunian plains.

"I am not, O Emperor, a new comer into the halls of kings. It was my fortune to be born a king's nephew and to be reared in a manner worthy of my race: but I am not altogether well versed in war and its confusions. From the first I have been passionately fond of literature and have spent my time in the study thereof, and thus it has been till now my lot to be always far from the clash of arms. It seems therefore unwise of me to continue to lead a life full of danger for the sake of the royal dignity, when neither danger nor dignity is a thing that I enjoy. No danger, since that new and strange sensation perturbs my thoughts; not the royal dignity, since possession of it has, according to the general law, brought satiety.

"Therefore, if some landed property could be secured to me, bringing in a yearly income of not less than twelve cwt. of gold, I should consider that more valuable to me than my kingship: and I am willing on those terms to hand over to thee the sovereignty of the Goths and Italians. I think that I shall thus be happier as a peaceful tiller of the soil than as a king immersed in kingly cares, no sooner out of one danger than into another. Send me then as speedily as possible a commissioner to whom I may hand over Italy and all that pertains to my kingship".

The letter gave supreme delight to the Emperor, and obtained the following reply.

"I heard long ago by common fame that you were a man of high intelligence, and now I find by experience that this is true. You show your wisdom in declining to await the arbitrament of war, which has plunged some men who staked their all upon it into terrible disasters. You will never have occasion to repent having turned us from an enemy into a friend. You shall receive all the property that you ask for, and, in addition, your name shall be inscribed in the highest rank of Roman nobility.

"I now send Athanasius and Peter to exchange the needful ratifications, and in a very short time Belisarius will come to complete the transaction thus settled between us".

Athanasius was the brother of Alexander who was sent the year before as ambassador to Athalaric. The duties entrusted to him and to Peter were mainly to settle the boundaries of the new *Patrimonium* which was to be assigned to Theodahad, to put the compact in writing, and to secure it by oaths given and taken; Belisarius was sent for in all speed from Sicily to receive charge of the fortresses, arsenals, and all the machinery of government from the royal trafficker. These arrangements were probably made towards the end of the year 535.

When the ambassadors arrived at the Gothic Court they found the mood of Theodahad strangely altered. To understand the reason of the change we must look again at the affairs of Dalmatia. We left Mundus the Gepid there, holding the retaken capital, Salona, for Justinian. A large Gothic army under the command of Asinarius and Grippas entered the province, apparently about the middle of autumn, and approached Salona. Maurice the son of Mundus, on a reconnoitering expedition, approached too near the main body of the Gothic army and was slain. Maddened with grief, the old barbarian, his father, fell upon the Gothic host. Though he attacked in too loose order he was at first successful, and broke the ranks of the foe, but pressing on too hotly in pursuit, he was pierced by the spear of one of the fugitives and fell dead. His fall stopped the onward movement of his troops. Both armies dispersed, and neither dared to appropriate the prize of war, the city of Salona; the Romans having got altogether out of hand since the death of their general, and the Goths misdoubting both the strength of the walls and the loyalty of the citizens.

It was some slight consolation to the Romans that these reverses robbed of its terrors an old Sibylline prophecy which had been much of late in the mouths of men. This prophecy, couched in mysterious characters, which are a marvel upon the page of Procopius, had been thus interpreted:

First Rome reconquers Afric. Then the World
Is with its progeny to ruin hurled.

Belisarius' capture of Carthage had seemed to bring the end of the world alarmingly near. But now the battle of Salona reassured men's minds. It was not the world and all its inhabitants, but only *Mundus* and his too daring son, with whose fate the oracle was full.

The fortune of the Roman arms in Dalmatia was soon retrieved. Constantian, who held the office of *Comes Stabuli* in the imperial household, was sent with a well-equipped army to recover Salona, which had been entered by the Goths. Having apparently the entire command of the sea, he sailed northwards from Epidamnus (Durazzo), and was soon to be seen in the offing from the coast of Epidaurus (a little south of the modern Cattaro). The panic-stricken Gothic general Grippas, who was informed by his scouts that myriads of Romans were approaching by sea, evacuated Salona and pitched his camp a little to the west of that city. Constantian sailed some hundred miles or so up the gulf and anchored at the island of Lissa, memorable to this generation for the naval battle fought there between the Italians and Austrians in 1866. Finding from his scouts that Salona was deserted he landed his troops, occupied it in force, repaired its ruinous walls, and posted 500 men to occupy the narrow pass by which it was approached from the west. After seven days of tarriance, the two Gothic generals, with that feebleness and absence of resource which mark the barbarian strategy in the earlier stages of this war, simply marched back again to Ravenna.

Dalmatia and Liburnia (or the *province* of Illyricum), which had for the most part followed the fortunes of Italy for a century and a half since the death of Theodosius, were thus permanently recovered by the State, which we must in this connection call the *Eastern* Empire, although it was, to a loyal Roman, simply the Empire, one and undivided. From this time forward the eastern coast of the Adriatic, though subject to Avar invasions, Slavonic migrations, Bosnian kingships, maintained a more or less intimate political connection with Constantinople, till the conquests of the Venetians in the tenth century brought it back once more into the world of Italian domination.

But these were the far-reaching results of the expedition of Mundus. We have to do with the more immediate effects of the early disasters of the imperial forces on that feeble and futile thing, the mind of King Theodahad. That royal student, if versed in the 'Republic' of Plato, had not laid equally to heart the more popular philosophy of Horace. At least he conspicuously disobeyed the precepts of that familiar ode in which 'the mortal Dellius' is exhorted to preserve a temper 'serene in arduous and reasonable in prosperous' circumstances. As pusillanimous as he had shown himself at the news of the successes of Belisarius, so intolerably arrogant did he become when the tidings reached him of the death of Mundus and his son. When the ambassadors who arrived about the same time as the news (probably somewhere about December 535) ventured to claim the fulfillment of his solemn promise to surrender the kingdom, he flatly refused. Peter spoke somewhat plainly as to the royal faithlessness. Theodahad petulantly answered, "The privilege of ambassadors is a holy thing, but it is conceded on the supposition that it be not abused. It is admitted that the person of an ambassador who seduces the wife of a citizen of the country to which he is accredited is not sacrosanct; and I shall not scruple to apply the same principle to an ambassador who insults the King". Peter and Athanasius made a spirited reply: "0 ruler of the Goths, you are seeking by flimsy pretexts to cover unholy deeds. An ambassador may be watched as strictly as his entertainer pleases, and therefore the talk about injury to female honor is altogether beside the mark. But as for what the ambassador says, be it good or bad, the praise or blame for it rests solely on him who sent him. The ambassador is a mere mouthpiece, and to him attaches no responsibility for his words. We shall therefore say all that we heard from the lips of the Emperor: and do you listen patiently, for if you become excited you will perhaps commit some outrage on our sacred character. We declare then that the time is come for you loyally to fulfill your compact with the Emperor. Here is the letter which he wrote to you. The notes which he has addressed to the chief men among the Goths we shall hand to no one but themselves only."

However, the Gothic nobles who were present authorized the ambassadors to hand over their letters to Theodahad. These dispatches congratulated the Goths on the near prospect of their absorption in the great polity of Rome, a state with whose laws and customs they had long ago become acquainted [in their capacity of *Foederati*]; and Justinian promised that they should find their dignity and credit increased, not diminished, by the change.

This was not, however, the view which the Gothic nobles took of the situation. Whatever their secret contempt for the weakly truculent character of their King, they were ready to second him heartily in his present mood of defiance to the Empire. Both sides therefore prepared for that which was now to be really "a truceless war".

In these preparations the winter of 535-536 wore away, and the second year of the great Gothic War commenced.

CHAPTER II.

BELISARIUS AT CARTHAGE AND AT NAPLES.

When the news of the double-dyed treachery of Theodahad reached the Court of Constantinople orders were dispatched to Belisarius to proceed with all speed to Italy and push the war against the Goths to the uttermost. He was, however, hindered for some weeks from obeying these orders, by a sudden call to another post of danger; a call which well illustrates the precarious and unenduring character of Justinian's conquests and the inherent vices of Byzantine domination.

It was a few days after Easter, in the year 536, probably therefore about the 30th or 31st of March, when a single ship rounded the headland of Plemmyrium, passed the fountain of Arethusa, and reached the landing-place of Syracuse. A few fugitives leaped on land and hastened to the presence of Belisarius. Chief among them was the Eunuch Solomon, in whose keeping, two years before, he had left the fortress and city of Carthage guarded by a triumphant Roman army. What causes had brought a man placed in such height of power, and a brave and prudent soldier, into so great disaster?

Not his wars with the declared enemies of the Empire, though it is worth our while to notice even here how Justinians conquests really paved the way for the barbarians. The Vandals had reared a kingdom in North Africa, semi-civilized, it, is true, but which, if left to itself, would have become wholly civilized, and which meanwhile was strong enough to keep the wild sons of the desert in check. Now, the Vandals overthrown, the Moors came on. They pushed their forays far into the African province; in hosts of 30,000 and 50,000 at a time they invaded Numidia and Byzacene; they loudly complained that the promises by which they had been lured into the Roman alliance had been left unfulfilled; and when Solomon ventured to remind the chiefs that he held their children as hostages for their good behavior they replied, "You monogamist Romans may fret about the loss of your children. We who may have fifty wives apiece if it so pleases us, feel no fear that we shall ever have a deficiency of sons".

In two battles the Eunuch-Governor had defeated his Moorish antagonists. But still the Moorish chief Iabdas remained encamped on the high and fruitful table-land of Mount Auras, thirteen days' journey from Carthage, and from thence at every favorable opportunity swept down into the plain, pillaging, slaying, leading into captivity; nor had Solomon, though he led one expedition against him, yet been able to dislodge him thence.

Thus had events passed till the Easter of 536, and then the real, the tremendous danger of the Eunuch's position was suddenly revealed to him, in the shape of an almost universal mutiny of the Roman soldiers. We call them Roman in accordance with the usage of the times, because they served that peculiar political organization at Constantinople which still called itself the Roman Republic, and because the banners under which they marched to battle still bore the world-known letters S.P.Q.R. But, as has been already hinted, probably not one soldier out of a hundred in the imperial army could speak Latin, and many of them may have hardly known sufficient Greek to find their way about the streets of Constantinople. They were Heruli from the Danube, Isaurians from the Asiatic highlands, Huns from the steppes of Scythia, Armenians from under the shadow of Ararat, anything and everything but true scions—of the old Oscan and Hellenic stocks whose deeds are commemorated by Livy and Thucydides.

These men, Teutons many of them by birth, and Arians by religious profession, having been permitted to marry the Vandal widows whose husbands they had slain, had expected to settle in comfort upon the Vandal lands, and live thenceforward in peace, under some loose bond of allegiance to the Emperor, as the new lords of Africa. Not such, however, was the intention of the bureaucracy of Constantinople. The usual! swarm of *Logothetae*, of *Agentes in rebus*, of *Scriniarii*, settled down upon the province, intent upon sucking the last available *aureus* out of it for the public treasury. The lands of the conquered Vandals were all deemed to have reverted to the state, and if the husband of a Vandal widow, whether he were soldier or civilian, cultivated them, it must be under the burden of a land-tax revised every fifteen years, so strictly as to make him virtually tenant at a rack-rent under the tax-gatherer. In many cases, not even on these unfavorable terms was the occupancy of the land assigned to the soldiers. Here, then, were plentiful materials for a quarrel. On the one hand, a number of hot-blooded, stalwart men, flushed with the pride of conquest, each one with a remembrancer of his wrongs for ever at his ear, reminding him, "Such an estate or such a villa belonged to me when I was the wife of a Vandal warrior, yet thou who hast conquered Vandals art thyself landless". On the other side, the Eunuch-Governor and the official hierarchy, pleading the law of the State, the custom of the Empire. "It was reasonable that the slaves, the ornaments, the portable property, should be the spoil of the soldiers. But the land, which once belonged to the Roman Empire, must revert to the Emperor and the Commonwealth of Rome, who called you forth as soldiers, trained you, armed you, paid you, not in order that you should conquer these lands for yourselves, but that they might become public property and furnish rations not for you only, but for all the soldiers of the Empire". Thus was the African land-question raised. But there was also a religious difficulty. Many of the soldiers in the late army of Belisarius, especially the martial Heruli, were Arians. The Vandal priests who still remained in Africa found access to these men, and inflamed their minds with a recital of the religious disabilities to which they, the conquerors as much as the conquered, were subject. The prohibition of Justinian was positive. No baptism nor any other religious rite was to be performed by or upon any man not holding the full, orthodox, Athanasian faith. The time of Easter was drawing nigh, at which it was usual to baptize all the children who had been born in the preceding year. No child of a Herulian would be admitted to the holy font, no Herulian himself would be permitted to share in the solemnities of Easter, unless he first renounced the creed of his forefathers, the creed which had perhaps been brought to his rude dwelling on the Danubian shore by some Arian bishop, disciple or successor of the sainted Ulfilas.

As the evil genius of the Empire would have it, there was yet a third element of disaffection cast into the African cauldron. The Vandals whom Belisarius carried captive to Byzantium had been enrolled in five regiments of cavalry, had received the honorable name of "Justinian's Vandals" and had been ordered to garrison the cities of Syria against the Persians. The greater part proceeded to their appointed stations and faithfully served the Empire which had robbed them of their country. But four hundred of them, finding themselves at Lesbos with a favoring wind, hoisted their sails, forced the mariners to obey their orders, and started for Peloponnesus first and then for Africa. Arrived at the well-remembered shore, they ran their ships aground, landed, and marched off for the uncaptured stronghold of Mount Aurasius. Here they received a message from the soldiers at Carthage who contemplated mutiny, soliciting their assistance, which, after solemn oaths and promises given and received, they agreed to furnish to the mutineers. So, when Easter drew on, all was ripe for revolt.

The mutineers agreed among themselves that Solomon should be slain in the great Basilica of Carthage on Good Friday, and that this crime should be the signal for the insurrection to break out. They took little care about secrecy: the guards, the shield-bearers, many even of the household servants of the Eunuch, were in the plot, but none betrayed it, so great was the longing of all for the Vandal lands. So, unsuspecting evil, sat Solomon in the great Basilica, while the ceremonies went forward which commemorated the death of Christ, and which were meant to be signalized by his own. The conspirators gathered round him. Each man, with frowns and gestures of impatience, motioned to his neighbor to do the deed of blood, but none could bring himself with his own arm to strike the blow. Either the sanctity of the place, or old loyalty to their general, or else the still unstifled voice of conscience, prevented any from volunteering for the service; and they had not taken the precaution of selecting the arch-murderer before they entered the sacred building. When the words '*Ite, jam missa* est' came from the lips of the officiating prelate, they hastened from the Basilica, each cursing the other for his cowardice and softness of heart. "Tomorrow", said they, "in the same place the deed shall be done". On the morrow Solomon again sat in the great Basilica; again his would-be murderers assembled round him, again the same invisible influence stayed their hands. When the service was over they foamed out into the Forum, a disappointed and angry crowd. The epithets 'Traitor', 'Coward', 'Faint-heart' were freely bandied about among them, so freely that, feeling sure that their design must now be generally known, the chief of the plot left the city and began freebooting in the country districts.

When Solomon discovered the danger with which he had to deal, he went round to the soldiers' quarters and exhorted those who were still remaining in the city to abide faithful to the Emperor. For five days the mutiny seemed to have been checked, but at the end of that time, when the soldiers within the city saw that their revolted comrades were pursuing their career of ravage outside unchecked, it burst out with fresh fury. The soldiers collected in the Hippodrome, and shouted out the names of Solomon and the other chief authorities in the state, loading them with every kind of coarse abuse. Theodore the Cappadocian, apparently the most popular of Solomon's officers, was sent by him to harangue them in soothing terms. Not a word of his soft eloquence was listened to; but believing him to be secretly opposed to Solomon and his policy, the mutineers with loud shouts acclaimed him as their leader. Theodore appears to have been a man of staunch loyalty, but he humored the whim of the rebels for a few hours, in order to favor Solomon's escape. With loud and tumultuous shouts the mutineers, self-constituted guards of Theodore, escorted him to the palace of the Prefect. There they found another Theodore, captain of the guards, a man of noble character and a skilled soldier, but for the moment unpopular with these rebels. Him they slew, and having thus tasted blood, they dispersed themselves through the city, killing every man whom they met, Roman or Provincial, who was suspected of being a friend of Solomon, or who had money enough about him to make murder profitable. They entered all the houses which were not guarded by the few still loyal soldiers, and carried off all the portable plunder that they found there. At length night came on, and the mutineers, stretched in drunken sleep in the streets and forums of the city, rested from their orgie of rapine. Then Solomon and his next in command, Martin, who had been cowering for refuge all day in the chapel of the Governor's palace, stole forth to the house of Theodore the Cappadocian. He pressed them to take food, though sadness and fear had well-nigh deprived them of appetite, and then had them conveyed to the harbor. A little company of eight persons embarked in a boat belonging to one of the ships under Martin's command. These eight persons were Solomon, Martin, five officers of the Eunuch's household, and—most important of all in our eyes—the Councilor Procopius, to whom we owe the whole of this narrative. After rowing in an open boat for nearly forty miles, the fugitive Governor and his suite reached Missua, on the opposite (eastward) shore of the bay of Tunis, a place which was apparently used as a kind of supplemental port, owing to the original harbor of Carthage having become too small for its trade.

At Missua they felt themselves in comparative safety, and from hence the Eunuch dispatched Martin to Valerian and the other generals commanding in Numidia, on the west of the Carthaginian province, to warn them of the mutiny, and to endeavor, under the shelter of their forces, to win back by gold or favor as many as possible of the mutineers to their old loyalty. He also wrote to Theodore, giving him a general commission to act for the imperial interests in Carthage as might seem best at the time, and then Solomon himself, probably taking some ship of war out of the roadstead at Missua, set sail for Syracuse with Procopius in his train, and, as we have seen, arrived there in safety to claim the assistance of Belisarius.

Meanwhile the insurgents, who had by this time found that Theodore the Cappadocian would not lend himself to their seditious designs, assembled on the plains of Bulla, a short distance to the south of Carthage, and there chose out Stutza, one of the body-guard of Martin, and acclaimed him as their king. Stutza, if not endowed with any great strategic talents, was a man of robustness and hardihood. He found under his standards no fewer than 8000 revolted soldiers. These were soon joined by 1000 Vandals, partly the recent fugitives from Constantinople, partly those who had escaped the notice of the conquering host two years before. They were further joined by that usual result of anarchy in the Roman state, a large number of slaves. The united host aimed at nothing less than driving out the imperial generals and making themselves lords of the whole northern coast of Africa. They at once marched to Carthage (which it is hard to understand why they should ever have quitted), and called upon Theodore to surrender the city. Josephus, one of the literary attendants of Belisarius, who happened to have just arrived at the capital, was sent to persuade them not to resort to any further acts of violence; but Stutza showed the soldier's disdain of the scribe and the mutineer's contempt of the rules of civilized warfare by at once putting him to death. Despair at this ruthless deed filled the hearts of the scanty defenders of Carthage, and they were on the point of surrendering the city to the insurgents.

Such was the state of affairs when in an hour all was changed by the arrival of Belisarius. He sailed from Syracuse with one ship, probably the same which had brought the Eunuch, and with one hundred picked men of his body-guard on board. It was twilight when he arrived. The mutineers were encamped round the city, confident that on the morrow it would be theirs. Day dawned: they heard that Belisarius was inside the walls: awed by the mere name of the mighty commander, they broke up their camp and commenced a disorderly retreat, or rather flight, never halting till they reached the city of Membressa on the Bagradas, fifty-one miles south-west from the capital. Here they at length ventured to encamp; and here the terrible Belisarius came up with them, having only 2000 men under his standards, whom by gifts and promises he had persuaded to return to their former loyalty. As Membressa itself was unwalled, neither army dared to occupy it. Belisarius seems to have crossed the Bagradas, which is not a rapid though a pretty copious stream, without opposition, and encamped near to its banks. The mutineers, whose army must have been five times as large as his, pitched their camp on an elevated spot, difficult of access. Both commanders, according to classic custom, harangued their men, or at least the Thucydidean historian whom we are following thinks proper to represent them as thus encouraging their troops. Belisarius, while deploring the hard necessity which compelled him to take up arms against the men who had once echoed his own password, declared that they had brought their ruin on themselves by their unholy deeds, and that the devastated fields of Africa, and the corpses of the comrades slain by them, men whose only crime was their loyalty, demanded vengeance. He was persuaded that the newly-raised tyrant Stutza would want that confidence in himself and in the prompt obedience of his troops which alone ensures success. And he ended with a maxim of which his own career was to afford a signal verification: "It is not by the mass of combatants but by their disciplined courage that victories are won".

Stutza enlarged on the ingratitude which, after *they* had undergone the toils of war, had given to idle non-combatants the fruits of victory. After the one gleam of freedom which they had enjoyed during the last few weeks, a return to slavery would be ten times bitterer than their previous condition. If indeed even to live as slaves would be granted them,—but after the dangerous example which they had set, they must expect, if vanquished, to suffer unutterable punishments, perhaps to expire in torment. They could die but once: let them die, if need were, free warriors on that battlefield. Nay, rather, let them conquer, as they must do, a foe so greatly their inferior in numbers, and whose troops in their secret hearts were only longing to share their freedom.

After all this eloquence the battle was hardly a battle. The mutineers, finding that the wind blew strongly in their faces, and fearing that their spears would thus fail to penetrate, endeavored to make a flank movement, and so to get to windward of the enemy. Belisarius did not give them time to execute this maneuver, but ordered his men to come to close quarters at once while the mutineers were still in disorder. This unexpected attack threw them into utter confusion. They fled in headlong rout, and did not draw bridle till they reached Numidia. The Vandals, less demoralized than the disloyal soldiers, for the most part refused to fly, and died upon the field of battle. Belisarius' army was too small to venture with safety upon a long pursuit, but the camp of the enemy was given up to be plundered by them. They found it richly furnished with gold and silver, the spoil of Carthage; utterly deserted by the men, but full of women, the original abettors of the war, who had now, probably in obedience to the laws of Mars, to contract a third marriage, with their new conquerors. The rebellion appeared sufficiently crushed to justify Belisarius in returning to Sicily, especially as there was a danger that the example set by the Carthaginian insurgents might be followed by the army stationed there. Accordingly, leaving his son-in-law Ildiger and Theodore of Cappadocia in charge of the African capital, he sailed away to Syracuse.

The interest which the mutiny at Carthage possesses for us consists in the light which it throws on the character of Belisarius, and the ascendency which he exercised over a greedy and licentious soldiery. Its course after he disappears from the scene must be described as briefly as possible.

The Roman generals in Numidia, five in number, finding Stutza with his band close to their frontier, marched hastily against him, thinking to crush him before he could reform his scattered army. He advanced, however, into the space between the hostile ranks, and delivered a short and spirited harangue, the result of which was that the generals found themselves deserted by their troops, who went over in a body to the insurgents. The generals took shelter in a neighboring church, surrendered on the promise of their lives being spared, and were all slain by Stutza, a man without pity and without faith.

The mutiny having thus become more formidable than ever, Justinian took a step which he would have done well to take sooner. He sent his nephew, the best of the nobles of the imperial house, the gentle and statesman-like Germanus, with a sufficient supply of treasure to discharge the soldiers' arrears of pay, which had evidently been accumulating for some time; and with instructions to pursue a policy of conciliation towards the insurgents, declaring that the Emperor only desired the good of his brave soldiers, and would severely punish all who had injured them. The man and the policy were so well matched that Germanus, who at first found under the imperial standard only a third of the troops entered on the African muster-rolls, had soon under his command a larger number of soldiers than followed the fortunes of Stutza. The rebels lost heart and fled again into Numidia. A battle ensued at a place called *Scalae Veteres*, the site of which does not appear to have been identified. The fight was desperate and confused. Rebels and loyalists were so like one another in outward appearance, that the troops of Germanus were obliged to be continually asking for the password, in order to distinguish friend from foe. The horse of Germanus was killed under him; but in the end his standards triumphed. Stutza fled: the rebel camp was sacked by the victorious imperialists, who in the fury of plunder refused to listen even to the restraining voice of the general. A squadron of Moors who had been hovering on the outskirts of the battle, the professed allies of the insurgents, but waiting to see which side was favored by Fortune, now joined the Emperor's forces in a headlong chase of the defeated soldiers.

With the battle of Scalae Veteres the military rebellion was at an end. Stutza with some of the Vandals succeeded in escaping to Mauritania, where he married the daughter of one of the Moorish chiefs. Solomon, who on the departure of Germanus was sent to resume the government of Africa, expelled the Moors from Numidia as well as from the Carthaginian province, and for four years ruled these regions in peace and prosperity. In 543 some acts of ill faith on the part of the Romans roused the hitherto loyal Moors of Tripoli and Tunis into insurrection. The chief, Antalas, long a faithful ally of the Romans, headed the movement: and in one of the first battles of the war, the Eunuch Solomon, deserted by a large body of his troops, who accused him of parsimoniously withholding from them their share of the spoils, fell into the hands of the enemy and was slain. His nephew Sergius, a young man of swaggering demeanor, ignorant of the art of war, unpopular with the generals for his arrogance, with the soldiers for his cowardice and effeminacy, with the provincials for his avarice and lust, was entrusted with the government of the province, which under his sway went rapidly to ruin.

And now for a brief space Stutza reappeared on the scene, cooperating with Antalas, and laboring not altogether in vain to combine with the Moorish invasion a revival of the old military mutiny. Sergius prosecuted the war with feebleness and ill-success. John the son of Sisinniolus, his best subordinate, was so disgusted by the governor's arrogance that he ceased to exert himself in the imperial cause. And after every defeat which Sergius sustained, after every successful siege by the Moors, a number of soldiers joined the standards of Stutza, who doubtless still harangued as volubly as eight years ago on the grievances of the army and the rapacity of the officials.

At length Justinian, though by this time he was heartily weary of his Western conquests and the endless cares in which they involved him, sent a few soldiers and many generals to do their utmost towards finishing the war in Africa. Among the generals was Areobindus, a descendant probably of the great Aspar, all-powerful under Marcian and Leo in the middle of the previous century. He was himself allied to the imperial house, having married Justinian's niece. Under Areobindus, John the son of Sisinniolus was willing to fight, and not only willing but eager. There was only one man in the world whom he hated more than Sergius, and that was the upstart Stutza. The hatred was mutual, and each of these men had been heard to say, that if he could only kill the other he would himself cheerfully expire. The double prayer was, practically, granted. A slender army of the imperialists—for Sergius moodily refused his cooperation—met the Moorish king and the veteran mutineer on the plain below Sicca Veneria, on the confines of the African and Numidian provinces, about 100 miles south-west of Carthage. Before the battle commenced, John and Stutza, instinct with mutual hatred, rode forth between the two armies to try conclusions with one another in single combat. An arrow from the bow of the imperial general wounded Stutza in the groin. He fell to the earth mortally wounded, but not dead. The mutineers and the army of the Moors swept across the plain, and found him lying under a tree, gasping out the feeble remains of life. Full of rage they dashed on, overpowered the scanty numbers of the imperialists, and turned them to flight. John's horse stumbled as he was galloping down a steep incline: while he was vainly endeavoring to mount, the enemy surrounded and slew him. In a few minutes Stutza died, happy in hearing that his great enemy had fallen. In the first moment of the flight John had said, "Any death is sweet now, since my prayer that I might slay Stutza has been granted".

The events of this campaign induced Justinian at last to remove Sergius from the government of Africa and send him to prosecute the war in Italy. After murders, insurrections, changes of ruler which it is not necessary to relate here another John, distinguished as the brother of Pappus, was appointed *Magister Militum*, and sent to govern Africa (for some years after 546). Under his administration the province again enjoyed some years of tolerable tranquility, and the Moors were brought into order and subjection. But from decade to decade, the fine country which had once owned the sway of the Vandals sank deeper into ruin. Many of the provincials fled to Sicily and the other islands of the Mediterranean. The traveler, in passing through those regions which had once been most thickly peopled, now scarcely met a single wayfarer. Languishing under barbarian inroads, imperial misgovernment, and iniquitous taxation, the country was ripening fast for the time when even Saracen invasion should seem a relief from yet more intolerable evils.

Or rapid survey of events in Africa has carried us fully ten years beyond the point which we have reached in the history of Italy. We go back to Belisarius, landing at Syracuse, on his return voyage from Carthage in April or May 536. The fears which were entertained of a repetition in Sicily of the mutinies of Carthage proved groundless; or, if there had been disaffection, the soldiers at the mere sight of a born ruler like Belisarius at once returned to their accustomed obedience. He was able to administer the best antidote to mutiny, employment. Leaving sufficient garrisons in Syracuse and Palermo, he crossed from Messina to Reggio, and planting his standard on the Italian soil, was daily joined by large numbers of the inhabitants.

Belisarius was now in Magna Graecia, that region which, in the seventh century before the birth of Christ, was so thickly sown with Hellenic colonies that it seemed another Hellas. Down to the time of the wars of Rome with Pyrrhus and the Tarentines (*BC* 281-272) this Grecian influence had lasted unimpaired. How far it had in the succeeding eight centuries been obliterated by the march of Roman legions, by the foundation of Roman colonies, by the formation of the slave-tilled *latifundia* of Roman proprietors, there are perhaps not sufficient materials to enable us to decide. Certainly the Byzantine reconquest was both easier and more secure in Calabria and Apulia than in any other part of Italy. One cause of this was that there were fewer Goths in the south than in the north.

Possibly another cause may have been that still existing remembrances of the golden age of Magna Graecia took the sting out of the taunt, "They are but Greeklings", which was sometimes applied, not by Goths only, but by Italian provincials, to the invaders from Byzantium. To trace out the remains of this lingering Hellenic feeling, and to distinguish them from the undoubted and considerable influence exerted on Southern Italy by the Greeks of Constantinople from the sixth century to the twelfth, would be an interesting labor; but it is one which lies beyond our present province.

Belisarius received an accession to the his ranks, which showed the weakness of the national feeling of the Goths. No less a personage than Evermud, the son-in-law of Theodahad, who had been entrusted with a detachment of troops to guard the Straits, came with all his retinue into the Roman camp, prostrated himself at the feet of Belisarius, and expressed his desire to be subject to the will of the Emperor. His unpatriotic subserviency was rewarded. He was at once sent to Constantinople, that haven of rest and luxury, which all Romanized Goths languished to behold, and there received the dignity of Patrician and many other rewards from the hand of Justinian.

The Roman army marched on unopposed and supported by the parallel movement of the fleet, through the province of Bruttii and Lucania. They crossed the wide bed of the Silarus; they entered the province of Campania. Still no Gothic army disputed the passage of any river, nor threatened them from any mountain height. At length they reached a strong city by the sea, defended by a large Gothic garrison, the city of Neapolis, the modern Naples. Before this place Belisarius was to tarry many days.

Naples nd

The modern city of *Naples* is divided into twelve *quartieri*. It is built along a winding and beautifully irregular shore-line, of which it occupies four miles in length, varying in breadth from one mile to two and a-half, according to the nature of the ground. The *Neapolis* of the Roman Empire occupied a space only a little overlapping one of the twelve modern *quartieri*, that of S. Lorenzo. It formed an oblong about 1000 yards in length by 800 in breadth. Apparently we have no means of stating its exact population at any period of the Empire; but, if we conjecture it at a twelfth of the population of the modern city, we shall probably be exaggerating rather than depreciating the number of its inhabitants.

It is thus evident that the modern traveler must unclothe himself of many of his remembrances of the existing city of Naples in order to form anything like an accurate idea of the place which Belisarius besieged. It may be well to proceed by the method of rejection, and to indicate the chief points, conspicuous in a modern panorama of Naples, which we must eliminate in order to obtain the true value of the ancient Neapolis. Starting, then, from the western extremity, from Posilippo and the Tomb of Virgil, we come first to the houses which look upon the long drives and shrubberies of the Riviera di Chiaia. We see at a glance that these are modern. They no more belong to the classical, or even the mediaeval, city than the Champs Elysées of the French capital belong to the Lutetia of Julian or the Paris of the Valois kings. But two natural strongholds arrest the eye as we move onwards towards the city: on the right the little fortress-crowned peninsula of Castello dell' Ovo, on the left the frowning ridge of the all-commanding Castle of St. Elmo. With the first we have already made acquaintance. The site of the villa of Lucullus, the luxurious gilded cage of the deposed Augustulus, the shrine of the sainted Severinus, it suggests interesting speculations as to who may have been its occupants when the trumpets of Belisarius sounded before its walls, but it is emphatically no part of the city of Neapolis.

Saint Elmo brings vividly before us the differences between ancient and modern warfare. From the fourteenth century onwards (at least till the most recent changes in the science of gunnery deprived it of its importance) it was emphatically the stronghold of Naples. He who held that, tyrannous crest of rock virtually held the town. And yet in the wars of the Romans and the Goths this magnificent natural fortress seems to have been absolutely unimportant. The nearest houses of Neapolis were about three-quarters of a mile distant from the base of Saint Elmo, and in those days of catapults and balistae this distance would seem to have been enough to rob even such an eminence of its terrors; otherwise we must surely have heard of its being occupied by Belisarius.

We move forwards to the east, still keeping tolerably near the shore. The far-famed Theatre of San Carlo, the Bourbon Palace with its rearing horses in bronze, the massive Castel Nuovo, and the two harbors below it, all these are outside of the ancient city. Outside of it too is the quaint and dingy Largo del Mercato, that most interesting spot to a lover of mediaeval Naples, where market-women chatter and chaffer over the stone once reddened with the blood of Conradin, where a poet's ear might still almost hear the gauntlet of the last of the Swabians ring upon the pavement, summoning his Aragonese kinsman to the age-long contest with the dynasty of Anjou. All this is Naples, but not Neapolis. Where then is the ancient city?

Turn back towards the north-west, strike the busy street of the Toledo about a third of the way up on its course from the sea. Here at limits of length we are, not at, but near, the site of the classical city, whose western wall once ran parallel to the Toledo at a distance of about 150 yards to the right. The Piazza Cavour (Largo delle Pigne) and Strada Carbonara lie a little outside of the northern boundary of Neapolis. Castel Capuano (near the modern railway station) marks its extreme eastern point. The southern wall ran along a little range of higher ground (now nearly levelled with the plain below it), at a distance of some two or three hundred yards from the coastline, from the Church of the Annunziata to the University. One suburb on the west perhaps once extended about half-way from the western wall of the ancient city to the Toledo, and another on the south may probably have filled up in a similar way the interval between the city and the sea.

The block of ground thus indicated once stood out, difficult as it is now to believe it, somewhat abruptly above the surrounding plain. Even now, looking at it on the map, we can trace in it the handiwork of the Roman surveyors. Its three broad *Decuman* streets running from east to west (Strada Nilo, Strada dei Tribunali, and Strada Anticaglia) intersected by twenty-three *Cardines* running from north to south, still, notwithstanding the alterations made in them to gratify the Neapolitan passion for church building, exhibit an appearance of regularity and rectangularity conspicuously absent in the other part of the city, the haphazard growth of the Middle Ages. Roman remains have at various times been discovered under almost the whole of the space denoted above, but nothing is now left for the lover of Roman antiquity to gaze upon save two Corinthian columns of the Temple of the Dioscuri built into the church of S. Paolo Maggiore, and some faint traces of the ancient Theatre lingering in the yards and cellars of the Strada Anticaglia.

Fortunately we have an excellent aid to the imagination in endeavoring to bring before the mental vision the Neapolis which Procopius gazed upon. The neighboring town of Pompeii is very similar in dimensions and shape, and was probably very similar in character. Only we must suppose that nearly five centuries—centuries upon the whole rather of the decay of art than of its development—had passed over the *Tablina* and the *Triclinia* of the buried city to make it correspond with its surviving neighbor. The heathen temples must be imagined to have fallen somewhat into decay, and several Christian basilicas must be allowed to have grown up under their shadow. The fact that the four oldest parish churches in Naples—S. Giovanni Maggiore, Santi Apostoli, S. Giorgio Maggiore, and S. Maria Maggiore—all belong to the district whose confines we have traced, is an interesting confirmation of the truth of its antiquity.

Belisarius stationed his fleet in the harbor, where they were beyond the range of the projectiles of the enemy. A Gothic garrison stationed in the suburb (possibly the suburb between the city and the sea) at once surrendered to the invaders. Then a message was sent to the Roman general asking him if he would consent to receive a deputation of some of the principal inhabitants of the city, anxious to confer with him for the public welfare. He consented, and the deputation, with one Stephanus at its head, appeared before of him. Stephanus pleaded the hard case of the Roman citizens of Naples, summoned by a Roman army to surrender their town, and prevented from doing so by a Gothic garrison. Nor were even these Gothic soldiers free agents. Their wives and children were in the hands of Theodahad, who would assuredly visit upon them any fault which the garrison might commit towards him. In these cruel circumstances the citizens begged Belisarius not to press upon them his summons to surrender. After all, it was not there, but under the walls of Rome, that the decisive engagement would have to be fought. If Rome were reduced to the Emperor's obedience, Neapolis must inevitably follow its example. If the general were repulsed from Rome, the possession of a little city like Neapolis would avail him nothing.

Belisarius coldly thanked the orator for his of advice as to the course of the campaign, but announced his intention of conducting the war according to his own notions of military expediency. To the Roman inhabitants he offered the choice of freedom to be achieved by his arms; or slavery, they themselves fighting to keep the yoke upon their necks. He could hardly doubt what in such circumstances their choice would be, especially as the prosperous condition of the loyal Sicilians showed that he was both able and willing to keep the promises which he made in the name of the

Emperor. Even to the Goths he could offer honorable terms. Let them either enter his army and become the servants of the great Monarch whom the civilized world obeyed, or, if they refused this proposal, on the surrender of the city they should march out unharmed (it is to be presumed with the honors of war), and depart whither they would.

Stephanus, whose patriotism had been quickened by the promise of large rewards to himself if he could bring about the surrender of the city, strove earnestly to induce his fellow-citizens to accept the terms of Belisarius. He was seconded in these efforts by a Syrian merchant named Antiochus, long resident in Neapolis, a man of great wealth and high reputation. Two orators however, named Pastor and Asclepiodotus, also men of great influence in the city, stood forth as the advocates of an opposite policy, one of loyalty to the Goths and resistance to Byzantium. If we are perplexed at finding professed rhetoricians and men of letters (one of whom bears a Greek name) championing the cause of the barbarians, we may remember the life-long loyalty of Cassiodorus to the house of Theodoric, and may conjecture that other men of like training to his had been induced to enter the Gothic service. Some of these, like the two rhetoricians now before us, may have had statesmanship enough to see that the so-called 'Roman liberty' which was offered to the Italians would mean only a change of masters, and that change not necessarily one for the better.

By the advice of Pastor and Asclepiodotus, the offered demands of the Neapolitans were raised so high that in their opinion Belisarius would never grant them. A memorandum containing these demands was presented by Stephanus to the General, who accepted them and confirmed his acceptance by an oath. On the news of this favorable reply the pressure in favor of surrender became so strong that the Gothic garrison alone would not have ventured to resist it. The common people had begun to stream down towards the gates with the intention of opening them: but then the two orators 'whose sentence was for open war' gathered the Goths and the principal Neapolitans together and again harangued them in support of their views: "The mob have taken this thought of Pastor and surrender into their minds and are eager to execute it. But we, who deem that they are rushing headlong to ruin, are bound to consult you, the leaders of the state, and to put our thoughts before you, the last contribution that we can make to the welfare of our country. You think that, because you have the promise and the oath of Belisarius, you are now relieved from all further danger of the horrors of war. And if that were so, we should be the first to advise you to surrender. But how can Belisarius guarantee your future security? He is going to fight the nation of the Goths under the walls of Rome. Suppose that he does not gain the victory: you will have the Gothic warriors in a few days before your gates breathing vengeance against the cowardly betrayers of their trust. And on the other hand, if he wins, even on that most favorable supposition you will have to make up your minds to the permanent presence of an imperial garrison in your town. For the Emperor, though he may be much obliged to you for the moment for removing an obstacle out of his path, will not fail to make a note of the fact that the Neapolitans are a fickle and disloyal people, not safe to be trusted with the defence of their city. No: depend upon it, you will stand better both with friends and foes if you do not lightly surrender the trust committed to your hands. Belisarius cannot take the city: the magnitude of the promises which he makes to you is the plainest proof of that. You have strong walls and an abundant supply of provisions. Only stand firm for a few days and you will see the cloud of war roll away from your borders". With this the orators brought forward some Jews to vouch for the fact that Neapolis was well provisioned for a siege. The Israelite nation were always in favor of the tolerant rule of Theodoric and his successors as against the narrow bigotry of Byzantium. Apparently, in this instance, they were able to speak with authority, being the merchants by whose aid the needful stores of provision had been procured. The result of the harangue of the two orators, backed by the assurances of the Hebrews, was that the party of surrender was outvoted, and Belisarius, sorely vexed at the delay, but unwilling to leave so strong a place untaken in his rear, had to set about the siege of Neapolis.

The citizens, having resolved in a stubborn defence appealed to Theodahad for assistance. But Theodahad, utterly unready for war, allowed the precious winter months to slip without making any preparation for war, and was now seeking to diviners and soothsayers for knowledge as to the future which he had done nothing to mould. The manner of divination concerted between him and a Jewish magician, was ridiculous enough to have been practiced by any Roman augur. Thirty hogs were shut in three different pens. One was labeled 'Troops of the Emperor', another 'Goths', and the 'last Romans'. The unfortunate animals were then left for a certain number of days without food. When the pens were opened. it was found that the Gothic hogs had all perished save two, that of the Roman animals half had died and the remaining half had lost all their bristles, while the Imperialists were nearly all alive and seemed to have suffered nothing from their captivity. The inference was obvious. The Gothic race was doomed to almost utter extermination; the provincials of Italy should suffer cruel hardships and the loss of all their property, but half of the nation should survive the war; while the Byzantine invaders alone should emerge from it fat and flourishing, after this augury of the hogs, Theodahad felt himself even less prepared than before to send effectual succor to the Neapolitans.

The citizens, however, were making so good a defence that it seemed as if they might be able to do without reinforcements. The steepness of the approaches to the walls, the narrow space between them and the sea, which left no room for the evolutions of troops, and possibly some defect in the harborage which made it difficult for the ships to approach near enough to hurl projectiles into the city, all made the task of Belisarius one of unusual difficulty. He had cut off the aqueduct which brought water from Serino, in the valley of the Samnite river Sabatus, into Neapolis; but there were so many excellent wells within the enclosure that the inhabitants scarcely perceived any diminution of their water-supply. As day passed on after day and still no breach was made in the walls, and many of his bravest soldiers were falling in the useless assaults, Belisarius, chafing at the delay, began bitterly to repent that he had ever undertaken the siege. It was still perhaps only June, but twenty days of the siege had already elapsed, and at this rate it would be winter before he met Theodahad and the great Gothic host under the walls of Rome.

At this crisis, when he was on the point of giving the order to the soldiers to collect their aqueduct. baggage and raise the siege, one of his body-guard, an Isaurian named Paucaris, brought him tidings which gave him a gleam of hope. One of his fellow-countrymen, a private soldier, clambering, as these Isaurian mountaineers were in the habit of doing, up every steep place that they could scale, had come to the end of the broken aqueduct. Curious to see the *specus* or channel along which the water had once flowed, he had entered through the aperture, which had been imperfectly closed by the defenders of the city, and crept for some distance along the now waterless conduit. At length he came to a part of its course where it was taken through the solid rock, and here, to save labor, the diameter of the *specus* was smaller, too small for a man in armor to creep through it. Yet he deemed that the hole might be widened sufficiently to remove this difficulty, and that it would then be possible to penetrate by this forgotten passage into the city itself. Belisarius at once perceived the importance of the discovery, and sent some Isaurians, with the utmost secrecy, under the guidance of their countryman to accomplish the desired excavation. They used no axe or hammer, that they might not alarm the enemy. Patiently, with sharp instruments of steel they filed away at the rock, and at length returned to the General, announcing that there was now a practicable passage through the aqueduct.

But before attempting by this means the assault of the city, Belisarius determined to make one more effort to persuade the inhabitants to surrender. Sending for Stephanus, he said to him (in words which remind us of a well-known utterance of our own Duke of Wellington), "Many are now the cities that I have seen taken, and I am perfectly familiar with all that goes on at such a time,—the grown men slain with the edge of the sword; the women suffering the last extremity of outrage, longing for death but unable to find one friendly destroyer; the children driven off into bondage, doomed to sink from an honorable condition into that of half-fed and ignorant boors, slaves of the very men whose hands are red with the blood of their parents: and besides all this, the leaping flames destroying in an hour all the comeliness of the city. I can see as in a mirror, my dear Stephanus, your fair city of Neapolis undergoing all these horrors which I have beheld in so many of the towns that I have taken; and my whole soul is stirred with pity for her and her inhabitants. She is a city of old renown. They are Romans and Christians, and I have many barbarians in my army, hard to restrain at any time, and now maddened by the loss of brethrens and comrades who have fallen in the siege. I will tell you honestly that you cannot escape me. he plans which I have made are such that the city must fall into my hands. Be advised by me, and accept an honorable capitulation while you can. If you refuse, blame not Fortune, but your own perversity for all the miseries that shall come upon you". With tears and lamentations Stephanus delivered to his fellow-citizens the message of Belisarius; but they, confident in the impregnability of their city, still abjured every thought of surrender.

As there was no possibility of avoiding the assault, Belisarius proceeded to make his plans for it as perfect as possible. At twilight he chose out four hundred men whom he placed under the command of Magnus, a cavalry officer, and Eunes, a leader of the Isaurians. Though we are not expressly told that it was so, there seems some reason to suppose that the half of this force commanded by Eunes was itself of Isaurian nationality; and no doubt both Paucaris and the original discoverer of the passage took part in the expedition. The men were fully armed with shield, breastplate, and sword, and two trumpeters went with them. The whole secret of the plan was then disclosed to Magnus and Eunes; the spot was indicated where they were to enter the aqueduct, and from whence with lighted torches they and their four hundred were to creep stealthily into the city. Meanwhile the Roman host was kept under arms ready for action, and the carpenters were set to work preparing ladders for the assault.

At first the General had to endure a disappointment. Fully one half of the aqueduct party—the non-Isaurian half if our conjecture be correct—when they had crept for some distance through the dark channel, declared that the deed was too dangerous, and marched back to the entrance, the reluctant and mortified Magnus at their head. Belisarius, who was still standing there surrounded by some of the bravest men in the army, had no difficulty in at once selecting two hundred volunteers to take the place of the recreants; and his gallant step-son Photius, claiming to be allowed to head the expedition, leapt eagerly into the aqueduct. The General thought of Antonina, and forbade her son to venture through the channel; but the example of his bravery and the bitter taunts of Belisarius so stung the waverers, that they too returned into the aqueduct, thus apparently raising the numbers of the storming party to six hundred.

Fearing that so large a detachment might make some noise which would be heard by the Gothic sentinels, the General ordered his lieutenant Bessas to draw near to the walls and engage their attention. Bessas harangued them accordingly in his and their native tongue, enlarging on the rich rewards of the imperial service, and advising them to enter it without delay. They replied with taunts and insults; but the object was gained. In the storm of the debate, amid all the crash of Teutonic gutturals, any muffled sounds from the region of the aqueduct passed unheeded.

The storming party were now within the circuit of the walls of Neapolis, but they found themselves penetrating further than they wished; and how to emerge into the city was as yet by no means apparent. A lofty vaulted roof of brick was over their heads. They seem to have been standing in what would have been a great reservoir had the aqueduct been still flowing. Despair seized the heart of those who had already entered the place, and the column of soldiers still pressing on from behind made their situation each moment more perilous. At length those in front saw a break in the vaulting above them, by the break the outlines of a cottage, by the cottage an olive-tree. It was hopeless for armed soldiers to climb up that steep reservoir-side; but one brave fellow, an Isaurian doubtless, laid aside helmet and shield, and with hands and feet scrambled up the wall. In the cottage he found one old woman in a state of abject poverty. He threatened her with death if she stirred or shrieked. She was mute. He fastened a strong strap which he had brought with him to the stem of the olive-tree. His comrades grasped the other end, and one by one all the six hundred mounted without accident.

By this time the fourth watch of the night had begun. The storming party rushed to the northern ramparts, beneath which they knew that Belisarius and Bessas would be stationed, slew two of the sentinels who were taken unawares, and then blew a long blast on their bugles. At once the Byzantine soldiers placed the ladders against the walls and began to mount. Destruction! The ladders, which had been hurriedly made in the darkness by the army-carpenters, were too short, and did not reach to the foot of the battlements. They were taken down again, and two of them were hastily but securely fastened together. Now the soldiers could mount. They poured over the battlements. On the north side at any rate the city was won.

On the south, between the sea and the wall, the task of the assailants was somewhat harder. There, not the Goths, but the Jews kept watch; the Jews ever embittered against the persecuting Government of Constantinople, and now fighting with the courage of despair, since they knew that the part which they had taken in opposing the surrender had marked them out for vengeance. But when day dawned, and they were attacked in their rear by assailants from the other part of the city, even the Jews were obliged to flee, and the southern gates were opened to the Byzantines.

The besiegers on the east side, where no serious assault had been contemplated, had no scaling ladders, and were obliged to burn the gates of the city before they could effect an entrance. By this time the whole troop of semi-barbarians called the Roman army was pouring through the town, murdering, ravishing, plundering, binding for slavery, even as Belisarius had prophetically described. The Huns who were serving under the banners of the Empire, and who were no doubt still heathens, did not respect even the sanctity of the churches, but slew those who had taken refuge at the altars.

Then Belisarius collected his troops together, probably in the great Forum of the city, and delivered a harangue in which he besought them not to tarnish the victory which God had given them by unholy deeds. The Neapolitans were now no longer enemies, but fellow-subjects: "let them not sow the seeds of irreconcilable hatred by a bloody butchery in the first city which they had taken". With these words, and with the assurance that all the wealth which they could lay hands upon should be theirs, as the fitting reward of their valor, he persuaded the soldiers to sheathe their swords, and even to unbind their captives and restore wives to their husbands, children to their parents. Thus, says the historian, did the Neapolitans—those at least of them who escaped the massacre—pass in a few hours from freedom to slavery, and back again from slavery to freedom, and even to a certain measure of comfort. For they had succeeded in burying their gold and all their most precious property; and after the storm of war had passed they were able to recover it.

Eight hundred Gothic warriors were taken prisoners in the city. Belisarius protected them from outrage at the hands of his soldiery and kept them in honorable captivity, treating them in all respects like soldiers of his own.

The unhappy leaders of the war-party attested by their end the sincerity of their advice. Pastor, who was previously in perfect health, when he saw that the city was taken, received so violent a shock that he had a stroke of apoplexy which proved immediately fatal. Asclepiodotus with some of the nobles of the city presented himself boldly before Belisarius. Stephanus, in his grief at the calamities which had befallen his native city, assailed with bitter reproaches "that betrayer of his country, that wickedest of men, who had sold his city in order to curry favor with the Goths. Had the cause of the barbarians triumphed, Asclepiodotus would have denounced the patriots as traitors and hounded them to the death. Only the valor of Belisarius had delivered them from this calamity". With some dignity Asclepiodotus replied that the invective of Stephanus was really his highest praise, since it showed that he had been firm in his duty to those whom he found set over him. Now that by the fortune of war Neapolis had passed under the power of the Emperor, Asclepiodotus would be found as faithful a servant of the Empire as he had been of the Goths, while Stephanus at the first whisper of ill-fortune would be found veering back again from his new to his old allegiance.

We are not told what part Belisarius took in this quarrel The populace followed Asclepiodotus on his departure from the general's tent, assailed him with reproaches as author of all their miseries, and at length slew him and mangled his remains. Then seeking the house of Pastor, they would not for a long time believe his slaves who assured them of his death. Satisfied at last by the sight of his dead body, they dragged it forth from the city and hung it ignominiously on a gibbet. They then repaired to the quarters of Belisarius, told him what they had done, and craved pardon for the display of their righteous indignation, a pardon which was readily granted.

So ended the Byzantine siege of Naples. The only remembrance of it which, in the changed circumstances of the city, a modern traveler can obtain, is furnished by a few red arches which, under the name of Ponti Rossi, traverse one of the roads leading north-eastwards from the city, a little below the royal palace of Capo di Monte. At this point apparently the aqueduct which led into the city of Naples branched off from the main line which held on its course westwards to Puteoli and Baiae. Over these arches marched the hardy Isaurians on that perilous midnight adventure which resulted in the capture of Neapolis.

CHAPTER III.

THE ELEVATION OF WITIGIS.

The failure of the Gothic King to avert the fall of Neapolis exasperated beyond endurance the warlike subjects of Theodahad. His avarice and his ingratitude were known; his want of loyalty to the nation of his fathers was more than suspected. Rumors of his negotiations with Constantinople, even the most secret and the most discreditable of them, had reached the ears of his subjects, and now the worst of those rumors seemed to be confirmed by his desertion of the defenders of Neapolis, a desertion so extraordinary that mere incompetence seemed insufficient to account for it.

That which our ancestors would have called Assembly, a *Folc-mote*, an assembly of the whole gothic nation under arms, was convened, by what authority we know not, to deliberate on the perilous condition of the country. The place of meeting was forty-three miles from Rome. It has been hitherto impossible to discover any clue to the name given by Procopius, who says "The Romans call the place Regeta"; but the other indications afforded by him show that it was situated in the Pomptine Marshes, and in that part of them which the draining operations of Decius, who had apparently cleared out the old Decennovial Canal, had restored to productiveness, perhaps even to fertility.

Allusion has already been made to Theodoric's share in the promotion of this useful work, and to the palace bearing his name which crowned the heights of Terracina. If not that palace itself, yet at any rate the hill on which it stood, rose conspicuously on the southern horizon some fifteen miles from the Gothic meeting-place. The reason for choosing this spot was that, thanks to the draining operations just referred to, the vast plain furnished a plentiful supply of grass for the horses of the assembled warriors.

As soon as the nation met upon the plain of Regeta, it was clear that the deposition of Theodahad was inevitable, and that the only question was who should succeed him. The line of the great Theodoric was practically extinct (only a young girl, the sister of Athalaric, remained); and in the great necessity of the nation, they travelled beyond the circle not only of royal, but even of noble blood, to find a deliverer. A warrior named Witigis, not sprung from any illustrious house, but who had rendered himself illustrious by great deeds wrought against the Gepids in the war of Sirmium, was raised upon the buckler and acclaimed as king.

The pen of the veteran Cassiodorus was employed to draw up the document in which was announced to the Goths the elevation of a king, not chosen in the recesses of a royal bedchamber, but in the expanse of the boundless Campagna; of one who owed his dignity first to Divine grace, but secondly to the free judgment of the people; of one who knew the brave men in his army by comradeship, having stood shoulder to shoulder with them in the day of battle. His countrymen were exhorted to relinquish that attitude of fear and mutual suspicion which the rule of the craven Theodahad had only too naturally produced, and to work with one accord for the deliverance of their nation.

Witigis decided without hesitation that the dethroned monarch must die. He gave the word to a Goth named Optaris to follow Theodahad and bring him back, dead or alive. Optaris had the stimulus of revenge besides that of obedience to urge him to fulfill his bloody commission, since he had lost a bride rich and lovely, whose hand had been plighted to him, by Theodahad's venal interference on behalf of a rival suitor. Night and day he spurred on his steed. He came up with the flying King before he had reached Ravenna, threw him to the ground, and cut his throat as a priest would slay a sheep for sacrifice.

So vanishes the Platonist Ostrogoth, the remover of land-marks, the perjurer and the coward, from the page of history. It is not often that the historian has to describe a character so thoroughly contemptible as that of Theodahad.

Witigis on his accession to the throne found an utter absence of effective preparation to meet the enemy. The two enemies, we should rather say, since the Franks, in fulfillment of a secret compact with Justinian, were in arms against the Goths, and a considerable part of the army of Theodahad was stationed in Provence and Dauphiné, endeavoring to defend that part of the kingdom against the sons of Clovis. In these circumstances Witigis determined to retire for a time to Ravenna, not indeed evacuating Rome, since the gallant veteran Leudaris was to be left in charge of that city with 4000 picked troops, but withdrawing the bulk of his army to the stronger capital, and there at his leisure preparing for the defence of the kingdom. In a speech to the army he set forth the reasons for this course, the necessity for getting the Frankish war off their hands and so of reducing the number of their invaders, the difference between a withdrawal dictated by motives of high policy and a cowardly flight, and so forth. The most important point of all, the effect of such a movement on the Roman population, was thus slightly handled: "If the Romans be well affected towards us, they will help to guard the city for the Goths, and will not put Fortune to the proof, knowing that we shall speedily return. But if they are meditating any intrigue against us, they will do us less harm by delivering the city to the enemy than by continuing in secret conspiracy; for we shall then know who are on our side, and shall be able to distinguish friends from foes".

With these and similar arguments Witigis persuaded his countrymen to retire with the bulk of the army into North Italy. It is easy to see now, and surely it should have been easy to see then, that this was a fatal blunder. The Franks, as the events of the next few months were to prove, were fighting only for their own hand, and might easily be bought off by territorial concessions in Gaul. The real and only inevitable enemy was Belisarius, the daring strategist who was now at Neapolis, and who had come to the Italian peninsula to conquer it, the whole of it, for his master or to die.

All-important in this struggle was the attitude of the Roman population, not in Rome only, but over the whole of Italy. They could still look back on the peace and plenty which had marked the just reign of Theodoric. Though by no means welded into one nation with their Gothic guests, there was not as yet, we have good reason to believe, any impassable chasm between the two races; and if they could be persuaded to cast in their lot with the Teutonic defenders of their land, if they could practice the lesson which they had been lately learning, of substituting the name 'Italy' for 'the Empire'; above all, if they could be induced to think of Belisarius and his troops as Greek intruders into their country, the new Romano-Gothic people and fatherland might yet be formed. The example of the resistance of Neapolis showed that this was not a mere idle dream. But all these hopes would be blasted, all the great work of Theodoric and Cassiodorus would be unraveled, and the Ostrogoths would sink into the position of a mere countryless horde, themselves invaders of Italy rather than the invaded, if the general of Justinian could once get within the walls of Rome, if the name of that venerable city with its thirteen centuries of glory could once be his to conjure with, if the head and the members being again joined together he could display himself to the world as the defender of the Roman Empire, in Rome, against the barbarians.

The chance, if chance there was, of so defending the Gothic kingdom was thrown away. The unwise counsel of Witigis—who, it may be, could not believe himself a king till he had actually sat in Theodoric's audience-chamber at Ravenna—prevailed, and the Gothic host marched off northwards, leaving only Leudaris and his 4000 braves to hold the capital against Belisarius. Witigis took, indeed, some precautions, such as they were, to assure the fidelity of the citizens. He harangued Pope Silverius, the Senate, and the people of Rome, calling to their remembrance the great benefits which they had received from Theodoric; he bound them under most solemn oaths to be faithful to the Gothic rule; he took a large number of Senators with him as hostages for the loyalty of the rest. To force the subjects whom he was not defending to swear eternal allegiance to his rule was the work of a weak man; to hint that, if they did not, their innocent Mends should suffer for it, was the threat of a cruel one. This taking of hostages, though it might seem for the moment an easy expedient for securing the fidelity of an unguarded city, was essentially a bad security. If the bond were forfeited by the surrender of the city, to exact the penalty, namely, the death of the chief citizens of Rome, helpless and innocent, was to put an absolutely impassable barrier of hate between the Gothic King and the vast majority of the inhabitants of Italy.

On his arrival at Ravenna Witigis took part in a pageant which may have both amazed and amused his Gothic subjects. He, the elderly warrior, the husband of a wife probably of his own age, having divorced that companion of his humbler fortunes, proceeded to marry the young and blooming Matasuentha, sister of Athalaric and granddaughter of the great Theodoric. Reasons of state were of course alleged for these strange nuptials. An alliance with the royal house might cause men to forget the lowliness of the new King's origin; and the danger of his finding a rival to the crown in Matasuentha's husband, or even of her making over her rights, such as they might be, to the Emperor, was barred by her becoming the Lady of the Goths. But the marriage was against nature, and brought no blessing with it. The unfortunate girl, as weary of her elderly husband as Athalaric had been of his grey-headed tutors, chafed against the yoke, and made no secret of the fact that she loved not her consort; and he, divided between the pride of the low-born adventurer exalted to a splendid position, and the unhappiness of the husband who is unloved and who lives in an atmosphere of daily reproaches, lost any power which he may ever have possessed of devising measures for the deliverance of the Gothic nation from its peril.

Altogether, the elevation of Witigis was a mistake for the Gothic monarchy. It was the old and often repeated error of supposing that because a man till he has reached middle life has played a subordinate part with some credit, he will be able to rise to the sudden requirements of a great and difficult position; that respectability will serve instead of genius. Against a general, perhaps the greatest that the world has ever seen for fertility of resource and power of rapid combination, the Goths had given themselves for a leader a mere brave and honest blunderer, whose notions of strategy were like those which Demosthenes reproved in his Athenian countrymen, who, as unskillful pugilists, were always trying to parry a blow after it had been struck and always being surprised by its successor. Yet as, with all his incapacity, he was loyal to the nation, the nation was loyal to him, and during the three following years of his disastrous leadership they never seem to have entertained the thought of replacing him by a better commander.

Having now allied himself with the daughter of the murdered Amalasuntha, Witigis sent an embassy to Constantinople, urging, with some reason, that the cause of quarrel between the Emperor and the Goths was at an end. The vile Theodahad had paid the penalty of his crimes, a penalty which Witigis himself had exacted from him. The daughter of Amalasuntha sat on the Gothic throne. What more did Justinian require? Why should he not stop the effusion of blood and restore peace to Italy? This letter to the Emperor was supplemented by one to the orthodox bishops of Italy, calling upon them to pray for the success of the embassy; to the Prefect of Thessalonica, praying him to speed the two ambassadors on their way; and to the Master of the Offices at Constantinople, beseeching him to use his influence in favor of peace.

The letters relating to this embassy were prepared by Cassiodorus, and were perhaps among the latest documents which proceeded from his pen. Though he did not yet apparently retire formally from public affairs, he seems to have perceived at this point that the dream of his life was a hopeless one, that fusion between Goth and Roman was impossible, and consequently to have retired from all active participation in the conflict which must now be fought out to the bitter end, but in which nevertheless he could pray for the success of neither party.

The letters written in reply to Witigis have not been preserved; but there can be no doubt that such letters were received by the Gothic king, probably in the late autumn of 536, and they must have been to the intent that the war must now proceed, since nothing but unqualified submission would satisfy the demand of Justinian.

One of the first acts of the reign of Witigis was to buy off the opposition of the Franks by the cession of the Ostrogothic possessions in Gaul (Provence and part of Dauphiné) and by the payment of twenty hundredweight of gold. Negotiations for this purpose had been commenced by Theodahad, but were interrupted by his death. Childebert, Theudibert, and Chlotochar now divided among them the treasure and the towns ceded by the Goths, and concluded a secret alliance with them, promising to send some of their horde of subject nations to assist in the defence of Italy. More they durst not do, being desirous still to keep up the appearance of friendship with Byzantium.

In thus resuming the pacific policy of Theodahad towards the Franks,—a policy which enabled him to recall the general Marcias and many thousands of the bravest of the Goths to the south of the Alps, Witigis seems to have been only recognizing an inevitable necessity. His great error was in not making this concession earlier. If he could thus purchase the friendship of the Franks, and secure his northern frontier from their attacks, he ought to have done so at once, and thus to have avoided the necessity for the fatal abandonment of Rome.

CHAPTER IV

BELISARIUS IN ROME

The events described in the preceding chapter occupied the summer and autumn of 536. How Belisarius was occupied during this interval it is not easy to say. The notes of time given us by Procopius in this part of his narrative are indistinct; nor have we between the siege of Neapolis and the siege of Rome any of those little personal touches which indicate the presence of an eyewitness. Possibly the historian was still at Carthage, attached to the staff of the African army. If in Italy, he was perhaps engaged in administrative work in some one of the towns of Southern Italy, such as Beneventum, of which he gives at this point of his narrative a short account full of archaeological information. The name of the place, at first Maleventum, from the fierce winds which rage there as well as in Dalmatia, but afterwards changed to Beneventum, to avoid the ill sound of the other (for the Latins call wind *ventus* in their language)—the traditions of Diomed the founder of the city—the grinning tusks of the Calydonian boar slain by his uncle Meleager, still preserved down to the days of Procopius—the legend of the Palladium stolen by Diomed and Ulysses from the temple of Athené at Troy and handed on by the former to Aeneas—the doubt where this Palladium was then preserved, whether at Rome or Constantinople—all this archaeological gossip flows from the Herodotean pen of our historian with a fullness which suggests that to him the autumn of 536 was in after days chiefly memorable as the time of his sojourn at Beneventum.

It seems likely that Belisarius devoted the summer and autumn months of 536 to the consolidation of his conquests in Southern Italy. Cumae, that town by Lake Avernus of old Sibylline fame, which was the only fortress besides Neapolis in the province of Campania, was occupied by him with a sufficient garrison. Calabria and Apulia, as has been already said, offered themselves as willing subjects to the Byzantine Emperor. A hardy and martial people like the Goths, holding the central Apennine chain, might have given Belisarius some trouble by separating Apulia from Campania and intercepting the communications between the Adriatic and Tyrrhene seas; but this danger was removed by the convenient treachery of Pitzas the Goth, probably the same person as the Pitzias who was victor in the war of Sirmium. He now commanded in the province of Samnium, and brought over with him not only his personal followers, but at least half of the province, to the allegiance of the Emperor.

Thus, with scarcely a stroke struck, had nearly the whole of that fair territory which modern geography knows as the Kingdom of the Two Sicilies been lost to the Goths and recovered by the commonwealth of Rome. Belisarius might well pause for a few months to secure these conquests and to await the result of the negotiations which Witigis, evidently somewhat half-hearted about his resistance, had opened up with Constantinople. Besides, he had reason to expect that he would soon receive an important communication from the Bishop of Rome himself; and before the winter had fairly commenced that communication came. To understand its full importance we must rapidly turn over a few pages of Papal history.

It has been already said that, after the death of the unfortunate Pope John in the prison of Theodoric a succession of somewhat inconspicuous Popes filled the chair of St. Peter. Neither Felix III, Boniface II, nor John II did anything to recall the stirring times of the previous Felix or of Hormisdas: but the long duel with Constantinople had ended in the glorious triumph of Rome: and the hard fate of John I had warned the pontiffs that their time was not yet come for an open rupture with 'Dominus Noster' the King of the Goths and Romans, in his palace by the Hadriatic. A cordial theological alliance therefore with Byzantium, and trembling lip-loyalty to Ravenna, was the attitude of the Popes during these years of transition. There were the customary disputes and disturbances at the election of each Pontiff, varied by stringent decrees of the Roman Senate against bribery, by attempts on the part of the King's counselors to magnify his share in the nomination to the vacant see, and by one yet stranger attempt on the part of Pope Boniface to acquire the power of nominating his successor to the Pontificate—a power such as a servile parliament of the sixteenth century conferred on Henry VIII with reference to the English crown. This scheme, however, was too audacious to succeed. Boniface was forced, probably by the pressure of public opinion, to revoke and even to burn the decree of nomination. The chief interest of this event for posterity lies in the fact that the person who was to have been benefited by the decree was the adroit but restless and unprincipled deacon Vigilius, of whose later intrigues for the acquisition of the Papal throne, and sorrows when he had obtained the coveted dignity, we shall hear abundantly in the future course of this history.

Theologically this uneventful period has a conspicuous interest of its own, as being one of the great battle-fields of the assertors and impugners of the doctrine of Papal Infallibility. One of the usual childish logomachies of the East was imported into Rome by certain Scythian monks, who pressed, as a matter of life and death, the orthodoxy of the formula "One of the Trinity suffered in the flesh" as against the heretical "One *person* of the Trinity suffered in the flesh". Hormisdas, before whom the matter was at first brought, had showed the usual good sense of Rome by trying simply to crush out the unintelligible and unprofitable discussion. In doing so, however, he used words which certainly seemed to convey to the non-theological mind the idea that he regarded the phrase "One of the Trinity suffered in the flesh" as heretical. That phrase a later Pope, John II, under some pressure from Justinian that he might not seem to countenance Nestorianism, adopted, as agreeing with the apostolic teaching; and it has consequently ever since been considered strictly orthodox to use it. Here are obviously the materials for a discussion, very interesting to theologians. The literature of the Hormisdas controversy is already considerable, and it is quite possible that the last word has not yet been spoken regarding it.

The successor of John II, Pope Agapetus, during his short episcopate of ten months, saw, more of the world than many of his predecessors in much longer pontificates. After the mission of Peter and Rusticus had failed, through his own treachery and vacillation, King Theodahad determined to make one more attempt to assuage the just resentment of Justinian. Knowing the great influence which since the reunion of the Churches the Roman pontiff exerted over the Eastern Caesar, he decided that Agapetus should be sent to Constantinople on an embassy of peace. To overcome the natural reluctance of a person of advanced age, and in a position of such high dignity, to act as his letter-carrier on a long and toilsome winter journey, Theodahad sent a message to him and to the Roman Senate informing them that, unless they succeeded in making his peace with Justinian, the senators, their wives, their sons, and their daughters should all be put to the sword. Truly the instincts of self-preservation in the coward are cruel.

The Pope Agapetus entered Constantinople on the 20th February, 536, and was received with great demonstrations of respect by the Emperor and the citizens. In the fulfillment of Theodahad's commission, as we know, he met with no success. The Emperor replied,—and his reply is characteristic of the huckstering spirit in which he made war,—that after the great expenses to which his treasury had been put in preparing the expedition for Italy he could not now draw back, leaving its object unattained. But if Agapetus could not or would not effect anything on behalf of his Gothic sovereign he effected much for the advancement of his own and his successors' dignity; and this visit of his is a memorable step in the progress of the Papacy towards an Universal Patriarchate. The see of Constantinople was at this time filled by Anthimus, recently translated thither from Trebizond by the influence of Theodora, and strongly suspected of sharing the Eutychian views of his patroness. Agapetus sternly refused to recognize Anthimus as lawful Patriarch of Constantinople, on the double ground of the ecclesiastical canon against translations and of his suspected heresy. Justinian tried the effect, so powerful on all others, of the thunder of the imperial voice and the frown on the imperial brow. "Either comply with my request or I will cause thee to be carried away into banishment". Quite unmoved, the noble old man replied in these memorable words : "I who am but a sinner came with eager longing to gaze upon the most Christian Emperor Justinian. In his place I find a Diocletian, whose threats do not one whit terrify me". It must be recorded, for the credit of Justinian, that this bold language moved his admiration rather than his anger. He allowed the Bishop of Rome to question the Patriarch of Constantinople whether he admitted the two natures in Christ; and when the faltering answers of Anthimus proclaimed him a secret Monophysite, Justinian, who always assumed in public the attitude of an opponent of his wife's heresy, at once drove him from the see and from the city. A new prelate, Mennas, of undoubted Chalcedonian orthodoxy was consecrated by Agapetus. Technically the rights of the see of Constantinople may have been saved, but there was certainly something in the whole proceeding which suggested the idea that, after all, the so-called Patriarch of New Rome was only a suffragan bishop in the presence of the successor of St. Peter.

Much had Agapetus done, and more was he doing, to repress the reviving Eutychianism of the East—encouraged though it was by the favor of Theodora—when death ended his career. He died on the 21st of April, 536 (when Belisarius was on the point of returning from Carthage to Sicily), and his body, enclosed in a leaden coffin, was brought from Constantinople to Rome and buried in the Basilica of St. Peter. The new Pope, Silverius, is said to have been intruded into the see by the mere will of "the tyrant Theodahad", who, moved himself by a bribe, brought terror to bear on the minds of the clergy to prevent any resistance to his will. It is, however, strongly suspected that this suggestion of an election vitiated by duress is a mere afterthought in order to excuse the highly irregular proceedings which, as we shall hereafter see, were connected with his deposition. One fact, rare if not unique in the history of the Papacy, distinguishes the personal history of Silverius. A Pope himself, he was also the son of a Pope. He was the offspring, born in lawful wedlock, of the sainted and strong-willed Hormisdas, who of course must have been a widower when he entered the service of the Church. We fail, however, to find in the gentle and peace-loving Silverius any trace of the adamantine character of his dictatorial father. Not of a noble or independent nature, he appears to be pushed about by ruder men and women, Gothic and Roman, according to their own needs and caprices, and is at last hustled out of the way more ignominiously than any of his predecessors. Domineering fathers make not infrequently timorous and abject sons.

Such, then, was the Pope Silverius—for we now return to contemplate the progress of the imperial army—who, having sworn a solemn oath of fealty to Witigis, now, near the end of 536, sent messengers to Belisarius to offer the peaceful surrender of the city of Rome. It was not, however, with any chivalrous intention of throwing themselves into the breach, and doing battle for the commonwealth of Rome that this invitation was sent. Silverius and the citizens had heard, of course, full particulars of the siege and sack of Naples, and wished to avoid similar calamities falling upon them. Weighing one danger against another, they thought that they should run less risk from the wrath of the Goths than from that of the Byzantines, and therefore sent Fidelius, the late Quaestor of Athalaric, to invite Belisarius to Rome, and to promise that the City should be surrendered to him without a struggle. Belisarius gladly accepted the invitation, and leaving Herodian with a garrison of 300 foot-soldiers in charge of Naples, he marched by the Latin Way from Campania to Rome. While the Via Appia was the great sea-coast road to Rome, the Via Latina took a more inland course by the valley of the Liris and along the base of the Volscian hilla, a course in fact very nearly coinciding with that of the modern railway between Rome and Naples. Belisarius and his army passed therefore through the town of Casinum, and immediately under its steep hill, upon the summit of which a man who was to attain even wider fame than Belisarius had reared, amid the ruins of Apollo's temple, the mother-edifice of a thousand European convents. It was Benedict of Nursia, who, little heeding the clash of opposing races, and scarce hearing the tramp of invading armies, was making for *Monte Cassino* an imperishable name in the history of humanity.

When the Gothic garrison of Rome learned that evacuate Belisarius was at hand, and that the Romans were disposed to surrender the City, they came to the conclusion that against such a general, aided by the good-will of the citizens, they should never be able to prevail, and that they would therefore withdraw peaceably from Rome. Leuderis alone, their brave old general, refused to quit the post which had been assigned to him, but was unable to command the obedience of his soldiers, or to recall them to some resolution more worthy of the Gothic name. They therefore marched quietly out by the Flaminian Gate (on the site of the modern Porta del Popolo), while Belisarius and his host entered by the Porta Asinaria, that stately gate flanked by two semi-circular towers which, though walled up, still stands near the Porta San Giovanni and behind the great Lateran Basilica. Leuderis was quietly taken prisoner, and sent with the keys of the city to Justinian. So much for the infallible precautions which Witigis assured the Goths he had taken against the surrender of the city, the "numerous men and highly intelligent officer who would never allow it to fall into the hands of Belisarius".

The entry of the Byzantine troops into Rome took place on the 9th of December, 536. Thus, as Procopius remarks, after sixty years of barbarian domination, was the city recovered for the Empire.

Belisarius seems not to have taken up his abode in any of the imperial residences on the Palatine Hill, where the representative of the Byzantine Caesar might naturally have been expected to dwell, but, prescient of the coming struggle, to have at once fixed his quarters on the Pincian Hill. This ridge on the north of Rome, so well-known by every visitor to the modern city, who, however short his stay, is sure to have seen the long train of carriages climbing to or returning from the fashionable drive, and who has probably stood upon its height in order to obtain the splendid view which it affords of the dome of St. Peters, was not one of the original seven hills of the city, nor formed, strictly speaking, a part even of imperial Rome. Known in earlier times as the Collis Hortulorum, or Hill of Gardens, it occupied too commanding a position to be safely left outside the defenses, and had therefore been included within the circuit of the walls of Honorius, some of the great retaining walls of the gardens of M. Q. Acilius Glabrio having been incorporated with the new defenses. Here then, in the Domus Pinciana, the imperial General took up his abode. Albeit probably somewhat dismantled, it was doubtless still a stately and spacious palace, though it has now disappeared and left no trace behind. It was admirably adapted for his purpose, being in fact a watch-tower commanding a view all-round the northern horizon, from the Vatican to the Mons Sacer. From this point a ride of a few minutes on his swift charger would bring him to the next great vantage-ground, the Castra Praetoria, whose square enclosure, projecting beyond the ordinary line of the Honorian walls, made a tempting object of attack, but also a splendid watch-tower for defence, carrying on the general's view to the Praenestine Gate (Porta Maggiore) on the south-east of the city. Thus, from these two points, about a third of the whole circuit of the walls, and nearly all of that part which was actually attacked by the Goths, was visible.

That the city would have to be defended, and that it would tax all his powers to defend it successfully, was a matter that was perfectly clear to the mind of Belisarius, though the Romans, dwelling in a fool's paradise of false security, deemed that all their troubles were over when the 4000 Goths marched forth by the Flaminian Gate. They thought that the war would inevitably be decided elsewhere by some great pitched battle. It seemed to them obvious that so skillful a general as Belisarius would never consent to be besieged in a city so little defended by nature as was the wide circuit of imperial Rome, nor undertake the almost superhuman task of providing for the sustenance of that vast population in addition to his own army. Such, however, was the scheme of Belisarius, who knew that behind the walls of Rome his little army could offer a more effectual resistance to the enemy than in any pitched battle on the Campanian plains. Slowly and sadly the citizens awoke to the fact that their hasty defection from the Gothic cause was by no means to relieve them from the hardships of a siege. Possibly some of them, in the year of misery that lay before them, even envied the short and sharp agony of Neapolis.

The commissariat of the city was naturally one of the chief objects of the General's solicitude. From Sicily, still the granary of the State, his ships had brought and were daily bringing large supplies of grain. These were carried into the great warehouses (*horrea publica*), which were under the care of the *Praefectus Annonae*. At the same time the citizens, sorely grumbling, were set busily to work to bring into the city the corn and provisions of all kinds that were stored in the surrounding country.

Side by side with this great work went on the repair of the walls, which Belisarius found in many places somewhat ruinous. Two hundred and sixty years had elapsed since they were erected by Aurelian and Probus, one hundred and thirty since they were renewed by Honorius, and in the latter interval they may have suffered not only from the slow foot of time, but from the destroying hands of the soldiers of Alaric, of Gaiseric, and of Ricimer. Theodoric's steady and persevering labors had effected something, but much still remained to be done. Belisarius repaired the rents which still existed, drew a deep and wide fosse round the outer side of the wall, and supplied what he considered to be a deficiency in the battlements by adding a cross-wall to each, on the left hand, so that the soldier might dispense with the use of a shield, being guarded against arrows and javelins hurled against him from that quarter.

The walls and gates of imperial Rome, substantially the same walls which Belisarius defended, and many of the same gates at which the Goths battered, are still visible; and few historical monuments surpass them in interest. No survey of them has yet been made sufficiently minute to enable us to say with certainty to what date each portion of them belongs: but some general conclusions may be safely drawn even by the superficial observer. Here you may see the *opus reticulatum*, that cross-hatched brickwork which marks a building of the Julian or Flavian age; there the fine and regular brickwork of Aurelian; there again the poor debased work of the time of Honorius. A little further on, you come to a place where layers of bricks regularly laid cease altogether. Mere rubble-work thrust in anyhow, blocks of marble, fragments of columns; such is the material with which the fatal holes in the walls have been darned and patched; and here antiquaries are generally disposed to see the 'tumultuary' restorations of Belisarius working in hot haste to complete his repairs before Witigis or the later Totila should appear before the walls. In a few places the gap in the brickwork is supplied by different and more massive materials. Great square blocks of the black volcanic stone called *tufa*, of which the wall of Servius Tullius was composed, are the sign of this intrusive formation. Are these also due to the rapid restorations of Belisarius, or was it part of the original plan to make the now superseded wall of the King do duty, after nine centuries, in the rampart of the Emperor? We turn an angle of the walls, and we see the mighty arches of the interlacing aqueducts by which Rome was fed with water from the Tiburtine and the Alban hills, with admirable skill made available for the defence of the city.

We move onward, we come to Christian monograms, to mediaeval inscriptions, to the armorial bearings of Popes. At the south of the city we look upon the grand Bastion, which marks the restoring hand of the great Farnese Pope, Paul III, employing the genius of Sangallo. We pass the great gate of Ostia, that gate through which St. Paul is believed to have been led forth to martyrdom, and which now bears his name. The wall runs down sharply to the Tiber, at the foot of that strange artificial hill the Monte Testaccio; for half a mile it lines the left bank of the stream; then at the gate of Porto it reappears on the opposite side of the Tiber. Here it changes its character, and the change is itself a compendium of mediaeval history. The wall which on the eastern shore was Imperial, with only some marks of Papal repair, now becomes purely Papal; the turrets give place to bastions; Urban VIII, as name-giver to the rampart, takes the place of Aurelian. We see at once how dear 'the Leonine city' was to the Pontifical heart; we discern that St. Peter's and the Vatican have taken the place which in imperial Rome was occupied by the Palatine, in Republican Rome by the Forum, the Capitol, and the Temple of Concord.

As everywhere in Rome, so pre-eminently in our circuit of the wall, the oldest and the newest ages are constantly jostling against one another. At the east of the city we were looking at the *tufa* blocks hewn by the masons of Servius Tullius. Now on the west we see the walls by the Porta Aurelia showing everywhere the dints of French bullets hurled against them when Oudinot in 1849 crushed out the little life of the Roman Republic of Mazzini. For yet more recent history we turn again to our northern starting-point, and there, almost under the palace of Belisarius, we see the stretch of absolutely new wall which marks the extent of the practicable breach through which the troops of Victor Emmanuel entered Rome in September, 1870.

A first and even a second perambulation of the walls of Rome, especially on the outside, may hardly give the observer an adequate conception of their original completeness as a work of defence. It has been well pointed out by one of our German authorities that Aurelian's object in constructing it cannot have been merely to furnish cover for the comparatively small numbers of the *cohortes urbanae*, the ordinary city-guard, but that he must have contemplated the necessity of a whole army garrisoning the city and defending his work. For this reason we have in Aurelian's original line of circumvallation, and to some extent, but less perfectly, in the Honorian restoration of it, a complete gallery or covered way carried all-round the inside of the wall. Nowhere can this original idea of the wall be better studied than on the south-east of the city, in the portion between the *Amphitheatrum Castrense* and the Porta Asinaria, or, in ecclesiastical language, between the Church of Santa Croce and that of St. John Lateran. Here, if we walk outside, we see the kind of work with which the rest of our tour of inspection has already made us familiar, that is, a wall from 50 to 60 feet high, with square towers some 20 feet higher than the rest of the work, projecting from the circuit of the wall at regular intervals of 33 yards. If we now pass in, not by the Porta Asinaria, which is closed, but by its representative the modern Porta San Giovanni, we find ourselves looking upon a structure greatly resembling one of the great Roman aqueducts, and probably often taken for such by travelers. We can see of course the backs of the square towers, but between every two of these there are seven tall arches about 33 feet high. A window through the wall near the bottom of each of these corresponds with an opening outside about half-way up the face of the wall, and thus lets us see that the level of the ground inside is from 20 to 30 feet higher than outside, the apparent height of the wall inside being of course reduced by the same amount. In the wall behind the arches we can see the holes marking the places where the ends of two sets of rafters, one above the other, have rested. Moreover, the piers which separate the arches are pierced by another set of tall thin arches at right angles to the others. A glance at the accompanying engravings will give a clearer idea of the construction of the walls than a page of description. The meaning of all these indications evidently is that a corridor or covered way ran round the whole inner circuit of the wall of Aurelian, where that was finished according to the design of the imperial builder. This gallery was two stories high between the towers; a third story would be added where these gave the needful height. Besides these covered galleries, which were used for the rapid transfer of troops from one part of the circuit to another, there was the regular path at the top of the walls, partially protected by battlements, on which the defenders were doubtless mustered when actual fighting was going forward.

For our knowledge of the fortifications of the state of the city we are not entirely dependent on our present the eighth observation of the walls, battered as they have been by the storms of the Middle Ages, and still more grievously as they have suffered at the hands of restorers and modernizers in the last three centuries. The 'Pilgrim of Einsiedeln', as he is conventionally termed, a visitor to Rome in the eighth or ninth century, recorded the most noteworthy objects of the Eternal City in a MS. which is preserved in the monastery of Einsiedeln in Switzerland. Among other information, he gives us the precise number of the towers, the battlements, and the loopholes in each section of the wall, including even the sanitary arrangements rendered necessary by the permanent presence of a large body of troops. It has been generally supposed that the Einsiedeln Pilgrim himself counted the towers of the sacred city of St. Peter; but one of our best German authorities suggests, with great probability, that he is really transcribing some much earlier official document, possibly that drawn up by the architects of Honorius at the beginning of the fifth century.

While Belisarius is repairing the moldering walls and assigning to the rude cohorts of his many-nationed army their various duties in the anticipated siege, we may allow ourselves to cast a hasty glance over the city which he has set himself to defend. A hasty glance, for this is not the time nor the place for minute antiquarian discussion; yet a glance of some sad and earnest interest, since we know that this is the last time that Rome in her glory will be seen by mortal man. The things which have befallen her up to this time have been only slight and transitory shocks, which have left no lasting dint upon her armor—Alarics burning of the palace of Sallust, Gaiserics half-accomplished spoliation of the golden roof of the temple of Jupiter Capitolinus, some havoc wrought in the insolence of their triumph by the *foederati* of Ricimer. More destructive, no doubt, was the slow process of denudation already commenced by the unpatriotic hands of the Romans themselves, and only partially checked by the decrees of Majorian and Theodoric. Still, as a whole, Rome the Golden City, the City of Consuls and Emperors, the City of Cicero's orations, of Horace's idle perambulations, of Trajan's magnificent constructions, yet stood when the Gothic war began. In the squalid, battered, depopulated, cluster of ruins, over which twenty-eight years later sounded the heralds' trumpets proclaiming that the Gothic war was ended, it would have been hard for Cicero, Horace, or Trajan to recognize his home. Classical Rome we are looking on for the last time; the Rome of the Middle Ages, the city of sacred shrines and relics and pilgrimages, is about to take her place.

It is impossible not to regret that Procopius has allowed himself to say so little as to the impression made on him by Rome. He must have entered the city soon after his chief, travelling by the Appian Way, the smooth and durable construction of which moved him to great admiration. But of the city itself, except of its gates and walls in so far as these require description in order to illustrate the siege, he has very little to say. It is easy to understand his silence. Most authors shrink from writing about the obvious and well-known. It would perhaps be easier to meet with ten vivid descriptions of the Island of Skye than one of the Strand or Cheapside. But not the less is it a loss for us that that quick and accurate observer, the Herodotus of the Post-Christian age, has not recorded more of his impressions of the streets, the buildings, and the people of Rome. Let us endeavor, however, to put ourselves in his place, and to reconstruct the city, at least in general outline, as he must have beheld it.

Journeying, as it is most probable that Procopius did, by the Appian Way, he would enter Rome by the gate then called the Porta Appia, but now the Porta di San Sebastiano, one of the finest of the still remaining entrances through the wall of Aurelian, with two noble towers, square within and semicircular without, the upper part of which, according to a careful English observer, bears traces of the restoring hand of Theodoric. Immediately after entering the city, Procopius would find himself passing under the still-preserved Arch of Drusus; and those of Trajan and Verus, spanning the intra-mural portion of the Appian Way, would before long attract his notice. This portion of the city, now so desolate and empty of inhabitants, was then probably thickly sown with the houses of the lower order of citizens.

High on his left, when he had proceeded somewhat more than half-a-mile, rose the mighty pile known to the ancients as the Thermae Antoninianae, and to the moderns as the Baths of Caracalla. Even in its ruins this building gives to the spectator an almost overwhelming idea of vastness and solidity. But when Procopius first saw it, the 1600 marble seats for bathers were probably all occupied, the gigantic swimming-bath was filled with clear cold water from the Marcian aqueduct, the great circular *Caldarium*, 160 feet in diameter, showed dimly through the steam the forms of hundreds of bathing Romans. Men were wrestling in the Palaestra and walking up and down in the Peristyle connected with the baths. Polished marble and deftly wrought mosaics lined the walls and covered the floors. At every turn one came upon some priceless work of art, like the Farnese Bull, the Hercules, the Flora, those statues the remnants of which, dug out of these ruins as from an unfailing quarry, have immortalized the names of Papal Nephews and made the fortunes of the museums of Bourbon Kings.

And now, as the traveler moved on, there rose more and more proudly above him the hill which has become for all later ages synonymous with regal power and magnificence, the imperial Palatine. Not as now, with only a villa and a convent standing erect upon it, the rest, grass and wild-flowers, and ruins for the most part not rising above the level of the ground, the whole hill was crowded with vast palaces, in which each successive dynasty had endeavored to outshine its predecessor in magnificence. Here, first, rose the tall but perhaps somewhat barbarous edifice with which Severus had determined to arrest the attention of his fellow-provincials from Africa travelling along the Appian Way, in order that their first question about Rome might be answered by his name. Just below it was the mysterious Septizonium, the work of the same Emperor, the porch of his palace and the counterpart of his tomb, of whose seven sets of columns, rising tier above tier, three were yet remaining only three centuries ago, when the remorseless Sixtus V transported them to the Vatican. Behind the palace of Severus, on the summit of the Palatine, were visible the immense banqueting halls of the Flavian Emperors, Vespasian and Domitian; behind them again the more modest house of Tiberius, and the labyrinth of apartments reared by the crazy Caligula.

In what condition are we to suppose that all these imperial dwellings were maintained when the troops of the Eastern Caesar came to reclaim them for their lord? Certainly not with all that untarnished magnificence which they possessed before the troubles of the third century commenced; hardly even with the show of affluence which they may still have worn when Constantius visited Rome in 357. Two centuries had elapsed since then—two centuries of more evil than good fortune—centuries in which the struggle for mere existence had left the rulers of the State little money or time to spare for repairs or decorations. But nothing, it may fairly be argued, had yet occurred to bring these massive piles into an obviously ruinous condition. If the comparison may be allowed, these dwellings on the Palatine probably presented in the state apartments that dingy appearance of faded greatness which one sees in the country-house of a noble family long resident abroad, but externally they had lost nothing of the stateliness with which they were meant to impress the mind of the beholder.

If Procopius ascended to the summit of the Palatine he may perchance have seen from thence, in the valley of the Circus Maximus, between the Palatine and Aventine hills, a chariot-race exhibited by the General to keep the populace in good-humor.

Here the Byzantine official would feel himself to be at once at home. Whether he favored the Blue or the Green faction we know not (though his animosity against Theodora makes us inclined to suspect him of sympathy with the Greens), but to whichsoever he belonged he could see his own faction striving for victory, and would hear, from at any rate a large portion of the crowd, the shouts with which they hailed the triumph, or the groans with which they lamented the defeat, of their favorite color.

Continuing his journey, the historian passed under the eastern summit of the Palatine, and then beneath the Arch of Constantine, that Arch which stands at this day comparatively undefaced, showing how the first Christian emperor purloined the work of the holier heathen Trajan to commemorate his own less worthy victories. Emerging from the shadow of the Arch he stood before the Flavian Amphitheatre and looked up to the immense Colossus of Nero, that statue of the Sun-god 120 feet in height, towering almost as high as the mighty edifice itself, to which it gave its best-known name, the Colosseum. It is generally felt that the Colosseum is one of those buildings which has gained by ruin. The topmost story, consisting, not of arches like the three below it, but of mere blank wall-spaces divided by pilasters, must have had when unbroken a somewhat heavy appearance; while, on the other hand, no beholder of the still perfect building could derive that impression of massive strength which we gain by looking, through the very chasms and rents in its outer shell, at the gigantic circuit of its concentric ellipses, at the massive walls radiating upwards and outwards upon which the seats of its 87,000 spectators rested. Altogether there is a pathetic majesty in the ruined Colosseum which can hardly have belonged to it in its days of prosperity, and, as one is almost inclined to say, of vulgar self-assertion.

But if this be true of the Colosseum itself, it is not true of the surrounding objects. The great Colossus has already been referred to. It is now represented only by a shapeless and unsightly heap of stones which once formed part of its pedestal. The ugly conical mass of brickwork near the same spot, and known as the Meta Sudans, was a beautiful upspringing fountain thirty or forty feet high when Procopius passed that way.

Eastwards, on the Oppian hill, stretched the long line of the Thermae Titi, the baths reared by Titus above the vast ruins of the Golden House of Nero. Immediately in front of the Colosseum (on the north-west) was the double temple reared by Hadrian in honor of Venus and Rome, perhaps one of the most beautiful edifices in the whole enclosure of the city. It was composed of two temples placed back to back. In one was the statue of Venus the Prosperous (Venus Felix), looking towards the Colosseum, in the other Roma Eterna sat gazing towards her own Capitol. In the curvilinear pediment of the latter was a frieze, according to the opinion of some archaeologists representing Mars caressing Rhea Sylvia, and the wolf suckling their heroic offspring. Around the whole structure ran a low colonnade containing four hundred pillars.

The famous Sacred Way, where once Horace loitered, a well-marked street, not as now a mere track through the midst of desolation, led the historian up to the marble arch of Titus. Here he doubtless looked, as we may yet look, upon the representation of the seven-branched candlestick and the other spoils of Jerusalem, the strange story of whose wanderings he has himself recorded for us in his history of the Vandalic War.

Descending the slope of the Via Sacra, and having on his right the lofty Basilica of Constantine, whose gigantic arches (long but erroneously called the Temple of Peace) stand on their hill over against the Palatine, and seem to assert a predominance over its yet remaining ruins, Procopius now with each downward step saw the glories of the Roman Forum more fully revealed. On his left the temple of the Great Twin Brethren, three of whose graceful Corinthian columns still survive, a well-known object to all visitors to the Forum. Hard by, the fountain from which the celestial horsemen gave their horses to drink after the battle of Lake Regillus. Further on, the long colonnades of the Basilica of Julius, four law-courts under the same roof. On his right, the tall columns of the Temple of Antoninus and Faustina, perhaps already supporting the roof of a Christian shrine, though not the unsightly edifice which at present clings to and defaces them; the chapel of the great Julius, the magnificent Basilica of Emilius; and, lastly, those two venerable objects, centers for so many ages of all the political life of Rome, the Senate-house and the Rostra. The Senate was still a living body, though its limbs had long been shaken by the palsies of a timid old age; but the days when impassioned orators thundered to the Roman people from the lofty Rostra had long passed away. Yet we may be permitted to conjecture that Procopius, with that awe-struck admiration which he had for "the Romans of old time" gazed upon those weatherworn trophies of the sea and mused on the strange contradictoriness of Fate, which had used all the harangues of those impetuous orators as instruments to fashion the serene and silent despotism of Justinian.

At the end of the Forum, with an embarrassment of wealth which perplexes us even in their ruins, rise the Arch of Septimius Severus, the Temple of Concord, the Temple of Vespasian, the ill-restored Temple of Saturn. Between them penetrated the Clivus Capitolinus, up which once slowly mounted the car of many a triumphing general. Behind all stretched the magnificent background of the Capitoline Hill, on the left-hand summit of which stood the superb mass of the Temple of Jupiter Capitolinus, robbed by Gaiseric of half its golden tiles, but still resplendent under the western sun Then came the saddle-shaped depression faced by the long Tabularium: and then the right-hand summit of the Capitoline, crowned by the Temple of Juno Moneta.

We have supposed our historian to deviate a little from the straight path in order to explore to the uttermost the buildings of the Republican Forum; but as his business lies at the northern extremity of the city, he must retrace a few of his steps and avail himself of the line of communication between the Via Sacra and the Via Flaminia which was opened up by the beneficent despotism of the Emperors. That is to say, he must leave the Forum of the Republic and traverse the long line of the spacious and well-planned Fora of the Caesars. In no part is the contrast between ancient and modern Rome more humiliating than here. In our day, a complex of mean and irregular streets almost entirely destitute of classical interest or mediaeval picturesqueness, fills up the interval between the Capitoline and the Quirinal hills. The deeply cut entablature of the Temple of Minerva resting upon the two half-buried 'Colonnacce' in front of the baker's shop, the three pillars of the Temple of Mars Ultor, the great feudal fortress of the Tor de Conti, and that most precious historical monument the Column of Trajan, alone redeem this region from utter wearisomeness. But this space, now so crowded and so irregular, was once the finest bit of architectural landscape-gardening in Rome. The Forum of Vespasian, the Forum of Nerva, the Forum of Augustus, the Forum of Julius, the Forum of Trajan, a series of magnificent squares and arcades, opening one into the other, occupying a space some 600 yards long by 100 wide and terminating in the mighty granite pillars of the Temple of Trajan, produced on the mind of the beholder the same kind of effect, but on a far grander scale, which is wrought by Trafalgar Square in London or the Place de la Concorde in Paris. Let not the modern traveler, who, passing from the Corso to the Colosseum, is accosted by his driver with the glibly uttered words 'Foro Trajano' suppose that the little oblong space, with a few pillar-bases which he beholds at the foot of the memorable Column, is indeed even in ruin the entire Forum of the greatest of the Emperors. The column is Trajan's column doubtless, though

> 'Apostolic statues climb
> The imperial urn whose ashes slept sublime
> Buried in air, the deep blue sky of Rome,
> And looking to the stars'.

But the so-called 'Foro Trajano' is only a small transverse section of one member of the Trajanic series, the Basilica Ulpia. The column, as is known, measured the height of earth which had to be dug away from a spur of the Capitoline hill in order to form the Forum. Between it and the Basilica Ulpia rose the two celebrated libraries of Greek and Latin authors, and between these two buildings stood once, and probably yet stood in the days of Procopius, that' everlasting statue of brass which by the Senate's orders was erected in honor of Sidonius, Poet-laureate and son-in-law of an Emperor. In those Libraries Procopius, in the intervals of the business and peril of the siege, may often have wandered in order to increase his acquaintance with the doings of the Romans of old. What treasures of knowledge, now for ever lost to the world, were still enshrined in those apartments! There all the rays of classical Art and Science were gathered into a focus. More important perhaps for us, all that the Greeks and Romans knew (and it was not a little, though carelessly recorded) concerning the Oriental civilization which preceded theirs, and concerning the Teutonic barbarism which encompassed it, was still contained in those magnificent literary collections. There was the Chaldean history of Berosus, there were the authentic Egyptian king-lists of Manetho, there was Livy's story of the last days of the Republic and the first days of the Empire, there was Tacitus's full history of the conquest of Britain, all that Ammianus could tell about the troubles of the third century and the conversion of Constantine, all that Cassiodorus had written about the royal Amals and the dim original of the Goths. All this perished, apparently in those twenty years of desolating war which now lie before us. It may be doubted whether for us the loss of the *Bibliothecae Ulpiae* is not even more to be regretted than that of the Library of Alexandria.

Ammianus tells us that when the Emperor Constantius visited Rome he gazed with admiration on the Capitol, the Colosseum, the Pantheon, and the Theatre of Pompey, but still with admiration which could express itself in words. "But when", says the historian, "he came to the Forum of Trajan, that structure unique in all the world, and, as I cannot but think, marvelous in the eyes of the Divinity himself, he beheld with silent amazement those gigantic interfacings of stones which it is past the power of speech to describe, and which no mortal must in future hope to imitate. Hopeless of ever attempting any such work himself, he would only look at the horse of Trajan, placed in the middle of the vestibule and bearing the statue of the Emperor. 'That', said Constantius, 'I can imitate, and I will'. Hormisdas, a royal refugee from the court of Persia, replied, with his nation's quickness of repartee: 'But first, 0 Emperor, if you can do so, order a stable to be built as fair as that before us, that your horse may have as fine an exercising ground as the one we are now looking upon'."

Emerging from the imperial Fora, Procopius would now enter upon the Via Lata, broad as its name denotes, one of the longest streets, if not the longest, in Rome, and very nearly corresponding to the modern Corso. The Subura, which lay a little to the east of the Forum of Augustus, was once at any rate one of the most thickly peopled districts of Rome, and we shall perhaps not be wrong in assuming that in the regions east of the Via Lata, upon the Quirinal, Viminal, and Esquiline Hills, where the tall buildings of the Fourth Rome, the Rome of Victor Emmanuel and United Italy, are now arising, the humbler classes of the Second or Imperial Rome had chiefly fixed their abodes.

On the left side of the Via Lata, where the Third or Papal Rome has spun its web of streets thickest, all or nearly all was yet given up to pleasure. This was the true West End of Rome, the region in which her parks and theatres were chiefly placed. Here were the great open spaces of the Campus Martius and Campus Flaminius; here two racecourses, those of Flaminius and Domitian; here the great theatres of Pompey, of Balbus, and of Marcelus, and the Porticoes of the Argonauts and of Octavia. Altogether it was a region devoted to pleasure and idleness by the side of the tawny Tiber, and most unlike the closely-built and somewhat dingy quarters of the city which now occupy it.

As Procopius moved along the straight course of the Via Lata his eye would probably be caught by the airy dome of the Pantheon of Agrippa, hovering over the buildings on his left. He would thread the Arch of Claudius, would stand at the foot of the Column of Marcus Aurelius, and then pass beneath that Emperors Arch of Triumph. Two mighty sepulchers could then arrest his attention: the Tomb of Hadrian seeming by its massive bulk almost close at hand, though on the other bank of the Tiber; and the Mausoleum of Augustus rising immediately on his left, a rotunda of white marble below, a green and shady pleasance above, recalling, by its wonderful admixture of Nature and Art, the far-famed Hanging Gardens of Babylon.

And now at length his never-to-be-forgotten first view of Rome was drawing to a close. The soon-sinking sun of late autumn warned him, perchance, to quicken his pace. He bore off to the right: by some steep steps where the receivers of the public alimony were wont to cluster, he climbed the high garden-decked Pincian. He entered the palace, bowed low before Belisarius, lower yet before the imperious Antonina, and received the General's orders as to the share of work that he was to undertake in connection with the provisionment of the city. Such is an account, imaginary indeed, but not improbable, of the circumstances in which the soldier-secretary first entered and first beheld Rome reunited to the Roman Empire.

It remains for us briefly to notice the rising Christian importance of the Christian buildings of Rome, of though we will here dispense with the imaginary companionship of Procopius, whose somewhat skeptical temper, well acquainted with the subjects in dispute among Christians, but determined to say as little as possible about them, holding it to be proof of a madman's folly to enquire into the nature of God, would make him an uncongenial guest at the sacred shrines. Of the five great patriarchal churches of Rome, three were beyond the walls of the city, and one was on its extreme verge. The last, and at the period that we have now reached still the foremost in dignity, is St. John Lateran, or the Basilica of Constantine, the so-called Mother-Church of Christendom. It stands near the Asinarian Gate, on the Property which Fausta, the unhappy wife of Constantine, inherited from her father Maximian, and which had once belonged to the senatorial family of the Laterani; and it formed the subject of that real and considerable donation of the first Christian Emperor to the Bishops of Rome which later ages distorted into a quasi-feudal investiture of the Imperial City.

Upon the Vatican Hill, outside the walls of St. Peters, Aurelian, looking down upon the Tiber and the Tomb of Hadrian, rose the five long aisles, the semicircular apse, and the nearly square entrance-Atrium of the Basilica of St. Peter. The region immediately surrounding it was perhaps still called the Gardens of Nero. It is certain that the reason for placing the Basilica on that spot was that there was the traditional site of the martyrdom of the Apostle, as well as of the sufferings of the nameless Christian crowd who, dressed in cloaks covered with pitch and set on fire, served as living torches to light that throned Satan to his revels and his chariot-races on the Vatican-mount.

Outside the gate of Ostia, and also near the traditional scene of the martyrdom of the Apostle to whom it was dedicated, stood the noble Basilica of St. Paul. This edifice, commenced by Theodosius, completed by Honorius, and having received the finishing touches to its decorations at the hand of Placidia under the guidance of Pope Leo, subsisted with but little change to the days of our fathers. The lamentable fire of 1823, by which the greater part of it was destroyed, took from us the most interesting relic of Christian Imperial Rome. Happily the restoration, though it cannot give us back the undiminished interest of the earlier building, has been carried on with admirable fidelity to the original design.

This cannot be said of the Liberian Basilica, the great church now known as S. Maria Maggiore, which, standing high on the Esquiline Hill, looked down westwards on the crowded Subura, and northwards towards the palatial Baths of Diocletian. The outside of the building has sustained the extremity of insult and wrong at the hands of the tasteless pseudo-classical restorers of the eighteenth century; and the inside, though not absolutely ruined by them, though its mosaics are still visible and much of its long colonnade still remains, shows too plainly how unsafe were the treasures of Christian antiquity in the hands of the conceited architects of the Renaissance.

The last of the great Basilicas, that of the martyred S. Lawrence, one mile outside the Tiburtine Gate, has suffered less ravage at the hands of restorers. It was in the thirteenth century singularly re-arranged and transformed, its apse being pulled down and turned into a nave, and its original vestibule being turned into a choir: still we have substantially before us the same church which was surrounded by the Gothic armies in their siege of Rome. With that blending of the old and of the very new which at once charms and bewilders the visitor to Rome, we have here again an inscription recording the work of 'the pious mind of Placidia' under the guidance of Attila's Pope Leo, and in the crypt the just erected tomb of Pio Nono. The latter is so placed as to command a view of the slab of marble dyed red with the blood of the deacon Laurentius, martyr for the faith under the Emperor Claudius Gothicus. This marble slab was a favorite relic with the late Pontiff.

Besides these live great patriarchal churches there were twenty-eight parish churches, known by the technical name of Tituli, from which the Cardinal-presbyters of a later age took their ecclesiastical designations. Some of these which have been preserved to this day are more interesting than the churches of greater dignity, having by reason of their comparative insignificance escaped the hand of the Renaissance destroyer.

The main features, which were evidently common to all the Christian edifices of Rome in the fifth and sixth centuries, were (1) a long line of columns, not by any means always uniform or of the same order of architecture, and generally taken from the outside of some heathen temple; (2) a semicircular apse at the eastern end, in which the bishop or presbyter sat surrounded by his inferior clergy, as the Roman magistrate in the original Basilica sat surrounded by the various members of his 'officium'; (3) an arch in front of the apse, the idea of which was probably borrowed from the triumphal arches of the Emperors; (4) upon the arch, upon the apse, on the flat wall-space above the arches, in fact wherever they could conveniently be introduced, a blaze of bright mosaics, like those still preserved to us at Ravenna and in a very few of these Roman churches. The subjects represented are the Savior, the symbols of the four Evangelists, the twelve Apostles under the guise of sheep, the mystic cities Jerusalem and Bethlehem, the Jordan and the four rivers of Paradise, and other emblems of the same character.

The fact that the columns of these churches were as a rule taken from heathen temples must of course qualify to some extent the statement that the splendor of the city was undiminished when Procopius entered it. Temples, not merely abandoned to silence and solitude, but rudely stripped of their pillared magnificence, must in many places have offended the eye of a beholder more sensitive to beauty than to religious enthusiasm. Still upon the whole, and with this abatement, we may repeat our proposition that it was the stately Rome of Consuls and Emperors which men then looked upon, and which after the middle of the sixth century they never beheld again.

'Alas, for Earth, for never shall we see
That brightness in her eye she bore when
Rome was free.'

CHAPTER V.

THE LONG SIEGE BEGUN.

Vacillation and feebleness of purpose marked the counsels of Witigis, as the consequences of the fatal error which he had committed in abandoning Rome made themselves manifest to his mind. At first his chief desire was to wait till his forces should be strengthened by the return of Marcias with the considerable army which he had under his command for the defence of Gothic Gaul against the Franks. Then came tidings which showed that Belisarius felt his hold of Rome so secure that he might venture onwards into the Tuscan province. Bessas was sent to Narni, about fifty miles from Rome, the first strong position on the Flaminian Way. The inhabitants being well affected to the imperial cause, he occupied this post without difficulty. Constantine, the rival of Bessas in martial glory, was sent with some of the body guards of Belisarius, and other troops, among whom figured several Huns, in order to seize some positions yet further from the city. Spoleto, twenty-five miles further from Rome on the Flaminian Way, was occupied by a garrison. Etrurian Perugia on her lofty hill-top, some forty miles further north than Spoleto, but lying a little off the great Flaminian highway, was next taken possession of, and here Constantine fixed his headquarters. The troops which Witigis dispatched against Perugia were defeated, and their generals were sent as prisoners to Rome.

The tidings of these reverses roused Witigis to more vigorous action; but, strangely enough, after tarrying so long in order to be joined by the recalled troops from Gaul, he must now weaken himself still further by sending a division into Dalmatia. It is true that of the two generals dispatched on this errand, one, Asinarius, was sent round the head of the Adriatic Gulf, to gather round his standard the barbarians who dwelt in the districts which we now call Carniola and Croatia. But the other, Uligisal, who sailed straight to Dalmatia, must have taken with him some troops who could be ill-spared from the defence of Italy. It is not necessary to trouble the reader with the details of these ill-advised, and in the end resultless, operations on the east of the Adriatic. The Goths met with reverses, but succeeded for some time in closely investing Salona both by sea and land. he Dalmatian capital, however, fell not; and after a siege of uncertain duration, the Gothic soldiers probably recrossed the Adriatic to take part in the more urgent work of resisting Belisarius in Italy.

About this time word was brought to the Gothic King that the citizens of Rome viewed with impatience the presence and the exactions of the imperial army. That there was some foundation of truth for this statement will appear by a reference to the last chapter; but it was evidently much exaggerated, and it by no means followed that the citizens who grumbled the most bitterly at the general's preparations for the siege would lift a finger for the surrender of the city to the justly enraged Gothic army. However, the tidings kindled immediately a flame of hope in the feebly forecasting soul of Witigis: and now he, who had wasted precious months in purposeless inaction, thought every day an age till he had recovered possession of the abandoned city. With the whole armed nation of the Goths, (except the division that had been ordered to

Dalmatia) he marched southwards in hot haste along the Flaminian Way. The numbers of his army amounted, if we trust the estimate of Procopius, to 150,000 men. The historian evidently uses round numbers, and has probably exaggerated the size of the besieging host in order to increase the fame of Belisarius; but there can be no doubt that Witigis was followed by a very large army, outnumbering many times over the little band of the Imperialists. The proportions of infantry and cavalry are not stated, but we are told that the greater number, both of the horses and men, were completely encased in defensive armor.

Once started on his march, Witigis was tormented by a fond fear that Belisarius would escape him, and was earnest in his prayers by night and by day that he might behold the walls of Rome while yet the Imperial forces stood behind them. On the journey the army fell in with a priest who had just quitted the city, and who was brought with shouts to the King's tent. "Is Belisarius yet in Rome?" asked Witigis, breathless with anxiety. "Ay, and likely to remain there", was the answer of the priest, who had a better idea of the state of the game than his questioner.

Still, the Imperial general was for a moment perplexed by the tidings that so vast a host was rolling on towards him. It was not for his own position that he was in fear, but he felt that he could scarcely hold the latest conquests in Tuscany in the face of such an army. After some anxious deliberation he ordered Constantine and Bessas to garrison three towns only, and then to fall back on Borne. The three towns were Spoleto, Perugia, and Narni, all situated on the top of high hills, and therefore easily defended. Narni especially, built on

>'that grey crag where girt with towers
>The fortress of Nequinum lowers
>O'er the pale waves of Nar,'

and commanding the entrance to a deep and picturesque gorge spanned by the stately bridge of Augustus (one of whose arches still remains), struck the mind of the historian by the grand inaccessibility of its position. Bessas, who lingered somewhat over the execution of the orders of his chief, had the excitement of a successful skirmish with the vanguard of the Gothic army before he retired from this fortress to Rome.

Notwithstanding the fact that these strongholds were in the possession of the enemy, Witigis appears to have pushed on by the Flaminian Way which winds at their feet; and was soon standing with his 150,000 men at the Etrurian end of the Milvian Bridge over the Tiber, two miles from Rome. This bridge, so well-known under its modern name of Ponte Molle to the fashionable loungers in Rome, is in its present shape the handiwork of Papal architects; but the foundations of the piers are ancient, and the general appearance of the six arches with which it spans the stream is not probably very different from that which it wore in the days of Belisarius. A bridge whose name had often been in the mouths of the Roman people in stirring times, in the crises of Punic wars and Catilinarian conspiracies, it had earned yet greater fame two centuries ago (A.D. 312) by the bloody battle fought under its parapets between the soldiers of Constantine and those of Maxentius, a battle the result of which ensured the triumph of Christianity through the whole Roman world, and which has been for this reason commemorated by Raffaele and Romano with splendid strength in the Stanze of the Vatican.

Expecting that the Goths would attempt to cross the river here, and anxious to retard their progress, though without hope of finally preventing them from reaching the eastern bank of the river, Belisarius had erected a fortress on the Etrurian bank, and decided to pitch his camp close to the stream on the Latian side, in order to overawe the barbarians by this show of confidence. And, indeed, the ardor of the Goths was not a little chilled when they saw the castle above, and the tawny river before them. They bivouacked between Monte Mario and the Tiber for the night, postponing till the morrow the assault on the bridge-fort. The night, however, brought gloomy forebodings to other hearts than theirs. It seemed to the garrison impossible that the bridge could be effectually defended against that vast horde of men whose camp-fires filled the plain. Twenty-two soldiers of the Roman army, themselves of barbarian origin, horsemen in the troop of Innocentius, went over to the foes and informed them of the state of discouragement which prevailed in the garrison. As night wore on, the rest of the men on duty in the bridge-fort deserted their post. They did not dare to show themselves in Rome, but slunk away to Campania. When day dawned the Goths marched without difficulty through the empty guard-house, across the undefended bridge, and now they stood on the eastern bank of the Tiber with no natural obstacle between them and Rome.

Little dreaming of the cowardice of the garrison, Belisarius, who thought the barbarians were still on the other side of the river, sent 1000 picked horsemen to the bridge-end to reconnoiter for a suitable camping-ground. They fell in with a party of the Gothic horsemen who had just crossed the bridge, and an equestrian battle followed. Then, says the historian, Belisarius forgot for a moment the discretion which ought to be manifested by a general, and by exposing himself like a common soldier brought the Imperial cause into the extremest peril. Springing upon his charger he hurried to the place whence the clash of arms was heard, and was soon in the thickest of the fight. His horse, a noble creature, which did everything that a horse could do to carry its rider harmless through the fray, was well known to all the army. Dark-roan, with a white star upon its forehead, it was called by the Greeks Phalius, and by the barbarians in the army Balan. The deserters knew the steed and his rider, and strove to direct the weapons of the Goths against them. "Balan! Balan! Aim for the horse with the white star" was their eager exclamation. The cry was caught up by the Goths, scarce one of whom understood its meaning. But they knew that the horse with the white star must carry some personage of importance: and "Balan! Balan!" resounded from a thousand Gothic throats through the confused roar of the battle. All their bravest thronged to the place, some with lances, some with swords, striving to transfix or to hew down the horse and his rider. To right, to left, Belisarius dealt his swashing blows. The best men of his bodyguard gathered round him, some protecting his body and that of his horse with their shields, others thrusting back the onset of the barbarians by impetuous counter-charges. It was a true Homeric battle, in which all that was most martial in the two armies was drawn to a single point, and on one group of fighting men rested the whole fortune of the day. At length Roman arms and Roman discipline prevailed. After a thousand Gothic warriors of the foremost rank and many of the bravest men of the Roman general's household had fallen, the barbarians fled to their camp, and Belisarius emerged absolutely unwounded from the fray.

When the fugitives reached the Gothic camp their comrades poured out in support of them. The Romans retreated to a hill near at hand, and here again a battle of cavalry took place, in which the deeds of greatest daring were wrought by a certain Valentine, who served in the humble capacity of groom to the son-in-law of Belisarius. Alone the brave menial charged an advancing squadron of the Goths, and rescued his comrades from imminent peril. The advance of the barbarians was, however, too strong to be resisted, and at length the whole Roman army, with Belisarius at their head, were in full flight to the walls of the city. They reached the Pincian Gate, which, from that memorable day, was long afterwards known by the name of the Gate of Belisarius. Down the sides of the fosse swarmed the crowd of fugitives, but only to find to their despair the folding doors of the Porta Pinciana obstinately closed against them. The hoars voice of Belisarius was heard, loudly and with dosed threats calling to the sentinels to open the gate, but in vain. In that face, all covered with sweat, and dust and gore, they did not recognize, now that twilight was coming on, the countenance of the general whom they had so often seen serene in his hours of triumph: his voice they could not distinguish through the din of the refluent tide of war. Above all, the terrible rumor had reached their ears, brought by the first fugitives from the field, that Belisarius, after performing prodigies of valor, had been left dead upon the plain. This thought most of all unnerved them. They were left, it seemed, without a general and without a plan, and as they stooped forward from the round towers by the gate, to see by the fading light how went the fortune of the fight, they felt themselves to be doomed men whose only chance of safety lay in keeping fast the doors by which, if opened, Goth and Roman would enter together.

    This was the state of affairs, the Roman soldiers huddled together under the wall, so close to one the another that they could hardly move, their comrades above refusing to open the gates, the Goths just preparing to rush down the fosse and make an exterminating charge, when the lost battle was retrieved by the wise rashness of Belisarius. Collecting his men into a small but orderly army he faced round and made a vigorous charge upon the pursuing Goths. Already thrown into disorder by the ardor of their pursuit, unable by the fading light to discern the small number of their foes, and naturally concluding that a new army was issuing from the gates of Rome to attack them, the barbarians turned and fled. Belisarius wisely pursued them but a short distance, reformed his ranks, and marched back in good order to the gate, where he had now no difficulty in obtaining an entrance. Thus did the battle, which had commenced at dawn and lasted till dark, end after all not disastrously for the Imperial troops. By universal consent the praise of highest daring on that day was awarded to two men, to Belisarius on the side of the Romans, and on that of the barbarians to a standard-bearer named Visandus. The latter was conspicuous in the thickest of the fight round Belisarius and the dark-roan steed, and it was not till he had received his thirteenth wound that he ceased from the combat. His victorious comrades saw and passed on from what they deemed to be the corpse of their champion; but three days after, when they came at their leisure to bury their dead, a soldier thought saw signs of life in the body of Visandus and implored him to speak. Hunger and a raging thirst prevented him from doing more than make one gasping request for water. When that was brought him consciousness fully returned, and he was able to be carried into the camp. He lived after this many years, having achieved great glory among his countrymen by his prowess and his narrow escape from death.

    For Belisarius, not even yet were the labors and anxieties of this long day ended. He mustered the soldiers and the greater part of the citizens upon the walls, and ordered them to kindle frequent fires along their circuit and to watch the whole night through. Then he went round the walls himself, arranging who was to be responsible for the defence of each portion, and especially which generals were to be on guard at each of the gates. While he was thus engaged, a messenger came in breathless haste from the Praenestine Gate at the south-east of the city to say that Bessas, who was commanding there, had learned that the enemy were pouring in by the Gate of St Pancratius on the other side of the Tiber. Hearing this, the officers round him besought him to save himself and the army by marching out at some other gate. Unshaken by these disastrous tidings, Belisarius calmly said that he did not believe the report. A horseman, dispatched with all speed to the Trastevere, returned with the welcome news that the enemy had not been seen in that part of the city. Belisarius improved the opportunity by issuing a general order that under no circumstances, not even if he heard that the Goths were inside the walls, was the officer entrusted with the defence of one gate to leave it in order to carry assistance to another. Each one was to attend to his own allotted portion of work and leave the care of the general defence to the commander-in-chief.

The earnest work of the defence was interrupted by the comedy of a harangue from a Gothic chief named Wacis, who, by order of Witigis, drew near to the walls. With much vehemence he inveighed against the faithlessness of the Romans, who had betrayed their brave Gothic defenders and handed themselves over, instead, to the guardianship of a company of Greeks, men who had hitherto never been heard of in Italy except as play-actors, mimics, or vagabond sailors. Belisarius bade the men on the walls to treat this tirade with silent contempt: and in truth, after the deeds of that day, to revive the taunts which had passed current for centuries against Grecian effeminacy was an impertinence which refuted itself. None the less, however, did the Roman citizens marvel at and secretly condemn the calm confidence of success, the absolute contempt for his foe which was displayed on this occasion by Belisarius, so lately a fugitive from the Gothic sword. He understood the rules of the game, however, better than they, and having repaired the error of the morning, knew that no second opportunity of the same kind would be afforded by him to the enemy.

And now, at last, when the night was already far advanced, was the general, who had fasted from early morning, prevailed on by his wife and friends to take some care for the refreshment of his body, hastily snatching a simple meal.

This memorable day was the beginning of the First Siege of Rome by the Ostrogoths, the longest and one of the deadliest that the Eternal City has ever endured. It began in the early days of March 537, and was not to end till a year and nine days later in the March of 538. When morning dawned, the Goths, who entertained no doubt of an early success against so large and helpless a city, proceeded to entrench themselves in seven camps, six on the eastern and one on the western side of the Tiber. They did not thus accomplish a perfect blockade of the city, but they did obstruct, in a tolerably effectual manner, eight out of its fourteen gates. As frequent reference in the course of this history will be made to one or other of these gates, it will be well to give a list of them here, with their ancient and modern names, printing those that were obstructed by the Goths in italics.

Ancient Name.	Modern Name.	No. of Towers.
East bank of the Tiber :		
1. Porta Flaminia	P. del Popolo	51
2. *Porta Solaria*	P. Salara.	10
3. *Porta Nomentana* near to	P. Pia.	57
4. *Porta Tiburtina*	P. San Lorenzo.	19
5. *Porta Labicana*		

6. Porta Praenestina)	P. Maggiore	26
7. Porta Asinaria near to	P. San Giovanni	20
8. Porta Metrovia (or Metronia)	Closed.	20
9. Porta Latina	Closed.	12
10. Porta Appia	P. San Sebastiano.	49
11. Porta Ostiensis	P. San Paolo.	49, 35 to the Tiber.

West bank of the Tiber:

12. Porta Portuensis, near to	P. Portese.	29.
13. Porta Aureltal (or Sancti Pancratii)	P. SanPancrazio.	24 to the Tiber
14. Porta Cornelia (or Sancti Petri)	Destroyed (opposite Ponte S. Angelo).	16

381.

To give some idea of the distance of one gate from another the number of square towers between each pair of gates is added on the authority of the Pilgrim of Einsiedeln. The intervals between the towers varied from 100 to 300 and even 400 feet, the wider spaces being chiefly found on the west side of the Tiber.

Between the Flaminian and the Salarian gates stood the somewhat smaller Porta Pinciana, now closed, which was the scene of some hot encounters during the siege. It is possible that Procopius may have reckoned the Porta Pinciana as one of the fourteen gates belonging to the whole circuit of the walls, and one of the six gates on the eastern side of the Tiber that were blocked by the enemy. In that case we must treat the Labicana and Praenestina as one gate, which their close proximity to one another justifies us in doing. It seems more probable, however, that Procopius, who is generally very careful to denote the Pincian by the term gate-let, and who informs us that there were fourteen gates "besides certain gate-lets" did not mean to reckon the Pincian among the great gates of Rome.

The total circuit of the walls of Aurelian and Honorius was about twelve miles. The space blockaded by the Goths amounted probably to tent of the about two-thirds of this circumference. The camps of the barbarians were works of some solidity. Deep fosses were dug around them: the earth dug out of the fosse was piled on its inner face so as to make a high rampart, and a fence of sharp stakes was inserted therein. Altogether, as Procopius says, these Gothic camps lacked none of the defenses of a regular castle. A careful observer (Mr. Parker), who has had the advantage of several years' residence in Rome, considers that the traces of all these camps are still visible. Without venturing to pronounce an opinion on a question requiring such minute local knowledge, it will not be amiss to place before the reader the result of his investigations. In any event the Gothic camps must have been near the sites which he has assigned to them.

The first camp was placed within a stone's throw of the Porta Flaminia (to the north-east), in the grounds which formerly belonged to the villa of the Domitii. This camp was obviously required in order to obstruct the great northern road of Rome and to threaten the gate leading to it.

The second, probably the largest and most important of all, was erected in what are now the gardens of the Villa Borghese. The woods and shady coverts of this, which is one of the most beautiful of the parks surrounding the walls of Rome, make it now very difficult to get a clear view of the ground and to reconstruct in imagination the scene of so many terrible encounters. Still it is possible to behold the quickly-rising ground on which the camp was placed. The raised platform for the tents to stand upon (one of these tents was probably the royal pavilion of Witigis) and the cliffs around it are (says Mr. Parker) very visible. Clearly seen from it were doubtless the high walls of the city, the Pincian gate-let, and the Pincian gardens surrounding the palace in which Belisarius dwelt.

The third camp, concealed from view by modern walls, says Parker, lay on the left hand of th Via Nomentana, about half-way (or rather less) to the ancient church of St. Agnes outside the walls.

Rounding the sharp projecting angle of the Castra Praetoria we come to two camps, fourth and fifth, one on the north and one on the south of the Via Tiburtina. The fifth, says Parker, is very near to the great church and burial-ground of St. Laurence outside the walls, from which the cliffs of it are distinctly seen. The fourth is apparently placed by him only about a couple of hundred yards away near the Villa Santo Spirito. It may perhaps be doubted whether Parker is right in putting these two camps so near to one another.

The sixth, and last on this side of the river, is placed about half-a-mile from the south-eastern corner of the walls along the Via Praenestina.

On the other side of the Tiber the Goths built a camp to assure their hold upon the Milvian Bridge and to threaten the gates of St. Peter and St. Pancratius. We are told that it was in the Campus Neronis. It must have been therefore not far from where the Vatican palace now stands: but after the vast changes which the Popes, from the fifteenth century onwards, have made in that region, it would be futile now to look for its remains. Marcias, who had by this time arrived with the troops from Gaul, took the command of this trans-Tiberine camp. A Gothic officer was placed in charge of each of the other camps, Witigis having a general oversight of all on the east of the Tiber and the particular oversight of one, which, as has been before said, was probably that in the Borghese gardens.

On the Roman side Belisarius himself took the command of the portion of the wall between the Pincian gate-let and the Salarian gate; the part which was considered least secure, and where the Roman opportunities for a sally were the most inviting. The Praenestine Gate (Maggiore) was assigned to Bessas, the Flaminia (P. del Popolo) to Constantine. The last-named gate was blocked up with large stones (perhaps taken from the old wall of King Servius), so that it might not be possible for traitors to open it to the enemy. For, on account of the close proximity of the first Gothic camp, a surprise at this gate was considered more probable than at any other.

The building of the seven camps of the barbarians was a temporary expedient, and when the war was over the traces of them, except for the eye of an archaeologist, soon passed away. Not so, however, with the next operation resorted to by the Goths, which may be said to have influenced the social life of Rome, and through Rome the social life of the kingdoms of Western Europe, throughout the ten centuries which we call the Middle Ages. This operation was the cutting of the Aqueducts. A deed of such far-reaching importance requires to be treated of in a chapter by itself; nor will the reader possibly object to turn for a little space from the tale of barbarous battle to the story of the wise forethought of the Romans of ancient days the builders of the mighty water-courses which fed the Eternal City.

CHAPTER VI.

THE CUTTING OF THE AQUEDUCTS.

The least observant visitor to Rome is awed and impressed by the ruins of the Aqueducts. As he stands on the top of the Colosseum, or as he is carried swiftly past them on the railway to Naples, he sees their long arcades stretching away in endless perspective across the monotonous Campagna, and, ignorant perhaps of the valuable service which some of them yet render to the water-supply of Rome, he is only touched and saddened by the sight of so much wasted labor, by the ever-recurring thought of the nothingness of man. But when he comes to enquire a little more closely into the history of these wonderful structures, he finds, not only that the ignorance of scientific principles to which it was once the fashion to attribute their origin, did not exist; not only that the Popes of later days have succeeded in restoring a few of them so as to make them practically useful in quenching the thirst of the modern Roman: but also that the aqueducts have a curious and interesting history of their own which admirably illustrates the life and progress of the great Republic. As her fortunes mounted, so the arches rose, higher and higher. As her dominion extended, so those mighty filaments stretched further and further up into the hills. Like a hand upon the clock-face of Empire was the ever-rising level of the water-supply of Rome.

For four hundred and forty-two years, that is during the whole period of the Kings and for the Rome before the first two centuries of the Republic, the Romans were satisfied with such water as they obtain from the tawny Tiber; from the wells, of which there was a considerable number; from the unspringing fountains, many of which were the objects of a simple religious worship; and from the cisterns in which they collected the not very abundant rain-fall.

At length, in the year 312 *BC*, when the Second Samnite War was verging towards its successful conclusion, the great Censor Appius Claudius bestowed upon Rome her first great road and her first aqueduct, both known through all after ages by his name. He went for his water-supply seven miles along the road to Palestrina, to a spot now called La Rustica, about half way between Rome and the hills, and hence, by a circuitous underground channel more than eleven miles long, he brought the water to the city. Not till it got to the Porta Capena, one of the old gates of the city on its southern side, did it emerge into the light of day, and then it was carried along arches only for the space of sixty paces. Thus, according to our modern use of the term, it might be considered as rather a conduit than an aqueduct. It has been remarked upon as an interesting fact that Appius Claudius, the first Roman author in verse and prose, the first considerable student of Greek literature, was also the first statesman to take thought for the water-supply of Rome. And further, that he whose censorship was marked by a singular coalition between the haughtiest of the aristocracy and the lowest of the commons, and who was suspected of aiming at the tyranny by the aid of the latter class, carried the water to that which was not only physically but socially one of the lowest quarters of Rome, the humble dwellings between the Aventine and the Caelian hills.

Forty years later, a much bolder enterprise in hydraulics was successfully attempted, when the stream afterwards known as the *Anio Vetus* was brought into the city by a course of 43 miles, at a level of 147 feet above the sea, or nearly 100 feet higher than the Aqua Appia. The last public act of the blind old Appius Claudius (the builder of the first aqueduct) had been to adjure the Roman Senate to listen to no proposals of peace from King Pyrrhus so long as a single Epirote soldier remained on the soil of Italy. Eight years later, when the war with Pyrrhus had been triumphantly concluded, Manius Curius, the hero of that war, signalized his censorship by beginning to build the second aqueduct, the spoils won in battle from the King of Epirus furnishing the pay of the workmen engaged in the operation. He died before the work was finished, and the glory of completing it belonged to Fulvius Flaccus, created with him duumvir for bringing the water to Rome.

This time the hydraulic engineers went further afield for the source of their supply. They looked across the Campagna to the dim hills of Tivoli—

'To the green steeps whence Anio leaps
In sheets of snow-white foam'

and daringly determined to bring the river Anio himself, or at least a considerable portion of his waters, to Rome. At a point about ten miles above Tivoli, near the mountain of S. Cosimato, the river was tapped. The water which was drawn from it was carried through tunnels in the rock, and by a generally subterranean course, till, after a journey as before stated of forty-three miles, it entered Rome just at the level of the ground, but at a point (the Porta Maggiore) where that level was considerably higher than the place where the Appian water crept into the city. Four generations passed before any further addition was made to the water-supply of Rome. Then, after the lapse of 128 years, the Marcian water, best of all the potable waters of Rome, was introduced into the city by the first aqueduct, in the common acceptation of the term, the first channel carried visibly above ground on arches over long reaches of country. Its source was at thirty-eight miles from Rome in the upper valley of the Anio, between Tivoli and Subiaco. Here lay a tranquil pool of water emerging from a natural grotto and of a deep green color, whence came the liquid treasure of the Marcia. The changes in the conformation of the valley make it difficult to identify the spot with certainty, but it is thought that the furthest east of three springs known as the Acque Serene is probably the famous Marcia. From a spot close to this, the Marcia-Pia aqueduct, constructed by a company in our own days, and named after Pope Pius the Ninth, now brings water to the city. The original Marcian aqueduct was built two years after the close of the Third Punic War, and the work was entrusted by the Senate, not this time to a Censor, but to the Praetor Urbanus, the highest judicial officer in Rome, who bore the name of Q. Marcius Rex. The aqueduct had a course of sixty-one miles, for seven of which it was carried upon arches, and it entered the city at 176 feet above the sea-level. The cost of its construction was 180 million sesterces, and it carried water into the lofty Capitol itself, not without some opposition on the part of the Augurs, who, after an inspection of the Sibylline books, averred that only the water of the Anio, not that of any spring adjacent to it, might be brought into the temple of Jupiter.

Only nineteen years had elapsed, but years of continued conquest, especially in the Spanish peninsula, when in BC 125 another aqueduct, smaller, but at a slightly higher level, was added to the water-bringers of Rome. This was the *Aqua Tepula*, thirteen miles in length, of which only six were subterranean, and entering Rome at a height of 184 feet above the sea-level. Servilius Caepio and Longinus Ravilla were the Censors to whom the execution of this work was entrusted. They resorted to a new source of supply, not utilizing this time either springs or streams in the Anio valley, but journeying to the foot of the conical Alban Mount (Monte Cavo), which rises to the south-east of Rome, and there wooing the waters of the tepid springs which bubbled up near the site of the modern village of Grotta Ferrata.

Another century passed, the century which saw the rise of Marius, Sulla, and the mighty Julius. Absorbed in foreign war and the factions of the Forum, Rome had no leisure for great works of industry, and did not even preserve in good condition those which she already possessed. At length in the year *BC* 33, three years before the battle of Actium, M. Vipsanius Agrippa, the ablest of the ministers of Augustus, bestirred himself on behalf of the water-supply of the vastly expanded city. He restored the Appia, the Anio Vetus, and the Marcia, which had fallen into ruins, but he was not satisfied with mere reconstruction. The same hand which gave the Pantheon and its adjoining baths to the citizens of Rome gave them also two more aqueducts, the Julia (BC 33) and the Aqua Virgo (BC 19).

The *Julia* bore the name of its builder, who, himself of the plebeian Vipsanian gens, had been adopted, by reason of his marriage with the daughter of Augustus, into the high aristocratic family of the Caesars. Its source was near that of the Tepula, but a little further from Rome. Apparently, in order that it might impart some of its fresh coolness to that tepid stream, its waters were first blended with it and then again divided into another channel, which flowed into Rome at an elevation four feet above the Tepula (188 feet above the sea-level). These two aqueducts, the Tepula and the Julia, are carried through the greater part of their course upon the same arcade with the Marcia.

'Like friends once parted,
Grown single-hearted,
They plied their watery tasks.'

And, as a rule, wherever in the neighborhood of Rome the *specus* (so the mason-wrought channel is termed) of the Marcia is descried, one sees also first the Tepula and then the Julia rising above it.

This work, however, did not end Agrippa's labors for the sanitary well-being of Rome. The Julia, though twice as large as the Tepula, was still one of the smaller contributors of water to the city. Fourteen years after its introduction Agrippa brought the Aqua Virgo into Rome. This splendid stream, three times as large as the Julia, was exceeded in size only by the Anio Vetus and the Marcia, among the then existing Aqueducts. To obtain it he went eight miles eastward of Rome, almost to the same spot where the great Censor had gathered the Aqua Appia. The Aqua Virgo derived its name from the story that when the soldiers of Agrippa were peering about to discover some new spring, a little maid pointed out to them a streamlet, which they followed up with the spade, thus soon finding themselves in presence of an immense volume of water. This story was commemorated by a picture in a little chapel built over the fountain.

The Virgo was not, like all the more recent aqueducts, brought into Rome at a high level. In fact it was only fifteen feet higher than the Appia, as might have been expected from the nearness of origin of the two streams. Its course is perfectly well known, as it is still bringing water to Rome, and is in truth that one of all the aqueducts which shows the most continuous record of useful service from ancient to modern times. It comes by a pretty straight course, chiefly underground, till within about two miles of Rome; then it circles round the eastern wall of the city, winds through the Borghese gardens, creeps by a deep cutting through the Pincian hill, and enters Rome under what is now the Villa Medici. In old days it was carried on to the Campus Martius and filled the baths of its founder Agrippa. It still supplies many of the chief fountains of the city, especially the most famous of all, the Fountain of Trevi. When the stranger steps down in front of the blowing Tritons and takes his cup of water from the ample marble basin, drinking to his return to the Eternal City, he is in truth drinking to the memory of the wise Agrippa and of the little maid who pointed out the fountain to his legionaries.

The contribution made by Augustus himself to the water-supply of Rome was a less worthy one than those of his son-in-law. "What possible reason", says Frontinus, "could have induced Augustus, that most far-sighted prince, to bring the water of the Alsietine Lake, which is also called Aqua Augusta, to Rome I cannot tell. It has nothing to recommend it. It is hardly even wholesome, and it does not supply any considerable part of the population [because of the low level at which it enters the city]. I can only suppose that when he was constructing his Naumachia he did not like to use the better class of water to fill his lake, and therefore brought this stream, granting all of it that he did not want himself to private persons for watering their gardens and similar purposes. However, as often as the bridges are under repair and there is a consequent interruption of the regular supply, this water is used for drinking purposes by the inhabitants of the Trans-Tiberine region". So far Frontinus. The work was altogether of an inglorious kind. The quantity supplied was small, less even than that in the little Aqua Tepula. The quality, as has been stated, was poor, the source of supply being the turbid Lago di Martignano among the Etrurian hills on the north-west of Rome. And though it started at a pretty high level (680 feet above the sea), after a course of a little more than twenty-two miles it entered Home on a lower plane than all the other aqueducts, lower even than the modest Appia, only about twenty-one feet above the level of the sea.

The frenzied great-grandson of Augustus, the terrible Caligula, side by side with all his mad prodigality did accomplish great work for the water-supply of Rome. He began, and his uncle Claudius finished, the two great aqueducts which closed the ascending series of Rome's artificial rivers, the Claudia and the Anio Novus. Thus by a singular coincidence the work which had been begun by a Claudius, the blind Censor of the fifth century of Rome, was crowned by another Claudius, not indeed a direct descendant, but a far distant scion, of the same haughty family, when the city was just entering upon her ninth century.

The two works, the Claudia and the Anio Novus, seem to have been proceeded with contemporaneously, and they travelled across the Campagna on the same stately series of arches, highest of all the arcades with whose ruins the traveler is familiar. They were, however, works of very different degrees of merit. The Claudia drew its waters from two fountains, the Caerulus and the Curtius, among the hills overhanging the Upper Anio, not many hundred yards away from the source of the Marcia. And the water which it brought to the citizens of Rome was always considered second only in excellence to the Marcia itself.

The construction of the Anio Novus, on the other hand, was another of those unwise attempts of which one would have thought the hydraulic engineers of the city had had enough, to make the river Anio, that turbid and turbulent stream, minister meekly to the thirst of Rome. The water was taken out of the river itself from a higher point than the Anio Vetus, indeed four miles higher than the fountains of the Claudia, but that did not remedy the evil. The bad qualities of the Aqua Alsietina did little harm, beyond some occasional inconvenience to the inhabitants of the Trastevere, because it lay below all the other aqueducts. But of the thick and muddy Anio Novus, flowing above the other streams and mixing its contributions with theirs, like some tedious and loud-voiced talker, whenever they were least desired, of this provoking aqueduct a wearied Imperial water-director could only say, "It ruins all the others". The length of its journey to the city was more than fifty-eight miles, that of the Claudia more than forty-six, and the arcade upon which they together crossed the plain was six miles and four hundred and ninety-one paces in length. The Anio Novus entered the city two hundred and fourteen feet above the level of the sea, the Claudia nine feet lower.

Thus were completed the nine great aqueducts of Rome; the aqueducts whose resources and machinery are copiously explained to us by the curator, Frontinus. Without troubling the reader with the names of some doubtful or obscure additions to the list, it must nevertheless be mentioned that the Emperor Trajan, in the year 109-110, brought the water of the Sabatine Lake to Rome. This lake was immediately adjoining to the (much smaller) Lacus Alsietinus from which Augustus had drawn his supply. Trajan, however, did not fritter away the advantage of his high fountain-head as Augustus had done, but brought his aqueduct right over the hill of the Janiculum. Here in the days of Procopius its stream might be seen (till Witigis intercepted it) turning the wheels of a hundred mills. Here now its restored waters may be seen gushing in magnificent abundance through the three arches of Fontana on the high hill of S. Pietro in Montorio.

In the following century the excellent young Emperor Alexander Severus obtained a fresh supply from the neighborhood of the old city of Gabii, about four miles south-east of the source of the Aqua Virgo. Little is known of the size or the course of the Aqua Alexandrina, whose chief interest for us is derived from the fact that it is practically the same aqueduct which was restored by the imperious old Pope, Sixtus V, and which is now called, after the name which he bore "in religion", Aqua Felice. A more complete contrast is hardly presented to us by history than between the first founder and the restorer of this aqueduct, between the young, fresh, warm-hearted Emperor, only too gentle a ruler and too dutiful a son for the fierce times in which he lived, and the proud and lonely old Pope, who bent low as if in decrepitude till he had picked up the Papal Tiara, and then stood erect, just and inflexible, a terror to the world and to Rome.

With Alexander Severus the history of the aqueducts closes. In the terrible convulsions which marked the middle of the third century there was no time or money to spare for the embellishment of the city. When peace was restored Diocletian and his attendant group of Emperors were to be found at Milan, at Nicomedeia, anywhere rather than at Rome. Constantine was too much engrossed with his new capital and his new creed to have leisure for the improvement of the still Pagan city by the Tiber. And two generations after the death of Constantine the barbarians were on the sacred soil of Italy, and it was no longer a question of constructing great works, but of feebly and fearfully defending them.

The amount of careful thought and contrivance which was involved in the construction and maintenance of these mighty works can be but imperfectly estimated by us. Ventilating-shafts, or 'respirators' as they are sometimes called, were introduced at proper intervals into the subterraneous aqueducts in order to let out the imprisoned air. At every half mile or so the channel formed an angle, to break the force of the water, and a reservoir was generally placed at every such corner. The land for fifteen feet on each side of the water-course was purchased from the neighboring owners and devoted to the use of the aqueduct. Injury from other buildings and from the roots of trees was thus avoided, and the crops raised on these narrow strips of land contributed to the sustenance of the little army of slaves employed in the maintenance of the waterway. Of these at the end of the first century there were 700, constituting two *familiae*. One *familia*, consisting of 240 men, had been formed by that indefatigable water-reformer, the Sir Hugh Middleton of Rome, Vipsanius Agrippa, by him bequeathed to Augustus, and by Augustus to the State. The other and larger body (460 men) had been formed by Claudius when he was engaged in the construction of the two highest aqueducts, and by him were likewise presented to the State. The command of this little band of men was vested in the *Curator Aquarum*, a high officer, who in the imperial age was generally designated for the work of superintending the water-supply. In earlier times this work had not been assigned to any special officer, but had formed part of the functions of an Aedile or a Censor.

Outside the walls there were a certain number of reservoirs (*piscinae*), in which some of the aqueducts had the opportunity of clearing their waters by depositing the mud or sand swept into them by a sudden storm.

Inside the city there were 247 'castles of water', heads or reservoirs constructed of masonry, in which the water was stored, and out of which the supply-pipes for the various regions of Rome were taken. For, in theory at least, no pipe might tap the channels of communication, but all must draw from some *castellum aquae*. This provision, however, was often evaded by the dishonesty of the servile watermen, who made a profit out of selling the water of the state to private individuals. A vast underground labyrinth of leaden pipes, in Old Rome as in a modern city, conveyed the water to the cisterns of the different houses. The lead for this purpose was probably brought to a large extent from our own island, since we find traces of the Romans at work in the lead-mines of the Mendip Hills within six years of their conquest of Britain. As Claudius was the then reigning Emperor, the cargoes of lead so shipped from Britain to Rome would be usefully employed in distributing the new water-supply brought to the higher levels by the Anio Novus and Aqua Claudia. One thousand kilogrammes of these leaden pipes were sent, unchronicled, to the melting-pot five years ago by one proprietor alone. But by carefully watching his opportunities, the eminent archaeologist Lanciani has succeeded in rescuing six hundred inscribed pipes from the havoc necessarily caused by all building operations in the soil intersected by them; and these six hundred inscriptions, classed and analyzed by him, throw a valuable light on the aquarian laws and customs of Imperial Home.

It has been said that fraud was extensively practised by the slaves in the employment of the *Curator Aquarum*. It may have been some suspicion of these fraudulent practices which caused the Emperor Nerva to nominate to that high place Sextus Julius Frontinus. This man, energetic, fearless, thorough, and equally ready to grapple with the difficulties of peaceful and of warlike administration, reminds us of the best type of our own Anglo-Indian governors. For three years (AD 75-78) he successfully administered the affairs of the province of Britain, as the worthy successor of Cerealis, as the not unworthy predecessor of Agricola. The chief exploit that marked his tenure of office was the subjugation of the Silures, the warlike and powerful tribe who held the hills of Brecknock and Glamorgan. Twenty years later, and when he was probably past middle life, Nerva, as has been said, delegated to him the difficult task of investigating and reforming the abuses connected with the water-supply of the capital. The treatise which he composed during his curatorship is our chief authority on the subject of the Roman aqueducts. Containing many careful scientific calculations and many useful hints as to the best means of upholding those mighty structures, it is an admirable specimen of the strong, clear common-sense and faithful attention to minute detail which were the characteristics of the best specimens of Roman officials.

The attention of Frontinus was at once arrested by the fact that in the *commentarii* or registers of the water-office there was actually a larger connected quantity of water accounted for than the whole water-amount which, according to the same books, appeared to be received from the various aqueducts. This slip on the part of the fraudulent *aquarii* caused the new Curator to take careful measurements of the water at the source of each aqueduct: and these measurements led him to the astounding result that the quantity of water entering the aqueducts was greater than the quantity alleged to be distributed through them by nearly one half. Some part of this difference might be due to unavoidable leakage along the line of the aqueducts: but far the larger part of it was due to the depredations of private persons, assisted by the corrupt connivance of the *aquarii*. When a private person had received a grant of water from the State, the proper course was for him to deposit a model of the pipe which had been conceded to him in the office of the Curator, whose servants were then directed to make an orifice of the same dimensions in the side of the reservoir, and permit the consumer to attach to it a pipe of the same size. Sometimes however, for a bribe, the *aquarius* would make a hole of larger diameter than the concession. Sometimes, while keeping the hole of the right size, he would attach a larger pipe which would soon be filled by the pressure of the water oozing through the wall of the reservoir. Sometimes a pipe for which there was absolutely no authority at all would be introduced into the reservoir, or yet worse into the aqueduct before it reached the reservoir. Sometimes the grant of water, which was by its express terms limited to the individual for life, would by corrupt connivance, without any fresh grant, be continued to his heirs. At every point the precious liquid treasure of the State was being wasted, that the pockets of the *familia* who served the aqueduct might be filled. It was probably some rumor of this infidelity of the *aquarii* to their trust, as well as a knowledge of the lavish grants of some of the Emperors, which caused Pliny to say, a generation before the reforms of Frontinus, "The Aqua Virgo excels all other waters to the touch, and the Aqua Marcia to the taste; but the pleasure of both has now for long been lost to the city, through the ambition and avarice of. the men who pervert the fountains of the public health for the supply of their own villas and suburban estates".

These then were the abuses which the former governor of Britain and conqueror of the Silures was placed in office to reform; and there can be little doubt that, at any rate for a time, he did reform them and restore to the people of Rome the full water-supply to which they were entitled. What was that water-supply, stated in terms with which we are familiar? What was the equivalent of the 24,805 *quinariae* which Frontinus insisted on debiting to the account of the *aquarii* at Rome In attempting to answer this question we are at once confronted by the difficulty, that though Frontinus has given us very exact particulars as to the dimensions of the pipes employed, he has not put beyond the possibility of a doubt the rate at which the water flowed through them, and which may have been very different for different aqueducts.

M. Bondelet, a French scholar and engineer of the early part of this century, after enquiring very carefully into the subject, came to the conclusion that the value of the *quinaria* was equivalent to a service of sixty cubic metres per day. Lanciani, going minutely over the same ground, slightly alters this figure, which he turns into 63'18 cubic metres, or 13,906 gallons a day. If we may rely on this computation, the whole amount of water poured into Rome at the end of the first century by the aqueducts, before Trajan and Alexander Severus had augmented the aquarian treasures of the city by the watercourses which bore their names, was not less than 344,938,330 gallons per day. Adopting the conjecture, in which there seems some probability, that the population of Rome in its most prosperous estate reached to about a million and a halt this gives a supply of 230 gallons daily for each inhabitant.

In our own country at the present day the modem consumption of water in our large towns varies between twenty and thirty gallons per head daily, and in one or two towns does not rise above ten gallons. What the supply may have been in the London of the Plantagenets and Tudors, before the great water-reform of Sir Hugh Middleton, we have perhaps no means of estimating; but it is stated, apparently on good authority, that in 1550 the inhabitants of Paris received a supply of only one quart per day, and nine-tenths of the people were compelled to obtain their supply direct from the Seine.

The estimate of the contents of the aqueducts as given above is that which has hitherto obtained most acceptance. It is right, however, to mention that a recent enquirer throws some doubt on Rondelet's calculations. From some observations made by him on the diameter and the gradient of the channel of the Aqua Marcia he reduces the average velocity of the streams, and consequently the volume of water delivered by them, by more than one half. The value of the *quinaria* on this computation descends to about 6000 gallons a day, the total supply of the nine aqueducts in the time of Frontinus to 148,000,000 gallons, and the allowance per head per day to one hundred gallons. Even so, however, the Roman citizen had more than three times the amount provided for the inhabitants of our English cities by the most liberal of our own municipalities.

This last consideration brings us to the question of what could have been done with all this wealth of water so lavishly poured into the Eternal City. The sparkling fountains with which every open space was adorned and refreshed, the great artificial lakes, on which at the occasion of public festivals mimic navies fought and in which marine monsters sported, are in part an answer to our question. But the Thermae, those magnificent ranges of halls in which the poorest citizen of Rome could enjoy, free of expense, all and more than all the luxuries that we associate with our misnamed Turkish Bath, the *Thermae*, those splendid temples of health, cleanliness, and civilization, must undoubtedly take the responsibility of the largest share in the water-consumption of Rome. We glanced a little while ago at the mighty Baths of Caracalla, able to accommodate 1600 bathers at once. Twice that number, we are told, could enjoy the Baths of Diocletian, those vast baths in whose central hall a large church is now erected, large, but occupying a comparatively small part of the ancient building. It is true that this was the most extensive of all the Roman Thermae; but the Baths of Constantine on the Quirinal, of Agrippa by the Pantheon, of Titus and Trajan above the ruins of the Golden House of Nero, were also superb buildings, fit to be the chosen resort of the sovereign people of the world; and all (with the possible exception of the Baths of Titus) were still in use, still receiving the crystal treasures of the aqueducts, when Belisarius recovered Rome for the Roman Empire

Now, in these first weeks of March 537, all this splendid heritage of civilization perished of the as in a moment. The Goths having thus arranged their army destroyed all the aqueducts, so that no water might enter from them into the city. The historian's statement is very clear and positive: otherwise we might be disposed to doubt whether the barbarians burrowed beneath the ground to discover and destroy the Aqua Appia, which is subterraneous till after it has entered the circuit of the walls. One would like to be informed also how they succeeded in arresting these copious streams of water without turning the Campagna itself into a morass. The waters which came from the Anio valley may perhaps have been diverted back again into that stream, but some of the others which had no river-bed near them must surely have been difficult to deal with. Possibly the sickness which at a later period assailed the Gothic host may have sprung in part from the unwholesome accumulation of these stagnant waters.

But our chief interest in the operation, an interest of regret, arises from the change which it must have wrought in the habits of the Roman people. Some faint and feeble attempts to restore the aqueducts were possibly made when the war was ended: in fact one such, accomplished by Belisarius for the Aqua Trajana, is recorded an inscription[1]. But as a whole, we may confidently state that the imperial system of aqueducts was never restored. Three in the course of ages were recovered for the City by the public spirit of her pontiffs, and one (the Marcia) has been added to her resources in our own days by the enterprise of a joint-stock company; but the Rome of the Middle Ages was practically, like the Rome of the Kings, dependent for her water on a few wells and cisterns and on the mud-burdened Tiber. The Bath with all its sinful luxuriousness, which brought it under the ban of philosophers and churchmen, but also with all its favoring influences on health, on refinement, even on clear and logical thought, the Bath which the eleven aqueducts of Rome had once replenished for a whole people, now became a forgotten dream of the past. As we look onward from the sixth century the Romans of the centuries before us will be in some respects a better people than their ancestors, more devout, less arrogant, perhaps less licentious, but they will not be so well-washed a people. And the sight of Rome, holy but dirty, will exert a very different and far less civilizing influence on the nations beyond the Alps who come to worship at her shrines than would have been exerted by a Rome, Christian indeed, but also rejoicing in the undiminished treasures of her artificial streams. Should an author ever arise who shall condescend to take the History of Personal Cleanliness for his theme (and historians have sometimes chosen subjects of less interest for humanity than this), he will find that one of the darkest days in his story is the day when the Gothic warriors of Witigis ruined the aqueducts of Rome.

CHAPTER VII.

THE GOTHIC ASSAULT.

An immediate effect of the cutting off of the water-supply was to endanger the regular delivery of the rations of flour to the soldier, and the citizens. Now that the water of Trajan's aqueduct no longer came dashing down over the Janiculan hill, the corn-mills which it had been wont to drive were silent. An obvious suggestion would have been to use beasts of burden to supply the needed power. But unfortunately, in order to effect the necessary economy of provisions, all beasts of burden, except the horses needed for warlike purposes, had been slain. Therefore, with his usual fertility of resource, Belisarius contrived to make water take the place of water. Stretching ropes across the Tiber from bank to bank near the Elian Bridge he moored two skiffs side by side at a distance of two feet apart, placed his mill-stones on board and hung his water-wheel between the skiffs, where the current of the river narrowed by the interposition of the bridge was strong enough to turn it and move the machinery. The Goths heard of this contrivance from the deserters who still came over to them, and succeeded in breaking the water-wheels by throwing huge logs, and even the carcasses of slain Romans, into the stream. Belisarius however by fastening to the bridge strong iron chains which stretched across the river, not only preserved his water-mills from these obstructions, but also, which was more important, guarded the city against the peril of a sudden attack by the boats' crews of the barbarians The water-mills of the Tiber thus invented by Belisarius continued to be used in Rome down to our own day, but are now apparently all superseded by mills driven by steam.

The watchful care of Belisarius did not even neglect to take into consideration the *cloacae*, the great sewers, of Rome; but as the mouths of all of them opened into the Tiber, in that part of it which was within the circuit of the walls, no special provision against a hostile surprise appeared to be necessary in this quarter.

Just at this time, when men's minds were on the stretch, waiting for the mighty duel to begin, came the tidings of an incident, trifling and yet tragical, which the superstitious in either army might easily regard as an omen of success to the one and of disaster to the other. Some Samnite lads, keeping their sheep on the slopes of the Apennines, beguiled the tedium of their occupation by choosing out two of their sturdiest, naming one Witigis and the other Belisarius, and setting them to wrestle for the victory. As Fate would have it, Witigis was thrown. Then said the boys in sport, 'Witigis shall be hanged'. They had tied him up to a tree, meaning to cut him down again before he had received any serious harm, when suddenly a wolf from the mountains was upon them and they fled. The poor boy, abandoned to his fate, died in agony. But when the story was noised abroad through Samnium, people read in it an indication of the predestined victory of Belisarius, and took no steps for the punishment of the youthful executioners.

Still, notwithstanding omens and auguries, the citizens of Rome were by no means satisfied with the turn that things were taking. With their food doled out to them in strict daily rations, with only water enough for drinking (supplied by the river and the wells), and none whatever for the sadly remembered delights of the Bath, unwashed and short of sleep (since to each man his turn for sentry duty at night seemed constantly recurring); above all, with the depressing feeling that all these sacrifices were in vain, and that those myriads of the Goths whom they saw burning their villas and ravaging the pleasant places all around the city must soon be within its walls, they began to murmur against Belisarius. Speeches were made in the Senate, not loud but full of angry feeling, against the general who had ventured to hold Rome with such an utterly inadequate force, and who was bringing the loyal subjects of the Emperor, guiltless of any wrong, into such extremity of peril by his rashness.

Witigis, who was informed by the deserters Gothic of this change of feeling, tried to turn it to account by sending an embassy to Belisarius, headed by a certain Albes. In the presence of Speech of the Senate and the Generals, Albes delivered an harangue in which, not uncourteously, he suggested to Belisarius that courage was one thing and rashness another. "If it is courage that has brought you here, look forth from the walls, survey the vast multitude of the Goths. You will have need of all your courage in dealing with that mighty host. But if you now feel that it was mere rashness that has led you hither, and if at the same time you are awakened to the thought of all the miseries which you are inflicting on the Romans by your opposition to their lawful ruler, we come to offer you one more opportunity of repentance. The Romans lived in all comfort and freedom under the rule of the good King Theodoric. Now, through your undesired interposition, they are suffering the extremity of misery, and their King, the King both of Goths and Italians, is obliged to encamp outside the walls, and practice all the cruel acts of war against the people whom he loves. We call upon you therefore to evacuate the city of Rome; but as it is not our wish to trample on the fallen we concede to you the liberty of marching forth unmolested and of taking with you all your possessions".

The spirit of the Gothic King was a good deal changed by the events of the last few days. On his march to Rome his only fear had been lest Belisarius should escape his dreadful vengeance. Now he was willing to offer him all the honors of war if only he would march out of the city which he ought never to have been allowed to enter. It may be doubted whether Witigis was wise in showing so manifestly his desire for the departure of the imperial General. The Senate, as we know, had begun to take a very gloomy view of the prospects of the defence. Such a speech as that of Albes would tend to reassure many a waverer, by showing him that the Goths, in their secret hearts, felt no great confidence of victory.

Belisarius in reply said, that the prudence or imprudence of his plan of campaign was his own affair, and he did not intend to take the advice of Witigis concerning it. "But I say to you that the time will come when you shall long to hide your heads under the thorns of the Campagna and shall not be able to do so. When we took Rome we laid hands on no alien possession, but only undid that work of violence by which you seized upon a city to which you had no claim. If any one of you fancies that he is going to enter Rome without a struggle he is mistaken. While Belisarius lives he will never quit his hold of this city"

So spoke Belisarius. The Roman Senators sat mute and trembling, not daring to echo the proud words of the General, nor to repel the accusations of the ambassadors upbraiding them with their treachery and ingratitude. Only Fidelius, aforetime Quaestor under Athalaric and now Praetorian Prefect under Belisarius, answered his late lords with words of scorn and banter. The ambassadors on their return to the camp were eagerly questioned by Witigis, what manner of man Belisarius was, and how he received the proposal for an evacuation of the city. To which they replied that he seemed to be the last man in the world to be frightened by mere words. Accordingly, Witigis set about the task of convincing him by more efficacious arguments.

Having counted the courses of masonry in the walls, and thus formed as accurate an estimate as possible of their height, the Goths constructed several wooden towers of the same height as the walls, running on wheels placed under their four corners, and with ropes fastened to them, so that they could be drawn by oxen. On the highest platform of the towers were ladders, which could be used if necessary to scale the battlements. In addition to the towers the Goths also made ready eight battering-rams. Procopius gives us a detailed description of this engine of war, Roman, as it is generally supposed, in its origin, but now borrowed from the Romans by the barbarians. They also prepared fascines, of the boughs of trees and the reeds of the Campagna, which they could throw into the fosse, so filling it up and preparing the way for the advance of their warlike engines.

On his side Belisarius armed the towers and battlements with a plenteous supply of the defensive engines of the period, the *Balista*, that magnified bow, worked by machinery, which shot a short square arrow twice the distance of an ordinary bow-shot and with such force as to break trees or stones; and the *Onager* or Wild Ass, which was a similarly magnified sling. Each gate he obstructed with a machine called a *Lupus*, which seems, from the somewhat obscure description of Procopius, to have been a kind of double portcullis, worked both from above and below, and ready to close its terrible wolf-jaws upon any enemy who should venture within reach of its fangs.

The general disposition of the army of Belisarius, which amounted in all to but 5000 men, was the same as that mentioned in a previous chapter. Bessas the imperialist Ostrogoth, and Peranius the *Iberian prince* from the shores of the Caspian, commanded at the great Praenestine Gate. At the Salarian and Pincian Gates Belisarius himself took charge of the fight; at the Flaminian, Ursicinus, who had under him a detachment of infantry known as "The Emperor's Own". They had, however, little to do in the battle which is about to be described, as the Flaminian Gate stood on a precipitous piece of ground and was too difficult of access for the Goths to assault it.

More astonishing was it to Procopius that the wall a little to the east of the Flaminian Gate should also have been left unassaulted by the Goths. Here, to this day, notwithstanding some lamentable and perfectly unnecessary Restorations of recent years, may be seen some portions of the Muro Torto, a twisted, bulging, overhanging mass of *opus reticulatum*. It looks as if it might fall tomorrow (and so, as we shall see, thought Belisarius), but it has stood in its present state for eighteen centuries. But the story of this piece of wall and the superstitions connected with it is so curious that Procopius must tell it in his own words:

"Between the Flaminian Gate and the gate-let next in order on the right hand, which is called the Pincian, a part of the wall split asunder long ago of its own accord. The cleft however did not reach to the ground, but only about half-way down. Thus it did not fall, nor receive any further damage, but it so leaned over in both directions that one part seems within, the other without the rest of the enclosure. From this circumstance the Romans have from of old called that part of the wall, in their own language, *Murus Ruptus*. Now when Belisarius was at the first minded to pull down this bit and build it up again, the Romans stopped him, assuring him that Peter (the

Apostle whom they venerate and admire above all others) had promised that he would care for the defence of their city at that point. And things turned out in this quarter exactly as they had expected; for neither on the day of the first assault, nor during any subsequent part of the siege, did the enemy approach this portion of the wall in force, or cause any tumult there. We often wondered that in all the assaults and midnight surprises of the enemy, this part of the fortifications never seemed to come into the remembrance either of besiegers or besieged. For this reason no one hath since attempted to rebuild it, but the wall remains to this day cleft in two. So much for the *Murus Ruptu.*

The reader will probably feel, in perusing this passage, that Procopius himself, though rather a Theist than a Christian, and not always constant even to Theism, was puzzled whether to accept or reject the legend of St. Peter's guardianship of the *Muro Torto*. He shows the same attitude of suspended belief towards the Sibylline Oracles and many other heathen marvels which are recorded in his pages.

Constantine, removed by Belisarius from the Porta Flaminia, was placed in charge of the riverside wall and the Bridge and Tomb of Hadrian. Paulus commanded at the Pancratian Gate on the other side of the Tiber: but here too, on account of the difficulty of the ground, the Goths attempted nothing worthy of note. A striking contrast this to one of the very last sieges of Rome, that under General Oudinot in 1849, when the Porta S. Pancrazio was riddled with hostile bullets. In consequence of the frequent skirmishes in that quarter the whole Janiculum was then covered with mounds, now grass-grown and peaceful-looking, under which French and Italian soldiers, slain in those dreary days, slumber side by side.

The preparations of the Goths being completed, on the eighteenth day of the siege, at sunrise, they began the assault. With dismay the Romans, clustered on the walls, beheld the immense masses of men converging to the City, the rams, the towers drawn by oxen moving slowly towards them. They beheld the sight with dismay, but a smile of calm of scorn curved the lips of Belisarius. The Romans could not bear to see him thus trifling as they thought in the extremity of their danger implored him to use the *balistae* on the walls before the enemy came any nearer; called him shameless and incompetent when he refused: but still Belisarius waited and still he smiled. At length, when the Goths were now close to the edge of the fosse, he drew his bow and shot one of their leaders, armed with breastplate and mail, through the neck. The chief fell dead, and a roar of applause at the fortunate omen rose from the Roman ranks. Again he bent his bow and again a Gothic noble fell, whereat another shout of applause from the walls rent the air. Then Belisarius gave all his soldiers the signal to& discharge their arrows, ordering those immediately around him to leave the men untouched and to aim all their shafts at the oxen. In a few minutes the milk-white Etrurian oxen were all slain, and then of necessity the towers, the rams, all the engines of war remained immovable at the edge of the fosse, useless for attack, only a hindrance to the assaulting host. So close to the walls, it was impossible for the Goths to bring up other beasts of burden, or to devise any means to repair the disaster. Then men understood the reason of the smile of Belisarius, who was amused at the simplicity of the barbarians in thinking that he would allow them to drive their oxen close up under his battlements. Then they recognized his wisdom in postponing the reply from the *balistae* till the Goths had come so near that their disaster was irreparable.

The towers and the rams had apparently been intended specially for that part of the wall close to the Pincian Gate. Foiled in this endeavor, Witigis drew back his men a little distance from the fosse, formed them into deep columns, and ordered them not to attempt any farther assault on that part of the walls, but so to harass the troops by incessant discharges of missile weapons as to prevent Belisarius from giving any assistance to the other points which he meant to assail, and which were especially the Porta Praenestina and the Porta Aurelia.

During this time sharp fighting was going on at the other gate which was under the immediate command of Belisarius, the Porta Salaria. Here for a little while the barbarians seemed to be getting the advantage. A long-limbed Goth, one of their nobles and renowned for his prowess in war, armed (as perhaps their common soldiers were not) with helmet and breastplate, left the ranks of his comrades and swung himself up into a tree from which he was able to discharge frequent and deadly missiles at the defenders of the battlements. At length, however, one of the *balistae* worked by the soldiers in the tower on the left of the gateway, more by good fortune than good aim, succeeded in striking him. The bolt went right through the warriors body and half through the tree: thus pinned to the tree-trunk he was left dangling between earth and heaven. At this sight a chill fear ran through the Gothic ranks, and withdrawing themselves out of the range of the *balistae* they gave no more trouble to the defenders of the Salarian Gate.

The weight of the Gothic assault was directed against the Praenestine Gate, the modern Porta Maggiore. Here they collected a number of their engines of attack, towers, battering-rams, and ladders: and here both the hoped-for absence of the great general and the dilapidated state of the wall inspired some reasonable hope of victory. The neighborhood of the Porta Maggiore is to this day one of the most interesting portions of the wall of Rome. Here you see the two stately arches which spanned the diverging roads to Labicum and Praeneste. Above them you read the clear, boldly-carved inscriptions which record the constructions of Claudius, and the restorations of Vespasian and Titus. Between them stands the curious tomb of the baker Eurysaces, which bore the sculptured effigies of the baker and his wife and a quaint inscription (still legible) recording that in this bread-basket the fragments of Marcus Vergilius Eurysaces and his excellent wife are gathered together. High above run the channels of the Anio Novus and the Aqua Claudia. Hard by at a lower level the Julia, Tepula, and Marcia, and yet lower the Anio Vetus enter the city. This intersection of the aqueducts gave the Porta Praenestina a strength peculiar to itself, and caused it to take an important place in the fortifications of the later emperors.

When the Goths assaulted Rome the Praenestine and Labican Gates did not show the same fair proportions which they displayed in the days of Claudius, and which they have recovered by the judicious restoration effected in 1838. By the operations of the military engineers of Aurelian and Honorius the Labican Gate was closed and the usual round towers were erected, flanking the gate, which enclosed and concealed from view till our own times the Tomb of Eurysaces. The high line of the aqueduct wall still remained (as it does to this day), but it had fallen much out of repair, and the real line of defence seems to have been a lower wall running parallel to it at a distance of less than 100 yards and skirting the line of the Via Labicana. Between these two walls, which ran thus side by side for about 500 yards, a strip of land was enclosed which was used in old days a menagerie for the wild beasts that were about to be employed in the shows of the amphitheatre. To use the words of Procopius, "It chanced that the [true] wall in that quarter had in great part crumbled away, as the bricks no longer cohered well together. But another low wall had been drawn round it on the outside by the Romans of old, not for safety's sake, for it had neither towers nor battlements nor any other of the appliances for defence, but on account of unseemly luxury, that they might there enclose in cages the lions and other beasts [or the amphitheatre. For which cause also they called it the Vivarium, for that is the name given by the Romans to a place where beasts of ungentle nature are wont to be kept.

To the *Vivarium* then the Goths directed the weight of their columns and the larger number of their engines of war. The objective point was well chosen. The ground was level and afforded easy access to the assailants. There was, it is true, a double wall, but the inner one, as the Goths well knew, was decayed and ruinous, and the outer one, though in better preservation, was low and undefended by towers or battlements. But the fatal fault of the attack was that in the narrow space between the two walls there was no room for the barbarians to maneuver, and of this fault Belisarius determined to avail himself. By this time he had hastened with the most valiant men of his little army to the place, but he set few defenders on the ramparts and offered little opposition to the strokes with which the Goths battered a breach in the wall of the *Vivarium*. When this was accomplished, when he saw them pouring in, in their multitudes, to the narrow enclosure, he sent Cyprian and some of the bravest of his troops to man the real wall, formed of the arcades of the aqueducts. The unexpected strength of this opposition caused some dismay in the hearts of the Goths, who had thought their work would be at an end when they had penetrated within the first enclosure. Then, when they were all intent upon the hand-to-hand encounter with the defenders of the wall, Belisarius ordered the Praenestine Gate to be thrown open. Behind it he had massed his troops armed with breastplate and sword; no javelin or pilum to encumber them with its needless aid. They had little to do but to slay. Panic seized the Goths, who sought to pour out of the *Vivarium* by the narrow breach which they had effected, and many of whom were trampled to death by their own friends. They thought no more of valor but of flight, says the historian, each man as best he could. The Romans followed and slew a great number before they could reach the distant Gothic camp. Belisarius ordered the engines of war collected by the assailants to be burned, and the red flames shooting up into the evening sky carried terror to the hearts of the fugitives. A similar sally from the Salarian Gate met with like success.

Meanwhile, however, on the north-west of Rome, at the Porta Aurelia (opposite the Castle of Sant' Angelo), the Goths had been much nearer to achieving victory. Here, as has been said, Constantine, withdrawn for this purpose from the Flaminian Gate, had charge of the defence of the city. Two points were especially threatened, the Porta Aurelia and the stretch of river-side wall between it and the Porta Flaminia. This bit of wall had been left somewhat weak, the river seeming here sufficient defence, nor did Belisarius feel himself able to spare a large number of men for its protection. But Constantine, seeing that the enemy were preparing to cross the stream and attack at this place, rushed off himself to defend it. He was successful. When the Goths found that their landing was not unopposed, and that even this piece of wall had defenders, they lost heart and gave up the attempt. These movements, however, occupied precious time, and when, probably about noon, Constantine returned to the Porta Aurelia, he found that important events had taken place in his absence.

The whole course of the attack and defence in that quarter was determined then, as it has been in so many subsequent struggles, by

'The Mole which Hadrian reared on high'

the tomb, the fortress, the prison, of Sant' Angelo. Procopius shall describe it for us, for his is still the fullest account which we possess of the mighty Mausoleum in its glory:

"The tomb of Hadrian the Roman Emperor is outside the Porta Aurelia, distant from the wall about a bow-shot, a memorable sight. For it is made of Parian marble, and the stones fit closely one into another with no other fastening. It has four equal sides, each about a stone's throw in length, and in height overtopping the wall of the city. Above there are placed statues of men and horses made out of the same stone [Parian], and marvelous to behold. This tomb then the men of old, since it seemed like an additional fortress for their city, joined to the line of fortification by two walls reaching out from the main circuit of the fortifications. And thus the tomb seemed like a citadel protecting the gate".

From this description and a few hints given by travelers who saw the Mausoleum in the Middle Ages, archaeologists have conjecturally reconstructed its original outline. A quadrangular structure of dazzling white marble, each side 300 Roman feet long and eighty-five feet high, it had upon its sides inscriptions to the various Emperors from Trajan to Severus who were buried within its walls. At the corners of this structure were equestrian statues of four Emperors. Above, two circular buildings, one over the other, were surrounded with colonnades and peopled with marble statues. Over all rose a conical cupola whose summit was 300 feet above the ground, so that it might be said of this Mausoleum as of the City in the Revelation, 'The length and the breadth and the height of it were equal'. Visitors to the gardens of the Vatican may still see there a bronze fir-cone, eight feet high, which according to tradition once surmounted the cupola of Hadrian's Tomb.

Towards this tomb-fortress, then, swarmed the Gothic bands from their camp in the Neronian gardens. They had no elaborate engines like their brethren on the other side of the river, but they had ladders and bows in abundance, and hoped easily to overpower the scanty forces of the defenders. A long colonnade led from the Elian Bridge to the great Basilica of St. Peter, sheltered by which they approached close under the walls of the Tomb before they were perceived by the garrison. They were then too near for the *balistae* to be used against them with effect, the bolts discharged by those unwieldy engines flying over the heads of the assailants. The arrows shot from the bows of the Imperial soldiers could not pierce the large oblong shields of the Goths, which reminded Procopius of the enormous bucklers that he had seen used in the Persian wars. Moreover, the quadrangular shape of the building which they had to defend put the garrison at a disadvantage, since, when they were facing the foe on one side, they continually found themselves taken in rear by the assailants on the opposite quarter. Altogether, things looked ill for the defenders of the Tomb, till a sudden instinct drove them to the statues; that silent marble chorus which stood watching the terrible drama. Tearing these down from their bases and breaking the larger figures into fragments, they hurled them down upon the eager Gothic host.

At once the exultation of the latter was turned into panic. They drew back from the avalanche of sculpture. They retreated within range of the *balistae*. The garrison plied these engines with desperate energy, and with shouts discharged their arrows also against the enemy, whose shields now no longer formed the compact *testudo* which had before resisted their missiles. At this moment Constantine appeared upon the scene and turned repulse into defeat. The Tomb of Hadrian was saved, but at a price which would have caused a bitter pang to the artistic Emperor who raised and adorned that mighty mausoleum.

Thus, on both sides of the Tiber, the confident onset of the Goths had ended in utter failure. The battle, which began with early dawn, lasted till evening twilight. All night long the flare of the burning engines of the Goths reddened the sky. All night rose the contrasted clamors of the two armies; from the battlements of the city, the cheers and the rude songs in which the Romans praised the fame of their hero-general; from the Gothic camps the lamentation for the fallen, the groans of the wounded, the hurrying steps of men rushing to and fro to bring aid to their agonizing comrades.

It was asserted by the Romans, and, according to Procopius, admitted by the Gothic leaders, that on this day 30,000 of the barbarians were stretched dead upon the field, beside the vast numbers of the wounded.

CHAPTER VIII.

ROMAN SORTIES.

After the Gothic assault was repulsed, Belisarius sent a messenger to Justinian with a letter announcing the victory and praying for reinforcements. The letter, which was probably composed by Procopius himself, is worth reading, especially as it helps us to understand the light in which the invasion of Italy was regarded at Constantinople. "The King shall enjoy his own again" was the key-note of all the Imperial proceedings both at Carthage and at Rome. It was not a young and vigorous nationality, with a fair prospect of an honorable career, that Justinian and his generals seemed to themselves to be suppressing. It was simply an inalienable right that they were asserting, a right that generations of barbaric domination could not weaken, the right of the *Imperator Romanus* to Rome and to every country that her legions had once subdued.

"We have arrived in Italy" (said Belisarius) "in obedience to your orders, and after possessing ourselves of a large extent of its territory have also taken Rome, driving away the barbarians whom we found there, whose captain, Leuderis, we lately sent to you. Owing, however, to the large number of soldiers whom we have had to detach for garrison duty in the various towns of Italy and Sicily which we have taken, our force here is dwindled to 5000 men. The enemy has come against us with an army 150,000 strong; and in the first engagement, when we went out to reconnoiter by the banks of the Tiber, being forced, contrary to our intention, to fight, we were very nearly buried under the multitude of their spears. Then, when the barbarians tried a general assault upon our walls with all their forces and with many engines of war, they were within a little of capturing us and the city at the first rush. Some good fortune however (for one must refer to Fortune not to our valor the accomplishment of a deed which in the nature of things was not to be expected) saved us from their hands.

"So far however, whether Valor or Fortune have decided the struggle, your affairs have gone as well as could be desired, but I should like that this success should continue in days to come. I will say without concealment what I think you ought now to do, knowing well that human affairs turn out as God wills, but knowing also that those who preside over the destinies of nations are judged according to the event of their enterprises, be that event good or bad. I pray you, then, let arms and soldiers be sent to us in such numbers that we may no longer have to continue the war on terms of such terrible inequality with our enemies. For it is not right to trust everything to Fortune, since if she favors us at one time she will turn her back upon us at another. But I pray you, O Emperor, to let this thought into your mind, that if the barbarians should now vanquish us, not only shall we be driven out of your own Italy and lose our army too, but deep disgrace will accrue to us all as the result of our actions. We shall certainly be thought to have ruined the Romans who have preferred loyalty to your Empire above their own safety. And thus even the good luck which has attended us so far will prove in the end calamitous to our friends. If we had failed in our attempts on Rome, on Campania, or on Sicily, we should only have had the slight mortification of not being able to appropriate the possessions of others. Very different will be our feelings now when we lose what we have learned to look upon as our own, and drag those who have trusted us down into the same abyss of ruin.

"Consider this too, I pray you, that it is only the good-will of the citizens which has enabled us to hold Rome for ever so short a time against the myriads who besiege it. With a wide extent of open country round it, with no access to the sea, shut off from supplies, we could do nothing if the citizens were hostile. They are still animated by friendly feelings towards us, but if their hardships should be greatly prolonged it is only natural that they should choose for themselves the easier lot. For a recently formed friendship like theirs requires prosperity to enable it to endure: and the Romans especially may be compelled by hunger to do many things which are very contrary to their inclination.

"To conclude: I know that I am bound to sacrifice life itself to your Majesty, and therefore no man shall force me, living, from this place. But consider, I pray you, what kind of fame would accrue to Justinian from such an end to the career of Belisarius"

The effect of this letter was to accelerate the preparations already made for reinforcing the gallant band in Rome. Valerian and Martin had been sent, late in 536, with ships and men to the help of Belisarius, but, fearing to face the winter storms, had lingered on the coast of Aetolia. They now received a message from the Emperor to quicken their movements; and at the same time the spirits of the general and the citizens were raised by the tidings that reinforcements were on their way to relieve them.

On the very next day after the failure of the Gothic assault the unmenaced gates of Rome opened, and a troop of aged men, women, and children, set forth from the city. Some went out by the Appian Gate and along the Appian Way, others went forth by the Porta Portuensis and sailed down the Tiber to the sea. They were accompanied by all the slaves, male and female, except such of the former as Belisarius had impressed for the defence of the walls. Even the soldiers had to part with the servants who generally followed them to war. In thus immediately sending the useless mouths out of Rome Belisarius showed his prompt appreciation of the necessities of his position. He had repelled an assault; he would now guard as well as he might against the dangers of a blockade. Had Witigis been as great a master as Belisarius of the cruel logic of war, he would undoubtedly have prevented the Byzantine general from disencumbering himself of the multitude, who by their necessities would have been the most effectual allies of the Goths inside the city. Imperfect as was the Gothic line of circumvallation, it is impossible to believe that more than 100,000 warriors, including a large body of cavalry, could not by occupying the main roads have prevented at least some of a large and defenseless multitude from escaping, and have driven them back within the walls of Rome. But, in fact, all of them, without fear or molestation, reached the friendly shelter of the cities of Campania, or crossed the straits and took refuge in Sicily.

The fact seems to have been that, except by a series of brave and blundering assaults upon the actual walls of the city, the Goths, or perhaps we should rather say the Gothic King, had no notion how to handle the siege. One right step indeed he took, in view of the now necessary blockade. Three days after the failure of the assault he sent a body of troops to Portus, which they found practically undefended, notwithstanding its massive wall (the ruins of which are still visible), and it was at once occupied by them with a garrison of 1000 men. Procopius is of opinion that even

300 Roman soldiers would have been sufficient to defend Portus, but they could not be spared by Belisarius from the yet more pressing duty of watching on the Roman ramparts. The occupation of Portus caused great inconvenience to the Romans, although they still remained in possession of Ostia and the neighboring harbor of Antium. From Portus (which since the second century had practically displaced Ostia as the chief emporium of Rome) merchants were accustomed to bring all heavy cargoes up the Tiber in barges drawn by oxen, for which there was an excellent towpath all along the right bank of the river. From Ostia, on the other hand, merchandise had to be brought in skiffs dependent on the favor of the wind, which, owing to the winding character of the river, seldom served them for a straight run from the harbor to the city.

Besides the occupation of Portus, Witigis could bethink him of no better device to annoy the Romans than the cruel and senseless one of murdering their hostages. He sent orders to Ravenna that all the Senators whom he had confined there at the outbreak of the war should be put to death. A few escaped to Milan, having had some warning of their impending fate. Among them were a certain Cerventinus, and Reparatus a brother of the deacon Virgilius, who was in a few months to become Pope. The others all perished, and with them went the Goth's last chance of ruling the Roman otherwise than by fear. Meanwhile the Gothic blockade, into which the siege was resolving itself, was of the feeblest and most inefficient kind. Leaving all the praise of dash and daring to the scanty bands of their enemies, the Goths clung timidly to their unwieldy camps, in which no doubt already pestilence was lurking. They never ventured forth by night, seldom except in large companies by day. The light Moorish horsemen were their especial terror. If a Goth wandered forth into the Campagna alone, to cut fodder for his horse or to bring one of the oxen in from pasture, he was almost sure to see one of these children of the desert bearing down upon him. With one cast of the Moor's lance the Goth was slain, his arms and his barbaric adornments were stripped from him, and the Moor was off again full speed towards Rome before the avenger could be upon his track.

Belisarius on the other hand, organized his defence of the city so thoroughly as to leave as little as possible to the caprice of Fortune. To prevent his own little band of soldiers from being worn out by continual sentinel-duty, especially at night, and at the same time to keep from starvation the Roman proletariat, all of whose ordinary work was stopped by the siege, he instituted a kind of National Guard. He mixed a certain number of these citizen soldiers with his regular troops, paying each of them a small sum for his daily maintenance, and dividing the whole amalgamated force into companies, to each of whom was assigned the duty of guarding a particular portion of the walls by day or by night. To obviate the danger of treachery, these companies were shifted every fortnight to some part of the circuit at a considerable distance from that which they last guarded. After the same interval the keys of every gate of the city were brought to him, melted down and cast afresh with different wards, the locks of course being altered to suit them. The names of the sentinels were entered upon a list which was called over each day. The place of any absent soldier or citizen was at once filled up, and he was summoned to the general's quarters to be punished, perhaps capitally punished, for his delinquency. All the night, bands of music played at intervals along the walls, to keep the defenders awake and to cheer their drooping courage. All night too, the Moors, the terrible Moors, wore instructed to prowl round the base of the walls, accompanied by bloodhounds, in order to detect any attempt by the Goths at a nocturnal escalade.

About this time a curious attempt was made, which shows that there was still an undercurrent of the old Paganism in the apparently Christian and Orthodox City. The little square temple of Janus, nearly coeval with the Republic, still stood in the Forum in front of the Senate-house and a little above the *Tria Fata* or temple of the Fates. The temple was all overlaid with brass; of brass was the double-faced statue of Janus, seven and a-half feet high, which stood within it, looking with one face to the rising and with one to the setting sun; of brass were the renowned gates which the Romans of old shut only in time of peace, when all good things abounded, and opened in time of war. Since the citizens of Rome had become zealous above all others in their attachment to Christianity, these gates had been kept equally shut whether peace or war were in the land. Now, however, some secret votaries of the old faith tried, probably under cover of night, to open these brazen gates, that the god might march out as of old to help the Roman armies. They did not succeed in opening wide the massive doors, but they seem to have wrenched them a little from their hinges, so that they would no longer shut tightly as aforetime; an apt symbol of the troubled state of things, neither settled peace nor victorious war, which was for many centuries to prevail in Rome. This evidence of still existing Paganism must have shocked the servants of the pious Justinian; but owing to the troublous state of affairs no enquiry was made as to the authors of the deed.

At length, on the forty-first day from the commencement of the siege, the long-looked-for reinforcements under Martin and Valerian arrived in Rome. They were but 1600 men after all, but they were cavalry troops, hardy horsemen from the regions beyond the Danube, Huns, Sclavonians, and Antes; and their arrival brought joy to the heart of Belisarius, who decided that now the time was come for attempting offensive operations against the enemy. The first sallying party was Belisarius under the command of Trajan, one of the body-guard of the General, a brave and capable man. He was ordered to lead forth 200 light-armed horsemen from the Salarian Gate, and to occupy a little eminence near to one of the Gothic camps. There was to be no hand-to-hand fighting; neither sword nor spear was to be used; only each man's bow was to discharge as many arrows as possible, and when these were exhausted the soldiers were to seek safety in flight. These orders were obeyed. Each Roman arrow transfixed some Gothic warrior or his steed. When their quivers were empty, the skirmishers hastened back under the shelter of the walls of the city. The Goths pursued, but soon found themselves within range of the *ballistae*, which were in full activity on the battlements. It was believed in the Roman camp that 1000 of their enemies had been laid low by this day's doings.

A second sortie under Mundilas and Diogenes and a third under Wilas, all three brave guardsmen of Belisarius, were equally destructive to the enemy, and the result was achieved with equally little cost to the troop, 300 strong in each case, by whom the sortie was effected.

Seeing the success of these maneuvers, Witigis, who had not yet apprehended the difference of training and equipment between his countrymen and the Imperialists, thought he could not do better than imitate them. Victory was evidently to be had if a general made his army small enough: and he accordingly sent 500 horsemen with orders to go as near as they could to the walls, without coming within range of the *ballistae*, and avenge upon the Romans all the evils which they had suffered at their hands. The Goths accordingly took up their position on a little rising ground; and Belisarius, perceiving them, sent Bessas with 1000 men to steal round and take them in rear. The Goths soon found themselves overmastered: many of them fell; the rest fled to their camp and were upbraided by Witigis for their cowardice.

"Why could not they win a victory with a handful of men as the troops on the other side did?" So did the clumsy workman quarrel with his tools. Three days after he got together another band of 500 men, picking them from each of the Gothic camps that he might be sure to have some valiant men among them, and sent them with the same general directions, "to do brave deeds against the enemy" When they drew near, Belisarius sent 1500 horsemen against them under the newly-arrived generals Martin and Valerian. An equestrian battle ensued. Again the Goths, hopelessly outnumbered, were easily put to flight, and great numbers of them were slain.

Not in the Gothic camp only did this uniform success of the Imperial troops, apparently on the most different lines of encounter, excite much and eager questioning: the Roman citizens, whose former criticisms had given place to abject admiration, attributed it all to the marvelous genius of Belisarius. In the Pincian Palace, however, the question was earnestly debated by the friends of the General. Upon this occasion it was that Belisarius expressed that opinion which has been already quoted, that the superiority of the Imperial army in mounted archers was the cause of its unvarying victories over the Goths, whether the battles were fought by larger or smaller bodies of men.

The repeated and brilliant successes of the Imperial troops were almost as embarrassing to Belisarius as to the Gothic King, though in a different way. They fostered both in officers and soldiers such an overweening contempt of the barbarians, that now nothing would satisfy them but to be led forth to a regular pitched battle under the walls of Rome, and make an end once for all of the presumptuous besiegers. The method which Belisarius preferred, and which was far safer, was to wear out the barbarians by an incessant succession of such movements as Shakespeare indicates by "alarums, excursions". He dreaded putting Fortune to the test with the whole of his little army at once. He found, however, at last that to keep that army at all in hand it was necessary (as it had been at the battle of Sura) to yield to their wish in this thing; and he indulged the hope that their confidence of victory might be one powerful factor in the process which would enable him to secure it. Still he would have made his grand attack somewhat by way of a surprise, but was foiled in this endeavor by the information given by deserters to the Goths. At length, therefore, he resigned himself to fight a regular pitched battle with full notice on either side. The customary harangues were delivered by each commander. Belisarius reminded his soldiers that this battle was one of their own seeking, and that they would have to justify the advice which they had ventured to give, and to maintain the credit of their previous victories, by their conduct on that day. He bade them not spare either horse or javelin or bow in the coming fray, since all such losses should be abundantly made up to them out of his military stores. The purport of the speech of Witigis—if Procopius's account of it be not a mere rhetorical exercise—was to assure his brethren in arms that it was no selfish care for his crown and dignity which made him the humble suitor for their best assistance on that day. "For the loss of life or kingship I care not; nay, I would pray to put off this purple robe today if only I were assured that it would hang upon Gothic shoulders tomorrow. Even Theodahad's end seems to me an enviable one, since he died by Gothic hands and lost life and power by the same stroke. But what I cannot bear to contemplate is ruin falling not only on me but on my race. I think of the calamity of the Vandals, and imagine that I see you and your sons carried away into captivity, your wives suffering the last indignities from our implacable foes, myself and my wife, the granddaughter of the great Theodoric, led whithersoever the insulting conqueror shall please to order. Think of all these things, my countrymen, and vow in your own hearts that you will die on this field of battle rather than they shall come to pass. If this be your determination, an easy victory is yours. Few in number are the enemy, and after all they are but Greeks and Greek-like people. The only thing which keeps them together is a vain confidence derived from some recent disasters of ours. Be true to yourselves, and you will soon shatter that confidence and inflict a signal punishment upon them for all the insults that we have received at their hands".

After this harangue Witigis drew up his army in line of battle, the infantry in the middle, the cavalry on either wing. He stationed them as near as might be to the Gothic camps, in order that when the Romans were defeated, as he made no doubt they would be, owing to their enormous inferiority in numbers, their long flight to the shelter of their walls might be as disastrous to them as possible. Belisarius on his side determined to make his real attack from the Pincian and Salarian Gates. At the same time a feigned attack towards the Gothic camp under Monte Mario was to be made from the Porta Aurelia and the neighborhood of the Tomb of Hadrian. The object of this feigned attack was of course to prevent the large number of Goths on the right bank of the Tiber from swarming across the Milvian Bridge to the assistance of their brethren. Strict orders were, however, given to Valentine, who commanded the troops in this quarter, on no account to advance really within fighting distance of the enemy, but to harass him with a perpetual apparent offer of battle never leading to a decided result.

In further pursuance of the same policy the General accepted the service of a large number of volunteers from among the mechanics of Rome, equipped them with shield and spear, and stationed them in front of the Pancratian Gate. He placed no reliance on the services of these men for actual fighting, utterly unused as they were to the art of war, but he reckoned, not without cause, on the effect which the sight of so large a body of men would have in preventing the Goths from quitting their camp under Monte Mario. Meanwhile, the orders to the mechanic-volunteers were, not to stir till they should receive the signal from him, a signal which he was fully determined never to give.

The battle, according to the original plan of Belisarius, was to be fought entirely with cavalry, the arm in which he knew himself to be strongest, many of his best foot-soldiers, who were already well-skilled in horsemanship, having provided themselves with horses at the expense of the enemy, and so turned themselves into cavalry. He feared too the instability of such infantry as he had, and their liability to sudden panics, and therefore determined to keep them near to the fosse of the city walls, there to act simply as a slight support for any of the cavalry who might chance to be thrown into confusion. The plan intention was changed at the last moment—the General was in a mood that day for receiving advice from all quarters—by the earnest representations of two valiant Asiatic highlanders, Principius, a Pisidian, and Tarmutus, an Isaurian, whose brother Eunas commanded the contingent of those hardy mountaineers. These men besought him no further to lessen the numbers of his gallant little army by withdrawing the foot-soldiers, the representatives of those mighty legions by which 'the Romans of old' had won their greatness, from active service. They asserted their conviction that if, in recent engagements, the infantry had done something less than their duty, the fault lay not with the common soldiers but with the officers, who insisted on being mounted, and who were, too often, only looking about for a favorable moment for flight. Thus the troops were discouraged, because they felt that the men who were giving them orders did not share their dangers. But if Belisarius would allow these horsemen officers to fight that day with the horsemen, and would allow them, Principius and Tarmutus, to share on foot the dangers of the men under their command, and with them to advance boldly against the enemy, they trusted with God's help to do some deeds against them that the world should know of. Belisarius for long would not yield. He loved the two valiant highlanders: he was loth to run the risk of losing them: he was also loth to run the risk of losing his little army of foot-soldiers. At length, however, he consented. He left the smallest possible number of soldiers to guard, with the help of the Roman populace, the machines on the battlements and at the gates: and placing the main body of his infantry under the command of Principius and Tarmutus, he gave them orders to march behind the cavalry against the enemy. Should any portion of the cavalry be put to flight they were to open their ranks and let them pass through, themselves engaging the enemy till the horsemen had time to reform.

It was felt on both sides that this was to be a decisive trial of strength. Witigis had put in battle array every man of his army available for service, leaving in the camps only the camp-followers and the men who were disabled by their wounds. Early in the morning the hostile ranks closed for battle. The troops in front of the Pincian and Salarian Gates soon got the upper hand of the enemy, among whose clustered masses their arrows fell with terrible effect. But the Gothic multitudes were too thick, and the men too stout-hearted for even this slaughter to produce complete rout. As one rank of the barbarians was mown down, another pressed forward to supply its place. Thus the Romans, who had slowly pressed forward, found themselves by noon close to the Gothic camp, but surrounded still by so compact a body of their foes that they began to feel that any pretext which would enable them to return in good order under the shelter of their walls would be a welcome thing. The heroes of this period of the struggle were an Isaurian guardsman named Athenodorus and two Cappadocians, Theodoret and Georgius, who darted forth in front of the Roman line and with their spears transfixed many of the enemy. Thus again the men who came from the rough sides of Mount Taurus showed themselves conspicuous among the most warlike spirits of the Imperial army.

While this hot strife was being waged on the north-east of the city, strange events were taking place on the other side of the river in the Neronian plain under Monte Mario. Here the Gothic general Marcias had been enjoined by his King to play a waiting game, and above all things to watch the Milvian Bridge in order that no Romans should cross by it to succor their countrymen. The Romans, it will be remembered, had received a similar order from their general, and it might therefore have been expected that there would be no battle. But as the day wore on, it chanced that one of the feigned assaults of the Roman troops was turned into a real one by the sudden giving way of the Gothic ranks. The flying Goths were unable to reach their camp, but turned and reformed upon one of the hills in the neighborhood of the Monte Mario. Among the Roman troops were many sailors and slaves acting the soldier for the first time, and ignorant of discipline. Possibly, though this is not expressly stated, some of the mechanic crew who were stationed in front of the Pancratian Gate joined in the pursuit. At any rate the successful Romans soon became quite unmanageable by their leaders. The loudly-shouted commands of their general, Valentine, were unheard or disregarded. They did not concern themselves with the slaughter of the flying Goths. They did not press on to seize and cross the Milvian Bridge, in which case their opportune assistance to Belisarius might almost have enabled him to end the war at a stroke. They only occupied themselves with the plunder of the Gothic camp, where silver vessels and many other precious things (evidences of the enriching effect of the long peace on the Ostrogothic warriors) attracted their greedy eyes. The natural consequence followed. The Goths, so long left unmolested, and leisurely reforming on Monte Mario, looked on for a time quietly at the plunder of their camp. Then taking heart from their long reprieve, and reading the signs of disorder in the hostile forces, they dashed on with a savage yell, leaped the ramparts of their camp, and scattered the invaders of it like chaff before the wind. Silver vessels and golden trappings, all the spoils for the sake of which the greedy crew had sacrificed the chance of a splendid victory, were dashed in terror to the ground, while the slaves and sailors dressed up in military garb fled on all sides in utter rout and confusion from the camp, or fell by hundreds under the Gothic sword. The day's fighting on the Neronian Plain had been a series of blunders on both sides, but the eventual victory rested with the side which made fewest, Marcias and his Goths.

At the same time the fortunes of the Imperial army on the north-east of the city began to decline. The Goths, driven to bay at the rampart of their camp, formed a *testudo* with their shields and succeeded in withstanding the Roman onset, and in slaying many men and horses. The smallness of the attacking army became more and more terribly apparent both to itself and the enemy; and at length the right wing of the Gothic cavalry, bending round, charged the Romans in flank. They broke and fled. The cavalry reached the ranks of the supporting infantry, who did not support them, but turned and fled likewise; and soon the whole Roman army, horse and foot, generals and common soldiers, were in headlong flight toward the city walls.

Like Nolan at the charge of Balaklava, Principius and Tarmutus atoned by a brave death for the disastrous counsels which in all good faith they had given to the General. With a little knot of faithful friends they for a time arrested the headlong torrent of the Gothic pursuit, and the delay thus caused saved numberless lives in the Imperial army. Then Principius fell, hacked to pieces by countless wounds, and forty-two of his brave foot-soldiers fell around him. Tarmutus with two Isaurian javelins in his hand long kept the enemy at bay. He found his strength failing him, and was just about to sink down in exhaustion, when a charge of his brother Ennes, at the head of some of his cavalry, gave him a few moments' relief. Then plucking up heart again, he shook himself loose from his pursuers and ran at full speed (he was ever swift of foot) towards the walls of the city. He reached the Pincian Gate, pierced with many wounds and be dabbled with gore, but still holding his two Isaurian javelins in his hand. At the gate he fell down fainting. His comrades thought him dead, but laid him on a shield and bore him into the City. He was not dead, however : he still breathed; but two days afterwards he expired of his wounds, leaving a name memorable to the whole army, but especially to his trusty Isaurian comrades.

The soldiers who had already entered the City shut the gates with a clash, and refused to let the fugitives enter, lest the Goths should enter with them. Panic-stricken, and with scarcely a thought of self-defense, the defeated soldiers huddled up under the shelter of the walls, their spears all broken or cast away in the flight, their bows useless by reason of the dense masses in which they were packed together. The Goths appeared in menacing attitude at the outer edge of the fosse. Had they poured down across it, as they were at first minded to, they might have well-nigh annihilated the army of Belisarius. But when they saw the citizens and the soldiers within the City clustering more thickly upon the walls, afraid of the terrible ballistae they retired, indulging only in the luxury of taunts and epithets of barbarian scorn hurled at the beaten army.

The events of the day had fully justified the intuitive judgment of Belisarius. The besieged, though terrible in skirmishes and sudden excursions, were too few in number for a pitched battle. "The fight" says Procopius, "which began at the camps of the barbarians ended in the trench and close to the walls of the City".

After this disastrous day the Imperial troops reverted to their old method of unexpected sallies by small bodies of troops, and practiced it with much of their former success. There is something of a Homeric, something of a mediaeval character in the stories which Procopius tells us of this period of the siege. No masses of troops were engaged on either side. Infantry were unused, save that a few bold and fleet-footed soldiers generally accompanied the horsemen. Single combats between great champions on horseback on either side were the order of the day.

Thus in one sally the general Bessas transfixed three of the bravest of the Gothic horsemen in succession with his spear, and with little aid from his followers put the rest of their squadron to flight. Thus also Chorsamantis, a Hun and one of the body-guard of Belisarius, in a charge on the Neronian Plain pursued too far, and was separated from his comrades. Seeing this the Goths closed round him, but he, standing on his defence, slew the foremost of their band. They wavered and fled before him. Drawing near to the walls of their camp and feeling that the eyes of their fellows were upon them, they turned, for very shame that so many should be chased by one. Again he slew their bravest, and again they fled. Thus he pursued them up to the very gates of the camp, and then returned across the plain unharmed. Soon after, in another combat, a Gothic arrow pierced his left thigh, penetrating even to the bone. The army surgeons insisted upon a rest of several days after so grave an injury, but the sturdy barbarian bore with impatience so long a seclusion from the delights of battle, and was often heard to murmur, "I will make those Gothic fellows pay for my wounded leg". Before long the wound healed and he was out of the doctors' hands. One day at the noontide meal, according to his usual custom, he became intoxicated, and determined that he would sally forth alone against the enemy, and, as he said over and over again to himself in the thick tones of a drunkard, "make them pay for my leg" Biding down to the Pincian Gate he declared that he was sent by the General to go forth against the enemy. The sentinels, not daring to challenge the assertion of one of the body-guard of Belisarius, and perhaps not perceiving his drunken condition, allowed him to pass through the gate. When the Goths saw a solitary figure riding forth from the city their first thought was "Here comes a deserter" but the bent bow and flying arrows of Chorsamantis soon undeceived them. Twenty of them came against him, whom he easily dispersed. He rode leisurely forward to the camp. The Romans from the ramparts, not recognizing who he was, took him for some madman. Soon he was surrounded by the outstreaming Goths, and after performing prodigies of valor fell dead amid a ring of slaughtered enemies, leaving a name to be celebrated for many a day in the camp-fire songs of his savage countrymen.

In reading this and many similar stories told us by Procopius we are of course bound to remember that we do not hear the Gothic accounts of their own exploits, accounts which might sometimes exhibit a Gothic champion chasing scores of flying Byzantines. But after making all needful abatement on this account, we shall probably be safe in supposing that the balance of hardihood, of wild reckless daring, was on the side of the Imperial army. Though the members of it called themselves Romans they were really for the most part, like Chorsamantis, barbarians, fresher from the wilderness than the Ostrogothic soldiers, every one of whom had been born and bred amid the delights of Italy. And the stern stuff of which the Imperial soldiers were made was tempered and pointed by what still remained of Roman discipline, and driven by the matchless skill of Belisarius straight to the heart of the foe.

On another occasion, the general Constantine, perhaps desiring to vie with the achievements of his rival Bessas, sallied out with a small body of Huns from the Porta Aurelia and found himself surrounded by a large troop of the enemy. To preserve himself from being attacked on all sides he retreated with his men into one of the narrow streets opening on Nero's Stadium. Here his men, dismounting, discharged their arrows at the enemy, who menaced them from the opposite ends of the street. The Goths thought, "Their quivers must soon be empty, and then we will rush in upon them from both sides and destroy them" But such was the deadly effect of the Hunnish missiles that the Goths found before long that their number was reduced more than one half. Night was closing in. They were seized with panic and fled. The pursuing Huns still aimed their deadly arrows at the backs of the flying foe. Thus, after effecting a frightful slaughter among the Goths, Constantine with his 'Massagetic' horsemen returned in safety to Home that night.

At another time it befell that Peranius, the general who came from the slopes of Caucasus, headed a sortie from the Salarian Gate. It was at first successful, and the Goths fled before the Romans. Then, when the sun was going down, the tide of battle turned. An Imperial soldier flying headlong before the Goths fell unawares into an underground vault prepared by ' the Romans of old' as a magazine for corn. Unable to climb the steep sides of the vault, and afraid to call for help, he passed all night in that confinement, in evil case. Next day another Roman sortie, more successful than the last, sent the Goths flying over the same tract of country, and lo! a Gothic soldier fell headlong into the same vault. The two companions in misfortune began to consult as to their means of escape, and bound themselves by solemn vows each to be as careful for his companion's safety as his own. Then they both sent up a tremendous shout, which was heard, as it chanced, by a band of Gothic soldiers. They came, they peeped over the mouth of the vaults and asked in Gothic tongue whoever was shouting from that darksome hole. The Goth alone replied, told his tale, and begged his comrades to deliver him from that horrible pit. They let down ropes into the vault, the ropes were made fast, they hauled up a man out of the pit, and to their astonishment a Roman soldier stood before them. The Roman—who had sagaciously argued that if his companion came up first no Gothic soldiers would trouble themselves to haul up him—explained the strange adventure and besought them to lower the ropes again for their own comrade. They did so, and when the Goth was drawn up he told them of his plighted faith, and entreated them to let his companion in danger go free. They complied, and the Roman returned unharmed to the City. As Ariosto sings of Ferrau and Rinaldo, when those fierce enemies agreed to roam together in search of Angelica who was beloved by both of them,—

'Oh loyal knights of that long vanished day!
Their faiths were two, they wooed one woman's smile,
And still they felt rude tokens of their fray,
The blows which each on other rained erewhile:
Yet through dark woods by paths that seemed to stray
They rode, and each nor feared nor harboured guile.'
(Orlando Furioso, 1. 22.)

A breath of the age of chivalry seems wafted over the savage battlefield, as we read of the vow between the two deadly enemies in the vault so loyally observed, and we half persuade ourselves that we perceive another aura from that still future age when men everywhere, recognizing that they have all fallen into the same pit of ruin and longing for deliverance, shall listen to the voice of the Divine Reconciler, "Sirs, ye are brethren : why do ye wrong one to another?"

The month of June was now begun. The combatants had reached the third month of the siege and had finished two years of the war. A certain Euthalius had landed at Tarracina bringing from Byzantium some much-needed treasure for the pay of the soldiers. In order to secure for him and for his escort of 100 men a safe entrance at nightfall into the city, Belisarius harassed the enemy through the long summer's day with incessant expectations of attack, expectations which, after the soldiers had taken their midday meal, were converted into realities. As usual the attacks were made on both sides, from the Pincian Gate and over the Neronian Plain. At the former place the Romans were commanded by three of Belisarius's guards, the Persian Artasines, Buchas the Hun, and Cutila the Thracian. The tide of war rolled backwards and forwards many times, and many succors poured forth both from the City and from the Gothic camp, over both of which the shouts and the din of battle resounded. At length the Romans prevailed, and drove back their foes. In this action the splendid contempt of pain shown by Cutila and by a brother-guardsman Arzes greatly impressed the mind of Procopius. Cutila had been wounded by a javelin which lodged in his skull. He still took part in the fight, and at sunset rode back with his comrades to the city, the javelin nodding to and fro in his head with every movement of his body. Arzes had received a Gothic arrow at the angle of the eye and nose, which came with such violence that it almost penetrated to the nape of his neck. He too rode back to Rome, like Cutila apparently heedless of the weapon which was shaking in the wound.

Meanwhile things were going ill with Martin and Valerian, who commanded the Imperial troops on the Neronian Plain. They were surrounded by large numbers of the enemy, and seemed on the point of being overwhelmed by them. At this crisis—it was now growing late—an opportune charge under Buchas the Hun, withdrawn for this purpose from the sortie on the other side of the city, saved the day. Buchas himself performed prodigies of valor. For a long time he alone, though still but a stripling, kept twelve of the enemy at bay. At length one Goth was able to deal him a slight wound under the right arm-pit, and another, a more serious wound, transversely, through the muscles of the thigh. By this time, however, he and his men had restored the fortunes of the Imperial troops. Valerian and Martin rode up with speed, scattered the barbarians who surrounded Buchas, and led him home between them, each holding one of his reins.

The object of all this bloody skirmishing was attained. Euthalius with the treasure, creeping along the Appian Way, stole at nightfall, unperceived, into the City. When all were returned within the walls, the wounded heroes were of course attended to; and Procopius, insatiable in his desire to widen his experience of human life, seems to have visited the surgical wards. The case of Arzes, who was looked upon as one of the bravest men in the household of Belisarius, gave the surgeons much anxious thought. To save the sight of the eye they held to be altogether impossible; but moreover they feared that the laceration of the multitude of nerves through which the arrow must be drawn, if it were extracted, would cause the death of the patient. A physician, Theoctistus by name, pressed his finger on the nape of his neck and asked if that gave him pain. When Arzes replied that it did, Theoctistus gave him the glad assurance, "Then we shall be able to save your life and your eye too". At once cutting off the feather end of the arrow where it projected from the face, the surgeons dissected the comparatively insensitive tissues at the end of the neck till they grasped the triangular point of the arrow, and drawing it out endways gave the patient but little pain and left him with his eye uninjured and his face unscarred. The cases of Cutila and Buchas terminated less favorably. When the javelin was drawn from the head of the former he fainted. Inflammation of the membranes of the brain set in, followed by delirium, and he died not many days after. Buchas also died after three days, of the terrible hemorrhage from his wounded thigh. The physicians assured Procopius that had the lance penetrated straight in, his life might have been preserved, but the transverse wound was fatal.

The deaths of these heroes filled the Roman army with sorrow, which was only mitigated by the sounds of lamentation arising from the Gothic camp. These bewailings, not previously heard after much fiercer encounters, were due to the exalted rank of the warriors who had fallen by the sword of Buchas.

Such were some of the sallies and skirmishes which occurred in this memorable siege. Sixty-nine encounters in all took place, and Procopius wisely remarks that it is not needful for him to give the details of all of them. He himself, as we shall soon see, left the scene of action for a time; and for some months of the remainder of the siege we miss the minute descriptive touches (though some readers may find them tedious) which reveal the personal presence of the historian in the earlier acts of the great drama.

CHAPTER IX.

THE BL0CKADE

In the terrible struggle of the Thirty Years' War there was a memorable interlude when Gustavus Adolphus and Wallenstein watched one another for eleven weeks before the walls of Nuremberg, the Swede in vain attempting to storm the entrenchments of the Bohemian, the Bohemian hoping that famine and pestilence would force the Swede to move off and leave Nuremberg to his mercy. That 'Campaign of Famine' was virtually a drawn game. Gustavus was forced to evacuate his position, but Wallenstein's army was so weakened by hunger and disease that he had to leave the famine-stricken city unattacked.

Somewhat similar to this was the position of the two armies that now struggled for the possession of Rome. It was clear that the Goths could not carry the defenses of the City by simply rushing up to them in undisciplined valor with their rude engines of war, and seeking to swarm over them. It was equally clear that the little band of Belisarius could not beat off the enemy by a pitched battle on the plains of the Campagna. The siege must therefore become a mere blockade, and the question was which party in the course of this blockade would be soonest exhausted. In the course of the Crimean War a Russian diplomatist uttered the famous saying, "My master has three good generals, and their names are January, February, and March". Even so in the dread conflict that was impending, two spectral forms, each marshalling a grim and shadowy army, were to stalk around the walls of the City and the six camps of the Goths. They would fight on both sides, but the terrible question for Belisarius and for Witigis was, to which side would they lend the more effectual aid. The names of these two invisible champions were Limos and Loimos (Famine and Pestilence).

Recognizing the changed character of the siege, Witigis took one step which he would have done well to have taken three months before, towards completing the blockade of Rome. About three and a-half miles from the city there is a point now marked by a picturesque mediaeval tower called Torre Fiscale, where two great lines of aqueducts cross one another, run for about 500 yards side by side, and then cross again. The lofty arcade of the Anio Vetus and Claudia is one of these lines, running at first to the south of its companion, then north, and then south again. The other is the arcade of the Marcian, Tepulan, and Julian waters, which has been used by Pope Sixtus V as the support of his hastily-constructed aqueduct, the Aqua Felice. Even now, in their ruined state, these long rows of lofty arches, crossing and recrossing one another, wear an aspect of solemn strength; and were a battle to be fought over this ground today they might play no unimportant part in the struggle of the contending armies. Here then the Goths, filling up the lower arches with clay and rubble, fashioned for themselves a fortress, rude perchance, but of considerable strength. They placed in it a garrison of 7000 men, who commanded not only the Via Latina (which was absolutely close to the aqueducts), but also the Via Appia (which runs nearly parallel to the Latina at about a miles distance), so effectually that the transport of provisions to Rome along either of those roads seems to have become practically impossible.

When the citizens saw these two great roads to the south blocked, discouragement began to fill their hearts. They had long looked forward to the month of Quintilis—that month which also bore the name of the great Julius, and in which they had celebrated for a thousand years the victory of the Lake Regillus—as the month of their deliverance from the Goths; and indeed a Sibylline prophecy of the Sibyl was in circulation among the remnant of the Patricians which intimated not very obscurely that this should come to pass. Yet Quintilis with its burning heat had come, was passing away, and still the yellow-haired barbarians clustered about the walls. So long as the crops stood in the Campagna some slight mitigation of the impending famine was afforded by bands of daring horsemen who rode forth at nightfall, hurriedly reaped the standing ears, laid them on their horses' backs, and galloped back to Rome to sell the furtive harvest at a high price to the wealthy citizens. But now even this resource was beginning to fail, and all the citizens, rich and poor alike, were being reduced to live on the grass which, as Procopius remarks, always, in winter and summer alike, covers with its green robe the land of the Romans. For animal food the resource of the moment was to make a kind of sausage out of the flesh of the army mules which had died of disease. Thus was the General, Limos, beginning to show himself in great force on the side hostile to Rome.

Belisarius, who was already sorely harassed by the daily increasing difficulties of commissariat, had the additional vexation of receiving, one day, an embassy from the hunger-stricken Romans. They told him in plain words that the patriotism and the loyalty to the Empire, on which they prided themselves when they opened to him the gates of the city, now seemed to them the extremity of foolishness. They felt that they were

'Cursed with the burden of a granted prayer'

and longed for nothing so much as to be put back into the same happy state they were in, before a soldier from Byzantium showed his face among them. But that now could never be. Their estates in the country round were wasted. The city was so shut up that none of the necessaries of life could enter it. Many of their fellow-citizens were already dead; and upon these they thought with envy, wishing that they could be laid quietly underground beside them. Hunger made them bold to speak thus to the mighty Belisarius. Hunger made every other evil that they had ever endured seem light. The thought of death by hunger made any other mode of death seem a delightful prospect. In one word, let him lead them forth against the enemy, and they promised that he should not find them fail from his side in the stress of battle.

With a haughty smile and a profession of equanimity which masked his real discouragement, Belisarius replied: "I have expected all the events that have occurred in this siege, and among them some such proposal as this of yours. I know what the populace is fickle, easily discouraged, always ready to suggest impossible enterprises, and to throw away real advantages. I have no intention, however, of complying with your counsels, and so sacrificing the interests of my master and your lives as well. We do not make war in this way by a series of ill-considered, spasmodic efforts. War is a matter of calm and serious calculation, and my calculations of the game tell me that to wait is our present policy. You are anxious to hazard all upon a single throw of the dice, but it is not my habit to take any such short cuts to success. You announce that you are willing to go with me to battle. Pray when did you learn your drill? Have you never heard that a certain amount of practice is necessary to enable men to fight; and do you imagine that the enemy will be kind enough to wait while you are learning how to use your weapons? Still, I thank you for your readiness to fight, and I praise the martial spirit which now animates you. To explain to you some of my reasons for delay, I will inform you that the largest armament ever sent forth by the Empire has been collected by Justinian out of every land, and is now covering the Ionian Gulf and the Campanian shore. In a few days I trust they will be with us, relieving your necessities by the supplies which they will bring, and burying the barbarians under the multitude of their darts. Now retire. I forgive you for the impatience which you have shown, and I proceed to my arrangements for hastening the arrival of the reinforcements".

Having with these boastful words revived the spirits of the Romans, the General dispatched the trusty Procopius to Naples to find out what truth there might be in the rumours of coming help. The historian set out at nightfall, escorted by the guardsman Mundilas with a small body of horse. The little party stole out of the Porta San Paolo, escaped the notice of the Gothic garrison at Torre Fiscale, and felt themselves, before long, past the danger of pursuit by the barbarians. Procopius then dismissed his escort and proceeded unattended to Naples. Soon the General's wife Antonina followed him thither, under the escort of Martin and Trajan, partly in order that Belisarius might know that she was in a place of safety, but also that her considerable administrative talents might be employed in organizing expeditions of relief. Certainly they did not find that vast Byzantine host darkening all the bays of Magna Graecia of which Belisarius had bragged to the Roman populace. But they did find in Campania a considerable number of unemployed cavalry; they also found that it was possible safely to diminish some of the Campanian and Apulian garrisons, and above all, as the Romans had command of the sea, it was easy to collect a goodly number of well-loaded provision-ships. Procopius alone, before he was joined by Antonina, had forwarded five hundred soldiers to Rome, together with a great number of provision-ships, which possibly unloaded their cargoes at Ostia.

During the time, probably lasting four months (July to November), that Procopius was engaged on this important mission, we miss (as has been already remarked) all the minutely graphic touches of his pen as to the siege of Rome, and these are not compensated by much that is interesting as to his stay at Neapolis. He saw there the remains of a fine mosaic picture of Theodoric which had been set up in that monarch's reign. Apparently the cement with which the little colored stones were fastened to the wall was badly made. The head had fallen shortly before Theodoric's death; eight years after, the breast and belly had fallen, and Athalaric had died a few days afterward. The fall of the part representing the loins had preceded only by a little space the murder of Amalasuntha. And now the legs and feet had also fallen, evidently showing that the whole Gothic monarchy was shortly to come to an end.

It was at this time also that Procopius studied the volcanic phenomena of Vesuvius, whose sullen caprices he describes very much in the language that would be used by a modern traveler. When he was there the mountain was bellowing in its well-known savage style, but had not yet begun to fling up its lava-stream; though this was daily expected. The upper part was excessively steep, the lower densely wooded. In the summit there was a cave so deep that it seemed to reach down to the very roots of the mountain, and in that cave, if one dared to bend over and look in, one could see the fire. People still kept alive the remembrance of the great eruption of 472, even as they now speak with awe of the eruption which occurred exactly fourteen centuries later, and point out to the traveler the wide-wasting desolation caused by the "lava di settanta due" In that earlier eruption the light volcanic stones were carried as far as Constantinople, so alarming the citizens that an annual ceremony (something like the Rogations in the Church at Vienne) was instituted for deliverance from this peril. By another eruption the stones were thrown as far as Tripoli in Africa. But Vesuvius upon the whole had not an evil reputation. The husbandmen had observed that when it was in a state of activity their crops of all kinds were more abundant than in other years: and the fine pure air of the mountain was deemed so conducive to health that physicians sent consumptive patients to dwell upon its flanks.

Leaving Procopius and Antonina at Naples, we return with their escorts to Rome. Great joy was brought to the citizens when Mundilas reported that the Appian Way was practically clear by night, the Goths not venturing to stir far from their aqueduct fortress after sunset. Belisarius hence inferred that while still postponing a general engagement he might adopt a somewhat bolder policy with the enemy, a policy which would make them besieged as well as besiegers. Martin and Trajan, after they had escorted Antonina on the road to Naples, were directed to take up their quarters at Tarracina. Gontharis and a band of Herulians occupied the yet nearer post of Albano, situated, like Tarracina, on the Appian Way, but at only one-fourth of the distance from Rome.

Albano, it is true, was before long taken by the Goths, but the general policy of encompassing, harassing, and virtually besieging the besiegers remained successful. Magnus, one of the generals of cavalry, and Sinthues, another of the brave guardsmen of Belisarius, were sent up the Anio valley to Tibur. They occupied and repaired the old citadel which stood where Tivoli now stands, surrounded by the steaming cascades of Anio, and, from this coign of vantage, by their frequent excursions grievously harassed the barbarians, whose reserves were perhaps quartered not far from the little town. In one of these forays Sinthues had the sinews of his right hand severed by a spear-thrust, and was thus disabled from actual fighting ever after.

On the southern side of Rome the Basilica of St. Paul, connected by its long colonnade with the Ostian Gate of the city (where stands the pyramid of Caius Cestius), and protected on one side by the stream of the Tiber, furnished a capital stronghold, but one which, from religious reasons, the Goths had hitherto refrained from including in their sphere of operations. The orthodox Belisarius was troubled with no such scruples. All the Huns in his army—the Huns were still heathen—were sent thither under the command of Valerian to form& a camp between the Basilica and the river. Here they could both obtain forage for their own horses and grievously interfere with the foraging excursions of the Goths from their fortress at Torre Fiscale. In truth, hunger, as the result of all these operations of Belisarius, was now beginning to tell severely on the unwieldy Gothic host. And not Hunger only: the other great general, Pestilence, began to lay his hand heavily on the barbarians. He was present in all their camps, but in none more terribly than in the new one between the Aqueducts. At length that stronghold had to be abandoned, and the dwindled remnant of its defenders returned to the camps nearer Rome. The deadly malaria had communicated itself also to the Huns in their trenches by S. Paolo, and they too returned to Rome. Already we seem to perceive in the sixth century the phenomenon with which we are so familiar in the nineteenth, that the malaria is more fatal in the solitary Campagna than in the crowded city.

So the autumn wore on, both armies suffering terrible privations, but each hoping to outlast the other. Probably about the month of October, Antonina returned to her fond and anxious husband. At least, on the 18th of November we find her taking part in a strange transaction, the particulars of which are preserved for us with dramatic vividness by the old Papal biographer. To understand it we must turn back a page or two in the tedious history of the Monophysite controversy. It will be remembered that the venerable Pope Agapetus during his visit to Constantinople in 536 had convicted Anthimus, the Byzantine Patriarch, of Monophysite heresy, had brought about his deposition from his see, and had Theodora consecrated Mennas in his room. The Empress Theodora, who clung to her Monophysite creed as passionately as if it had been some new form of sensual gratification, set her heart on the reversal of this deposition; and seeing the influence exerted over her husband's mind by the successors of St. Peter, determined that Anthimus should be recalled by the mediation of the Roman Pontiff. To the restless and intriguing intellect of the Empress the torrents of noble blood which were being shed in desperate conflict round the walls of the Eternal City meant merely that she was a little nearer to or a little further from the accomplishment of her project for having her own Bishop reinstated in his see. With this view she sent letters to the new Pope, Silverius, urging him to pay a speedy visit to Constantinople, or, failing in that act of courtesy, at least to restore Anthimus to his old dignity. Silverius, when he read the letters, said, "Now I know that this woman will compass my death"; but trusting in God and St. Peter he returned a positive refusal to recall the heretic who was justly condemned for his wickedness.

Finding Silverius inflexible, Theodora listened to the offer which had been already made by the archdeacon Vigilius, who was at this time acting as *Apocrisiarius*, or, in the language of later times, Nuncio of the Roman Bishop at the Imperial Court. This man, who, it may be remembered, was the expectant legatee of the Papal dignity, if Pope Boniface II had obtained the power to will away that splendid heritage, now offered full compliance with all Theodora's demands in favor of the Monophysites, and in addition, it is said, a bribe of 200 pounds weight of gold if he were enthroned instead of Silverius in the chair of St. Peter. The Empress therefore addressed a letter to the Patrician Belisarius directing him to find some occasion against Silverius to depose him from the Pontificate, or, if that were impossible, to force him to repair to Constantinople. The noble Belisarius, who had little liking for the task, and had enough upon his hands in the defence of Rome without plunging into the controversy concerning the Two Natures, had perhaps lingered in the fulfillment of this odious commission. Now, if our reading of the course of events be correct, Antonina, anxious to win the favor of Theodora, having returned from her successful mission to Campania, urged her unwilling husband to execute the commands of their patroness.

A letter was produced, written in the name of Silverius and addressed to King Witigis, offering to open the Asinarian Gate to the Goths. There was this much of plausibility in the alleged treason, that the Lateran Church is close to the Asinarian Gate, and possibly it might seem not inconsistent with the office of a Christian bishop to end the frightful sufferings of his flock even by such an act of disloyalty as this. The contemporaries, however, of Silverius seem to have entirely acquitted him of responsibility in this matter: and even the names of the forgers of the document are given by one historian. They were, Marcus, a clerk, probably employed at the General's headquarters, and a guardsman named Julian.

With this letter in his hand, Belisarius sent for Silverius and urged him to avert his own ruin by obeying the mandates of the terrible Augusta, renouncing the decrees of Chalcedon and entering into communion with the Monophysites. For a moment Silverius seems to have wavered. He left the palace, withdrew from the dangerous Lateran, shut himself up in the church of St. Sabina on the desolate Aventine, and there took counsel with his friends what he should do. Photius, the son of Antonina, was sent to lure him from his retreat by promises of safety.

The Pope went once to the Pincian, notwithstanding the advice of his friends "to put no confidence in the oaths of the Greeks" He returned that time in safety though still unyielding; but going a second time with a heavy heart and fearing the malice of his enemies, he was, Liberatus tells us, "seen by his friends no more". The expressive silence of this historian corresponds with the fuller details given by the, perhaps later, Papal biographer: "At the first and the second veils" (such were the semi-regal pomp and seclusion which he great General maintained) "all the clergy were parted from him. Then Silverius, entering with Vigilius only into the Mausoleum, found Antonina the Patrician's wife lying on a couch, and Vilisarius [Belisarius] sitting at her feet. And when the Patrician's wife saw him, she said to him: Tell us, Lord Pope Silverius, what have we done to thee and to the Romans that thou shouldest wish to betray us into the hands of the Goths? While she was yet speaking the sub-deacon John, District-visitor of the first Region, stripped the pallium from his shoulders and led him into a bed-room. There he stripped him, put on him the monastic dress, and concealed him. Then Sixtus the sub-deacon, District-visitor of the sixth Region, seeing him already turned into a monk, went forth and made this announcement to the clergy: The Lord Pope has been deposed and made a monk. Then they, hearing this, all fled; and Vigilius the Archdeacon received Silverius as if into his protection, and sent him to banishment in Pontus"—or rather, as Liberatus tells us, to Patara in Lycia. Assuredly the first-fruits of the restored Imperial dominion in Italy were bitter for the Roman Bishops who had so large a share in bringing about the change. That a Pope, the son of a Pope and a great Roman noble, should have the pallium torn from him and be thrust forth into obscure exile at the bidding of a woman, and that woman the daughter of an actress and a circus-rider, was a degradation to which the Arian Theodoric and his successors had never subjected the representative of St. Peter.

We will anticipate the course of the narrative by a few months in order to finish the story of Silverius. When he arrived at Patara his wrongs stirred the compassion of the Bishop of that city, who sought an audience with the Emperor and said, "Of all the many kings who reign in the world not one has suffered such cruel reverses of fortune as this man, who, as Pope, is over the whole Church". Justinian, who was perhaps ignorant of his wife's machinations, ordered that Silverius should be carried back to Rome and put on his trial. If the letters attributed to him were genuine, he should still have the choice of the episcopate of any other city but Rome; if forged, he should be restored to the Papal throne. Vigilius—so his enemies asserted—terrified by the return of his rival, sent a message to Belisarius, "Hand over to me Silverius; else can I not pay the price which I promised for the popedom". The unhappy ex-pontiff was transferred to the custody of two of the body-guard of Vigilius, and by them taken to the desolate island of Palmaria, where, being fed on the bread of adversity and the water of affliction, he expired on the 21st of June, 538. Posterity reverenced him as a martyr, and many sick persons were cured at his tomb.

We return to the siege of Rome. The month of December was now reached. Fresh troops, whose numbers were considerable when compared with the little band of Belisarius, though not when compared with the still remaining multitudes of the besiegers, had been dispatched from the East, and were collecting in the harbors of Southern Italy. There were at Naples 3000 Isaurians under Paulus and Conon, at Otranto 800 Thracian horsemen under John, and 1000 other cavalry under Alexander and Marcentius. There had already arrived in Rome by the Via Latina 300 horsemen under Zeno; and the 500 soldiers (perhaps infantry) collected by Procopius were still in Campania waiting to enter Rome.

Of the fresh generals who thus appear upon the scene, the only one of whom we need take special notice is John. He was the nephew of Vitalian, and from that relationship might have been supposed to be not a safe servant for Justinian, by whom Vitalian had been murdered. But we can discern no evidence of his being regarded with suspicion on this account. He was a skillful general and a stout-hearted soldier, absolutely incapable of fear, and able to vie with any of the barbarians in the endurance of hardship and in contentment with the coarsest fare. Either a cruel disposition, or, possibly, mere love for the gory revel of battle, had procured for him the epithet of *Sanguinarius*, under which he appears in the Papal Biography. Next to Bessas and Constantine, he was probably the most important officer now in the Imperial service in Italy, and, as we shall see hereafter, his fame was viewed with some jealousy by Belisarius. Although there were other officers bearing the same popular name, to prevent the tedious repetition either of his gory epithet or of his relationship to Vitalian, he will in these pages be called simply John, the others being distinguished by their peculiar epithets.

The large number of troops under Paulus and Conon were ordered to sail with at speed to Ostia. John, with his 1800 horsemen, to whom were joined the 500 soldiers raised by Procopius, marched along the Appian Way, escorting a long train of wagons laden with provisions for the famishing citizens of Rome. If the enemy should attack them their purpose was to form the wagons in a circle round them and fight behind this hastily raised barrier. No such attack, however, appears to have been made. The Goths at this time were thinking of embassies and oratory rather than of cutting off the enemy's supplies. It was no small disappointment to John and his troops to find Tarracina destitute of Roman forces. They had reckoned on meeting there Martin and Trajan, whom Belisarius had a few days before withdrawn into the city. However, favored perhaps in part by the fight which was at the same time going on round the walls of Rome, both divisions of the army, by sea and land, arrived safely at Ostia, with all the stores of corn and wine with which they had freighted their ships and piled their wagons. The Isaurians dug a deep ditch round their quarters in the harbor-city, and the troops of John placed themselves in laager' (to use the phrase with which South African warfare has made us familiar) behind their wagons. Meanwhile to divert the attention of the barbarians from the movements of the relieving armies Belisarius had planned a fresh sortie. The story of these sallies is becoming monotonous, from their almost uniform success, but we are nearing the end of the catalogue. The main attack was to be made this time from the Porta Flaminia, a gate which had been so fast closed up by Belisarius that the Goths had practically come to regard it not only as unable, but also as containing for them no menace of a sally. Now, however, the General removed by night the large masses of stone (taken very likely from the *agger* of Servius Tullius) with which he had filled it up and drew up the great body of his troops behind it. A feigned attack made by 1000 horsemen under Trajan and Diogenes, issuing from the Pincian Gate, distracted the attention of the Goths, and caused them to pour out from the neighboring camps in chase of the flying Romans. When they were in all the confusion of pursuit, Belisarius ordered the Flaminian Gate to be opened and launched his well-drilled troops against the unsuspecting foe. The Romans charged across the intervening space, and were soon close up to the ramparts of that which we have called the First Gothic Camp, nearest of all the camps to the walls of Rome. A steep and narrow pathway which led to the main gate of the camp was held for a time, in Thermopylae fashion, by a courageous and well-armed barbarian, but Mundilas, the brave guardsman, at length slew the Gothic Leonidas and suffered no one to fill his place. The Roman soldiers pressed on, and swarmed round the ramparts of the camp, but, few as were the defenders within it, they were kept for some time at bay by the strength of the works. "For the fosse" says our historian, "was dug to a great depth, and the earth taken out from it, being all thrown to the inside, had made a very high bank which served the purpose of a wall, and was strongly armed with very sharp stakes and many of them". Then one of the household guard of Belisarius, an active soldier named Aquilinus, catching hold of a horse's bridle leaped upon its back, and was carried by its spring right over the rampart into the camp. Here he slew many of the Goths, but gathering round him they hurled upon him a shower of missiles. The horse was killed, but the brave and nimble Aquilinus escaped unhurt, and leaping down from the wall, joined on foot the stream of Roman soldiers who were pouring southwards from the Gothic camp towards the Pincian Gate, where the barbarians were still pursuing the flying troops of Trajan.

A shower of arrows in their rear slew many of the Goths: the survivors looked round and halted: the lately flying Romans also turned: the Goths found themselves caught between two attacks; they lost all cohesion and fell by hundreds. A few with difficulty escaped to the nearest camps, the occupants of which kept close and dared not stir forth to help them. In this battle, successful as were its main results for the Romans, Trajan received a wound which was well-nigh fatal. An arrow struck his face, a little above his right eye, in the angle formed by the eye and the nose. The whole of the iron tip, though long and large, entered and was hidden in the wound: the wooden part of the arrow, not well joined to the iron, fell to the earth. Notwithstanding his wound Trajan went on pursuing and slaying, and no ill results came of it. "Five years after" says the historian, "the arrow-tip of its own accord worked its way to the surface and showed itself in his face. For three years it has protruded a little from the surface. Everyone expects that in course of time it will work out altogether. Meanwhile Trajan has suffered no inconvenience from it of any kind".

The result of this sally was to strike deep discouragement into the hearts of the barbarians. "Already" said they to one another, "we are as much the besieged as the besiegers. Famine and Pestilence are stalking through all our camps. New armies, we cannot tell how large, are on their way from Constantinople, and the terrible Belisarius, who knows that only a few of us are left to represent the many myriads who sat down before Rome, is actually daring to assault us in our camps, one of which he has all but taken". In some kind of assembly, which the historian calls their Senate, they debated the question of raising the siege, and decided on the desperate expedient of an appeal to the justice and generosity of Byzantium, while sending an embassy to Rome to plead their cause with Belisarius. The embassy consisted of an official of high rank in the Gothic state but of Roman lineage (one who occupied in fact nearly the same position formerly held by Cassiodorus, but whose name Procopius has not recorded), and with him two Gothic nobles. The arguments used by the Gothic envoy and the replies of Belisarius, which are probably in the main correctly reported by the historian, himself present at the interview, may best be presented in the form of a dialogue.

Gothic Envoys. This war is inflicting upon both the combatants indescribable miseries. Let us each moderate our desires, and see if some means cannot be found of bringing it to an end. The ruler should think not merely of the gratification of his own ambition, but also of the happiness of his subjects, and that assuredly is not being promoted on either side by the continuance of the war. We suggest that the conference be not conducted by means of studied orations on either side, but that each party say out that which is in their minds without preparation, and that if anything be said which seems improper, exception be taken to it at once.

Belisarius. I shall interpose no hindrance to the dialogue proceeding as ye propose: but see that ye utter words that are just and that tend towards peace.

Gothic Envoys. We complain of you, O Romans, that you have taken up arms without cause against an allied and friendly people: and we shall prove our complaint by facts which no man can gainsay. The Goths came into possession of this Gothic land not by violently wresting it from the Romans, but by taking it from Odovacar, who, having over-turned the Emperor of that day, changed the constitutional government which existed here into a tyranny. Now Zeno who was then Emperor of the East was desirous to avenge his colleague on the usurper and to free the country, but was not strong enough to cope with the forces of Odovacar. He therefore persuaded our ruler Theodoric, who was at that very time meditating the siege of Byzantium, to forego his hostility to the Empire in remembrance of the dignities which he had already received in the Roman State, (those namely of Patrician and Consul), to avenge upon Odovacar his injustice to Augustulus, and to confer upon this country and his own people the blessings of a just and stable government. Thus then did our nation come to be guardians of this land of Italy. The settled order of things which we found here we preserved, nor can any man point to any new law, written or unwritten, and say that was introduced by Theodoric. As for religious affairs, so anxiously have we guarded the liberty of the Romans that there is no instance of one of them having voluntarily or under compulsion adopted our creed, while there are many instances of Goths who have gone over to yours, not one of whom has suffered any punishment. The holy places of the Romans have received the highest honor from us, and their right of sanctuary has been uniformly respected. The high offices of the State have been always held by Romans, not once by a Goth. We challenge contradiction if any of our statements are incorrect. Then, too, the Romans have been permitted by the Goths to receive a Consul every year, on the nomination of the Emperor of the East. To sum up. You did nothing to help Italy when, not for a few months but for ten long years, she was groaning under the oppression of Odovacar and his barbarians: but now you are putting forth all your strength upon no valid pretext against her rightful occupants. We call upon you therefore to depart hence, to enjoy in quiet your own possessions and the plunder which during this war you have collected in our country.

Belisarius (in wrath). You promised that you would speak briefly and with moderation, but you have given us a long harangue, full of something very like bragging. The Emperor Zeno sent Theodoric to make war upon Odovacar, not in order that he himself should obtain the kingship of Italy (for what would have been the advantage of replacing one tyrant by another?), but that the country might be restored to freedom and its obedience to the Emperor. Now all that Theodoric did against the usurper was well done, but his later behavior, in refusing to restore the country to its rightful lord, was outrageously ungrateful: nor can I see any difference between the conduct of a man who originally lays hands on another's property, and his who, when such a stolen treasure comes into his possession, refuses to restore it to its true owner. Never, therefore, will I surrender the Emperor's land to any other lord. But if you have any other request to make, speak on.

Gothic Envoys. How true is all that we have advanced every member of this company knows right well. But, as a proof of our moderation, we will relinquish to you the large and wealthy island of Sicily, without which your possession of Africa is insecure.

Belisarius (with sarcastic courtesy). Such generosity calls for a return in kind. We will freely grant permission to the Goths to occupy the whole of Britain, a much larger island than you offer to us, and one which once belonged to the Romans as Sicily once belonged to the Goths.

Gothic Envoys. Well then, if we talk about adding Naples and Campania to our offer, will you consider it?

Belisarius. Certainly not. We have no power to grant away the lands of the Emperor in a manner which he might not approve of.

Gothic Envoys. Or if we pledged ourselves to pay a certain yearly tribute to your master?

Belisarius. No, not so. We can treat on no conditions but those which secure that the Emperor shall have his own again.

Gothic Envoys. Come then: allow us to send ambassadors to the Emperor to treat about all the matters in dispute, and let there be a cessation of hostilities on both sides for a fixed period, to give the ambassadors time to go and return.

Belisarius. Be it so. Never shall my voice be raised against any proposition which is really made in the interests of peace.

And thereupon the ambassadors returned to the Gothic camp to make arrangements for the coming truce. Thus ended this memorable interview between the representative of Caesar and the servants of the Gothic King. Memorable, if for no others, assuredly for us, the dwellers in that well-nigh forgotten island whose sovereignty Belisarius tossed contemptuously to the Goths as a reply to their proposed surrender of Sicily. Would that we had a Procopius to tell us what was passing at that moment in 'the island much larger than Sicily, which had belonged aforetime to the Romans!' Three years before, as we are told, Cerdic, the half-mythical ancestor of King Alfred and of Queen Victoria, had died (if indeed he had ever lived), perchance in some palace rudely put together on the ruins of the Roman Praetorium at Winchester. His people had been for near twenty years pausing in their career of conquest, during that mysterious interval, or even refluence of the Saxon wave, which legend has glorified by connecting it with the great deeds of Arthur. In the far north, ten years after this time, King Ida was to rear upon the basaltic rock of Bamborough, overlooking the misty flock of the Fame Islands, that fortress which was to be the capital of the Bernician kingdom, and which narrowly missed being the capital of England itself and rivaling the world-wide fame of London. When we have said this we have told nearly all that is known of the deeds of our fathers and the fortunes of our land during this central portion of the sixth century after Christ.

The negotiations for a truce, and the consequent slackening of the vigilance of the Goths, came at the most opportune moment possible for the plans of Belisarius. Vast quantities of corn, wine, and provisions for the relief of the hunger-stricken City were collected at Ostia, but a murderous struggle would have been necessary to cover their entrance into Rome. On the very evening of the day of conference Belisarius, accompanied apparently by his wife and attended by 100 horsemen, rode to Ostia to meet the generals who were in command of the Isaurians at that port. He encouraged them by the tidings of the negotiations that had been commenced, urged them to use all possible diligence in the transport of the provisions to Rome, and promised to do all in his power to secure them a safe passage. With the first grey of the morning he returned to the City, leaving Antonina behind to consult with the generals as to the best means of conveying the stores. The only practicable towpath—as was before said—ran along the right bank of the river, and was commanded by the Gothic garrison of Portus. Moreover, the draught-oxen were half dead with hunger and hardship. In these circumstances Antonina and the generals decided to trust to sails and oars alone. They selected all the largest boats belonging to the navy at Ostia, fitted each one with rude battlements of tall planks to protect the rowers from the arrows of the enemy, freighted them with the cargoes of provisions, and began their perilous voyage. A considerable part of the army accompanied them along the left bank of the river by way of escort, but several of the Isaurians were also left at Ostia to guard the ships. Apparently the wind blew from the south-west, for wherever the stream pursued a straight course their sails were full and all went pleasantly; but in the windings of the river they had to resort to their oars, and hard was the toil needed to traverse these portions of the stream.

Strangely enough, the Goths, though no truce was formally concluded, offered no opposition to this proceeding, though they must have known that that day's work, if successful, would undo, in great measure, the results of the last six months of blockade. The garrison at Portus lay quiet, marveling at the ingenuity of the Romans, and saw the heavy barges sail almost under the towers of their fortress. The Goths in the six camps lay quiet too, partly comforting themselves with the assurance that the Romans would never get their city revictualled in that way, partly thinking that it was not worthwhile to imperil the results of the conference and lose the longed-for truce by any hostile action which might offend the terrible Belisarius. So they let their opportunity slip. The barges passed and repassed till all the stores were safely transported to Rome. The ships then returned to Constantinople with all speed to avoid the peril of storms, the winter solstice being now reached. A few Isaurians, under the command of Paulus, were left at Ostia, but the great mass of the new soldiers entered Rome in safety.

When the Goths had quietly looked on at all these important operations, they might just as well have at once recognized the hopelessness of their task and marched away from Rome. They still clung however, or rather perhaps their King alone still clung, to the expedient of a truce and an embassy, and to the hope of obtaining favorable terms from the justice of Justinian. It was arranged that Gothic ambassadors should be sent under Roman escort to Constantinople, that a truce for three months should be concluded between the two armies to give the embassy time to go and return, and that hostages of high rank should be given on both sides. The Gothic hostage was a nobleman named Ulias; the Roman hostage was Zeno, a cavalry officer who, as was before stated, had recently entered Rome by the Latin Way.

In the whole course of these negotiations the Goths had been thoroughly outwitted by Belisarius. Nothing had been said about the question of revictualling Rome; and Belisarius had quietly decided that question in his own favor, under the very eyes of the puzzled barbarians. Neither does anything seem to have been said expressly as to the case of either army ceasing to occupy all its positions in force, a case which soon arose. Shut off from the coast by the Byzantines' command of the sea, and having, very likely, failed to maintain the Roman roads in good condition, the Goths found great difficulty in provisioning the garrisons at some of their distant posts. Under the stress of this difficulty they withdrew their garrisons from Portus, from Centumcellae (the modern Civita Vecchia), and from Albanum. As fast as each square was thus left vacant on the chess-board, Belisarius moved up a piece to take possession of it. The Goths, who found themselves thus ever more and more hemmed in by the Roman outposts, sent an embassy of angry complaint to Belisarius. "Was this in accordance with the terms of the armistice? Witigis had sent for the Goths in Portus to come to him for a temporary service, and Paulus and his Isaurians had marched in and taken possession of the undefended fortress. So, too, with Albanum and Centumcellae. All these places must be given back to them or they would do terrible things". Belisarius simply laughed at their threats, and told them that all the world knew perfectly well for what reason those fortresses had been abandoned. The truce still formally continued, but both parties eyed one another with jealousy and distrust.

By the new reinforcements which had been sent poured into Rome, Belisarius found himself at the head of so large a number of troops that he could even spare some for distant operations. He therefore dispatched John at the head of 800 horsemen to the mountains of the Abruzzi. Two other bodies of troops, amounting to 1200 in all, were to follow his motions and adapt their movements to his, but, perhaps for reasons of commissariat, not to occupy the same quarters. One of these supporting armies was commanded by Damian, nephew of Valerian, and his troops were drawn from that general's army. The orders given to John were to pass the winter at Alba [Fucentia], a city about seventy miles from Rome, in the heart of the Apennines and near to the little lake of Fucinus. Here he was to rest, not disturbing the Goths so long as they attempted no hostile operation. The moment that he perceived the truce to be broken, he was to sweep like a whirlwind on the territory of Picenum, between the Apennines and the Adriatic, to ravage the Gothic possessions (scrupulously respecting those of the Romans), to collect plunder from every quarter, and to carry off their women and children into slavery. All this could be easily effected, since the men of the district were all serving in the Gothic armies. He was to take every fortress that threatened his route, leaving none to molest his rear, and he was to keep his plunder intact till the time came for dividing it among the whole army. "For it is not fair" said Belisarius, with a laugh, "that we should have the trouble of killing the drones and that you should divide all the honey".

Two events relieved the tedium of the siege during the early months of the year 538: the visit of the Archbishop of Milan and the quarrel between Belisarius and Constantine. Datius, the Ligurian Archbishop, came at the head of a deputation of influential citizens to entreat Belisarius to send a small garrison to enable them to hold their city (which had apparently already revolted from the Gothic King) for the Empire. They enlarged on the populousness and wealth of Mediolanum, the second city of Italy, its important position (eight days' journey from Bavenna and the same distance from the frontiers of Gaul), and the certainty that Liguria would follow whithersoever its capital might lead. Belisarius promised to grant their request as soon as possible, and meanwhile persuaded Datius and his companions to pass the winter with him in Rome.

The quarrel with Constantine, in which Procopius sees the hand of Nemesis resenting the uniform prosperity of the Imperial cause, arose out of small beginnings. certain Presidius, one of the leading citizens of Ravenna, having some cause of complaint against the Goths, determined to flee to the Imperial army. Leaving Ravenna on pretence of hunting, he passed through the Gothic lines (this happened just before Witigis started for the siege of Rome) and made his way to the army which under Constantine was then quartered at Spoleto. Of all his possessions he was able to bring with him nothing but two daggers in golden scabbards set with precious stones. The fame of the refugee from Ravenna and his jeweled poniards reached the ears of Constantine, who sent one of his guards named Maxentiolus to the church outside the walls, where Presidius had taken refuge, to demand the daggers in the General's name. Presidius was forced to submit to this spoliation, but hastened to Rome to lay his complaint before the General. In the turmoil of the Gothic assault and the Roman sorties, he found for long no suitable opportunity for stating his case; but now that the truce had been proclaimed he sought and obtained an audience with the General, before whom he laid his complaint. Belisarius had other reasons for censuring his lieutenant; but at present he confined himself to a gentle remonstrance with Constantine, and the expression of a wish that he would abstain from such acts of rapacity. The Fate which was brooding over the covetous general prevented him from "leaving well alone". He must needs taunt Presidius, whenever he met him, with the loss of his daggers, and ask him what he had gained by complaining to Belisarius. At length the refugee could bear it no longer; but one day when Belisarius was riding through the Forum he seized his horse's bridle and cried out with a loud voice, "Are these the far-famed laws of Justinian, that when a man takes refuge with you from the barbarians ye should spoil him of his goods by force?" The General's retinue shouted to him to let go the horse's bridle, but he clung to it, repeating his cries and passionate appeals for justice, till Belisarius, who knew the rightness of his cause, promised that the daggers should be restored to him.

The next day there was an assembly of the generals in a chamber of the palace on the Pincian. Constantine was there, and Bessas and Valerian. There was also present Ildiger, son-in-law of Antonina, who had lately come to Rome with a large troop of horsemen from Africa. Before all this assembly Belisarius related what had occurred on the previous day, blamed the unjust deed of Constantine, and exhorted him to make a tardy reparation for his fault by restoring the daggers to their owner. "No" replied Constantine, "I will do nothing of the kind. I would rather throw the daggers into the Tiber than give them back to Presidius". Belisarius asked him with some warmth if he remembered who was his general. "In everything else" said Constantine, "I am willing to obey you, since the Emperor orders me to do so, but as for the matter that you are now talking about I will never obey you". Belisarius ordered the guards to enter. "To kill me, I suppose" said Constantine. "No" was the answer, "but since your armor-bearer Maxentiolus by force took these daggers away, by force to compel him to restore them". Constantine, however, believing that his death was decided upon, determined to do some memorable deed while he yet lived, and drawing the dagger which hung at his side stabbed Belisarius in the belly. Wounded, but not fatally, the General staggered back, and clasping Bessas in his arms interposed the portly form of the Ostrogoth between himself and the assassin. He then glided out of the chamber. Constantine, mad with rage, was on the point of following him, but Ildiger seized him by the right hand and Bessas by the left, and they together pulled him in an opposite direction. Then the guards entered, and with much difficulty wrested the dagger from the furious officer. He was dragged off to a place of confinement in the palace, thence, after some days, to another house, and eventually was put to death by the order of Belisarius.

The execution of a lieutenant who had so grossly insulted his superior officer and attempted his life does not appear to be a deed difficult to justify. Procopius remarks, however, that "this was the only unholy action which Belisarius ever committed, and it was unlike his usual disposition. For he generally showed great gentleness in his dealings with all men. But, as before remarked, it was fated that Constantine should come to a bad end". This reflection convinces us that we have not heard the whole story, and that the affair of the jeweled poniards was rather the pretext than the cause of the death of Constantine. In the *Anecdota*, that Scandalous Chronicle written in the old age of Procopius, he informs us that when all Constantinople was talking about the gallantries of Antonina and the punishment inflicted on her lover by Belisarius, Constantine, in his condolence with the injured husband, said, "It is not the young man but the lady that I should punish in such a case". Antonina heard of the saying and treasured up her wrath till an occasion was found for wreaking it upon the injudicious officer.

Not long after this affair, the Goths attempted to enter the City by guile. Agricola's aqueduct, the Aqua Virgo, is so constructed, for engineering reasons, as to form a long circuit round the east and north of the City. The course which it now pursues is almost entirely in the rear of the Gothic position, but there seems reason to think that in 538 it passed through the Gothic lines, that it touched the Wall of Aurelian near the Salarian Gate, and was then carried for some distance round the Wall on a low arcade only some three or four feet in height. However this may be, there is no doubt that then as now it burrowed under the Pincian Hill, and emerged into a deep well-like chamber communicating with one of the palaces on that eminence. That palace was then the Pincian Palace inhabited by Belisarius. The dwelling which now rises immediately above the receptacle of the Aqua Virgo is the Villa Medicis, the home of the French Academy. A strong argument is thus furnished in favor of identifying the two sites. From the Pincian the water was carried, then as now, to the Campus Martius, the fountain of Trevi, and the neighborhood of the Pantheon; in fact the aqueduct ran right into the very heart of Rome.

A party of Goths, during this treacherous truce-time, determined to attempt an entrance into the City by this aqueduct, which of course, like all the others, was now only a tunnel bare of water. With lighted torches they groped their way through the *specus*, which is about six feet high by a foot and a half wide. They crept along unopposed, perhaps for a distance of one or two miles, till at last they were actually within the City, and close to the foot of the steps leading to the very palace of Belisarius. Here they found their further progress barred by a newly-erected wall. This wall had been built by command of Belisarius soon after his entry into the City. The wary General, who knew every move that his enemy ought to make upon the board, was not going to allow Rome to be taken from him as he had taken Naples from the Goths, by stealing through an aqueduct. Foiled in their present purpose, the Goths broke off a bit of stone from this wall as a record of their perilous expedition, and returned to tell Witigis how near they had been to success and why they had missed it. But while the explorers were moving along torches through the small part of the Aqua Virgo which was above ground, the flash of their torches through a chink in the walls attracted the attention of a sentinel, stationed perhaps in the fosse somewhere near the Pincian Gate. He talked to his comrades about this mysterious light, seen only a foot or two above the surface of the earth; but they only laughed at him, telling him that he must have seen a wolfs eyes gleaming through the darkness. However, the story of the sentinel and his wonderful light reached the ears of Belisarius. In a moment its true meaning flashed upon him. "This is no wolf" he said to himself; "the Goths are trying the aqueduct". At once he sent the guardsman Diogenes with a body of picked men to examine the channel. We must suppose that they took down part of the obstructing wall, and so entered the *specus*. They saw the place where the stone had been chipped off which was shown to Witigis. They pressed on: they found everywhere the droppings from the Gothic flambeaux, and at length discovered some Gothic lamps. It was clear that the enemy had been trying by these means to steal into Rome. The Goths soon perceived that Belisarius was acquainted with their adventure, and the design, which Witigis had discussed in a council of war, of following up the quest opened by the exploring party, was promptly abandoned.

During the remainder of the three months of nominal truce two more attempts upon the City were made, or at any rate planned, by the barbarians. One was upon the Pincian Gate, and was arranged for the hour of the midday meal, when but few soldiers were likely to be behind the battlements. The Goths were coming on in loose order, with ladders to mount the walls and fire to burn the gate. But not even in truce-time were the walls ever left quite bare of guards. Fortunately, it was then the turn of the gallant Ildiger to keep watch. He saw the loosely marshaled band advancing, at once divined their traitorous design, sallied out with his followers, easily changed their disorderly advance into an equally disorderly retreat, and slew the greater number of them. A great clamor was raised in Rome; the Goths saw that their design was discovered, and all returned to their camps.

The next scheme was of a baser kind, and was worthy of the confused brain from which it sprung. It has been said that the wall of the City between the Tomb of Hadrian and the Flaminian Gate was low and destitute of towers, the military engineers of Aurelian having thought that the river would here be a sufficient protection. Witigis therefore argued thus with himself: "If I could only lull to sleep the vigilance of the Roman sentinels on that piece of wall, a strong detachment of my army might cross the river in boats, climb the wall, and open the gates of the City to the rest of the army, who shall be all waiting outside". He therefore took into his pay two Romans, probably of the laboring class, who dwelt near the great basilica of St. Peter. They promised to take a large skin of wine to these sentinels about nightfall, offer them refreshment, keep them drinking and talking till far into the night, and when they were too drunk to observe anything, throw an opiate, with which Witigis provided the traitors, into their cups. The infamous scheme was revealed to Belisarius by one of its intended instruments, who revealed also the name of his accomplice. The latter under torture confessed the criminal intention, and surrendered the opiate which he had received from Witigis. Belisarius cut off the nose and ears of the unhappy traitor,—these barbarous mutilations were becoming part of the penal code of Constantinople,—and sent him mounted on an ass to the Gothic camp to tell his dismal tale to his royal confederate. When the barbarians saw him they recognized that God did not bring their plans to a successful issue, and therefore that they would never be able to capture the City.

By these two attempts (if we may trust the statement of Procopius, who probably throws more blame on the Goths than they deserve) the three months' truce was broken to justify Belisarius in commencing a campaign of retaliation. He sent letters to John ordering him to begin the operations in Picenum which had been arranged between them. John marched with his two thousand horsemen through the settlements of the Goths, burning, plundering, wasting all that belonged to the enemy. Ulitheus, the aged uncle of Witigis, dared to meet him in battle, but was slain, and almost his whole army fell with him. After this, none would face him in the field. Pressing on through the country on the eastern slopes of the Apennines, he came to the fortresses of Urbino and Osimo, neither of them garrisoned by a large force of Goths, but both strong by their natural position. According to the orders of Belisarius he should have reduced each of these fortresses before proceeding further, but the cry of his army and his own military instinct both directed a bold forward movement to Rimini. To that city by the Adriatic he accordingly marched, and such was the terror of the Goths that he carried it at the first assault. It is true that he had not here, as in the cases of Urbino and Osimo, to attack a high hill fortress, for Rimini, though surrounded with walls, lies in a wide plain at the mouth of the Marecchia; and the supremacy by sea which the Byzantines possessed would have made it a difficult city for the Goths to hold against a united attack by sea and land.

But whatever the cause, here was the victorious army of John in possession of an important city two hundred miles in the rear of the Gothic army, and only thirty-three, a single days march, from their capital, Ravenna. John had rightly calculated that this step of his would lead to the raising of the siege of Rome. The Goths, thoroughly alarmed for the safety of their capital, began to chafe at every day spent in sight of those walls which, as they felt, they never should surmount. Their King too had his own reasons for sharing their impatience when it began to be whispered that his young wife Matasuentha, proud and petulant, and never forgiving her lowly-born husband for the compulsion which had brought her to his side in wedlock, had sent secret messages to John at Rimini congratulating him on his success, and holding out to him hopes that she would betray the Gothic cause if he would accept her hand in marriage.

So it came to pass that when the three months of truce had expired, although no tidings had about been received from the ambassadors, the Goths resolved to abandon their blockade of Rome. It was near the time of the Vernal Equinox, and 374 days from the commencement of the siege, when they carried this resolution into effect. At dawn of day, having set all their seven camps on fire, the dispirited mass of men began to move northward along the Flaminian Way.

The Romans, who saw them departing, were for some time in doubt whether to pursue them or rather "to make a bridge of gold for a retreating foe". The absence of so many of their cavalry in Picenum was a reason for leaving them unmolested. But Belisarius hastily armed as large a force as he could muster, both of horse and foot, and when half the Gothic army had crossed the Milvian Bridge he launched his soldiers forth from the Flaminian Gate, and made a furious attack on the Gothic rear. Mundilas, the escort of Procopius, conspicuous in so many previous battles, wrought great deeds of valor in this, fighting four barbarians at once and killing them all. Longinus, an Isaurian, was also among the foremost in the fight, which, having been for some time doubtful, ended in the flight of the barbarians. Then followed a terrible scene, Goth struggling with Goth for a place upon the bridge and for a way of escape from the devouring sword. Many fell by the hands of their own comrades, many were pushed off the bridge, and, encumbered by the weight of their armor, sank in the stream of the Tiber. Few, according to the account of Procopius, succeeded in struggling across to the opposite shore, where the other half of the army stood awaiting them. In this statement there is probably some exaggeration, but there can be no doubt that the well-timed attack of Belisarius inflicted a severe blow upon the retreating enemy. The joy of the Romans in their victory was alloyed by grief for the death of the valiant Longinus.

So ended the long siege of Rome by Witigis, a siege in which the numbers and prowess of the Goths were rendered useless by the utter incapacity of their commander. Ignorant how to assault, ignorant how to blockade, he allowed even the sword of Hunger to be wrested from him and used against his army by Belisarius. He suffered the flower of the Gothic nation to perish, not so much by the weapons of the Romans as by the deadly dews of the Campagna. With heavy hearts the barbarians must have thought, as they turned them northwards, upon the many graves of gallant men which they were leaving on that fatal plain. Some of them must have suspected the melancholy truth that they had dug one grave, deeper and wider than all, the grave of the Gothic monarchy in Italy.

CHAPTER X.

THE RELIEF OF RIMINI.

The utter failure of the Gothic enterprise against Rome did not, as might have been expected, immediately bring about the fall of Ravenna. Unskillful as was the strategy of the Ostrogoths, there was yet far more power of resistance shown by them than by the Vandals. In three months the invasion of Africa had been brought to a triumphant conclusion. The war in Italy had now lasted for three years, two more were still to elapse before the fall of the Gothic capital announced even its apparent conclusion.

These two years were passed in somewhat desultory fighting, waged partly in the neighborhood of Milan and partly along the course of the great Flaminian Way. Leaving the valley of the Po for the present out of our calculations, we will confine our attention to the long struggle which wasted the Umbrian lands, traversed by the great north road of Italy which bore the name of Proconsul Flaminius. t had been always an important highway. By it the legions of Caesar had marched forth to conquer Gaul, and had returned to conquer the Republic. The course of events in the fifth and sixth centuries which made Rome and Ravenna both, in a certain sense, capitals of Italy, gave to the two hundred and thirty miles of road between those capitals an importance, political and military, such as it had never possessed before.

Notwithstanding some slight curves, we may think of this road as running due north and south, since Ravenna is in almost precisely the same longitude as Rome: and at the point of the history which we have now reached the fortresses to the right of it are for the most part in the hands of the Emperor's generals, while nearly all those on the left are held for the Gothic King. This was the manner in which the latter disposed of his forces. At Urbs Vetus, the modern Orvieto, were 1000 men under the command of Albilas. At Clusium, that tomb of old Etruscan greatness, 1000 under Gelimer. At Tuder, now Todi, which also still preserves the memory of Etruria by its ancient walls, there were 400 Goths under Uligisalus. Fiesole, which from her high perch looks down upon Florence and the vale of Arno, was another Gothic stronghold, but we are not told by how many men it was occupied. Osimo, which similarly overlooks Ancona and the Adriatic, was held by 4000 picked troops under Visandus, and here, the advance of Belisarius was to be checked by a more stubborn resistance than was maintained by any of the other Gothic garrisons. At Urbino were stationed 2000 Goths under Morras. Mons Feletris (the high rock of S. Leo and the original capital of the mediaeval principality of Montefeltro) was occupied by 500 Goths, and Cesena by the like number. All of these places were high city-crowned hills of the kind with which not only the traveler in Italy but the student of pictures painted by the Umbrian masters is so familiar. They all bring back to the memory of an Englishman those graphic lines of Macaulay,

'Like an eagle's nest
   Perched on the crest

Of purple Apennine.'

Such were the Gothic strongholds.

On the other side the Romans held Narni, Spoleto, Perugia, and, across the central mountain-chain, Ancona and Rimini.

A glance at the map will show how the combatants were ranged, as if for one vast pitched battle, along the line of the Flaminian Way: and posts held by each party: Orvieto, seventy-four miles of Rome, garrisoned by Goths; Rimini, within thirty-three miles of Ravenna, garrisoned by Romans. If we may be permitted to take a simile from chess, each player has one piece pushed far up towards the enemy's line, threatening to cry check to the king, but itself in serious danger if not strongly supported. Belisarius had no mind to leave his piece so dangerously advanced. By a brilliant display of rashness, and it must be added of insubordination, John, with his 2000 Isaurian horsemen, had advanced to Rimini; and now the commander-in-chief, wanting the Isaurians for other service, ordered them to withdraw from that perilous position. Summoning his son-in-law Ildiger, and Martin (the veteran of the Vandal war and the sharer in the flight of Solomon), who had come out with the recent reinforcements to Italy, he put 1000 horsemen under their command and gave them a commission to take his orders to John. These orders were that he should withdraw with all his troops from Rimini, leaving in it a small garrison of picked soldiers drawn from the too numerous defenders of Ancona, which had been taken possession of by Conon at the head of his Thracians and Isaurians. The very smallness of the garrison at Rimini would, Belisarius hoped, induce the Goths to pass it by unmolested; while, on the other hand, two thousand cavalry soldiers, the flower of the Isaurian reinforcements, would offer a tempting prize to the enemy, to whom they would, if left at Rimini, soon be compelled to surrender by shortness of provisions.

Ildiger and Martin, whose watchword was speed, soon distanced the barbarian army who were marching in the same direction, but who were an unwieldy host, and were obliged to make a long circuit whenever they came near a Roman fortress. As many of our actors have to traverse the same Flaminian Way in the course of the next their few years, it may be well briefly to describe the journey of these two officers, though assuredly they, in their breathless haste, took not much note of aught beside castles and armies.

Issuing forth from Rome by the Flaminian Gate (Porta del Popolo), and after two miles' journey crossing the Tiber by the Ponte Molle, they would keep along the high table-land on the right bank of that river till they reached the base of precipitous Soracte—

'Not now in snow',

but which

'from out the plain
Heaved like a long-swept wave about to break,
And on the curl hung pausing'

Soon after Soracte was left behind, they would pass through the long ravine-girdled street of Falerii (near Civita Castellana), and then at Borghetto, thirty-eight miles from Rome, would cross the Tiber again and strike into the Sabine hills. The town, which is called in inscriptions *splendidissima civitas Ocricolana* now represented by the poor little village of Otricoli, at a distance of forty-five miles from Rome, might possibly receive them at the end of their first day's journey.

Next day they would fairly enter the old province of Umbria, exchange greetings with the friendly garrison of Narni, high up on its hill, and gaze down on the magnificent bridge of Augustus, whose single arch still stands so proudly in the ravine through which Nar's white waters are rolling. Perchance on a still summer's day they might hear the roar of the cascades of Velinus as they rode out from the city of Interamnia (Terni). The second day's journey of forty miles would be ended as they wound up the hill of Spoleto and entered the strong fortress built upon its height by King Theodoric. They are still mounting up the valley of the sulphurous Nar, and are now in the heart of what was formerly one of the most prosperous pastoral regions of Italy. The softly-flowing Clitumnus, by which perchance Virgil once walked, viewing with a farmer's admiring eye the cattle in its meadows, accompanies them when they start on their next day's journey, and they pass almost within sight of Mevania, which, like Clitumnus, nourished the far-famed; milk-white oxen that were slain for sacrifice on Rome's great days of triumph.

On this their third day's march they would pass the low-lying city of Fulginium, now Foligno. They might look down the valley of the Topino, past the hill on which now stand the terraced sanctuaries of Assisi, to the dim rock where the stronghold of Perugia was held by the faithful soldiers of the Emperor. But their course lies up the stream in a different direction. It is here that they begin to set themselves definitely to cross the great chain of the Apennines, whose high peaks have long been breaking the line of their northern horizon. Past the city and market which bore the name of the great road-maker Flaminius, they ride, ascending ever, but by no severe gradient, till they reach the upland region in which Nucera, Tadinum, Helvillum are situated, and see rising on their left the sharp serrated ridge at the foot of which, on the other side, lies the ancient Umbrian capital of Iguvium. They are breathing mountain air, and, if it be now the month of June, the snow is still lingering in patches on the summits of the Apennines; but the road is good, and easily passable everywhere, even by a large and encumbered army. And here, it may be on the summit of the pass just beyond the place where the waters divide, these flowing southwards to the Tiber, those northwards and eastwards towards the Adriatic, our horsemen end their day's journey; a long and toilsome one, for we have supposed them to travel on this day fifty-six miles. At the place where they halt for the night there is a posting station, with a sword for its sign. This sign might have been of prophetic import, for here probably, upon the crest of the Apennines, on the site of the modern village of Scheggia, was fought, fourteen years later, the decisive battle between the chosen Gothic champion and the lieutenant of the Byzantine Emperor.

The fourth morning dawns, and the flying column must be early in their saddles, for they suspect that there is tough work awaiting them today. Down through the narrow gorge of the Burano, over at least one bridge whose Roman masonry still endures to our own days, they ride for two hours till they reach the fair city of Cales, situated on the flanks of the precipitous Monte Petrano. And now at last, at the station which goes sometimes by the name of Intercisa, sometimes by that of Petra Pertusa, and which is twenty-three miles from their morning's starting-point, they find their onward course checked, and recognize that only by hard fighting can they win through to bear the all-important message to Rimini. For what happened at Intercisa we need not draw upon our imaginations, since we find ourselves here again under the guidance of Procopius. This is his description of Petra, a description evidently the result of personal observation:

"This fortress was not built by the hands of man, but was called into being by the nature of the place, for the road is here through an extremely rocky country. On the right of this road runs a river, fordable by no man on account of the swiftness of its current. On the left, near at hand, a cliff rises, abrupt and so lofty that if there should chance to be any men on its summit they seem to those at its base only like very little birds. At this point, long ago, there was no possibility of advance to the traveler; the rock and river between them barring all further progress. Here then the men of old hewed out a passage through the rock, and thus made a doorway into the country beyond. A few fortifications above and around the gate turned it into a natural fortress of great size, and they called its name Petra (Pertusa)"

The slight additional fortifications which the place received from the hand of man have disappeared, but the natural features of the Passo di Furlo—so the passage is now called—precisely correspond to this description of Procopius. Coming from Cagli on the south, one enters a dark and narrow gorge, as grand, though not as long, as the Via Mala in Switzerland, and sees the great wall of rock rising higher and higher on the left, the mountain torrent of the Candigliano foaming and chafing angrily below. At length, when all further progress seems barred, the end of a tunnel is perceived; we enter, and pass for 120 feet through the heart of the cliff. Emerging, we find the mountain pass ended: we see a broad and smiling landscape before us, and looking back we read upon the northern face of the rock the following inscription, telling us that the passage was hewn at the command of the founder of the Flavian dynasty, seventy-six years after the birth of Christ:

IMP . CAESAR . AVG
VESPASIANVS . PONT . MAX
TRIB . POT . VII . IMP. XVII. P.P. COS. VIII.
CENSOR . FACIVND . CVRAVIT

An inscription, probably of similar purport, over the southern end of the tunnel has been obliterated.

Of course to our generation, which has seen the St. Gothard and the Mont Cenis pierced by tunnels twelve miles in length, or even to the generation before us which beheld the galleries hewn in the rock for the great Alpine roads of Napoleon and his imitators, this work has nothing that is in itself marvelous. But when we remember that the Romans were unacquainted with the use of gunpowder, and consequently, as blasting was impossible, every square inch of rock had to be hewn out with axe and chisel, we shall see that there is something admirable in the courage which planned and the patience which accomplished so arduous a work.

Before this mountain gateway, additionally fenced and guarded by some few towers and battlements, and provided with chambers for the accommodation of the sentinels, Ildiger and Martin, with their thousand travel-stained horsemen, appeared and summoned its garrison to surrender. The garrison refused: and for some time the Roman horsemen discharged their missiles to no purpose. The Goths attempted no reply, but simply remained quiet and invulnerable in their stronghold. Then the Imperialist troops—among whom there were very probably some sure-footed Isaurian highlanders—clambered up the steep hillside and rolled down vast masses of rock on the fortress below. Wherever these missiles came in their thundering course they knocked off some piece of masonry or some battlement of a tower. In the tunnel itself, the Goths would have been safe even from this rocky avalanche: but they were in the watch-towers, and it was perhaps too late to seek the tunnel's shelter. Utterly cowed, they stretched forth their hands to such of the Imperialist soldiers as still remained in the roadway, and signified their willingness to surrender. Their submission was accepted. They promised to become the faithful servants of the Emperor, and to obey the orders of Belisarius. A few, with their wives and children, were left as the Imperialist garrison of the fortress: the rest appear to have marched under the banner of their late assailants onward to Rimini. Petra Pertusa was won, and the Flaminian Way was cleared, from Rome to the Adriatic.

If there was yet time the successful assailants would probably push on in order to spend the night in comfortable quarters at Forum Sempronii. It is a journey of nine miles down the broadening valley of the Metaurus. To every loyal Roman heart this is classic ground, for here Livius and Nero won that famous victory over Hasdrubal, which saved Italy from becoming a dependency of Carthage. One of the high mountains that we have passed on our left bears yet the name of Monte Nerone in memory of the battle. What more immediately concerns the soldiers of Justinian is that the side valley, the mouth of which they are now passing, leads up to Urbino, thirteen miles off, and that Morras with his 2000 Goths holds that place for Witigis. But the barbarians seem to be keeping close in their rock-fortress, and without molestation from their foraging parties, Ildiger and Martin reach the friendly shelter of Forum Sempronii. This place, of which there are still some scanty ruins left about a mile from its successor and strangely disguised namesake, Fossombrone, was in Roman times an important centre of trade and government, a fact which is vouched for by the large collection of inscriptions now preserved at the modern city. Next day, the fifth of their journey according to our calculations, the horsemen would travel, still by the banks of the Metaurus and under the shade of its beautiful groves of oak. Sea-breezes and touch of coolness in the air warn them that they are approaching the Adriatic; but still, if they look back over the route which they have traversed, they can see the deep cleft in the Apennine wall caused by the gorge of Petra, a continuing memorial of the hard-fought fight of yesterday. At the end of sixteen miles they reach the little city by the sea which bears the proud name of the Temple of Fortune (Fanum Fortunae). Its modern representative, Fano, still keeps its stately walls, mediaeval themselves, but by the quadrangular shape of their enclosure marking the site of their Roman predecessors: and we can still behold the Arch of Augustus, added to by Constantine, under which in all probability rode the horsemen of Ildiger.

Southwards from Fano the great highway runs along the seashore to Sena Gallica (Sinigaglia) and Ancona, which latter place is distant forty miles from the Fane of Fortune. To Ancona the two officers proceed, turning their backs for a moment on Rimini. They collect a considerable number of foot-soldiers at Ancona, went back with them to Fano, and then, turning northwards and passing through the little town of Pisaurum, traverse the forty-four miles which separate Rimini from Fano. They reach Rimini on the third day after leaving Ancona, the ninth (according to our conjectural arrangement of their journey) since their departure from Rome.

Rimini is now a tolerably bright and cheerful Italian city, with a considerable wealth of mediaeval interest. The great half-finished church (instinct with the growing Paganism of the early Renaissance), which bears the name of 'The Temple of the

Malatestas' and which shows everywhere the sculptured elephant, badge of that lawless house, everywhere the intertwined initials of Sigismund and his mistress Isotta,—the chapel in the market-place, where a Saint Anthony of Padua, distressed that men would not hearken to him, preached to the silent congregation of the fishes,—the house of Francesca da Rimini, where she read the story of Lancelot with her ill-fated lover, and 'that day read no further'—these are some of the chief spots hallowed by the associations of the Middle Ages. But the classical interests of the city are at least equally strong. Here, in the market-place, is the little square *suggestus* on which, so men say, Julius Caesar sprang to harangue his troops after the passage of the Rubicon. Here is a fine triumphal arch of Augustus, perhaps somewhat spoiled by the incongruous additions of the Middle Ages, but still bearing on its two fronts, the faces, in good preservation, of Jupiter and Minerva, of Venus and Neptune. Above all, here still stands the Roman bridge of five stately arches spanning the wide stream of the Marecchia. Two slabs in the parapet of this bridge, which the *contadino*, coming in to market, brushes with his sleeve, record, in fine and legible characters, that the bridge was begun in the last year of Augustus and finished in the seventh year of Tiberius. Below the parapet, on the centre-stones of the arches, are yet visible the Augur's wand, the civic wreath, the funeral urn, and other emblems attesting the religious character of the rites with which the Imperial bridge-maker (Pontifex Maximus) consecrated his handiwork.

When Ildiger and Martin stood before John in the Praetorium at Ariminum and delivered the message of Belisarius, that general flatly refused to obey it. It is difficult to understand how John could have excused to himself such a violation of that implicit obedience which is the first duty of the soldier: but the one defect in the military character of Belisarius—a defect which parts him off from the general whom in many respects he so greatly resembles, Marlborough—was his failure to obtain the hearty and loyal cooperation of his subordinate officers. There may have been a strain of capricious unreasonableness in his own character to produce this result: or it may have been due to the fact that he was too obviously guided in important affairs by the whims and the animosities of Antonina.

Whatever the cause, John refused to part with the 2000 horsemen under his command, or to evacuate Rimini. Damian also, his lieutenant, elected to abide with him. All that Ildiger and Martin could do was to withdraw the soldiers who belonged to the household of Belisarius, to leave the infantry brought from Ancona, and to depart, which they did with all speed.

Before long, Witigis and his army stood before the walls of Ariminum. They constructed a wooden tower high enough to overtop the battlements and resting on four strong wheels. Taking warning by their experience at the siege of Rome, they did not, this time, avail themselves of oxen to draw their tower, but arranged that it should be pushed along by men inside, protected from the arrows of the foe. A broad and winding inside—perhaps not unlike that which leads to the top of the Campanile of St. Mark's at Venice—enabled large bodies of troops to ascend and descend rapidly. On the night after this huge machine was completed, they betook themselves to peaceful slumber, making no doubt that next day the city would be theirs; a belief which was fully shared by the disheartened garrison, who saw that no obstacle existed to hinder the progress of the dreaded tower to their walls. Not yet, however, would the energetic John yield to despair. Leaving the main body of the garrison to the walls in their usual order, he secretly sallied forth at dead of night with a band of hardy Isaurians, all supplied with mattocks and trenching tools. Working with a will, but in deep silence, the brawny mountaineers succeeded, before daybreak, in excavating a deep trench in front of the tower: and, moreover, the earth which they had dug out from the trench being thrown up on the inside interposed the additional obstacle of a mound between the besiegers and their prey. Neither trench nor mound seems to have gone all round the city, but they sufficiently protected a weak portion of the walls, against which the Goths had felt secure of victory. Just before dawn the barbarians discovered what was being done, and rushed at full speed against the trenching party; but John, well satisfied with his night's work, retreated quietly within the city.

At day-break Witigis, who saw with sore heartache the hated obstacle to his hopes, put to death the careless guards whose slumbers had made it possible to construct it. He still determined, however, to try his expedient of the tower, and ordered his men to fill up the trench with fascines. This they did, though under a fierce discharge of stones and arrows from the walls. But when the ponderous engine advanced over the edge of the trench, the fascines bent and cracked under its weight, and the impelling soldiers found it impossible to move it further. Moreover, were even the trench surmounted, the heaped-up mound beyond would have been an insuperable difficulty. As the day wore on, the weary barbarians, fearing lest the tower should be set on fire in a nocturnal sally, prepared to draw their ineffectual engine back into their own lines. John saw the movement, and longed to prevent it. He addressed his soldiers in kindling words, in which, while complaining of his desertion by Belisarius, he urged upon his men the thought that their only chance of seeing again the dear ones whom they had left behind, lay in their own prowess, in that supreme crisis of their fate when life and death hung upon a razors edge. He then led nearly his whole army forth to battle, leaving only a few men to guard the ramparts. The Goths resisted stubbornly, and, when evening closed in, succeeded in drawing back the tower; but the contest had been so bloody, and they had lost in it so many of their heroes, that they determined to try no more assaults, but to wait and see what their ally, Hunger, whose hand was already making itself felt upon the besieged, would do towards opening the gates.

Not long after the successful repulse of the Gothic attack on this Umbrian sea-port, her rival the sea-port of Picenum, Ancona, all but fell a prey to a similar assault. Witigis had sent a general named Wakim to Osimo with orders to lead the troops assembled in that stronghold to the siege of the neighboring Ancona. The fortress of this city was very strong, situated probably on the high hill where the cathedral now stands, looking down on the magnificent harbor. But if the Roman castellum was strong, the town below it was weak and difficult to defend. Conon, one of the generals of Isaurians recently dispatched from Constantinople, either from a tender-hearted desire to protect the peaceful citizens, or from a wish to distinguish himself by performing that which seemed impossible, included not the fortress only but the city in his line of defence, and drew up his forces on the plain about half-a-mile inland from the city.

Here he professed to entrench himself, "but his trench", says Procopius contemptuously, "winding all-round the foot of the mountain, might have been of some service in a chase after game, but was quite useless for war". The defenders of this line soon found themselves hopelessly outnumbered by the Goths. They turned and fled towards the castle. The first comers were received without difficulty, but when the pursuing Goths began to be mingled with the pursued, the defenders wisely closed the gates. Conon himself was among those who were thus shut out, and who had to be ignominiously hauled up ropes let down from the battlements. The barbarians applied scaling ladders to the walls, and all but succeeded in surmounting them. They probably would have succeeded altogether but for the efforts of two brave men, Ulimun the Thracian and Bulgundus the Hun, the former in the bodyguard of Belisarius, the latter in that of Valerian, who by mere chance happened to have recently landed at Ancona. These men kept the enemy at bay with their swords till the garrison had all re-entered the fort. Then they too, with their bodies hacked all over, and half-dead from their wounds, turned back from the field of fight.

Procopius does not say what became of the city of Ancona, but it was probably sacked by the enemy.

We hear but little of the doings of Belisarius while these events were passing. His scheme for gradually and cautiously reducing the district which lay nearest to Rome, before advancing northwards, was rewarded by the surrender of Tuder and Clusium. The four hundred Goths who occupied the former place and the thousand Goths in the latter surrendered at the mere rumor that his army was approaching, and having received a promise that their lives should be spared, were sent away unharmed to Sicily and Naples.

But now the arrival of fresh and large reinforcements from Constantinople in Picenum drew Belisarius, almost in spite of himself to the regions of the Adriatic, and forced him to reconsider the decision which he had formed, to leave the mutinous general at Rimini to his fate.

At the head of this new army sent forth from Constantinople was the Eunuch Narses, a man destined to exert a more potent influence on the future fortunes of Italy than even Belisarius himself. He was born in Persarmenia—that portion of Armenia which was allotted to Persia at the partition of 384—and the year of his birth was probably about 478. As the practice of rearing boys for service as eunuchs in the Eastern Courts had by this time become common, it is quite possible that he was not of servile origin. But whatever his birth and original condition may have been, we find him in middle life occupying a high place in the Byzantine Court. After filling the post of *Chartularius*, or Keeper of the Archives of the Imperial Bed-chamber, an office which he shared with two colleagues and which gave him the rank of a *Spectahilis*, he rose (some time before the year 530) to the splendid position *of Praepositus Sacri Cubiculi*, or Grand Chamberlain. He thus became an Illustris, and one of the greatest of the Illustres, standing in the same front rank with the Praetorian Prefects and the Masters of the Soldiery, and probably, in practice, more powerful than any of these ministers, as having more continual and confidential access to the person of the sovereign.

It has been already stated that in the terrible days of the insurrection of the NIKA the Eunuch Chamberlain rendered essential service to his master. While the newly proclaimed Emperor Hypatius was sitting in the Circus receiving the congratulations of his friends and listening to their invectives against Justinian, Narses crept forth into the streets with a bag in his hand filled from the Imperial treasury, met with some of the leaders of the Blue faction, reminded them of old benefits of Justinian's, of old grudges against the Greens, judiciously expended the treasures in his bag, and finally succeeded in persuading them to shout "Justiniane Imperator Tu vincas". The coalition of the two factions was dissolved and the throne of the Emperor was saved.

This then was the man, hitherto versed only in the intrigues of the cabinet, or at best in the discussions of the cabinet, whom Justinian placed at the head of the new army which was sent to Italy to secure the conquests of Belisarius. What was the Emperor's motive in sending so trusty a counselor but so inexperienced a soldier, a man too who had probably reached the sixth decade of his life, on such a martial mission? The motive, as we shall see, was not stated in express terms to the Eunuch: perhaps it was not fully confessed by the Emperor even to himself. But there can be little doubt that there was growing up in the Imperial mind a feeling that the splendid victories of Belisarius might make of him a dangerous rival for the Empire, and that it was desirable to have him closely watched, but not seriously hampered, by a devoted partisan of the dynasty, a man who from his age and condition could never himself aspire to the purple. Like an Aulic counsellor in the camp of Wallenstein, like the Commissioners of the Convention in the camp of Dumouriez, was Narses in the praetorium of Belisarius.

A great council of war was held at Firmum (now Fermo), a town of Picenum about forty miles south of Ancona and six miles inland from the Adriatic. There were present at it not only the two chiefs Belisarius and Narses, but Martin and Ildiger, Justin the Master of the Soldiery for Illyricum, another Narses with his brother Aratius (Persarmenians like the Eunuch Narses, who had deserted the service of Persia for that of Byzantium), and some wild Herulian chieftains named Wisand, Alueth, and Fanotheus. The one great subject of discussion was, of course, whether Rimini should be relieved or left to its fate. To march so far northwards, leaving the strong position of Osimo untaken in their rear, seemed like courting destruction for the whole army. On the other hand, the distress of the defenders of Rimini for want of provisions was growing so severe that any day some terrible tidings might be expected concerning them. The opinion of the majority of the officers was bitterly hostile to John. By his rashness, his vanity, his avaricious thirst for plunder, he had brought a Roman army into this extremity of danger. He had disobeyed orders, and not allowed the commander-in-chief to conduct the campaign according to his own ideas of strategy. They did not say "Let him suffer the penalty of his folly" but the conclusion to be drawn was obvious.

When the younger men had blurted out their invectives against the unfortunate general, the grey-headed Narses arose. Admitting his own inexperience in the art of war, he urged that in the extraordinary circumstances in which they Rimini were placed, even an amateur soldier might be listened to with advantage. The question presented itself to his mind in this way. Were the evil results which might follow from one or other of the two courses proposed, of equal magnitude? If Osimo were left untaken, if the garrison of Osimo were allowed to recruit itself from without, still the enterprise on that fortress might be resumed at some future time, and probably with success. But if Rimini were allowed to surrender, if a city recovered for the Emperor were suffered to be retaken by the barbarians, if a gallant general, a brave army were permitted to fall into their cruel hands, what remedy could be imagined for these reverses? The Goths were still far more numerous than the soldiers of the Emperor, but it was the consciousness of uniform disaster which cowed their spirits and prepared them for defeat. Let them gain one such advantage as this, so signal, so manifest to all Italy, they would derive new courage from their success, and twice the present number of Imperial soldiers could not beat them. "Therefore" concluded Narses, "if John has treated your orders with contempt, most excellent Belisarius, take your own measures for punishing him, since there is nothing to prevent your throwing him over the walls to the enemy when once you have relieved Rimini. But see that you do not, in punishing what I firmly believe to have been the involuntary error of John, take vengeance on us and on all loyal subjects of the Emperor"

This speech, uttered by the most trusted counselor of Justinian, and coming from one who loved the besieged general with strong personal affection, produced a great effect upon the council; an effect which was increased by the reading of the following letter, which, just at the right moment of time, was brought by a soldier who had escaped from the besieged town and passed unnoticed through the ranks of the enemy.

"John to the Illustrious Belisarius, Master of the Soldiery.

Know that all our provisions have now long ago been exhausted, and that henceforward we are no longer strong enough to defend ourselves from the besiegers, nor to resist the citizens should they insist on a surrender. In seven days therefore, much against our will, we shall have to give up this city and ourselves to the enemy, for we cannot longer avert the impending doom. I think you will hold that our act, though it will tarnish the luster of your arms, is excused by absolute necessity"

In sore perplexity, Belisarius, yielding to the wishes of the council of war, devised the following almost desperate scheme for the relief of Rimini. To keep in check the garrison of Osimo a detachment of 1000 men were directed to encamp on the sea-coast, about thirty miles from the Gothic stronghold, with orders vigilantly to watch its defenders, but on no account to attack them. The largest part of the army was put on ship-board, and the fleet, under the command of Ildiger, was ordered to cruise slowly towards Rimini, not outstripping the troops which were to march by land, and when arrived, to anchor in front of the besieged city. Martin, with another division, was to march along the great highway, close to the coast, through Ancona, Fano, and Pesaro. Belisarius himself and the Eunuch Narses led a flying column, which was intended to relieve Rimini by a desperate expedient if all the more obvious methods should fail.

Marching westwards from Fermo they passed through Urbs Salvia, once an important city, but so ruined by an onslaught of Alaric that when Procopius passed through it he saw but a single gateway and the remains of a tesselated pavement, attesting its former greatness. From thence they struck into the heart of the Apennines, and in the high region near Nocera descried the great Flaminian Way coming northwards from Spoleto. Keeping upon this great highway they recrossed the Apennine chain, but before they were clear from the intricacies of the mountains, and when they were at the distance of a day's journey from Rimini, they fell in with a party of Goths who were casually passing that way, possibly marching between the two Gothic strongholds of Osimo and Urbino. So little were the barbarians thinking of war that the wounds received from the arrows of the Romans were the first indications of their presence. They sought cover behind the rocks of the mountain-pass, and some thus escaped death. Peeping forth from their hiding-places, they perceived the standards of Belisarius; they saw an apparently countless multitude streaming over the mountains—for the army was marching in loose order by many mountain pathways, not in column along the one high road—and they fled in terror to the camp of Witigis, to show their wounds, to tell of the standards of Belisarius and to spread panic by the tidings that the great general was on his march to encompass them. In fact, the troops of Belisarius, who bivouacked for the night on the scene of this little skirmish, did not reach Rimini till all the fighting was over; but its Gothic besiegers expected every moment to see him emerge from the mountains, march towards them from the north, and cut off their retreat to Ravenna.

While the Goths were thus anxiously looking towards the north, suddenly upon the south, between them and Pesaro, blazed the watch-fires of an enormous army. These were the troops of Martin, who had been ordered by Belisarius to adopt this familiar stratagem, to make his line appear in the night-time larger than it actually was. Then, to complete the discouragement of the Goths, the Imperial warships, which indeed bore a formidable army, appeared in the twilight in the harbor of Rimini. Fancying themselves on the point of being surrounded, the soldiers of Witigis left their camp, filled as it was with the trappings of their barbaric splendor, and fled in headlong haste to Ravenna. Had there been any strength or spirit left in the Roman garrison, they might, by one timely sally, have well-nigh destroyed the Gothic army and ended the war upon the spot; but hunger and misery had reduced them too low for this. They had enough life left in them to be rescued, and that was all. Of the relieving army, Ildiger and his division were the first to appear upon the scene. They sacked the camp of the Goths and made slaves of the sick barbarians whom they found there. Then came Martin and his division. Last of all, about noon of the following day, Belisarius and the Eunuch appeared upon the scene. When they saw the pale faces and emaciated forms of the squalid defenders of Rimini, Belisarius, who was still thinking of the original disobedience to orders which had brought about all this suffering, could not suppress the somewhat ungenerous taunt, "Oh, Joannes! you will not find it easy to pay your debt of gratitude to Ildiger for this deliverance". "No thanks at all do I owe to Ildiger, but all to Narses the Emperor's Chamberlain" answered John, who either knew or conjectured what had passed in the council of war at Fermo regarding his deliverance.

Thus were sown the seeds of a dissension which wrought much harm, and might conceivably have wrought much more, to the affairs of the Emperor.

CHAPTER XI.

DISSENSIONS IN THE IMPERIAL CAMP.

The relief of Rimini greatly strengthened the party of Narses at the council-table of the Imperial generals. It was indeed the arm of Belisarius that had wrought that great achievement, but the directing brain, as John asserted, and as most men in the army believed, was the brain of the Imperial Chamberlain. Accordingly friends and flatterers of this successful amateur general gathered round him in large numbers, with their unwise yet only too gratifying suggestions. "It was surely" they said, "beneath his dignity to allow himself to be dragged about, as a mere subordinate officer, in the train of Belisarius". When the Emperor sent a minister of such high rank, the sharer of his most secret counsels, into the field, he must have intended him to hold a separate command, to win glory for himself by his great actions, and not merely to help in gathering fresh laurels for the brow of the already too powerful Master of the Soldiery. The suggestion that he should himself be general-in-chief over a separate army was one which would meet with ready acceptance from the bravest of the officers and the best part of the troops. All the Herulian auxiliaries, all his own bodyguard, all John's soldiers and those of Justin, all the men who followed the standards of the other Narses and his brother Aratius, a gallant host amounting in all to fully 10,000 men, would be proud to fight under the deliverer of Rimini, and to vindicate for Narses at least an equal share with Belisarius in the glory of the recovery of Italy. An equal, or even henceforward a greater share; for the army of Belisarius was so weakened by the detachment of soldiers doing garrison-duty in all the towns from Sicily to Picenum, that he would have to follow rather than to lead in the operations which were yet necessary to finish the war".

These insidious counsels, urged at every possible opportunity, bore their expected fruit in the mind of the Eunuch, elated as he was by his great success in the affair of Rimini. Order after order which he received from Belisarius was quietly disregarded, as not suited to the present posture of affairs; and the General was made to feel, without the possibility of mistake, that, though he might advise, he must not presume to command, so great a personage as the Praepositus of the Sacred Bed-chamber. When Belisarius understood that this was really, the position taken up by Narses he summoned all the generals to a council of war. Without directly complaining of the spirit of insubordination which he saw creeping in among them, he told them that he saw their views did not coincide with his as to the present crisis. The enemy, in his view, were still essentially stronger than their own forces. By dexterity and good-luck the Goths had hitherto been successfully outgeneraled; but, let them only redeem their fortunes by one happy stroke, the opportunity for which might be offered them by the over-confidence of the Imperial officers, and, passing from despair to the enthusiasm of success, they would become dangerous, perhaps irresistible. To the mind of Belisarius the present aspect of the theatre of war brought grave anxiety. With Witigis and thirty or forty thousand Goths at Ravenna, with his nephew besieging Milan and dominating Liguria, with Osimo held by a numerous and gallant Gothic garrison, with even Orvieto, so near to Rome, still in the possession of the enemy, and with the Franks, of old so formidable to the Romans, hanging like a thunder-cloud upon the Alps, ready at any moment to sweep down on Upper Italy, there was danger that the Imperial army might soon find itself surrounded by foes. He proposed therefore that the host should part itself into two and only two strong divisions, that the one should march into Liguria for the relief of Milan, and the other should undertake the reduction of Osimo and such other exploits in Umbria and Picenum as they might find themselves capable of performing. We are led to infer, though the fact is not expressly stated, that Belisarius offered to Narses and the generals of his faction the choice of undertaking independently either of these alternative operations.

When the speech of Belisarius was ended, Narses said curtly, and with little deference to the General's authority, "What you have laid before us is doubtless true as far as it goes. But I hold that it is quite absurd to say that this great army is equal only to the accomplishment of these two objects, the relief of Milan and the reduction of Osimo. While you are leading such of the Romans as you think fit to those cities, I and my friends will proceed to recover for the Emperor the province of Aemilia [in other words, the southern bank of the Po from Piacenza to the Adriatic]. This is a province which the Goths are said especially to prize. We shall thus so terrify them that they will not dare to issue forth from Ravenna and cut off your supplies, an operation which they are sure to undertake if we all march off together to besiege Osimo"

So spoke Narses, and thus forced Belisarius to fall back on his Imperial commission, which gave him the supreme and ultimate responsibility for the movements of the whole army of Italy. That this authority was not impaired by recent changes was proved by a letter from the Emperor, which he read to the council, and which ran as follows:

"We have not sent our chamberlain Narses to Italy to take the command of the army. For we wish Belisarius alone to lead the whole army, whithersoever it may seem best to him; and it behoves you all to follow him in whatsoever makes for the good of our Empire".

So ran the letter of Justinian, which seemed at first sight entirely to negative the claims of Narses clause in to an independent command. But, as the Eunuch pointed out, a singular limitation was contained in the last clause, "you are to follow him in whatsoever makes for the good of our Empire". "We do not think", said Narses, "that your present plan of campaign is for the good of the Empire, and therefore we decline to follow you". The clause had possibly been introduced in order to guard against the contingency of Belisarius aspiring to the purple. Or perhaps, now as in the case of Odovacar's embassy to Constantinople, it seemed to the guiding spirits in the Imperial Chancery a stroke of statesmanship to put forth an ambiguous document which might be interpreted by each side according to its own inclination. The Empire by the Bosporus was already developing those qualities which we, perhaps unfairly, term Oriental.

For the moment some kind of compromise seems to have been patched up. Peranius, with a large army, was sent to besiege Orvieto, which, from its nearness to Rome, was admitted by all to be a point of danger. Belisarius, with the rest of the army, moved off to attack Urbino, which was a day's journey to the south of Rimini. Narses and John, and the other generals of that party, followed or accompanied Belisarius; but when they came in sight of the city, the disaffected generals encamped on the west, leaving Belisarius and his adherents to sit down on the eastern side.

Urbino, the Athens of Italy, as she was called in the short but glorious summer of her fame, acquired imperishable renown under the rule of the princes of the house of Montefeltro in the fifteenth century. The influence exerted on Italian Literature by the fostering care of these princes is known to all scholars; but in the history of Painting the name of their little capital is of mightier meaning, since the utmost ends of the earth have heard the fame of Raffaelle of Urbino. Now, she is again not much more than she was in the days of Belisarius, a little bleak fortress looking forth upon the bare horizon of Umbrian hills, herself highest of them all. No river has she of her own, but is reached by a steep ascent of five miles from the fair valley of the Metaurus. This was the city to which, in the autumn of 538, Belisarius sent ambassadors, promising all kinds of favors to the garrison if they would anticipate their inevitable fate by a speedy surrender. Strong in their belief of the impregnability of their fortress, in the good store of provisions which they had accumulated within its walls, and in the possession of an excellent spring of water, the garrison refused to surrender, and haughtily bade the ambassadors to depart from the gates immediately.

Seeing that Belisarius was bent upon reducing Narses and the place, by a tedious blockade if that were needful, Narses and John decided to take their own course. John had slightly attempted Urbino before, on his first entry into Picenum, and had found it impregnable. Since then a much larger garrison and stores of provisions had been introduced. Why linger any longer on these bleak highlands, winter now approaching, and success well-nigh impossible? They broke up their camp on the west of the city, and marched away, intent upon their favorite scheme of the annexation of the Aemilia.

The garrison, seeing that half their enemies had marched away, flouted and jeered those who remained. The city, though it did not stand on a precipitous cliff like others of these Umbrian fortresses, was nevertheless at the top of an exceedingly steep hill; and only on the north side was the approach anything like level. On this side Belisarius proposed to make his attack. ordered his soldiers to collect a quantity of trunks and boughs of trees, and out of these to construct a machine which they called the Porch. The trunks being fixed upright, and the boughs, perhaps still covered with leaves, being wattled together to form the sides, the machine, worked by soldiers within, was to be moved along the one level approach to the city, and the soldiers under its shelter were to begin battering at the wall. But no sooner had they reached the vicinity of the fortress, than, instead of being met by a shower of arrows, they saw the battlements thronged with Goths stretching out their right hands in the attitude of suppliants and praying for mercy. This sudden change in the attitude of the garrison, lately so bent on resistance to the death, was caused by the mysterious failure of their one hitherto copious spring. It had for three days fallen lower and lower, and now, when the soldiers went to draw water, they obtained nothing but liquid mud. Without a spring of water defence was impossible, and they did wisely to surrender. The characteristic good-fortune of Belisarius had prevailed. Urbino was his, and some of its late defenders appear to have taken service in the Imperial army.

The news of the speedy surrender of Urbino brought not only surprise but grief to the heart of Narses, who was still quartered at Rimini. He urged John to undertake the reduction of the strong city of Cesena, twenty miles inland on the Emilian Way. John took scaling ladders, and attempted an assault. The garrison resisted vigorously, slaying many of the assailants, among them Fanotheus, the King of the wild Herulian auxiliaries of the Empire. John, whose temper was impatient of the slow work of a siege, pronounced this, as he had pronounced so many other cities under whose walls he had stood, impregnable, and marched off for the easier exploit of overrunning the Emilian province. The ancient city of Forum Cornelii (now Imola) was carried by surprise, and the whole province was recovered for the Emperor; an easy conquest, but probably not one of great strategic value.

The winter solstice was now past, and the new year, 539, begun. The heart of Belisarius was still set upon what he knew to be the necessary task of the capture of Osimo; but he would not in the winter season expose his troops to the hardships of a long encampment in the open country while he was blockading the city. He therefore sent Aratius, with the bulk of the army, into winter quarters at Fermo, with orders to watch the garrison of Osimo and prevent their wandering at will over Picenum: and he himself marched with a detachment of moderate size to Orvieto, which had been for many months besieged by Peranius, and the garrison of which were hard pressed by famine.

Albilas their general had long kept up their spirits by delusive hopes of coming reinforcements, but they were already reduced to feed upon hides steeped in water to soften them: and when they saw the standards of the mighty Belisarius under their walls, they soon surrendered at discretion. It was well for the Roman cause that the blockade had been so complete, for, to an assault, the rock-built city of the Clanis would have been, in the judgment of Belisarius, quite inaccessible.

It was now nine months since the raising of the siege of Rome. The progress of the Imperial arms since that time had not been rapid, but it had been steady. Rimini had been relieved, Urbino taken, the Aemilia reannexed to the Empire, Orvieto, that dangerous neighbor to Rome, reduced. Now, however, in the early months of 539, the Imperial arms sustained a terrible reverse in the reconquest of Milan by the Goths. To understand the course of Rome, of events which led up to this disaster, we must go back twelve months, to the early part of 538, shortly after the conclusion of the three months' truce between Belisarius and Witigis. The reader may remember that at that time Datius, the Archbishop of Milan, made his appearance in Rome, at the head of a deputation, entreating Belisarius to send troops to rescue the capital of Liguria from the barbarians. The General, perhaps unwisely, complied, thus in appearance committing the same faults, of advancing too far and extending his line of defence too widely, which he had blamed in the case of his subordinate John, when that officer occupied Rimini. After the siege of Rome was raised he sent one thousand troops to escort Datius back to his diocese. The little army was composed of Isaurians under Ennes, and Thracians under Paulus. Mundilas, whose Praetorium was sentinelled by a few picked soldiers from Belisarius's own bodyguard, commanded the whole expedition, which was also accompanied by Fidelius, formerly Quaestor under Athalaric, now Praetorian Prefect of Italy under Justinian, and the most important civil functionary in the restored province.

The expedition sailed from Porto to Genoa. There the soldiers left the ships, but took the ships' boats with them on wagons, and by their means crossed the river Po without difficulty. Under the walls of Pavia (Ticinum) they fought a bloody battle with the Goths, in which the Imperial arms triumphed. The fugitive barbarians were only just able to close the gates of their city in time to prevent it from being taken by the conquerors. It would have been an important prize; for Pavia, even more perhaps than Ravenna, was the treasury and arsenal of the Gothic monarchy. The exultation of Mundilas at his victory in the field was damped by the disappointment of not occupying Pavia, and yet more by the death of the Illustris, Fidelius, who had tarried behind to offer his devotions in a church near the field of battle. On his departure, his horse fell with him : the Goths perceived his helpless condition, and sallying forth from the city slew the recreant official, whom they doubtless considered a traitor to the house of Theodoric.

When the expedition arrived at Milan, the city, thoroughly Roman in its sympathies, surrendered itself gladly into their hands. Bergamo, Como, Novara, and other towns in the neighborhood, followed the example of the capital, and were garrisoned by Roman troops. In this way Mundilas reduced his own immediate following in Milan to three hundred men, among whom, however, were his two capable officers, Paulus and Ennes.

On hearing of the defection of Milan, Witigis dispatched a large army, under the command of his nephew Uraias, for its recovery. Uraias was one of the favorite heroes of the Gothic nation, as brave and energetic as his uncle was helpless and timid. He was not the only enemy by which the re-Romanised city was threatened. Theudibert, King of the Franks, intent, as his nation used ever to be, on turning the calamities of Italy to profit, but not wishing at present openly to quarrel with the Emperor, ordered, or permitted, ten thousand of his Burgundian subjects to cross the Alps and to encamp before Milan, holding himself ready to disavow the action of the invaders should it suit his purpose to conciliate the Court of Byzantium. By these two armies, the Frankish and the Gothic, Milan was, in the spring months of 538, so closely invested that it was impossible to carry any food into the city. The little band of three hundred Thracians and Isaurians being quite inadequate to guard the wide circuit of the city-walls, Mundilas was forced to call upon the citizens themselves to man the ramparts.

When Belisarius heard that Uraias had formed the siege of Milan, he sent two generals, Martin and Uliaris, with a large army, to relieve the beleaguered city. Martin had shared with Ildiger the perils of his bold dash through Umbria, and Uliaris had taken, apparently, a creditable part in the expedition for the relief of Rimini; but neither officer now behaved in a manner worthy of his former reputation. When they reached the river Po, they encamped upon its southern bank, and there remained for a long time timidly consulting how they should cross the stream.

A messenger dispatched by Mundilas, Paulus by name, stole through the ranks of the besiegers, swam across the river, and was admitted to the tent of the generals. With burning words he told them that their delay was ruining the cause of the Emperor, and that they would be no better than traitors if they allowed the great city of Mediolanum, wealthiest and most populous of all the cities of Italy, her great bulwark against the Franks and all the other Transalpine barbarians, to fall into the hands of the enemy. The generals promised speedy assistance, a promise with which Paulus, returning by night through the ranks of the enemy, gladdened the hearts of his fellow-citizens. But still they sat, week after week, in unaccountable hesitation, cowering by the southern bank of the great river.

At length, in order to justify themselves to Belisarius, they wrote him a letter saying that they feared their forces were insufficient to cope with the great armies of the Goths and Franks that were roaming through the plains of Liguria, and begging him to order John and Justin to march from the neighboring province of Aemilia to their aid. Such an order was sent to those generals, who openly refused to obey any command of Belisarius, saying that Narses was their leader.

In these wretched delays, the fruit of cowardice and of insubordination, more than six months must have passed from the first investment of Milan. At length Narses, having received a letter from Belisarius frankly setting before him the dangers which his insubordinate policy was preparing for the Empire, gave the required order. John began collecting boats upon the Venetian coast to enable the army to make the passage of the river, but was attacked by fever—apparently a genuine, not a feigned attack—and when he recovered, the opportunity was lost.

For, in the meantime, the disgracefully abandoned defenders of Milan had been undergoing terrible privations. They were reduced at last to eat dogs and mice and such creatures as no man had ever thought of before in connection with the idea of food. The besiegers, who knew how matters stood with them, sent ambassadors, calling on Mundilas to surrender the city, and promising that the lives of all the soldiers should be preserved. Mundilas was willing to agree to these terms if the citizens might be included in the capitulation; but the enemy, indignant at the treachery of the Milanese, avowed that every one of them should perish. Then Mundilas made a spirit-stirring address to his soldiers, exhorting them to seize their arms and burst forth with him in one last desperate sally. He could not bear, by looking on, to make himself a partaker in the dreadful deeds which would assuredly be done against these unhappy subjects of the Emperor, whose only crime was having invited him within their walls. "Every man" said he, "has his appointed day of death, which he can neither hasten nor delay. The only difference between men is that some meet this inevitable doom gloriously, while others, struggling to escape from it, die just as soon, but by a coward's death. Let us show that we are worthy of the teaching of Belisarius, which we have all shared, and which makes it an impiety for us to be anything else but brave and glorious in our dying. We may achieve some undreamed of victory over the enemy: and if not we are nobly freed from all our present miseries".

The exhortation was in vain. The soldiers, disheartened by the hardships of the siege, could not rise to the height of the desperate courage of their leader, and insisted on surrendering the city to the Goths. The barbarians honorably observed towards the soldiers the terms of the capitulation, but wreaked their full vengeance on the wretched inhabitants of Milan. All the men were slain, and these, if the information given to Procopius was correct, amounted to 300,000. The women were made slaves, and handed over by the Goths to their Burgundian allies in payment of their services. The city itself was razed to the ground: not the only time that signal destruction has overtaken the fair capital of Lombardy. All the surrounding cities, notwithstanding their Imperial garrisons, had to open their gates to the foe; but we do not read that they shared the same terrible fate. Liguria was once again part of the Gothic monarchy.

Reparatus, the Praetorian Prefect, and successor of Fidelius, fell into the hands of the Goths, and, not being included in the army's capitulation, was cut up by the barbarians into small pieces, which were then contemptuously thrown to the dogs. Cerventinus his brother—the two were also brothers of Pope Vigilius—had shared the flight of Reparatus from Ravenna. More fortunate than his brother, he now escaped from the doomed city, and making his way through Venetia, bore the terrible tidings to Justinian. Martin and Uliaris, returning from their inglorious campaign, brought the same tidings to Belisarius, who received them with intense grief and anger, and refused to admit Uliaris to his presence. In his letter to the Emperor he doubtless laid the blame disaster of the fall of Milan on the divided counsels by which for the last twelve months his arm had been paralyzed. Justinian, among whose many faults cruelty was not included, inflicted no signal punishment on any of the blunderers by whom his interests had been so grievously injured, but took now the step which he should have taken on the first news of the dissensions of the generals, by sending to Narses a letter of recall, and formally constituting Belisarius Generalissimo of the Imperial forces in Italy.

Narses accordingly returned with a few soldiers to Constantinople. The wild Herulians who had come in his train refused to serve under any other leader, marched off into Liguria, sold their captives and their beasts of burden to the Goths, took an oath of perpetual friendship with that nation, marched through Venetia into Illyria, again changed their minds, and accepted service under the Emperor at Constantinople. An unstable and brutish people, and one for which Procopius never spares a disparaging word when an opportunity of uttering it is afforded by the course of his narrative.

CHAPTER XII.

SIEGES OF FIESOLI AND OSIMO.

The war had now lasted four years, and it was over a ruined and wasted Italy that the wolves of war were growling. The summer of 538 was long remembered as the time when Famine and her child Disease in their full horror first fell upon Tuscany, Liguria, and the Aemilia. The fields had now been left for two years uncultivated. A self-sown crop, poor but still a crop, sprang up in the summer of 537. Unreaped by the hand of man, it lay rotting on the ground: no plough stirred the furrows, no hand scattered fresh seed upon the earth, and in the following summer there was of course mere desolation. The inhabitants of Tuscany betook them to the mountains, and fed upon the acorns which they gathered in the oak-forests that cling round the shoulders of the Apennines. The dwellers in the Aemilia flocked into Picenum, thinking that the nearness of the seaboard would at least preserve them from absolute starvation;

Procopius marked the stages of decline in this hunger-smitten people, and describes it in words which were perhaps meant to remind the reader of Thucydides' description of the Plague of Athens. First the pinched face and yellow complexion surcharged with bile; then the natural moisture dried up, and the skin, looking like tanned leather, adhering to the bones; the yellow color turning to a livid purple, and the purple to black, which made the poor famine-stricken countryman look like a burned-out torch; the expression of dazed wonder in the face sometimes changing to the wild eyes of the maniac;—he saw and noted it all. As is always the case after long endurance of hunger, some men, when provisions were brought into the country, could not profit by them. However carefully the nourishment was doled out to them, in small quantities at a time as one feeds a little child, still in many cases their digestions could not bear it, and those who had survived the famine died of food.

In some places cannibalism made its appearance. Two women dwelt in a lonely house near Rimini, and were wont to entice into their dwelling the passers-by, whom they slew in their sleep, and on whose flesh they feasted. Seventeen men had thus perished. The eighteenth started up out of sleep just as the hags were approaching for his destruction. With drawn sword he stood over them, forced them to confess all their wickedness, then slew them.

Elsewhere the famine-wasted inhabitants might be seen streaming forth into the fields to pluck any green herb that could be made available for food. Often when they had knelt down for this purpose their strength would not serve them to pull it out of the ground. And so it came to pass that they lay down and died upon the ungathered herbage, unburied, for there was none to bury them, but undesecrated, for even the birds of carrion found nothing to attract them in those fleshless corpses.

One little story told by Procopius brings vividly before us the misery caused in Italy by the movements of the hostile armies. When the historian accompanied Belisarius on his march over the Apennines for the relief of Rimini, he saw a child which was suckled and watched over by a goat. The mother of this child, a woman of Urbs Salvia, had fled before the approach of John's army—the liberating army—into the province of Picenum. In her flight she had been for a moment, as she supposed, parted from her new-born babe; but either death or captivity had prevented her from returning to the place where she had laid it down. The babe, wrapped in its swaddling-clothes, lifted up its voice and wept. A she-goat which was near ran to it, and pitying its cry, nourished it as she would have nourished her own little one, and guarded it from all other animals. When the inhabitants of Urbs Salvia found that John's army had friendly thoughts towards them, they returned to their homes; but among them was not the mother of the child. One after another of the women offered to give suck to the child, but it refused all nourishment save that of its four-footed nurse; and she with loud bleatings and gestures of anger claimed the child as her own charge. It was therefore left to the care of the goat, and named, like the outcast prince of Argos, Aegisthus, "the goat's child". Procopius, as has been said, saw this marvel on his way through Urbs Salvia. The goat was at the time at some little distance from her charge, but when Procopius and his friends pinched it and made it cry, she came bounding towards it with a bleat of distress, and standing over it, signified with butting horn that she would guard it against all assailants.

Notwithstanding the cruel exhaustion of Italy, the parties were still too evenly matched for the struggle to come to an end: Witigis, who by his tardy and resourceless policy reminds us not a little the Saxon Ethelred, began to cast about him for allies, a step which, if he had taken it three years ago, might perhaps have saved him from ruin. The Franks were too utterly untrustworthy; the Lombards, to whose King Wacis he sent an embassy offering great gifts as the price of his alliance, refused to break with Byzantium. He therefore called an assembly of the elders, and there setting forth the difficulties of his situation, asked for the advice of his subjects. After long deliberations and many idle suggestions, a proposal was made which was fitted to the present state of affairs. It was pointed out by one of the Gothic statesmen that the peace which Justinian concluded on the accession of Chosroes in 531 was the true cause of the disasters both of the Vandal and the Gothic monarchies. Had the Caesar of Constantinople not felt secure of attack from the Persian King, he had never dared to employ the matchless skill of Belisarius on the banks of Libyan rivers and under the walls of Umbrian towns. It was therefore proposed and decided to send ambassadors to Chosroes to stir him up, if possible, to a renewal of hostilities against the Roman Empire. The ambassadors chosen were not Goths, whose nationality might have prevented them from traversing in safety the wide provinces of the East, but two priests of Liguria, probably Arian by their creed though Roman by speech and parentage, who for the promise of a large sum of money undertook this hazardous enterprise. One of these assumed the style of a bishop to give weight to his representations, and the other accompanied him as an ecclesiastical attendant.

The journey of these men to the Persian Court of course occupied a considerable time, and the full results of their mission were not apparent for more than a year after the period which we have now reached. The mere rumor, however, that negotiations were being opened between the Goths and the Persians made Justinian, who knew the weakness of his eastern frontier, so anxious to close the Italian war that he at once sent home the Gothic envoys, who for a twelvemonth had been waiting in his ante-chambers, suffering all those heart-breaking delays which seem to be engendered by the very air of Constantinople. Now they were bidden to return, offering to the Goths a long truce on terms which should be beneficial to both the combatants. Belisarius, however, who throughout this stage of the proceedings overruled with little hesitation the decisions of his master, refused to allow the Gothic envoys to enter Ravenna till the sanctity of the persons of ambassadors had been vindicated by the return of Peter and Athanasius, the Emperor's envoys to Theodahad, who, for nearly four years, had been kept in unjustifiable captivity. They returned, and as a reward of their devotion were promoted to high offices in the Empire. Athanasius was made Praetorian Prefect of Italy in the room of Reparatus, slain at Milan; and Peter, the brave and outspoken disputant with Theodahad, was hailed as Illustrious Master of the Offices, and received the embassies of foreign rulers in the palace-hall of Byzantium.

In these negotiations the winter and early spring of 539 wore away. In May 539 Belisarius addressed himself to the capture of the two fortresses which still held out for the Goths south of Ravenna: and such was the strength of position, perched upon their almost inaccessible heights, that all the rest of the year was consumed upon the task. The two fortresses were Faesulae and Auximum, represented by the modern towns of Fiesole and Osimo, the one overlooking the gleaming Arno, the other beholding the blue Adriatic upon its horizon.

Every Italian traveler knows the little Tuscan town to which we climb for our finest view of the dome of Brunelleschi and the tower of Giotto, pausing in our ascent to visit the villa of the Magnificent Lorenzo, and thinking of Milton's conversations with Galileo as we gaze upon

> 'The moon whose orb
> Through optic glass the Tuscan artist viewed
> At evening from the top of Fiesole.'

Instead of all this cluster of enchanting sights and memories, what had the Faesulae of the sixth century to show? She had, no doubt in greater extent, that stupendous Etruscan wall, the mere fragments of which make the Roman ruins by the side of it look like the handiwork of pigmies. She had the high fortress or Arx, a thousand feet above the Plain of Arno, where the friars of St. Francis' order now kneel for worship; the Temple of Bacchus, which was perhaps even then turned into a Christian basilica; and the Theatre, on whose stone seats we may still sit and imagine that we see from thence the couriers of Belisarius or Witigis spurring their steeds along the Cassian Road below. She had perhaps some remembrance of the day, six centuries ago, when Petreius defeated Catiline under her cliffs. More probably, her inhabitants yet pointed to the spot, near to her walls, where the vast horde of Radagaisus was surrounded and starved into submission by Stilicho.

Fiesole was held by a body of Gothic troops, of whose numbers we are not informed. To compel their surrender, Cyprian, one of the old officers who had fought under Belisarius at the siege of Rome, and Justin, one of the new arrivals under Narses, were sent with some of their own soldiers (probably cavalry) and a band of Isaurian auxiliaries, together with five hundred of the regular infantry, who still represented, though faintly, the old Roman legion. John, now again obedient to the orders of Belisarius; another John, whose mighty appetite procured him in the camp the nickname of the Glutton; and Martin, apparently forgiven for his disgraceful failure before Milan, were sent with a large body of troops to cover the siege of Fiesole and to hover about the upper waters of the Po. If possible, they were to intercept the communications of Uraias with Ravenna; if that were impossible, and if he should march to the relief of his uncle Witigis, they were to keep up an active pursuit of his army. These generals found the town of Tortona (then called Dertona), by the bank of the Po, a convenient basis of operations. As it was unwalled, it could be easily occupied by them; but by the command of Theodoric it had been plentifully supplied with houses suitable for the quartering of troops, and these were now taken advantage of by the generals who came to overthrow his kingdom. After a few skirmishes the siege of Fiesole settled down into a mere blockade. The Roman soldiers were unable to scale the heights on which the city stood, but they could easily surround them and see that no provisions were brought into Fiesole. Pressed by famine, the garrison called on Witigis, who ordered his nephew Uraias to advance to their assistance. Uraias with a large army marched to Pavia, crossed the Po, and sat down over against John and Martin, at a distance of some seven miles from their camp at Tortona. Neither party was willing to begin the fight. The Romans felt that their end was gained if they prevented Uraias from attacking the besiegers of Tortona. The Goths feared that one lost battle would shatter the last hope of their monarchy. Both armies therefore resumed that waiting game which they had played before the fall of Milan, and for which the Lombard plain (as we now call it) is so eminently adapted.

While this was the position of affairs, a new enemy swept like a torrent down the ravines of the Alps of St. Bernard, an enemy whose advent for a time changed the whole aspect of the war in Upper Italy. "The Franks", says Procopius, "seeing the mischief which Goths and Romans were inflicting on one another, and the length to which the war was being protracted, began to take it very ill that they should obtain no advantage from the calamities of a country of which they were such near neighbors. Forgetting, therefore, the oaths which they had sworn and the covenants which they had ratified only a short time before with both kingdoms—for this nation is the most slippery of all mankind in its observance of its plighted word—they marched into Italy to the number of 100,000 men under the guidance of their King Theudibert. A few horsemen armed with spears surrounded the person of their King: all the rest fought on foot, having neither bow nor spear, but each with a sword and shield and one axe. The iron of this axe is stout, sharp, and two-edged; the handle, made of wood, is exceedingly short. At a signal given they all throw these axes, and thus at the first onset are wont to break the shields of the enemy and slay his men.

When the Goths heard that this new host under Theudibert's own command was descending from the passes of the Alps, they trusted that the Franks were about to throw their weight into the opposite scale to that of the Empire, and that the hard struggle of the last four years was at length to be terminated by their co-operation. The Franks took care not to undeceive them so long as the Po had still to be crossed, but marched as a friendly force, harming no one, through Liguria. Having entered Pavia, having been allowed quietly to obtain possession of the bridge at the confluence of the Ticino and the Po, they threw off all disguise, and slaying the Gothic women and children whom they found there, cast their dead bodies into the stream, as an offering to the unseen powers and as the first-fruits of the war. Procopius assures us that this savage deed had really a religious significance, "since these barbarians, Christians though they be, preserve much of their, old creed, still practicing human sacrifices and other unhallowed rites, by which they seek to divine the future". Thin as the varnish of Christianity was over the Frankish nation, "the eldest daughter of the Catholic Church", it is hardly possible that this statement can be literally true. There were many Alamanni, doubtless, and other men of tribes confessedly still heathen, in the wild horde which clustered round the horse of King Theudibert; and it may have been some of these who performed the religious part of the rite, the Christian Franks only sharing in the brutal butchery which preceded it.

When the Gothic sentinels on the bridge saw the horrid deed perpetrated by these savages, they fled without striking a blow. The Franks proceeded towards Tortona; the main body of the Gothic army, still believing in their friendly intentions, advanced to meet them, but were soon undeceived by the storm of flying axes, swung by Frankish hands, laying their bravest low. In their consternation they turned to flee, and fled right through the Roman camp, never stopping till they reached Ravenna.

When the Imperial troops saw the flight of the Goths, deeming that Belisarius must certainly have arrived, must have conquered, and must be now pursuing, they advanced, as they supposed, to meet him. They too were cruelly undeceived, and being easily routed by the vast host of the Franks, fled across the Apennines, some into Tuscany to join the besiegers of Fiesoli, others to Osimo to tell the grievous tidings to Belisarius. The Franks, having thus won an easy victory over both armies, and sacked both camps, rioted for some time in the enjoyment of all the good things that they found there. When these came to an end, having no proper commissariat, and, like the brutish barbarians that they were, having no skill for aught but mere ravage of the country in which they found themselves, they fell short of provisions. The large draught-oxen of Liguria furnished them for a time with beef, but their only drink was the water of the great river. The combination proved injurious to the digestion of the greedy soldiers, and diarrhea and dysentery soon scourged the army of Theudibert, a third part of which, so it was reported, fell victims to these diseases.

Belisarius was filled with anxiety for the fate of the besiegers of Fiesole when he heard of the Frankish invasion. He wrote a letter to Theudibert charging him with conduct which the basest of mankind could scarcely have been guilty of, in violating his sworn and written promise to join in a league against the Goths, nay more, in actually turning his arms against the Empire. He warned him that the wrath of the Emperor for such a wanton outrage would not be easily turned aside, and recommended him to take care lest, in his light-hearted search after adventures, he fell himself into the extreme of peril. The letter reached Theudibert just at a time when his fickle soldiers were loudly complaining of the loss of so many thousands of their comrades by disease. The purpose of his soul was changed, and he vanished across the Alps with the remainder of his host as speedily as he came, having done nearly as much mischief and reaped as little advantage as Charles VIII, the typical Frank of the fifteenth century, in his invasion of Italy. Thus already is the melancholy strain begun which for a thousand years and more was to be the dirge of Italy. Already might a truly statesmanlike Roman see the mistake which had been made in rejecting—for merely sentimental reasons—the wise policy of Theodoric and Cassiodorus, that policy which would have made the Roman the brain and the Ostrogoth the sword-arm of Italy. Might that scheme have had fair play,—

> Then, still untired,
> Would not be seen the armed torrents poured
> Down the steep Alps, nor would the hostile horde
> Of many-nationed spoilers from the Po
> Quaff blood and water, nor the stranger's sword
> Be her sad weapon of defence, and so,
> Victor or vanquished, she, the slave of friend or foe.

While these events were passing in the north and west of Italy, Belisarius was prosecuting, with less success than had hitherto fallen to his lot, the slow siege of Osimo. This little city, which stands on a hill 900 feet above the sea, is ten miles south of Ancona, and about nine west of the Adriatic shore. Few travelers now climb up to its difficult height except those who may be disposed to take it on their way, when making pilgrimage to the Holy House of the Virgin brought, as the story goes, by angels from Nazareth and deposited on the neighboring hill of Loretto. The journey leads us through one of the fairest districts of Italy; a fertile undulating land, each height crowned with its own village, a stronghold in former days. We meet the stalwart peasants of La Marca driving their milk-white oxen in their antique chariot-like carts. Each cart is adorned with some picture of virgin or saint, or, for those who do not soar so high, of wife or sweetheart, rudely painted, but testifying to that yearning after the beautiful in Art which is the Italian's heritage. At length the road mounts steeply upward. After a toilsome ascent we stand upon the mountain crest of Osimo and survey the wide panorama.

Almost at our feet lies Castelfidardo, where, in 1860, Lamoricière, commanding the soldiers of the Pope, sustained a crushing defeat at the hands of the general of Victor Emmanuel. The curving coast of Ancona on the north, the Adriatic filling up the eastern horizon, the long line of the Apennines on the west, and their king the Gran Sasso d'Italia in the dim south, may all be seen from our airy watch-tower. In the Palazzo Pubblico of the town we find abundant evidence of its vanished greatness. Here are many inscriptions, belonging to the age both of republican and imperial Rome, betokening the pride of the Auximates in their city, once like Philippi in Macedonia, "a chief city in that country and a colony".

The gens *Oppia* seems for some time to have supplied the chief persons of the miniature senate, but all, of whatever family, proudly claim the title of "Decurio of the Roman colony of the Auximates", that word Decurio being still a badge of honor, not yet the branded mark of servitude. Looking at these tombs we recall with interest the words of Caesar, who tells us that at the beginning of the Civil War, the *Decuriones of Auximum* sent a message to the Senatorial general who commanded the garrison, "that neither they nor their fellow-townsmen could endure that after all his services to the Republic, Caius Caesar the general should be excluded from their walls". In the years, nearly six hundred, which had passed since that important resolution was formed, Auximum had generally played its part with credit, as the leading city of Picenum. Ancona, which now far surpasses it in importance, was then its humble dependent, bearing to it nearly the same relation that Ostia bore to Rome or Piraeus to Athens.

Auximum was garrisoned by some of the noblest and most martial of the Goths, who rightly looked upon it as the key of Ravenna. The Roman troops were quartered in huts all-round the foot of the hill; and the garrison saw a chance of success by making a charge at evening upon a portion of the host while Belisarius was still engaged with his body-guard in measuring the ground for the camp. The attack was bravely repelled, and the garrison retired, but the moment they stood again on their precipitous hill-top the battle again inclined in their favour. Night fell: a number of the garrison, who had gone out to forage the day before, returning, found the camp-fires between them and Auximum. A few managed to steal through the lines of the Romans into the city, but the greater number took refuge in some woods near, and were there found by the besiegers and killed.

Reluctantly Belisarius, having carefully surveyed the ground, came to the conclusion that the place being absolutely unapproachable all round, except by a steep ascent, was invulnerable to any sudden stroke, and must be blockaded. The blockade took him seven months, months of weariness and chafing delay, during which the Frank was descending into Lombardy, the Courts of Ravenna and Ctesiphon were spinning their negotiations for alliance, and the position of the Empire under the grasping policy of Justinian was becoming every day more full of peril.

There was a green patch of ground not far from the walls of Osimo which was the scene of many a bloody encounter. Each party by turns resorted to it to obtain forage for their horses and cattle, sometimes, in the case of the hard-pressed garrison, to pluck some herbs by which men could allay the pangs of hunger; and each party when thus engaged was of course harassed by the enemy. Once the Goths, seeing a number of Romans on the foraging-ground, detached some heavy wagon-wheels from their axles and rolled them down the hill upon their foes: but the Romans easily opened their ranks and let the wagon-wheels thunder past them into the plain, guiltless of a single besieger's life. In reading of these naive expedients of the Goths for inflicting injury on their foes, one feels that they were but overgrown schoolboys, playing the game of war with a certain heartiness and joviality, but quite ignorant of the conditions of success.

Their next move, however, showed a little more tactical skill. They stationed an ambuscade in a valley at some little distance from the town, by judicious appearance of flight drew the Romans towards it, and then with their combined forces inflicted heavy loss on the besiegers. The misfortune of the position was that the Romans who remained in the camp could plainly see the ambuscade, and shouted to their comrades not to venture further in that direction: but in the din of battle the shouts were either unheard or supposed to be shouts of encouragement, and thus the Gothic stratagem succeeded.

While Belisarius was brooding over this disappointing day's work, his secretary, the literary Procopius, approached him with a suggestion drawn from his reading of the war-books written by 'the men of old'. "In ancient times" said he, "armies used to have one note on the bugle for advance, another for recall. It may be that your troops, largely recruited from among the barbarians, are too untutored to learn this difference of note, but at least you may have a difference of instrument. Let the light and portable cavalry-trumpet, made as it is only of wood and leather, be always used to sound the advance: and when the deep note of the brazen trumpet of the infantry is heard, let the army know that that is the signal for retreat". The general adopted his secretary's suggestion, and calling his soldiers together delivered a short harangue in which he explained the new code of signals, at the same time cautioning them against headlong rashness, and assuring them that, in the skirmishing kind of warfare in which they were now engaged, there was no shame in retreat, or even in flight when the exigencies of the position required it. Of those exigencies the general must be the judge, and he would give the signal for retreat, when he deemed it necessary, by a blast from the infantry trumpet.

In the next skirmish at the foraging-ground under the new tactics the Romans were victorious. One of the swart Moorish horsemen from Mount Atlas seeing the dead body of a Goth covered with gold armor—haply such as Theodoric was buried in at Ravenna—began dragging him from the field by the hair of his head. A Goth shot an arrow which pierced the spoiler through the calves of both of his legs. Still, says

Procopius, the Moor persisted in dragging the golden-armored hero by his hair. Suddenly the trumpet of retreat was heard, and the Romans hurried back to the camp carrying off with them both the Moor and his prize. The garrison, who were beginning to be hard pressed with hunger, resolved to send messengers to Ravenna to claim the help of their King. The letters were written and the messengers prepared. Upon the first moonless night the Goths crowded to the ramparts and uttered a mighty shout, which made the besiegers think that a sally was in progress or that assistance was arriving from Ravenna. Even Belisarius was deceived, and fearing the confusion of a nocturnal skirmish he ordered his soldiers to keep quiet in their quarters. This was exactly what the barbarians desired, since it enabled their messengers to steal through the Roman lines in safety. The letter which they delivered to Witigis was worded in that independent tone which the German warriors feared not to adopt to their King. "When you placed us, 0 King, as a garrison in Auximum, you asserted that you were committing to us the keys of Ravenna and of your kingdom. You bade us hold the place manfully, and you promised that you with all your army would promptly move to our assistance. We, who have had to fight both with hunger and Belisarius, have been faithful to our trust, but you have not lifted a finger to help us. But remember, that if the Romans take Auximum, the keys of your house, there is not a chamber therein from which you will be able to bar them". Witigis read the letter, heard the messengers, sent them back to buoy up the beleaguered garrison with hopes of speedy assistance, but took not a single step in fulfillment of his promise. He was afraid of John and Martin, hovering over the valley of the Po: he was perhaps more justly afraid of the difficulty of provisioning his troops on the long march into Picenum. To the Romans who had possession of the sea, and who could import all that they needed from Sicily and Calabria, this difficulty was far less formidable than to him. Still, if the relief of Osimo was dangerous, its reduction meant certain ruin. Anything would have been better than to let his brave soldiers, trusting to his plighted word, starve slowly on their battlements, while he himself, like another Honorius, skulked behind the lagoons of Ravenna.

After these events came the mad torrent of the Frankish invasion, bringing equal consternation to Goths and Romans, and affording to Witigis something more than a mere pretext for the postponement of his promise. The garrison of Osimo of course knew nothing of this invasion; and Belisarius, informed of the previous embassy by deserters, watched the fortress with added diligence to prevent any second-message from being sent. In these circumstances, the Goths, bent on bringing their case again before their King, began to parley with a certain Burcentius, a soldier (probably an Armenian) who had come to Italy with Narses the Less, and who was stationed in a lonely place to prevent the foraging expeditions of the garrison. Large moneys in hand and the promise of more on his return from Ravenna induced this man to turn traitor and to bear the Second letter of the Goths to Witigis. The letter ran thus: "You will best inform yourself as to our present condition by enquiring who is the bearer of this dispatch. For it is absolutely impossible for any Goth to get through the enemy's lines. Our best food is now the herbage which grows near the city wall, and even this cannot be obtained without the sacrifice of many lives. Whither such facts as these tend we leave to be judged of by you and all the Goths in Ravenna".

To this short and pathetic letter Witigis returned a long and shifty answer, laying the blame of his past inactivity on Theudibert and the Franks; promising now with all speed to come to the assistance of his brave soldiers, and beseeching them to continue to act worthily of the reputation for valor which had caused him to single them out from all others as the defenders of his kingdom.

With the King's letter and many pieces of Gothic gold in his girdle, Burcentius returned to his station by the foraging-ground. His six days' absence was easily explained to his comrades. He had been seized with illness, and had been obliged to spend those days, off duty, in a neighboring church. At a suitable time he gave the King's letter to the garrison, who were greatly encouraged thereby, and persevered many days longer in their diet of salad, ever hoping that the trumpet of Witigis would be heard next day beneath their walls.

Still the slothful and cowardly King came not. Once more the Goths employed the services of the traitor Burcentius, who this time bore a letter from them saying that they would wait five days, no longer, and would then surrender the city. Again Burcentius returned after his opportune illness, bringing yet further flattering words and false hopes from the Nithing (as Saxons would have called him) in his palace at Ravenna. Again they were duped, and waited on in the extremity of hardship, resisting all the kind and coaxing words of Belisarius, to whom it began to be a matter of life and death to get the siege speedily ended.

Utterly perplexed by this extraordinary pertinacity of the Goths, and longing to find out its cause, the General discussed with his subordinate Valerian, whether it would be possible to capture some prisoner of distinction and extort from him the desired knowledge. Valerian mentioned that he had in his train some Slovenes from the banks of the Danube, and that these men were wont to crouch behind some small rock or shrub and stealing forth from thence to capture unwary travelers, either Romans, or barbarians of another tribe. This savage accomplishment, as it seemed, might now be turned to useful account. A tall and powerful Slovene was chosen and told that he should receive a large sum if he would capture a living Goth. He went forth accordingly in the dim morning twilight, and, bending his stalwart limbs into the smallest possible compass, hid behind a bush close to the foraging-ground. Thither came soon a Gothic noble to pick some herbs for his miserable meal. He cast many a look towards the Roman camp, to see if danger threatened him from thence, but suspected nothing of his nearer foe. While he was stooping down, suddenly the Slovene was upon him, grasped him tightly round the waist, and in spite of his struggles carried him into the camp to Belisarius. The prisoner, when questioned as to the cause of his countrymen's extraordinary pertinacity, revealed the history of the last two messages to Ravenna, and pointed to Burcentius as the bearer of them. The wretched Armenian confessed his guilt, and was handed over to his comrades to be dealt with according to their& pleasure. The pleasure of these barbarians was that he should be burned alive in the full sight of the garrison, his employers. "Thus" says Procopius, "did Burcentius reap the fruit of his greediness for gain".

Still the indomitable Goths would not surrender the fortress which had been confided to them by the faithless Witigis—faithless, but yet their king, Belisarius therefore determined to cut off their supply of water, and thus force them to a capitulation. There was outside the city, but near the walls, a cistern constructed of massive masonry, from which the Goths used to draw water, each excursion for the purpose being a sortie, which had to be effected hurriedly and by stealth. The General's design was to break down the masonry of this cistern sufficiently to prevent any large accumulation of water therein, as the Goths would never have time to wait and fill their amphorae from the slowly-running stream. Drawing up all his troops in battle array and threatening the town with an attack, he kept the garrison occupied while five Isaurians, equipped with axes and crowbars, stole into the cistern. They were, however, perceived by the garrison, who guessed their errand, and assailed them with a cloud of missiles. The strong vaulted roof over their heads, placed there by the builders of the cistern to keep its waters from the noon-day sun, proved to the Isaurians an effectual shelter. Hereupon the garrison issued forth to dislodge them. So fierce was their onset that the besiegers' line wavered before them. Belisarius rushed to the spot, by voice and gesture exhorting them to stand firm. While he was thus engaged an arrow from a Gothic bow came whizzing towards him, and would certainly have inflicted on him a fatal wound in the belly, had not one of his guards, named Unigat, seeing the General's danger, interposed his hand and in it received the hostile weapon. The faithful guardsman was forced to quit the field in agony, and lost for the remainder of his days the use of his hand; but the General's life was saved:—his narrowest escape this, since he rode the dark roan charger on the first day of the siege of Borne. At the same time, seven Armenian heroes (soldiers of Narses the Less and Aratius) did great deeds of valor, charging uphill against the Goths, dispersing their forces on the level ground, and at length, about noon-day, turning the battle, which had begun at dawn and seemed at one time likely to be a Roman defeat, into a Roman victory. Great, however, was the disappointment of Belisarius when he found that all this bravery had been wasted. The Isaurians, emerging from the cistern, were obliged to confess that in six hours of labor they had not been able to loosen a single stone. "For the masons of old time", says the historian, "put such thoroughly good work into this as into all their other buildings, that they yielded not easily either to time or to the hand of an enemy". This remark, which is fully confirmed by all that we see of the earlier work of the Romans in our own land, is perhaps meant as a covert criticism on the ostentatious but unenduring edifices of Justinian.

Thus foiled in his attempt to destroy the cistern, Belisarius, regardless of those general instincts of humanity which have endeavored to formulate themselves under the title of "The Laws of War", resolved to poison the well. The bodies of dead animals, poisonous herbs, and heaps of quicklime were thrown by his orders into the cistern. Still, however, the brave garrison held out, drawing their water from one tiny well in the city, and looking forth daily for the Gothic banners on the northern horizon.

At length the end of this tedious siege came from an unexpected quarter. The garrison of Fiesole, unable to endure their hardships longer, surrendered to Cyprian and Justin, on condition that their lives should be spared. Bringing their new prisoners with them, the generals marched to Osimo The sight of their captive fellow-countrymen, aided by the remonstrances of Belisarius, broke down the long endurance of the defenders of the capital of Picenum, and they offered to surrender if they might march forth with all their possessions to join their countrymen at Ravenna. Belisarius was earnestly desirous to end the siege at once, before an alliance which he dreaded between Franks and Goths should have had time to consolidate itself. On the other hand, he was reluctant to allow so many noble Goths, the bravest of the brave, to swell the ranks of the defenders of Ravenna; and his soldiers loudly murmured that it was monstrous, after subjecting them to the hardships of a siege, and such a siege, to deprive them of a soldier's heritage, the spoil. At length the two parties came to a fair arrangement. The Goths were to surrender half their property to the besiegers, taking a solemn oath to conceal nothing, and were allowed to retain the other half. So satisfied were they with these terms, and probably also so exasperated at the faithlessness of their King, that they appear to have actually taken service under the standards of the Emperor. There were evidently still many Goths to whom only two relations towards the Empire suggested themselves as possible, hostile invasion of its territory, or settlement as *foederati* within its borders. The siege of Osimo had lasted, according to one authority, seven months. It probably began in May, 539, and ended in December of the same year.

CHAPTER XIII.

THE FALL OF RAVENNA.

Osimo being taken, Belisarius collected all his energies for the siege of Ravenna. Ravenna, defended by a power having command of the sea, would have been practically impregnable; Ravenna, beleaguered by land and by sea, had delayed Theodoric for three years before its walls, and had at length only surrendered on a capitulation which, if faithfully observed, would have left Theodoric but half a victory. Belisarius therefore, while making all his preparations for a siege, determined not to leave untried the path of negotiation, which in the present state of the Emperor's affairs, with Persia menacing and the Franks eager for mischief, might shorten this dangerous last act of the drama. The Franks, as the General had been informed, were sending their embassy to Witigis, proposing an alliance for the reconquest and division of Italy; and Belisarius sent his ambassadors to confront them there, and argue against Metz for Constantinople. At the head of the Imperial embassy was Theodosius, an officer of high rank in the semi-regal household of Belisarius, but whose guilty intimacy with Antonina, the mistress of that household, had already been spoken of by his retinue under their breath, and was at a later period to be blazed abroad in court and marketplace, and to exercise a disastrous influence on the fortunes and character of the uxorious General.

As was before said, Belisarius was not trusting wholly to negotiation. Magnus and Vitalius, with two large bodies of troops, were sent to operate on the two banks of the Po, and to prevent provisions from its fertile valley being introduced into Ravenna. Their efforts were marvelously seconded by a sudden failure of the waters of the river, which caused the Gothic flotilla, prepared for the transport of provisions, to be stranded on the banks and to fall a prey to the Roman soldiers. In a very short time the river resumed its usual course, and navigable once more, served the purposes of the besiegers as it had failed to serve those of the besieged. It was therefore in a city which was already feeling some of the hardships of scarcity, if not yet of actual famine, that the envoys of Belisarius and of Theudibert set forth their commissions.

The Franks declared that their master was even now sending 500,000 warriors over the Alps, whose hatchets flying through the air would soon bury the Roman army in one heap of ruin. Theudibert had heard with sorrow of the sufferings of his good friends the Goths at the hands of the Romans, the natural and perfidious enemy of all barbarian nations. He offered them therefore victory if they would accept his companionship in arms, and a peaceable division of the land of Italy between them; or, on the other hand, if they were mad enough to choose the Roman alliance, defeat, ignominious defeat, to be shared with their bitterest and most irreconcilable foes.

The ambassadors of Belisarius had an easy task in enlarging on the faithlessness of the nation of Clovis. The present depressed condition of the Thuringians and Burgundians showed too plainly what an alliance with this all-grasping nation foreboded to those who were foolish enough to enter into such a compact. The corpses of all the brave Gothic warriors lately slain upon the banks of the Po attested the peculiar Frankish manner of helping distressed allies. What god they could invoke, or what pledge of fidelity they could give that had not already been forsworn and violated by them, the ambassadors could not conjecture. This last proposition, that the Goths should share all their lands with the Franks, was the most impudent of all their proceedings. Let Witigis and his subjects once make trial of it, and they would find, too late, that partnership with the insatiable Frank meant the loss of all that yet remained to them.

When the ambassadors had finished their harangues, Witigis conferred with the leading men of the nation as to their proposals. Would that the debates of this Gothic *Witenagemote* had been preserved for us! We can, however, only record the result of their deliberations, which was, that the Emperors offers should be accepted and the Frankish envoys dismissed. Parleys as to the terms of peace followed; but Belisarius, less generous or more wary than the Gothic King, when similar negotiations were going forward two years previously under the walls of Rome, refused to relax by a single sentinel the rigor of his blockade of Ravenna. Ildiger commanded the flying columns which maneuvered on each bank of the Po, while Vitalius was sent into Venetia to force or persuade the cities in that province to resume their allegiance to the Empire. During this pause in the contest the large magazines of provisions collected in Ravenna were destroyed by fire. In the Roman army it was generally believed that this was brought about by the bribes of Belisarius. The Goths differed in opinion from one another, some attributing the disaster to a stroke of lightning, others to domestic treachery, in connection with which the name of Matasuentha, the ill-mated wife of Witigis, was freely mentioned. They scarcely knew which explanation of the event should fill them with the gloomier forebodings, since one indicated the faithlessness of man, the other the anger of Heaven.

The brave and loyal Uraias, hearing of the blockade of Ravenna, was about to march to its assistance with 4000 men, partly natives of Liguria, partly Goths whom he had drawn from garrison duty in the various fortresses of the Cottian Alps. Unfortunately on their march the troops heard that the garrisons of these fortresses, at the instigation of Sisigis, the general upon the Frankish frontier, were surrendering themselves wholesale to a guardsman of Belisarius named Thomas, who had been sent with quite a small body of troops to receive them into the Imperial allegiance. Anxious for the safety of their wives and children, the soldiers of Uraias insisted on retracing their steps westward. They were too late: John and Martin, who were still stationed in the upper valley of the Po, hurried to the Cottian forts before them, took the very castles in which the families of these soldiers were lodged, and carried them into captivity. With such precious pledges in the hands of the Romans, the barbarians refused to fight against them. They suddenly deserted the standards of Uraias, and seeking the encampment of John begged to be admitted as foederati into the Imperial service. Baffled and powerless, Uraias was obliged to retire with a few followers into the fastnesses of Liguria. Thus all hope of assistance from him for the blockaded city was at an end.

About this time, probably early in the year 540, came two senators from Constantinople, Domnicus and Maximus, bearing the Emperor's offer of terms of peace. These terms were unexpectedly favorable to the Goths. Witigis was to be allowed to retain the title of King and half the royal treasure, and to reign over all the rich plains to the north of the Po; the other half of the royal treasure and all Italy south of the Po, with Sicily, were to be reunited to the Empire Such concessions, at this late period of the struggle, might well seem almost absurd to one who watched the fortune of the game in Italy alone. But the Emperor knew well the other and terrible dangers which threatened his dominions. A swarm of ferocious Huns were about to burst upon Illyria, Macedon, and Thrace, extending their ravages up to the very suburbs of Constantinople. Even more formidable than these transitory marauders was the more deeply calculated advance of the Persia potentate, Chosroes was moving to battle, stirred thereto in part by the representations of Witigis, in part by his own hereditary hatred of the Empire: and in June of this year he was to fall, with the pitiless fury of an Oriental despot, on the wealthy and luxurious city of Antioch. Decidedly Justinian had good reason for wishing to have his matchless general and as many as possible of his soldiers recalled from Italy. Decidedly he was right in offering easy terms to the Goths; and Italy might possibly have been spared some centuries of misery could those terms have formed the basis of a peace.

The obstacle came not from the Goths, who gave a joyful assent to the proposals of the ambassadors, his It came from Belisarius, who had set his heart on ending the Italian war with a complete and dramatic success, and on leading Witigis, as he had already led Gelimer, a captive to the feet of Justinian. He refused to be any party to the proposed treaty; and the Goths, fearing some stratagem, would not accept it without his counter-signature. Murmurs were heard in the tents of the Imperial captains against the presumption of the General who dared to disobey the orders which proceeded from the sacred presence-chamber of the Emperor, and who was bent on prolonging the war for sinister purposes of his own. Knowing that these injurious reports were flying about the camp, Belisarius called a council of war, at which he invited the presence of the ambassadors. He said to his discontented subordinates, with apparent frankness: "No one knows better than myself the great part which chance plays in war, and how a cause apparently quite hopeless will sometimes revive, and prove after all victorious. By all means let us take the best possible advice in debating so important a subject as the proposed treaty. Only one thing I must protest against. No man must hold his peace now, and then lie in wait to censure me after the event. Let everyone speak his opinion now, on the question whether we can recover the whole of Italy, or whether it is wiser to abandon part of it to the barbarians; and, having spoken it, let him stand by it like a man". Thus adjured, the generals without exception stated that they thought it politic to let the treaty of peace go forward, upon the proposed conditions. Belisarius desired them to sign a paper to that effect, and they signed it.

While these deliberations were going: on in the Imperial camp, the scarcity was growing into famine within the city. Sore pressed by hunger, yet determined not to surrender unconditionally to the Emperor, fearing, above all things, to be transported from their own beloved Italy to the distant and unknown Constantinople, the Goths conceived the extraordinary idea of offering to their victor, Belisarius, the Empire of the West. Even Witigis supported this proposal, and besought the great General to accept the proffered dignity. The scheme had a certain brilliant audacity about it, and was the most striking testimony ever offered to the strategical genius of Belisarius. Yet it probably seemed less strange and (if we may use the word by anticipation) less romantic to contemporaries than it does to us. All the traditions of the Ostrogoths, except for the thirty years of Theodoric's reign, pointed to the Empire as the natural employer of armies of Gothic *foederati*. Even Theodoric, in his mode of working the machinery of the state, had shown himself an Emperor of the West in everything but the name. A Teutonic kingdom in Roman lands was still a comparatively new and untried thing, while an Empire fought for by Gothic arms was a familiar conception.

The feelings with which Belisarius received this startling proposition were probably of a mingled kind. As Procopius says, "he hated the name of an usurper with perfect hatred, and had bound himself by the most solemn oaths to the Emperor to attempt no revolution in his lifetime". He probably looked upon himself as the destined successor of his master, should he survive Justinian, and he knew what ruin the revolutionary attempts upon the purple, made by successful generals, had wrought for the Empire. On the other hand, he saw that a feigned compliance with the wishes of the Goths would at once open to him the gates of Ravenna, and, possibly, the thought was not altogether absent from his mind that it might be desirable at any moment to turn that feigned compliance into reality.

In order to keep his hands clear, he ordered the generals of the party which still called itself anti- Belisarian to disperse in various directions in order to obtain provisions for the army. These generals were John and Bessas, Narses the Less, and Aratius; and they were accompanied by Athanasius, the recently-appointed Praetorian Prefect of Italy. Before they went, he convoked another council of generals and ambassadors, and asked them what they would think of the deed if he succeeded in saving all Italy for the Empire and carrying all the Gothic nobles, with their treasures, captive to Constantinople. They replied that it would be a deed past all praise, and bade him by all means to accomplish it if he could. He then sent private messengers to the Goths offering to do all their will. The Gothic envoys returned with their vague talk of peace for the multitude and their secret proposals for Belisarius's own ear. He willingly stipulated that the persons and property of the Goths should be held harmless, but postponed till after the entry into Ravenna, the solemn oath (the coronation-oath, as we should term it), by which he was to pledge himself to reign as the impartial ruler of Goths and Romans alike. The suspicions of the barbarians were not excited even by this postponement. They imagined that he was hungering and thirsting for empire, and never supposed that he himself would throw any difficulties in the way of winning it.

Of all the many dramatic situations in the life of the great general—and they are so many as to excite our marvel that no great poet has based a tragedy on his story—the most dramatic was surely his entry into Ravenna in the spring of 540. The Roman fleet, laden with corn and other provisions, had been ordered to cast anchor in the port of Classis. Thus, when the gates were opened to admit Belisarius, he brought with him plenty to a famine-stricken people. Then he rode through the streets of the impregnable Queen of the Lagoons, with the Gothic ambassadors by his side, and the all-observing Procopius in his train. Much did the secretary ponder, as he rode, on one of his favorite themes of meditation, that hidden force—he will not call it Providence, and perhaps dare not call it Fate—which loves to baffle the calculations of men, and give the race not to the swift, the battle not to the strong, but to the objects of its own apparently capricious selection. The streets were crowded with tall and martial Goths, far surpassing in number and size the Roman army, and through them marched the little band of Belisarius, undersized, mean-looking men, but conquerors. The Goths, still confiding in what the new Emperor of the West would do for them, felt not nor admitted the shame; but the quick instinct of the women told them that their husbands were disgraced by such an ending to the war. They spat in the faces of the barbarians, and, pointing to the insignificant-looking men who followed the ensigns of the *Senatus Populusque Romanus*, "Are these the mighty heroes", said they, "with whose deeds you have terrified us? Are these your conquerors? Men can we call you no longer, who have been beaten by champions such as these"

The exact time when Belisarius dropped the mask and let the barbarians see that he was not their Emperor, but still only the general of Justinian, is not clearly indicated. Probably the process of disillusion was a gradual one. At the moment of his triumphal entry he doubtless allowed himself to be saluted as Caesar, but any thoughts which he may have entertained of keeping his promise to the Goths and actually assuming the purple vanished.

His honour rooted in dishonour stood,
And faith unfaithful, kept him falsely true.

On one point, however, he did keep the compact to which he had sworn. There was no plunder of the city, and the Goths were allowed to retain all their private property. But the great hoard of the kings, stored up in the palace, all that the wisdom of Theodoric and the insatiate avarice of Theodahad had accumulated, was carried away to Constantinople. Some of it may perchance have remained in the treasure-vaults of the palace of the Eastern Caesars till Baldwin and Dandolo with their Franks and Venetians, the soldiers of the Fourth Crusade, wrenched open the doors of those mysterious chambers, nearly seven centuries after the accession of Justinian. Witigis himself was treated courteously, but kept for the present in ward, till he could be taken in the conquerors train to Constantinople. Some of his greatest nobles were selected to accompany him. The mass of the Gothic warriors, at least such of them as dwelt south of the Po, were told to return to their own lands. The Roman soldiers and the men of Roman extraction thus became actually the majority in the former capital of the Goths.

In this way did the strong and stately city of Ravenna come again under the sway of a Roman Caesar, the stronghold of whose dominion in Italy it was destined to remain for two centuries, till Aistulf the Lombard in 752 reft it from Byzantium, to be himself despoiled of it a few years later by Pepin the Frank. and many others, surrendered at once to the Imperial forces on hearing of the fall of Ravenna. Verona and Pavia seem to have been the only cities of any importance still held by the unsubdued Gothic warriors. In Verona the command was vested in a brave chief named Ildibad, nephew of Theudis, King of the Visigoths in Spain. This man refused to transfer his allegiance to the Emperor, though Belisarius, by detaining his children captives in Ravenna, had it in his power to put sore pressure upon him. In Pavia the noble Uraias, nephew of Witigis, still commanded.

When the hope that Belisarius would play an independent part as Emperor of the West faded from the hearts of the Gothic warriors, the bravest of them flocked to Pavia and sought an audience with Uraias. With tears such as valiant men may shed, they thus addressed him: "Of all the evils which have befallen the nation of the Goths you, O Uraias! are the chief cause, through your very worthiness. For that uncle of yours, so cowardly and so unfortunate in war, would long ago have been thrust aside by us from the throne, even as we thrust aside Theodoric's own nephew Theodahad, if we had not looked with admiration on your prowess, and believed that you were in truth at the helm of the state, leaving only the name of kingship to your uncle. Now is our good-nature shown to have been folly, and the very root of all the evils that have come upon us. Hosts of our best and bravest, as you know, 0 dear Uraias! have fallen on our Italian battlefields. Our proudest nobles, with Witigis and the Gothic hoard, are being carried off to Constantinople by Belisarius. You and we alone remain, a feeble and miserable remnant, and we too shall soon, if we live, share the same fate. But we can die, O Uraias! and it is better for us to die than to be carried captive with our wives and our little ones to the uttermost ends of the earth. Be you our leader, and we shall do something worthy of our renown before we find a grave in Italy"

Uraias replied, that he too, like them, preferred death to slavery, but that the kingship he would not take, since he would seem to be setting himself up as a rival to his uncle. He strongly advised them to offer it to Ildibad, a man of bravery and might, and one whose relationship to Theudis, the Visigothic King, might at this crisis prove serviceable to their cause. The advice seemed good to the Gothic warriors, who at once repaired to Verona and invested Ildibad with the purple robe of royalty. Though accepting the kingly office, he urged his new subjects not yet to abandon all hope of persuading Belisarius to fulfill his plighted word and ascend the Western throne by their assistance, in which event Ildibad would willingly return into a private station. One more effort accordingly they made to shake the loyalty of their conqueror. All Italy knew that he was under orders to leave Ravenna; to take charge of the Persian war, said some, accused by his brother generals of treasonable designs, said others. There was some truth in both assertions. Justinian needed Belisarius on the banks of the Euphrates, but he also feared him in the palace at Ravenna. The Gothic envoys appeared in the presence of Belisarius: they reproached him for his former breach of faith; they upbraided him as a self-made slave, who did not blush to choose the condition of a lackey of Justinian when he might, in all the dignity of manhood, reign as Emperor of the West over brave and loyal warriors. They besought him even yet to retrace his steps. Ildibad would bring his new purple and gladly lay it at the feet of the monarch of the Goths and Italians. Reproaches and blandishments were alike in vain. The Roman General refused to strike a single stroke for Empire in the lifetime of Justinian. The Envoys returned to Ildibad. Belisarius, in obedience to his masters orders, quitted Ravenna; and with his departure, which coincided with the end of the fifth year of the war, ended the first act of the Byzantine reconquest of Italy.

At this point also we take our final leave of one whose name has been of continual occurrence through many chapters of this history, the late Praetorian Prefect, Cassiodorus. Since the election of King Witigis he had not, apparently, taken any conspicuous part in public affairs. Amid the clash of arms his persuasive voice was silent: and with the two races, Goth and Roman, exasperated against one another by memories of battle, massacre, and the privations of terrible sieges, he recognized but too plainly that the labor of his life was wasted. The united commonwealth of Goths and Romans was a broken bubble, and he might as easily call up Theodoric from the grave as recall even one of the days of that golden age when Theodoric was king.

Something, however, might yet be done to save the precious inheritance of classical antiquity from the waves of barbaric invasion which were now too obviously about to roll over Italy, from Byzantium's mercenaries, the Lombard and the Herul, as well as from the Frankish neighbor who had learned with too fatal aptitude the road across the Alps. This service—and it was the greatest he could have rendered to humanity—Cassiodorus determined to perform while he passed the evening of his life in monastic seclusion in his native Bruttii, at his own beloved Scyllacium.

It was probably in the year 539 or 540 that the veteran statesman laid aside the insignia of a Praetorian Prefect and assumed the garb of a monk. The chief reason for choosing the earlier year, and for supposing Cassiodorus not to have continued till the bitter end in the service of Witigis, is that had he been present on the memorable day when Belisarius and his men entered Ravenna, he would probably have met and conversed with Procopius. In that case his noble character, and the important part which he had played for a generation in the Ostrogothic monarchy, would surely have impressed themselves on the mind of the historian, and prevented that strange omission which he has made in writing so fully about Theodoric's kingdom and never mentioning the name of Cassiodorus.

In any event the late chief minister was close upon the 60th year of his age when he retired to Squillace. His mind during the last few dreary years had been ever more and more turning to the two great solaces of a disappointed man, Literature and Religion. After he had completed the collection of his Various Epistles he had, upon the earnest entreaty of his friends, composed a short treatise on the Nature of the Soul. The philosophy of this treatise is not new, being chiefly derived from Plato: and the philology, as displayed in some marvelous derivations at the outset of the treatise, if new, is not true. But there are some striking thoughts in this little essay, as, for instance, on the ineffable love which the soul bears to her dwelling-place the body, fearing death for its sake though herself immortal, dreading the body's pain from which she cannot herself receive any injury. But the most interesting passage, coming from so old and astute a statesman as Cassiodorus, is one in which he naively attempts to describe the outward signs by which we distinguish evil men from the good.

"The bad man's countenance, whatever be its natural beauty, always has a cloud resting upon it. In the midst of his mirth a deep and secret sadness is always waiting to take possession of him, and appears on his countenance when he deems himself unobserved. His eye wanders hither and thither, and he is ever on the watch to see what others think of him. His conversation is by fits and starts: he takes up one subject after another and leaves his narratives unfinished without apparent cause. He has a look of worry and preoccupation in his idlest hours, and lives in perpetual fear when none is pursuing him. Seeking greedily for all the pleasures of life, he is incurring the penalty of eternal death; and endeavoring to prolong his share of this world's light he is preparing for himself the shades of eternal night"

Was Cassiodorus when he drew this striking picture describing the way in which the memory of the murdered Amalasuntha tormented the soul of Theodahad?

"The good man, on the other hand, has a certain calm joyousness in his countenance, earned by many secret tears. His face is pale and thin, but suggests the idea of strength. A long beard gives venerableness to his aspect: he is very clean, without a trace of foppery. His eyes are clear, and brighten naturally when he addresses you. His voice is of moderate tone, not so low as to be akin to silence, nor swoln into the harsh bluster of the bully. His very pace is ordered, neither hurrying nor creeping. He does not watch another's eye to see how it is regarding him, but holds simply straightforward on his way. Even the natural sweetness of his breath distinguishes him from the evil man, who seeks to hide the fumes of wine by the sickening scent of artificial perfumes".

The time was now come for Cassiodorus openly to enter that monastic state towards which, as we can perceive from this ideal portraiture of a good man, his own aspirations had for some time been tending. Leaving the lagunes of Ravenna, the pine-wood and the palace of the Ostrogothic kings, where so many of the hours of his middle life had been spent, he returned to his first love, his own ancestral Scyllacium, its hills, its fish-ponds, its wide outlook over the Ionian sea. Here upon his patrimonial domain he founded two monasteries. High up on the hill, and perhaps surrounded by the walls of the older and deserted city, was placed the secluded hermitage of

Castellum, destined for those who preferred the solitary life of the rigid anchorite to the more social atmosphere of the monastic brotherhood. The latter and more popular type of convent was represented by the monastery of Vivarium, situated by the little river Pellena, and on the edge of the fish-ponds of which Cassiodorus has already given us so picturesque a description. Here the old statesman erected for the monks, who soon flocked round him, a building which, though not luxurious, was better supplied with the comforts of life than was usual with institutions of this kind, at any rate in the first fervor of monasticism. These are the terms in which Cassiodorus himself describes the place, in a treatise dedicated to his monks:

"The very situation of the Vivarian monastery invites you to exercise hospitality towards travelers and the poor. There you have well-watered gardens and the streams of the river Pellena, abounding in fish, close beside you. A modest and useful stream, not overwhelming you by the multitude of its waters, but on the other hand never running dry, it is ever at your call when needed for the supply of your gardens. Here, by God's help, we have made in the mountain caverns safe receptacles for the fish which you may catch from the stream. In these they can swim about and feed and disport themselves, and never know that they are captives, till the time comes when you require them for your food. We have also ordered baths to be built, suitably prepared for those who are in feeble health; and into these flows the fair transparent stream, good alike for washing and for drinking. We hope therefore that your monastery will be sought by strangers rather than that you will need to go elsewhere to seek delight in strange places. But all these things, as you know, pertain to the joys of the present life, and have nought to do with the hope of the future which belongs to the faithful. Thus placed here, let us transfer our desires to those things which shall cause us to reign there with Christ".

Again, after describing in attractive terms the happy labors of the *antiquarii* in the copying-room of the monastery, he goes on to speak of the permitted luxury of comely book-binding, and of his mechanical contrivances for promoting the regular employment of the monastic day. "To these we have also added workmen skilled in covering the codices, in order that the glory of the sacred books may be decked with robes of fitting beauty. Herein we do in some sort imitate that householder in our Lord's parable who, when he had asked the guests to his supper, desired that they should be clothed in wedding garments. By these workmen we have caused several kinds of binding to be all represented in one codex, in order that the man of taste may choose that form of covering which pleases him best. We have also prepared for your nocturnal studies mechanical lamps, self-trimming and self-supplied with oil, so that they burn brightly without any human assistance. And in order that the division of the hours of the day, so advantageous to the human race, may not pass unobserved by you, I have caused one measurer of time to be constructed in which the indication is made by the sun's rays, and another, worked by water, which night and day marks regularly the passage of the hours. This is also of use in cloudy days, when the inherent force of water accomplishes what the fiery energy of the sun fails to perform. Thus do we make the two most opposite elements, fire and water, concur harmoniously for the same purpose". From these few passages it will be seen what was the spirit in which Cassiodorus founded his monastery of Vivarium. Religion and learning were to be the two poles upon which the daily life of the community revolved. He himself tells us that he had earnestly striven to persuade Pope Agapetus to found a great theological school at Rome, like those which were then flourishing at Alexandria and Nisibis. The wars and tumults which had recently afflicted the kingdom of Italy made the fulfillment of this design impossible; and Cassiodorus thereupon resolved that his own retirement from the field of political life should be the commencement of a vigorous and sustained effort to stem the tide of ignorance and barbarism which was flowing over Italy. Hitherto the monk retiring from the world had been too much inclined to think only of the salvation of his own individual soul. Long hours of mystic musing had filled up the day of the Egyptian anchorite. Augustine and Cassian, men so widely divergent in their theological teaching, had each contributed something towards the introduction of healthy work into the routine of the monastic life; and Benedict, with whose life and career we shall soon have to concern ourselves in greater detail, had wisely ordained in his rule that a considerable part of the day should be devoted to actual toil. Still, all this had reference only to manual labor. It was the glory of Cassiodorus that he, first and preeminently, insisted on the expediency of including intellectual labor in the sphere of monastic duties. Some monks, he freely admitted, would never be at home in the cloister library, and might better devote their energies to the cloister garden. But there were others who only needed training to make them apt scholars in divine and human learning, and this training he set himself to give them. This thought—may we not say this divinely suggested thought?—in the mind of Cassiodorus was one of infinite importance to the human race. Here, on the one hand, were the vast armies of monks, whom both the unsettled state of the times and the religious ideas of the age were driving irresistibly into the cloister; and who, when immured there with only theology to occupy their minds, became, as the great cities of the East knew too well, preachers of discord and mad fanaticism. Here, on the other hand, were the accumulated stores of two thousand years of literature, sacred and profane, the writings of Hebrew prophets, Greek philosophers, Latin rhetoricians, perishing for want of men at leisure to transcribe them. The luxurious Roman noble with his slave-amanuenses multiplying copies of his favorite authors for his own and his friends' libraries, was an almost extinct existence. With every movement of barbarian troops over Italy, whether those barbarians called themselves the men of Witigis or of Justinian, some towns were being sacked, some precious manuscripts were perishing from the world. Cassiodorus perceived that the boundless, the often wearisome leisure of the convent might be profitably spent in arresting this work of denudation, in preserving for future ages the intellectual treasure which must otherwise have inevitably perished. That this was one of the great services rendered by monasticism to the human race, the most superficial student of history has learned: but not all who have learned it know that the monk's first decided impulse in this direction was derived from Theodoric's minister Cassiodorus.

The veteran statesman seems to have wisely abstained from making himself actual Abbot of either of his two monasteries. To have done so would have plunged him into a sea of petty administrative details and prevented him from thinking out his schemes for the instruction of the men who had gathered round him.

Cassiodorus (as has been said) was probably about sixty years of age when he retired from Ravenna and when this 'Indian summer' of his life, so beautiful and so full of fruit for humanity, began. His own writings after this time were copious, and though they have long since ceased to have any scientific value, they are interesting as showing the many-sided, encyclopedic character of the attainments of him who had been all his life a busy official. A voluminous commentary on the Psalms was the work on which he probably prided himself the most, and which is now the most absolutely useless. In the so-called "*Historia Tripartita*" he and his friend Epiphanius wove together, somewhat clumsily, into a single narrative the three histories of Church affairs from the Conversion of Constantine to the days of Theodosius II given by Socrates, Sozomen, and Theodoret. In the *'Complexiones'* he comments upon the Epistles, the Acts of the Apostles, and the Apocalypse: and here it may be remarked in passing, that he includes the Epistle to the Hebrews among the writings of the Apostle Paul, apparently without a suspicion that this had not always been the received view in the Roman Church. In his book "*De Institutione Divinarum Litterarum*" from which some quotations have already been made, he gives his monks some valuable hints how to study and how to transcribe the Holy Scriptures and the writings of the Fathers. Some precepts for the regulation of their daily life are also included herein, and upon the whole the book seems to approach nearer to the character of the 'Rule of Cassiodorus' than any other that he has composed. In the "*De Artibus ac Disciplinis liberalium Litterarum*" he treats of the seven liberal arts, which are Grammar, Rhetoric, Dialectic, Arithmetic, Music, Geometry, and Astronomy. It is characteristic of the writer that Rhetoric and Dialectic, the two great weapons in the armory of a Roman official, are treated of at considerable length, while of the other five arts only the slenderest outline is furnished.

Lastly, when the veteran statesman had already reached the ninety-third year of his age, he composed for his faithful monks a somewhat lengthy treatise on Orthography. They said to him, "What does it profit us to know what the ancients wrote or what your sagacity has added thereto, if we are entirely ignorant how we ought to write these things, and through want of acquaintance with spelling cannot accurately reproduce what we read in our own speech?". He accordingly collected for their benefit the precepts of ten grammarians, ending with his contemporary Priscian, as to the art of orthography. One of the greatest difficulties even of fairly educated Romans at that day seems to have been to distinguish in writing between the two letters *b* and *v*, which were alike in sound. This difficulty, which is abundantly illustrated by the errors in inscriptions in the Imperial age, is strenuously grappled with by Cassiodorus, or rather by the authors from whom he quotes, and who give long and elaborate rules to prevent the student from spelling *libero* with a *v*, or *navigo* with a *b*.

Amid these literary labors, in the holy seclusion of Squillace, we may suppose Cassiodorus to have died, having nearly completed a century of life. Even in 573, when he wrote his treatise on Orthography, he had already long overpassed the limit of time prescribed for the present volume. It was then twenty years after the final overthrow of the Ostrogothic monarchy. The Lombards had been in Italy five years. Narses was dead, Alboin was dead, Justinian's successor had been for eight years upon the throne. Yet still the brave and patient old man, who had once been the chief minister of a mighty realm, toiled on at his self-imposed task. The folly of his countrymen, the hopelessly adverse current of events, had prevented him from building up the kingdom of Italy: they could not prevent him from conferring a priceless gift on mankind by rescuing the literature of Rome from the barbarians for the benefit of those barbarians' progeny.

CHAPTER XIV

AFFAIRS AT CONSTANTINOPLE

The year 540 was a memorable one for the monarchy of Justinian, both by its disasters and its triumphs. In June of that year, not many weeks after the fall of Ravenna, the troops of Chosroes entered Antioch. Heavily had the citizens of that fair and luxurious city, for near three centuries the inviolate capital of Syria, the place where the disciples were first called Christians, to pay for the taunts and gibes which, confiding in the strength of their walls, they had leveled at the haughty King of the fire-worshippers. Men, women, and children were mixed in one promiscuous carnage; long and stately streets were turned into smoking ruins; the sad remnant of the population which had laughed at Julian and rebelled against Theodosius was carried away into captivity beyond the Euphrates, beyond the Tigris, and there in the new city of Chosroantiocheia pined in vain for the groves of Daphne and the streams of Orontes, themselves the living monuments of their tyrant's triumph.

But also in the same year, and very shortly after these terrible tidings reached Constantinople, the ships bearing Belisarius with his captives and the Gothic hoard cast anchor in the Golden Horn. There was no regular triumph, as there had been when the Vandal King was led through the streets of the City. The jealous timidity of the Emperor was aroused, and he feared to grant the soldiers and the populace so tempting an opportunity for shouting *"Belisarie Imperator tu Vincas"*, and placing the brilliant General on the throne of the studious and secluded monarch. But though the formal pageant was withheld, none the less must the day when the successor of Theodoric prostrated himself in the purple presence-chamber of the Caesars have been felt as a real triumph for Belisarius. Then might the Byzantines see Witigis and his wife, the grand-daughter of the great Amal, followed by a long train of Gothic warriors whose stately frames and noble countenances filled even the exacting Justinian with admiration. With them came the children of the gallant Ildibad, unwilling hostages on behalf of the newly-crowned King. The vessels of gold and silver, and all the ponderous magnificence of the great Gothic hoard, were exhibited to the wondering Senators, though not to the multitudes outside the palace. Then Witigis having made his prostration was raised by the Emperor and received the title of Patrician. After he had spent two years at the capital, honored by the friendship of the Emperor, the old Gothic King died. A man apparently who in his younger and hungrier days had done the State some service; but when his countrymen gave him a palace and a crown and a royal bride as rewards for the deliverance which they expected at his hands, he replied, by his acts or rather by his utter absence of acts, in the words of Horace's wealthy soldier, 'Let him fight battles who has lost his all' His young wife, Matasuentha, soon after his death married Germanus, at that time the favorite nephew of Justinian. What mattered to her the ruin of her people and the downfall of the edifice erected by the wise patience of her illustrious grandfather? She had seen Constantinople, that Paradise of all degenerate Teutons, she had been able to copy the dresses of the crowned circus-dancer Theodora, she was even admitted into the family of the Dardanian peasants who swayed the destinies of the Empire.

As for Belisarius himself, the man who had brought two kings to the footstool of Justinian; who had subdued the two races of most terrible renown in the wars of the preceding century, the Goths and the Vandals; who had again, as it seemed, united to the Empire its severed Western portion, his name and fame were in the mouths of all men. Though the well-earned triumph had been denied him, every day that he showed himself in the streets of Constantinople was in fact a triumph. It was a pleasure of which the Byzantines never tired, to see him ride through the city from his palace to the Agora. Before him went troops of tall Vandals and Goths, of swarthy Moors the wiry sons of the desert. All had at one time or another felt his conquering sword, yet all delighted to sound his praises. Behind him rode some of his own domestic bodyguard, itself a little army of 7000 men when all were mustered; each horse a stately charger, each man nobly born and of noble aspect, and one who had done great deeds fighting in the foremost ranks with the enemy. In the course of this history we have heard continually of the exploits performed by this 'spearman' or that 'shield-bearer' of Belisarius. No wonder that the astonished Senators of Rome had said, 'One household alone has destroyed the kingdom of Theodoric,' when they marked the great part played by the body-guard of the General, in the world-famous defence of Rome.

The central figure of this brilliant cavalcade, Belisarius himself, was of mighty stature, with well-proportioned limbs and a countenance of manly beauty. Though, as we have seen, he had not the power of attaching to himself the loyal devotion of his officers of highest rank, his affability with the multitude, his tender care over the common soldier, even his desire to mitigate the horrors of war for the peasants of the invaded lands, were the theme of universal praise. He visited his wounded soldiers, doing all that money could do to assuage their sufferings. The successful champions received from his own hand armlets of costly metal, or chains of gold or silver. If a brave but needy warrior had lost his horse or his bow in the combat, it was from the private stores of the General that the loss was supplied. No soldier, where Belisarius commanded, was permitted to straggle from the high road and tread down the growing crops of grass or of corn. Even the fruit hanging ripe from the trees was safe from depredation when he marched past with his men. All provisions were paid for on a liberal scale, and thus, like our own Wellington on his march from the Pyrenees to Paris, he made even the greed of the peasant the most effectual helper of his commissariat.

His military character, as it had thus far revealed itself, has been sufficiently indicated by his deeds. His one distinguishing quality was resourcefulness. Nothing seemed to daunt or perplex him; and whatever move his antagonist might make, he was always ready with the reply. He was bold to the very verge of rashness, when only by audacity could the game be won; but when time was on his side, he could delay like Fabius himself. Strong, and even terrible, when sternness was required, yet with a disposition naturally sympathetic, temperate at the banquet, for 'no man ever saw Belisarius intoxicated', chaste in morals and faithful to his wedded wife through all the license of a camp, he anticipates, in some features of his character, the ideals of knight errantry and Christian soldiership, the Sir Galahad and the Bayard of chivalry, the Gustavus and the Havelock of the modern age.

Such was Belisarius in the midsummer of his greatness and renown, at the thirty-sixth year of his age, a year younger than Napoleon at Austerlitz, four years older than

Hannibal at Cannae. Unfortunately, the happiness of his lot was only in outward seeming. Even while he strode through the Agora of Constantinople, followed by the yellow-haired giants from Carthage or Ravenna, his heart was brooding sadly over the thought that the wife whom he loved with such passionate devotion no longer cared for him, and that all her affection seemed to be reserved for a shaven monk at Ephesus.

The whole story of the infidelities of Antonina, infidelities told with a cruel zest in the *Anecdota* of Procopius, need not be repeated here. The backstairs-gossip of a palace does not become worthy material for history, because it happens to relate to the wrongs of a warrior and a statesman. It is enough to say that the wife of Belisarius, though she had already reached or passed middle life, unmindful of her conjugal duty was passionately in love with her handsome chamberlain, Theodosius, and adopted child of herself and her husband. At Carthage and at Syracuse Belisarius saw and heard enough to rouse his suspicions: but he put the terrible thought away from him, and even consented, as we have seen, to put to death (ostensibly for another offence) the officer, Constantine, who had expressed an opinion unfavorable to the honor of Antonina. So the years had gone by, Theodosius holding a place of honor and trust in the General's palace, passionately loved by its mistress, and Belisarius the only person therein who was ignorant of his dishonor. When the whole party returned to the capital, Theodosius felt that the risk which he was running was too terrible, and retired to Ephesus, where he entered a convent. Antonina made no attempt to conceal her wild grief at his departure, and actually persuaded Belisarius to join her in entreating the Emperor to command his return.

At length, in the spring of 541, all his preparations being completed, Belisarius started for the East to try conclusions with Chosroes. On the eve of his departure, Photius, son of Antonina, driven to despair by the machinations of his unnatural mother against his life, laid before the General convincing proof of her past unfaithfulness. He proved to him also that Theodosius, who had refused to leave his convent in obedience to the Emperor's orders, was in reality only waiting for the moment of Belisarius's departure to return to Constantinople and resume the interrupted intrigue. Now at length the emotion of jealousy, so long kept at bay, took full possession of the General's soul.

He made Photius his confederate, and devised with him a scheme for separating the guilty lovers and imprisoning Theodosius. Then he started for the field; but with a mind distracted by these bitter thoughts, and hampered by the necessity of keeping open his communications with his step-son, he failed to achieve any brilliant success over Chosroes. The plan, however, devised between him and Photius was at first successfully executed. Antonina was kept in harsh durance, and her lover was carried off to a fortress in Cilicia, the very name of which was known only to Photius. So far the avengers of the injured honor of the husband had succeeded; but now Theodora appeared upon the scene, her aid being invoked by the guilty but furious wife; and whenever Theodora condescended to intervene, all laws human and divine must give way before her To understand the Empress's motives for interfering, obviously on the wrong side, in this wretched matrimonial dispute, we must turn to the political history of the times and take note of another event which signalized this year 541, the fall of John of Cappadocia.

It will be remembered that in the terrible insurrection of the Nika, the fury of the populace had been especially directed against two ministers of the Emperor, Tribonian the quaestor, and John of Cappadocia the Praetorian Prefect. Both had bowed before the storm, but both, soon after the suppression of the revolt, had been restored to their old offices. Tribonian had probably learned the lesson that the ministers of a king must at least seem to do justice. At any rate, his courteous demeanor, his honeyed words, and the vast learning of which he was undoubtedly master, caused the people to acquiesce patiently in his subsequent tenure of office, and he died, a few years after the time which we have now reached, at peace with all men. Far different was the career of his early partner in unpopularity, the coarse-fibred, ignorant, but singularly able John of Cappadocia. For eight years this remorseless tyrant was the ruling spirit in the internal administration of the Empire. When it came to a question of foreign policy, such as the Vandal expedition, which he would fain have dissuaded Justinian from undertaking, he might be, and was outvoted: but when a new tax had to be levied, or a provincial governor too chary of the fortunes of his subjects to be reprimanded, the voice of John was supreme. He had essentially the slave-driver's nature, the harsh bullying voice, the strong clear brain, the relentless heart, which enable a man in authority to get the maximum of work out of those below him, if they have no choice but to obey. Such a man with the powers of a Grand Vizier was invaluable to Justinian, whose expensive and showy policy required that a great number of harsh and even cruel deeds should be done, though personally his not unkind disposition and his studious nature would have shrunk from the doing of them.

Of any such scruples the hard heart of the Cappadocian felt not a trace. As pitiless as he was quick-witted, a man who lived for the gratification of his lusts, and who believed in nothing else, except in a sorcerer's spells, John was both cruel himself and the cause of cruelty in others. He erected the stocks and the rack in a secret chamber of the Prefect's palace, and there tortured those whom he suspected of concealing their wealth from him, till they had given up the uttermost farthing. One old man, Antiochus by name, was found when he was loosed from the ropes to have died under the severity of the torture. What the Prefect was doing himself in the capital, his minions, emulous of his cruelty, were doing in all the provinces of the East. One in particular, also named John, and surnamed Baggy-cheek from the fat and flabby cheeks which made his face hideous, laid waste the province of Lydia and the city of Philadelphia with his cruel exactions. A certain Petronius possessed a valuable jewel which had been handed down to him by his ancestors. Of this jewel the Governor was determined to obtain possession; whether for the Emperor's treasury or his own, who shall say? The owner was put in irons; was beaten with rods by stalwart barbarians; still he refused to part with the inheritance of his fathers. He was shut up in a mule-stable and compelled to spend his days and nights in that filthy dwelling. All his fellow-citizens bewailed, but none were able to help him. The Bishop of Philadelphia, timidly venturing on some words of remonstrance, backed by an appeal to the sacred writings, was assailed by such a torrent of abuse, for himself, for his office, for the holy books, as might only have been rivaled in the lowest stews of Constantinople. The Bishop wept, but Petronius, seeing that he had fallen into the hands of a monster who feared neither God nor man, sent to his house for the jewel, handed it to the tax-collector, and was permitted to depart, after he had given several pieces of gold to his tormentors as a fee for their labors in chastising him.

Sadder yet was the history of Proclus, a retired veteran, whom the tyrant assailed with a demand for twenty *aurei*, which the unfortunate soldier did not possess. The exactors thought that he merely feigned poverty, and blunted all their instruments of torture on his miserable frame. Wearied out at length he said, "Very well, then, come home with me and I will give you the twenty *aurei*". On the road he asked leave to tarry for a few minutes at a wayside inn. His oppressors waited outside, but as he was long in returning, they broke into the chamber and found the poor wretch hanging by a cord from a hook. Indignant at being thus outwitted by a man who had dared to die instead of satisfying the tax-gatherer, they cast his body into the Agora to be trodden under foot of men, and appropriated to the Imperial treasury the slender fortune which might otherwise have sufficed, and not more than sufficed, for the costs of his burial.

The collector of the public revenue is always and everywhere spoken against, and we generally read the stories of his wrongdoing with some abatement for probable exaggeration. But in this case the most grievous tales of oppression come to us, not from the oppressed provincials, but from a leading member of the Civil Service, from the Somerset House (so to speak) of Constantinople; and the remarkable but unconcerted agreement between Joannes Lydus and Procopius gives great additional value to the testimony of each.

The daily life of the master-extortioner John of Cappadocia is painted by these writers in vivid colors, too vivid indeed and too horrible to be reproduced here. The official palace in which he abode had been built by one of his most virtuous predecessors, Constantine, some seventy years previously, in the reign of Leo, and was then a modest well-proportioned dwelling, such as suited the chief minister of a well-ordered state. It was adorned—and here we get an interesting glimpse of the arts of the Fifth Century—by a picture in mosaic representing the installation of its founder. A later Prefect, Sergius, had added a large upper story, which somewhat spoilt the proportions of the building, and in these upper rooms John of Cappadocia spent his nights and days, wallowing in all kinds of brutal and sensual indulgences.

Sea and land were ransacked to supply the materials for his gluttony, and while he reclined at the banquet, with his head covered with a veil to look like a king upon the stage, and while troops of the most degraded of mankind of both sexes shared his orgies, the grave and reverend members of his staff, men who had enrolled themselves in the *officium* of the Prefect, believing that they were entering a learned and honorable profession, were compelled to wait upon him at table, like the basest of menials, doing his bidding and that of the shameless crew by whom he was surrounded. If any one dared to thwart the will of the tyrant in this or any other matter, he was handed over to the rough chastisement of John's barbarian men-at-arms, "men with wolfish souls and wolfish names".

So passed the Cappadocian's evening, in flagitious and obscene orgies prolonged far into the night. When his troop of parasites had left him and he had to seek his bed-chamber, then the timidity of the bully showed itself. He knew that he had many enemies (one especially, mightiest and most unscrupulous of them all), and in spite of his thousands of bodyguards he could never shake off the haunting fear that he should wake up to see some barbarian's eyes gleaming at him from under shaggy eye-brows and the knife raised to strike him to the heart. He started up at intervals to peep out from under the eaves of his dwelling, looking this way and that way at every avenue leading to the palace. Thus with fitful and broken slumbers the night wore away. But when morning came, the fears, the half-formed resolutions of amendment made in the night, had all vanished. He perhaps bethought him that it was well to cultivate his popularity with the mob; for this man, whose hand was so heavy on wealthy senators and Christian bishops, had a certain following among the lowest of the populace, particularly among the Green faction and the brawny Cappadocian porters, his countrymen. Accordingly, dressed in a robe of vivid green, which made more conspicuous the paleness of his sodden face, he would rush through the Agora courting the salutations and the applause of the multitude. Then back to the palace to spend the morning in schemes for amassing money by extortion, the evening in devices for squandering it on bodily delights: and so day was added to day in the life of the Praetorian Prefect of the East.

The man, though enslaved to bestial pleasures, had yet some stirrings of ambition, and probably some intellectual qualities which made him fit to rule: and he had a fixed persuasion that he would one day be chosen Emperor. It was a natural thing for a Praetorian Prefect, already so near the summit of the State,—
'Lifted up so high,
To scorn subjection, and think one step higher
Would set him highest'

He wore already a cloak dyed in the purple of Cos, but differing from the Emperor's in that it reached only to the knees, while the Emperors swept the ground; and the gold lace with which the Prefect's was trimmed was of a different and less conspicuous shape. When the Praetorian Prefect entered the room in the palace where the Senate was assembled, the chief officers of the army rose from their seats and fell prostrate before him. The etiquette was for him to raise them and assure them by a kiss, of his good-will to the military power. A minister thus highly distinguished might, as has been said, think the last step an easy one, and yet practically we do not find in the history of the Empire that it was often made. Officers of the guard and ministers of the household were hailed Imperator more often than Prefects of the Praetorium.

In the case of John of Cappadocia the coming elevation was not a matter of political calculation but of superstitious belief. Though he feared not God nor regarded man, he had great faith in the power of sorcerers and soothsayers; and the prediction with which these men flattered him, "Thou shall be wrapped in the mantle of Augustus", sank deep into his heart. Often might he be seen kneeling the whole night through on the pavement of a Christian church, dressed in the short cloak of a priest of Jupiter, and not engaged, so men said, in Christian, devotions, but muttering some Pagan prayer or spell, which, as he hoped, would save his life from the assassin's dagger, and make the mind of the Emperor yet more pliable in his hands than it was already.

But it was the Emperor only, not his more quick-witted wife, whose mind submitted to the ascendancy of the Cappadocian. Utterly insensible as Theodora was to the distinction between right and wrong, her artistic Greek nature felt keenly the difference between the beautiful and the uncomely; and the coarse, clumsy profligacy of the Prefect filled her with disgust. He courted the favor of the Green faction to whom she had vowed a life-long enmity. She read doubtless his designs on the Imperial succession, and knew that, if they prospered, the days of Justinian's widow would be numbered. Thus it came to pass that, early in the career of John of Cappadocia, Theodora was his declared foe. At the time of the sedition of the Nika she had counseled his disgrace, and we may fairly conclude that his second tenure of office, though it lasted eight years, was one long struggle for power between the Emperor's minister and his consort. There is one notable instance, that of Richelieu, in which such a struggle has terminated in the minister's favour; but generally speaking, however indispensable the counselor may seem, the final victory rests with the wife.

When Belisarius returned from the Gothic war, his popularity and his renown were wormwood to the jealous Prefect, who laid many an unsuccessful snare for his rival. Belisarius started for his Eastern campaign; but his wife, a far more dangerous foe, remained behind. Antonina, who had set her heart on obtaining the favor of Theodora, and knew that John's destruction would be the surest means to that end, devised a scheme for his ruin, so dishonorable that even the brutal Prefect wins a moment's sympathy when we see him thus ensnared. The one amiable feature in his character was his fondness for his only child Euphemia, a young and modest girl, who must assuredly have been brought up out of sight and hearing of her father's orgies. With this child Antonina cultivated an apparent friendship, and, after many visits had established seeming intimacy, she one day burst out into angry complaints of the way in which the Empire was now governed. "See what an ungrateful master Justinian has been to Belisarius. After extending the bounds of the Roman Empire further than it had ever reached before, and bringing two kings with all their treasures captive to Constantinople, what thanks has my husband received?". Other words were added to the same effect. Euphemia, who, young as she was, shared her father's enmity to Theodora, delighted at this prelude, replied, "Dear lady, the fault is surely yours and your husband's. You could make an end of all this, but will not, and seem to be satisfied with things as they are". "We are powerless" said Antonina, "by ourselves. Our strength lies only in the camp, and unless someone in the cabinet seconds our efforts, we can do nothing; but if your father would help us, by God's blessing we might perhaps accomplish something worth telling of".

All this conversation was duly reported to John of Cappadocia, who, thinking that now at last the words of the soothsayers were coming true and that by the arms of Belisarius he was to be seated on the throne of the Caesars, fell headlong into the trap prepared for him and pressed for an immediate interview with Antonina, at which they might arrange their plans and exchange oaths of secrecy and fidelity. Apparently in order to gain time to communicate with Theodora, Antonina replied that an interview in the capital would be inexpedient and dangerous, but that on her approaching departure to join her husband at the camp, John could safely pay her a valedictory visit at the suburb which marked the first stage of her journey. The deceived Prefect willingly accepted the invitation. And yet the very scene of their meeting might have suggested thoughts of prudence. It was a country house of Belisarius, but it was named Rufinianum, having no doubt once belonged to the aspiring Prefect of Arcadius, who mounted the platform to be saluted as Emperor, and descended from it a mutilated and dishonored corpse.

All these arrangements were duly communicated to Theodora, and by her to the Emperor. Narses the Eunuch and Marcellus Captain of the House-hold Troops were sent with a considerable number of troops to listen, and if they heard treasonable words to arrest the traitor. Theodora arrived at the country house where she was to pass the night, and whence she was to start on the morrow. John of Cappadocia came there too, having, so it was said, received and disregarded a message from Justinian—"Have no secret interview with Antonina". At midnight they met, the deceived and the deceiver, apparently in the garden of the palace. Behind a low fence crouched Narses and Marcellus with some of their followers. The Cappadocian began open-mouthed about the plot, binding himself and seeking to bind Antonina by the most terrible oaths to secrecy. When they had heard enough, the spies arose and came towards John to arrest him. He uttered a cry: his own guards rushed to the spot, and a struggle followed in which Marcellus was wounded, but not mortally, by a soldier ignorant of his rank. In the scuffle John escaped. Men thought that even then, if he had gone straight to Justinian and appealed to the Imperial clemency, he might still have retained his office; but by fleeing to a church for refuge he left the field free to Theodora, who made his ruin sure. Having been seized in the church, he was degraded from his dignity of Prefect and taken to the city of Cyzicus, on the southern shore of the Sea of Marmora, where he was forced to assume the priestly office, changing his name from John to Peter. It was noted by those who were present at in the sacred ceremony, that a priestly robe not having been specially prepared for the unwilling candidate, the garment of a clerical by-stander was borrowed for the purpose, that the name of this by-stander chanced to be Augustus, and that thus the promises of the sorcerers to the Prefect were literally fulfilled, since he had been "wrapped in the mantle of Augustus".

By the favor of the Emperor, who had not yet of lost his kindly feeling towards him, the new-made priest was allowed to retain a sufficient portion of his vast and ill-gotten wealth to excite the sore envy of his fellow citizens. The murder of a highly unpopular bishop of Cyzicus, of which crime John was unjustly accused, afforded a pretext to the Commissioners of the Senate to inflict upon him a terrible punishment. The former Consul, Patrician, and Prefect was stripped naked, like the meanest criminal, grievously scourged, and compelled to recite in a loud voice all the misdeeds of his past life. Then, with no possessions but one rough mantle, bought for a few pence, he was shipped on board a vessel bound for the coast of Africa. At what port soever the ship touched he was constrained to go on shore and beg for a crust of bread or a few obols from the passers-by. Such was the fall of the man whose wealth had been counted by millions, and who had once been practically lord of Asia. Still, even in his abject misery, he cherished his old dreams of coming empire, and in fact, after seven years of exile, he was, upon the death of Theodora, recalled by her husband to the capital. He regained, however, none of his former honors, but spent the rest of his life in obscurity, and died a simple presbyter.

The help which Antonina had given to the Empress in this deadly duel with the Prefect made the former one of the most important personages in the State. Theodora was not ungrateful, and her influence, now all-powerful, was thrown enthusiastically into the scale on behalf of her new ally. Hence, to go back to the dreary domestic history of Belisarius, it is easy to understand why the General was prevented from inflicting punishment on his faithless wife. Antonina's petition for help reached the ears of Theodora. She was herself delivered from her prison, Photius was tortured (but in vain) to make him reveal the place where Theodosius was confined, and then thrown into a dark dungeon. He made two attempts to flee, after each of which Theodora caused him to be dragged away from the Holy Table itself, under which he had taken refuge. At length, however, he escaped to Jerusalem, where, taking the habit of a monk, he, by a life of obscurity and hardship, succeeded in evading the further persecutions of his unnatural mother and her Imperial ally.

The Empress at length succeeded in discovering the retreat of Theodosius, and, as if she were performing the most meritorious of actions, restored him to the arms of Antonina. Belisarius, cowed and spirit-broken by the malice of two wicked women, was forced humbly to beg forgiveness from the wife who had so deeply wronged him. Tortures, banishment, loss of property, were the punishments showered upon the unhappy dependents of Belisarius and Photius, who had sided with their masters against the adulteress. The guilty intimacy of Antonina and her lover was soon dissolved by the death of Theodosius, who fell a victim to an attack of dysentery; but from this time onwards the General was made to feel that he was an outcast from the Imperial favor, and that only as Antonina's husband was he to expect even toleration at the hands of Theodora.

Such was the reward which services, perhaps the most brilliant and the most faithful which ever were rendered by a subject to his sovereign, received at the Court of Byzantium.

The year 541, which saw the fall of John of Cappadocia, was also memorable in the history of the Roman State, as witnessing the death of that venerable institution, which had survived the storms of ten centuries and a half, the Roman Consulship. For some years the nominations to this high office had been scanty and intermittent. There were no consuls in 531 and 532. The Emperor held the office alone in 533, and with a colleague in 534. Belisarius was sole consul in 535. The two following years, having no consuls, of their own, were styled the First and the Second after the Consulship of Belisarius. John of Cappadocia gave his name to the year 538, and the years 539 and 540 had again consuls, though one only for each year. In 541 Albinus Basilius sat in the curule chair, and he was practically the last of the long list of warriors, orators, demagogues, courtiers, which began (in the year 509 *BC*) with the names of Lucius Junius Brutus and Lucius Tarquinius Collatinus. All the rest of the years of Justinian, twenty-four in number, were reckoned as 'Post Consulatum Basilii'. Afterwards, each succeeding Emperor assumed the style of consul in the first year of his reign, but the office, thus wholly absorbed in the sun of Imperial splendor, ceased to have even that faint reflection of its former glory, which we have traced in the fifth and sixth centuries. The pretext for abolishing a dignity so closely connected with the remembrance of the heroic days of the Roman State was, that the nobles upon whom it was conferred frittered away their substance in pompous shows exhibited to the people. The real reason doubtless was that precisely by means of those glorious associations it kept alive in the minds of men some remembrance of the days when the Emperor was not all in all, nay, was not yet even heard of. Consuls, as the centuries rolled on, had found their power encroached upon and limited by the Dictators, who seemed to be imperatively called for by the disorders of the Roman State. The temporary figure of the Dictator had given way to the Imperator, the Princeps invested with Tribunician powers, the undefined All-ruler who was yet only first citizen in the commonwealth, the wonderful Republican Autocrat whom Julius and Augustus had imagined and had bodied forth. Gradually the Imperator had become more of a king and less of a citizen, till under Diocletian the adoring senators, the purple sandals, all the paraphernalia of Eastern royalty, marked him out as visibly supreme. Still, many remains of the old Roman constitution, especially the venerable magistracy of the Consulship, subsisting side by side with the new dominion, bore witness to the old order out of which it sprang. Now, the last remains of the withered calyx fell away, and the Imperial dignity exhibits itself to the world, an absolute and undisguised autocracy. The Emperor is the sole source of power; the people have not to elect, but to obey.

CHAPTER XV.

THE ELEVATION OF TOTILA.

No stronger proof of the superiority of Belisarius, both as a general and a ruler, could be afforded than the disasters which befell the Imperial cause in Italy after his departure. There can be little doubt that Justinian's chief reason for recalling him was the fear that he might listen to some such proposition as that made to him by the Goths during the siege of Ravenna and might claim independent sovereignty. The fact that he was not sent against Chosroes till the spring of 541 proves that jealousy was Justinian's main motive, and heavily was he punished for that jealousy by the subsequent course of the war. Italy appeared to be recovered for the Empire when Belisarius entered Ravenna in triumph. Six months more of the great General's presence in the peninsula would probably have turned that appearance into a reality. But as it was, the stone of Sisyphus had only just touched the topmost angle of the cliffs. When Belisarius went, it thundered down again into the plains. The struggle had all to be fought over again, and twelve years of war, generally disastrous to the Imperial arms, had to be encountered before Italy was really united to the Roman Commonwealth.

The officers who accompanied Belisarius on his return to Constantinople were Ildiger his son-in-law, Valerian, Martin, and Herodian. All of these generals except Herodian, who was speedily sent back to Italy, distinguished themselves in the Persian war.

The chiefs of the army who were left in Italy were John the nephew of Vitalian, John 'the Glutton', Bessas the Goth, Vitalius, and Constantian 'the Count of the Imperial Stables'. The last two had commanded in Dalmatia, till the cessation of the Gothic resistance in that quarter allowed them to be transferred to Italy.

Among all these generals there was none placed in supreme command. Constantian as commandant of Ravenna, and Bessas, either at this time or soon after governor of Rome, were placed in two of the most prominent positions in the country. John's military record was the most brilliant, and probably with all his faults he would, if appointed General-in-chief, have soon brought the war to a successful termination. But no—the studious Emperor was not going to encounter again the same agony of jealous apprehension which had caused each successive bulletin from Belisarius to be like a stab in his heart. Forgetful therefore of the fine old Homeric maxim,

"Ill is the rule of the many: let one alone be the ruler"

he left the generals with an equality of authority to hold and govern Italy each according to his own ideas. Naturally, these ideas were in each case to plunder as much and to fight as little as possible. The bonds of discipline were soon utterly relaxed, and the rapacious, demoralized army of the Emperor became formidable to the peaceful provincials, but to no one else.

Now too the power of that terrible engine of oppression, the Byzantine taxing-system, began to make itself felt in Italy. Justinian's first care with all his conquests was to make them pay. With an extravagant wife, a pompous and costly court, with that rage for building which seems to be engendered by the very air of Constantinople, with multitudes of hostile tribes hovering round his frontiers who required constant bribes to prevent them from exposing the showy weakness of his Empire, with all these many calls upon him Justinian was perpetually in need of money; and the scourge, the rack, the squalid dungeon, as we have seen in the last chapter, were freely used in order to obtain it. That odious analogy to a great Roman household which had now thoroughly established itself in the once free commonwealth of Rome, and which made the Emperor a master and his subjects slaves, seemed to justify any excess of rapine. If we could scrutinize the heart of the Dardanian peasant's son who sat on the throne of the Caesars, we should probably find that his secret thought was something like this : "It is the business of my generals to conquer for me new provinces. The inhabitants of those provinces become my slaves, and must pay whatever I command them. It is my privilege to spend the money which I condescend to receive from them exactly for such purposes as I choose"

With these high notions of prerogative in his mind, Justinian became one of the most ruinous governors to his Empire that the world has ever seen. The reader need not be reminded of the dreary story of fiscal oppression which in Constantinople, in Africa, in Lydia, has already met his view. The eighteen new taxes with fearful and unheard-of names, the stringently-exercised rights of preemption, the cruel *angaria* which, like the French *corvées*, consumed the strength of the peasant in unremunerated labor, all these made the yoke of the Emperor terrible to his subjects. And yet, as was before pointed out, notwithstanding this extreme rigor in collecting the taxes, the reproductive expenditure of the Empire was not attended to : the aqueducts were not kept up, the *cursus publicus* or public post, the best legacy received from the flourishing days of the Empire, was suffered to fell into irretrievable ruin. Everywhere the splendor of the reign of Justinian— and there was splendor and an appearance of prosperity about it—was obtained by living upon the capital of the country. Everywhere, by his fiscal oppression as well as by his persecuting attempts to produce religious conformity, he was preparing the provinces of the East, pale, emaciated, and miserable, for the advent of the Moslem conquerors, who, within a century of his death, were to win the fairest of them, and were to hold them even to our own day.

In order to deal with the fiscal questions arising in the newly-recovered provinces, Justinian appears to have created a special class of officers, who bore the name of Logothetes, and whose functions correspond to those which with us are exercised by an auditor or comptroller. Doubtless some such machinery was necessary to enable the Emperor to take up the financial administration of two great countries, somewhat entangled by the supremacy of Vandal and Ostrogothic kings (however true it might be that the subordinate officers in the revenue department had remained Roman), and also to appraise at their just value, often to reduce, the large claims which the soldiers by whom the conquest had been wrought would make against the Imperial treasury. Some such machinery was necessary, but it should have been worked with a due regard to the eternal principles of justice and to the special and temporary expediency of winning the affections of a people who for two generations had not seen the face of an Imperial tax-gatherer.

Both justice and expediency, however, were disregarded by the freshly appointed Logothetes, and especially by the chief of the new department. This man, Alexander by name, received the surname 'the Scissors', from a bitter joke which was current about him among the oppressed provincials, who declared that he could clip the gold coins that came into his hands without injuring their roundness, and reissue them without risk of detection. He, like all the other Logothetes, was paid by the results of his work, receiving one-twelfth of all that by his various devices he recovered for the Imperial Treasury. From a very humble station in life he soon rose to great power and accumulated enormous wealth, which he displayed with vulgar ostentation before the various classes of men whom his exactions were grinding into the dust.

The first of these classes were the soldiers, for the Logothete was the natural enemy of the soldier, and Justinian deemed himself now secure enough in his hold on Italy to kick down the ladder by which he had risen. Every offence against the public peace—and the wild swarms of Huns, Isaurians, Heruli, whom Belisarius had brought into Italy, when his strong hand was removed, no doubt committed many such offences—had to be atoned for by a heavy fine to the Imperial treasury, one-twelfth of which went into the coffers of Alexander the Logothete. The endeavor to punish was praiseworthy, but it would have been wise to employ some sharp military punishment in cases of signal offence, and above all, to make the generals feel that they were responsible for the good conduct of their men, rather than to create the general feeling that while the Logothete was rolling in wealth the soldiers whose stout hearts had reconquered Italy were shrinking into a poor, despised, and beggared remnant, and would undertake no more daring deeds for the Emperor who had requited them with such ingratitude.

Not in Italy only, but throughout the Empire, another form of embezzlement practiced by the Logothetes told terribly upon the efficiency of the army. The system of payment of the soldiers at this time was one of advance according to length of service. The young soldier received little, perhaps nothing besides his arms and his rations. The man who had seen some years' service and who was half way up on the rolls of the legion was more liberally dealt with. The veteran who would shortly leave the ranks received a very handsome salary, out of which he was expected to provide for his superannuation fund and to leave something to his family. Of course, promotion to these more favored positions depended on the retirement or death of those who occupied them. But the Logothetes, intent on curtailing the soldier's allowances for the Emperor's profit and their own, hit upon the expedient of keeping the highly paid places full of phantom warriors. A veteran might have died a natural death, retired from the service, or fallen in battle, but still his name was borne on the rolls of his legion; and thus an excuse was afforded for keeping the middle-aged and elderly combatant still upon the lowest scale of pay. Procopius hints that Justinian himself connived at a system so grossly unfair to the soldiers and so absurdly deceptive as to the real strength of the army.

Among the various frivolous pretences for abridging the soldier's pay or cancelling his right to promotion we hear with surprise that one was derived from their Greek nationality. "They were called Greeks, as if it was quite out of the question for one of that nation to show anything like high courage". This passage shows us, what we might have expected, that these exactions were tried more frequently on the docile native soldier than on the fiery and easily unsettled barbarian auxiliary. It also brings before us the officials of the great monarchy by the Bosporus, men who were themselves Greek in their names, their language, and their ideas, still acting the part of pure-blooded Roman governors, and affecting to speak of the men who were in fact their countrymen with the old Roman disdain, the disdain which was not altogether unreasonable in the conquerors of Pydna and Cynoscephalae.

Having filled the soldiery with a burning sense of wrong, Alexander proceeded to alienate thoroughly as possible the Roman inhabitants of Italy, whose good-will had so greatly aided the progress of Belisarius. All Italians who had had any pecuniary transactions with the Gothic kings, or had held office under them, were called upon to produce a strict account of all moneys had and received, even though such moneys had passed through their hands forty years ago in the early days of Theodoric. Very possibly the easy-tempered King and his Gothic nobles had not been served with absolute fidelity by the sharp Italian officials. "But what concern is that of yours?" they naturally enquired. "It is not the Emperor who suffered : nay, rather, we might have thought that we were serving the Emperor by every *aureus* that we withheld from the most powerful of his foes". But now was again exemplified the elasticity which marked all the reasonings of the Imperial cabinet on the subject of the Gothic domination in Italy. When that domination appeared to be hopelessly overthrown, Byzantium reverted to the theory which it had so often played with, that Theodoric and his successors had been the lawful governors of Italy under Anastasius, Justin, and Justinian, that they had been by no means usurpers, but regular vicegerents, and therefore that an action for embezzlement would lie in the Emperor's name against all officials of the Ostrogothic Kings who had not faithfully discharged their trust. But this theory was not popular in Italy; and enforced as it was by grasping Logothetes, regardless of all principles of justice as to the kind of evidence which they required for transactions long past and forgotten, it swelled the chorus of discontent which was arising in all parts of the peninsula against the tyrant who had been hailed as a deliverer.

By all these causes the smoldering embers of the Gothic resistance were soon fanned into a flame. When Belisarius left Italy, Ildibad held only one city, Pavia, and had but one thousand soldiers. Before the year was ended, all Liguria and Venetia, that is all Italy north of the Po, recognised his sway, and an army of considerable size (largely composed of deserters from the Imperial standard) was under his orders. All the generals but one watched this sudden development of the Gothic power with apathy. Vitalius alone, who was lately commanding in Dalmatia and now in Venetia, moved with his hordes of Herulian auxiliaries against Ildibad. A great battle followed near Treviso—not many miles from the little trembling colony of salt-manufacturers at Venice—and this battle was disastrous for the Imperialists. Vitalius himself with difficulty escaped. Theudimund son of Maurice and grandson of Mundus the Gepid, a young lad who thus represented three generations of Imperial defeat, was in imminent peril of his life, but just succeeded in escaping, along with Vitalius. Visandus, King of the Heruli, lay dead upon the field.

The tidings of this victory, which were soon carried to Constantinople, made the name of Ildibad of great account in the mouths of all men. Domestic dissensions, however, soon cut short a career which promised to be of great brilliance. Uraias the nephew of Witigis could forget, his wife could not, that the Gothic crown had been offered to him and that Ildibad reigned by virtue of his refusal. This lady, who was conspicuous among all her countrywomen for beauty and for the wealth which she lavishly displayed, was one day proceeding to the baths with much barbaric pomp of raiment and retinue. At the same moment the wife of Ildibad happened to pass, in mean attire and with scant attendance; for Ildibad had lost his possessions as well as his children by the fall of Ravenna, and there had been no time as yet to form another royal hoard. The wife of the chief who would not reign offered no obeisance to the wife of the actual King, and even allowed it to be seen that she was jeering with her attendants at that honorable poverty. The insult, and the burning tears with which his wife told the tale, maddened the heart of Ildibad. He began to traduce his benefactor, accusing him of disloyalty to the national cause, and before long caused him to be assassinated.

From that day Ildibad's hold on the hearts of his countrymen was gone, and he also soon fell a victim to the hand of the assassin. One of his guards, named Wilas, a Gepid by birth, was betrothed to a young maiden whom he loved with passionate ardor. During his absence on some military duty, the King, either from forgetfulness or caprice, conferred the hand of the damsel on another of his followers. From the moment that he heard the tidings, Wilas, maddened with the wrong, vowed his master's death; and he found many willing accomplices, for the blood of Uraias cried for vengeance. There came a day when Ildibad was feasting right royally in his palace, with all his guards in bright armor standing round him. The King stretched forth his hand to grasp some delicate morsel; but, overcome apparently by the wine that he had drunk, fell forward on the couch. Wilas saw his opportunity, stepped forward, drew his sword, and severed his master's neck at one blow. With amazement and horror the bystanders saw the head of Ildibad roll upon the festive board, even while his fingers yet clutched the morsel that was never to be eaten. Nothing is said as to any punishment of the murderer.

The death of Ildibad occurred about May, 541, a year after the departure of Belisarius and six years from the commencement of the war. He was succeeded by Eraric the Rugian, whose precarious royalty was, however, never fully acknowledged by the remnant of the Gothic nation. It will be remembered that a part of the Rugian people had followed the standards of Theodoric into Italy and had shared his victories and his revenge over their deadly enemy Odovacar. Notwithstanding the subsequent treachery of Frederic their King, the bulk of the little nation remained faithful subjects of the Ostrogothic royalty, but though they loyally did his bidding in battle they remained a separate nationality, marrying only the women of their own tribe, and probably having justice administered by their own chiefs. This fragment of a nation, in the distress and discouragement of their Gothic friends, aspired to give a king to the whole confederacy: a pretension almost as audacious as if in the party disputes at the close of the reign of Queen Anne the Huguenot refugees had signified their willingness to place one of their number on the throne of Great Britain.

Eraric reigned only five months, during which time he performed not a single noteworthy action against the enemy, but devoted his chief energies to those illusory negotiations with Constantinople which were the natural resource of a barbarian king doubtful of the loyalty of his subjects. He called together a general assembly of the Goths, and proposed to them to send ambassadors to Justinian, offering peace upon the same terms which had been suggested to Witigis: all Italy south of the Po to be the Emperor's, the rest to belong to the Goths. The assembly approved, and the ambassadors set forth on their journey; but it is scarcely necessary to state that they bore also a secret commission by virtue of which Eraric offered to sell his people and the whole of Italy to Justinian upon the usual terms, the Patriciate, a large sum of money, and a splendid establishment at Constantinople. But in the mean time the hearts of all the Gothic people, sore for the loss of Ildibad, from whose mighty arm they had expected deliverance, and impatient at the feeble gropings after a policy of this Rugian kinglet whom accident had set over them, were turning with more and more of hope and loyalty to one still remaining scion of the house of Ildibad. This was his nephew Baduila, a man still young for command, but one whose courage and capacity had already much talked of at the council-table and the banquet. At the moment of his uncle's murder he was in command of the garrison at Treviso: and when he heard the tidings of that lamentable event, thinking that it was all over with Gothic freedom, he sent, messengers to Ravenna offering to surrender his stronghold on receiving pledges from Constantian for the safety of himself and his soldiers. The offer was gladly accepted, the day for the surrender fixed, the Roman generals looked upon Treviso as already theirs, when the whole aspect of the case was changed by a deputation from the discontented Goths offering the crown to Baduila. The young chief told them with perfect openness all that had passed between him and Constantian, but agreed, if the Rugian adventurer were removed before the day fixed for his capitulation, to cancel his agreement with Ravenna and to accept the dangerous honor of the kingship. The negotiations of Eraric with the Emperor, both those which were avowed and those which were only suspected, no doubt hardened the hearts of the Gothic patriots against him and quickened their zeal: and thus it came to pass that in the autumn of 541, long before the messengers had returned from Constantinople, Eraric had been slain by the conspirators and the young Baduila had been raised on the shield as King.

The unanimous testimony of the coins of the new King proves that Baduila was that form of his name by which he himself chose to be known. From some cause, however, which has not been explained, he was also known even to the Goths as Totila, and this name is the only one which seems to have reached the ears of the Greek historians. It is useless now to attempt to appeal from their decision, and the name Totila is that by which he will be mentioned henceforward in this history.

The new King wielded the Ostrogothic scepter for eleven years, a longer period than any of hi predecessors since the great Theodoric. Coming to the help of his countrymen when their cause seemed sunk below hope, he succeeded in raising it to a height of glory such as even under Theodoric himself it had scarcely surpassed. Though almost the last, he was quite the noblest flower that bloomed upon the Ostrogothic stem, gentle, just, and generous, as well as a valiant soldier and an able statesman. Though he first appears before us, engaged in somewhat doubtful transactions, breaking his agreement with Constantian and counseling the death of Eraric, he is upon the whole one of the best types of the still future age of chivalry that the Downfall of the Empire can exhibit: and in fact we may truthfully say of him in the words of Chaucer—

"He was a very perfect gentle knight".

The tidings of the ill-success of the Imperial arms and of the death of Eraric were conveyed to Justinian, who sent a severe reprimand to the generals for their supineness and misgovernment. Stung by this rebuke, having assembled a council of war at Ravenna, at which all the chief generals were present as well as Alexander the Logothete, they resolved to besiege Verona, the key to Totila's Venetian province, and as soon as that city was taken to press on to Pavia and extinguish the Gothic monarchy in its last asylum. The plan was strategically sound, and its failure was only due to the really ludicrous rapacity of the generals. An army of 12,000 men, under the command of eleven generals, advanced into the wide and fertile plains south of Verona, where their cavalry could operate with great advantages against the enemy. Moreover, a nobleman of the province of Venetia named Marcian, who dwelt near to Verona and favored the Imperial cause, sent word to the generals that he had bribed one of the sentinels to open a gate of that city to the Imperial forces. The generals, not feeling absolutely sure that this offer was made in good faith, invited volunteers for the dangerous task of commanding a small picked force, which should advance in front of the army and be admitted under cover of night within the walls of Verona. No one was willing to undertake the duty but Artabazes, a Persian, who in the Eastern campaign of 541 had attached himself to the fortunes of Belisarius and had been sent by him to serve in the Italian war. Having selected one hundred and twenty of the bravest men in the army he advanced at dead of night to the walls, and was admitted inside the gate by the sentinel, faithful in his treachery: his followers then slew the surrounding guards and mounted to the battlements. The Goths, finding out what had happened, threw up the game, retired through the northern gate to one of the hills overlooking the town, and there passed the night.

With the smallest fraction of military capacity the important city of Verona would now have been recovered for the Emperor. But the eleven generals, having started with the bulk of the army at the appointed time, began, when they were still five miles distant, to dispute as to the division of the spoil. The quarrel was at length adjusted, but meantime the sun had risen, and there was broad daylight over the old amphitheatre, over the swirling Adige, over the streets and market-places of Verona. The Goths from their hill-side took in the whole position of affairs, and saw by what an insignificant band they had been ousted from the city. Bushing in again by the northern gate, of which they had not given up possession, they drove Artabazes and his band to take refuge behind the battlements of the southern portion of the wall. At this moment the Roman army and the eleven generals arrived under the walls and found all the gates barred, and all the circuit of the city, except one small part, occupied by their foes. Vainly did Artabazes and his friends shout to them for help. They withdrew with all speed, and the little band whom they thus left to their fate had no resource but to leap headlong from the battlements. The greater number were killed by the fall. A few who had the good-fortune to alight on smooth soft ground escaped. Among these latter was Artabazes, who, when he reached the camp, inveighed bitterly against the cowardice and incapacity of the generals, which had brought so promising an enterprise to disaster.

Recognizing the failure of their design to reconquer Venetia, the whole army crossed the Po and mustered again near Faventia, a town on the Emilian Way, about twenty miles south-west of Ravenna. This place still survives in the modem Faenza, a bright little city of the plain, nestling under the shadow of the Apennines. Its early advances in the ceramic art have made the name of *faience* familiar to all French dealers in earthenware.

When Totila learned what had passed at Verona he set forth with his whole army in pursuit of the Roman generals. So dwindled, however, was the Gothic force, that those words 'the whole army' still described a force of only five thousand men. While he was still on the northern bank of the Po, Artabazes, who had not ridden in vain beside Belisarius to battle, and who is the only soldier whose deeds shed a brief luster across this part of the annals of the Imperial army, implored his brother generals to attack the barbarians in the act of crossing, so that they might have only one part of the Gothic force to deal with at once. He truly said that they need not trouble their minds about the alleged in-gloriousness of such a victory. In war success was everything, and if they defeated the foe, men would not narrowly scrutinize the means by which they had overcome. But the generals, having each his own scheme for conducting the campaign, could accept no common plan of action, not even the obvious one suggested by Artabazes, but remained inactive in the plain of Faenza, for which course they had, it must be admitted, one excuse, in that they thereby barred the Emilian Way against the southward progress of the invader.

Here then Totila, having crossed the Po without opposition, met the many-generalled forces of the enemy. In a most spirit-stirring speech he called upon his soldiers for one supreme effort of valor. He did not dissemble the difficulties of their situation. The Romans if defeated could take shelter in their fortresses, or could await reinforcements from Byzantium; but they had no such hope. Defeat for them meant ruin, the utter ruin of the Gothic cause in Italy. But, on the other hand, victory earned that day would bring with her every promise for the days to come. Blundering and defeat had reduced the army of the Goths from two hundred thousand men to one thousand, and their kingdom from the fair land of Italy to the single city of Ticinum. But then, one victory gained by the gallant Ildibad had multiplied their numbers five-fold, and had given them for one city all the lands north of the great river. Another victory now, with the blessing of God on their endeavours, with the favor and sympathy of all the Italians wearied out by the exactions of the Byzantine tax-gatherers, might restore to them all that they had lost. And such a victory they might surely win against the recent dastards of Verona.

After this harangue Totila selected three hundred men, who were to cross the river at a point two miles and a-half distant and fall upon the rear of the enemy when the battle was joined. Then the two armies set themselves in battle array; but before the fight began, one of those single combats in which the barbarians in both armies delighted, and which seem more congenial to the instincts of mediaeval chivalry than to the scientific discipline of the old Imperial legion, occupied the attention of both armies. A Goth, mighty in stature and terrible in aspect, Wiliaris by name, completely armed, with helmet and coat of mail, rode forth into the space between the two armies, and, Goliath-like, challenged the Romans to an encounter. All shrank from accepting the challenge except the gallant Persian, Artabazes. Couching their spears at one another the two champions spurred their horses to a gallop. The Persian's spear penetrated the right lung of the Goth. Instant death followed, but the spear in the dead man's hand, having become jammed against a piece of rock below him, prevented him from falling and gave him still the erect attitude of life. Artabazes pressed on to complete his victory, and drew his sword to smite his enemy through his coat of mail, but in doing so, by some sudden swerve of his horse, his own neck was grazed by the upright spear of the dead Wiliaris. It seemed a mere scratch at first, and he rode back in triumph to his comrades : but an artery had been pierced, the blood would not be stanched, and in three days the gallant Artabazes was numbered with the dead. Thus did a dead man slay the living.

While Artabazes, out of the reach of bow-shot, was vainly endeavoring to stanch his wound, the battle was going ill with the Romans. Totila's three hundred men appearing in the rear were taken for the vanguard of another army, and completed the incipient panic. The generals fled headlong from the field, one to take refuge in one city, another in another. Multitudes of the soldiers were slain, multitudes taken prisoners and sent to a place of safety; and all the standards fell into the hands of the enemy, a disgrace which, Procopius assures us, had never before befallen a Roman army.

Totila now found himself strong enough to strike boldly across the Apennines, probably taking, not the Flaminian but the Cassian Way, and so try to gain a footing in Tuscany. With this view he sent a detachment of soldiers to besiege Florence. Fiesole, on its inaccessible height, he probably deemed too difficult for his little army. Justin, who had distinguished himself in these regions three years before, was now commandant of the Imperial garrison of Florence; but, fearing that he was too weak in men and provisions to hold out long, he sent messengers by night to Ravenna to ask for relief. A force, probably a strong force, was sent to his aid under the command of his old friend and colleague Cyprian, together with John and Bessas. At the approach of this large body of troops the Goths raised the siege of Florence and retreated northwards up the valley of the Sieve, which still bears in popular usage the name by which Procopius calls it, the valley of Mugello. It was thought unadvisable by the Imperial generals to risk an engagement with their whole force in the gorges of the mountains, and it was decided that one of their number, with a picked body of troops, should seek out and engage the Goths, while the rest of the army followed at their leisure. The lot fell on John the venturesome and precipitate, who, nothing loth, pushed on up the rocky valley. The Goths had stationed themselves on a hill, from which they rushed down with loud shouts upon the foe. There was a little wavering in the Roman ranks. John, with loud shouts and eager gestures, encouraged his men, but one of his guardsmen, a prominent figure in the ranks, was slain; and in the confused noise of the battle it was rumored that John himself had fallen. Then came wild panic : the Roman troops swept down the valley, and when they met the solid squadrons of their fellow-soldiers, and told them the terrible tidings of the death of the bravest of the generals, they too caught the infection of fear and fled in disgraceful and disorderly flight. Many were slain by the pursuing Goths. Some having been taken prisoners, were treated with the utmost kindness by the politic Totila, and even induced in large numbers to take service under his standard. But others went galloping on for days through Italy, pursued by no man, but bearing everywhere the same demoralizing tidings of rout and ruin, and rested not till they found themselves behind the walls of some distant fortress, where they might at least for a time breathe in safety from the fear of Totila.

Such, according to Procopius, was the battle, or rather the headlong rout, of Mugello. He was not an eye-witness of the scene, and one is inclined to conjecture that he has overrated the element of mere panic and underrated the strategic skill of the Goths, who had apparently posted themselves on some coign of vantage among the hills from which they could inflict deadly injury on the foe, themselves almost unharmed. But, whatever were the details of the fight, it seems to have opened the whole of Central and Southern Italy to Totila. Cesena, Urbino, Montefeltro, Petra Pertusa, all those Umbrian fortresses which it had cost Belisarius two years of hard fighting to win, were now lost to Justinian. Totila pressed on into Etruria. There no great fortress seems to have surrendered to him, and he would not repeat the error of Witigis by dashing his head against the stone walls of Rome. He therefore crossed the Tiber, marched southwards through Campania and Samnium, easily took Beneventum, and razed its walls, that no Byzantine host might shelter there in time to come. The stronghold of Cumae with a large store of treasure fell into his hands. In the same place was a little colony of aristocratic refugees, the wives and daughters of the Senators. Totila treated them with every mark of courtesy, and dismissed them unhurt to their husbands and fathers, an act of chivalry which made a deep impression on the minds of the Romans. All the southern provinces of Italy, Apulia, Calabria, Bruttii, and Lucania, were overrun by his troops. Not all the fortresses in these parts were yet his, but he collected securely and at his ease both the rent of the landowner and the revenue of the Emperor.

The oppressions of the Logothetes had revealed to all men that one great motive for the Imperial reconquest of Italy was revenue; and Totila, by anticipating the visit of the tax-gatherer, stabbed Justinian's administration in a vital part. The barbarian auxiliaries could not be paid: desertions from the Imperial standard became more and more frequent; all the prizes of valor were seen to glitter in the hand of the young Gothic hero, who, encouraged by his marvelous success, determined to wrest from the Emperor the first fruits of Belisarius's campaigns in Italy. He sat down before the walls of Naples, which was held by a garrison of a thousand men, chiefly Isaurians, under the command of Conon.

This sudden transformation of the political scene took place in the summer of 542. And what meanwhile were the Imperial generals doing? Without unity of action or the semblance of concerted plan they were each cowering over the treasure which they had succeeded in accumulating, and which was stored in the several fortresses under their command. Thus Constantian had shut himself up in Ravenna; John, not slain but a fugitive from Mugello, in Rome; Bessas at Spoleto; Justin at Florence (which had not, after all, fallen into the hands of the Goths); and his friend Cyprian at Perugia. Like islands these high fortresses occupied by the Imperial soldiers stand out above the wide-spreading sea of Gothic reconquest. Even the victorious Totila will not be safe till he has reduced them also to submission.

The terrible news of the re-establishment of the Gothic kingdom in Italy filled Justinian with sorrow at the thought of all his wasted men and treasure. Not yet, however, was he brought to the point of entrusting the sole command to Belisarius: that remedy still seemed to him worse than the disease. He would end, however, the anarchy of the generals by appointing one man as Praetorian Prefect of Italy, who should have supreme power over all the armies of the Empire within the peninsula. This was a wise measure in itself, but the holder of the office was badly chosen. Maximin, the new Prefect , was quite inexperienced in war, of a sluggish and cowardly temper; and though the generals under him, Herodian the commander of the Thracians and Phazas nephew of Peranius, who came from the gorges of the Caucasus and commanded a brave band of Armenian mountaineers, knew somewhat more about the business of war, their martial energy was deadened by the feebleness of their chief.

This new appointment was made apparently in the autumn of 542. The timid Maximin, afraid to face the unquiet Adriatic in November, lingered, upon one pretence or another, on the coast of Epirus. All the time the distress of Conon and the beleaguered garrison of Naples was growing more severe. Demetrius, another officer of the old army of Belisarius, who had been dispatched from Constantinople after Maximin, perhaps to quicken his movements, sailed to Sicily and there collected a large fleet of merchantmen, which he filled with provisions, hoping by the mere size of his armament to overawe the Goths and succeed in revictualling Naples. Had he sailed thither at once his bold calculation would probably have been verified : but unfortunately he wasted time in a fruitless journey to Rome, where he hoped to enlist volunteers for the relief of the besieged city. The discontented and demoralized soldiers refused to follow his standard, and after all he appeared in the Bay of Naples with only his provision-ships and the troops which he himself had brought from Constantinople.

When the fleet of Demetrius was approaching the bay a little boat appeared, in which sat his namesake, another Demetrius, a Cephalonian seaman whose nautical skill had been of the highest service to Belisarius in his Italian and African voyages. This man was now Financial Administrator of the city of Naples for the Emperor. He had good reason to wish for the success of his namesake the general, since when Totila first summoned the citizens to surrender he had assailed the stately and silent barbarian with such a torrent of voluble abuse as only a foul-mouthed Greek could utter. He had now come, at great hazard of his life, to inform the general of the distress of the beleaguered city and to quicken his zeal for its relief.

But, during the ill-advised journey to Rome, Totila also had obtained information of the movements and character of the relieving squadron. He had prepared a fleet of cutters, lightly loaded and easily handled, and with these he dashed into the fleet of heavy merchantmen as soon as they had rounded the promontory of Misenum and entered the Bay of Naples. The unwieldy and feebly-armed vessels were at once steered for flight. All of the ships, all of their cargoes, most of the men on board, were taken. Some of the soldiers were slain; a few who were on board the hindermost vessels of the fleet were able to escape in boats. Among these fugitives was Demetrius the general. His namesake, the unhappy sailor-orator, fell into the hands of Totila, who ordered his abusive tongue and the hands that had been probably too greedy of gold to be cut off, and then suffered the miserable man to go whither he would. A cruel and unkingly deed, not worthy of the gallant Totila.

Meanwhile the Prefect Maximin arrived with all his armament in the harbor of Syracuse. Having reached the friendly shore he would not again leave it, though all the generals sent messages urging him to go to the assistance of Conon. But, at length, fear of the Emperor's wrath so far overcame his other fears that he sent his whole armament to Naples under the command of Herodian, Demetrius, and Phazas, tarrying himself quietly at Syracuse. By this time the winter was far advanced and sailing was indeed dangerous. A tremendous storm sprang up just as the fleet entered the Bay of Naples, Phazas the Armenian seems to have at once abandoned all hope, and fled before the storm. The rowers could not draw their oars out of the water, the deafening roar of the wind and waves drowned the word of command if any officer had presence of mind enough to utter it, and, in short, all the ships but a very few were dashed on shore by the fury of the gale. Of course in these circumstances their crews fell a helpless prey to the Goths who lined the coast.

Herodian and Phazas with a very few others escaped. Demetrius, this time, fell into the hands of the enemy. With a halter round his neck he was led in front of the walls of the city, and was then compelled—but a man who called himself the countryman of Regulus should not have yielded to such compulsion—to harangue the citizens in such words as Totila dictated. The speech was all upon the necessity of surrender, the impossibility of resisting the Goths, the powerlessness of the Emperor, whose great armament had jus been shattered before their eyes, to prepare another for their deliverance. Cries and lamentations filled all the city when the inhabitants, after their long sufferings bravely borne, heard such counsels of despair coming from the lips of a Roman general standing in such humiliating guise before them. Totila, who knew what their frame of mind must be, invited them to the battlements and there held parley. He told them that he had no grudge in his heart against the citizens of Naples, but, on the contrary, would ever remember their fidelity to the Gothic crown and the stout defence which they had made against Belisarius seven years before, when every other city in Italy was rushing into rebellion. Neither ought they on their part to bear any grudge against him for the hardships which the siege had caused them, and which were all part of the kindly violence by which he would force them back into the path of happiness which they had quitted. He then offered his terms: leave to Conon and his soldiers to depart whithersoever they would, taking all their possessions with them, and a solemn oath for the safety of every Neapolitan citizen.

The terms were generous, and both citizens and soldiers, pressed by hunger and pestilence, were eager to accept them. Loyalty to the Emperor, however, made them still consent to the surrender only in the event of no help reaching them within thirty days. Totila, with that instinct of repartee which shone forth in him, and which was more like a Greek than a Goth, replied, "Take three months if you will. I am certain that no succors in that time will arrive from Byzantium". And with that he promised to abstain for ninety days from all attacks upon their fortifications, but did not repeat the blunder of Witigis, in allowing the process of revictualling to go forward during the truce. Disheartened and worn out with famine, the citizens surrendered the place long before the appointed day, and Naples (May, 543) again became subject to Gothic rule.

On becoming master of the city, Totila showed a thoughtful kindness towards the inhabitants, such as, in the emphatic words of Procopius, could have been expected neither from an enemy nor a barbarian. To obviate the evil consequences of overfeeding after their long abstinence, he posted soldiers in the gates and at the harbor with orders to let none of the inhabitants leave the city. Each house was then supplied with rations of food on a very moderate scale, and the portion given was daily and insensibly increased till the people were again on full diet.

Conon and his soldiers were provided with ships, which were ordered to take them to any port that they might name. Fearing to be taunted with their surrender if they went to Constantinople, they elected to be taken to Rome. The wind, however, proved so contrary that they were obliged to return on shore. They feared that the Gothic King might regard himself as now absolved from his promises and might treat them as foes. Far from it: he summoned them to his presence, renewed his promises of protection, and bade them mingle freely with his soldiers and buy in his camp whatever they had need of. As the wind still continued contrary, he provided them with horses and beasts of burden, gave them provisions for the way, and started them on their road for Rome, assigning to them some Gothic warriors of reputation by way of escort. And this, though his own heart was set on taking Rome and he knew that these men were going to swell the ranks of her defenders.

In conformity with his uniform policy (borrowed perhaps from the traditions of Gaiseric), he then dismantled the walls of Naples, or at least a sufficient portion of them to make the city, as he believed, untenable by a Roman army. For he preferred ever to fight on the open plain, rather than to be entangled in the artifices and mechanical contrivances which belong to the attack and defence of besieged cities.

About this time an event happened which showed in a striking light the policy of Totila towards the Italians. A countryman of Calabria appeared in the royal tent, demanding justice upon one of the Gothic King's body-guard who had violated his daughter. The offence was admitted, and the offender was put in ward till Totila, should decide upon his punishment. As it was generally believed that this punishment would be death, some of the men of highest rank in the army came to implore the King not to sacrifice for such a fault the life of a brave and capable soldier. With gentle firmness Totila refused their request. He pointed out that it is easy to earn a character for good-nature by letting offenders go unpunished, but that this cheap kindness is the ruin of good government in the state, and of discipline in the army. He enlarged on his favorite theme, that all the vast advantages with which the Goths commenced the war had been neutralized by the vices of Theodahad; and on the other hand, that, by the Divine favor and for the punishment of the rapine and extortion of their foes, the Gothic banner had in a marvelous way been raised again from the dust in which it had lain drooping. Now, then, let the chiefs choose which they would have, the safety of the whole Gothic state or the preservation of the life of this criminal. Both they could not have, for victory would be theirs only so long as their cause was good. The nobles were convinced by his words, and no murmurs were heard when, a few days after, the ravisher was put to death and his goods bestowed on the maiden whom he had wronged.

Such was the just rule of the barbarian King. Meanwhile the so-called Roman officers, shut up in their several fortresses, seemed intent only on plundering the country which they could not defend. The generals feasted themselves at gorgeous banquets, where their paramours, decked with the spoils of Italy, flaunted their mercenary beauty. The soldiers, dead to all sense of discipline, and despising the orders of such chiefs, wandered through the country districts, wherever the Goths were not, pillaging both *villa* and *praedium,* and making themselves far more terrible to the rural inhabitants than the Goths from whom they professed to defend them. Thus was the provincial, especially he who had been a rich provincial, of Italy in evil case. Totila had appropriated his lands and was receiving the revenues which they furnished, and all his moveable property was stolen from him by the soldiers of John or Bessas.

The state of the country became at length so intolerable that Constantian, the commandant of Ravenna wrote to the Emperor that it was no longer possible to defend his cause in Italy; and all the other officers set their hands to this statement. Of this state of discouragement among his enemies Totila endeavored to avail himself by a letter which he addressed at this time to the Roman Senate. "Surely", he said, "you must in these evil days sometimes remember the benefits which you received, not so very long ago, at the hands of Theodoric and Amalasuntha. Dear Romans, compare the memory of those rulers with what you now know of the kindness of the Greeks towards their subjects. You received these men with open arms, and how have they repaid you? With the griping exactions of Alexander the Logothete, with the insolent oppressions of the petty military tyrants who swagger in your streets. Do not think that as a young man I speak presumptuously, or that as a barbarian king I speak boastfully when I say that we are about to change all this and to rescue Italy from her tyrants. I make this assertion, not trusting to our own valor alone, but believing that we are the ministers of Divine justice against these oppressors, and I implore you not to side against your champions and with your foes, but by such a conspicuous service as the surrender of Rome into our hands to wipe out the remembrance of your past ingratitude"

This letter was entrusted to some of the captive Romans, with orders to convey it to the Senate. John forbade those who read the letter to return any answer. Thereupon the Gothic King caused several copies of the letter to be made, appended to them his emphatic assurances, sealed by solemn oaths, that he would respect the lives and property of such Romans as should surrender, and sent the letters at night by trusty messengers into the City. When day dawned the Forum and all the chief streets of Rome were found to be placarded with Totila's proclamation. The doers of the deed could not be discovered, but John, suspecting the Arian priests of complicity in the affair, expelled them from the City.

Finding that this was the only answer to his Rome and appeal, Totila resolved to undertake in regular form the siege of Rome. He was at the same time occupied in besieging Otranto, which he was anxious to take, as it was the point at which Byzantine reinforcements might be expected to land, in order to raise the standard of the Empire in Calabria. He considered, however, that he had soldiers enough for both enterprises, and, leaving a small detachment to prosecute the siege of Otranto, he marched with the bulk of his army to Rome.

Now at length did Justinian, with grief and sighing, come to the conclusion that only one man could cope with this terrible young Gothic champion, and that, even though the Persians were pressing him hard in the East, Belisarius must return to Italy.

But, before we begin to watch the strange duel between the veteran Byzantine General and the young Gothic King, before we turn the pages which record another and yet another siege of Rome, we must devote a little time to the contemplation of the figure of one who, more powerfully than either Belisarius or Totila, moulded the destinies of Italy and Western Europe. The great Law-giver of European monasticism died just at this time. Let us leave for a space the marches and counter-marches of Roman and Barbarian, and stand in spirit with the weeping monks of Monte Cassino by the death-bed of Benedict of Nursia.

CHAPTER XVI

SAINT BENEDICT
(480 – 547)

By devious ways, and through a tangle of forgotten or but half-remembered names, we are come to a broad highway trodden by the feet of many reverent generations and made illustrious by some of the best-known figures in the history of mediaeval Christianity. Even in the annals of monasticism the saintly Severinus of Noricum, the studious Cassiodorus of Squillace, are but faintly remembered; but everyone who knows anything of the spirit of the Middle Ages is familiar with the name of Benedict of Nursia. His face and the faces of his sister Scholastica, and his pupils Maurus and Placidus, portrayed by some of greatest painters whom the world has known, look softly down from the walls of endless Italian galleries. His great monastery on Mount Cassino was for centuries, scarcely less than Rome and Jerusalem, the object of the reverent homage of the Christian world. More than either of those two historic cities did it enshrine a still existing ideal for the formation of what was deemed the highest type of human character. In the ninth century the great Emperor Charles ordered an enquiry to be made, as into a point requiring abstruse and careful research, "Whether there were any monks anywhere in his dominions who professed any other rule than the rule of Saint Benedict".

And so it continued to be, till in the thirteenth century those great twin brethren, Francis and Dominic, rose above the horizon, and the holiness of the reposeful Monk paled before the more enthusiastic holiness of the Friar. But during the intervening centuries, from the ninth to the thirteenth, all Western-monks, from Poland to Portugal and from Cumberland to Calabria, looked with fond eyes of filial obedience and admiration to that Campanian hill on which their founder had fixed his home and of which a monastic Isaiah might have prophesied, "From Cassino shall go forth the law, and the word of the Lord from the mountain of Benedict".

The life of Saint Benedict was written in Latin by Pope Gregory the Great, whose birth-year was perhaps the same as the death-year of the Saint. Such a book, the biography of the greatest Monk, written by the greatest Pope, obtained of course a wide and enduring popularity in the West; and in order that the East might share the benefit, a later pope, Zacharias, translated it into Greek. It is entitled "The Life and Miracles of the Venerable Benedict, Founder and Abbot of the Monastery which is called (of) the Citadel of the Province of Campania". As we might have expected from the title, supernatural events occupy a large place in the narrative, and we find ourselves at once confronted with one of those problems as to the growth of belief which so often perplex the historian of the Middle Ages. We have not here to deal with the mere romancing of some idle monk, manufacturing legends for the glory of his order about a saint who had been in his tomb for centuries. Pope Gregory was all but a contemporary of St. Benedict, and he professes to have derived his materials from four disciples and successors of the Saint, Constantine, Valentinian, Simplicius, and Honoratus. In these circumstances the merely mythical factor seems to be excluded from consideration; and there is something in the noble character of Gregory and of the friends of Benedict which makes a historian unwilling to adopt, unless under absolute compulsion, the theory of a pious fraud. Yet probably not even the most absolutely surrendered intellect in the Catholic Church accepts all the marvels here, recorded as literally and exactly true. It is useless to attempt to rationalize them down into the ordinary occurrences of everyday life. Yet in recounting them one would not wish to seem either to sneer or to believe. Our best course doubtless is to give them in Pope Gregory's own words, studying them as phenomena of the age, and remembering that whatever was the actual substratum of fact, natural or supernatural, this which we find here recorded was what one of the greatest minds of the sixth century, the architect of the medieval Papacy and the restorer of the Christianity of Britain, either himself believed or wished to see believed by his disciples.

In the high Sabine uplands, nearly two thousand feet above the sea-level, under the shadow of the soaring Monti Sibellini, which are among the highest peaks of the Apennine range, lies the little city of Norcia, known in Roman days as the *municipium* of Nursia, and familiar to diligent students of the Aeneid as 'frigida Nursia'.

A little stranded city, apparently, in its sequestered Apennine valley: its nearest point of contact with the world of politics and of war would be Spoleto, about twenty miles to the west of it on the great Flaminian Way, and Spoleto was eighty miles from Rome. Here then in "frigid Nursia", about four years after Odovacar made himself supreme in Italy, was born to a noble Roman a son who received the prophetic name of Benedict, "the blessed one". He was sent as a boy to Rome to pursue his studies, and when there he probably saw the statues of Odovacar overthrown and the Forum placarded with the proclamations of the new ruler of Italy, Theodoric. But the young Nursian was thinking, not of the rise and fall of empires, but of the salvation of his own soul. He was horrified by what he saw of the wickedness of the great city; he feared that if he became imbued with what there passed for wisdom he too should one day rush headlong into all its vices: he elected rather to be poor and ignorant, and decided on quitting Rome and assuming the garb of a monk. He set out for "the desert" that is, for the wild, thinly-peopled country, by the upper waters of the Anio, and (pathetic evidence of the still tender years of the fervid anchorite) the faithful nurse who had come with him to Rome insisted on following him to his retirement.

Before they reached the actual mountain solitudes they came to the little town of Efide (the modern village of Affile), and there finding many devout men who listened with sympathy to his sorrows and aspirations, he yielded to their advice and consented to take up his abode near them, in some chamber attached to the church of St. Peter. While he was dwelling here the first exhibition of his miraculous powers made him famous through all the surrounding district and drove him into yet deeper solitude. His faithful nurse had borrowed from some neighbors a sieve to sift some corn with, and this sieve, made not of wood but earthenware, had been carelessly left on the table, by a fall from which it was broken in two. The nurse wept over the broken implement, and the youthful saint, taking the fragments from her hand and retiring for prayer, found when he rose from his knees the sieve so restored that no trace of the fracture could be discerned. So great was the admiration of the inhabitants at this marvel that they hung up the miraculous sieve at the entrance of the church, and there it remained for many years, till it perished, like many more precious treasures, in the waves of the Lombard invasion.

The fame of this miracle brought to Benedict more visitors and more of the praise of this world than he could bear. His mind reverted to its original design, he determined to be absolutely unknown, and flying secretly from his nurse, he crossed the little ridge of hills which separates Affile from Subiaco and from the deep wild gorge of the Anio. Subiaco, the Sublacus or Sublaqueum of the Romans, derives its name from the lakes which had been formed there by Nero, whose stately villa was mirrored in those artificial waters.

We have already had occasion to notice it in connection with the story of the Roman aqueducts. It was about three miles above the place where the turbid waters of the Anio Novus were diverted from the river-bed into the aqueduct which bore that name, and some twelve miles above the more serene and purer fountains of the Claudia and the Marcia. Situated about forty-four miles from Rome, in a precipitous and thickly-wooded valley, Sublaqueum was the sort of place which an artistic Emperor like Nero, who tried to make a solitude even round his golden house in Rome, might naturally resort to in the First Century, even as Popes made it the scene of their *villeggiatura* in later centuries, and even as artists from all countries now throng to it to transfer to their canvas the picturesque outlines of its rocks, its woods, and its castles. But during the convulsions of the Fifth Century, when wealthy pleasure-lovers were few, it might easily sink into solitude and decay: and hence no doubt it was that when Benedict, somewhere about the year 495, sought its recesses, a few rough peasants and some scattered anchorites formed its whole population, and his retirement thither could be spoken of by his biographer as a retreat into the desert.

Here he was met by a monk named Romanus, who, hearing of his desires after a solitary life, bestowed upon him the monastic habit and led him to a narrow cave at the foot of a hill, where the delicately nurtured youth spent the next three years, hidden from the eyes of all men, and with the place of his retreat known only to the faithful Romanus. This only friend dwelt in a monastery not far off, on the table-land overlooking the river. With pious theft he abstracted a small portion from each monastic meal, and on stated days hastened with his store to the brow of the hill. As no path led down to the cave of the recluse, the basket of provisions was tied to the end of a long rope, to which a bell was also attached, and thus the slowly-lowered vessel by its tinkling sound called the Saint from prayer to food. "But one day the Ancient Enemy [the Devil], envying the charity of one brother and the refreshment of the other, when he saw the rope lowered, threw a stone and broke the bell. Romanus, however, still continued to minister to him at the stated hours.

After a time, from some unexplained cause, the ministrations of Romanus ceased, and the Saint, insensible to the wants of the body, might easily have perished of hunger. But a certain Presbyter living a long way from Subiaco, having prepared for himself a hearty meal for the next day, the festival of Easter, saw the Lord in a night vision and heard him say, "While thou art preparing for thyself these delicacies, a servant of mine in a cavern near Sublaqueum is tortured with hunger". The Presbyter rose at once and set off on that Easter morning with the provisions in his hand. Up hill and down dale he went, till at last, scrambling down the face of the precipice, he found the cave where dwelt the holy man. After they had prayed and talked together for some time the Presbyter said to the Hermit, "Rise and let us eat: today is Easter-day". Benedict, who in his solitude and his perpetual fastings had long lost count of Lent and Easter-tide, said, "An Easter-day to me truly, since I have been allowed to look upon thy face". The other answered, "In very truth this is the Easter-day, the day of the

Resurrection of the Lord, upon which it becomes thee not to keep fast. Eat then, for therefore am I sent, that we may share together the gifts of the Lord Almighty". So they ate and drank together, and after long converse the Presbyter departed.

It was soon after this that some shepherds of the neighborhood discovered the cave, and found what they at first supposed to be a wild beast coiled up among the bushes. When they found that a man, and a holy man, was enveloped in that garment of skins, they listened eagerly to his preaching: and from this time forward he was never left in want of food, one or other of the shepherds bringing him such victuals as he needed, and receiving in return, from his lips, the message of eternal life.

After the unnatural calm and utter absorption in the contemplation of heavenly things which had marked the Saint's first sojourn in the cave, there came a storm of terrible temptation. In those years of abstraction the dreamy child had grown into a man, with the hot blood of Italy in his veins; and his imprisoned and buffeted manhood struggled hard for victory. Soft birdlike voices sounded in his ears, the form of a beautiful woman rose before his eyes, everything conspired to tempt him back from that dreary solitude into the sweet world which he had quitted before he knew of its delights. He had all but yielded to the temptation, he had all but turned his back upon the desert, when a sudden thrill of emotion recalled him to his old resolve. Bent on punishing the rebellious body which had so nearly conquered the soul, he plunged naked into a dense thicket of thorns and nettles, and rolled himself in them till all his skin was torn and smarting. The pain of the body relieved the anguish of the soul, and, according to the lovely poetical fancy of after ages, when seven centuries later his great imitator St. Francis visited the spot, the thorns which had been the instrument of St. Benedict's penance were miraculously turned to roses.

From a hint which the Saint himself has given us, we may infer that his own mature judgment condemned his early impetuosity in facing while yet a boy the hardships and temptations of an anchorite's life in the wilderness. He says in the first chapter of his Rule, 'Hermits are' [by which he evidently means ' should be'] men who are not in the first fervor of their noviciate, but who having first learned by a long course of monastic discipline and by the assistance of many brethren how to fight against the Devil, afterwards step forth alone from the ranks of their brethren to engage him in single combat, God himself being their aid against the sins of the flesh and thoughts of evil.

The fame of the young Saint was now spread abroad throughout the valley, and the inmates of the convent of Varia (now Vicovaro), about twenty miles lower down the stream, having lost their abbot by death, besought Benedict to come and preside over them. Long he refused, feeling sure that his ways of thinking and acting would never agree with theirs. For these monks evidently belonged to that class which he in after days described as "the evil brood of the Sarabaitae". This name, of Egyptian origin, denoted those who had turned back from the rigor of their monastic profession while still wearing the monastic garb. "Their law", as he said, "is the gratification of their own desires. Whatever they take a fancy to they call holy: the unlawful is that to which they feel no temptation".

These men, in a temporary fit of penitence and desire after better things, chose Benedict for their his Abbot, and he at length yielded to their will. But soon the passion for reform died away. They found it intolerable to be reprimanded at each little deviation to the right hand or to the left from the path of ascetic virtue.. Angry words were bandied about in whispers, as each accused the other of having counseled the mad design of making this austere recluse from the wilderness their Abbot. At length their discontent reached such a height that they resolved on poisoning him. When the cup containing the deadly draught was offered to the reclining Abbot he, according to monastic usage, made the sign of the cross in act of benediction. The moment that the holy sign was made, as if a stone had fallen from his hands, the cup was shivered to pieces and the wine was spilt on the ground. Perceiving at once the meaning of the miracle, Benedict arose and addressed the pallid monks with serene countenance: "Almighty God pity you, my brethren. Why have ye designed this wickedness against me? Said I not unto you that my ways and yours could never agree? Go and seek an Abbot after your own heart, for me ye shall see here no more". And with that he arose and returned to the wilderness.

But Benedict's fame was now so far spread abroad that it was impossible for him any longer to lead the life of an absolutely solitary recluse. During the first twenty years of the sixth century (*AD* 501-520), men anxious to commence the monastic career under his training were flocking to him from all parts of Italy. So numerous were these that he established no fewer than twelve monasteries in the neighborhood of Subiaco; to each of which he assigned a superior, chosen from among his intimate friends. While probably exercising a general superintendence over all these religious houses, he himself dwelt with a few of his friends in a small house reared above his cave, the predecessor of the present *Convento del Sacro Speco* at Subiaco.

Now too the nobles of Rome began to bring him their sons for education, and for dedication if they should still after needful probation desire it, to the untroubled life of a coenobite. The most celebrated among these noble novices were Maurus and Placidus, sons of Aequitius and the Patrician Tertullus. They came about the year 523, Placidus a mere child, Maurus a bright, earnest lad, already able to enter into some of the thoughts of his revered master and to be the instrument of his rule over the brethren. In the splendid series of frescoes by Signorelli and Sodoma which line the cloisters of the great Benedictine monastery of Monte Oliveto, none is more interesting than that which depicts the arrival of young Maurus and Placidus, brought by their fathers, richly dressed and with a long train of horses and servants and all the state of a Roman noble as imagined by a mediaeval painter. Almost pathetic are the immediately following pictures, in which the little heads are already marked with the tonsure and the youthful faces already wear an aspect of too reposeful, unboyish holiness.

One of the most noteworthy and perplexing miracles of the Saint is connected with these, his young disciples. One day the little Placidus having gone to draw water from the neighboring lake, stooping too far forward fell in and was swept by the swift current far from the shore. Benedict, who was praying in his cell, suddenly called out, "Brother Maurus! run! That child has fallen into the water and is being carried away by the stream". Maurus asked and received a hurried blessing, hastened to the margin of the lake, ran over its surface with rapid course, not perceiving that he trod on water, pulled his companion up by the hair, and hastily returned. When he had reached the shore he looked back over the lake and then saw for the first time, with trembling, what he had done. He returned and related the event to Benedict. "It is a miracle" said he, "granted to thee as a reward of thy prompt obedience". "Not so" said the youth, "it is a miracle wrought by thy prayers". The friendly controversy was settled by the testimony of the rescued Placidus, who declared that when he was being drawn out of the water he saw the hood of Benedict waving above him, and felt that it was by Benedict's arm that he was delivered.

The rivalry between the monks and the parish priests, between the regular and the secular clergy, as they were afterwards called, which was to reappear in so many forms in after ages, already began to show itself. Florentius, the priest of a neighboring church, filled with jealousy at the increasing fame and influence of the Saint, endeavored by slander and misrepresentation to draw away his disciples from following him. As years went on and still the fame of Benedict increased, while Florentius remained obscure, the character of the priest underwent an evil change, and from slanderous words he proceeded to murderous deeds. He sent, according to a not uncommon custom, a piece of bread to Benedict as a token of brotherhood. The morsel was, however, a poisoned one, or at least the Saint believed it to be so, though, as he commanded a crow which was accustomed to feed out of his hand to bear it away into a desert place and there deposit it where it could be found of no man, it is difficult to see what evidence existed of the wicked designs of Florentius. The next step taken by the priest, who sent seven women of evil life to the monks' cells, was so outrageous and threatened such ruin to the community if this was to be the permitted manner of warfare, that Benedict resolved to withdraw from the conflict, and, leaving his twelve monasteries under the rule of their respective heads, sought a new home for himself and his chosen friends fifty miles to the southward, in the countries watered by the Liris. We may fairly conjecture that the enmity of Florentius was not the sole cause that urged him to this migration. His was one of those characters which require solitude, leisure, liberty, in order to attain their true development. At Subiaco he found himself no longer a recluse, but the centre of a great system of administration, his name a battle-cry, himself the leader of a party. Leaving those to strive and conquer who would, he bowed his head to the storm and again sought the freedom of the desert. Scarcely, however, had he started on his southward journey when a messenger from the faithful Maurus reached him with the tidings of the death of his enemy. The balcony on which Florentius was standing, to watch and to gloat over the departure of his foe, had given way, and the wicked priest had been killed by his fall. Benedict burst into loud lamentations over his death, inflicted penance on the messenger, who seemed to exult in the tidings which he bore, and continued his journey towards the Campanian lands. Evidently the enmity of Florentius, though it might be one cause, was not the sole cause of the great migration.

The new home of the Father of Monks was erected upon a promontory of high table-land, just upon the confines of Latium and Campania, which then overlooked the Via Latina, as it now overlooks the modern railway between Rome and Naples, from a point a little nearer to the latter city than to the former. Here, round the Citadel of Campania, grew the shady groves in which, two hundred years after Constantine, a rustic multitude, still, after the manner of their forefathers, offered their pagan sacrifices to the statue of Apollo. At the command of Benedict the statue was ground to powder, the woods were cut down, and where the altar of the Far-darting god had stood, there rose, amid much opposition from unseen and hellish foes, two chapels to St. Martin and St. John, and, hard by, the new dwelling of the Coenobites. It was a memorable event in the history of the valley of the Liris, which turned the obscure *Castrum Casinum* into the world-renowned, the thought-moulding, the venerated monastery of Monte Cassino

The migration from the Anio to the Liris occurred about 528, and fifteen years were passed by the Saint in his new citadel-home. The record of these years, as of those passed at Subiaco, is chiefly a record of miracles. Some of the chief characteristics of this miraculous history may be here briefly touched upon.

Least interesting to us, because most obviously artificial in their character, are those wonders recorded of the Saint in which there is an obvious desire to emulate the miraculous deeds of Elijah and Elisha. When Benedict goes forth into the fields with his disciples to work, and by his prayers restores the dead son of a peasant to life; when he heals a leper; when a miraculous supply of oil bubbles up in the cask and runs over on the convent floor; when he provides the monks of Subiaco with an easily-accessible spring of sweet water, we feel that whether to the Saint himself or to his biographers, the idea of these supernatural occurrences was suggested by what they had read in the Books of Kings.

Childish as some of them may seem to us, there is a greater psychological interest in those stories which describe the Saint as struggling for victory against the wiles and stratagems of the Devil. The Power of Evil is almost uniformly spoken of by Gregory as "the Ancient Enemy" (*antiquus hostis*), and the minute acquaintance which is shown with his works and ways, the comparative ease with which his plots are foiled and himself brought to confusion, remind us rather of the way in which a hostile politician is spoken of by the admirers of his rival than of the dark and trembling hints dropped in the Hebrew and Christian Scriptures concerning the mysterious Being who for ever sets his will against the will of the Most High. When the monastery was being built at Cassino hard by the old idolatrous grove, the *'antiquus hostis'* continually appeared to the fathers in their dreams; he filled the air with his lamentations; he once stood in bodily presence before the Saint, with flaming eyes, calling "Benedict! Benedict", and when he refused to answer, cried out "Maledict! not Benedict. what hast thou to do with me? Why wilt thou thus persecute me?" A stone which the builders wished to raise to its place in the new building was made immovable to all their efforts by reason of the Ancient Enemy sitting upon it, till Benedict by his prayers caused him to depart. The kitchen of the monastery appeared to the brethren to be on fire, and the work of building was interrupted by their causeless panic, till again by the prayers of the Saint their eyes were opened, and they saw that the imagined fire was no fire at all, but only a figment of the Ancient Enemy. At one time the Enemy appeared in the strange guise of a veterinary surgeon, and, visiting one of the monks who was drawing water, afflicted him with some strange disorder of a hysterical kind, which was cured by a sharp buffet from the hand of Benedict. At another time a monk was afflicted with an unaccountable love of roving, which always led him to go forth from the monastery just when the brethren were engaged in prayer. Admonitions from his own abbot (for he was not under the immediate supervision of Benedict) were in vain. The Saint, being sent for to heal him, clearly perceived a little black boy tugging at the fringe of the monk's habit, and thus coaxing him to leave the chapel. The Saint saw it, and on the following day his friend Maurus also saw it; but to the eyes of Pompeianus, abbot of the monastery, the black imp remained invisible. Sharp strokes of the rod corrected the wandering spirit of the monk, who thenceforward sat quietly in the chapel to the end of the service.

We are here, manifestly, in presence of the Medieval figure of the Devil. This is the being who, according to the belief of the Middle Ages, furnished the design for the Bridge of St. Gotthard and for the Cathedral of Cologne; the being who is always on the point of outwitting, but is generally in the end outwitted by, the sons of men; the being at whom Luther, monk in heart if reformer in brain, threw his inkstand when he sat in the little chamber at the Wartburg.

Are we not justified in saying that this conception of the character of man's unseen Foe has more than an accidental connection with the monastic system with whose birth it is contemporaneous? Assuredly those protracted fasts, those long and lonely vigils of anchorite and coenobite, had something to do with bringing the Devil of the Middle Ages into the field of human imaginings.

Some of the histories recounted of the Saint Social bring vividly before us the social conditions of the the age in which he lived, conditions of which probably no one had a wider or more accurate knowledge than the Superior of a great Monastery. Into that safe fold came men from all ranks and all stations in life, the lofty and the lowly, some seeking shelter, some solace, some rest from the hopeless distractions of a turbulent age; and the spiritual father was bound to listen to the tale of each, to sympathize with the sorrows of all. St. Benedict himself in his rule, while insisting on the duty of the abbot's avoiding all respect of persons, hints at the difficulty of its fulfillment. "Let good deeds and obedience be the only means of obtaining the abbot's favor. Let not the free-born man be preferred to him who was a slave before he entered the convent, unless there be some other reason for the preference". Distinguished merit may lead to promotion out of the order of seniority, "but if otherwise, let each keep his proper place [in that order], since, whether slaves or free, we are all one in Christ, and, under the same Lord, wear all of us the same badge of service".

In St. Benedict's case, Goth and Roman, peasant and noble, the son of the tax-ridden *Curialis*, and the son of the lordly *Defensor*, were all subject to his equal sway. Near to his monastery, and in some measure subject to his oversight, dwelt two noble ladies who had vowed themselves to a life of holiness. A monk, of lower social condition, who performed menial offices for these ladies, was often vexed by the sharp words which they used towards him, mindful rather of the past difference in their positions, than of their present equality in Christ. On hearing the good man's complaints St. Benedict visited the ladies, and told them that if they did not keep their tongues in better subjection he should be compelled to excommunicate them. Peevish and froward, however, and probably suffering in health by reason of the change from a palace to a cell, the noble ladies abated none of their scolding words. In no long time they both died, and were buried within the precincts of the church. There was a strange sight seen by their nurse, when she attended, according to custom, to bring an oblation for her dead mistresses, at the solemnization of the mass. When the Deacon called out "Let all who do not communicate depart", two dim figures were seen to rise out of the floor and steal away from the sacred building. Seeing this happen more than once, and remembering the threatened excommunication of the Saint, which evidently had power beyond the limits of this life, the faithful nurse sought the cell of Benedict and told him the marvelous tale. He gave her an oblation from his own hand to offer on their behalf, in proof that he no longer excommunicated them. The oblation was duly made, and thereafter the souls of the harassed harassers had peace.

Once, at evening, the venerable Father was sitting at table, partaking of the bread and cooked vegetables which formed his frugal repast. Opposite him, according to the rule of the monastery, stood a young monk, holding the lamp and ready to do the Abbot's bidding. It chanced that he who upon this evening performed this lowly duty was a young noble, son of one of the Imperial Defensors, whose father therefore was one of the most important personages in the state. Suddenly the thought flashed through his mind, "Who is this man who sits here eating his evening meal, upon whom I am waiting like a slave, holding the lamp, handing him the dishes? And what am I, I the Defensor's son, that I should condescend to such drudgery?". Not a word did the young noble utter, but the Saint, who read his proud thought, said suddenly, with voice of stern rebuke, "Seal up thy heart, my brother. What is that which thou art saying? Seal up thy heart". He called in the other brethren, bade the young man hand the lamp to them and retire for an hour of silent meditation. The monks afterwards asked the culprit what he had done to awaken such wrath in the Saint's mind. He told them, not what he had done, but what he had thought; and they all recognized that nothing could escape the venerable Benedict, in whose ear men's thoughts sounded like spoken words.

Whatsoever among the miracles attributed to the founder of Cassino we may feel bound to reject, we can hardly refuse to him an extraordinary, perhaps a supernatural power of reading the human heart. The story just told is one of the most striking instances of this power. Other cases are recorded, as when he rebuked some monks who, contrary to the rule, had partaken of refreshment in a religious woman's house, outside of the monastery, when he reminded another monk of an offence which he had himself forgotten, the acceptance of some handkerchiefs from the inmates of a nunnery to whom he had been sent to preach,—or when he detected the dishonesty of a young monk who, when entrusted with two bottles of wine for the use of the monastery, had delivered one only.

This power of penetrating the secret thoughts of those who came into his presence was remarkably exemplified in St. Benedict's interview with Totila; an interview which took place, probably, in the year 542, when the Gothic King was on his march to the siege of Naples. Pope Gregory, as the champion of orthodoxy and of the Roman nationality, naturally represents the Arian and barbarian King somewhat less favorably than he deserves. Still, even in the Papal narrative (which it will be well to give in a literal translation), something of the nobleness of Totila's character may be discerned.

"*Chapter XIV. How the feigning of King Totila was discovered.*

In the times of the Goths, Totila their King having heard that the holy man possessed the spirit of prophecy, and being on his way to the monastery halted at some distance and sent word that he would come to him. Having sent this message, as he was a man of unbelieving mind, he determined to try whether the man of God really possessed the prophetic spirit. There was a certain sword-bearer of his, named Riggo, to whom he lent his [purple] buskins and ordered him to put on the royal robes and to go, personating him, to the man of God. To aid the deception he also sent three counts, who before all others were wont to attend upon his person, namely Vuld [or Vultheric], Kuderic, and Blidi. These were to keep close by the side of Riggo, to whom he assigned other guards and other marks of honor, with the intention that by these and by the purple raiment he might be taken for the King. When this same Riggo, thus arrayed and thus accompanied, had entered the monastery, the man of God was sitting afar off. But seeing him coming, as soon as his voice could be heard he cried out, saying, "Put off, my son, put off that which thou wearest; it is not thine". Thereat Riggo fell straightway to the earth, struck with terror because he had presumed to mock so great a man; and all who had come with him to the man of God groveled on the ground. Then arising, they did not dare to approach, but hurrying back to their King told him how speedily they had been detected"

"Chapter xv. Of the Prophecy which was made concerning the same King.

Then, in his own person, the same Totila approached the man of God, but when he saw him sitting afar off he did not dare to come close, but cast himself upon the ground. Then, when the man of God had twice or thrice said to him "Rise", but still he did not dare to raise himself from the earth, Benedict the servant of Jesus Christ condescended himself to approach the prostrate King and cause him to arise. He rebuked him for his past deeds, and in few words told him all that should come to pass, saying,

> "Much evil hast thou done,
> Much evil art thou doing.
> Now at length cease from sin.
> Thou shalt enter Rome:
> Thou shalt cross the sea.
> Nine years shalt thou reign,
> In the tenth shalt thou die."

When he had heard these words, the King, vehemently terrified, asked for his prayers and withdrew; and from that time forward he was less cruel than aforetime. Not long afterwards he entered Rome, and crossed to Sicily. But in the tenth year of his reign, by the judgment of Almighty God, he lost his kingdom with his life.

Moreover, the priest of the church of Canusium was sent to visit the same servant of God, by whom, for his meritorious life, he was held in great affection. And once when they were talking together concerning the entry of King Totila and the destruction of the city of Rome, the priest said, "By this King that city will be destroyed so that it shall be no more inhabited". To whom the man of God made answer, "Rome shall not be exterminated by the barbarians, but, wearied with tempests, lightnings, whirlwinds, and earthquakes, it shall consume away in itself". The mysteries of which prophecy are now made clearer than the daylight to us, who see in this city, walls shattered, houses thrown down, churches destroyed by the whirlwind, and the great edifices of the city loosened by long old age falling around us in abounding ruin". So far Pope Gregory.

These two scenes, the unmasking of the false King and the prediction of the future fortunes of the true one, are vividly portrayed, not only by Signorelli at Monte Oliveto, but also by Spinello Aretino on the walls of the large square sacristy at San Miniato. Especially well rendered is the dismay of the detected impostor. Riggo's knees are loosened with terror, and he turns sick with fear as he meets the stern mildness of Benedict's gaze and hears that voice of command, "My son, put off, put off that which thou wearest, for it is not thine".

Within a year, probably, from the interview with Totila, St. Benedict was dead. The little that has got to be told about him is a history of farewells. First came the death of his sister Scholastica. She had been from infancy dedicated to the service of God, and had apparently inhabited a cell not far from his monastery, first at Subiaco and then at Monte Cassino. Once a year the Saint used to come and visit his sister in her cell, which, though of course outside the gates of the monastery, was within the limits of the modest monastic estate. When the time for the last yearly visit was come, Benedict with a little knot of his disciples went down to his sister's cell and spent the whole day in religious conversation and in singing with her the praises of the Most High. The evening was come; they were seated at supper; it was time for Benedict to depart, but still the stream of conversation, which perhaps deviated sometimes from the near joys of heaven to the far distant past of their common infancy in upland Nursia, seemed unexhausted. Scholastica pressed her brother to stay that they might on the morrow resume their celestial converse. "What dost thou ask me, my sister", said he; "I can by no means pass the night outside of my cell". At this time the evening sky was bright and clear, and not a cloud was visible. Scholastica clasped her hands tightly together and bowed her head in silent prayer. After a time she looked up again. The lightning was flashing, the thunder was pealing, and such torrents of rain were descending, that neither Benedict nor his companions could stir across the threshold of the cell. "Almighty God have pity on thee" said Benedict. "What is this that thou hast done?". "My brother", she answered, "I asked thee and thou wouldest not hear. Then I asked my Lord, and he heard me. Now depart if thou canst: leave me alone and return to thy monastery". Benedict recognised and bowed to the divine answer to prayer. He passed the night in his sister's cell, and they cheered one another with alternate speech upon the joys of the spiritual life. In the morning he departed to his own cell, and three days after, when he was standing therein, lifting up his eyes he saw a white dove rising into the sky. Then he knew that his sister Scholastica was dead, and sent some of the brotherhood to bring her body and lay it in the prepared sepulcher, where it should wait a little season for his own.

It was not long, apparently, after this event that the Saint received a visit from his dear friend Servandus, the head of a neighboring monastery founded by Liberius the Patrician, probably the same with whom we have already made acquaintance as the faithful servant of Odovacar and Theodoric. After spending the evening in that kind of conversation which was the highest mental enjoyment of these venerable men, they retired to rest. Benedict in the topmost chamber of a tall tower overlooking all the buildings and courtyards of the monastery, his guest in a lower story of the same tower, the disciples of both below. Benedict rose, while all others still slept, before the appointed hour of vigils (two o'clock in the morning). While he stood at his window and looked south-eastwards over the Campanian plain, suddenly the darkness of the night was scattered; a radiance as of the sun filled the deep Italian sky, and under that strangely flashing light it seemed to him that the world was made visible as it was to Christ upon the Specular Mount, all illumined by one ray only from the sun. While he was still fixing his earnest gaze on that heavenly radiance, behold a sphere of fire, in which he saw the soul of his friend Germanus, Bishop of Capua, being borne by angels to heaven. Thrice with a loud voice he called on Servandus, sleeping below, to arise and see the marvel: but when Servandus stood beside his friend at the window, the fiery sphere had vanished, the vision of the world was ended, and only

"The few last rays of that far-scattered light"

were yet discernible. St. Benedict sent a brother at once to Capua to enquire as to the welfare of the Bishop, and learned that on that same night, at the very moment of the heavenly vision, Germanus had given up the ghost.

And now did Benedict's discourse often turn upon his own approaching end, telling those about him under the seal of confidence when it should be, and sending word to his absent disciples by what signs they should be made certain of his decease. Six days before his death he ordered his grave to be dug. After this he was seized with a sharp attack of fever, which grew daily more severe. On the sixth day he bade his disciples carry him into the oratory, fortified himself for death by receiving the body and blood of the Lord, and then, leaning his weak limbs upon the arms of his disciples, he stood with his hands upraised to heaven, and thus passed away in the act and attitude of prayer.

That same day two of his disciples, one in his cell at Monte Cassino and another in a distant monastery, saw the same vision. To each it seemed that a pathway strewn with bright robes and gleaming with innumerable fires stretched eastwards from Benedict's cell and upwards into the depth of heaven. Above stood a man of venerable aspect and radiant countenance, who asked them if they knew what that pathway was which they beheld. They answered, "No"; and he replied," This is the path by which Benedict, beloved of God, hath ascended up to heaven"

He was buried side by side with his sister in the place where he had overthrown the altar of Apollo, and within the walls of the new oratory of St. John.

Returning now to the line of thought indicated at the beginning of this chapter, if we ask why has the fame of St. Benedict so entirely eclipsed that of all other Western monks, the answer is undoubtedly furnished to us by the one literary product of his life, his *Regula*. This *Rule*, extending only to seventy-three short chapters (many of them very short), and not probably designed by its author for use much beyond the bounds of the communities under his own immediate supervision, proved to be the thing which the world of religious and thoughtful men was then longing for, a complete code of monastic duty. Thus by a strange parallelism, almost in the very year when the great Emperor Justinian was codifying the results of seven centuries of Roman secular legislation for the benefit of the judges and the statesmen of the new Europe, St. Benedict on his lonely mountain-top was unconsciously composing his code for the regulation of the daily life of the great civilizers of Europe for seven centuries to come. The chief principles of that code were labor, obedience, and a regulated fervor of devotion to the Most High. The life prescribed therein, which seems to us so austere, so awfully remote from the common needs and the common pleasures of humanity, seemed to him, and was in reality, gentle and easy when compared with the anchorite's wild endeavors after an impossible holiness, endeavors which had often culminated in absolute madness, or broken down into mere worldliness and despair of all good. It is therefore in no spirit of affectation that Benedict in his Preface to the Rule uses these remarkable words: "We must therefore establish a school of service to our Lord, in which institution we trust that nothing rough and nothing grievous will be found to have been ordained by us"

It is, however, the man himself rather than the vast system almost unconsciously founded by him that it has seemed necessary at this point to bring before the mind of the reader. St. Benedict died only ten years before the extreme limit of time reached by this volume. Later on, when we have to deal with the history of the Lombard domination in Italy, our attention will be attracted to the further fortunes of Monte Cassino, ruined, restored, endowed with vast wealth, all by the same Lombard conquerors. For the present we leave the followers of the Saint engaged in their holy and useful labors, praying, digging, transcribing. "The wilderness and the solitary place shall be glad for them, and the desert shall rejoice and blossom as the rose". The *scriptorium* of the Benedictine monastery will multiply copies not only of missals and theological treatises, but of the poems and histories of antiquity. Whatever may have been the religious value or the religious dangers of the monastic life, the historian at least is bound to express his gratitude to these men, without whose life-long toil the great deeds and thoughts of Greece and Rome might have been as completely lost to us as the wars of the buried Lake-dwellers or the thoughts of Paleolithic Man. To take an illustration from St. Benedict's own beloved Subiaco, the work of his disciples has been like one of the great aqueducts of the valley of the Anio,—sometimes carried underground for centuries through the obscurity of unremembered existences, sometimes emerging to the daylight and borne high upon the arcade of noble lives, but equally through all its course bearing the precious stream of ancient thought from the far-off hills of time into the humming and crowded cities of modern civilization.

CHAPTER XVII.

THE RETURN OF BELISARIUS.

At the point where we left the narrative of the fight for the possession of Italy the struggle had been proceeding for nine years. We had reached the spring months of 544. Totila, in the two years and a-half of his kingship, had beaten the Imperial generals in two pitched battles by land, and in one engagement by sea had opened to himself the Flaminian Way by the capture of Petra Pertusa, could march freely from one end of Italy to the other, had taken Naples and Benevento, and was threatening the southern port of Otranto. The Roman generals, without concert or courage or care for their master's interests, were shut up in Rome, in Ravenna, in Spoleto, and a few other still untaken strongholds, more intent on plundering the wretched Italians than on defending the Imperial cause.

At this point of the struggle the Emperor, with a heavy heart, recognized the truth of what all his subjects had doubtless for many months been saying, that the only hope of saving any part of his Italian conquests lay in employing the man who had first effected them. Belisarius, now no longer Master of the Soldiery, but only Count of the Sacred Stable, was to be relieved from the comparatively useless work of superintending the Imperial stud and sent to reconquer Italy. But the Belisarius who came back to the peninsula in 544 to measure swords with Totila was a different man from the triumphant and popular hero who had sailed away from Ravenna in the spring of the year 540. First came the certainty of Antonina's unfaithfulness, the attempt to punish her, the sacrifice of his brave helper Photius, the unworthy and hollow show of reconciliation forced upon him by the imperious Theodora; a reconciliation which left husband and wife still strangers to one another, rival and hostile powers though dwelling in the same palace. These events, the bitter fruit of the year 541, had already aged and saddened Belisarius. Then in the year 542 he lost even the semblance of his master's favor, and became an utterly broken and ruined man.

It was in that year that a pestilence, one of the most terrible that have ever devastated the East, visited Constantinople. It arose in Egypt, and in its leisurely course sought out and ravaged every corner of the Roman and Persian worlds, not sparing the new barbarian kingdoms. For four months it hung heavily over Constantinople, the number of deaths rising at one time to five thousand daily. The markets were deserted, all ordinary crafts were abandoned, the cares of tending the patients in their terrible delirium and of burying the dead overtaxed the energies of their unstricken relatives. The work of burial had at length to be undertaken by the Emperor, who employed all the household troops for the purpose. Even so, it was impossible to dig graves fast enough to supply the terrible demand, and at length they were satisfied with stacking the corpses in a large and deserted fortress, which was roughly roofed over when it would hold no more. A sickening odor filled all Constantinople when the wind happened to set towards the city from this horrible charnel-house.

Justinian himself was one of those who were struck down by this terrible pestilence, and for a time it seemed that he, like the great majority of those attacked, would fall a victim to the disease. The situation of Theodora was full of peril. The victims of her cruelty and avarice had left avengers who were all eager for her blood. The life of that weak, plague-stricken, probably delirious patient was all that intervened between her and death at the hands of an infuriated populace; unless, indeed—and this seemed the desperate woman's only chance of retaining life and power—the imminent death of her husband could be concealed long enough to give her time to assemble the senate in the palace, and to have some pliant nephew, or some popular general, who would promise to make her his wife, clothed in the purple and presented to the Romans in the amphitheatre as the new Augustus.

Such were the calculations of Theodora, as, under that form of government, they were sure to be the more or less avowed calculations of every ambitious and childless Empress. There was still, however, the army to be reckoned with, that supposed embodiment of the Roman people in arms by which in old time the title Imperator had been exclusively conferred. The Eastern army was jealous and uneasy. A rumor reached it that Justinian was already dead: and at a hastily-summoned military council some generals were heard to mutter that if a new Emperor were made at Constantinople without their consent they would not acknowledge him. Suddenly the whole aspect of affairs was changed by the unlooked-for recovery of Justinian. The ulcer, which was the characteristic mark of the disease, probably began to suppurate freely, and the other dangerous symptoms abated: such, at least Procopius tells us, was the almost invariable course of the malady in the small number who recovered. Now were all other voices hushed in a chorus of servile loyalty to Justinian and Theodora; and the officers who had been present at that dangerous council hastened to clear themselves of suspicion by each accusing someone else of treason to the present occupants of the throne. Two parties soon declared themselves. On the one side were John surnamed the Glutton, and Peter; on the other, Belisarius and a general named Buzes, a greedy and self-seeking man, but one who had held the high offices of Consul and *Magister Militum per Orientem*.

Theodora ordered all the generals to repair to the capital, caused a strict enquiry to be made into the proceedings at the so-called treasonable council, and decided, whether rightly or wrongly we cannot say, that Belisarius and Buzes had acted in opposition to her interests. Her vengeance on Buzes was swift and terrible. Summoning him to the women's apartments in the palace, as if she had some important tidings to communicate, she ordered him to be bound and conveyed to one of her secret dungeons. "Dark, labyrinthine, and Tartarean" says Procopius, were the underground chambers in which she immured her victims. Here, in utter darkness, unable to distinguish day from night, with no employment to divert his thoughts, dwelt for twenty-eight months the former Consul and Master of the Host. Once a day a servant entered the prison, forbidden to hear or utter a word, and cast his food down before the captive as to a dumb brute, dumb as a brute himself. Thus he remained, men generally supposing him to be dead and not daring to mention his name, till Theodora, taking pity on his misery, in the third year of his imprisonment released him from his living tomb. Men looked upon him with awe, as if he had been the ghost of Buzes. His sight was gone and his health was broken, but we hear of him again, three years after his liberation, as commanding armies and as a person of importance at the Imperial court.

As for Belisarius, it was not thought desirable to proceed to such extreme lengths in his punishment, and there was probably even less evidence against him than against Buzes of having discussed the succession to the throne in a treasonable manner. There was, however, a charge, which had been vaguely hanging over him for years, of having appropriated to himself the lion's share of the treasures of Gelimer and Witigis, and having brought only a remnant of those treasures into the palace of the Emperor. His recent Eastern campaigns, too, though they had not added greatly to his fame, were reported to have added unduly to his wealth. The law or the custom which regulated the division of such booty was perhaps not book very clearly defined, and it might be urged with some reason that such splendid successes as those of Belisarius, achieved against such overwhelming odds, made him an exception to all rules. It is admitted, however, by Procopius that his wealth was enormous and worthy of the halls of kings; and from the way in which the subject is handled by this historian, for so many years his friend and follower, we may fairly infer that this charge was substantially a just one. The chief blot upon the character of Belisarius, as upon the character of the general who in modern times most resembles him, Marlborough, was avarice. Unlike Marlborough, however, he was lavish in the spending, as well as greedy in the getting of money. His avarice was the child of ostentation rather than of mere love of hoarding. To see himself surrounded by the bravest warriors in the world, to look at their glittering armor, to feel that these men were his dependants, and that the world said that his household alone had delivered Rome, this was the thought dearest to the heart of Belisarius. For this he labored and heaped up treasure, not always perhaps regarding the rule of right.

All this splendor of his, however, was now shattered at a blow. If it was not safe to shut up Belisarius in a Tartarean dungeon, it was safe to disgrace him, and it was done thoroughly. The command of the army of the East was taken from him and given to his old lieutenant, Martin, the same who galloped with Ildiger along the Flaminian Way, bearing the General's message to Rimini, the same who was sent with Uliaris to relieve Milan, and who failed so disgracefully in his mission. Not only was the command taken from Belisarius, but, by an unusually high-handed exercise of power, his splendid military household was broken up. All those valiant life-guardsmen, both horse and foot-soldiers, taken from the master whom they had served with such loyal enthusiasm, were divided by lot among the rival generals and the eunuchs of the palace. The glittering armor and gay accoutrements of course went with the wearers. Some portion of the treasure of the chief, that which he had brought home from the Eastern campaign, was conveyed by one of the Empress's eunuchs to her own palace. All the band of devoted friends who had hitherto crowded round the steps of Belisarius were now forbidden even to speak to him. As Procopius, himself no doubt one of these forcibly silenced friends, has said, "A bitter sight in truth it was, and one that men would have scarce believed possible, to see Belisarius walking about Byzantium as a common man, almost alone, deep in thought, with sadness in his face, ever fearing death at the hands of an assassin".

All this time Antonina dwelt with him in the same house as a stranger, mutual resentment and suspicion separating the hearts that had once been so fondly united. Now came out the better side of Theodora's character in the scheme which she devised to reconcile these two divided souls, and at the same time to repay some part of her debt of gratitude to Antonina by restoring to her the love of her husband. Those who prefer it may accept the theory of Procopius, that the whole humiliation of Belisarius had been contrived by the cruel ingenuity of the Empress for the sole purpose of bringing him helpless and a suppliant to his wife's feet. To me it seems more probable that the disgrace of the General was, at least in appearance, justified by his questionable conduct concerning the treasure; that it was partly caused by the unslumbering jealousy of Justinian, and partly by Theodora's resentment for some incautious words of his at the military council; but that the idea of introducing Antonina's name into the settlement of the dispute, and reconciling Belisarius by one stroke both to his wife and to the Emperor, was due to some unextinguished instinct of good in the heart of the cruel Empress, and should not be set down against her on the page of history.

One morning Belisarius went early to the palace, as was his wont, attended by a few shabbily-dressed followers. The Imperial pair appeared to be in no gracious mood towards him; the *valetaille* of the palace, taking the cue from their masters, flouted and insulted him. After a day thus drearily spent, dispirited and anxious, he returned to his palace, looking this way and that, to see from which side the dreaded assassins would rush forth upon him. "With this horror at his heart he went into his chamber and sat there upon the couch alone, revolving no noble thoughts in his heart, nor remembering the hero that he once had been, but dizzy and perspiring, full of trembling despair, and gnawed with slavish fears and mean anxieties". So writes Procopius, somewhat forgetful of the difference between physical and moral courage, and, for private reasons of his own, unnecessarily severe on these

'Fears of the brave and follies of the wise'

Antonina was walking up and down in the atrium, feigning an attack of indigestion, apparently longing to comfort her lord, but too proud to do so unasked. Then, just after sunset, came a messenger from the palace, named Quadratus, who, rapidly crossing the court, stood before the door of the men's apartment and called in a loud voice, "A message from the Empress". Belisarius, who made no doubt that this was the bearer of his death-warrant, drew his feet up on the couch and lay there upon his back, with no thought of self-defense, expecting death. His hopes revived at the sight of the letter which Quadratus handed to him, and which ran thus:

"Theodora Augusta to the Patrician Belisarius.

What you have done to us, good Sir, you know very well. But I, on account of my obligations to your wife, have resolved to cancel all these charges against you for her sake, and to make her a present of your life. Henceforward, then, you may be encouraged as to the safety of your life and property, but it rests with you to show what manner of husband you will be to her in future".

A rapture of joy thrilled the heart of Belisarius as he read these words. Without waiting for the departure of the messenger he ran forth and fell prostrate before Antonina. He kissed her feet, he clasped her robe; he called her the author of his life and his salvation; he would be her slave, her faithful slave henceforward, and would forget the name of husband. It was unheroic, doubtless, thus to humble himself at the feet of the woman who had so deeply wounded his honor; but it was love, not fear, that made him unheroic. It was not the coward's desire of life, it was the estranged lover's delight in the thought of ended enmity that unmanned Belisarius. For two years he had bitterly felt that

'To be wroth with one we love
Both work like madness in the brain'

And now that a power above them both had ended this agony, he forgot the dignity of the Patrician and the General in the almost hysterical rapture of the reconciled husband.

That reconciliation was an abiding one. Whatever were the later sins of Antonina, we hear no more of discord between her and Belisarius, rather of his infatuation in approving of all her actions. But the friends who had helped the injured husband in his quarrel found themselves the losers by this 'renewing of love'. Photius, obliged to hide himself in the squalid habit of a monk at Jerusalem, called in vain for aid to his mighty father-in-law. Procopius probably found his career of promotion stopped by the same disastrous reconciliation, and now began to fashion those periods of terrible invective which were one day to be stored in the underground chambers of the *Anecdota*, menacing ruin to the reputations of Antonina, of Theodora, of Justinian, even of the once loved Belisarius.

Out of the sequestered property of the General the munificent Empress made a present to her husband of thirty hundred-weight of gold, restoring the rest to its former owner. In order that her family might become possessed of the rest by ordinary course of law, she began to arrange a marriage between her grandson Anastasius and Belisarius's only daughter Joannina.

The entreaties of Belisarius that he might be allowed once again to lead the Eastern army against Chosroes were disregarded, partly on account of the remonstrances of Antonina, who passionately declared that she would never again visit those countries in which she had undergone the cruel indignity of arrest and imprisonment. The 'respectable' but not 'illustrious' office of 'Count of the Sacred Stable' was conferred upon him, to show that he was again received into some measure of Imperial favor. When it became more and more clear that the divided and demoralized generals in Italy would never make head against Totila, the Emperor graciously assigned him the task of repairing all the blunders that had been committed in that land since he left it four years previously. At the same time a promise (so it is said) was exacted from him that he would ask for no money from the Imperial treasury for the war, but would provide for its whole equipment at his own expense. Thus feebly supported by his master, with his splendid band of household troops dispersed among the eunuchs of the palace, with his own spirit half broken by all the sorrows and humiliations of recent years, he was not likely to threaten the security of Justinian, nor to be heard of as Emperor of the West. Whether this needy and heart-broken man would cope effectually in war with the young and gallant Totila was another question, and one which will be answered in the following chapters.

CHAPTER XVIII.

THE SECOND SIEGE OF ROME.

Belisarius, on receiving the charge of the Italian war, tried to persuade some of the soldiers enlisted for the Persian campaign to serve under his banners, but the magic of his name was gone, and all refused. He therefore had to spend some time moving to and fro in Thrace, where, by a large expenditure of money—his own money probably—he succeeded in raising some young volunteers.

Vitalius, whose commands had been hitherto chiefly in Dalmatia and Venetia, and who now held the high position of *Magister Militum per Illyricum*, met him at Salona; but the united forces of the two generals numbered only 4000 men. The first expedition directed by them was a decided success. The garrison of Otranto, hard pressed by the besieging Goths, had consented to surrender on a certain day if no help arrived previously. Valentine, whom the reader may perhaps remember as the groom of Photius who was raised from the ranks as a reward for his splendid bravery during the siege of Rome, was now sent by sea to relieve the outworn and enfeebled defenders of Otranto, and to substitute fresh and vigorous soldiers in their place. Arriving only four days before the stipulated day of surrender, and falling suddenly on the unsuspecting Goths, he succeeded in cutting his way through them to the citadel. The disappointed besiegers shortly after raised the siege and returned to Totila. Valentine also, having accomplished his commission and having left a whole year's supply of provisions in the lately beleaguered town, returned to Salona. Belisarius now moved up the coast to Pola in Istria, and from thence crossed to Ravenna. His own opinion was in favor of an immediate march to Rome, but Totila's forces were interposed in a menacing manner along the back-bone of Italy from Campania to Calabria, and Vitalius persuaded him against his better judgment to make Ravenna his base of operations; Ravenna, which alike in the days of Honorius, of Odovacar, and of Witigis, had been proved to be admirable as a hiding-place, but poor as a basis for offensive war.

Totila meanwhile, who, by means of a fictitious deputation bearing letters professedly written in the name of the Roman commander of Genoa and asking for help, had cleverly, if somewhat unscrupulously, obtained information as to the real size of the new army of reconquest, felt that he could afford to despise it, and proceeded in a leisurely manner to tighten his grasp on Rome. Tivoli was taken, owing to some dispute between the inhabitants and the Isaurian garrison, and all the citizens, as we hear with regret, were put to the sword, the massacre being accompanied by circumstances of unusual atrocity. The Tiber was watched to prevent provisions being borne down its stream into the city: and a fleet of small swift sailing ships, stationed at Naples and the Lipari Islands, captured nearly all the vessels which from the south sought to make the harbor of Ostia, bringing corn to Rome.

Belisarius, on entering Ravenna, (an entry how unlike that moment of supreme triumph when he marched into the same city four years previously), delivered an address to the inhabitants, Gothic as well as Roman, in which, while freely admitting the mistakes that had been made since his departure from Italy, he expressed the Emperor's unabated kindness and love towards all his subjects of whatever race, and earnestly entreated them to use all their influence with their friends to induce them to leave the service of the 'tyrant' Totila. The harangue, however, fell flat upon the listeners, who had learned in the last few years how little the kindness of the Roman Emperor was better than the tyranny of the barbarian. No defections from Totila's army resulted from this appeal.

Thorimuth, one of the guardsmen of Belisarius—we again begin to hear of the military household of the General—was next sent into the province of Aemilia, to try his fortune with the cities in that rich and populous district Vitalius with his Illyrian troops accompanied him, and for a time their efforts were successful. Fort after fort surrendered, and they were able to take up a strong position (probably their winter-quarters) in the important city of Bologna. Then a strange event took place, and one which well illustrates the intrinsic worthlessness of these Justinianic conquests. The Illyrians determined that they would serve no longer in Italy, and, withdrawing with swift secrecy from Bologna, marched back into their own land. The Emperor was very wroth, but after their ambassadors had set their case before him he could hardly retain his anger. They had in fact two excellent reasons for deserting. They had served for years in Italy without receiving any pay from the bankrupt treasury; and a great army of Huns was at that very moment wasting their homes and carrying off their wives and children into slavery. Totila, hearing of the defection of the Illyrians, tried to intercept the retreat of Vitalius and Thorimuth, but was out-generalled and sustained a trifling defeat. None the less, however, had Bologna, and probably the whole province of Aemilia, to be evacuated by the Imperial troops.

The same brave guardsman Thorimuth, with two comrades Ricilas and Sabinian, was next sent at the head of 1000 men to relieve the garrison of Osimo, which rock-cradled city was now being held as stubbornly for the Emperor as, six years before, it had been held for Witigis. They succeeded in entering the city by night, and apparently in supplying it with some fresh store of provisions. Ricilas however, in a fit of drunken hardihood, threw away his life in a fight which he had foolishly provoked, and from which he was somewhat ignobly trying to escape. Then came the necessary work of withdrawing from the city, in order not to aid the blockaders by adding to the number of mouths to be fed within its walls. Totila was informed by a deserter when the withdrawal was to take place, occupied an advantageous position about three miles from Osimo, fell upon them in the confusion of their midnight march, slew two hundred of them, Thorimuth and Sabinian in the number, and captured all their baggage and beasts of burden. The rest of the relieving army escaped across the mountains to Rimini.

Procopius forgets to inform us of the after-fortunes of the garrison of Osimo. They must, however, have surrendered, eventually, to the Goths, since seven years later the place was undoubtedly held by Gothic soldiers.

The next exploit of Belisarius was a clever reconstruction of the defenses of Pesaro. This little Hadriatic city, eighteen miles south of Rimini, had, together with her sister city of Fano, been dismantled by Witigis in order to prevent its occupation by the Byzantines. The gates had been destroyed and half of the circuit of the walls pulled down. Now, however, Belisarius, who was anxious to secure the town for the sake of the good foraging-ground for cavalry which surrounded it, sent messengers by night to take exact measurements of the height and width of the gateways. Gates made to fit these openings and bound with iron were then sent by sea from Ravenna, and were soon erected by the soldiers who had been recently commanded by Thorimuth. The walls were rebuilt in any fashion, stones or clay or any other material that was at hand being used for the purpose, and Pesaro was once more a walled city, which Totila assaulted, but assaulted in vain.

A twelvemonth had now elapsed since Belisarius received the charge of the Italian war, and what results had he to show? Otranto and Osimo relieved, and Pesaro refortified: this was not a very splendid account of a year's work of the famous Belisarius: and against these successes had to be set Tivoli captured and the strings of the net drawn perceptibly tighter round Rome by the leisurely operations of the contemptuous Totila. Belisarius keenly felt the impotence to which he was reduced, and broke his promise to Justinian to ask for no money for the war,—if such a promise was ever made,—by sending to Constantinople the following piteous epistle:

"I have arrived in Italy, 0 best of Emperors! in great want of men, of horses, of arms, and of money. A man who has not a sufficient supply of these will hardly, I think, ever be found able to carry on war. It is true that after diligent perambulation of Thrace and Illyria I was able to collect some soldiers there; but they are few in numbers, wretched in quality, have no weapons in their hands worth speaking of, and are altogether unpracticed in fighting. As for the soldiers whom I found in this country, they are discontented and disheartened, cowed by frequent defeats, and so bent on flight when the foe appears that they slip off their horses and dash their arms to the ground. As for making Italy provide the money necessary for carrying on the war, that is impossible; to so large an extent has it been reconquered by the enemy. Hence we are unable to give to the soldiers the long over-due arrears of their pay, and this consciousness of debt takes from us all freedom of speech towards them. And you ought, Sire! to be plainly told that the larger part of your nominal soldiers have enlisted and are now serving under the banners of the enemy. If then the mere sending of Belisarius to Italy was all that was necessary, your preparations for the war are perfect: but if you want to overcome your enemies you must do something more than this, for a General without subordinates is nothing. First and foremost, it behoves you to send me my own guards, both mounted and unmounted; secondly, a large number of Huns and other barbarians; and thirdly, money to pay them withal".

This letter, so pathetic, but yet so outspoken, was sent to Constantinople by the hands of John the nephew of Vitalian, who solemnly promised a speedy return. Everything, however, seemed to combine against the unfortunate commander of the Italian war. John saw a favorable opportunity for advancing his own interests by a brilliant marriage, and while Belisarius languished at Ravenna, the Byzantine populace were admiring a splendid pageant, the wedding festival of John and the daughter of Germanus, the great-niece of the Emperor Justinian.

So the year wore on. Belisarius felt more keenly than ever the mistake which he had made in shutting himself up in Ravenna, far from Rome, the real key of the position. Leaving Justin (who seems to have quitted his charge at Florence or possibly had been unable to hold that city against the Goths) to take the chief command at Ravenna, the General recrossed the Adriatic to form a new army at Durazzo. There, in course of time, he was met by the bridegroom John, raised doubtless above all fear of rebuke for his tardiness by the splendor of his new connection. With him came the Armenian General Isaac, and they brought under their standards an army, apparently a considerable army, of Romans and barbarians.

Meanwhile Totila, in this year 545, was steadily steady advancing, strengthening his position in Central Italy, tightening his grip on Rome.& Fermo and Ascoli, two cities of Picenum, were taken; Spoleto, perhaps the most important city on the Flaminian Way, was surrendered by its governor Herodian; men said too easily surrendered, because Herodian feared an investigation which Belisarius was about to institute into some irregularities of his past life. Assisi (how little did the men of that day think of the wealth of associations which in after ages would cluster round the name!) was more loyally defended for the Emperor by the valiant Goth, Siegfried, but he was slain in a sally and Assisi opened its gates to Totila. The neighboring citadel of Perugia still held out, but its garrison was weakened and discouraged by the assassination of their brave commander Cyprian by one of his bodyguard, who, if Procopius's story be correct, was bribed by Totila to commit this crime. Uliphus, the murderer, took refuge in Totila's camp. We shall meet with him once again, in the last days of the war, and mark his punishment.

At length, in the autumn probably of 545, Totila marched to Rome and formally commenced the siege of the city. Both in the Campagna and everywhere else throughout Italy he was careful to respect the property of the tillers of the soil. All that he expected of them was that they should pay into his hands the rent which the Colonus would otherwise have remitted to his patron, and the taxes which the free husbandman (if such there were) would have paid to the Imperial logothete. No money was to be sent to Constantinople; all that would have gone thither was to go to the Gothic King; and in return for this, the corn and the cattle of the peasant were to be left untouched, the honor of his wife and his daughter to be held inviolate. Such was the motto of Totila, and it is not surprising that the Italian peasant viewed with indifference, if not with actual pleasure, the extension of his kingdom, nor that his own army, paying for everything which it consumed, lived in comparative comfort, while Famine was coming ever nearer and nearer before the eyes of the inhabitants of the beleaguered City.

A sally, against the orders both of Bessas the Commandant of Rome and of Belisarius himself, had been undertaken by Artasires the Persian and Barbarian the Thracian (two of the General's guardsmen whom he had sent to Rome in order to keep up the spirits of the inhabitants), but had completely failed, and great discouragement was the result. Already perhaps a movement was being begun to escape from the hardships of a long siege by an early surrender. At least we are told that Cethegus, a man holding the rank of Patrician and *Princess Senatus*, was brought before a council of generals, charged with treasonable designs. Nothing apparently could be proved against him, but he was permitted, or ordered, to depart from Rome, and repaired to Civita Vecchia.

The year 546 had probably begun when Belisarius, still unable himself to repair to the scene of action, sent Valentine to Porto, at the mouth of the Tiber, to assist the troops which were posted there under the command of Innocentius in harassing the besieging army, and to clear the river for the passage of provision-ships up to Rome. With Valentine was sent Phocas, one of the General's mounted guards, and an exceedingly brave and capable soldier. They had five hundred men under their command. It was decided that these new troops should make an attack upon the camp of the enemy, which was to be seconded by a simultaneous sally from the city. Bessas however, the Imperial Commandant of Rome, though warned of the intended movement, refused to allow any of the three thousand men under his command to join in it. The attack therefore, though fairly successful, achieved nothing, and the assailants returned to Porto neither the better nor the worse for what they had done. They sent an upbraiding message to Bessas, and warned him that on a given day and hour they would repeat the attack, which they implored him to support by a vigorous sortie. Bessas, however, whose understanding of his duty seems to have been entirely summed up in the modern phrase 'masterly inactivity', again refused to imperil any of his men for such an enterprise. A deserter from the army of Innocentius warned Totila of the coming attack, and consequently, when the Imperialist troops issued from the walls of Porto, they soon found themselves in a Gothic ambuscade. Most of the five hundred fell, and their leaders with them. So perished the brave groom of Photius, whom we first saw stemming the tide of battle which surged round Belisarius and his dark roan horse, hard by the Milvian Bridge. Since then his name has been much in the mouths of men. Now his aforetime master, an emaciated and heart-broken monk, kneels beside the cradle at Bethlehem, and he lies upon the desolate Campagna, outside the walls of Porto, cloven by a Gothic broadsword.

Soon after this, some ships laden with corn for the Roman people were sent by Pope Vigilius, who was at this time, for reasons which will afterwards appear, residing in the island of Sicily. The Goths saw the ships coming, and guessing their errand arranged an ambush, probably from that side of the Tiber which washes the Isola Sacra, between Porto and Ostia. The Romans from their battlements saw the whole stratagem—everyone who has climbed the bell-tower of Ostia or of Porto knows how far the sight can travel over that unbroken alluvial plain—and made vigorous signs, by waving their garments and pointing with their hands, to prevent their friends from choosing that channel and urge them to land at some other point of the coast. Unfortunately the signals which were meant to discourage were interpreted as enthusiastic encouragement and acclamation. The corn-ships came sailing on, right into the Portensian channel, and close past the Gothic ambuscade. They were at once boarded, their cargoes appropriated for the Gothic army, and a bishop who was on board, and whose name by a curious coincidence happened to be also Valentine, was straitly interrogated as to the position of affairs in Sicily. Detecting him in returning false answers to his questions, the King, with a flash of barbarian rage blazing out from beneath the restraints of reason and self-discipline, ordered the lying ecclesiastic's hands to be cut off and let him go whither he would.

About this time, two years after the re-appointment of Belisarius, the important city of Placentia, one of the keys of the Emilian Way, was surrendered to the Goths after nearly a year's siege, in which the defenders had endured terrible hardships from famine, being at length reduced, it was whispered, to feed upon human flesh. The reduction of the important city of Placentia was a great gain to Totila, who could now move his troops freely between Pavia, the heart of the Gothic resistance, and the valleys of the Arno and the Tiber.

By this time in Rome also the pressure of famine was beginning to be sorely felt, and the citizens—perhaps without the knowledge, perhaps against the wish of Bessas—decided to send an embassy to Totila, to see if terms could be arranged for a truce, and for the eventual, surrender of the City, if help came not by a given day. The envoy chosen was the deacon Pelagius, a man who had resided long in Constantinople on terms of close friendship with the Emperor, who had recently returned to Rome with large stores of wealth, which he had generously employed in relieving the distresses of the poorer citizens. Nine years after this time, on the death of Vigilius, he was to be installed in the chair of St. Peter. Already during the long absence of Vigilius he wielded an influence little less than Papal in the Eternal City.

Totila received the generous deacon with great outward show of reverence and affection, but before he began to set forth his request, addressed him with courteous but decided words:

"We Goths feel as strongly as the Romans the duty of showing every possible respect to the office of an ambassador. In my opinion, however, that respect is better shown by an early and frank statement of what can and what cannot be conceded, than by any number of honeyed words, holding out hopes which the speaker does not mean to gratify. Let me therefore at once and plainly tell you that there are three things which it is useless for you to request. On any other subject I will hear you gladly, and if possible grant your petition.

"The first is pardon for the inhabitants of Sicily. It is impossible for us to forget the flourishing condition of that island, the very granary of Rome, which Theodoric, in reliance on the honor of its people and in answer to their earnest request, consented to leave unoccupied by Gothic garrisons. What was the reward of this generous confidence? As soon as the Imperial armament appeared in the offing, an armament which it was easily within their power to have resisted, they sent no tidings of its approach to the Goths, they did not occupy one of the strong places in the island, but at once, like runaway-slaves seeking a new master, they crowded down to the shore with suppliant hands and said: 'Our cities are yours, we are faithful subjects of the Emperor'. This was the turning-point in the fortunes of our nation. It was from this island that the enemy sallied forth as from a fortress to occupy any part of Italy that they pleased. It was by the assistance of the Sicilians that they gathered those vast stores of corn which enabled them for a whole year to stand a blockade in Rome. These are not injuries which the Goths can ever forget: therefore ask for no pardon for the Sicilians.

"The second point is the preservation of the walls of Rome. Behind these walls our enemies sheltered themselves for a year, never venturing to meet us in the open field, but wearing out our noble army by all sorts of tricks and clever surprises. We should be fools to allow this kind of stratagem to be practiced against us hereafter: and moreover, the citizens of Rome will gain by the demolition of their walls. No more deadly assaults, no more of the yet deadlier blockades for them in future. Safe and quiet in their unwalled city they will await the arbitrament of battle, which will be waged on some other field between the opposing armies.

"The third point is the surrender of the slaves who have fled to us from their Roman owners. We have received these men on a solemn promise that we will never give them up to their former masters. We have allowed them to stand alongside of us in the battle. If after all this we were to abandon them to the mercy of their lords, you yourselves would know that there was no reliance to be placed on the promises of men so faithless and so ungrateful."

Such in substance was the speech of Totila, a speech which, though too vindictive in its reference to the Sicilians, contained much unanswerable argument from the Gothic stand-point. The Deacon Pelagius did not attempt to answer it, but made a short and ill-tempered speech to the effect that courtesy to an ambassador was only a mockery if he had no chance of obtaining what he asked for. For himself he would rather receive a slap in the face and return to those who sent him with some one of his requests granted, than be received with ever so great a show of politeness and return unsuccessful. He declined to make any request whatever to Totila, in face of the prohibition to touch on the three reserved points, and would only remark that if the King determined to wage a truceless war on the unhappy Sicilians, who had never borne arms against him, there was little hope of mercy for the Romans in whose hands he had seen the spear. He would have nothing more to do with the embassy, but would leave the matter in the hands of God, who was not unaccustomed to punish those who behaved themselves arrogantly towards a suppliant. With heavy hearts the Roman citizens saw Pelagius return from the mission which his own peevishness had made a fruitless one. In large numbers they thronged to the house—perhaps the Pincian Palace, perhaps one of the old Imperial Palaces overlooking the Forum—which served as a Praetorium, and where abode the representatives of the Emperor. The council of officers before whom they laid their sad case was presided over by Bessas and Conon; Bessas the Thracian Ostrogoth who had defended the Porta Maggiore against his countrymen in the earlier siege, Conon the leader of Isaurians, who three years before had found himself forced by pressure, such as the citizens were now bringing to bear, to surrender Naples to Totila. In terms of abject misery the citizens of Rome put up their prayer to these iron-hearted men. "We do not appear before you as your fellow-countrymen, as members of the same great commonwealth, as men who willingly received you within our walls, and have fought side by side with you against a common enemy. Forget all this: imagine that we are captives taken in war, imagine that we are slaves. Yet even the slave is fed by his master. And only for this do we pray, for food enough to keep us alive. If you cannot or will not do this, manumit us, give us leave to depart hence, and so save yourselves the trouble of digging graves for your servants. If that again be impossible then kill us outright. Sudden death will be sweet in comparison with this lingering torture, and you will be quit of many thousand murmuring Romans by one blow".

Bessas and the generals round him gravely replied to this passionate outburst, that they could adopt none of the three courses suggested: that it was quite impossible to supply rations to the non-combatant dwellers in Rome, that it would be prejudicial to the Emperors interests to allow the citizens to depart, and that to kill them all would be an unholy deed. Belisarius and the new army from Constantinople would reach Rome before long, and they must patiently await their arrival.

It was evidently the determination of Bessas and his brother officers, who, it must be remembered, were for the most part men of barbarian origin themselves, to look with absolute indifference on the misery of the mere citizens of Rome, nay, even to trade upon it for their own advantage. A large supply of corn had been accumulated in the magazines, but this was all strictly reserved for the soldiers. A wealthy Roman, however, might buy at famine prices from a soldier such part of his ration as he did not require, nay, it was believed that even Bessas and Conon were not above enriching themselves by this ungenerous traffic. The quotations in this terrible market rose and rose, till at last the Roman patrician had to pay at the rate of four hundred and forty-eight shillings for a quarter of wheat. The less wealthy middle-class citizens paid a fourth of this price for bran; and, made Spartans by necessity, looked upon the coarse bread into which it was baked as the sweetest and most delicate of food. Animal food was of course hardly ever to be procured. Once some men of the life-guard of Bessas found an ox outside the walls, which they sold for the comparatively moderate price of £30 sterling. Fortunate was the Roman deemed who came upon the carcase of a horse or other beast of burden, and could thus once more have the delight of chewing flesh.

For the great mass of needy citizens the staple article of food was the nettles which grew freely under the walls and in the many ruined temples and palaces of Rome. To prevent the leaves from stinging the lips and throat, they were cooked with great care, and in this way a tantalizing semblance of nourishment was given to the craving stomach. These nettles before long became the universal food of all classes. No more *aurei* were left in the girdle even of the patrician, no household goods which he could barter for food, and, worst of all, even the soldiers' rations were growing scantier, so that neither buyers nor sellers existed to form a market. The flesh of the citizens was all wasted away, their skin was dark and livid, they moved about like specters rather than men, and many while still walking among the ruins and chewing the nettles between their teeth suddenly sank to the earth and gave up the ghost.

One unhappy Roman, the father of five children, found himself surrounded by his little ones, who plucked at his robe and uttered those two terrible words, "Father! Bread!". A sudden and terrible serenity came over his face, and he said to them, "My children! follow me". They followed in the hope that he had some unknown store of food. He walked rapidly to one of the bridges over the Tiber, mounted the parapet, veiled his face with his robe, his children all the while looking on, and plunged headlong in the stream. Death, even a coward's death, leaving his little ones alone with their misery, was better than hearing any longer that heart-rending cry.

At length, when creatures generally deemed unfit for food, such as dogs and mice, had become unattainable luxuries; when men were staying the hunger-pang with the most loathsome substances; when stories of cannibalism were becoming more and more frequent and well-authenticated, and when still Belisarius came not; at length the hard heart of Bessas relented, and he agreed for a large sum of money to allow the non-combatants to leave Rome. A few escaped unhurt through the enemy's outposts. Many were pursued and slain. Yet more perhaps died of the effects of the famine, on the road or on ship-board, before they had arrived at their journey's end. "To so low a point" says Procopius, thinking doubtless of the four fateful letters which were once carried in triumph round the world, "to so low a point had fallen the fortunes of the Senate and the People of Rome!"

What meanwhile delayed the advance of Belisarius to the relief of the beleaguered city? In the council of war which was held at Durazzo he had earnestly pleaded that this was the most pressing duty of the Imperial generals, and that in order to effect it they should embark the whole army on ship-board, when with a favoring breeze they might in five days reach the mouth of the Tiber. His rival John, on the other hand, pointed to the insecure tenure by which the Goths held Calabria and the South of Italy, and maintained that their true policy was to land at one of the southern ports, receive those countries back again into the Imperial allegiance, and then by a rapid march through Samnium and Campania take Totila in the rear and raise the siege of Rome. As neither general could convince the other, and Belisarius could not force the husband of Justinian's great-niece to obey him, a compromise was agreed upon, which was perhaps worse than either plan pursued singly. While Belisarius and the Armenian Isaac with one part of the troops set sail for the Tiber, John with the remainder was to prosecute the campaign in Calabria and, as soon as might be, meet his comrades under the walls of Rome.

Belisarius first set sail for the Tiber, and meeting with contrary winds, was forced to take shelter in the harbor of Otranto. The Goths, who had returned to the siege of that place, fled when they saw his fleet approaching, and halted not till they reached

Brindisi, at the distance of fifty miles. From thence they sent messengers to tell their King of the invasion of Calabria. Totila sent word to them to hold on as long as they could, but meanwhile relaxed not the vigilance of his blockade of Rome. Soon the wind changed, and Belisarius, after a favorable voyage, reached Portus at the mouth of the Tiber.

Soon afterwards John crosses the Adriatic Gulf, and, as good luck would have it, landed not far from Brindisi. A Gothic scout who had been taken prisoner begged for his life, and promised in return to guide him to the enemy. "First of all" said the Imperial General, "show me where the horses pasture". Accordingly the man led him to a green plain where the horses of the Goths were feeding. On each horse's back leaped a Byzantine foot-soldier, and then they galloped to the camp of the unsuspecting foe. An utter rout followed, and this defeat opened the whole province of Calabria to the Imperialists. Canusium opened its gates to them, and hither came Tullianus son of Venantius, long ago governor of Bruttii and Lucania under Theodoric. Tullianus fearlessly spoke of the oppressions wrought by the Emperors generals in Italy, oppressions which had compelled the inhabitants of these provinces, much against their will, to accept the yoke of the Goths, Arians and barbarians though they were, as the less intolerable of the two evils. Now, however, if John would promise to prevent the ravages of his soldiery, Tullianus would use his influence to obtain the speedy submission of the two provinces. The promise was given, and by the good Bruttii and offices of Tullianus, Bruttii and Lucania were recovered speedily recovered for the Empire.

Here, however, John's advance towards Rome stopped. Three hundred horsemen sent by Totila towards to Capua were sufficient to check his further progress, notwithstanding the urgent messages of Belisarius, who bitterly complained that he who had been allowed to select the bravest men in the army, "and all of them barbarians", should allow himself to be checked by a little body of three hundred men. The qualification thus emphasized by Belisarius shows clearly enough how little the citizens of the Roman Empire had to do with winning the Empire's battles. John now turned southward and inflicted a crushing defeat on Recimund, who with an army of Goths, Moors, and deserters from the Imperial ranks, was holding Reggio for Totila, to prevent any succors being sent from Sicily to the mainland. But this victory had little effect on the main course of the war. While the great duel was going on around the towers of Rome, John in his Apulian camp was only a listless spectator of the agony of the Empire.

The narrative now turns to Belisarius, who, from Porto as his base of operations, is about to make an attempt for the relief of Rome. At the risk of a little repetition it will be well to give a somewhat detailed description of the two harbors of Rome, which, after several alternations of prosperity and decay, are both now practically deserted, Portus and Ostia.

Let us take Ostia first, though it makes the less conspicuous figure in our present narrative. It is situated on the south of the Tiber, on the left bank, that is to say, of the left-hand channel of the stream. The excavations of recent years have been fruitful in results for the archaeologist, and it may be doubted whether any other ruins, except those of Pompeii, enable us more vividly to reproduce the actual appearance of a Roman city. We see the broad road lined with tombs, leading up to the city-gate: we see the narrow streets paved with large flat stones on which the wheel-marks of the Roman *biga* are yet visible : we see the semicircular area and columns of a theatre : we see the steps and part of the portico of the stately Temple of Vulcan : we see the chambers of an Imperial palace in which Antoninus Pius perhaps spent his summers, and among them one little chapel, dedicated, probably in the second century, to the worship of Mithras, the Eastern Sun-god. Almost more interesting, as enabling us more vividly to picture the commercial life of the city, are the magazines, in one of which are still to be found some dozen or so of *dolia*, earthenware hogsheads once filled with wine or oil, now empty and buried up to their necks in the fine sand of the Tiber. Here too is a well-preserved gateway once leading into a courtyard lined with warehouses, and bearing on the keystone of the arch the sculptured resemblance of a Roman *modius (*peck-measure*)*, as a reminder, perhaps, to the merchant, of the duty of giving just measure to all his customers. Not far off is a stone on which some public notice, possibly for the regulation of the market, has been affixed. Everywhere we feel that we are tracing the lineaments of a great city of commerce, though one that has been dead for centuries.

One thing disappoints us in Ostia, and yet in our disappointment helps to explain its present desolation. We miss the sea. We have read in Minucius Felix how at Ostia the three friends Alteration who were about to hold high converse on Fate and Providence and the nature of the gods, first walked along the yielding sand, and watched the boys playing "duck and drake" with their smooth stones rebounding from the Mediterranean waves. We have read how three centuries later Monica and Augustine sat upon the same shore and gazed over the same expanse of sea, as the mother talked with her recovered son of the joys of the heavenly kingdom. But the Ostia of today gives us no help in picturing either of these scenes. The sea has retreated to a distance of three miles from its walls: we see only the flat and desolate Campagna, the muddy Tiber, the grass-grown mounds of the deserted city.

Now let us leave Ostia and turn our steps to Portus. A ferry-boat takes us across the Fiumara, as the broad, sluggish, turbid southern channel of the Tiber is called. Then a walk of two miles across the sandy expanse of the Isola Sacra brings us to the northern channel. The island called the Isola Sacra, which is now, owing to the recession of the coast-line, five or six times as large as it was in the days of Procopius, was then, though solitary, fair as the garden of Venus, full of roses and all fragrant flowers, says an enthusiastic geographer of the fourth century. Now, a few low trees provide the inhabitants with fire-wood, and a poor and coarse grass affords pasture to the not always inoffensive herds of buffaloes. A celebrated temple stood here dedicated to the Great Twin Brethren, but even its site is now forgotten. At the end of the path however, just opposite Porto, we come to the ancient tower which marks the spot where once stood the church of Saint Hippolytus, the cathedral church of Portus, separated from the city by the Tiber channel, and rightly named after the most famous bishop of that see, whose great work, a *Refutation of all Heresies*, has in our own day been recovered for ecclesiastical literature.

Again crossing in a ferry-boat the waters of the Tiber, but this time the northern channel, we reach the village of Porto Moderno. The modern successor to Portus as a Mediterranean harbor is the little town of Fiumicino, two miles further down the stream. There we find a small wooden pier projecting into the sea, a few ships discharging their cargoes, a row of tall lodging-houses, all filled during a few weeks in spring by the crowd of bathers from Rome, all empty and deserted in September from fear of the everywhere brooding malaria. Here, in this so-called Porto Moderno, which was really called into existence by Pope Gregory IV a few years before the birth of

Alfred the Great, hard by the then ruined Portus of the Emperors, there are a modernized church, a mediaeval castle, in one room of which are collected the Latin inscriptions discovered in the neighborhood: not much else to interest the archaeologist, except a fallen column, once no doubt forming part of the elder Portus, on which, rudely carved perhaps by the knife of one of his soldiers, appear five letters of the name of the glorious Vandal, Stilicho.

We take a few steps northwards and find ourselves looking upon a piece of water which as it recedes from us becomes shallower, changes into rushes, into marsh, into firm land. We soon observe a certain regularity about its sides, and find that it is in fact a regular hexagon, each side nearly 300 yards long. Yes, this is the celebrated hexagonal harbor of Trajan. Long rows of massive warehouses, in which were stored the rations of Egyptian and Sicilian corn for all the people of Rome, were once mirrored in its waters : even yet some huge blocks of masonry remain to show how solid was their building. The greatest ships of the ancient world, ships of commerce and of war, laden with corn or with legions, have glided in by the deep canal which is now represented only by a little brook that a child could step over, and have maneuvered easily in the capacious dock which is now a reedy fish-pond. At each angle of the hexagon rose a column, crowned with a statue. On our right hand, full fronting the opening by which the ships entered the basin, stood a colossal statue of the founder himself, the mighty Emperor Trajan. Now, almost on the same spot, one may see the neat villa of the present owner of Portus and Ostia and all the intervening and surrounding country, the Prince Torlonia. A fine herd of horses grazes on the margin of the pool: the frogs fill the air with their harsh melody: other signs of life there are none.

Outside of the hexagonal basin, that is to the north-west of it, was formerly the yet larger harbor of Claudius, with a pier curving round to the north-east, the work of Theodoric. This is now even more blended with the desolate Campagna than the work of Trajan. The name of Claudius is great at Portus as it is in the valley of the Anio. It was from this port that his fleet sailed for the conquest of the almost 'world-severed' island of Britain. The northern channel which he cut for the river had the double effect of making the new harbor possible and of removing the inundations with which Father Tiber had been wont to visit the city of his sons. A fair inscription, which was found some fifty years ago in the excavations of Cardinal Pallavicini and has been placed by his orders on the side of the modern carriage-road to Porto, records these beneficent labors of the dull-witted Emperor.

We have yielded perhaps too long to the melancholy fascination of these scenes, once filled with the lively hum of commerce, echoing to the voice of sailors from every country on the Mediterranean, and now abandoned to the bittern and the cormorant. We must return to the sixth century and look upon them as they were seen by Belisarius. Ostia in his time was no doubt far fallen from her former greatness, impoverished by five centuries of competition with the superior advantages of Portus; but it was still a considerable commercial city: and Portus, except so far as the war itself had injured its commerce, was probably well-nigh as busy as in the days of Claudius. The great magazines stood there, all waiting for the corn-supplies of the Roman people, if only the light cruisers of Totila would allow them to be filled. The walls with which Constantine had enclosed the city and harbor, now mere grass mounds over which the horses gallop in their play, were then defensible fortifications, probably from twelve to fifteen feet high. Within the enclosure of these walls, which were about a mile and a-half in length, and flanked by the river and the sea, lay the army of Belisarius, who now again, as in his earlier campaigns, was accompanied by the martial Antonina. It is important to remember the difference between the position of the combatants in 537 and in the present siege. Then, Ostia was held by the Romans, and Portus was a Gothic stronghold. Now, Portus is the one place of vantage left to the Romans in the neighborhood of the capital, and Ostia is occupied by a Gothic garrison.

The town of Portus was nineteen Roman miles from Rome. About four miles above it, where the river was narrowest, Totila had caused a boom to be placed to block the passage of ships bearing provisions to the starving City. This boom consisted of long beams of timber lashed together and forming a kind of floating bridge. It was protected by a wooden tower at either end, and was yet further strengthened by an iron chain stretched across from shore to shore a little below it, in order to prevent the boom from being broken by the mere impact of a hostile vessel.

The counter-preparations of Belisarius were very complete. Having lashed together two broad barges, he erected a wooden tower upon them sufficiently high to overtop the bridge. Trusting nothing to chance, he had the measurements of the bridge taken by two of his soldiers who feigned themselves deserters. To the top of the tower a boat was hoisted filled with a combustible mixture, pitch, sulphur, rosin, an anticipation of the dreaded 'Greek fire' of later ages. Surrounding the barges, and partly towing them, was a fleet of two hundred swift cutters laden with corn and other necessaries for the starving Romans, but also bearing some of the bravest of his soldiers, and turned into ships of war by high wooden ramparts on the decks, pierced with loop-holes for the archers. Detachments of infantry and cavalry were also stationed at all the points of vantage on the bank to support the operations of the ships, and especially to prevent any advance of the enemy upon Portus.

Having made these preparations, Belisarius entrusted the defence of the sea-port, containing as it did all his stores, his reserve troops, and above all his wife, to Isaac of Armenia, with a solemn charge that come what might, and even should he hear that Belisarius himself had fallen before the foe, under no conceivable circumstances was he to leave the post thus committed to him. At the same time he sent word to Bessas to support his movements by a vigorous sortie from the city against the Gothic camps. This message however, like so many others of the same kind, failed to shake the 'masterly inactivity' of the governor of Rome. The Goths had full leisure that day to concentrate their whole attention on the operations of Belisarius.

With some labor the rowers urged the laden cutters up the river. The Goths, confiding in the strength of their bridge and chain, remained quiet in their camps. Soon they found out their error. The archers from the cutters dealt such havoc among the Gothic guards on either shore that resistance was quelled and they were able to sever the chain and sail on in triumph up to the bridge. Now the Goths perceived the danger and swarmed down upon the bridge. The fighting here became terrific. Belisarius, watching his opportunity, steered the floating tower close up to the Gothic fort commanding the north end of the bridge, which stood close to the water's edge. The boat laden with Greek fire was set alight and skillfully thrown into the very middle of the fort, which was at once wrapped in flames. In the conflagration two hundred of the Gothic garrison, headed by Osdas, the bravest of the brave, all perished. Encouraged by this success, the archers on board, the *dromones,* sent a yet thicker shower of arrows at the Goths on the shore. Terror seized the barbarian ranks; they turned to flee;

the Romans began to hew the timbers of the bridge to pieces; the revictualling of the hungry city seemed already accomplished.

Seemed only. By one of those tricks of Fate upon which our historian delights to moralize, the very moment when he seemed to have won her, Victory flitted away out of the grasp of Belisarius. A rumor, perhaps a premature rumor, of the success of the mornings operations, especially of the severing of the chain, reached the ears of Isaac at Portus. Forgetful of his general's solemn charge, and only envious at having no share in the glory of the triumph, he sallied forth with a hundred horsemen, crossed the Insula Sacra, and suddenly attacked the Gothic garrison of Ostia, who were commanded by the gallant Roderic. In the first skirmish Roderic was wounded, and his soldiers, whether from fear or guile, turned and fled. The Imperialists entered the camp, and found a store of money and other valuables therein, which they began to plunder. While they were thus engaged the Goths returned in greater numbers, easily overpowered the hundred Romans, slew the greater number of them, and took the rest, among whom was Isaac himself, prisoners.

The mere failure of this foolish attack would have been in itself no great disaster. But as adverse Fortune would have it, a messenger escaped from the field and bore the tidings to Belisarius at the bridge, "Isaac is taken". "Isaac taken" thought the General: "then Portus and Antonina are taken too". At this thought, says the historian, "he was bewildered with fear, a thing which had never happened to him in any previous peril". Yet even this bewilderment is for us the most convincing proof that they were chains of love, not of fear, which yet bound him to Antonina. He at once gave the signal for retreat, in the hope that by a speedy return he might surprise the victorious barbarians and rescue Portus from their grasp. When he reached the seaport (which it is to be remembered was only four miles from the scene of action), found all safe there, and recognized by what folly of his subordinate and what misreading of the game by himself he had been cheated out of an already-assured victory, he was seized with such deep chagrin, that his bodily strength, perhaps already weakened by the unwholesome air of the Campagna, quite broke down. He sickened with fever, which at one time caused his life to be despaired of, and for some months he was unable to take any active share in the conduct of the campaign.

Two days after this battle Roderic the governor of Ostia died, and Totila, enraged at the loss of his brave comrade, put his feeble Armenian captive to death—a deed not worthy of his fame.

Meanwhile, in Borne, there was a daily increasing demoralization among the soldiers of the garrison. Procopius attributes this entirely to the avarice of Bessas, who according to him was so intent on his traffic in corn at famine-prices to the few still remaining citizens, that he neglected all the duties of a general, and purposely refused to co-operate with Belisarius, knowing that the more the siege could be prolonged, the richer he would grow. It is almost certain that there is some exaggeration here. Bessas was a sufficiently capable soldier to know that if no watch were kept on the walls the city would be taken, and that then even the treasure for the sake of which he had committed so many crimes would with difficulty be saved from the enemy. Perhaps the true explanation of his conduct is this. He saw the fame which Belisarius had acquired by his year-long defence of Rome and determined to rival it. The secret of that success had been the refusal to spend the strength of the soldiers on useless sorties, and Bessas showed that he had laid that lesson to heart. But there were two reasons for his failure. In Totila he had to deal with a very different adversary from the blundering

Witigis, with an adversary who was also determined to waste none of his strength on useless assaults, who never hurried himself, but who by a slow, patient, scientific blockade consumed the life of Rome. And, what was even more important, the noble heart of Belisarius had saved him from that crime of callous indifference to the sufferings of non-combatants which Bessas forsooth gloried in, as showing his soldier-like disregard of all that did not bear on the success of the great game, but which really lost him the great game itself. No doubt he enriched himself by sales of corn at famine-prices to the Senators. None of these barbarian and semi-barbarian generals of Byzantium had any refined feelings of honor where money was concerned. But this can hardly have been his sole thought. He had a plan for the defence of Rome which he thought he could work out independently of the welfare or the sufferings of the citizens. And in that thought he was wrong even from the military point of view. Without the loyal help of the great mass of citizens it was impossible to keep the vast circuit of the walls effectually guarded, and one unguarded spot, on one dark night, might make all other precautions useless.

So much by way of necessary protest before quoting the words of Procopius. "Neither in the attack on the bridge, nor at any previous time, would Bessas assist as he was required to do. For he had still some corn stored up, since the supplies previously sent to Rome by the magistrates of Sicily had been intended both for the soldiers and the citizens; but he, giving forth a very small quantity to the citizens, kept the largest part concealed, nominally on behalf of the soldiers, but really that he might retail it to the Senators at a high price. Of course therefore the end of the siege was the thing which he least desired. By his transactions in corn Bessas was growing ever richer, since the necessity of the buyers allowed him to fix the price according to his own fancy. Being wholly immersed in this business, he took no thought as to the watch upon the walls or any other measure of precaution, but if the soldiers chose to be remiss he allowed them to be so. Hence there were but few sentinels on the walls, and those very careless about their duty. The sentinel on guard at any given time might indulge, if he pleased, in long slumbers, since there was no one set over him to call him to account. There were none to go the rounds, as aforetime, to challenge the sentinels and ascertain what they were doing. Nor could any of the citizens assist in this work of vigilance; for, as I have said, those who were now left in the City were very few in number and terribly reduced in strength".

According to the view suggested above, these last words of the historian contain the gist of the whole matter. The rest of the description does but portray the condition of a garrison demoralized by being set to perform a duty hopelessly beyond their powers.

The Asinarian Gate—by which it may be remembered Belisarius entered Rome in December 536—yet stands, with its two round towers, behind the Church of the Lateran, one of the finest monuments of the great defensive work of Aurelian and Honorius. The gateway itself is blocked up, and the mediaeval Porta S. Giovanni, a few yards to the east of it, now opens upon the great highway to Albano, Capua, and Naples. Notwithstanding this alteration, however, there is still a lofty and well-preserved piece of the ancient wall, and nowhere do we find a better specimen than here, of the galleries through which the sentinels went their rounds, of the loopholes through which the archers shot, of the battlements by which the more exposed warriors above were partially defended. Upon this part of the wall there was a *vigilia* of four Isaurian soldiers, who, tired of the siege, disgusted with their failing food, and mindful very probably of the kindness with which Totila had treated them after the capture of Naples, resolved to betray the City to the Gothic King. Letting themselves down by ropes from the battlements, they sought the camp of the barbarians and unfolded their design to Totila. He thanked them warmly, offered them large sums of money if the City should be put in his power, and sent two of his guards to view the place where the Isaurians kept watch. The men climbed up by the ropes, inspected the fortifications, heard all that the Isaurians had to say, and returned to report favorably of the project.

There was something about the Isaurians' demeanor, however, which had roused the King's suspicion, and a second and even a third visit from them (their return being each time accompanied by some of his own followers to examine the walls) was necessary before he would trust his army in their hands. This extreme caution on the part of the daring Totila had well-nigh proved fatal to the scheme. It chanced that the Roman scouts brought as captives into the City ten Gothic soldiers, who, being interrogated as to what Totila was meditating next, were foolish enough or disloyal enough to disclose, what had now become the talk of the camp, that he hoped to get possession of the city by the help of some Isaurians Happily, however, Bessas and Conon paid no further attention to the story, which was perhaps too vague to guide them to the very Isaurians who were meditating treason.

When the third deputation, headed by a kinsman of Totila himself, had returned, reporting favorably of the Isaurians'' proposal, the King at length made up his mind to accept the venture. At nightfall the whole Gothic host, fully armed, was drawn up outside the Asinarian Gate. Four Goths, men conspicuous for valor and strength, mounted by ropes to the place where the friendly Isaurians were on guard, the other Roman sentinels being all wrapped in slumber. As soon as they were within the walls they hastened to the gateway. With rapid well-directed blows from their axes they severed the great bar of wood which kept the gates closed, and shattered the iron locks, the keys of which were of course in other keeping. The work must have been speedily done, for the noise of blows like those would break the sleep of even the most over-wearied sentinels. Then they opened wide the gates, and without difficulty or opposition, without striking a blow except at bolts and bars, the whole Gothic army marched in.

After all, it seemed, the hundred and fifty thousand warriors who in the long siege left their bones under the grass of the Campagna had not died in vain. The 'hoarded vengeance' of ten years might at length be reaped. The Goths were again in Rome.

CHAPTER XIX.

ROMA CAPTA.

When the Goths had entered by the Asinarian Gate, Totila, still fearful of some treachery, caused them all to halt in good order till day-light dawned. Meanwhile, universal uproar and confusion reigned in the panic-stricken City. The three thousand Imperial soldiers streamed out of the Flaminian Gate, even as the Gothic garrison had done ten years before. Bessas and Conon were mingled with the crowd of fugitives, not being compelled by any exaggerated sense of honor to die upon the scene of their discomfiture. The best proof that Bessas was indeed taken unawares is furnished by the fact that all the treasure which he had accumulated at the cost of so much human suffering was left behind in his palace and fell into the hands of the Gothic King. Before the night had ended a messenger came in haste to tell the King of the flight of the Governor and his army. "Excellent tidings!" said Totila. "No! I will not pursue after them. What more delightful news could anyone wish for than to hear that his enemies are fleeing?". Of the Roman nobles, a few who were fortunate enough to possess horses accompanied the flight of the army: the rest sought shelter in the various churches. Among the refugees we find the names of Decius and Basilius, the former perhaps descended from the Emperor and from the great Decii of the Republic, the latter probably the same nobleman whom we have already taken note of as the last Roman Consul. Among the suppliants at the altars the names of Maximus, Olybrius, and Orestes also remind us, truly or falsely, of men eminent in the struggles of the preceding century.

When day dawned, Totila proceeded to St Peter's basilica to return thanks to God for his victory. His soldiers roamed through the city, slaying and plundering. One horror usually accompanying the sack of a captured city was absent. No Roman maid, wife, or widow suffered the least insult from any of the Gothic soldiery, so strict were the orders of Totila on this point, and so little did his subjects dare to disobey him.

The plunder of the Roman palaces was, however, freely permitted to them, on the somewhat ambiguous condition that the most valuable of the property—meaning probably silver, gold, and jewels—was to be brought to the King to form the nucleus of a new great Gothic hoard.

Thus then, amid the noise and confusion of the plunder of a mighty city, amid the shouts of the slayers and the groans of the dying, Totila proceeded to the great basilica on the Vatican. Arrived there, he found the deacon Pelagius awaiting him, bearing a roll of the Sacred Scriptures and expressing in every gesture the humility of a suppliant. "Spare thine own subjects, 0 our Master!!" said the submissive ecclesiastic. With a scoff which he could not forbear at the haughty demeanor of Pelagius on the occasion of their last meeting, Totila said, "Now, then, thou art willing to make requests of me". "Yes" said Pelagius, "since God hath made me thy slave. But spare thy slaves, Master! Henceforward". Totila listened to the request, and at once sent messengers all through the City, saying that, though the plunder might continue, no more blood was to be shed. Already, twenty-six soldiers and sixty citizens had fallen under the swords of the Goths. The smallness of these numbers points rather to the depopulation of the City than to the humanity of the conquerors. Procopius was informed that only five hundred citizens were left in Rome, the greater part of whom had fled to the churches; nor does there seem any reason for supposing that he has underestimated this number, notwithstanding the vast contrast with the many myriads who once thronged the streets of the Eternal City.

The condition of the survivors of the Roman people was so miserable that death from the Gothic broadsword might seem in comparison scarcely an evil to be dreaded. Proud Senators and their delicately nurtured wives, clothed in the garb of peasants and of slaves, wandered about from house to house, knocking at the doors and craving from the charity of the Gothic warriors a morsel of food to keep the life within them. Among these abject suppliants was one whose tale seems to carry us back for two generations. Rusticiana, the daughter of Symmachus and the widow of Boethius, yet lived, and in these darkest days of her country she had distinguished herself by the generosity with which she had devoted her wealth to the relief of her starving fellow-citizens. She too was now a humble petitioner for a morsel of bread. When the Goths discovered who she was, many of them clamored that she should be slain, the chief crime of which she was accused being that she had given money to the Roman generals as the price of their consent to the destruction of the statues of Theodoric. Her resentment against the sovereign who had put her husband and father to death is easily understood : but it is not probable that either Belisarius or Bessas would require much persuasion to induce them to sanction the destruction of the visible emblems of the great Ostrogoth. True or false as the story might be, Totila refused to allow Rusticiana to be molested on account of it, and gave strict orders that the venerable lady should be treated with all courtesy. We hear nothing more concerning her, and with this incident the family of Boethius passes out of history.

On the day after the capture of the City, Totila addressed two very different harangues to two very different audiences. The Goths were all gathered together, surely in the same Forum which once echoed Cicero's denunciations against Catiline, and Antony's praises of the murdered Julius: and here their King congratulated them on an event which he almost described in Cromwell's words as "a crowning mercy" so urgently did he insist on the truth that it was not by human strength, but by God's manifest blessing on the righteous cause, that the victory had been won. "At the beginning of the war, 200,000 valiant Goths, rich in money, in arms, in horses, and with numbers of prudent veterans to guide their counsels, lost empire, life, liberty, to a little band of 7000 Greeks. Now, from more than 20,000 of the same enemies, a scanty remnant of the nation, poor, despised, utterly devoid of experience, had wrested the great prize of the war. Why this difference? Because aforetime the Goths, putting justice last in their thoughts, committed, against the subject Romans and one another, all sorts of unholy deeds: but now they had been striving to act righteously towards all men". In this resolution, even at the risk of wearying them, he besought them to continue. For if they changed, assuredly God's favour towards them would change likewise, since it is not this race or that nation, as such, on whose side God fights, but He assists all men everywhere who honor the precepts of eternal righteousness.

It is not without a feeling of pain that we pass from the Forum to the Senate House, and listen to the bitter words with which the Gothic King; rebuked the cowering Senators of Rome. He reminded them of all the benefits which they had received at the hands of Theodoric and Athalaric; how these Kings had left in their keeping all the great offices of state and had permitted them to accumulate boundless wealth; and yet after all this they had turned against their benefactors and brought Greeks into the common fatherland. "What harm did the Goths ever do you? And now tell me, what good have you ever received from Justinian the Emperor? Has he not taken away from you almost all the great offices of state? Has he not insulted and oppressed you by means of the men who are called his Logothetes? Has he not compelled you to give an account to him of every solidus which you received from the public funds even under the Gothic Kings? All harassed and impoverished as you are by the war, has he not compelled you to pay to the Greeks the full taxes which could be levied in a time of profoundest peace?". With words like these, the boldness of which astonishes us in a subject of Justinian, though he does put them into the mouth of a Gothic King, did Totila lash the wincing Senators even as an angry master scolds his slaves. Then, pointing to Herodian, the former Roman General, and to the four Isaurian deserters, "These men" he said, "strangers and aliens, have done for us what you our fellow-citizens failed to do. Herodian received us into Spoleto, the Isaurians into Rome. Wherefore they, our friends, shall be received into the places of trust and honor, and you henceforward shall be treated as slaves". Not a single Senator dared to make an answer to this torrent of upbraiding. Pelagius, however, soothed the wrath of Totila, begged him to have compassion on the fallen, and obtained from him a promise of kinder treatment than his speech had foreshadowed. The Deacon, who had evidently acquired considerable influence over the mind of Totila, was now (after solemnly swearing speedily to return) sent to Constantinople, in company with a Roman orator named Theodore, to propose terms of peace.

The letter which they bore was in the following words: "I shall keep silence about the events which have happened in the City of the Romans, because I think you will have already heard them from other quarters. But I will tell you shortly why I have sent these ambassadors. I pray you to secure for yourself and to grant to us the blessings of peace. You and I have excellent memorials and models in Anastasius and Theodoric, who reigned not long ago, and who filled their own lives and those of their subjects with peace and all prosperity. If this request should be consented to by you, I shall look upon you as a father, and gladly be your ally in whatsoever expedition you may meditate". The written courtesies of the letter were supplemented by a verbal threat, that if the Emperor would not consent to peace, the Eternal City should be razed to the ground, and Totila, with his triumphant Goths, would invade the provinces of Illyricum. The only reply, however, which Justinian deigned to make to either courtesies or threats was that Belisarius had full powers for the conduct of the war and any proposals for peace must be addressed to him.

Meanwhile the war in Lucania, under the guidance of Tullianus, who had gathered the peasants of the province round him, was being prosecuted with some vigor. Three hundred Antae, wild mountaineers from the hills of Bosnia, were holding the fastnesses of the Apennines against all comers, and successfully repulsed some followers of Totila who were sent to dislodge them. The Gothic King was desirous to transfer his operations to the South of Italy, but feared either to weaken his army by leaving a garrison in Rome, or to give Belisarius, still lying sick at Portus, the chance of recovering it if left ungarrisoned. In these circumstances, from no blind rage against the prostrate City, but simply as a matter of strategy, he decided to make it untenable and uninhabitable. He threw down large portions of the walls, so that it was roughly computed that only two-thirds of the line of defence remained standing. He was about to proceed to burn all the finest buildings in Rome, and turn the City by the Tiber into a sheep-walk, when ambassadors were announced who brought a letter from Belisarius.

"Fair cities" said the General, "are the glory of the great men who have been their founders, and surely no wise man would wish to be remembered as the destroyer of any of them. But of all cities under the sun Rome is confessed to be the greatest and the most glorious. No one man, no single century reared her greatness. A long line of kings and emperors, the united efforts of some of the noblest of men, a vast interval of time, a lavish expenditure of wealth, the most costly materials and the most skillful craftsmen of the world, have all united to make Rome. Slowly and gradually has each succeeding age there reared its monuments. Any act, therefore, of wanton outrage against that City will be resented as an injustice by all men of all ages, by those who have gone before us, because it effaces the memorials of their greatness, by those who shall come after, since the most wonderful sight in the world will be no longer theirs to look upon. Remember too, that this war must end either in the Emperor's victory or your own. If you should prove to be the conqueror, how great will be your delight in having preserved the most precious jewel of your crown. If yours should turn out to be the losing side, great will be the thanks due from the conqueror for your preservation of Rome, while its destruction would make every plea for mercy and humanity on your behalf inadmissible. And last of all comes the question what shall be your own eternal record in history, whether you will be remembered as the preserver or the destroyer of the greatest city in the world".

Belisarius, in writing this letter, had not miscalculated the temper of his antagonist. Totila read it over and over again, laid its warnings to heart, and dismissed the ambassadors with the assurance that he would do no further damage to the monuments of the Eternal City. He then withdrew the greater part of his troops to Mount Algidus, a shoulder of the high Alban mount, about twenty miles south-east of Rome, and marched himself into Lucania to prosecute the war against John and his eager ally Tullianus. The Senators had to follow in his train, unwilling hostages. Their wives and children were sent to the chief cities of Campania. Rome herself, though not ruined, was left without a single inhabitant.

The archaeologist who reads how narrowly Rome thus escaped destruction at the hands of Totila may, at first, almost regret that he was prevented from carrying his purpose into effect. There would then, so he thinks, have been one mighty conflagration, in which all that was of wood must have perished, but which the mighty walls of temple and palace would assuredly have survived. Then the City would have become a wilderness of grass-grown mounds, amid which the shepherd of the Campagna might have wandered while his goats nibbled the short grass in the halls of Emperors and Consuls. The successive sieges by Lombard, Norman, and German, the havoc wrought by ignorant feudal barons, the yet worse havoc of statue-hunting Papal Nephews, the slow but ceaseless ruin effected by the 'little citizens' of Rome, whose squalid habitations burrowed into the foundations of temple and forum and theatre, the detestable industry of the lime-kilns, which for ten centuries were perpetually burning into mortar the noblest monuments of Greek and Roman art,—all this would have been avoided, and the buried city might have lain hidden for twelve centuries, till another Layard or another Schliemann revealed its wonders to a generation capable of understanding and appreciating them.

But no: this could never have been. The religious memories which clustered around Rome were too mighty to allow of her ever being thus utterly deserted. If Rome herself in the plenitude of her power could not obliterate Jerusalem, much less could the Northern barbarians cause Rome to be forgotten. The successor of St. Peter must inevitably have come back to the tombs of the Fisherman and the Tent-maker; pilgrims from all the countries of the West must have flocked to the scenes of the saints' martyrdoms; convents and hostelries must again have risen by the Tiber; and in the course of centuries, if not of a few generations, another city, not very unlike the Rome of the Middle Ages, would have covered the space of the marble-strewn sheep-walk left by Totila.

CHAPTER XX.

THE RE-OCCUPATION OF ROME.

After the capture of Rome a space of a month or two elapsed marked by no great operations on either side. Totila, as has been said, marched into Lucania dragging the Senators in his train. By their orders the peasants (*coloni*) upon the senatorial estates laid down their arms, and Lucania was for a time recovered by the Goths. The Senators were then sent to rejoin their wives and children in the cities of Campania, where they dwelt under a strong Gothic guard. Totila pitched his camp first on the high hill of "windy Garganus" jutting out into the Adriatic Sea. Here, according to Procopius, he occupied the very same lines of entrenchment which had been defended by the troops of Hannibal during the Second Punic War.

Spoleto, which had been won by the treachery of Herodian, was lost to the Goths by the treachery of Martian, a feigned deserter who won the favour of Totila, obtained the command of the fortress which had been made out of the amphitheatre adjoining the town, and handed it over to some Imperial troops invited thither from Perugia. By the loss of this position the Goths' free use of the Flaminian Way was doubtless somewhat interfered with.

John sallied forth from his stronghold at Hydruntum and occupied Tarentum, which, though situated on the sea-coast, by its position at the head of its own gulf afforded nearer access into the heart of Apulia. He prudently narrowed his line of defence, abandoning all that part of the town which lay outside the isthmus, and here took up a position of considerable strength. Totila, as a countermove, quartered four hundred men at Acherontia, a high hill-city on the borders of Lucania and Apulia, a well-chosen position for the overawing of both provinces. He then marched away towards the north, to menace Ravenna, but was soon recalled by tidings as unwelcome as they were unexpected.

For the space of six weeks or more after its evacuation by Totila, Rome had been left, we are told, absolutely empty of inhabitants. Few comparatively of the cities and towns in her worldwide dominion had to pass through this strange experience of an absolute cessation of the life which had beat in them for centuries. This breach in the continuity of her history, short as it was, makes Rome the companion in adversity of Eburacum and Deva and the other 'waste Chesters' of England, and puts her to that extent in a different category from cities like Paris, Lyons, and we may perhaps add Augsburg and Cologne, in which the daily routine of civil life has gone on without interruption from the first or second century after Christ till modern days.

As soon as Belisarius was able to rise from the bed on which his fever had prostrated him at Portus, he was possessed with a desire to see for himself the extent of ruin at Rome; and then there gradually took shape in his mind a scheme for the recovery of the City, so bold and original that it at first seemed like a dream of delirium, but was soon recognized by those who beheld its accomplishment as a master-stroke of genius. His first reconnaissance of the City, made with only one thousand soldiers, was interfered with by the Goths from Mount Algidus, who were, however, defeated in the skirmish which followed. On his second visit, made with all the troops under his command, except a small garrison left at Portus, the march was accomplished without any such interruption. He had decided in his own mind that the rents in the line of defence made by Totila, though great, were not irreparable. All his own soldiers, and all the people from the country round who flocked into Rome, attracted both by the spell of her undying name and by the abundant market for provisions which the General immediately established there, were set to work to rebuild the breaches in the walls. There was no lime; there could be no pretence of regularity in the work. Great blocks of tufa from the old wall of Servius, where these were nigh at hand, where they were not, rubble of any kind that could be had, were thrust into the interstices. The fosse which had been dug for the first siege was fortunately still unfilled, and a rough palisade of stakes was now added to the fosse. So eagerly did all work that in the space of fifteen days the whole circuit of the walls was in some fashion or other repaired; only the gates which Totila had destroyed could not be replaced for want of skilled workmen in the City. So great and so rapid a work of national defence, accomplished by the willing labor of soldiers and citizens, had perhaps never been seen, since Dionysius in twenty days raised those mighty fortifications which we still see surrounding, but at how great a distance, the dwindled city of Syracuse.

When Totila heard the news of the re-occupation of Rome he marched thither with all the speed of anger and mortification. His army bivouacked along the banks of the Tiber, and at sunrise on the day after their arrival, with wrath and clamor attacked the defenders of the wall. The battle lasted from dawn till dark, and was fought with all the obstinacy which the one party could draw from their rage, the other from their despair. To make up for the absence of gates, Belisarius stationed all his bravest champions in the gateways, there, like Horatius, to keep the foe at bay by the might of their arms alone. His less trustworthy troops, and perhaps some of the civic population, were ranged upon the walls, and from their superior elevation dealt deadly damage on the barbarians. When night fell the besiegers withdrew from the attack, forced to confess to one another that it was a failure. While they were tending their wounded, and repairing their broken weapons, the Romans were further strengthening their defence by planting caltrops (*tribuli*) in all the gateways. These instruments, minutely described by Procopius, were made of four spikes of wood or iron, so fastened together at one end that however the *tribuli* was thrown, there would always be three of the spikes resting securely on the ground and the fourth projecting upwards—an effectual precaution, as Robert Bruce proved at Bannockburn, against a charge of hostile cavalry.

Next day the Goths again made a fierce assault, and were again repulsed. The besieged made a vigorous sally, but pursuing too far were in some danger of being surrounded and cut to pieces. They were rescued, however, by another sally ordered by Belisarius, and the barbarians retired.

Some days passed, and again the Goths rushed with fury to the walls. Again the Roman champions sallied forth—from the absence of gates it was probably hard to resist without making a sortie—and again they got the best of the conflict. The standard-bearer of Totila fell stricken by a mortal blow, and the royal ensign drooped in the dust. Then followed a Homeric combat round the dead man's body. The barbarians by a sword-stroke through the wrist succeeded in rescuing the left hand, which still grasped the standard, and was adorned with a gay armlet of gold. The rest of the body was seized and stripped of its armor by the Romans, who retired with little loss to the City, while the Goths fled in disorder.

It was too clear that Rome was indeed lost. The fateful City was again held by the invincible General, and all the past labors of the barbarians were in vain. Bitterly did the Gothic chiefs now reproach their King for not having either razed the City to the ground or occupied it in force. A few weeks before they had all been chanting the praises of the wise, the unconquered King, who took city after city from the Romans, and then marring their defenses, sprang forth again like a hero to fight in the open field. Such however, as the historian sadly remarks, is the inconsistency of human nature, and it is not likely that men will ever act more nobly.

Slowly and reluctantly did Totila leave his rival in undisputed possession of the great prize. He retreated to Tivoli, breaking down all the bridges over the Tiber to prevent Belisarius from following him. The city and citadel of Tibur which the Goths had before destroyed were now rebuilt by them, and received their arms and their treasure. If Rome could not be retaken, at least Belisarius might be kept in check from this well-placed watchtower. Possibly while the bulk of the Gothic army took up its quarters on the hill, in sight of the Sibyl's Temple and within hearing of the roar of Anio, their King may have lodged in the vast enclosure in the plain below, a city rather than a palace, which goes by the unpretending name of "the Villa of Hadrian"

Meanwhile Belisarius, free from molestation, caused gates to be prepared and fitted into the empty archways round Rome. They were bound with iron and fitted with massive locks, the keys of which were sent to Constantinople. Amid all his anxieties Justinian could once more feel himself Emperor of Rome. And so (May, 547) ended the twelfth year of the war and the third year of the second command of Belisarius.

There are times when the Muse of History seems to relax a little from the majestic calm with which she tells the story of the centuries. A smile appears to flicker round her statuesque lips as she tells of Cleon forced to go forth to war against Sphacteria, and returning, contrary to the expectation of all men, with his three hundred Spartan prisoners; of the Genoese besieging Venice, and themselves sealed up in Chioggia; of the leaders of the Fourth Crusade setting out to fight with the infidels and destroying the Christian Empire of Constantinople. With even such a quiver of amusement in her voice does she describe Belisarius slipping, like a hermit-crab, into the shattered shell of Empire which was called Rome, and making it in so few days into a fortress which he could hold against all the onsets of the angry Totila. It seems doubtful, however, whether the exploit was worth all the trouble and risk which attended it. The importance now attached to the possession of Rome was chiefly a matter of sentiment: its reoccupation had little practical effect on the fortunes of the war.

It may be fairly inferred, from the not very Roman precise information given us by Procopius, that at this time the north and centre of Italy were almost entirely in the possession of the Goths. The only exceptions appear to have been Ravenna and Ancona on the northern Adriatic, Perugia in Tuscany, Spoleto in Umbria, and Rome with her neighbor Portus. Samnium, Campania, and Northern Apulia were for the most part strongly held by the Goths. Calabria was so far dominated by the ports of Otranto and Taranto that it might be considered as a possession of the Emperor's. In Lucania, the hostile family of Venantius were perpetually endeavoring to rekindle the flames of loyalty to the Empire. Bruttii probably, and Sicily certainly, obeyed the generals of the Emperor.

One reason for the languid and desultory character of the war was the determination of the Emperor to spend no more money upon it than he could possibly help. From the slender remains of loyal Italy, Belisarius had to squeeze out the funds necessary for the support of his own army and that of John, not neglecting, it is to be feared, to add to his own stores in doing so. Another cause was the evident want of hearty co-operation between the two generals, due to the fact that one belonged to the party of Germanus and the other to that of Theodora, at the court of the Emperor. This discord between John and Belisarius was referred to with satisfaction by Totila in a long harangue which he delivered to his soldiers before marching off to form the siege of Perugia. In it he frankly admitted that he knew that they looked upon him with dissatisfaction for not having hindered the re-occupation of Rome; confessed, in substance if not in express words, that this was a blunder; but pleaded that he had not shown himself deaf to the teachings of experience, and urged that the step taken by Belisarius was one of such extreme rashness, that, though it had been justified by success, he could not, by the laws of war, have been expected to anticipate it.

Not long after this harangue the Gothic King lost his other great prize of war, the Senator-hostages in Campania. John, who had for some time been vainly besieging Acherontia, made a sudden dash into that province, marching night and day without stopping. He had reached Capua, and might have effected his purpose without bloodshed, had not Totila, with a kind of instinctive apprehension of some such design, also sent a detachment of cavalry into Campania. The Gothic horsemen, who had been marching rapidly, reached Minturnaa (close to the old frontier of Latium and Campania and about forty miles from Capua), but were in no fit state for marching further that day. The least fatigued of the horsemen—about four hundred in number—were mounted on the freshest of the horses and pushed forward to Capua, where they stumbled unawares upon the whole of John's army. In the skirmish that ensued this little band was naturally worsted. The survivors, few in number, galloped back to Minturnae, scarcely able to describe what had befallen them, but the streaming blood, the arrows yet fixed in the wounds, told the tale of defeat plainly enough. Hereupon the whole body of cavalry retreated in all haste from Minturnae, and when they reached Totila, gave him an exaggerated account of the number of the enemy, in order to excuse their own precipitancy.

John meanwhile proceeded, unhindered, to liberate the Senators and their wives from captivity. Of the senatorial ladies and their children he found the tale complete: but many of the fathers and husbands had escaped to Belisarius at Portus, and consequently needed no deliverance. There was one Roman noble, Clementinus by name, who fled to a church in Capua for refuge from the unwelcome rescuers. He feared the vengeance of the Emperor for his too ready surrender to the Goths of a fort in the neighborhood of Naples, and absolutely refused to accompany the army of John. Another Roman, Orestes by name, who had filled the office of Consul, and whom we heard of at the capture of Rome as a refugee at the altar of St. Peter's, longed to accompany the array of deliverance, but could not, being unable to find a horse to bear him to their camp. All the rescued prisoners were straightway sent to the safe harborage of Sicily, together with seventy Roman soldiers, formerly deserters to the army of Totila, who had now returned to their old allegiance.

Great was the vexation of Totila when he learned that he had lost these valuable hostages. Determining at least to be revenged, and knowing that John, who had retreated into Lucania, would carefully watch all the roads leading to his camp, he marched rapidly along the rugged heights of the Apennines, till at nightfall he was close to the camp of the enemy. He had ten thousand men with him, John but one thousand. If he could but have restrained his impatience till daybreak, he might have enclosed his enemy as in a net: but in his rage and haste he gave the signal for attack at once, and thereby lost much of the advantage of his superiority in numbers. About a hundred of the Romans were slain, some of them still only half-awake, but the rest escaped. Among the latter were John and the Herulian chief Arufus, who seems to have been his right hand in this enterprise. Among the few prisoners was an Armenian general, Gilacius by name, who, though in the service of the Emperor, knew no tongue but his native Armenian. The soldiers, fearful in the confusion of the night of killing one of their own friends, asked him who he was, to which he could make no reply but *Gilacius Strategos* (Gilacius the General), over and over again repeated. By often hearing the honorable title *Strategos*, he had just succeeded in learning the name of his own dignity. The Goths, who soon perceived that he was no officer of theirs, took him prisoner; and we regret to find that, not many days after, the unfortunate Oriental, who knew neither the Greek nor the Latin nor the Gothic language was put to death by his Teutonic captors. John with the reremains of his army succeeded in reaching Otranto, and again shut himself up in that stronghold.

For two years after this skirmish no event of great importance occurred, but, as far as we can judge from the not very lucid narrative of Procopius,. the Imperial cause slowly receded. Justinian sent indeed fresh troops to Italy, but only in driblets, and commanded by incapable generals. Incapable through want of self-restraint was the fierce Herulian Verus, who was constantly in a state of intoxication. He landed at Otranto, marched with his three hundred followers to Brindisi, and encamped near to that town. Seeing his force thus encamped in an undefended position, Totila exclaimed, "One of two things must be true. Either Verus has a large army, or he is a very unwise man. Let us go, either to make trial of his strength or to punish him for his folly". He advanced, easily routed the little band commanded by thedrunken Herulian, and would have driven them into the sea but for the sudden and accidental appearance of Byzantine ships in the offing, bearing Warazes and eight hundred Armenians.

Incapable, from utter lack of courage and every soldierly quality, was Valerian, who had held the high post of *Magister Militum* in Armenia, but was transferred to Italy with more than one thousand men to cooperate with John and Belisarius. He lingered for months at Salona, afraid of the storms of the Adriatic. Then, when a council of war was held at Otranto, and a march northwards into Picenum was resolved upon, he would not face the perils and hardships of the march, but took ship again and sailed tranquilly to Imperialist Ancona, where he shut himself up and hoped for better days. Evidently he was one of those generals whose chief care is to keep their own persons out of the stress of battle.

The only interest of these two campaigns lies in the defence of Roscianum (now Rossano). The story of this place takes us back—it is true, by a circuitous route—to the very dawn of Hellenic history. At the westernmost angle of that deep hollow in the foot of Italy which is named the Gulf of Tarentum stood, in the eighth century before the Christian era, the mighty Achaian city of Sybaris. The wealth derived from the splendid fertility of her soil (though now her ruins lie hidden in a fever-haunted morass), as well as from a profitable commerce with the shepherds on the Apennines behind their city, enabled the aristocrats of Sybaris early to acquire that reputation for unbounded luxury which has made their name proverbial. It was Smindyrides, a citizen of Sybaris, who was the first utterer of the complaint concerning the crumpled rose-leaf in his bed, and who declared that the sight of a peasant working in the fields overwhelmed him with fatigue. The neighbor and rival of Sybaris was the city, also populous and powerful, of Crotona, which stood at the south-east angle of the Gulf of Tarentum. Thither, in the sixth century before Christ, fled the languid aristocrats of Sybaris, expelled by a popular rising, and by a tyrant the child of revolution. That tyrant, Telys, insolently demanded the surrender of his enemies, but the demand was refused by the citizens of Crotona, trembling indeed before the power of Sybaris, but nerved to great deeds in the cause of hospitality by the exhortations of their guide and philosopher, Pythagoras. In the battle which ensued, the multitudinous host of the Sybarites was defeated by the army of the southern city, commanded by the mighty Milo of Crotona, famous for ever as an athlete, and yet also a disciple of Pythagoras. The Crotoniates advanced, sacked the rival city, and, so it is said, turned the river Crathis over its ruins, that none might know where Sybaris had stood.

All this happened in the year 510 BC, the same year in which, according to tradition, the Tarquins were driven from Rome.

Nearly seventy years later (BC 443) the Athenians, on the earnest entreaty of the descendants of the Sybarites, sent a colony to the desolate spot; and in the near neighborhood of the obliterated city rose the new settlement of Thurii, best known in history from the fact that Herodotus was one of its original colonists and spent his old age within its walls. But either because the mouth of the river Crathis had become unnavigable, or for some other reason, it had been found necessary to establish the docks and harbor of Thurii close to the promontory of Roscia, twelve miles south of the old city. In the hills, some seven or eight miles west of these docks, the Romans built a strong fortress which bore the name of Roscianum, and is represented by the modern city of Rossano, with an archbishop and twelve thousand inhabitants.

In Roscianum was now collected a considerable number of wealthy and noble Italians, refugees from that part of Italy which was occupied by the barbarians. Conspicuous among them was Deopheron, son of Venantius and brother of Tullianus, a member of a family animated by bitter hostility to the Gothic rule. John had sent from his army for the defence of Roscianum three hundred Illyrians, under the command of Chalazar the Hun, an excellent soldier, who seems to have been recognized as head over the whole garrison. Belisarius had only been able to spare one hundred foot-soldiers for the same service.

Early in 548 Belisarius, who with his martial wife had sailed round to Crotona, sent a further detachment of soldiers to relieve Roscianum. They met, apparently by accident, a smaller force sent by Totila to attack it. In the skirmish which followed the Goths were completely defeated and fled, leaving two hundred of their number dead upon the plain. While the victors were lapped in all the security of success, leaving the passes unguarded, pitching their tents wide at night, and wandering afar for forage by day, suddenly Totila, with three thousand men, burst upon them from the mountains. Vain was the might of Phazas, the brave Iberian from Caucasus, upon whose quarters the blow first descended, to turn the tide of battle. He fell fighting bravely in the midst of a band of heroes. Much fear came upon the Romans when they knew him to be dead, for they had expected great exploits from him in the future. Barbatian, one of the body-guard of Belisarius, who had shared the command with Phazas, fled with two of his comrades from the field, and brought the grievous news to his master. Belisarius, who seems to have been alarmed for the safety of Crotona itself, leaped on shipboard, probably Antonina accompanied him, and sailed for Messina, which, so fair was the wind, he reached in one day, though distant ninety miles from Crotona.

Hard pressed by Totila after this ineffectual attempt to relieve them, the garrison at length agreed to surrender Roscianum if no help should reach them by the middle of summer (548). The appointed day had just dawned, when they saw on the horizon the friendly sails of the Byzantine ships. Belisarius, John, and Valerian had met in council at Otranto, and had decided to send a fleet to the help of the beleaguered city. The hopes of the garrison being raised by this sight, they refused to fulfill their compact. A storm, however, arose, which the captain dared not face on that rock-bound coast, and the ships returned to Crotona. Many weeks passed, and again the Byzantine ships appeared in the offing. The barbarians leaped upon their horses and moved briskly along the shore, determined to dispute the landing. Totila placed his spearmen here, his bowmen there, and left not a spot unoccupied where the enemy could land. At that sight the Romans' eagerness for the fight vanished. They let down their anchors; they hovered about, beholding the docks and Roscianum from afar: at length they weighed anchor and sailed back to Crotona.

Another council of war was held. The generals resolved to try to effect a diversion. Belisarius was to revictual Rome, the others were to march into Picenum and attack the besieging armies there. It was upon this occasion that Valerian distinguished himself by not marching, but sailing to the friendly shelter of Ancona. But all these operations were in vain. Totila refused to be diverted from the siege of Roscianum; and the unfortunate garrison, who had only been tantalized by all the attempts to succor them, sent Deopheron and a Thracian life-guardsman of Belisarius named Gudilas to cry for Totila's mercy on their unfaithfulness. To Chalazar the Hun, whom he looked upon as the chief deceiver, the King showed himself unpitying. He cut off both his hands and inflicted on him other shameful mutilations before he deprived him of life. The rest of the garrison were admitted to the benefit of the old capitulation. The lives of all, and the property of as many as chose to accept service under the Gothic standard, were left uninjured. The result was that all the late defenders of Roscianum, but eighty, gladly enlisted with the barbarians. The eighty loyal soldiers made their way in honorable poverty to Crotona. Not one of the Italian nobles lost his life, but the property of all was taken from them.

Belisarius had now been for more than four years in Italy, and, chiefly on account of the miserable manner in which his efforts had been seconded by his master, he had but a poor account to render of his exploits during that time. "He had never really grasped the land of Italy during this second command" says Procopius, who cannot forgive the triumph of Antonina, and who seems to delight in trampling on the fragments of his broken idol. "He never made a single regular march by land, but skulked about from fortress to fortress, stealing from one point of the coast to another like a fugitive; and thus he really gave the enemy boldness to capture Rome, and one might almost say the whole country". His one really brilliant exploit, the re-occupation of Rome, had not, as we have seen, materially affected the fortunes of the war. It was time certainly that he should either be enabled to achieve something greater, or else quit Italy altogether. Antonina accordingly set out for Constantinople to obtain from her patroness an assurance of more effectual succor than the Imperial cause in Italy had yet received. When she arrived she found that an event had occurred which changed the whole aspect of affairs at the court of Justinian. On the 1st of July, 548, Theodora, the beautiful and the remorseless, died, after a little more than twenty-one years of empire. When we read that the cause of her death was cancer, of an exceptionally virulent type, even our remembrance of the misdeeds of Theodora is well-nigh swallowed up in pity for her fate.

Antonina, on arriving at Constantinople and hearing of the death of her Imperial friend, once decided on the necessary changes in her tactics. For the last six or seven years tedious negotiations had been carried on between the two ladies for the marriage of a grandson of Theodora with Joannina, only child of Belisarius, and heiress of all his vast wealth Long had Antonina, while seeming to consent to this match, secretly opposed it. And now, though her daughter's heart was entirely given to her young betrothed, perhaps even her honor surrendered to him, the cold schemer relentlessly broke off the engagement. We hear nothing more of the fate of either of the lovers; but it seems probable that the daughter of Belisarius died before her father.

As for the Italian expedition, Antonina recognized the impossibility of now obtaining from the parsimonious Emperor the supplies of men and money without which success was impossible. Germanus, noblest and most virtuous of all the Emperor's nephews, would be now indisputably the second person in the state, and if any laurels were to be gathered in Italy they would without doubt be destined for him. She confined herself therefore to petitioning the Emperor for the lesser boon of the recall of her husband, and this favor was granted to her. Early in the year 549 Belisarius returned to Constantinople, with wealth much increased but glory somewhat tarnished by the events of those five years of his second command.

Justinian, upon whom the hand of Chosroes was at that time pressing heavily, had some thought of employing him again in the Persian War, but though he was named Master of the Soldiery *per Orientem* we find no evidence of his having again taken the field for that enterprise. He also held the rank of general of the household troops and he took precedence of all other Consuls and Patricians, even those who had held these dignities for a longer period than himself.

To end our notice of the career of the great General it will be necessary to travel a little beyond the period properly covered by this volume. In the year 559 great alarm was created in the provinces of Moesia and Thrace by the tidings that the Kotrigur Huns had crossed the frozen Danube. What relation the tribe who were called by this uncouth name may have borne to the countrymen of Attila it might be difficult to say. They seem to have acknowledged a closer kinship with the Utigur Huns who dwelt alongside of them north of the Danube than with any other race of barbarians; but the attitude of the two clans to one another was not friendly, and the favor shown by the authorities at Constantinople to the Romanizing Utigurs was one of the pretexts upon which the more savage Kotrigurs took up arms against the Empire.

Under the command of their King Zabergan the horde of savage horsemen swept across the ill-defended plains of Moesia and through the Balkan passes into Thrace. Thence, like Alaric of old, Zabergan sent one division of his army southwards to the cities of Greece, the inhabitants of which were dwelling in fancied security. Another division ravaged the Chersonese, and hoped to effect a passage into Asia. The third division dared to move towards the Imperial City itself. To their own astonishment doubtless they found their progress practically unopposed. The wall of Anastasius, the breakwater which has so often turned back the tide of barbaric invasion, was not at this time in a state capable of defence. Earthquakes had leveled parts of it with the ground, and the Emperor, who had dispatched conquering expeditions to Carthage and Rome, and imposed his theological definitions on a General Council, wanted either the leisure or the money needful for the obvious duty of repairing this line of fortifications. Over the crumbling heaps pressed King Zabergan and his seven thousand horsemen. Wherever they went they spread terror and desolation. Two captives of illustrious rank fell into their hands,—Sergius, the *Magister Militum per Thracias*, and Ederman, son of that Grand Chamberlain Calopodius whose name twenty-seven years before had been uttered with shouts of execration by the Green party in the Hippodrome at Constantinople. On the ordinary inhabitants of this district—the Rome Counties as we should say of the Byzantine Empire—the hand of these savage spoilers fell very heavily. A vast crowd of captives were dragged about with them in their wanderings. Nuns torn from the convent had to undergo the last extremity of outrage from their brutal conquerors. Pregnant women, when the hour of their distress came upon them, had to bring forth their little ones on the highway, untended, unpitied, and unsheltered from the gaze of the barbarians. The children born in these terrible days were left naked on the road as the squalid host moved on to some fresh scene of devastation, and were a prey to dogs and vultures.

Amid such scenes of terror the savage Kotrigurs reached the little village of Melantias on the river Athyras, eighteen miles from Constantinople, a point on the road to Hadrianople about seven miles further from the capital than the celebrated suburb of San Stefano, to which in our own time the invaders from across the Danube penetrated. There was universal terror and dismay in the sovereign city, and men eagerly asked one another what force there was to resist the invader. The mighty armies of the Empire, which in her prosperous days had amounted to six hundred and forty-five thousand men, had dwindled in the time of Justinian to one hundred and fifty thousand. And of this diminished force some were in Italy, some in Spain; some were watching the defiles of the Caucasus, and some were keeping down the Monophysites in Alexandria. The number of real fighting men available for the defence of the capital was so small as to be absolutely contemptible. There Swas, however, a body of men, the so-called *Scholarii*, the Household Troops of the Empire, who, like the life-guards of a modern sovereign, should have been available for the defence not only of the palace, but of the capital also. But eighty years of indiscipline had ruined the efficiency of a body of troops which under Theodosius and his sons had contained many men, of barbarian origin indeed, but the bravest soldiers in the army. Zeno, we are told, had commenced the downward course by filling the ranks of the *Scholarii* entirely with his own pampered Isaurian countrymen. Since then the process of decay had continued. To wear the gorgeous costume of a *scholarius*, to have access to the palace, and to be employed about the person of the Emperor had seemed so desirable to the rich citizens of Constantinople that they had offered large sums to have their names entered on the muster-rolls. The Emperors, especially Justinian, hard pressed for money, had gladly caught at this means of replenishing their coffers: and thus it came to pass that at this crisis of the nation's need a number of splendidly-dressed luxurious citizen-soldiers, entirely unused to the hardships and the exercises of war, were, with one exception, all that could be relied upon to beat back the wild hordes of Zabergan.

That exception was a little body of veterans, not more than three hundred in number, who had served under Belisarius in Italy. To them and to their glorious commander all eyes were now turned. The Emperor, now probably in the seventy-seventh year of his age, and no longer sustained by the proud spirit of the indomitable Theodora, was seized, apparently, with such fear as had prostrated him during the insurrection of the Nika. He gave orders that all the vessels of gold and silver should be stripped from the churches in the suburbs and carried within the City. He bade the *Scholarii*, and even the Senators themselves, assemble behind the gates of the wall with which Theodosius II had encompassed Constantinople. And, last mark of the extremity of his fear, he consented to invest Belisarius with the supreme command, notwithstanding the unslumbering jealousy with which he regarded the greatest of his servants.

Belisarius, who seems, notwithstanding his illustrious offices, to have been virtually living in retirement since his return from Italy, accepted the charge laid upon him and donned the breastplate and helmet which had been for ten years unworn. Though still only in middle life (for, if our computation of his birth-year be correct, he was but fifty-four, and he cannot possibly have been more than two or three years older), he seemed to those around him already outworn with age. The terrible anxieties of even his most triumphant campaigns, the strain of the long siege of Rome, the fever at Portus, above all the exquisite misery of the quarrel with Antonina, had aged him before his time.

But with the familiar sensation of the helmet and the breastplate worn once more came back much of the martial energy of former days. Leaving perhaps the dainty *Scholarii* to man the walls of Constantinople, he went forth with his three hundred veterans, with all the horses that he could collect from the Circus and from the Imperial stables, and with a crowd of rustics eager to taste what they supposed to be the pleasures of war under the command of the unconquered Belisarius. The General accepted their service, determining to avail himself of their numbers to strike terror into the enemy, but to give them no chance of actually mingling in the fray. He pitched his camp at the village of Chettus, bade the peasants draw a deep ditch round it, and, as of old at the relief of Rimini, kindled his watch-fires on as broad a line as possible, that the barbarians might form an exaggerated idea of his numbers. Seeing that his veterans were indulging in too contemptuous an estimate of their enemy, and already counting the victory as won, he addressed them in a military harangue, in which he explained that while he fully shared their conviction that victory was possible, it was so only on the condition of strict obedience to his orders. Nothing but Roman discipline strictly observed could enable their little band to triumph over the savage hosts of Zabergan.

Still intent on deceiving the enemy as much as possible, he ordered his rustic followers to cut down trees and trail them about in the rear of every column of his troops, so raising a cloud of dust which masked their movements, and gave them the appearance of a mighty multitude. Then, when two thousand of Zabergan's horsemen advanced towards him, by a skillful disposition of his archers in an adjoining wood, he so galled the enemy with a well-directed shower of arrows on both flanks, that he compelled them to narrow their front and charge him at that part of his line where he knew that his hardy veterans would repel them. And during the whole time of the engagement the rustics and the citizens of Constantinople were ordered, not to fight, but to keep up such a shouting and such a clash of arms against one another as might convey to the minds of the barbarians the idea that a desperate encounter was going on somewhere near them.

These tactics, quaint and almost childish as they victory seem to us, proved successful. The advancing Huns were vigorously repulsed by the handful of Italian veterans; they were dismayed by the shouting and the clash of arms; they turned to fly, and in flight forgot their Parthian-like accomplishment of discharging arrows at a pursuing foe. Belisarius did not dare to follow them far lest he should reveal the weakness of his little band; but four hundred slaughtered Huns, and the hot haste in which Zabergan returned to his camp, sufficiently showed that victory rested with the Imperial troops. Constantinople at any rate was saved. The Huns marched back to the other side of the wall of Anastasius, and renounced the hope of penetrating to the capital. The victory might have been made a decisive one had Belisarius been continued in the command, but as soon as Constantinople was delivered from its pressing danger, that jealousy of the great General, which had become a second nature with the aged Emperor, resumed its sway. Belisarius was curtly and ungraciously ordered to return to the City, and the Kotrigurs, as soon as they heard that he was no longer with the army, ceased to retreat. The rest of the Hunnish campaign need not here be described. It was ended by the payment of a large sum of money by Justinian, nominally as ransom for Sergius and the other captives, but really as a bribe to induce the Kotrigurs to return to their old haunts by the Danube. Their hostile kinsmen the Utigurs fell upon them in their homeward march, and inflicted upon them such grievous slaughter that they never after ventured on an invasion of the Empire. Both of these offshoots of the great Hunnish stock were in fact soon uprooted and destroyed by the irruption of the terrible Avars.

Belisarius on his return to Constantinople was hailed with shouts-of joy by the common people, who beheld in him their deliverer from all the horrors of barbarian capture. For a little time his appearance in the streets and in the Forum was as veritable a triumph as when he returned from the siege of Ravenna. Soon, however, the jealous temper of the sovereign, the calumnies of the courtiers, the envy of the nobles, who seem never to have been reconciled to his rapid elevation, prevailed over the enthusiasm of the populace, and Belisarius became again, as he had been for ten years previously, a man who, though possessed of wealth, of renown, and of nominal rank, was devoid of any real influence in State affairs.

Three years after his victory over Zabergan, Belisarius was accused& of connivance at a conspiracy against the life of Justinian. The conspiracy, which was set on foot by one Sergius, (a person of obscure rank, and not to be confounded with the *Magister Militum* who had been taken captive by the Huns), was apparently an affair of no political importance, a mere villainous scheme to murder a venerable old man during his siesta : and being revealed by a loquacious confederate to an officer of the Imperial house-hold, was suppressed without difficulty. In their fall, however, the detected murderers endeavored to drag down the great General. They declared that Belisarius himself had been aware of the existence of the conspiracy, and that his steward, Paulus by name, had taken an active part in their deliberations. The accused men being arrested, and probably put to the torture, confessed that Belisarius was privy to the plot. On the fifth of December the Emperor convoked a meeting of the Senate, to which he proceeded in state, accompanied by the Patriarch Eutychius. He ordered the confessions to be read in the presence of the assembly. Belisarius, on hearing himself accused, showed not so much of indignation as of misery and self-abasement. Justinian, though his anger was hot against the accused General, suffered him to live, but took away his guards and his large retinue of servants, and ordered him to remain in his house under surveillance. This state of things lasted for seven months. On the nineteenth of July in the following year the veteran General was restored to all his former honors and emoluments, and received again into the favor of Justinian, who had probably satisfied himself that the accusation which he had previously believed was a mere calumny invented by ruined and desperate men.

Nearly two years after this, Belisarius died, preceding his jealous master to the grave by about eight months. His wife Antonina, according to one late and doubtful authority, also survived him, but retired after his death into religious seclusion. His property, that vast wealth for the sake of which he had endured so much humiliation and allowed so many stains to rest on his glory, was appropriated, perhaps after the death of his widow, to the necessities of the Imperial Treasury.

Such, as far as we can now ascertain it, is apparently the true story of the disgrace of Belisarius and his final restoration to the favor of Justinian. But another story, that which represents him as blinded and reduced to beggary, and sitting as a mendicant at the gates of Constantinople, or even of Rome, has obtained very wide currency, partly through the genius of Marmontel, who naturally laid hold of so striking a reverse of fortune to give point to the romance of *Belisaire*. The authority for this story is of the poorest kind, and dates only from the eleventh or twelfth century. It is a very probable suggestion that in the five or six hundred years which intervened between the hero's death and the first appearance of this story in literature, popular tradition had confounded his reverses with those of his contemporary John of Cappadocia, who was really reduced to beggary, but not to blindness. Yet the idea of so terrible a fall from so splendid a position has fastened itself too deeply in the popular mind to be ever really eradicated, let it be disproved as often as it may. In the future, as in the past, for one reader who knows of the capture of Gelimer or the marvelous defence of Rome, there will be ten who associate the great General's name with the thought of a blind beggar holding a wooden box before him, and crying in pathetic tones "*Date obolum Belisario'*

CHAPTER XXI.

THE THIRD SIEGE OF ROME.

Belisarius left the Imperial cause in Italy capture of in a miserable condition. The garrison of Perugia, who for three years and more, notwithstanding the murder of the gallant Cyprian had resisted the arms and the solicitations of Totila, were now overmastered, and before Belisarius reached Constantinople that high Etrurian fortress, taken by storm, not yielding to a surrender, had passed into the power of the Goths.

At Rome, the soldiers who had been placed in charge of the recovered City, with long arrears of pay due to them from the treasury, could endure no longer the spectacle of Isaurian Conon, their commandant, renewing as they believed the greedy game of the corn-traffic by which he and Bessas had enriched themselves during the second siege, and thus thriving upon their misery. Having risen in mutiny and slain their general they sent some of the Roman clergy as their ambassadors to Constantinople, claiming a full amnesty for their crime and discharge of the arrears of pay due to them from the State. Should these demands not be complied with, they declared that they would at once surrender the City to the Goths. Of course the Emperor had no choice but to comply, and to promise to pay from his exhausted treasury the money kept back by fraud and reclaimed by massacre.

This mutiny occurred several months before the recall of Belisarius. Now, after that event, Totila began to press the garrison of Rome more vigorously than he had done for the past two years. The cause which suddenly endowed the ancient capital of the world with so great importance in his eyes was a singular one, namely, his suit for the hand of a Frankish princess. Ever since the death of Clovis, and preeminently since the break of the Gothic war, the Frankish Kings had been advancing steadily towards a position of greater legitimacy than any of the other barbarian royalties; and this pretension of theirs had been upon the whole acquiesced in by the Eastern Emperor, anxious above all things to prevent the weight of the Frankish battle-axe from being thrown into the scale of his enemies. Thus Justinian had formally sanctioned the cession made by the Ostrogoths of the south-east corner of Gaul to the Franks, and in doing so must inevitably have waived any shadow of claim which the Empire might still have been supposed to possess to the remaining nine-tenths of Gaul, the territory wrested from Syagrius, Alaric, and Godomar. Secure in this Imperial recognition of their rights and in the loyal support which, as professors of the Athanasian form of Christianity, they received from the Catholic clergy, the Frankish partnership of kings clothed the substance of their power with more of the form of independent sovereignty than any of the Teutonic conquerors, whether at Toulouse or at Ravenna, had yet cared, or dared, to assume. Sitting in the Emperor's seat in the lordly amphitheatre of Arles, the long-haired Merwing watched the chariot-race and received the loyal acclamations of the people. Now too the sons of Clovis began to coin golden money bearing their own image and superscription, whereas hitherto all the barbarian monarchs (including, says Procopius, even the King of Persia himself) had been content to see their effigy on coins of silver, while upon the *solidi* of the nobler metal appeared the rude resemblance of the Caesar of Byzantium. It is singular to find already working in the middle of the sixth century a thought as to the superior legitimacy of Frankish conquest, which was not to bear fruit in visible deeds till two hundred and fifty years later, when Frankish Charles was hailed by the people of Rome as Imperator and Augustus.

While these ideas of a right, in some way differing from the mere right of conquest, were working in the minds of the bishops and counselors of the Frankish Courts, came Totila's messengers to one of the kings of the Franks, probably Theudebert of Metz, asking on behalf of their master for his daughter's hand in marriage. The Frankish King refused the request, saying that that man neither was nor would ever be King of Italy who, having once been in possession of Rome, could not hold it, but destroyed a part of the city and abandoned the rest to his enemies. What became of Totila's matrimonial suit in after days we know not: but at any rate the taunt stung him to the quick, and he determined that the world should recognize him as master not only of Italy, but of Rome.

The garrison of Rome now consisted of three thousand picked soldiers commanded by Diogenes, one of the military household of Belisarius, who had distinguished himself in sallies and on the battlements during the first siege of Borne. Under his able generalship the utmost force of the garrison was put forth to repel the foe. Assault after assault was repulsed, and the baffled Totila was obliged to convert the siege into a blockade. Having taken Porto, he was able to make this blockade more rigorous than any which had preceded it. On the other hand, in the very depth of her recent fall, the Eternal City found a new source of safety. Diogenes had sown great breadths of land within the walls with corn. The great City, once brimming over with human life and filled in Horace's days with the babble of all human tongues, was now a little, well-ordered, and prosperous farm. In the summer of 549, when Totila stood before her walls, the golden ears were waving to the wind on the heights of the lordly Palatine and along the by-ways of the crowded Suburra.

Notwithstanding this advantage, however, the desperate bankruptcy of Justinian's government played the game of Totila. Either the arrears stipulated for by the murderers of Conon had not been sent, or they had not been fairly divided among the soldiers. The little band of Isaurians who kept guard at the Porta San Paolo (the archway which spans the road to Ostia) deeply resented the withholding of their pay, which, as they declared, was now several years in arrears. Deeply too had sunk into their hearts the story of the splendid rewards given by Totila to those of their countrymen who three years before had betrayed the City to the Goths. Even now from the walls they could see these men arrayed in splendid armor riding side by side with the Gothic captains. Accordingly they opened secret negotiations with the besiegers, and promised on a certain night to open the Gate of St. Paul. Totila, who knew that he could reckon on no such sleepy supineness among the besieged as had enabled him to effect his previous entry, resorted to a stratagem. When the fated night came, he put a party of trumpeters on board two little boats, and ordered them, before the first watch was over, to creep up the river and blow a loud blast from their trumpets as near as possible to the centre of the City. They did so. The Romans, not doubting that an attack was being made by the way of the river (perhaps just below the northern end of the Aventine Mount), left their various posts and all hurried to the threatened quarter. Meanwhile the Isaurian deserters opened the Pauline opened to Gate, and the Gothic host, without trouble or loss of life, found themselves once more inside the City.

Of the garrison, many were slain by the Gothic soldiers in the streets, some fled northwards and eastwards, and succeeded in escaping from the sword of the barbarians; some, probably the most warlike of the host, headed by the brave Diogenes, rushed forth by the Porta San Pancrazio and along the Aurelian Way, hoping to reinforce the garrison which at Centumcellae (Civita Vecchia) was defending the last stronghold now left to the Empire in Central Italy. Totila, who anticipated this movement, had stationed a party of his best warriors in ambush on this road. The fugitives rushed headlong into the snare, and a fearful slaughter of them followed, from which only a very few escaped to Civita Vecchia. Among the few, however, was he whom Totila most desired to capture, their valiant leader Diogenes.

One of the bravest soldiers, first of Belisarius and then of Diogenes, a cavalry officer named Paul (who like his great namesake was a native of the province of Cilicia), collected a band of four hundred horsemen, and with them occupied the Tomb of Hadrian and the bridge of St. Peter which was commanded by it. Statueless, battered by the storm of war, and bereft of nearly all its Imperial adornment, but still

> 'A tower of strength
> That stood four-square to every wind that blew'

rose the mighty Mausoleum. As soon as day dawned, the Goths advanced to the attack of the fortress, but owing to the peculiar character of the ground, could effect nothing, and perished by handfuls in the narrow approaches, where their crowded masses were exposed without cover to the shower of the Roman missiles. Seeing this, Totila at once called off his men, forbade all direct assault upon the Tomb, and gave orders to wait the surer work of hunger. Through the rest of that day and the following night the gallant followers of Paul remained without food. The next day they determined to kill some of the horses and feed upon their flesh; but repugnance to the strange banquet kept them till twilight still unfed. Then they said one to another, "Were it not better to die gloriously than to linger on here in misery, and surrender after all?" They resolved accordingly to burst forth suddenly upon the besiegers, to slay as many of them as possible, and die, if they must die, in the thick of the battle. These strong men then, with sudden emotion, twined their arms around one another, and kissed one another's faces with the death-kiss, as knowing that they must all straightway perish. Totila, seeing these gestures from afar and reading their import, sent to offer honorable terms of surrender. Either the garrison might depart unharmed to Constantinople, leaving their horses and arms behind them, and having taken an oath never again to serve against the Goths; or, if they preferred to keep their military possessions, and would enter his service, they should be treated in all things as the equals of their conquerors and new comrades. The despairing soldiers heard this message with delight. At first they were all for returning to Constantinople: then when they bethought them of the shame and the danger of returning unarmed and on foot over all the wide lands that intervened between them and the Emperor, and remembered how that Emperor had broken his share of the compact by leaving their pay so long in arrear, they changed their minds and elected to serve under the standards of the gallant Totila. Only two men remained faithful to the Emperor, Paul himself, and Mindes the Isaurian. They sought the King's presence and said, "We have wives and children in our native land, and without them it is not possible for us to live. Send us therefore to Byzantium". Totila knew them for true men, and giving them an escort and necessaries for the journey, started them on their road. There were still three hundred Roman soldiers, refugees at the various altars in the City. To them also Totila offered the same terms, and all accepted service under him.

There was no talk now of destroying, but only of keeping and embellishing Rome. Totila caused abundance of provisions to be brought into the City. The scattered remnants of the Senatorial families were brought back from their Campanian exile and bidden to inhabit their old homes without fear. As many as possible of the buildings which he himself had hewn down and burned with fire were raised up again. And when the Gothic King sat in the podium of the Circus Maximus, dressed in his royal robes, and gave the signal for the charioteers to start from the twelve *ostia*, he doubtless remembered the taunt of the Frankish King, and felt with pardonable triumph that he was now at least undoubted King of Italy.

Totila then sent a Roman citizen named Stephen to Constantinople to propose terms of peace and alliance between the two nations, which had now been for near fifteen years engaged in deadly struggle: but the Emperor, immersed in theology and still unwilling to own himself defeated, did not even admit the ambassador to an interview. On hearing of this rebuff Totila marched first to Centumcellae and summoned it to surrender, offering the garrison the same terms which had been granted to the defenders of Hadrian's Tomb. Diogenes replied that it was not consistent with his honor to surrender the stronghold entrusted to him, for so little cause shown, but that if by a given day he had received no succors from his master, Centumcellae should be evacuated. Thirty hostages were given on each side for the fulfillment of this compact, the Goths being bound not to attack during the stipulated interval, and the Romans not to defend beyond it; and then the Gothic army, accompanied by the Gothic fleet, consisting of four hundred cutters and many larger vessels captured from the Imperialists, moved off to the south.

Vengeance upon ungrateful Sicily was the great desire of Totila's heart, as it had been three years before when he forbade the Roman deacon Pelagius even to name her pardon. Some work, however, had yet to be done on the mainland. Reggio, which was under the command of Thorimuth, one of the former defenders of Osimo, was assaulted, but so bravely defended that the siege had to be turned into a blockade. Tarentum was easily taken. In the north, Rimini, once so stubbornly defended by John, was now betrayed into the hands of the Goths. From Ravenna, Verus the Herulian, whose drunken hardihood had once moved the mirth of Totila, made another of his wild sorties, in which he fell with many of his followers.

Just at the end of 549, or the beginning of 550, Reggio fell, the garrison being compelled by famine to surrender. Even before this town, nearly the last stronghold left to the Empire in Southern Italy, had been won, Totila had crossed the Straits of Messina into Sicily. His campaign here was one of plunder rather than conquest. All the chief cities of the island, Messina, Syracuse, Palermo, seem to have resisted his arms; and only four fortresses, the names of which are not given, submitted to him. But far and wide through the island the villas of the Roman nobles bore witness to the invader's presence. The whole of the year 550 and (apparently) part of 551 were occupied by these devastations. At the end of that interval the King, collecting all his booty, large troops of horses and herds of cattle, stores of grain, fruit, and every other kind of produce of which he had despoiled the Sicilians, loaded his ships with the plunder and returned to Italy. It was said that he had been partly persuaded to to abandon Sicily by his own Quaestor, a citizen of Spoleto named Spinus, who had the misfortune to be taken prisoner at Catana. This man, of Roman, not Gothic kin, persuaded his captors to consent to his being exchanged for a noble Roman lady who had fallen into Totila's hands. They at first scouted the idea of so unequal a bargain, but consented upon his promising to do his best to induce Totila to depart from the island. On being liberated he painted to his master in lively colors the danger that the Imperial armament then assembling on the other side of the Adriatic might make a sudden swoop upon the coast in the neighborhood of Genoa and carry off the Gothic women and children tranquilly abiding in those northern regions and supposed to be out of the reach of war. Totila listened to the advice, which was probably sound enough, with whatever motive given, and desisting from his work of plunder, returned to his true base of operations in Italy, leaving garrisons in his four Sicilian fortresses.

Meantime the appointed day for the surrender Diogenes of Centumcellae had come and gone. Diogenes hearing, as everyone else in Italy had heard, rumors of the great army collected in Dalmatia under the Emperor's nephew Germanus, considered himself absolved from his promise, and refused to surrender the Mediterranean fortress. The thirty hostages who had been mutually given and received, returned in safety to their friends. Of the further fortunes of the valiant governor we have no information. Centumcellae was certainly surrendered to the Goths, probably not later than the spring of 551: but Procopius has omitted to tell us the story of its final surrender and to inform us—what we would gladly have known—whether Diogenes experienced the generosity or the hot wrath of Totila.

All these expectations, however, of help from Byzantium were for the present disappointed. Belisarius was recalled, as we have seen, early in 549. During all the rest of that year and the next, and until the middle of 551, nothing effectual was done for the relief of the Italians, who were still loyal to the Empire. Strange weakness and vacillation marked the counsels of the Emperor. The elderly Patrician Liberius, formerly ambassador from Theodahad to Justinian, a man of pure and upright character but quite unversed in war, was appointed to the command of the relieving army. Then his appointment was cancelled. Some months afterwards he was again appointed, and actually set sail for Syracuse, where he succeeded in effecting some temporary relief for the city, straitly besieged by the Goths. He had accomplished this work, and had sailed away to Palermo, before he learned that the wavering Emperor had again revoked his commission and entrusted the command of the Sicilian army to Artabanes the Armenian prince, though, as we shall shortly see, he had little reason for trusting his loyalty. The ships of Artabanes were dispersed by a fierce storm while they were rounding the promontories of Calabria, but the General himself with one ship succeeded in making his way through the tumultuous seas to the island of Malta.

Then for a time all other names were merged in the renown of Germanus, the nephew of Justinian, who collected a great army at Sardica, and from whom all men either hoped or feared a triumphant ending to the Italian war. How these expectations were disappointed, and what were some of the causes of the strange but not inexplicable vacillation of Justinian during these years of Totila's victorious progress, must be told in the next chapter.

CHAPTER XXII.

THE EXPEDITION OF GERMANUS.

The noblest and probably the eldest-born of the character nephews of the childless Emperor, he who, as far as anyone could be said to inherit in an elective monarchy, might be called the heir-presumptive of Justinian, was Germanus. An active and warlike general, he had struck terror into the Slavonian marauders by the striking success of his campaign against them in the year of his uncle's accession. He had afterwards, as we have seen, been successfully engaged in quelling the mutiny in Africa. In his civil career he had equally won the approbation of his countrymen. Of a grave and dignified demeanor, both in the Palace and the Forum, yet ever ready to listen to the cry of the needy, and willing to give freely or to lend large sums without interest as the nature of the case required; an upright judge, a gracious and courteous host, keeping open house every day for the foremost citizens of Byzantium, yet studiously separating himself from the factions of the Circus and the Agora; such, according to Procopius (who, after his quarrel with Belisarius, transferred all his devotion to the Imperial nephew), was the warrior and statesman Germanus. By his wife Passara, who had died several years before the time which we have now reached, he had two sons, Justin and Justinian. The former was Consul in 540, the year of the fall of Ravenna, and while clothed with that dignity followed his father to battle against Chosroes. The latter, like his brother often employed against the Slavonian and Gepid troublers of the Empire, was also a valiant soldier and the useful lieutenant of his father.

But Germanus, though thus richly endowed with all qualities which should have made him a pillar of the throne of Justinian, perhaps we should rather say, because endowed with those qualities, was annoyed by a perpetual, if petty, persecution on the part of the Empress Theodora. The military talents of his sons were seldom made use of; those who wished to stand well at Court avoided his friendship; his daughter remained unmarried till the rough soldier John dared to incur a temporary displeasure for the sake of so brilliant an alliance and married the great-niece of the Emperor. The most recent grievance of Germanus had reference to the wealth of his lately deceased brother Boraides, who, leaving to his widow and only daughter so much only as was absolutely necessary to prevent his testament from being declared invalid, directed that all the rest of his large property should pass to Germanus. This disposition was probably made in order to strengthen the claims of that branch of the family on the succession to the Imperial throne: and, probably for the very same reason, Justinian, or Theodora, intervening, ordered that the widow and daughter should be the sole legatees.

The death of Theodora might have been expected at once to place her enemy Germanus in a position of undisputed eminence at Court. Just at this time, however, some of the stored-up resentments of earlier years fermented into a conspiracy which well-nigh brought about the ruin of Germanus. There were at Constantinople two natives of Persarmenia, princes of the Arsacid line, who had risen high in the Imperial service, but each of whom had his own bitter grievance against Justinian and Theodora. Artabanes, who in 545 stabbed the usurper Gontharis at Carthage and restored Africa to the Emperor, claimed one reward for his conspicuous services, the hand of Justinian's niece Praejecta, whom he had both avenged and rescued by his daring deed. She, in her gratitude, was willing, nay, eager thus to reward him, but there was one fatal obstacle. Artabanes had a wife already, whom he had put away and well-nigh forgotten, but who, now that his fortunes were brightening, showed no sign of forgetting him. This woman sought the succor of Theodora, whose chief redeeming virtue it was that she could not close her ears to the cry of a woman in distress. Theodora insisted upon Artabanes taking back his long discarded wife, and gave Praejecta to another husband. The tall, stately, silent Armenian rose high in the favor of the Emperor; he became Magister Militum in Praesenti, General of the Foederati, and at last Consul; but all these honors and emoluments could not deaden his sense of the wrong which he conceived himself to have endured, in that he had lost the woman whom he loved and was daily in the company of the woman whom he hated.

While Artabanes, as all men knew, was thus brooding over his matrimonial grievance, his fellow-countryman Arsaces diligently fanned the flame of his resentment. The reasons for the discontent of Arsaces were more discreditable than those which had alienated Artabanes. He had been detected in treasonable negotiations with Chosroes, and had been punished, not by the sentence of death which he richly deserved, but by a slight flogging and by being paraded through the City on a camel with the marks of his chastisement still upon him. This clemency was wasted on the fierce Oriental, and he now was forever at the ear of Artabanes, accusing him of inopportune bravery, and timidity which a woman would be ashamed of. "You slew Gotharis though he was your friend and you were a guest at his banquet. And now you scruple about killing Justinian, the hereditary enemy of your race, and him who has done you this grievous wrong. And yet to anyone who will reflect on the matter for a moment, the assassination of Justinian will seem to be a very simple and easy action, and one that no one need fear to attempt. There he sits till far into the night in his unsentinelled library, with a few doting priests around him, wholly intent on turning over the precious rolls which contain the Christian oracles. You have nothing to fear from the relatives of the Emperor. Germanus, the most powerful of them all, is smarting under wrongs more grievous even than ours; and he and his gallant young sons, I doubt not, will eagerly join in our conspiracy". By such arguments as these, Artabanes was at length induced to enter into the plot, which was then communicated to another Armenian, Chanaranges by name, a handsome and volatile young man, who had no particular grievance against the Emperor, but was willing to join with a light heart in this glorious scheme for murdering an unguarded and elderly man in the midst of his theological studies.

The next step was to secure the adhesion of Germanus and his family, and for this purpose the elder son Justin, a youth with the first manly down upon his lips, was sounded by Arsaces. After swearing a tremendous oath that he would reveal what was about to be told him to no man save his father only, the young man was first artfully reminded of all the grievances which his father, his brother, and he had received at the hands of Justinian, ending with the crowning injustice of withholding from them the inheritance of his uncle Boraides. "Nor", said Arsaces, "are these injuries likely soon to come to an end. Belisarius, your enemy, is ordered home from Italy. He is reported to be even now half-way through Illyria. When he comes, you will find that you are treated even more contemptuously than before". And with that, Arsaces in a whisper revealed to him the design to kill his uncle the Emperor; and gave the names of Artabanes and Chanaranges as already privy to the plot.

The young Justin turned giddy with contending emotions as the deed, so wicked and yet opening up the possibility of such a welcome change in his condition, was disclosed to him; but the nobler passion of horror at the crime prevailed, and in a few curt words he told the tempter that neither he nor his father could ever be accomplices in such a deed. He then departed and told his father what he had heard. Germanus, perplexed at the tidings and seeing danger round him on every hand, violated his son's oath by unfolding the whole matter to his friend Marcellus, Captain of the Palace-guards.

Marcellus was a man of somewhat austere character, careless of money, of pleasure, and of popularity, but a lover of justice; one whom his natural taciturnity and almost churlishness of temper made a singularly faithful confidant. The advice, the dangerous advice, as it proved, which he gave, was not to hurry the conspirators into crime, nor to run the risk of a counter-accusation by making an immediate disclosure to the Emperor, but to draw them on to a confession of their villainy in the presence of an unsuspected witness, and thus to make certain that punishment should fall only on the guilty. This treacherous scheme of unmasking treachery was accordingly adopted. The young Justin was told to re-open the negotiations which he had abruptly closed. Arsaces was now dumb concerning the plot, but Chanaranges, full of eagerness for the conspiracy, desired nothing better than to have a conversation first with Justin and then with his father respecting it. On a given day, therefore, he repaired by appointment to the palace of Germanus. In the *triclinium* where they met, a thick muslin curtain hung from the ceiling to the floor, veiling the couch on which the master of the house was wont to recline at the banquet. It veiled also, though Chanaranges knew it not, the crouching form of Leontius, a man with the highest reputation for justice and truthfulness—according to the standard of Byzantium in the sixth century—who had been selected, apparently with no reluctance on his part, for the honorable office of eaves-dropper.

This was the purport of the conversation of Chanaranges as to the plans of the conspirators. "We have reflected that if we slay Justinian while Belisarius is still on his way to Constantinople, we shall be no nearer our purpose of setting you, 0 Germanus! on the throne. For Belisarius will then certainly collect an army in Thrace to avenge the murder of the Emperor, and when he appears before the gates of the City we shall have no means of repelling him. We must therefore wait till he has actually arrived, and is closeted with the Emperor in the palace. Then, late in the evening, we will resort thither with daggers in our hands and slay Justinian, Belisarius, and Marcellus all at once. After that we can dispose of matters as we will".

When Marcellus heard from Leontius of this atrocious proposition, he still, for some mysterious other reason, postponed reporting it to the Emperor. Germanus however, truly perceiving that the mere fact of listening unmoved to such a conversation must subject him to the most odious imputations, took two other great officials into his confidence. These were Constantian, late general in Dalmatia and governor of Ravenna, and Buzes, the unhappy ex-consul who had been kept for twenty-eight months in a dark dungeon by Theodora, but who appears to have been still loyal to her Imperial spouse.

Tidings soon came of the near approach of the returning Belisarius. Then at length the taciturn Marcellus informed his master of the danger impending over both their lives. Artabanes and some of his confidential officers were put to the torture, and the Senate was summoned to the Palace to read and to deliberate upon the depositions thus obtained. Of course the names of Germanus and Justin were among the first mentioned by the criminals in their agony. When these names were read out, many faces in the assembly were turned with horror and amazement to Germanus; and it seemed as if nothing could save him from immediate condemnation. When he told the whole story, however, and called on Marcellus, Leontius, Constantian, and Buzes as vouchers for its truth, the tide of opinion turned, and the Senate by an unanimous vote acquitted Germanus and his son of all evil designs against the Republic.

Not so, however, the Emperor. When the Senators went in to the Presence Chamber to report the result of their deliberations, he burst into a torrent of angry invective against his nephew for his tardiness in bringing him tidings of the plot. Two of the nobles, in order to curry favour with the Emperor, affected to sympathize with his views, and thus hounded him on to yet more violent expressions. The rest of the Senate stood trembling and silent, ashamed to condemn and afraid to acquit Germanus. At this crisis the stern rugged character of Marcellus shone forth in all its nobleness. He loudly asserted that all the blame, if blame there was, for the delay must rest upon his shoulders; that Germanus had consulted him at the earliest possible moment, and that he from motives of policy had insisted that Justinian should not then be told of the plot. He thus at length succeeded in mollifying the wrath of the Emperor against his nephew, earning himself great praise from all men for his fearless truthfulness.

The clemency of Justinian's nature was shown in a conspicuous manner towards those who had planned his murder. Artabanes was for the time deprived of his office, but, as we have seen, received next year an important command in Sicily. All the conspirators were kept for a time in honorable confinement in the Palace, not in the public gaol, and even this punishment was probably not of long duration.

A ruler who knew that his life was in danger from plots such as that of Arsaces might be excused for some vacillation in the choice and the promotion of his generals. Other cares were also pressing upon the wearied brain of Justinian, and making even the recovery of Italy seem a light matter in comparison with them. The sneer of the Armenian about the midnight hours spent in turning over theological treatises in the company of doting priests was not undeserved. Justinian was now, and had been for the last five years, deep in the controversy of 'The Three Chapters'. When Pope Vigilius, who had been summoned to Constantinople for this very purpose, together with the other Roman refugees, the Patrician Gothigus at their head, pressed upon him the necessity of a vigorous effort for the deliverance of Italy, he replied, in substance, that the affairs of Italy should have his attention when he had succeeded in reconciling the contradictions of Christians as to their common faith. A long adjournment certainly of his performance of the humbler duties of a ruler.

There were also other wars going on in the Empire, some much nearer home than that of Italy, which distracted the energies of Justinian. The eternal contest with Persia was at this time transferred to the eastern end of the Black Sea, to the region now known as Mingrelia, where from 549 to 557 what was called the Lazic war was being waged with varying fortunes, but upon the whole with a preponderance of success on the side of the Romans.

North of the Danube there was discontent, and a dangerous spirit of enterprise abroad among the fierce neighbors of the Empire. Where the Drave and the Theiss flow into the Danube, the Gepidae and Lombards were fiercely disputing with one another, imploring the intervention of Justinian, and then joining to attack his general when he invasion of entered their land. Further east in the country which we now call Wallachia, the Slavonians, long despised and comparatively harmless, were becoming a terrible scourge of the Empire. In the year 549 three thousand of these barbarians crossed the Danube, marched to the Hebrus, defeated Roman armies more numerous than their own, took captive the Roman General Asbad—one of the sumptuously-equipped *Candidati*, the pampered guardsmen of the Emperor—and after cutting off long strips of skin from his back, burned the miserable man alive. Then they pressed on to Topirus on the coast of the Aegean, nearly opposite the isle of Thasos, and only twelve days' journey from Constantinople. They drew forth the garrison by a feigned flight, took the city, ransacked its treasures, slew the men to the number of fifteen thousand, and carried off all the women and children into captivity. Thus they spread throughout Illyria and Thrace, ravaging the lands and torturing the inhabitants with fiendish cruelty. The terrible punishment of impalement, with which the Danubian lands have since been fatally familiarized, inflicted by men of another race than the Slavonian, now makes its appearance, and is described by Procopius with ghastly accuracy and vivid power. At length, drunk with their debauch of blood, the Slavonians retreated across the Danube, driving the endless files of their weeping captives before them, and leaving all Thrace and Illyria full of unburied corpses.

Two more invasions of these barbarians followed in the next year. It was thought by some that Totila had hired them to harass Justinian and prevent his attending to the affairs of Italy: but men who had been able to gratify their savage passions with so little labor or danger to themselves were not likely to require much pressing to undertake another raid into the feebly-defended Empire.

It will thus be seen that there was some reason why Justinian (stripped as he was by death of his bold and strenuous partner Theodora) should hesitate and delay and waver in his counsels with reference to the war in Italy. The name of Germanus as commander-in-chief for this war had been proposed shortly after the recall of Belisarius. Then the Emperor changed his mind and appointed the elderly and unwarlike Liberius. This appointment, as we have seen, had soon been cancelled, again made and again revoked. Now, probably at the beginning of 550, Justinian, while sending Artabanes to Sicily, took the bold and wise step of declaring Germanus, as Belisarius had been declared, commander with absolute powers for the whole war against Totila and the Goths. He gave him a large army, and instructions to add to it by raising new levies in Thrace and Illyria. More to the surprise of his councilors, he unloosed his purse-strings and sent his nephew a large store of treasure. To this Germanus, whose heart was set on restoring Italy, as he had already restored Africa after the rebellion of Stutza to the obedience of the Empire, added large sums from his own private fortune. The fame of so popular a commander, and the unwonted abundance of money at head-quarters, soon attracted large numbers of eager recruits, especially from among the barbarians of the Danube. All these flocked to Sardica (now the Bulgarian capital, Sophia), where Germanus had set up his standard. His son-in-law, the valiant and unscrupulous John, was of course with him. With him too were his martial sons Justin and Justinian, eager to embrace the long-desired opportunity of showing their prowess in war. There was Philemuth King of the Heruli, who had fought under Belisarius in his first Italian command: and there—a name of ill-omen for the Roman power in Italy—were one thousand heavy-armed soldiers of the Lombard nation.

The most potent, however, of all the allies of Germanus, the one who most daunted the hearts of the Goths, already dispirited at the thought of so great a commander coming against them, was his newly-wedded wife. This was none other than Matasuentha, widow of King Witigis and granddaughter of the great Theodoric. Again was the Amal princess married to a husband considerably older than herself; but there are some slight indications that this union was more to her taste than that with the humbly-born Witigis. At any rate, she was now a member of the Imperial family, and, as her countryman Jordanes proudly records, a legitimate Patrician. The three references made to this marriage by the Gothic historian, who wrote within two years after its consummation, show the great importance attached to it by his nation, and entirely confirm the statement of Procopius as to the depression which came over the soldiers of Totila at the thought of fighting with one who was now in a certain sense a member of the family of the great Theodoric.

Both hopes and fears, however, springing out of the appointment of Germanus to the supreme command were alike to be proved vain. The first of the two Slavonic invasions of the year 550, in which the marauders penetrated as far as Naissus in Servia, alarmed the Emperor, who sent orders to Germanus to suspend his westward march and succor Thessalonica, which was threatened by the barbarians. The terror of his name, and the remembrance of the great deeds which he had wrought twenty years before in the Danubian lands, sufficed to turn the Slavonians from their purpose and to divert their march into Dalmatia. In two days more the army would have resumed its interrupted journey towards Italy: but suddenly Germanus was attacked by disease—possibly a fever caught during his marches over the corpse-strewn valleys of Thrace—and after a very short illness he died.

The picture drawn of this prince has necessarily been taken from the pages of his partisan Procopius, who very likely has painted in too bright colors the character of his patron: but after making all necessary allowance for this partiality, it seems impossible to deny that here was a man of great gifts, of many noble qualities, and of splendid possibilities. As with a rising English statesman who dies before he attains 'Cabinet-rank', the premature death of Germanus has prevented him from leaving a great name in history. Had it fallen to his lot to defeat Totila, to restore the Western Empire, to bequeath its crown to a long line of descendants boasting a combined descent from Theodoric and Justinian, the name of Germanus might be at this day one of the most familiar land-marks on the frontier line between ancient and modern history.

In a few lines we must trace the subsequent history of the family of Germanus, since that is now the sole remaining branch of the family of Theodoric. After the death of her husband, Matasuentha bore a son, who was named after his father, Germanus. In this infant the hopes of Jordanes were centered when he wrote his Gothic history. It has been suggested that there was a scheme on the part of a nationalist Italian party headed by Vigilius to proclaim this infant as heir to Theodoric, or Emperor of the West, and obtain his recognition by Justinian, wearied out as he was by the war. The *'De Rebus Geticis'* of Jordanes is thus supposed to have been a sort of political pamphlet written in the interest of this combination. The theory is an ingenious one, but seems to lack that amount of contemporary evidence which would make it anything more than a theory. In any case, however, it is interesting to note that we have now reached the date of the composition of the treatises of Jordanes, with the contents of which we have become so familiar. The death of Germanus and the birth of his posthumous son are the last events of importance recorded by that writer, and it is clear that both the *'De Regnorum Successione'* and the *'De Rebus Geticis'* or, as Mommsen prefers to call them, the *'Romana et Getica Jordanis'*, were written in the year 551.

As for Germanus Postumus, the child of Matasuentha, he appears to have played a respectable, if not a highly distinguished part, as a great nobleman of Constantinople. His daughter married Theodosius, son of the Emperor Maurice; and the tumults which ended the reign of that Emperor, the popularity of Germanus caused him to be spoken of as a suitable candidate for the Imperial purple. The rumor of such a project nearly cost him his life, owing to the suspicious fears of Maurice. On the fall of that Emperor, the fierce and illiterate soldier who succeeded him, Phocas, made a show of offering the diadem to Germanus, but the latter, knowing well how precarious would be the life of an Emperor elected under such conditions, wisely declined the proffered dignity. When the cruel character of the tyrant who thereupon ascended the throne had exhibited itself, and his unfitness for the diadem was made clear to all men, Germanus made two attempts to dethrone him, by reviving the old loyalty of the Blue Faction to the house of Maurice, and appealing to the compassion of the populace on behalf of Constantina, widow of that Emperor. The first of these attempts cost him his official position, for he was ordered to cut off his hair and become a priest. The second cost him, and those on whose behalf he was conspiring, their lives. Constantina and her three daughters were slain with the sword upon the very spot where Maurice and his five sons had been put to death three years before; and Germanus with his daughter (the widow of the young Theodosius) were beheaded upon the little island of Prote in the Sea of Marmora, five miles south of Chalcedon. There, within sight of the towers and domes of Constantinople, associated for ever with the fame of Justinian, so often gazed upon with wonder by the young Theodoric, perished the two in whose veins flowed the blended blood of Emperor and King, the last descendants that History can discern of the glorious lineage of the Amala.

CHAPTER XXIII.

THE SORROWS OF VIGILIUS.

Before we sit as spectators to watch the last act of the drama of Imperial Restoration in Italy, we must study for a short time one of the most perplexed and entangled passages in Papal History, that which relates to the Pontificate of Vigilius. The story is made difficult partly by the fact that it is a battle-ground for the champions and the opponents of the doctrine of Papal Infallibility, a doctrine which a secular historian may claim the privilege of passing by in silence, refusing to be drawn by the course of his narrative into the attitude either of a denier or of a maintainer of its truth. But the character of Pope Vigilius himself, and the bitter theological controversies in which he was involved, and in which it was his fate to please neither of the two contending parties, cause the contemporary notices of his life to be obscure and contradictory beyond the ordinary quality even of ecclesiastical history.

Let us briefly recapitulate what has been already said concerning the early career of this Pontiff. That he belonged to one of the great official families of Rome is proved by the fact that the Senator Reparatus was his brother. Throughout his life we may perceive some indications that his natural sympathies were with the aristocracy and the Court, and that some of his difficulties arose from a vain attempt to reconcile these aristocratic instincts with the bold part which a Pope in the Sixth Century was expected to play on behalf of the people and the popular enthusiasm of the lesser clergy. His unsuccessful attempt to obtain the first place in the Roman Church by the mere nomination of Pope Boniface II (an attempt which perhaps indicates the disposition of the Roman nobles to make the Papacy the exclusive possession of their own order) left Vigilius in the humiliating position of a defeated intriguer. Henceforward he probably knew that he had no chance of obtaining the Pontificate by a fair vote of the clergy and people of Rome. The influence which, as an ecclesiastic, member of a great Roman family, he still possessed, and which was sufficient to obtain for him the important position of Nuncio (Apocrisiarius) at the Court of Constantinople, must therefore be used in a different and less open manner. In his official intercourse with the great personages of that Court he had abundant opportunity for observing how the heart of Theodora was set on the restoration of the Monophysites to high places in the Church, and how seldom that upon which Theodora had set her heart failed to be granted in the end by her Imperial consort.

Hence came those secret negotiations with the Empress which have been already referred to, and which led to the downfall of the unhappy Silverius. We view with some distrust the circumstantial statements of historians as to conversations and correspondence which must necessarily have been known to extremely few persons; but, according to these statements, the terms of the bargain were that Theodora should address a letter to Belisarius directing him to make Vigilius Pope, and should also present to the new Pontiff 700 lbs. weight of gold. Vigilius on his part undertook to overthrow the authority of the Council of Chalcedon, and to write to Theodosius, Anthimus, and Severus, the Monophysite Patriarchs of Alexandria, Constantinople, and Antioch, acknowledging them as brethren in the faith.

Armed with this letter from the all-powerful Theodora, Vigilius sailed for Rome and sought an interview with Belisarius. Handing him the Empress's mandate he promised the General 200 lbs. weight of gold as the price of his assistance in procuring the coveted dignity. The result of this interview was, if we are to believe the biographers, the accusation against Silverius, the summons to the Pontiff to appear in the Pincian Palace, Antonina's insolent demeanor, the pallium stripped from off the Pope's shoulders, and the coarse monastic garb hung round them in its stead.

This deposition of a Pope by the authority of the Emperor was a high-handed, probably an unpopular act; but there is no reason to doubt that it was acquiesced in by the clergy and people of Rome, and that Vigilius was regarded as his lawful successor. The accusation against Silverius was a political one. Not heterodoxy in doctrine, but a treacherous scheme for opening the gates of the City to the Goths, was the charge on account of which he met with such rough handling in the Pincian Palace; and of such an offence the Emperor or his deputy seems to have been considered a competent judge. The deposition of Silverius comes therefore under the same category with the deposition of the Byzantine Patriarchs, Euphemius and Macedonius; and is chiefly noteworthy as showing how dangerous to the independence of the Papacy was that Imperial authority which the Popes had with so light a heart brought back into the circle of Italian politics.

When the new Pope was firmly seated in his throne, the two authors of his elevation naturally called upon him to fulfill his share of the compact with each of them. Avarice made him unwilling to perform one of his promises; the loyalty to Chalcedon which seemed to nestle in the folds of the Papal pallium, indisposed him to perform the other. As we have seen, he pleaded to Belisarius that unless Silverius were surrendered to him he could not pay the promised purchase-money. Whether, upon the surrender and death of his predecessor, the two hundredweight of gold were transferred from the vaults of St. Peter's to the head-quarters of Belisarius, history does not inform us; but the Pope does seem to have attempted, in a half-hearted clandestine way, to fulfill his contract with Theodora. As for over-throwing the Council of Chalcedon, that was absurdly impossible; but he did write a letter addressed "To my Lords and dear Brethren in the love of Christ our Savior, the Bishops Theodosius, Anthimus, and Severus". In this letter he said, "I know that your Holinesses have already heard the report of my faith; nevertheless, to meet the wishes of my glorious daughter, the Patrician Antonina, I write these presents to assure you that the same faith which you hold I hold likewise, and have ever held. I know that your Brotherhood will gladly receive these things which I write. At the same time it is necessary that this letter should not be read by any one, but rather that your Wisdom should still profess to regard me as chief among your opponents, that I may the more easily carry through to the end the things which I now undertake. Pray God for me, my dear Brethren in Christ". To this letter was appended a confession of faith which, if not actually Monophysite, went, in the opinion of his contemporaries, perilously near to the edge of that heresy.

For a time this secret recognition of her partisans may have satisfied Theodora, but as the years went on and still Anthimus remained in exile and apparently under the ban of St. Peter, she pressed for a public fulfillment of the bargain by virtue of which Vigilius had become Pope. But Vigilius was now firm in his seat and could assume the attitude of unbending orthodoxy. The letter which he now sent was of this purport. "Be it far from me, Lady Augusta, that I should do this thing. Aforetime I spoke wrongly and foolishly: but now will I in no wise consent to recall a man that is an heretic and under anathema. And if it be said that I am an unworthy Vicar of the blessed Apostle Peter, yet what can be said against my holy predecessors Agapetus and Silverius, who condemned Anthimus?".

The anger of Theodora against her rebellious accomplice was quickened, and apparently justified, by the accusations which reached Constantinople, preferred by the Roman commonalty against their haughty and passionate Pope. It was not only the old charge of procuring the deposition and conniving at the death of Silverius that was now brought up against him. Other strange charges were made, which at least seem to indicate the violent temper of the aristocratic Pontiff. "We submit to your Piety", said the Roman messengers, "that Vigilius is a homicide. He was seized with such fury that he gave a blow on the face to his notary, who shortly after fell at his feet and expired. Also upon some offence committed by a widow's son he caused him to be arrested at night by his nephew Vigilius, son of the Consul Asterius, and beaten with rods till he died".

"On the receipt of these tidings" says the Papal biographer, "the Augusta [Theodora] sent Anthemius the Scribe to Rome with her orders and with special commission, saying: Only if he is in the Basilica of St. Peter refrain from arresting him. For if you shall find Vigilius in the Lateran or in the Palace [adjoining it], or in any church, at once put him on ship-board and bring him hither to us. If you do not do this, by Him who liveth for ever I will have you flayed alive. Then Anthemius the Scribe, coming to Rome, found him in the church of St. Cecilia on the 10th of the Kalends of December [22 November, 545J .... It was then his birthday, and he was distributing presents to the people: but Anthemius, arresting him, took him down to the Tiber and placed him on board ship. The common people followed him, begging in a loud voice that they might receive his prayers. When he had uttered his prayers all the people answered Amen, and the ship moved off. But when the Romans saw that the ship which bore Vigilius was really on her way, then they began to throw sticks, stones, and potsherds, and to shout: Hunger go with you: mortality be with you. You have wrought evil for the Romans: may you find evil wherever you go". Nevertheless, some men who loved him followed him forth from the church.

In this picture of a haughty and unpopular Pope, crouched to by the mob so long as he is still on shore, and the receiver of their missiles and their taunts as soon as his ship is under way, there is something which looks like the handiwork of a contemporary. Yet it is not very easy to fit in the details here given with what we know, of the life of Vigilius. He was certainly not taken straight to Constantinople and at once exposed to the wrath of Theodora. On the contrary, he seems to have spent the following year in Sicily, not in close custody, but an honored and important guest. From thence, as we have already seen, in the early part of 546 he dispatched a number of corn-ships to Rome, a charitable return for the muttered execrations of the crowd (which perhaps had not reached the ears of his Holiness)—"May hunger go with you and death overtake you".

This mysterious residence of a year in Sicily was ended by an invitation, not from Theodora, but from Justinian, in obedience to which Vigilius sailed for Constantinople, arriving at that city on the 25th January, 547. The petition previously urged by Theodora for the recognition of Anthimus seems now to have been tacitly dropped. The whole efforts, both of the Imperial pair and of all who were like-minded with them in the East, were now devoted to procuring the Pope's assent to the condemnation of the Three Chapters.

The theological controversy which is labelled by this strangely-chosen name is one of the paltriest and least edifying that even the creed-spinners of the Eastern Church ever originated. Gladly would a modern historian leave it undisturbed in the dust which, for a thousand years and more, has gathered over it. But this cannot be. Even as Monophysitism, by loosening the hold of the Empire on Syria and Egypt, prepared the path of the Companions of Mohammed, so the schism of the Three Chapters loosened the hold of the Empire an recovered Italy, and made smooth the path of the invading Lombards. As the student of the Thirty Years' War in Germany must compel himself to listen to the disputes between the Lutheran and the Reformed Churches; as the student of the history of Holland must have patience with the squabbles of Calvinists and Remonstrants; as the student of our own Civil War must for the time look upon Prelacy and Presbytery as opposing principles for whose victory or defeat the universe stands expectant; so must we, at any rate for a few pages, watch narrowly the theological sword-play between Emperor and Pope beside the graves of Theodore of Mopsuestia, Theodore and Ibas.

In the whispered conversations of Arsaces and Artabanes we caught a glimpse of the Emperor as he appeared at this time to his subjects, a grey-bearded theologian, sitting in the library of his palace till far on into the night, conversing with monks and bishops, and endlessly turning over with them the rolls of the Christian Scriptures or the Fathers' comments upon them. In these theological conferences Justinian discovered, or was taught to recognize, three defects in the proceedings of the venerated Council of Chalcedon.

1. Theodore, Bishop of Mopsuestia, was the teacher of Nestorius, and one of the strongest maintainers of the doctrine that the divine Logos, distinct from the human personality of Christ, dwelt therein as Jehovah dwelt in his temple at Jerusalem. This doctrine had been emphatically condemned at the successive Councils of Ephesus (431) and Chalcedon (451): but Theodore himself, whose death happened three years before the former Council, had been allowed to sleep quietly in his tomb and had hitherto escaped anathema. This omission Justinian now proposed to remedy. Theodore had been dead for more than a century, but his name must now be struck out of the diptychs, and his person and writings visited with the unsparing anathema of the Church.

2. Theodoret, Bishop of Cyrrhus in Syria (with whom we have already made some acquaintance as an ecclesiastical historian), was a friend and fellow-pupil of Nestorius, and therefore in the charitable judgment of the orthodox could easily be accused of sharing his heresy. Modern enquirers, however, incline to the conclusion that he was no Nestorian, but a man, clearer-sighted than some of his contemporaries, who began, earlier than they, the contest against the arrogant Monophysitism of the Alexandrian Church. However in this contest he had published treatises sharply attacking both Cyril, who was accounted orthodox, and the Council of Ephesus, to whose authority the whole Church bowed. Justinian did not seek for an anathema on the person of Theodoret, who after years of excommunication had been replaced in his bishopric by the Council of Chalcedon; but he claimed that these special writings against Cyril and against the Third Council should be branded as heretical, a claim which was legitimate according to the ecclesiastical ideas of the day, but which opened

an endless vista of future disputation if there was to be practically no 'Statute of limitations' in theological controversy.

3. Ibas of Edessa was, like the two last-named prelates, a Syrian bishop, and belonged to the school of Theodore of Mopsuestia. He, like Theodoret, had been deposed from his see during the short interval between the Third and Fourth Councils in which the Monophysites virtually reigned supreme in the Church; and like Theodoret, he had been reinstated by the Council of Chalcedon. The chief offence now alleged against him was a letter written by him to a certain Maris, Bishop of Hardaschir in Persia, in which he described the acts of the Council of Ephesus in a tone of violent hostility and denounced Cyril as a heretic. Although Ibas himself, even at this period of his life, does not seem to have fully accepted the teaching of Nestorius, and afterwards at the Council of Chalcedon joined in the anathema against that theologian, there can be no doubt that some of the expressions used in this letter wore a Nestorian color, and that if Cyril was to be venerated as a saint, it was hard to defend the orthodoxy of Ibas. What rendered the affair peculiarly difficult, and should have made Justinian peculiarly unwilling to disinter it from the oblivion in which it was entombed, was that the Council of Chalcedon itself, the venerable Fourth Synod, had listened to the reading of this semi-Nestorian epistle and allowed it to be entered upon its minutes without manifesting its disapproval; nay, that the Papal Legates had expressly declared, 'after the reading of this letter we pronounce Ibas orthodox, and give judgment that he be restored to his see'

These, then, were the three points in which the lawyer-like intellect of Justinian had detected imperfection in the proceedings of the Council of Chalcedon, and in which he considered that a tacit reversal of the action of that Council might be made, in order to conciliate the prejudices of the Monophysites. The object which he had in view, and which was that which Zeno and Anastasius had sought to obtain, was a desirable one. The deep and increasing alienation of the Monophysites of Egypt and Syria was, in the existing condition of the Church's relations to the State, a real danger to the Empire, a danger the full extent of which was manifested in the following century, when the hosts of Omar and Amru invaded those two provinces. But the expedient devised by Justinian, though not devoid of cleverness, was too small and subtle to succeed. The stern Monophysites of Alexandria were not to be drawn back into union with Constantinople by the excitement of hunting three heretics who had been dead for a century. And, on the other hand, Italy, Africa, and Gaul felt that when the Sacred Council of Chalcedon was touched the Ark of God was in danger. By whatever external professions of respect the insult might be veiled, the new ecclesiastical legislation was an insult to the authority of Chalcedon and was resented accordingly.

The attempt to procure the condemnation of the persons or the writings of these three Syrian theologians occupied the best energies of Justinian during ten years of his reign, and perhaps somewhat consoled him for the loss of the Monophysite partner of his throne, who died when he was but half-way through the battle. It was probably towards the end of 543, or early in 544, that 'Imperator Caesar Philochristus, Justinianus, Alamannicus, Gotthicus, Francicus, Gennanicus, Anticus, Alanicus, Vandalicus, Africanus, the pious, the fortunate, the renowned, the victorious, the triumphant, the ever-venerable, the august' issued in the name of the Father and the Son and the Holy Ghost his edict to the whole body of the Catholic and Apostolic Church. This edict is lost, but from a second edict which was published about eight years later, and which was probably a somewhat expanded edition of the first, we may form a conjecture as to its contents. This latter edict (which with its Latin translation fills fifty large octavo pages) begins by an elaborate statement of Christian doctrine according to the Creed of Nicaea. In ten short sections or 'chapters' the errors of the Arians, the Apollinarians, the Eutychians, and the Nestorians are stamped with the Imperial anathema. Then come the celebrated Three Chapters, of which for the next century the world was to hear more than enough. In the eleventh chapter, Theodore of Mopsuestia, his person, his writings, his defenders are all anathematized. In the twelfth the same stigma is affixed to the writings of Theodoret on behalf of Nestorius and against Cyril and the Council of Ephesus. In the thirteenth, everyone who defends the impious epistle of Ibas to the Persian heretic Maris, everyone who says that that epistle or any part of it is sound, everyone who refuses to anathematize it, is himself declared to be anathema. Then follows a long argument vainly endeavoring to prove that this 'impious epistle' met with no approval at the Council of Chalcedon. The question whether it be right to anathematize Theodore after his death is discussed, and decided in the affirmative on the authority of St. Augustine, and also on the ground that if the Church might not condemn heretics after their death, neither might she liberate after death those who, like St. Chrysostom, have passed away loaded with an unjust anathema. At length the Imperial theologian concludes with an appeal for reunion to the Monophysite sectaries: "If therefore, after this true confession of faith and condemnation of the heretics, any one shall separate himself from the holy Church of God for the sake of words and syllables and quibbles about phrases, as if religion consisted in names and modes of speech and not in deeds, such an one will have to answer for his love of schism, and for those who have been or shall be hereafter deceived by him, to the great God and our Savior Jesus Christ in the Day of Judgment. Amen"

Throughout the whole of this long edict is heard a tone of calm superiority which reveals the presence of the ecclesiastical legislator who deems that he is settling once and for ever the controversies that have distracted the Church. It does not need the repetition of the titles of Justinian to assure us that we are listening to the same mouth which gave forth the *Codex* and the *Institutiones*. But beside this, we may perhaps discern a spirit of rivalry with Pope Leo and an endeavor to imitate the style of the majestic *Tome* which had been accepted by all Christendom as the true definition of the faith with regard to the union of the two natures in Christ. If it was the hope of the Emperor that he might go down to posterity as the successful competitor of that great Pontiff, he has been signally disappointed. True, he did with infinite labor and difficulty persuade a General Council to ratify his censures against the three Syrians, but the prevalent feeling even of his own age was probably that he was meddling with matters beyond his range, as it must have been the earnest desire of his successors that he would have left the Three Chapters in oblivion.

The edict thus prepared in the Imperial cabinet was laid before the Patriarchs of the East. Constantinople, Antioch, Jerusalem, Alexandria all at length signed, some after much hesitation, and the first only on condition that if Rome did not agree his assent should be accounted as withdrawn. Once having signed, however, they were led by an instinct of self-preservation to compel their suffragan bishops to the same course, and thus it came to pass that before long, probably before the end of 544, all the dioceses of the East had condemned the Three Chapters. Not so, however, in the West. Everywhere, in Gaul, in Illyricum, in Italy, but pre-eminently in the province which had Carthage for its capital, a spirit of jealous alarm for the honor of the Fourth Council was aroused by the Imperial edict. Datius of Milan (the prelate whom we have seen actively promoting the restoration of his province to the obedience of Justinian) stoutly refused in Constantinople itself to append his signature to the edict, and returned to the West in order to arouse in the Pope the same spirit of opposition. The forced departure of Vigilius himself from Rome was perhaps really owing to this controversy; and according to one well-informed writer, the populace of Rome, instead of shouting out 'Hunger and mortality go with thee!' really exclaimed, 'Do not condemn the Three Chapters!'; and the Bishops of Africa, Sardinia, and Illyricum accosted him on his journey with a similar request. However this may be, it is evident that the increasing opposition of the Western Bishops to the Imperial theology made Justinian even more anxious to have the successor of St. Peter close to his own residence and amenable to his own powers of persuasion or terror. Vigilius received an imperative summons to Constantinople, set sail from Sicily, and arrived at the capital on the 25th of January, 547.

The Pope was received in that city, which he already knew so well, with every outward demonstration of respect. His first acts, however, seemed to show that the shouts of the Roman populace, 'Condemn not the Three Chapters!' were still ringing in his ears. He condemned Mennas, the Patriarch of Constantinople and all the other Bishops who had subscribed the Edict, to exclusion for four months from the Communion of the Church: and this ecclesiastical courtesy was repaid by Mennas with a sentence of precisely the same length upon the Bishop of Old Rome. According to Pope Gregory the Great, Vigilius at this time also laid his anathema on the Empress Theodora.

This mood of stern antagonism to the Court did not last for many months. Justinian seems to have tried both flattery and menaces to shake the decision of the Pontiff: and if the menaces of imprisonment and hardship elicited only the spirited reply, "You may keep me in captivity, but the blessed Apostle Peter will never be your captive". On the other hand the invitations to the Imperial Palace, the visits from great personages in the state, the entreaties that he would not disturb the harmony of anathema which existed everywhere but where his power prevailed, were more successful. Vigilius renewed friendly relations with the Patriarch Mennas. He summoned the Western Bishops who were in Constantinople to a series of conferences, in which he discussed with them the possibility of gratifying the wishes of the Emperor. At length, on the 11th of April 548, he published to the world the solemn *Judicatum*, in which, summing up as judge the result of these episcopal conferences, he declared that, acting in obedience to the Apostolic command, "Prove all things: hold fast that which is good", he had examined the writings of Theodore of Mopsuestia, and finding many things in them contrary to the faith, he anathematized him and all his defenders. Similarly did he anathematize those writings of Theodoret in which he attacked the propositions of St. Cyril. Also the impious epistle said to have been written by Ibas to Maris the Persian. But in all this, as Vigilius with fourfold emphasis asserted, no disrespect was intended to the Council of Chalcedon, and anathema was pronounced on any one who should seek to impair its eternal and unshaken authority.

This saving clause was not sufficient to induce the Bishops of the West to acquiesce in the *Judicatum*. All men who were undazzled by splendor and unterrified by the frowns of the Court could see that the new anathemas did deal a heavy blow at the authority and reputation of the Fourth Council. Even in Constantinople itself Datius of Milan, hitherto the trusty ally of the Pope, expressed his profound dissatisfaction with the *Judicatum*. It is true that Rusticus, a deacon and nephew of Vigilius, who was tarrying with his uncle at the capital, at first expressed unbounded enthusiasm on behalf of the *Judicatum*, busied himself in transmitting copies of it through the Empire, and declared that not only ought the name of Theodore of Mopsuestia to be anathematized, but his very bones dug up and cast out of holy ground. So too a young and restless ecclesiastic named Sebastian. Sebastian (also a deacon of the Roman Church), at first hailed the *Judicatum* as a direct message from Heaven. Soon, however, they were carried away with the tide of Western feeling, everywhere ebbing away from Vigilius and his new friends. They sent letters to Sicily, to Italy, to Africa, declaring that the Pope had betrayed the Council of Chalcedon; letters which, coming from Roman deacons and men of his immediate retinue, did infinite harm to the Papal cause. Vigilius, either in petulance or in self-defense, retaliated by deposing them and six of their 'fellow-conspirators' from their various offices in the Church.

These repressive measures could not silence the voice of real alarm and indignation in the Western Churches. Facundus, the African Bishop to whom we owe the fullest account of this tedious controversy, had been present at Constantinople through all the conferences which led up to the *Judicatum*, and had done his utmost to prevent its being issued. Returning now to his native province he gave such an account of the recent proceedings of the Pope that the Bishops assembled in Council resorted to the extreme measure of formally excommunicating the occupant of the Chair of St. Peter.

Vigilius saw that he had strained the allegiance of his Western suffragans too far, and with hesitation and awkwardness began to retreat. He asked Justinian's permission to withdraw the *Judicatum*, and the Emperor, who began to perceive that he and the Pope alone could not carry the whole Church with them, consented. It was decided that a General Council should be convened, and in order that the matter should be left open for that Council's decision, the Pope's Judicatum was to be considered as withdrawn. In private, however, the Pope had to swear to the Emperor that he would do his utmost to secure the condemnation of the Three Chapters, would enter into no secret compact with their defenders, and would disclose to the Emperor the name of anyone who should seek to draw him into any plots, on behalf of the Chapters or against the State. Justinian on his part swore that he would keep this engagement secret, and would not visit with the penalty of death the persons whom Vigilius under his compact might be compelled to denounce.

The proposed Council now occupied the minds of all the great dignitaries of Church and State at Constantinople. But as the months passed over, it became more and more clear that the Council would not heal the schism which Justinian had with so light a heart created. He was using his power with a heavy hand against his theological opponents, extruding Bishops their sees, especially in Africa, with a harshness which would have seemed more to befit an Arian Vandal than an Orthodox Emperor: but neither from Africa nor Illyria, from Italy nor Gaul would the Bishops come to do his bidding in Council by condemning the Three Chapters. The Eastern Bishops, more subservient and less fanatically Chalcedonian, were willing to do all that the Emperor required of them. Now then, if Vigilius was to fulfill his oath to the Emperor, he must take his place at the head of these Eastern Bishops, and formally anathematize the

Chapters which his own clergy and well-nigh all the Bishops of the West were passionately defending.

The situation was a cruel one, and might well make Vigilius curse the day when he began to intrigue for the Chair of St Peter. As if to complicate matters still further, the Emperor, without waiting for the assembling of the Council, put forth a second edict containing his authoritative definition of the essentials of the Christian faith, and anathematizing the Three Chapters. An assembly of all the Eastern and Western prelates who were at that time to be found in Constantinople was convened in the palace of Placidia, where the Pope was then dwelling. The professional jealousy of all the Bishops seems to have been aroused, and not even Theodore Bishop of Caesarea, the Emperor's chief adviser and right hand in all that concerned the condemnation of the Chapters, durst oppose the unanimous voice of the assembly, expressed by Datius of Milan and Vigilius of Rome, that an ecclesiastic who should celebrate mass in any of the churches where the Emperor's edict was publicly exhibited was a traitor to the brotherhood of the Church.

Notwithstanding this solemn prohibition, Theodore before many days were over solemnly celebrated mass in one of the contaminated churches, and prevailed upon Zoilus, Patriarch of Alexandria, who had been hitherto considered somewhat of a Papal partisan, to be present likewise. Indignant at this open act of disobedience to the successor of St. Peter, Vigilius, with the concurrence of Datius and twelve other Western Bishops, chiefly from Italian cities, published a solemn sentence of degradation from every ecclesiastical function against Theodore of Caesarea; and waxing bolder at the sound of their own voices, included in it also Mennas, Patriarch of Constantinople.

This daring blow, struck under the very eyes of the Emperor against his chief religious adviser and the ecclesiastical head of his own city, so exasperated Justinian that Vigilius and Datius found it necessary to fly for their lives to the asylum of the great basilicas. Vigilius chose for his place of refuge the Basilica of St. Peter, rightly judging that the sanctity of that place would be more efficacious than any other for the successor of the Apostle. Justinian however, who seems to have been in a state of frenzy at the insults offered to his vanity as a theologian and to his power as an Emperor, sent the Praetor to arrest him in the Basilica itself. This Praetor, the head of the City police, 'to whom' as the adherents of Vigilius indignantly asserted, 'thieves and murderers rightly belonged' came with a large number of soldiers bearing naked swords and bows ready strung in their hands. When he beheld them Vigilius fled to the altar, and clung to the columns on which it was supported. The deacons and other ecclesiastics who surrounded the Pope were first dragged away by the hair of their heads, and then the soldiers seized Vigilius himself, some by the legs, some by the hair, and some by the beard, and endeavored to pull him from the altar. Still, however, with convulsive grasp the Pope clung to the pillars, and still the soldiers strove to drag his tall and portly form away from the place of refuge. In the scuffle the pillars of the altar were broken, and the altar itself was only prevented by the interposed hands of the ecclesiastics from falling on the Pope's head and ending his Pontificate and his sorrows at one blow.

The sight of a chief of police and his satellites grasping the successor of St. Peter by the legs and trying to drag him forth from the shelter of St. Peters own basilica was too much for the religious feelings of the people of Constantinople. Loud and menacing murmurs arose from the spectators who had crowded into the church. Even some of the soldiers audibly expressed their disapproval of the work upon which they were engaged: and soon the Praetor with his retinue vanished from the sacred building, leaving Vigilius still under its safeguard.

The Emperor now tried another method. A deputation of the most important personages of postulate the Empire was sent to argue calmly with Vigilius Pope. and persuade him to abandon an attitude of needless hostility and distrust. The persons who composed this deputation are all of them interesting to us for other reasons. First and foremost was Belisarius (now probably in the forty-sixth year of his age), the instrument by whom Vigilius had been raised to the Papacy. With him came his fellow-patrician Cethegus, the exile from Rome, formerly Princeps of the Roman Senate, a man once accused of treachery to the Emperor, but now apparently restored to full Imperial favor. The other envoys were Justin the son of the lately-deceased Germanus, who had been Consul eleven years previously, and who now held the high office of Master of the Household; Peter, once the bold ambassador to Theodahad, now Patrician and Master of the Offices; and Marcellinus the Quaestor, apparently the same literary courtier of Justinian who under the title of Marcellinus Comes has, by his useful Chronicle, filled so many gaps in our knowledge of the history of the fifth and sixth centuries. This deputation was instructed to invite the Pope to come forth from his asylum on receiving a solemn oath for his personal safety, and to inform him that, if he would not accept these terms, measures should again be taken for his forcible removal. After some little bargaining as to the forms of the oath, Vigilius consented to these conditions. The memorandum containing the terms of agreement was laid upon a cross containing a fragment of the true wood of the Cross of Calvary, above the keys of St. Peter, and upon the iron grating which fenced in the altar of the Apostle. When all these arrangements had been made, to give greater efficacy to the compact the five noblemen took their 'corporal oath' for the safety of the Pontiff, and Vigilius, emerging from his hiding-place, returned to the palace of Placidia.

Notwithstanding all this solemn swearing, the situation of the Pope after his return became daily more intolerable. His servants and the ecclesiastics who remained faithful to him were publicly insulted; every entrance to the palace was blocked by armed men; he had reason to think that a violent attack was about to be made upon his person. After making a vain appeal to the Imperial envoys whose plighted oath was thus being violated, he quitted the palace again by night two days before Christmas-day. The shouts of the men-at-arms penetrated even into his bedchamber, and only this urgent terror, as he himself says, could have impelled him to the hardships and dangers of a nocturnal expedition. He fled this time, not to his old asylum at St. Peter's, but across the Bosporus to Chalcedon. There, in the renowned sanctuary of St Euphemia, in the very church where, just one century before, the great Council of the Six Hundred and Thirty Fathers had been held, the hunted Pope, the champion of that Council's authority, took refuge.

In such a place it would have been dangerous for the Emperor to repeat the scenes of violence which had profaned the basilica of St. Peter. After a month's interval he sent the same five noblemen who had composed the previous deputation, with an offer of new and perhaps more stringent oaths of protection if the Pope would again return to his palace. The answer of Vigilius was firm and dignified: "For no private or pecuniary reason have I sought shelter in this church, but solely in order to avert the scandal to the Church which was being perpetrated before all the world. If the Emperor is determined to restore peace to the Church, as she enjoyed it in the days of his uncle and pious predecessor, I need no oaths, but come forth from my asylum at once. If this be not his intention, oaths are also needless, for I shall not leave the basilica of St. Euphemia".

The Pope now proceeded, or threatened to proceed, to publish the excommunication of Theodore and Mennas, which had before been privately served upon them. On his part the Emperor sent by the hands of Peter the Referendarius a letter which Vigilius alleges to have been so full of insults and misstatements, that he is certain it can never have been written by the Emperor. This, however, is of course only a figure of speech to enable him to criticize it without open disrespect. There can be no doubt that it was Justinian's own composition, and we can easily imagine its purport—an unsparing exposure of the past vacillations, intrigues, and broken promises of the Roman Pontiff.

To this document and to the Emperors proposals for peace Vigilius replied by a long letter, the '*Encyclica*', containing his account of the controversies of the past year, and offering, upon receiving proper oaths for their safety, to send Datius of Milan and certain other of the ecclesiastics who shared his seclusion, to treat, with full powers from him, for the restoration of the peace of the Church. It is from this *Encyclica* that we derive the greater part of our information as to the embittered strife between Pope and Emperor.

That strife which for the past six months had assumed an acute type and had seemed likely to end in bloodshed, now relapsed into its tedious chronic condition. Death removed some of the combatants from the scene. Datius of Milan died in June; two months afterwards, Mennas of Constantinople. It was clear that Justinian had succeeded in tying a knot which only a Fifth General Council could untie, and to that Council, which at length on the fifth of May, 553, assembled in Constantinople, all eyes, at least the eyes of all Oriental Christians, were now directed. The Western prelates still kept aloof. It was one thing to summon them to Constantinople, and another thing to induce them to visit a capital where the venerable Datius, and Vigilius successor of St. Peter, had been treated with such discourtesy and had encountered so much actual peril.

The Emperor naturally desired that the presidency of the Council should be vested in the Bishop of Old Rome; and Eutychius the new Patriarch of Constantinople, a man apparently of gentler disposition than Mennas, voluntarily offered to concede the first place to Vigilius. The Pope,' however, did not choose to preside in a Council composed almost entirely of Eastern Bishops. For the matter in debate he perhaps cared little, but he rightly dreaded again placing himself in opposition to the general voice of the Western Church. There were long negotiations between Pope and Emperor as to the composition of the Council. Vigilius proposed that four Easterns and four Westerns should meet and that their decision should be accepted as final. Justinian was willing to concede that four Bishops from each of the three Eastern Patriarchates should meet Vigilius and three of the Bishops in his obedience; but this the Pope would not accept. Thus the negotiations broke down: and in truth a small committee of the kind indicated by these proposals would have been a poor substitute for the great ecclesiastical Parliaments which had met at Nicaea and Chalcedon.

Eventually when the Council, consisting of one hundred and thirty-nine Bishops from the East and six from the West, met in the Metropolitan Church of Constantinople, the throne prepared for Vigilius was vacant Some sittings were spent in fruitless endeavors to induce the Pope to join the assembled Prelates, Belisarius and

Cethegus being again vainly sent by the Emperor on this errand: and then the Council, under the presidency of Eutychius, proceeded to its main business. There was little discussion, apparently no opposition. The bishops had, probably, each already condemned the Three Chapters in their individual capacity, and now shouted 'Anathema to Theodore; long life to the Emperor' with edifying unanimity.

When Vigilius was invited to join the Council he replied with a demand for a delay of twenty days to enable him to prepare a written statement of his Judgment on the Three Chapters. The Emperor answered, with some justice, that it was not his individual sentence, but his voice and vote at the Council that was required; but the Pope persisted in his project, and by the 14th of May had drawn up a document called the *Constitutum*, containing his own judgment and that of nineteen Bishops of the West and deacons of Rome concerning the matters in dispute. In this document, while examining at great length the writings and severely condemning the errors of Theodore of Mopsuestia, and while reiterating his own profession of faith, so as to show that he himself was utterly untainted with Nestorianism, Vigilius condemned all the proceedings of those who were now agitating for the condemnation of the Three Chapters; grounding his opposition chiefly on the familiar arguments of the impropriety of anathematizing the dead, and the fact that, as far as Theodore and Ibas were concerned, the cause had been already decided in their favor at Chalcedon. He concluded in the tone of an autocrat of the Church, forbidding any person who held any ecclesiastical dignity whatever to put forth any opinion concerning the Three Chapters contrary to this *Constitutum*, or to raise any further question concerning them. Any action which might be taken by such ecclesiastical persons in opposition to this decree was declared beforehand to be made null and void "by the authority of the Apostolic See over which by the grace of God we preside".

The members of the Fifth Council, at whom of course this *Constitutum* was chiefly aimed, went on their way disregarding it; and at their seventh and last sitting, after completing all their other anathemas, struck the name of Vigilius out of the diptychs. This was done at the express and urgent entreaty of Justinian. Thus had the nephew of Justin, the mainstay of that Imperial house whose great glory it had once been to bring about the reconciliation with the Roman See, himself imitated the audacious act of Acacius, by excommunicating the successor of St. Peter.

Sentence of banishment was passed on all the opposers of the Fifth Council, and in this banishment Vigilius, already in a certain sense an exile, had doubly to share. He was conveyed to the little island of Proconnesus, near the western end of the Sea of Marmora, closely guarded, and given to understand that so long as he refused to accept the authority of the Fifth Council, he had no hope of revisiting Rome. Not only so, but the Emperor appears to have determined to order a new election to the Papal Chair, superseding Vigilius by a more pliable pontiff as Theodora had superseded Silverius by Vigilius. Under these hard blows, with the prospect of yet harder to come, and with his health undermined by that cruel disease the agony of which has crushed the strongest hearts, the spirit of Vigilius gave way. After six months of banishment he wrote a letter to the Patriarch of Constantinople, in which he lamented the misunderstandings which, by the instigation of the Devil, had arisen between himself and his brother bishops dwelling in the Royal City. Christ, the true Light of the World, had now removed all darkness from the writers mind and recalled the whole Church to peace. Following the noble example of St. Augustine, who feared not in his *Retractationes* to own the mistakes in his previous writings, Vigilius would now acknowledge that, having with renewed care examined the writings of Theodore of Mopsuestia, he found therein many things both blasphemous and absurd which he was now ready unhesitatingly to condemn. With equal clearness could he anathematize all that Theodoret had written against the true faith, against the Council of Ephesus, and the twelve chapters of Cyril. Lastly, he anathematized the letter, full of profane blasphemies, which Ibas was said to have written to the Persian heretic Maris. No point was left uncovered. The Pope had surrendered to his enemies at discretion.

Two months later, Vigilius addressed, probably to the Bishops of the West, a long *Constitutum*, in which, going over all the weary controversy, he in fact retracted whatsoever he had previously advanced as to the impropriety of condemning the Three Chapters. The only novelty in the document, and a perilous one, was a long piece of special pleading (which seems to have convinced no one either in its own or succeeding ages) on behalf of the proposition that the so-called letter of Ibas was never written by that ecclesiastic.

After this complete capitulation the Pope was suffered to return to Italy. Great events had meanwhile been happening there, events which made his return at this time eminently opportune. The Roman clergy had petitioned for his restoration, to which step Justinian may perhaps have given somewhat of the character of an act of amnesty; though indeed the Emperor had so completely vanquished the Pope, that no reason for quarrel any longer existed between them.

But Vigilius was not after all to see again the Church of the Lateran, for the sake of the first place in which he had done so many misdeeds and endured so many hardships. His health, which had been failing ever since his flight to Chalcedon, and which had no doubt suffered from his banishment to Proconnesus, now became rapidly worse. He could proceed no further on his way than to Sicily, and died there on the 7th January, 555. He was succeeded, after a vacancy of a little more than three months, by the deacon Pelagius, who had served under Vigilius at Constantinople through all the recent controversy, and had shared his hardships and his perils.

As far as Emperor and Pope were concerned, thus closed the controversy of the Three Chapters. Justinian had undoubtedly gathered all the laurels that could reward such a petty and ignoble contest. He, the amateur theologian, after a struggle as long as the siege of Troy, had imposed his definition of the right faith on all the four Christian patriarchates, and had bound those who believe in the infallibility of General Councils to accept it henceforward as an essential article of the Christian creed that the soul of Theodore of Mopsuestia suffers eternal torment. As a statesman his success was not perhaps equally brilliant. He did not by his maneuvers secure the loyalty of a single disaffected Monophysite; and he raised up a generation of bitter schismatics in Italy who were to persist for a century and a half, preferring even the rule of the savage Lombard to communion with the Church which anathematized the Three Chapters. As a guide and counselor of the Church the half-heathen Constantine certainly presents a fairer record than the highly-trained controversialist Justinian.

The unhappy Vigilius, in the course of this controversy, had to drink the cup of humiliation to the dregs. Deeply offending both parties, he has found champions in neither; and in consequence posterity has been perhaps unduly severe upon his memory. Travelling as he did at least four times from one point to the diametrically opposite point of the theological compass, he deeply injured the credit of the Roman See, which now passed through half a century of obscurity till the arising of the first and greatest Gregory. He must certainly be held to have been an unsuccessful general of the forces of the Papacy, but there is no proof that he was a coward, and his censors have perhaps hardly enough considered whether at his particular point in the campaign success was possible. For six years he had to dwell at the seat of the rival Patriarch, daily beholding the majesty of the Emperor and begirt by evidences of his power. To resist the commands of this omnipotent Caesar, from a modest dwelling within a mile or two of his palace, was a task which required much more hardihood than merely hurling spiritual thunderbolts from the Lateran or the Vatican at some unseen and unknown Frederick or Henry on the other side of the Alps.

Then the theological battle-field was ill-chosen for the interests of the Papacy. To say nothing of the dismal unreality of the controversy (though Vigilius was probably acute enough to perceive and to be disheartened by this unreality), there can be no doubt that the pedantic, lawyer-like mind of Justinian had detected a flaw in the proceedings of the Council of Chalcedon. His determination to publish his discovery to an admiring world placed Vigilius in a pitiable dilemma, one from which even a Leo or a Hormisdas would have found a difficulty in escaping. If he defended the Three Chapters he was looked upon as tainted with Nestorianism and false to the Council of Ephesus. If he condemned them he seemed to be dallying with the Monophysites and disloyal to the Council of Chalcedon. Certainly to adopt both courses alternately, and to do this twice over, was about as disastrous a policy as he could possibly have adopted. But even as to this vacillation the harshness of our censure would be abated if we grasped fully the enormous difficulty of his position. He, like Justinian, was striving, and could not but strive, for an unattainable object. The Emperor was compelled to struggle for the restoration of the old boundaries of the Roman Empire. The Pope was bound to wrestle for the preservation of the unity of the Christian Church. A decree against which they were powerless to contend had gone forth that the East and the West should be parted asunder, politically, religiously, and intellectually. But they knew not this; and the luckless Vigilius, laboring to prevent the Eastern and Western Churches from being rent asunder by this miserable question about the damnation of Theodore, was like a man who, standing on shipboard, reaches out his hand to a friend standing on the pier, and not unclasping it quickly enough, is swept from his place by the motion of the vessel and fells headlong into the sea.

But assuredly the wonderful political instinct of the Roman Church was at fault when she allied herself with Constantinople against Ravenna. Already have two Popes—Silverius and Vigilius—found the little finger of Justinian thicker than the loins of Theodoric.

CHAPTER XXIV.

NARSES AND TOTILA.

Immersed in theology and intent on the damnation of Theodore of Mopsuestia, Justinian would gladly have forgotten the affairs of Italy. Sixteen years ago he had sent his soldiers and his invincible General on an expedition which he perhaps hoped would prove, like the Vandal campaign, not much more than a military promenade. Victory had come far more slowly in Italy than in Africa, and in the very moment of his triumph the prize had slipped from his grasp and the whole work had to be done over again. Ever since Totila was raised upon the shields of the Goths, ill-success, scarcely varied by one or two streaks of good-fortune, had attended the Imperial arms, and now only four points on the coast—Ravenna, Ancona, Hydruntum, Crotona—owned allegiance to the Empire. As a source of revenue, the country for whose re-annexation such large sums had been expended was absolutely worthless; and on the other hand, whenever the Imperial wished to erect a new church or fortress in Thrace or Asia Minor to commemorate his name and to be described with inflated rhetoric in the *De Aedificiis* of Procopius, the finance-minister, if he were an honest man, was sure to remind him of the long arrears of pay due to the starving troops in Italy, and of the absolute necessity that any money that could be spared should be remitted to Ravenna. Thus it came to pass that Justinian already in 549 was sick of the very name of Italy, and would have been willing to sit down satisfied with its loss, but that, as already stated, Vigilius and the other Roman refugees incessantly pressed upon him with their petitions for help, and their not unreasonable complaints of the ruin which his policy, if it was to stop short at this point, would have brought upon them.

There was, then, to be another expedition to Italy. Germanus being untimely dead and Liberius hopelessly incapable, the question arose who should be the new commander of the forces. John the nephew of Vitalian, who had passed the winter of 550 at Salona, had the military talent necessary for the post, but, notwithstanding his recently-formed connection with the Imperial house, he was still too little superior to the other generals by character or position to make it probable that they would accord to him that unquestioning obedience, the want of which had already proved so fatal to the Emperor's interests.

In these circumstances Justinian decided to offer the command of the new Italian expedition to his Grand Chamberlain Narses, who eagerly accepted it. The choice of this man, an eunuch, in the seventy-fifth year of his age, one whose life had been spent in the enervating atmosphere and amid the idle labors of an Imperial presence-chamber, would have seemed the extremity of madness to the stout soldiers of the Republic by whom the title Imperator had first been worn. Yet, in truth, this choice proved to be another instance of Justinian's admirable knowledge of men, and great power (when he gave his intellect fair play) of adapting his means to the required ends. Narses (who lived for more than twenty years after the date we have now reached), though short in stature and lean in figure, evidently still possessed good health, and faculties quite undimmed by age. In his previous campaign in Italy, fourteen years before, he had shown no small strategic talent, and he had for ever secured the grateful affection of the stout soldier John, who would now willingly concede to him an obedience such as any other general would demand in vain. The two together, Narses as the wily much meditating brain, and John as the vigorous swiftly smiting arm, might be expected to do great deeds against even the gallant Totila. And throughout Italy, wherever the Roman armies might move, recovering cities or provinces for the Empire, the presence of a man who came straight from the Sacred Majesty of the Emperor, and had been for the past twenty years or more a Cabinet-minister (as we should say) of the highest rank, would command the unhesitating and eager obedience of all that official hierarchy whose instinct it was to obey, if it could only be assured that its orders came direct from Imperial Power.

The announcement that the Eunuch was to command the Italian army was received with a shout of applause by all who hoped to share in the expedition. Narses, unlike many previous eunuchs at the Imperial Court, had always been conspicuous for his free-handed generosity. Many a barbarian soldier of fortune had already found himself opportunely enriched by the Grand Chamberlain's favor. These longed to show their gratitude by the alacrity of their service; while to those who had not yet experienced his benefits the 'lively sense of favors to come' proved an equally powerful stimulus to action. With the zealous Catholics also throughout the Empire the appointment of Narses was in the highest degree popular, since his piety towards God and his devotion to the Virgin Mother were notorious throughout the Court, as they soon became notorious throughout the army. It was believed by his soldiers that the Illustrious *Cubicularius* had supernatural visitations from the Mother of God, and that she announced to him by some secret but well-known sign the favorable moment for his troops to move forward to battle. Such a belief was, in the existing temper of men's minds, by itself a powerful aid to victory.

Above all, Narses, as being one of the innermost governing council of the Empire, could ensure that his expedition should not be starved, as the second expedition of Belisarius had been starved, into failure. There was no talk now, as there had been then, of the General himself providing the sinews of war. The Imperial exchequer was now freely drawn upon. The long-standing arrears of the soldiers' pay were discharged. Liberal offers were made to all new-comers: and soon the usual motley host which called itself a Roman army was gathering round the Eunuch's standards, full of martial ardor for the fray, full of martial cupidity for the plunder of Italy.

It was a satire on the policy of Justinian that Narses, eager to reach Salona on the Adriatic coast and there assemble his army, was actually stopped at Philippopolis in Thrace by a horde of Hunnish savages—probably the Kotrigur Huns whose raids have been already alluded to—who had penetrated into the Empire and were ravaging far and wide the Thracian villages. Fortunately, however, for the Italian expedition, the Hunnish torrent parted itself into two streams, one of which pursued its journey towards Constantinople, while the other moved south-westward to Thessalonica. Between the two hordes Narses adroitly made his way across Macedonia to Salona, where he spent the remainder of the year 551 in organizing an army for the invasion of Italy.

The news that this supreme effort was to be made for his overthrow quickened the energy of Totila, and at the same time increased his efforts to win the favor of the Roman people. While closely pressing both by sea and land the siege of Ancona, in order that the Imperialists might have no base of operations in all the long interval from Ravenna to Crotona, he also, as has been already said, brought back many of the captive Senators to Rome, and encouraged them to repair the desolations which he had himself caused, and which, we are told, were most conspicuous in the part of the City that lay on the west of the Tiber. The King's care for the rebuilding of the City gained him some little favor from the Romans, who, in the estimation of Procopius, surpassed all other populations in love for their City and pride in its adornment; but the Senators, paupers and still feeling themselves like captives, wandered ghost-like amid the scenes of their vanished splendor, and had neither the spirit nor the resources to assist, themselves, in the work of restoration.

As we have seen in previous chapters, Totila had paid more attention to his fleet than any of the Ostrogothic Kings who preceded him, and was by no means disposed tamely to yield to Byzantium the dominion of the seas. Three hundred ships of war were sent by him to cruise off the western coast of Greece, omitting no opportunity of plundering and distressing the subjects of the Empire. Their crews ravaged the island of Corcyra and the little islets near it, landed in Epirus, and laid waste the territory round the venerable fane of Dodona and Augustus's more modern City of Victory, and then, cruising along the coast, fell in with and captured some of the ships that were carrying provisions to the army of Narses at Salona.

The siege of Ancona was, however, the chief operation in which Totila's forces were engaged: and that city, sore pressed both by sea and land, saw itself apparently on the eve of surrender to the Goths. Valerian, who seems to have been responsible for the government and defence of Ancona, was at this time staying at Ravenna, and finding himself unable to afford any effectual help with the forces which he had collected there, sent messengers to John at Salona with an earnest exhortation to avert the ruin to the Emperors affairs which must result from the capture of so important a sea-port. John was convinced, and ventured, in defiance of the express orders which he had received from the Emperor, to dispatch a squadron for the relief of Ancona. Valerian met him at Scardona on the coast of Ulyria, and concerted measures for the coming expedition, and soon the two generals, with fifty ships under their orders, crossed the Adriatic and anchored off the little town of Sena Gallica (the modern Sinigaglia), sixteen miles north-west of Ancona. On the other side the Goths had forty-seven ships of war, which they filled with some of their noblest soldiers and with which they sailed to meet the enemy, under the command of two admirals, Giblas and Indulph. The latter officer was one who had once been a soldier in Belisarius's own bodyguard, but, like so many of his comrades, disgusted by the Imperial ingratitude, had deserted to the standards of Totila. Scipuar, who had been joined in command with these two officers, remained with the rest of the army to prosecute the siege of Ancona by land.

Off Sinigaglia then the two fleets anchored, and both sides prepared for action. John and Valerian haranguing their troops insisted on the immense importance of raising the siege of Ancona and the hopelessness of their own position if they allowed the Goths on this day to obtain the command of the sea. Indulph and Giblas scoffed at the new audacity of the accursed Greeks who had at last ventured forth from the creeks and bays of Dalmatia in which they had so long been hiding. A feeble and unwarlike race, born to be defeated in battle, this sudden display of rashness on their part was the result of mere ignorance, but must be at once repressed by Gothic valor before it had time to grow to a dangerous height.

Notwithstanding these vaunting words, the Greeks, those children of the sea, who, from the days of Cadmus, had spread their sails to every breeze that ruffled the

Aegean, vanquished the Goths, those hereditary landsmen, whose forefathers had roamed for centuries in the Sarmatian solitudes. The wind was light, and as ship grappled ship the battle assumed the appearance of a hand-to-hand encounter by land rather than a sea-fight. But the Goths, deficient in that instinctive sympathy between the sailor and his ship which belongs to a nation of mariners, failed to keep their vessels at proper distances from one another. Here a wide-yawning interval invited the inroad of the enemy; there several ships close together became a terror to their friends, and lost all power of maneuvering. The orders of the generals became inaudible in the hubbub of angry voices as each Gothic steersman shouted to his fellow to leave him ampler sea-room. Intent on averting collision with their countrymen by poles and boat-hooks, the Goths were unable to attend to the necessities of the battle. Meanwhile the Imperial mariners, who had kept their ranks in perfect order, were perpetually charging into the gaps in the line of the barbarians, surrounding and cutting out the ships which were left defenseless, or keeping up a storm of missiles on those parts of the line where the hostile ships were thickly entangled with one another, and where the interlacing masts showed like net-work to the eye of a beholder. The barbarians fell into the torpor of despair, and saw the chance of victory float away from them without making an effort to turn the tide. Then to torpor succeeded panic, and they steered their ships for headlong flight, flight which delivered them yet more utterly into the hands of the Romans. Indulph indeed with eleven of his ships succeeded in escaping from the scene of action; but, despairing of further resistance by sea, landed his men in the first harborage and burned his ships to prevent their falling into the power of the enemy. All the other Gothic ships were either sunk or taken by the Romans, and Giblas himself was taken prisoner.

The Goths who had succeeded in escaping from the scene took the dismal tale of defeat to the army before Ancona, who at once raised the siege and retreated to the shelter of rock-built Osimo. John and Valerian then appeared upon the scene, occupied and perhaps plundered the recent Gothic camp, abundantly revictualled Ancona, and then returned to Salona and Ravenna respectively, having by this achievement struck a heavy blow at the power and yet more at the self-confidence of the Goths in Italy.

About the same time another disaster befell the Gothic cause. The respectable but feeble Liberius was removed from the government of Sicily, and Artabanes the Armenian was appointed in his stead. Avenger of Areobindus, governor of Carthage, Master of the Soldiery, aspirant to the hand of Justinian's niece, conspirator against Justinian's life, in all the varied phases of his career, whether loyal or disloyal, Artabanes had always shown courage and capacity; and he now abundantly justified the generous confidence reposed in him by the forgiving Emperor. He attacked the Gothic garrisons in Sicily with such vigor and blockaded so effectually those who would not meet him in the field that they were all speedily forced to surrender, and Sicily was lost to the Goths.

John, the governor of Africa, endeavored to rival the exploits of Artabanes by sending an expedition to subdue Corsica and Sardinia. These islands, on account of their long subjection to the Vandals, were looked upon as forming part of the African province and as naturally following its fortunes, but the result of the maritime supremacy of Totila during the last few years had been to annex them to the Ostrogothic kingdom. The armament which the Carthaginian governor now dispatched to Sardinia commenced in regular form the siege of Cagliari; but the Gothic garrison, which was a powerful one, sallied forth from the city and inflicted such a severe defeat on the besiegers that they fled headlong to their ships, and the reconquest of the two islands had to be for the time abandoned.

Notwithstanding this slight gleam of success, the defeat at Sinigaglia, which left the Imperial fleet mistress of the sea, and the loss of Sicily, threw Totila and his nobles into a state of deep dejection. We learn at this point of the story that their hold upon the north of Italy had for some years been insecure, if it had not been altogether lost. The Franks of the Sixth Century, according to Procopius, adopted the ungenerous policy of always turning their neighbors' troubles to profitable account, by seizing their most precious possessions when they were engaged in a life and death struggle with some powerful enemy. In pursuance of this policy Theudibert, grandson of Clovis, had descended into the valley of the Po (probably in the early years of Totila's heroic reign), and had annexed to his dominions, or at least had made subject to tribute, the three provinces of Liguria, Venetia, and the Cottian Alps, or, to speak in the language of modern geography, the whole of Piedmont and Lombardy. The Goths, knowing that it was hopeless for them to contend at once against the Empire and the Franks, acquiesced for a time in this usurpation, and even made a kind of league of amity with Theudibert, the question of the precise apportionment of his Italian territory being by common consent adjourned till the war with the Empire should be ended.

Gladly would Totila now have ended that war by some peaceful compromise. With Northern Italy in the power of the Franks, with Central and Southern Italy reduced well-nigh to a desert by seventeen years of war, he was prepared to relinquish all claim to the comparatively uninjured provinces of Sicily and Dalmatia, to pay a large tribute for the portion of Italy which was left to him, and to form a league of perpetual alliance with the Empire. It can hardly be doubted that for the Eastern Emperors themselves, from the mere Byzantine point of view, as well as for Italy and the world, such an arrangement would have been better than what was really in store for them if it was rejected,—the truceless enmity of the savage Lombard. But Justinian, even when most weary of his Italian enterprise, would listen to no proposals for abandoning *de jure* any one of his claims. He hated the very name of the Goths, and longed to extirpate them from the soil of the Empire. Thus all the many embassies of Totila, whatever the terms proposed, never returned with a message of peace.

About this time, however, the Emperor himself had recourse to an embassy in order to detach the Franks from the Gothic alliance. King Theudibert was now dead, having been accidentally killed while hunting wild bulls in a forest; and to his son Theudibald, a feeble and sickly youth, Leontius the senator, ambassador of Justinian, addressed his remonstrances and his requests. And certainly the complaints of their former ally, addressed to the Franks of that day, seem to have had some foundation in truth. "Justinian", said the ambassador, "would never have undertaken his enterprise against the Goths without the promise of your cooperation, for which he paid large sums of money. You refused your promised assistance and stood aside while we with vast labor and peril conquered the country, which you then most unjustly invaded, appropriating some of its provinces. We might blame, but we rather beseech you for your own sakes to depart out of Italy; for ill-gotten gains such as these will bring you no prosperity. You say that you are in alliance with the Goths: but the Goths have been your enemies from the beginning, and have waged against you one unceasing and unrelenting war. Just now, through fear, they condescend to be your flatterers, but if they once get clear of us, you will soon find out what is their feeling towards the Franks. The ambassador concluded by exhorting Theudibald to undo what his father had done amiss, by firmly renewing the former alliance between the Franks and the Empire.

Theudibald piteously replied that his father could not have been the clever robber of his neighbors' property whom the ambassadors described since he himself was by no means wealthy. He thought the Emperor would have been rather pleased than otherwise to see his enemies the Goths despoiled of three important provinces, and he could truly say that if he could be proved to have taken anything from the Empire he would straightway restore it. He then commissioned a Frank named Leudard to return as his envoy with Leontius to Constantinople; but nothing seems to have resulted from the visit of the ambassador.

With these negotiations the winter of 551 wore away. Early in the spring of 552 occurred the relief of Crotona, so long the base of the Imperial operations in the south of Italy. Its garrison, hard pressed by the Goths, sent a message to Artabanes, the governor of Sicily, that unless speedily relieved they must surrender the city. Artabanes at the time was unable to help them, but Justinian himself, hearing of their distress, sent orders to the detachment which guarded the pass of Thermopylae to set sail with all speed for Italy and raise the siege of Crotona. Strange to say, so great was their dispatch and so favorable the breezes that they appeared in the bay before the arrival of the day fixed for the surrender of the city. The sight of the ships filled the besiegers with terror. They fled in all directions, eastwards to Tarentum, and southwards to the very edge of the Straits of Messina; and the Gothic governors of some of the other towns of Southern Italy, Tarentum itself and the 'lofty nest of Acherontia' began to treat for the surrender of those places to the Imperial generals.

Deep discouragement everywhere was creeping over the hearts of the defenders of the throne of Totila, and meanwhile the great and well-equipped host which Narses had been so long preparing at Salona was at last on its way. The sum total of the Imperial army does not seem to be given us by our historian, but we hear something of the multifarious elements of which it was composed. The two armies of John and of his father-in-law Germanus formed the nucleus of the host, but besides these there was the other John, nicknamed the Glutton, with a multitude of stout Roman soldiers. There was Asbad, a young Gepid of extraordinary bravery, with four hundred warriors, all men of his own blood. There was Aruth, a Herulian by birth but Roman by training, by inclination, and by marriage, who led a large band of his countrymen, men who especially delighted in the perils of the fight. Philemuth, also a Herulian, perhaps of purer barbaric training, who had served in many previous campaigns in Italy, was followed by more than three thousand men of the same wild and wandering race, all mounted on horseback. The young Dagisthaeus, probably also of barbarian origin, was released from the prison into which he had been thrown on account of his miserable mismanagement of the war waged with Persia in the defiles of Mount Caucasus, and was allowed to have another chance of vindicating his reputation as a general and his loyalty as a subject of the Emperor. In the same army was to be found a Persian prince himself, Kobad, nephew of Chosroes, grandson and namesake of the great King who had waged war with Anastasius. This prince, whom in his youth conspirators had sought to seat on the throne of the Sassanids, had been condemned to death by his merciless uncle, and had been only saved by the humane disobedience of the General in Chief (or Chanaranges) to whom the murderous order had been entrusted, and who eventually paid for his compassion with his life. Many of his countrymen, refugees like himself from the tyranny of Chosroes, followed Kobad to the war in a strange land and in defence of a stranger's claims.

We have left to the last the most important in the eyes of posterity of all this motley horde of army of chieftains. Audoin, King of the Lombards, rode in the train of Narses at the head of two thousand five hundred brave warriors, who had for their personal attendants more than three thousand men also skilled in war. The mention of these two classes shows us that we are already approaching the days of the knights and squires of chivalry. We hear not much, it is true, of the actual deeds of Audoin in the following campaign, but his importance for us consists in the fact that he is the father of the terrible Alboin, who, sixteen years after the time which we have now reached, will on his own account be crossing the Alpine wall and descending with his savage horde into that fertile plain which thenceforward will to all ages be known as Lombardy. Thus continually do we see the Roman *foederatus* becoming the conqueror of Rome. Thus did Theodosius lead Alaric in his train over the Julian Alps and show him the road to Italy.

Huns in great numbers, squalid and fierce as ever, but useful soldiers when deeds of daring and hard endurance were needed, urged on their little steeds at the sound of the Imperial bugles. It was indeed a strange army to be charged with asserting the majesty of the Roman Empire and reuniting to it the old Hesperian land. Could a Cincinnatus or a Regulus have looked upon those wild tribes from beyond the Danube and those dark faces from beside the Euphrates, all under the supreme command of an eunuch from under the shadow of Mount Ararat, he would assuredly have been perplexed to decide whether they or the soldiers of Totila had less claim to the great name of Roman.

But ethnological considerations such as these were beside the mark. A common passion, the hope of the spoil of Italy, fused all these discordant nationalities into one coherent whole. The purse-strings of the Emperor were loosened; and over the whole army hovered the genius of the deep-thoughted Narses, willing to part freely with the treasures of his master, and his own, if only his shaking hand might pluck the laurels which had been denied, in the vigor of middle age, to the mighty Belisarius.

Imperial army marched round the head of the Adriatic Gulf: but when it came to the confines of Venetia it found the passage barred by order of the Frankish King. The real reason for this hostile procedure was that for the moment it seemed a more profitable course to keep, than to break, the oaths which the Franks had sworn to the Goths; but the pretext alleged, namely, the presence of the Lombard auxiliaries, foes to the Frankish name, in the army of Narses, had probably also some genuine force. Already these races, which for the following two centuries were to contest with one another the right to plunder Italy, eyed one another with jealous hostility, each foreseeing in the other an unwelcome fellow-guest at the banquet.

Nor were the Franks the only enemies who intervened between the Imperial host and the friendly shelter of Ravenna. More to the west, Teias, one of the bravest of the young officers of Totila, barred the way at Verona against any invader who should seek to enter by the Pass of the Brenner. At the same time, as he hoped, he had so obstructed the bridges over the intricate rivers and canals of Lombardy as to make it impossible for Narses to pass him without fighting a pitched battle.

Narses, as Totila was well aware, did not possess a sufficiently large flotilla to transport his army directly across the head of the Adriatic Gulf from the mouth of the Isonzo to Classis; but in his perplexity his skillful lieutenant, John, who was well acquainted with the country between Aquileia and Ravenna, suggested to him an expedient by which the few ships which he had might render signal service to the army. The scheme was this : for the soldiers to march close to the sea, where the country, intersected as it is by the mouths of the Piave, Brenta, Adige, and Po, would offer no field for the hostile operations of the Franks, and to use the ships, which were to accompany them within signaling distance, for the transport of the soldiers across the river-estuaries, perhaps also in some cases across the actual lagoons. This difficult operation was successfully effected; the flank, both of the Frankish generals and of Teias, was turned, and Narses with all his army reached Ravenna in safety. Justin, who had been left in charge of Ravenna by Belisarius, and Valerian, the recent victor at Sinigaglia, joined their forces, which were apparently not very numerous, to those of Narses.

After a tarriance of nine days at Ravenna there came an insulting message from Usdrilas, who was holding Bimini for the Goths: "After your vaunted preparations, which have kept all Italy in a ferment, and after trying to strike terror into our hearts by knitting your brows and looking more awful than mortal men, you have crept into Ravenna and are skulking there, afraid of the very name of the Goths. Come out, with all that mongrel host of barbarians to whom you want to deliver Italy, and let us behold you, for the eyes of the Goths hunger for the sight of you". Narses, on reading these words, laughed at the insolence of the barbarian, but set forward nevertheless with the bulk of his army, leaving a small garrison under Justin at Ravenna. On his arrival at Rimini he found that the bridge over the Marecchia—that noble structure of Augustus which was described in an earlier chapter—was effectually blocked by the enemy. While the soldiers of Narses, some of whom had crossed the river, were looking about for a ford convenient for the passage of the bulk of the army, Usdrilas, with some of his followers, came upon them. A skirmish followed, in which, by a rare stroke of good fortune, the Herulians in the Imperial army slew Usdrilas himself. His head, severed from his body, was brought into the camp of Narses, and cheered both General and soldiers by this apparent token of divine favor upon their enterprise. The General, however, determined not to stay to prosecute the siege of Rimini, but availed himself of the discouragement of the enemy, caused by the death of Usdrilas, to throw a pontoon bridge across the Marecchia and proceed on his march southwards. "For he did not choose", says Procopius, "to molest either Ariminum or any other post occupied by the enemy, in order that he might not lose time and fail in his most important enterprise by having his attention diverted to minor objects... After passing Ariminum [and, we may add, Fanum,] he departed from the Flaminian Way and struck off to the left. For the position of Petra Pertusa, which have described in a previous book of my history, and which is exceedingly strong by nature, having been occupied long before by the enemy, rendered the Flaminian Way altogether impassable to the Romans. Narses, therefore, being thus obliged to quit the shortest road, took that which was available".

We see, from this passage of Procopius, that again, as in previous stages of the war, the possession of Petra Pertusa (the Passo di Furlo) exercised an important influence on the movements of the combatants. As it was now in the hands of the Goths, Narses was compelled to leave the broad highway of Flaminius and to keep southwards along the Adriatic Gulf till he could find a road which would take him into the Via Flaminia at a point on the Romeward side of the Passo di Furlo. Such a road, as I read his movements, he found before he reached Sinigaglia. Taking a sharp turn to the right near the mouth of the Sena (Cesano), he would be brought, by a march of about thirty-six miles up the valley formed by that stream and across the uplands, to the town of Cales (Cagli). Here the Imperial army would be once more upon the great Flaminian Way, having in fact turned the fortress of Pertusa, but they would be still among narrow defiles, where the road is often carried by narrow bridges over rocky streams. An attack at this part of their course might have easily thrown the army into disorder, and we may be sure that Narses and his chief officers would breathe more freely when, after fourteen miles' march up a sharp ascent crossing and recrossing the torrent of the Burano, they came at length, at the posting-station Ad Ensem, to the crest of the pass, and saw a broader and less difficult valley spreading below them to the south. Somewhere in the neighborhood of this posting-station (represented by the modern village of Scheggia), Narses probably encamped and prepared for battle, being aware of the near neighborhood of the Gothic host. The words of Procopius, who states that the camp was pitched "upon the Apennine mountains" and yet "upon a level spot" describe with great accuracy the exact situation of Scheggia.

Meanwhile Totila, after receiving the news of the untoward events which had happened in Venetia, tarried for some time in the neighborhood of Rome to give the soldiers of Teias, now outflanked and useless, time to rejoin his standards. When all but two thousand of these had arrived he started upon the northward march, through Etruria and Umbria. His movements were quickened by hearing of the death of Usdrilas and the ineffectual attempt of the garrison of Rimini to arrest the progress of the invaders. Knowing that the pass of Furlo was blocked, he was probably uncertain as to the precise point at which Narses would seek to traverse the great Apennine wall that intervened between him and Rome. Scanning doubtless with eagerness every possible outlet through the mountains, he had reached the little town of Tadinum. Further north he had not been able to penetrate, before Narses arrived upon the crest of the pass.

Here then, upon the Flaminian Way, but high up in the heart of the Apennines, must be fought the battle which was to decide once and for ever the embittered quarrel between the nation of the Ostrogoths and Eastern Rome. The place is worthy to be the theatre of great events. It is close to the 'House of two Waters' from which flows on one side a stream that eventually swells the waters of the Tiber and passes out into the Tyrrhene Sea, on the other the torrent of the Burano, which pours itself through rocky defiles northwards to the Adriatic. The valley itself is a sort of long trough sloping gradually towards the south. On the eastern side, with their summits for the most part invisible from this point, rise some of the greatest mountains of the Apennine chain, snow-crowned Monte Cucco, Monte Catria with its grand buttress, Monte Corno, Monte Strega looking like a witch's hand with five skinny fingers pointing upward to the sky. On the opposite side of the valley, upon our right as we look towards Rome, rises a lower but more picturesque range of hills. These sharp serrated summits, so clearly defined against the sunset sky, are Monte S. Ubaldo and Monte Calvo, the mountains of Gubbio. At their base, hidden from us because on the other side of them lies the little city of Gubbio, dear to scholars for its precious Eugubine Tables which enshrine the language of ancient Umbria, and dear to painters for the frescoes of Nelli, one of the most reverent of the artists of Umbria.

The distance between Scheggia and Tadino is about fifteen miles, agreeing closely enough with the distance of one hundred stadia which, according to Procopius, intervened at first between the camps of the two generals. But a more precise identification of the site of the battle I am not able to furnish. I have no doubt that it was fought south of Scheggia and north of Tadino; but Procopius, whose campaigning days were over, and who was evidently not himself present at the battle, does not, I fear, enable us to fix the site more accurately than this.

As soon as Narses had encamped his army he sent an embassy to Totila, strongly recommending him to lay down his arms and abandon the hopeless task of resisting, with his handful of disorderly followers, the whole might of the Roman Empire. If, however, the ambassadors perceived him still bent on battle they were to ask him to name the day. Totila haughtily rejected the counsels of his foe, and when asked upon what day he proposed to fight, replied: "In eight days from this time". Narses suspected a stratagem and prepared for battle on the morrow. He had read his enemy's mind aright. On the very next day Totila suddenly appeared with his whole army and encamped at the distance of two bowshots from the Imperialists.

A hill of moderate height (probably an outlier of the main Apennine range) looked down upon both armies, and commanded a path by which the Imperial host might be taken in rear. The possession of this hill was at once seen to be a matter of great importance to either side, but Narses was beforehand with Totila in seizing this coign of vantage. Fifty picked foot-soldiers were sent to occupy it during the night, and when day dawned the Goths, from their encampment opposite, saw these men drawn up in serried array, and having their front protected by the bed of a torrent running parallel to the only path, before alluded to. A squadron of cavalry was sent to dislodge them, but the Romans kept their rank, and by clashing upon their shields, so frightened the horses of the Goths that they were able to lay low many an embarrassed rider with their spear-thrusts. The cavalry fell into helpless confusion, and retired discomfited. Again and again with fresh squadrons of horse did Totila attempt to dislodge them, but the brave Fifty kept their ground unbroken. The honors of this fight fell pre-eminently to two men, by name Paulus and Ausilas, who stepped forth, Horatius-like, before their comrades to bear the stress of battle. They laid their scimitars on the ground and drew their bows, slaying a horse or a man with each discharge, so long as there was an arrow in their quivers. Then drawing their swords they lopped off one by one the spear-heads which the Goths protruded against them. By these repeated strokes the sword of Paulus was at length so bent as to become quite useless. He threw it on the ground and, with his unarmed hands, seized and broke no fewer than four of the spears of the enemy. This desperate valor more than anything else daunted the Gothic assailants and compelled them to abandon their attempt upon the hill where the Fifty were posted. Paulus was rewarded after the battle by being made one of the guardsmen of Narses.

Now were the two main armies drawn up in battle array, and in that position they were harangued by their respective leaders Narses congratulated his troops on their evident superiority to the band of robbers and deserters who composed the Gothic host; a superiority which, by the Divine favor, was certain to bring them the victory. He reviled the soldiers in the hostile army as the runaway slaves of the Emperor, their King as a leader picked out of the gutter, and declared that it was only by tricks and thievish artifice that they had so long been able to harass the Empire. Lastly, he dwelt upon the ephemeral character of all the barbaric royalties, contrasting them with the settled order, the deep vitality, the *diuturnity* (if such a word may be allowed us) of the mighty Roman State. Totila, perceiving that a shiver of admiring awe ran through the Gothic lines at the sight of the mighty host of the Empire, called upon his comrades for one last effort of valor, a last effort, since Justinian, like themselves, was weary of the war, and, if discomfited now, would molest them no more forever. "After all, why should any soldier fly? The only motive could be love of life, and he was infinitely safer, to appeal to no higher motive, fighting in the ranks with the enemy than after he had once turned his back before them. Nor were they really the formidable host which they seemed. Huns, and Longobards, and Heruli, a motley horde got together from all quarters, like the miscellaneous dishes of a club-feast, they had no bond of unity, no instinct of cohesion. Their pay was the only inducement to fight that they could understand, and now that they had received that, it would not be surprising if, in compliance with the secret orders of their national leaders, they absolutely melted away from the ranks on the field of undesired battle"

Narses, who had evidently the superiority in numbers as well as in equipment, drew up his troops in the following order. In the centre he stationed his barbarian allies, the Lombards and the Heruli, and, as he was not over-confident of their stability, he directed them to dismount and fight on foot, in order that flight might not be easy if they were minded to fly. All his best Roman troops, with picked men from among the Hunnish barbarians, men who for their prowess had been selected as body-guards, he stationed on his left wing, where he himself and his lieutenant John were in command. This portion of the army was covered by the hill before described, which was held by the fifty valiant men, and which seems to have been 'the key of the position'. Under this hill, and at an angle with the rest of his line, Narses stationed two bodies of cavalry, numbering respectively one thousand and five hundred. The five hundred were to watch the Roman line and strengthen any part which might seem for the moment to be wavering. The thousand were to wait for the commencement of the action, and then to strain every nerve in order to get to the rear of the Goths, and so place them between two attacks. On the left wing were the rest of the Roman troops under John the Glutton, together with Valerian and Dagisthaeus. On each flank was a force of four thousand archers, fighting, contrary to the usual custom of Roman archers in those days, on foot. Looking at the tactics of the Roman general as a whole, we perceive an almost ostentatious disregard of what might happen to his centre. He was determined to conquer with the wings of his army, determined that Totila, not he, should make the attack, and that when the enemy attacked he should be outflanked and surrounded by the picked troops on his right and left. We have no particulars as to the Gothic order of battle. We know only that Totila drew up his troops in the same manner as the enemy had done, that, unlike Narses, he relied a good deal on the effect to be produced by his cavalry, and that he ordered his warriors to use no weapon but the spear, herein, according to Procopius, committing a fatal blunder, and, in fact, handing the game over to the Romans, whose soldiers, more elastic in their movements and trusted with greater freedom by their commanders, might thrust with the spear, transfix with the arrow, or hew down with the broad sword, each as he found he could fight most successfully.

There was a pause, a long pause, before the two armies encountered one another. It was for Totila to commence, and he, knowing that the last two thousand men of the army of Teias were on their way to join him, purposely postponed the signal. Various demonstrations filled up these waiting hours of the morning. Totila rode along his line, with firm voice and cheery countenance, exhorting his men to be of good courage. The Eunuch-General appealed not to the patriotism or the manhood of his miscellaneous horde of warriors, but to their avarice, riding in front of them and dangling, before their hungry eyes, armlets, twisted collars, and bridles, all of gold. "These", said he, "and such other prizes as these shall reward your valor if you fight well today".

Then rode forth Cocas (once a Roman soldier but now serving Totila) and challenged the bravest of the Imperial host to single combat. An Armenian, Anzalas by name, accepted the challenge. Cocas rode impetuously on, couching his spear, which he aimed at the belly of his antagonist. A sudden swerve of the Armenian, made at the right moment of time, saved his life and enabled him in passing to give a fatal thrust at the left flank of his antagonist. With a crash fell Cocas from his horse and a great shout from the roman ranks hailed this presage of victory.

Still the Gothic two thousand lingered, and in order further to pass the time, Totila, who had been practiced from his youth in all the arts of horsemanship, gratified the two armies with an extraordinary performance. Richly dressed, with gold lavishly displayed on helmet, mail, and greaves, with purple favors fluttering from his cheek-strap, his *pilum* and his spear, he rode forth on his high-spirited horse between the opposed squadrons. Now he wheeled his horse to the right, then sharply to the left. Anon he threw his heavy spear up to the morning breezes, stretched out his hand and caught it by the middle in its quivering fall. Then he tossed the spear from hand to hand, he lay back in his saddle he rose with disparted legs, he bent to one side, then to the other; he displayed in their perfection all the accomplishments of the Gothic *manége*. Strange anticipation of the coming dawn of chivalry! Strange but fatal contrast between the lithe form of the young barbarian hero, rejoicing in his strength, and the bowed figure of the withered and aged Eunuch whose wily brain was even then surely devising the athlete's overthrow. Still further to delay the battle, Totila sent a message to Narses inviting him to a conference; but the Eunuch declined the offer, saying that Totila had before professed himself eager for the fight, and now might have his wish.

At length, just at the time of the noonday meal, the expected two thousand arrived in the camp. Totila, who had drawn back his army within their entrenchments, bade them and the new-comers take food and don armor with all speed, and then led them forth precipitately, hoping to catch the Imperial host in the disorder and relaxation of the midday repast. Not so, however, was Narses to be outwitted. This sudden attack was the very thing which he had looked for, and to guard against its evil consequences no regular luncheon, no noontide slumber, had been permitted to his men. Their food had been served out to them while still under arms and keeping rank, as to the knights of a later day—

'Who drank the red wine through the helmet barred'.

Moreover, true to his policy of taking the Goths in flank, he had turned his straight line into a crescent, drawing back his barbarian centre and trusting to the eight thousand archers on his wings to give a good account of the enemy.

These tactics were completely successful. Totila's charge of horse failed to reach the Imperial center, and while they were engaged in this hopeless quest, the eight thousand archers kept up a murderous discharge of arrows on their flanks. The Lombards and Heruli also, whose disposition for fighting had been up to the last moment uncertain, threw themselves into the fray with unexpected eagerness, so that Procopius is doubtful whether they or their Roman fellow-soldier displayed the more brilliant valor.

For some time the Gothic mounted spearmen maintained the unequal fight, but when the sun was declining their heavy masses came staggering back towards the supporting infantry. It was not an orderly retreat; there was no thought of forming again and charging the pursuing foe. It seemed to the Romans that the hearts of the Goths had suddenly died within them, as if they had met with an army of ghosts, or felt that they were fighting against Heaven. The flight of the cavalry was so headlong and so violent that some of their own friends were trampled to death under their horsehoofs.

The contagion of fear imparted itself to the supporting infantry. They probably knew themselves outnumbered, they saw themselves outflanked, and they fled in irretrievable disorder. The Imperialists pressed on unpitying, slaying Gothic warrior and Roman deserter with equal fury. Some of the vanquished cried for quarter and obtained it at the time, but were soon after perfidiously slain by their captors. In all the Gothic army none were saved except by headlong flight.

And where the while was Totila, he of the gold-embossed shield and purple-fluttering spear? One account states that, being disguised as a common soldier, he was wounded by an arrow, shot at a venture, at the beginning of the fight, and that his departure from the field, together with the depression resulting from such an apparent sign of the anger of Heaven, caused the subsequent disorder. Another account, that which Procopius seems to have preferred, related that the Gothic King, still unwounded and possibly in mean disguise, fled at nightfall with four or five followers, on swift horses, from the battlefield. They were closely pursued by some Imperialist soldiers, ignorant of the rank of the fugitive. One of these, Asbad the Gepid, was about to strike Totila in the back with his spear. A young Goth belonging to the royal household cried out, "Dog! what mean you by trying to strike your own lord?". The incautious exclamation revealed the secret of Totila's identity, and of course Asbad thrust in his spear with all the greater vigor. Scipuar (the recent besieger of Ancona) wounded Asbad in the foot, but himself received a stroke which hindered his further flight. The companions of Asbad tarried to dress the wound of their fallen friend. Totila's companions, who thought they were still pursued, hurried him on, though mortally stricken and now scarcely breathing. At length, at the village of Caprae, thirteen miles from the battlefield, they stopped and tried to tend his wound. But it was too late; in a few minutes the hero's life was ended.

The traveler who is journeying from Gubbio to Tadino, when he is drawing near to the latter place, sees from the bridge over the Chiascio a little hamlet among the hills to the right, which bears the mar of Caprara. There seems no good reason for doubting that this is the place, formerly known as Caprae, to which the faithful Goths bore their pallid master, and where they laid him down to die.

According to the other story heard by Procopius, Totila was forced by the intolerable pain of his wound to quit the field of battle, and ride by himself to Caprae, but at that place was compelled to alight and have his wound dressed, in the course of which operation he died.

The Romans had no knowledge of the death of their great enemy till a woman of the Goths informed them of the fact, and offered to show them the grave. They disinterred the dead body, looked at the discolored features, saw that they were indeed those of Totila; then, without offering any further indignity to the corpse, they hurried off with the glad tidings to Narses, who was piously thanking God and the Virgin for the victory.

In the month of August messengers arrived to Constantinople bearing the tidings of victory, attesting them by the bloodstained robe and gemmed helmet of the Gothic king, which they cast at the feet of the Emperor in his stately Hall of Audience.

And thus ended the career of the Teutonic hero Baduila—for we must restore him his own name in death—a man who perhaps more even than Theodoric himself deserves to be considered the type and embodiment of all that was noblest in the Ostrogothic nation, and who, if he had filled the place of Athalaric or even of Witigis, would assuredly have made for himself a world-famous name in European History. If the Ostrogothic Kingdom of Italy might but have lived, Baduila would have held the same high place in its annals which Englishmen accord to Alfred, Frenchmen to Charlemagne and Germans to the mighty Barbarossa.

CHAPTER XXV

FINIS GOTHORUM. THE LAST OF THE GOTHS

The first care of Narses, after the battle was ended and he had expressed his thankfulness for the victory to Heaven, was to remove from Italy as speedily as possible some of the earthly instruments by whom the victory had been won. Of all his wild horde of *Foederati* none were more savage that the Lombards. Every peasant's cottage where they passed was given to the devouring flame, and the hapless women of Italy, torn even from the altars at which they had taken refuge, must needs gratify the lust of these squalid barbarians. By the gift of large sums of he persuaded these dishonoring allies to promise to return to their own land; and Valerian, with his nephew Damian, were sent with a body of troops to watch their journey through the Julian Alps, and to see that they did not deviate from the road to engage in the delightful work of devastation. This duty accomplished, Valerian commenced the siege of Verona, the garrison of which soon expressed their willingness to surrender. Now, however, the Frankish generals appeared upon the scene, and in the name of their master forbade Verona to be reunited to the Empire. Owing to the number of fortresses which they now held in Upper Italy, they considered all the land north of the Po to be in fact Frankish territory, and would suffer no city within its borders to surrender to the generals of Justinian. Not feeling himself strong enough to challenge this conclusion, Valerian moved off to the banks of the Po to prevent the Gothic army of Upper Italy from crossing that river and marching to the relief of Rome.

Meanwhile the little remnant of Goths who had escaped from the fatal field on which Totila fell had made their way to Pavia, where, even as it had been twelve years ago after the surrender of Ravenna, the last hope of their race was enshrined. By common consent Teias, son of Fritigern, the bravest of Totila's generals and a man probably still young or in early middle life, was acclaimed as King. The Gothic army was now deplorably weakened, not by deaths only, but probably by desertions also, for the full purse which Narses was ever displaying doubtless drew back many of the former soldiers of the Empire to their old allegiance. Teias accordingly strained every nerve to obtain a cordial alliance with the Franks, without which he deemed impossible to meet Narses in the open field. The royal treasure in the stronghold of Pavia was all expended in lavish gifts to Theudibald and his court to obtain this alliance. He Franks took the money of the dying Gothic nationality, and decided not to give it any assistance, but to let the Emperor and the King to fight out their battle to the end, that Italy might fall an easier prey to themselves.

For some time Valerian seems to have prevented Teias and his little army from crossing the Po; and meanwhile the surrender of Gothic fortresses was going on all over Italy. Narni and Spoleto opened their gates to Narses immediately after the battle of the Apennines. At Perugia a similar event to that which had brought the city into the power of the Goths restored it to the possession of the Emperor. The renegade soldier Uliphus, who eight years before had murdered Cyprian, had since then held Perugia for the Gothic King, having his old comrade and fellow-deserter Meligedius for his second in command. Meligedius now commenced secret negotiations for the surrender of the city to Narses. Uliphus and his party got scent of the intrigue, and endeavored to prevent it by force. A fight of the factions followed, in which Uliphus was killed; and his comrade then without difficulty handed over the Umbrian stronghold to an Imperial garrison.

At Tarentum, strangely enough, the negotiations for surrender which had been commenced by the Gothic governor were not quickened by the battle of the Apennines. Ragnaris had possibly some dim visions of himself wearing the crown of Totila, and he believed moreover that the Franks allied with the Goths would yet turn the tide of war. He accordingly repented of his promise to the besiegers, and began to cast about him for an excuse to get the hostages whom he had given back into his own power. He therefore sent to Pacurius, governor of Otranto, asking for a few Imperial soldiers to escort him to the latter city. Pacurius, suspecting no evil, fell into the snare, and sent him fifty soldiers, whom Ragnaris at once announced that he should hold as hostages till his hostages were surrendered. Pacurius, enraged, marched with the larger part of his army against Tarentum. The cruel and faithless Ragnaris slew the fifty involuntary hostages, but was himself routed in the battle which followed, and fled to Acherontia. Tarentum opened her gates to the standards of the Empire; and in Central Italy the extremely important position of Petra Pertusa speedily followed her example.

These various sieges and surrenders all over Italy Rome were probably going on throughout the summer and autumn of the year 552; but meanwhile the great prize, which every Imperial general was bound to strive for, had already been won upon the soldier-trampled banks of the Tiber. Having by his orders to Valerian secured himself from an irruption of Teias and his Goths from Upper Italy, Narses marched to Rome with a great army, chiefly composed of archers, and encamped before its walls. The Gothic garrison concentrated their strength on what might be called the city of Totila, a comparatively small space round the Tomb of Hadrian which the young King, after his first destruction of the City, had labored to rebuild and to fortify. The Goths were utterly unable to defend, and even the army of Narses was unable to invest, the whole circuit of the walls, and the fighting which went on was therefore on both sides of a detached and desultory character. At one point the attack was made by Narses himself, at another by John, at a third by Philemuth and his Herulians; but after all, the honors of the siege fell to none of these, but to Dagisthaeus, so lately the inmate of a prison, now again the leader of the legions. With a band of soldiers bearing the standards of Narses and of John, and carrying scaling-ladders, he suddenly appeared before an unguarded portion of the walls, applied his ladders to their sides, mounted his men on the battlements, and hastened at their head through the ruined City to open the gates to his brother generals. The Goths, at the sight of the Imperial soldiers, gave up all hope of holding the City, and fled, some to Porto, some to the Tomb of Hadrian; and even this, their fortress, was soon surrendered on condition that the lives of the garrison should be spared.

The two harbors of Porto and Civita Vecchia before long fell also into the hands of the Imperialists. The keys of Rome were again sent to Justinian; a ceremony which must have brought a smile to the lips of any philosophical observer who remembered that this was the *fifth* capture that Roma Invicta had undergone during the reign of this single Emperor, and who knew what a mere husk of the once glorious City was now dignified with the name of Rome.

Men remarked with wonder, and Procopius with his accustomed comments on the mutability of fortune, that Dagisthaeus had now taken the city which Bessas had lost, while in the East, in the gorges of Caucasus, Bessas had recovered the fortress of Petra which had been lost by the slothfulness of Dagisthaeus.

To the scanty remains of the Roman Senate and people the recovery of the Imperial City brought no good. They were dispersed over Italy, chiefly in Campania, and were lodged in fortresses garrisoned by Goths. The war had now become one of extermination between the two races, and the word went forth to slay them wherever they could be found. Maximus, the grandson of the Emperor, whose life had been spared after Totila's capture of Rome, now fell a victim to the rage of the barbarians; and Teias tarnished his fame as a warrior by putting to death three hundred lads of handsome appearance, sons of Roman nobles, whom Totila had selected really as hostages, but ostensibly as pages of his court, and had held in safe-keeping in Northern Italy.

Meanwhile the sands of Ostrogothic dominion were running low. With a war of extermination begun, and with the invading race reduced as it now was to a few thousand men, the end could not be long doubtful. The war dwindled down into an attempt on the one part to seize, and on the other to defend, the last remainder of the Gothic treasure. The great hoard at Pavia had nearly all gone to propitiate the faithless Franks; but there was still a yet larger hoard, collected by Totila, deposited in the old fortress of Cumae in Campania, hard by the Lake of Avernus and the Sibyl's Cave. This fortress was commanded by Aligern, the brother of Teias; with whom was joined Herodian, erewhile Roman governor of Spoleto, the greatness of whose crime against the Emperor kept him faithful to the Gothic King. In order to capture the treasure, Narses sent a considerable detachment of his army into Campania. While he himself remained in Rome, trying to bring back something of order into the wilderness-city, he sent John and Philemuth the Herulian into Tuscany to hold the passes and prevent Teias from marching southwards to the assistance of his brother. With much skill, however, Teias contrived, by making a great detour into Picenum and the Adriatic provinces, and twice crossing the Apennines, to march with his little army into Campania. Learning this, Narses summoned his generals from every quarter, John, Philemuth, Valerian, to join him in one great movement southwards, in order to crush out the last remains of Gothic nationality on the Campanian plains.

The rapidity of the movements of the Imperial generals seems to have frustrated the plans of Teias. He was in Campania indeed, but he had not, if I read his movements aright, effected a junction with his brother, nor succeeded in reaching Cumae. He had descended from the mountains near Nocera, some ten miles to the east of the base of Vesuvius, while Cumae, where his brother guarded the great hoard, lay westwards of Naples, fully fifteen miles on the other side of the great volcano.

Here, then, at length Narses and all the best generals of the Empire, with their large and many-nationed army, succeeded in bringing to bay the little troop which followed the last King of the Goths. The small stream of the Draco, now known as the Samo, marked the line between the contending armies, a stream unimportant in itself, but which, working its way between deep and steep banks, offered an effectual opposition to the free movements of cavalry. Behind them the Goths had the lofty mountain-range now known as the Monte S. Angelo which fills up the peninsula of Amalfi and Sorrento, before them the Sarno and the fertile plain which reaches to the base of Vesuvius, and in which are visible in the distance the green mounds of Pompeii.

In this little peninsula the army of Teias stood at bay for two months. Their ships still commanded the sea, and having communication with some harbor in their rear, probably Salerno or Stabia, they freely obtained all the provisions that they required. They had fortified the bridge over the Sarno with wooden towers, upon which they placed *balistae* and other engines of war, thus successfully barring the approach of the enemy. Every now and then, however, a challenge would be given or received, and a Gothic champion would stalk across the bridge to meet some Imperial warrior in single combat. At the end of the two months a traitorous admiral surrendered the Gothic command fleet to the enemy, who had been moreover collecting ships in large numbers from Sicily and all parts of the Empire. The Goths, whose situation was becoming desperate, fell back from their previous line, and took up their position in the Mons Lactarius, an outlier of the St. Angelo range which rises abruptly above the valley of the Sarno. They were safe for the time, since the army of Narses dared not follow them into that rocky region; but they soon repented of their retreat, finding only death by starvation awaiting them in the mountains. With a sudden resolve, and hoping to take the Imperial army by surprise, they rushed down into the plain, and a battle, the last pitched battle between the Ostrogoths and the armies of the Empire, began.

The Imperialists were to a certain extent caught unawares, but their discipline and superior numbers prevented them from being outmaneuvered. The legions and the bands of the *foederati* could not group themselves in their accustomed order, nor gather round the standards of their respective generals. Each man had to fight how he could and where he could, obeying not the commands of his officer but his own instincts of valor. The Goths dismounted from their horses and formed themselves into a deep phalanx, and the Romans, whether from policy or generosity, dismounted from their horses also and fought in the same formation. It was a battle between despair on the one side, and on the other raging shame at the very thought of being beaten by such a mere handful of antagonists. King Teias stood with a little band of followers in front of the Gothic ranks, and performed, in the judgment of the Greek historian, deeds worthy of the old days of the heroes. Covering his body with his broad Gothic shield he made a sudden rush, now here, now there, and transfixed with his spear many of his foes. Vainly meanwhile were the Roman lances thrust at him, and the Roman arrows did but bury themselves in his mighty buckler. When this, being full of arrows, became too heavy for his arm, an armor-bearer, deftly interposing a new shield, relieved him of the old one.

A third of the day had worn away in this strife of heroes, and now was the buckler of Teias heavy with the weight of twelve hostile arrows hanging from it. Without flinching by a finger's breadth from his post in the forefront of the battle, and standing like one rooted to the ground, the King, still dealing death around him, called eagerly to his squire for another shield. He came, he removed the arrow-laden shield and sought to interpose a fresh one, but in the moment of the exchange a javelin pierced the breast of Teias, and he fell mortally wounded to the ground.

When the Imperial soldiers saw that they had laid their great enemy low, they rushed to the corpse, cut off the head, and carried it along the line of battle to impart new courage to their comrades and strike panic into the hearts of his followers. Yet not even then were the Ostrogoths daunted. They fought on with the courage of despair till night descended; they renewed the battle next day with sore and savage hearts. At length in some pause of the strife, caused by the utter weariness of either army, the Goths sent a message to Narses that they perceived that God was against them, and if they could obtain honorable conditions they would renounce the war. Their conditions were these : —No service under the banners of the hated Empire; leave to depart from Italy and live as free men in some other kingdom of the barbarians; leave also to collect their moveable property from the various fortresses in which it was stored up, and take it with them to defray their expenses on the road.

Narses deliberated on this proposal in a council of war, and by the advice of John, unwilling to goad these men, already desperate, to utter madness, wisely accepted it. His only stipulations were that they should bind themselves to leave Italy and to engage in no future war against any part of the Roman Empire. One thousand Goths refusing to accept these terms, broke out of their camp, escaped the vigilance of the enemy, and under the command of Indulph (the general who commanded in the sea-fight off Sinigaglia) succeeded in marching across Italy to Ticinum. That city, as well as Cumae, held out for a few months longer against the troops of the Emperor, but the story of their final surrender will best be told in connection with the invasion of the Alamannic brethren, whose deeds and whose reverses, though they come in the order of time soon after the death of Teias, seem to belong to another cycle of narrative. All the other Goths—the remnant of that mighty host which, sixteen years before, marched as they thought to certain victory under the walls of Rome—made their way sadly over the Alpine passes, bidding an eternal farewell to the fair land of their birth.

They disappeared, those brave Teutons, out of whom, welded with the Latin race, so noble a people might have been made to cultivate and to defend the Italian peninsula. They were swallowed up in we know not what morass of Gepid, of Herulian, of Slavonic barbarism. There remained in Italy the Logothetes of Justinian.

PART ONE

BOOK I
THE VISIGOTHIC INVASION
INTRODUCTION.
SUMMARY OF ROMAN IMPERIAL HISTORY.

CHAPTERS
I. EARLY HISTORY OF THE GOTHS
II. JOVIAN, PROCOPIUS, ATHANARIC.
III. VALENTINIAN THE FIRST
IV. THE LAST YEARS OF VALENS
V. THEODOSIUS
VI. THE VICTORY OF NICAEA
VII. THE FALL OF GRATIAN
VIII. MAXIMUS AND AMBROSE
IX. THE INSURRECTION OF ANTIOCH
X. THEODOSIUS IN ITALY AND THE MASSACRE OF THESSALONICA
XI. EUGENIUS AND ARBOGAST
XII. INTERNAL ORGANISATION OF THE EMPIRE
XIII. HONORIUS, STILICHO, ALARIC
XIV. ALARIC'S FIRST INVASION OF ITALY
XV. THE FALL OF STILICHO
XVII. ALARIC'S THREE SIEGES OF ROME.
XVIII. THE LOVERS OF PLACIDIA
XIX. PLACIDIA AUGUSTA
XX. SALVIAN ON THE DIVINE GOVERNMENT

PART TWO

BOOK II
THE HUNNISH INVASION

I. EARLY HISTORY OF THE HUNS.
II. ATTILA AND THE COURT OF CONSTANTINOPLE.
III. ATTILA IN GAUL.
IV. ATTILA IN ITALY.

BOOK III
THE VANDAL INVASION AND THE HERULIAN MUTINY

I. EXTINCTION OF THE HUNNISH EMPIRE AND THE THEODOSIAN DYNASTY.
II. THE VANDALS FROM GERMANY TO ROME.
III. THE LETTERS AND POEMS OF APOLLINARIS SIDONIUS.
IV. AVITUS, THE CLIENT OF THE VISIGOTHS.
V. SUPREMACY OF RICIMER. MAJORIAN.
VI. SEVERUS II, THE LUCANIAN. ANTHEMIUS, THE CLIENT OF BYZANTIUM.

VII. OLYBRIUS, THE CLIENT OF THE VANDAL. GLYCERIUS, THE CLIENT OF THE BURGUNDIAN. JULIUS NEPOS, THE CLIENT OF BYZANTIUM. ROMULUS AUGUSTULUS, SON OF ORESTES.
VIII. ODOVACAR, THE SOLDIER OF FORTUNE.
IX. CAUSES OF THE FALL OF THE WESTERN EMPIRE.

PART THREE

BOOK IV
THE OSTROGOTHIC INVASION.

I. A CENTURY OF OSTROGOTHIC HISTORY.
II. THE REIGN OF ZENO.
III THE TWO THEODORICS IN THRACE
V. FLAVIUS ODOVACAR.
V. THE FRIGIAN WAR
VI. THE DEATH-GRAPPLE.
VII. KING AND PEOPLE.
VIII. THEODORIC AND HIS COURT
IX. THEODORIC'S RELATIONS WITH GAUL.
X. THEODORIC'S RELATIONS WITH THE EAST.
XI. THEODORIC'S RELATIONS WITH THE CHURCH.
XII. BOETHIUS AND SYMMACHUS.
XIII. THE ACCESSION OF ATHALARIC.
XIV. JUSTINIAN.
XV. BELISARIUS.
XVI. THE LOVERS OF AMALASUNTHA.

BOOK V
THE IMPERIAL RESTORATION
535—553

I. THE FIRST YEAR OF THE WAR
II. BELISARIUS AT CARTHAGE AND AT NAPLES.
III. THE ELEVATION OF WITIGIS.
IV. BELISARIUS IN ROME
V. THE LONG SIEGE BEGUN.
VI. THE CUTTING OF THE AQUEDUCTS.
VII. THE GOTHIC ASSAULT.
VIII. ROMAN SORTIES.
IX. THE BLOCKADE
X. THE RELIEF OF RIMINI.
XI. DISSENSIONS IN THE IMPERIAL CAMP.
XII. SIEGES OF FIESOLI AND OSIMO.
XIII. THE FALL OF RAVENNA.
XIV. AFFAIRS AT CONSTANTINOPLE
XV. THE ELEVATION OF TOTILA.
XVI. SAINT BENEDICT (480 – 547)
XVII. THE RETURN OF BELISARIUS.

XVIII. THE SECOND SIEGE OF ROME.
CHAPTER XIX. ROMA CAPTA.
XX. THE RE-OCCUPATION OF ROME.
XXI. THE THIRD SIEGE OF ROME.
XXII. THE EXPEDITION OF GERMANUS.
XXIII. THE SORROWS OF VIGILIUS.
XXIV. NARSES AND TOTILA.
XXV FINIS GOTHORUM. THE LAST OF THE GOTHS

PART FOUR

BOOK VI.
THE LOMBARD INVASION.

I. THE ALAMANNIC BRETHREN.
II. THE RULE OF NARSES.
III. THE LANGOBARDIC FOREWORLD
1. Early Notices of the Langobardi by Greek and Roman Writers.
2. The Saga of the Langobardi
3. War with the Heruli
4. War with the Gepidae.
IV. ALBOIN IN ITALY.
V. THE INTERREGNUM.
VI. FLAVIUS AUTHARI.
VII. GREGORY THE GREAT.
VIII. GREGORY AND THE LOMBARDS.
IX. THE PAPAL PEACE.
X. THE LAST YEARS OF GREGORY
XI. THE ISTRIAN SCHISM.

BOOK VII
THE LOMBARD KINGDOM
A.D. 600-744

I. THE SEVENTH CENTURY.
II. THE FOUR GREAT DUCHIES.
I. The Duchy of Trient (Tridentum).
II. The Duchy of Friuli (Forum Julii).
III. The Duchy of Benevento (Beneventum).
IV. The Duchy of Spoleto (Spoletium).
Note A. Ecclesiastical notices of the Lombards of Spoleto in the Dialogues of Gregory the Great. Life of St. Cetheus.
III. SAINT COLUMBANUS.
IV. THEUDELINDA AND HER CHILDREN.
V. THE LEGISLATION OF ROTHARI.
VI. GRIMWALD AND CONSTANS.
The Story of St. Barbatus.
VII. THE BAVARIAN LINE RESTORED.
VIII. STORY OF THE DUCHIES, CONTINUED.
IX. THE PAPACY AND THE EMPIRE.
X. THE LAWS OF LIUTPRAND.

XI. ICONOCLASM.
XII. KING LIUTPRAND.
XIII. POLITICAL STATE OF IMPERIAL ITALY.
XIV. POLITICAL STATE OF LOMBARD ITALY.

PART FIVE

BOOK VIII.
FRANKISH INVASIONS.

I. INTRODUCTION. THE MEROVINGIAN KINGS. EARLY FRANKISH HISTORY.
II. THE EARLY ARNULFINGS
III. PIPPIN OF HERISTAL AND CHARLES MARTEL
IV. DUKES OF BAVARIA
V. THE GREAT RENUNCIATION
VI. THE ANOINTING OF PIPPIN
VII. THE DONATION OF CONSTANTINE
VIII. THE STRUGGLE FOR THE EXARCHATE
IX. THE PONTIFICATE OP PAUL I (757-767).
X. A PAPAL CHAOS.
XI. THE PONTIFICATE OF STEPHEN III.
XII. RAVENNA AND ROME.
XIII. THE ACCESSION OF POPE HADRIAN.
XIV. END OF THE LOMBARD MONARCHY.

BOOK IX
THE FRANKISH EMPIRE
774-814

I. THE PONTIFICATE OF HADRIAN I.
Frankish and Byzantine Affairs,
II. THE PONTIFICATE OF HADRIAN I.
Italian Affairs.
III. TASSILO OF BAVARIA.
IV. TWO COURTS : CONSTANTINOPLE AND AACHEN
V. POPE AND EMPEROR.
VI. CHARLES AND IRENE.
VII. VENICE.
VIII. THE FINAL RECOGNITION.
IX. CAROLUS MORTUUS.
X. THE LIFE OF THE PEOPLE

Printed in Great Britain
by Amazon